THE ELEMENT
ENCYCLOPEDIA
OF MAGICAL
CREATURES

John &
Caitlín Matthews

THE ELEMENT ENCYCLOPEDIA OF MAGICAL CREATURES

the ultimate
a–z of fantastic beings
from myth and magic

HarperElement
An Imprint of HarperCollins*Publishers*
77–85 Fulham Palace Road,
Hammersmith, London W6 8JB

www.harpercollins.co.uk

HarperElement is a trademark of HarperCollins*Publishers* Ltd

The material in this book is taken from *The Element Encyclopedia of Magical Creatures*, first
published by HarperElement in 2005

This production 2013

© John and Caitlín Matthews 2005

John and Caitlín Matthews assert the moral right to be identified as the authors of this work

Text illustrations by Andrew Paciorek

A catalogue record of this book is available from the British Library

ISBN-13 978-000-793146-0

Printed and bound in England by
Clays Ltd, St Ives plc

Dedication

This book is dedicated to the loving,
wise and magical Dwina Murphy-Gibb

Contents

Foreword

The City of Gargoyles

We live in a city of gargoyles and fabulous beasts. Extraordinary creatures of all kinds cavort, peer and grapple on most of the walls wherever we walk around Oxford. We are daily familiar with the griffin, the cockatrice, the winged lion and many other magical creatures who guard the buildings of our city.

When we began this book, we were explorers who had yet to see their first phoenix, but we were astonished at the abundance of magical creatures and the worldwide similarities in the stories and themes that make animals and other beings kin to us all. We did not take a microscope or any dissecting tools with us, nor did we wear the sceptic's sharp-angled spectacles that make all objects under observation appear warped and foolish. Indeed, we did not start out to set ourselves up as any kind of experts. It has been love of all living things that has kept us on the road and helped us travel safely on the compass-point pathways that lead from north to south and from east to west. Some creatures showed themselves to us very generously, others were shy and retiring, and so we had to listen to what other people had reported about them. We hope that such second-hand sources do not amount to idle or damaging gossip, and that the creatures in question may retain their secret habitat free from molestation.

As you set out in these pages, we urge you to wander at will, rather than to read from A–Z. The magical creatures themselves will lead you to find the hidden country that is your unique imagination. We also believe that there are creatures we have not described because they have yet to come into being. As long as the land of imagination is allowed to remain, with such a rich source of fodder, extinction is not an option.

Of course, no book of this extent could be done without the help of all the students of mythical creatures who have gone before. We would like to acknowledge those who made our own researches easier, especially Jan Knappert, Carol Rose and J.C. Cooper, whose wonderfully rich works inspired us to hunt still further. Thanks also go to Emrys Matthews for help with the appearance of various creatures, especially the Vampire, Werewolf and Zombie, in the media, where so many of these have found a new home.

John & Caitlín Matthews
Oxford, 10 March 2005

The Element Encyclopedia of Magical Creatures

Introduction

The Zoology of the Imagination

'The zoology of our dreams is far poorer than the zoology of the Maker.'

Jorge Luis Borges,
The Book of Imaginary Beings.

Here are creatures of every possible kind. Creatures that hold up the world; creatures that destroy the world; creatures who are one half human, one half animal and sometimes even part god. Here are animals we think we know, but whose natures are magical; creatures who have strange characteristics such as faces in the middle of their bodies, animal heads, forelegs and back legs of different species. Here also are creatures that follow us, padding silently through the night; creatures that prey upon us, from the fearsome and terrible fire-breathing dragon, to the body of water that has a mind of its own and will leap up and chase you before gobbling you up. All are the product – in one form or another – of human imagination, from a time before thought was organized into word and word into text.

Curiously, it seems we have come full circle, since in our own time imagination responds more to visual stimuli rather than to ancient tales, and we are by no means bereft of creatures that enthral, scare and astonish us with their wonder. Film and TV are, for many of us, the first and most immediate source of myth and folktale – from the classic stop-frame animation of Ray Harryhausen, who gave us Medusa and Pegasus in *Jason and the Argonauts*, to Steven Spielberg's *Jurassic Park*, with its credible dinosaurs, we have gained an appetite for ever more wondrous creatures. Whether we think of the computer-animated adventures of the ogre *Shrek*, or the mythic creatures conjured up, and sometimes ridden, by Harry Potter and his friends at Hogwarts

Academy, we are not content simply to accommodate the creatures we have known from the past – we want more. The cinema has not been slow to satisfy this appetite and to stretch our imagination even further. George Lucas has given us a veritable menagerie of new species in his *Star Wars* universe – from Wookies to Bantha, from Rancor to Hutt. In addition, a legion of movies and TV shows such as *Buffy the Vampire Slayer, Angel* and *Ultraviolet*, numerous versions of *Dracula* and the *Blade* trilogy, have kept the history of Vampires and Werewolves fresh and alive in our dreams. These clearly demonstrate that we have not seen the last of the creatures that are to enter into creation.

The naming of animals is a primal task, one that God, in the Christian myth, gave to Adam in the Garden of Eden. Naming is a means of understanding more about an animal, for the name denotes the nature. Our collection is a wonderful menagerie where names have been arranged in alphabetical order for ease of consultation, but we urge you to read where your imagination prompts you, as it pleases you to explore, to learn more about Kkuuxuginaagits or the wonderfully onomatopoeic Toatoatavaya-o.

This book is a zoology of the imagination more than it is a natural history. It follows the myths of magical creatures wherever they show themselves, myths that are primal stories encoding understandings that we grasp by means of metaphor rather than with any literal-mindedness. Where will these creatures lead us?

The Supernaturals

Magical creatures and fabulous animals form part of the order of nature that we can call the supernaturals. The place of their existence is not in the physical world, but in the otherworldly realms that surround and permeate our own world. Because the Otherworld and our own everyday world overlap at different points, where time and place interface with timeless space, these are the points where we encounter its inhabitants. For example, the unicorn does not just live in times past because the stories we tell about it seem fabulous, it has its own timeless existence in the Otherworld. It can cross out of that realm and appear when it chooses and to whom it chooses.

Those who go in pursuit of the supernaturals must be prepared to follow them into other dimensions. It is only time and place-bound folk who deny their existence, because they have lost the flexibility and sense of adventure to go in quest of them. These otherworldly dimensions and the coordinates of transfer between realms have become less known and frequented in an age that is becoming sealed into one side of reality. This reserve or scepticism about other realms is not a problem that has arisen just in our time, as Shakespeare shows in *Henry IV*, where Hotspur rants about Glendower's arcane beliefs:

> '... *sometimes he angers me*
> *With telling me of the moldwarp and*
> *the ant,*

*Of the dreamer Merlin and his
    prophecies,
And of a dragon, and a finless fish,
A clip-wing'd griffin, and a moulten
    raven,
A couching lion, and ramping cat,
And such a deal of skimble-shamble stuff
As puts me from my faith.'*

Around us are many such muggles as Hotspur who are content to inhabit mundane reality, just as in the world of Harry Potter, where magicians are distinct from non-magicians. But we do not have to become magicians in order to explore the world of the supernaturals, though it does help to have a flexible imagination that is prepared to follow dreams, listen to traveller's tales and explore the ways in which we can encounter these magical creatures for ourselves.

Evolution and Memory

According to Darwinian theories of evolution, it is logical to consider animals as the forerunners of human life, to see all creatures as part of a huge family tree of living beings. Such scientific theories are seen as being at odds with the traditional stories and myths told about the creating creatures who take an active part in the formation of life, but the mythic imagination allows intelligence and wisdom to animals in ways that science discounts or ignores.

Darwin's evolutionary pronouncements encouraged people to see themselves as descendants of a long tree of life, but when he made his discoveries public in the 19th century some people were astounded and distressed to find that they might have ape forebears, or that they might themselves be 'monkey's uncles'. In our own time, in 21st-century USA, the gap between received scientific history and religious tradition still jars the pedestrian foot on the pavement of scientific progress. In that country, and elsewhere, some fundamentalist Christians doggedly deny the Darwinian theory of evolution of our descent through a chain of creatures, and continue to assert that human beings are the result of nothing less than a direct and discrete creation by God. What they make of the discovery of early hominids and other fossils is unknown to us, but this must be highly inconvenient evidence to such believers at the very least. (*See* 'Epilogue'.)

Natural historians tell us that our bodies bear the mark of our animal origins from the serpentine scales of our skins, the bovine horn of our nails and the animal hair that grows on our bodies, among a variety of other physiological and cellular similarities. But the link between people and animals is not merely an evolutionary connection. It is a fundamental mythic understanding that is shared by traditional societies: we are part of a sacred continuum of life that cannot be severed without supreme loss of meaning.

Introduction

In traditional reckoning, the passing of time is frequently marked by the listing of a sequence of living beings, including a succession of animals. A traditional Irish reckoning of lifetimes, goes like this:

> 'Three fields to a tree
> Three trees to a hound
> Three hounds to a horse
> Three horses to a human being
> Three human beings to a deer
> Three deer to an eagle
> Three eagles to a salmon
> Three salmon to a yew
> Three yews to an age of the world.'

This is not a measure of literal commensuration but a measurement of myth and memory. What is so salutary in this particular list is that human beings are located between horses and deer in mythic longevity.

The Shape of Story

In every culture throughout the world, there is a rich vein of animal myths and stories that are related to the primal beginnings of the world. These cycles of stories are often the very first stories ever told. In them, the wisdom and lore of the first animal beings relate how human beings should behave, revealing how things were first instituted. We see such animal story cycles from the unbroken oral traditions that pass through the classical, medieval and renaissance times, from the fables of Aesop to the animal stories of Rudyard Kipling's *Jungle Book* and *Just So* stories. Buddha used the Jataka animal tales to teach people about right behaviour. In these stories, it is the animals that are in charge.

The animals of such stories are not domesticated, tamed or subdued to the will of humans, nor are they anthropomorphized animals or storybook characters whose actions mimic humans. They are wise beings in their own right whose words and actions cause the world to come into being. They are almighty, omniscient and full of wisdom. Some are tricksters, like Coyote or Raven, who both involve themselves in the laying down of laws for humans and whose lateral thinking discovers useful tools for living such as fire or agriculture. They are guardians for those times when humans overstep the respectful mark whereby all living creatures can be threatened by destruction or they are animals who partake of humanity in some way, like the Centaurs who are the teachers of humanity, bringing music, art and other essential skills.

We live in a time where we most urgently need the wisdom of the animals and creating creatures. Although Darwinian theories of evolution have told us that human beings are the summit of the evolutionary ladder, at the top of the food chain, we need the salutary wisdom of the animals to put us in our place, to remind us that we too are animals – sometimes animals 'of little brain'. And like that supremely humble anthropomorphism Winnie the Pooh, a bear of little brain, with a little help from our animal advisors, we can sort out even the most troubling of problems.

Guardians of the Soul

In the *Vedas*, the Hindu god, Shiva, calls upon all the gods to help him overcome the invading *asuras* – 'the non-gods' or demons. They will be able to do this, he tells them, only if they are willing to leave off their godly forms and assume their animal nature. The gods are revolted by the idea and decline his invitation. We know from a wide range of world mythology how divinities have both humanoid as well as other animal forms – sometimes represented by their having animal heads on human bodies. A similar myth is told of the Olympian gods of Greece who fled the ravages of the monstrous Typhon by hiding themselves as animals among the Egyptian animal-headed gods so that they might not be noticed. This way of shape-shifting into animal form is not confined to gods alone.

From early times, we find the widespread notion that human beings have a multiple soul, part of which manifests in animal form. Shamanic traditions hold that in order to live in the most balanced way possible, it is necessary to discover the identity of this animal soul and meet it in dreams and visions, to dance with it in rituals, to wear parts of the animal in question, to keep attuned to its powers, to take its name or explore its nature in order to be fully at

one with our soul. When someone falls sick, a shaman sends out part of his own soul to journey into the spirit realms to find the animal nature of the person's soul and bring it back again. Cajoling, pleading, hunting, stalking, trapping and herding, the shaman uses all the skills of a real hunter to bring back the animal soul.

Magical creatures include all those animals that are the guardians of our animal soul. Among the Tzotzil-speaking Indians of Zinacanan in the highlands of Mexico, we find the belief that human beings have multiple souls, one of which is called the *chanul*. When the ancestors imbue unborn embryos with souls, they also install a shared soul in the embryo of an animal, so that when a Zinacanteco baby is born, then an ocelot or jaguar or coyote or opossum is also born. During childhood, the child discovers the animal with which it shares its soul. This companionship lasts throughout life, with the animal sharing its nature with the human.

In Central America, the animal guardian spirit is known as the *nagual*. To discover the destiny that the *nagual* gives an individual, he must go into the forest and sleep. In his dreams and visions, the *nagual* will come to him and the contract of his life will be set out. *Naguales* move invisibly, protecting and guarding those to whom they are attached. But individuals must know the right forms of prayer that are necessary to contact and receive help from the *naguales*.

In Greco-Roman mythology, which has underpinned so much of our literature and thought, the giant Titans are

Introduction

said to have attempted to slay Dionysus Zagreus. The god tried to escape by shape-shifting, but when he assumed a form of a bull the Titans killed and ate him. But the goddess Athena rescued his heart, which she fed to Zeus, allowing Dionysus to be reborn. Zeus then destroyed the Titans and from their ashes created mankind, thus ensuring that human nature included both immortal and titanic elements in its make-up.

In our own times, we have been reintroduced to the idea of the guardian animal spirit in the work of Philip Pullman. Pullman's *His Dark Materials* shows how each character in his alternative worlds has a *daemon* or guardian spirit in the form of an animal. This daemon is an essential part of the soul, directing, prompting, guarding and warning its human partner throughout life. Pullman's books reveal the horror of what it would be like to be parted from our daemonic counterpart. How can we continue to ignore our own daemons in a world that draws further away from common sense and the urgings of instinct? It is only when we accept and integrate the animal powers of our daemon that we can pass out of a fragmented and warring condition, so that our soul can be whole once more. Like the Hindu gods whom Shiva exhorts to find and enter their animal natures, so too it is our task to find our corresponding affinity in the animal world and embody its wisdom in our lives, for we have forgotten it for too long.

The Language of the Animals

One of the most impossible and exciting features of this book is the way in which magical creatures do not hold their form. Animals have a way of becoming humans, and humans animals. There is a good reason for this, and it is given in an Inuit poem, collected by the explorer, Knud Rasmussen:

> 'In the very earliest time,
> When both people and animals lived
>   on earth,
> A person could become an animal if
>   he wanted to,
> And an animal could become a human
>   being …
> All spoke the same language.'

The point at which human beings lost the ability to talk with animals is not known, but it remains a continuous thread in world folklore and myth. In the East, it was held that people 'eat the heart and liver of serpents, hoping thereby to acquire a knowledge of the language of the animals'. Some of the Turkic tribes of Asia had the custom of giving the tongues of different animals to children who were learning to talk in order to accelerate the process.

In the West, the myth tells us that on Midsummer's Eve, the serpents gathered together to spin a crown of ferns for their king. At their gathering they put their heads together and hissed glass wishing rings called snakestones, which would, if found, help people prosper in all

The Element Encyclopedia of Magical Creatures

enterprises. Pliny tells a similar story about 'the druid's egg', a stone which is engendered by knots of serpents and which has special powers. Fern seed was the ingredient that helped herdsmen and hunters not only become invisible but also learn what animals were saying. The ability to relearn the speech common to animals and humans was also required by shamans and magicians in order to bridge the worlds between the mundane and time-bound realms and the timeless Otherworld.

There are many characters in world myth that acquire the ability to speak and understand animal speech patterns. In the Welsh story of the Oldest Animals, it is a man called Gwrhyr Gwalstwad Ieithoedd (Long Man, Interpreter of Tongues) who alone can converse with animals. He leads King Arthur's nephew Culhwch to find the lost hero, Mabon, by following a string of animals who lead to his hiding place through time and memory.

The Brothers Grimm tell a Swiss story of an old man whose only son studies with a master who teaches him how to understand what dogs bark, birds sing and frogs croak. His father is incensed at what he sees as a waste of education and orders his son to be killed. The servants merely kill a deer, cutting out its eyes and tongue to give their master a token of the ordered death. Meanwhile the lad continues on his way. He goes among wild dogs that are ravaging the land; learning that they are bewitched into guarding a great treasure, he finds the way to discover it and so stop them barking. Later on he hears frogs discussing the

death of the pope and how the cardinals are now looking for a divine miracle in order to appoint a successor. As the hero enters the church where the cardinals sit in deliberation, two doves land on his shoulders and the clergy recognize him as pope. Ignorant of how to say his own papal investiture mass, the hero listens to what the doves coo to him and he echoes their words.

In the 'Narnia' books of C.S. Lewis, Prince Caspian lives in a time when people have forgotten that animals once could talk, but he learns how to seek them out and with their help restore his lost kingdom. We are in a similar time. This commonality of language is lost to many of us and we have become estranged from our creaturely kindred. We have become tame and forgotten our animal origins.

Monsters and the Role of the Monstrous

Some of the creatures appearing in this collection are what many would call monsters. But what makes a monster? A monster is seen to be any creature that deviates from the norm. Grotesque variations of the familiar are abhorrent and scary, as we understand when we view any unfortunate person born with a physical abnormality. We feel pity and compassion, but we are also greatly unsettled. But genetic malformations are in a different category to the true

Introduction

monster. Monsters are not one-off creatures; while they may make solitary appearances, they are actually legion.

Leonardo da Vinci wrote about the creation of imaginary animals,

'You cannot make any such animal without making its limbs bear some resemblance to those of other animals. If you want your dragon to look natural, then take the head of a mastiff or setter, the eyes of a cat, the ears of a porcupine, the nose of a greyhound, the eyebrows of a lion, the crest of an old cock and the neck of a turtle.'

It is this very *likeness to the normal* that skews our perception and aesthetic values, giving us the sense of the monstrous.

Monsters have the ability to show the unspoken or unexpressed. Indeed, that is what the word 'monster' derives from − a 'showing', 'omen' or 'miracle'. What we do not care to look at too closely, and what we gloss over in our own behaviour, is expressed by the monster who reflects our shadow. Indeed, cultures worldwide expressly use the monstrous as a threshold guardian of control, drawing on primordial or cultural monsters to patrol the limits as bogeymen. And fear is the bogeyman's chief weapon of control.

Any study of magical creatures shows how, with certain exceptions, some of them are automatically seen as monstrous by the Christian world, animals that symbolize evil, emanating from the devil, helping to oppose the lawful order of things. Monsters infest places, destroy crops, waste the land, persecute human inhabitants and threaten life itself. As Jacqueline Borsje writes,

'Monsters originally represent non-moral evil, the powers of Chaos. As Christian influence on the texts increases they seem to attain an extra dimension ... they also begin to personify moral evil.'

But this is not the primal function of monsters. They are not intrinsically or morally evil in themselves. They have another function.

We may see just how the idea of monsters and the monstrous has continued to invoke a deep response if we consider two of the seminal works of 19th-century fiction: *Frankenstein* by Mary Shelley and *Dr Jekyll and Mr Hyde* by Robert Louis Stevenson. Both are deeply rooted in the idea of the monstrous other, the aspect of nature that is not of us and therefore horrific. Each makes it clear that to create and let loose the monster within is every bit as terrifying as an encounter with a Black Dog or Dragon.

Monsters as agents of the primal chaos of creation underlie many world myths. Thus, we find Tiamat and her family in Assyrian myth, the Titans of

Greek myth, the giants and primeval monsters of Celtic, Polynesian and Australian myth. Without these monsters, there would be no earth, no seas, no rivers, no mountains. These titanic beings are world-shapers who live just below the surface of our imagination. Their function is to watch the by-ways and borders of the ordered world, threatening it with chaos, challenging its fixity with a shimmering power, ensuring that the civilized order is kept flexible and permeable to the changing influences of a creative power that has not yet ceased to flow. Monsters can therefore be seen as guardians of creative power whose purpose is to challenge the self-complacency of the seemingly changeless order that we so like to inhabit. Monsters bring out our heroic side, making us draw deep upon our own animal resourcefulness.

Back in pre-Christian myth, the slaying of the monster is a heroic task necessary to keep safe the boundaries of ordinary living. But while too much chaos can swamp us, too much certainty can also bring life to a dead end. In that perpetual shimmer of contact between our world and the world of monsters is an invisible gateway, an edge of excitement that incites us to quest, adventure and balance. Primarily, monsters help us maintain the balance of the universe.

Whose Account Counts?

In the exploration and classification of magical creatures, who decides what creature is real or unreal? Whose account is authoritative? The poem *The Six Blind Men and the Elephant* by the 19th-century American John Godfrey Saxe is a children's favourite, based upon a Sufi fable. As the six blind sages feel the unknown object before them with their questing hands, they try hard to determine what kind of beast it really is. As they each feel the side, tusk, trunk, leg, ear and tail of the elephant, the sages think they have found, respectively, a wall, a spear, a snake, a tree, a fan and a rope. The moral concludes:

> *'So oft in theologic wars,*
> *The disputants, I ween,*
> *Rail on in utter ignorance*
> *Of what each other mean.*
> *And prate about an Elephant*
> *Not one of them has seen!'*

Very many of the reporters of magical creatures are often as well equipped as the Six Men from Hindoostan above who have no notion of what they are talking about. Pliny the Elder, writing in the first century is perhaps the most notorious non-eye-witness of them all, relying upon the testimony of others to speak of animals that even the original observers did not linger to describe too carefully. What Pliny and others have observed

Introduction

(or not actually witnessed) is similar to the half-truths and observations that we make about all the animals around us in the natural world. One of the reasons we believe animals behave in certain ways is due to our lack of patience or to the rationalist or fabulist's fall-back which conveniently explains away why a thing is so. The real observer of the natural world soon learns a better truth, although may still not always understand what is being witnessed.

It is only recently, for example, that scientists have learned that whale-song is not just about communicating with other whales but about the practical ultrasonic mapping of coastlines and sea beds by which whales steer their course. Yet, within our own lifetime, we have heard the most fabulist explanations of whale-song which have inspired composers such as Alan Hovhaness (whose *And God Created the Whale* includes whale-voices with orchestral backing) or films like *Star Trek 4* where the very real environmental concerns of the 1980s impinge on the fictional future of the Galactic Empire.

The sources of this book are varied. Where possible we have gone to the first tellers of tales as much as to the more recent accounts. Many of these early reporters lived at a time when only the known world was mapped. The uncharted regions, as in many mariners' maps of the sea, sported monsters that kept people at bay. Some cultures maintained a policy of exclusion, allowing no foreigners to step into their territory, much as China did until only recently. Medieval explorers and travellers such as Marco Polo (*c.* 1250–1323) and

Sir John Mandeville (1300–72) returned with accounts of things unknown to Europeans, animals and customs that were indeed magical and fabulous. Whereas Marco Polo actually did travel to China and was in the service of Kublai Khan, Mandeville only travelled to the Middle East, although he reported creatures in regions beyond such as Africa and the Orient.

The main classical source which everyone in the ancient world consulted for matters of natural history were the writings of the philosopher Aristotle, who attempted to classify all animals in the 4th century BC. This, in turn, influenced another important work – the *Physiologus* which was not a book as such but rather a collection of lore compiled in the melting pot of ancient wisdom that was the city of Alexandria from a variety of classical and Biblical sources reinterpreted by Christian clerics. The word *physiologus* simply meant 'a naturalist'. Over many transcriptions of manuscripts, copyists misunderstood the phrase 'the naturalist says ...' as an actual person called Physiologus! This lore became the progenitor of the many medieval bestiaries that circulated across the centuries. These were, in the words of T.H. White, 'a kind of naturalist's scrapbook which has grown with the addition of several hands'. These beautifully illustrated bestiaries are a delight to behold, full of fantastic creatures that in many cases only the clerical imagination could devise.

Other important resources include the 3rd-century Roman historian Aelian, who wrote a *On the Characteristics of Animals* that included some far from

The Element Encyclopedia of Magical Creatures

natural creatures; the marvellous Herodotus, (*c.* 484 BC) whose skilful storytelling was only outstripped by his imagination; and the great Diodorus Siculus, (*c.* 44 BC) who wrote a *Universal History* in 40 volumes which covered the period from the creation to 60 BC and included many of the most strange and fascinating beasts.

While for the most part we referred to authoritative and well-researched sources, we also listened to that mischievous creature 'common report' which continues to tell tales of hearsay and amazing encounters between humans and magical creatures, such as the Yeti and the Loch Ness Monster, both of which have a well-attested lineage. We have always tried to use accounts by people who were indigenous to the countries and regions where such creatures have shown themselves. These myths have both the primacy of local report as well as a depth of metaphor and meaning. They also hold that humans and animals are part of a sacred continuum of life, not living in separate worlds.

Magical Creatures — An Extinct Species?

The extreme rationality of our time has led magical creatures to the very brink of extinction, engulfed in shoals of disbelief. Whenever such terrible times come round, there is usually a corresponding defence and rallying of forces. The magical creatures that once so occupied the imaginations of adult scholars of all ages, had become merely the stuff of children's stories, suitable for infants and fanciful people of little intelligence. Just when it seemed that all magical creatures were 'only imagination', the very imagination that society so spurns came to the rescue. In literature and in film, magical and fabulous creatures began to flourish and spread once more. From the monster movies of *Godzilla* and *King Kong* through to *Jurassic Park*, from the horror films of the *Wolf Man* through to the zombies of *Night of the Living Dead*, and the successive school terms of Hogwarts where Harry Potter and friends learn more about griffins, dragons and the practicalities of dealing with pixies, mandrakes and serpents.

Are there yet more magical creatures about whom we as yet know nothing, animals and other beings that are still about to reveal themselves? If we look at the evidences of cryptozoology websites dedicated to sightings of unknown animals, we find many new creatures everyday, such as the Moth Man, the Chupacabras (Goatsucker) and many others whom we don't yet rightly know. Not all the magical creatures were described by Pliny the Elder or the bestiaries of the *Physiologus*, nor are all species pinned down and classified by naturalists. Our evolutional history is still being written, as the Epilogue demonstrates; while in the realm of the imagination we have only to look at the species invented by the fertile mind of George Lucas in his

Star Wars films to see how new creatures continue to appear.

Despite our sophistication and civilization, our electric light and concrete roads, not all creatures are domestic, friendly, tamed or under our control. When darkness falls, when the sidewalks fall into shadow, on the lonely roadside, in the mountain passes, rustling in the trees, bubbling mysteriously in the waters, other creatures lurk. Some we do not see, some do not wish to be seen by, some make us hurry onwards.

We believe that life finds many forms and will seek its unfolding evolution in ways that we cannot yet dream. Despite its extent, this book is a work in progress, a report of magical creatures whose numbers increase and decrease on a daily basis. Those that we believe to be dead and gone are not really extinct – they merely slip sideways into the Otherworld to haunt our imaginations, choosing their moment of reappearance. New composites and creations have yet to appear, wondrous, fabulous, magical. As you close this book at the end of the day, laying your head upon your pillow, what magical creatures will dance out of the darkness to enter your dreams? For in our dreams and imaginations, there is no 'extinct' or 'yet-to-be', only an eternal present where all creatures exist.

THE ELEMENT ENCYCLOPEDIA OF MAGICAL CREATURES

A

A Bao a Qu

This strange creature originates on the Malay Peninsula. Described as having many tentacles and a soft smooth skin, it waits for unwary pilgrims at the bottom of the Tower of Victory in Chitor. Pilgrims come to climb this tower, each level representing a further stage on the journey towards enlightenment. As the pilgrim climbs, the creature grows stronger, changing colour and shape, drawing the life force from the unsuspecting victim. Supposedly, the creature will only attain a final form, and be fully alive, when a pilgrim reaches the top of the tower.

Aardvark

In African folklore, the aardvark or ant-bear is much admired because of its diligent quest for food and its fearless response to soldier ants. Hausa magicians make a charm from the heart, skin, forehead and nails of the aardvark, which they pound together with the root of a certain tree. Wrapped in a piece of skin and worn on the chest this gives the owner the power to pass through walls or roofs at night.

Aatxe

In Basque mythology of Spain, Aatxe was a spirit in the form of a bull. He haunts the caves and gorges of the Pyrenees Mountains, coming forth at night, especially during stormy weather, to trouble wayfarers.

Ababil

A race of enormous birds described in the Koran as dropping red clay bricks on the army of elephants sent by the king of Yemen to attack the city of Mecca in the year (571) when the Prophet Mohammed was born.

Abada

A type of small Unicorn reported to live in the lands of the African Congo. The Abada is seldom seen for it is a shy animal.

Abaia

In the mythology of Melanesia, the Abaia is a gigantic eel-like monster that lives at the bottom of a lake. It considers all of the fish in the lake its children and protects them furiously against anyone attempting to catch them. Those foolish enough to try are immediately overwhelmed by a tidal wave caused by the Abaia swishing its enormous tail.

Abath

Accounts of this animal were brought back by 16th-century European travellers to the Malay Peninsula. Described as female, with a single horn growing from its forehead, these were probably the result of a half-glimpsed Javan or Sumatran rhinoceros. Like the Unicorn, a powder made from the horn served both as an aphrodisiac and as an antidote to poison. However, since the Unicorn was invariably represented as male, and since there was only ever one in existence at any time, the Abath seems to have developed independently from the European myths of the one-horned creature. (*See also* Alicorn, Chio-Tuan.)

ABATWA

A race of tiny fairies who share the dwelling of the ants in parts of South Africa. They only occasionally reveal themselves – usually to children, wizards or pregnant women. To see one in the seventh month of pregnancy ensures the mother will give birth to a boy.

ABGAL

A kind of early form of the merman, the Abgal is mentioned in Sumerian mythology. It is one of a number of spirits, originally servants of Ea, the god of wisdom. Like the centaurs of Greek mythology who helped civilize humanity, the task of these beings was to teach the arts and sciences to humanity. They did this during the day while fasting, only stopping to eat at night. Early carved reliefs show them as men above the waist, fish below.

ABOMINABLE SNOWMAN

The Abominable Snowman is a name given to the Yeti which lives in the Himalayas.

ACAMAS

One of the names of the Cyclops in Greek Mythology.

ACEPHALI

In Greek mythology, the Acephali were human beings whose features were situated in their chests. They had no heads at all. According to the accounts of Herodotus and Josephus, the Acephali lived in Libya. They are similar to the Blemyahs.

ACHELOUS

In Greek mythology, Achelous was a river god who took three different shapes when he chose. He could take the form of a bull, a speckled serpent or a bull-headed man, like the Minotaur. He wrestled with Hercules for the hand of Dejanira and, while in the latter form, lost a horn. The blood that fell to the ground from the horn became the Sirens, while the horn itself was discovered by Naïads who took and filled it with flowers and fruit. Classical myth tells us that Achelous' horn was then presented to Plenty (Amalthea) who made it her cornucopia (the 'horn of plenty').

The Element Encyclopedia of Magical Creatures

ACHIYALABOPA

Among the Pueblo peoples of North America, stories are told of this fabulous animal – a bird with rainbow-coloured wings and feathers like knives. It is a celestial creature and may at one time have been considered responsible for the whole of creation.

ACTAEON

In Greek myth, Actaeon is one of the eight horses of the sun. Actaeon is described as pure white in colour, with flaring nostrils from which issue flame and smoke. The name Actaeon means 'effulgence', clearly referring to the powerful heat and light of the sun. At night, the horses browsed on magical herbs on the Islands of the Blessed; by day, the nymphs of time, the Horae, harnessed them to the chariot of the sun, which was driven by the god Helios. (*See also* Horse, Acthon.)

ACTHON

One of the four winged horses of the sun in Roman myth. The poet Ovid (43 BC–AD 17) lists Acthon together with Eous, Phlegon and Pyrios. These four were harnessed daily to the chariot of the sun and driven across the heavens by the charioteer Phaethon. (*See also* Horse.)

ADAR LLWCH GWIN

According to Celtic tradition, the Adar Llwch Gwin were giant birds, similar in kind to the Griffin, which were given to a warrior named Drudwas ap Tryffin by his fairy wife. The name derives from the Welsh words *llwch* ('dust') and *gwin* ('wine'). The birds were said to understand human speech and to obey whatever command was given to them by their master. However, on one occasion, when Drudwas was about to do battle with the hero Arthur, he commanded them to kill the first man to enter the battle. Arthur himself was delayed and the birds immediately turned on Drudwas and tore him to pieces.

ADARO

This strange being appears in the myths of the Solomon Islands in the western Pacific Ocean. He is clearly related to the merman, but unlike these familiar sea creatures, the Adaro has legs, attached to which are fins; a larger fin, similar to that of a shark, sprouts from his head. He also has fish gills and a sharp horn where his nose ought to be. The Adaro commands a huge army of flying fish, which savagely rend into pieces anyone foolish enough to invade his waters. The Solomon Islanders describe him as flying through the air, carried by his fish army or riding on the back of a rainbow during storms at sea.)

ADITI

In Hindu tradition, Aditi is the primordial entity from which all things come. She is shown in the form of a cow who nourishes every living thing. She gives her milk freely to all on the condition that humans behave to her as if they are her calves, like children to their mother. The injunction 'Do not injure Aditi the Cow,' is a warning to protect the whole of nature and the Earth itself.

ADLET

These monstrous creatures feature in the mythology of the Inuit people of Labrador and the Hudson Bay area. They are part of a curious creation myth, according to which a human woman cohabited with a red dog. Five of the children resulting from this union were dogs themselves, and these were sent across the sea to Europe where they founded the European races. Five other children were even more monstrous and turned upon the Inuit themselves, drinking their blood and rending them limb from limb.

AELLO

One of the Harpies of classical Greek and Roman myth.

AETERNAE

According to the legends that surround the life and deeds of Alexander the Great, the Aeternae were encountered on the northern plains of India when his army passed that way in the 4th century BC. They were described as having bony, saw-toothed protuberances sprouting from their heads, with which they attacked and wounded their enemies. They killed several of Alexander's soldiers who were unlucky enough to encounter them.

AETOLIAN BOAR

Also known as the Calydonian boar, this mighty beast appears in classical Greek mythology as a means of inflicting divine justice. The goddess Artemis sent the boar as a punishment to the people of the Aetolian region of Greece, who had failed to give her sufficient honour and sacrifice. After the boar had ravaged much of the country, the hero Meleager was given the task of hunting down and destroying the creature. Calling upon many of greatest heroes in the classical world, Meleager lead them on a long and savage hunt across the country. In the end, it was the huntress Atalanta who brought down the boar with an arrow, after which Meleager killed it with his spear. He then gave the prize of the carcass to Atalanta, but this caused a quarrel over the division of the spoils and in the ensuing battle Meleager himself was slain.

AFANC

A water monster found specifically in Welsh folklore tradition. Also known as the Addanc or Abhac, it preyed on unwary travellers. Early references, dating back to the Middle Ages, are vague about its shape and size, but later it came to be described as a giant beaver. The reason for this may be that the name Afanc comes from a local dialect word for beaver. On the river Conway in north Wales there is a whirlpool known as Llyn yr Afanc, and local stories tell of the capture of the monster, which was bound by iron chains and dragged from its home to a lake, Llyn Cwm Ffynnon.

The creature is also associated with Lake Bala, where a version of the Noah's Flood story is told. A man named Dwyfan suspected that the monster was going to cause a flood and built an ark to house all the animals he could find. The flood did indeed come, caused by the thrashing of the Afanc. Dwyfan and his wife Dwyfach were the sole survivors and they founded the British race. This story probably originated in the flash floods for which the area is famous. Later, it was said that the Arthurian hero Peredur (Percival) slew the Afanc in single combat, but stories were still told of it as late as the 19th century.

AFRIT/AFREET

A tribe of monstrous demons or djins found in Muslim and Arabic folklore. Described as gigantic in form, sometimes with cloven hooves and horns, it may well have added details to the description of the Devil in Christian mythology. Incredibly fierce and cruel, the Afrits stole unattended children and dragged them to their deaths. Usually found in desert lands, the people of Kenya spoke of them inhabiting muddy pools and shallow rivers, from which they leapt out without warning. According to biblical tradition, King Solomon once bound an Afrit with magic, and forced it to help him find the Shamir. Lord Byron, who travelled widely in the Middle East, was so fascinated by the stories of the Afrit that he included one in his poem 'The Giaour'.

> *Go – and with Gouls and Afrits rave;*
> *Till these in horror shrink away*
> *From Spectre more accursed than they.*

AGATHODEMON

A winged serpent from classical Greek and Gnostic traditions. It is especially associated with bringing good luck, and offerings of wine were made to this being to ensure good harvest of the vines. In later Greek tradition, small temples were set up to the Agathodemon, which at this point was now seen as a snake.

AGLOAOPHEME

The name of one of the Sirens in Greek and Roman mythology.

AGUANE

Female fairies living among the
Austrian Alps, in northern Italy and
the borders of Slovenia. They are
shapeshifters but their true form is that
of a beautiful young woman with long
hair and either goat's or horse's feet.
They are particularly known as guardians of rivers and mountain streams,
and it is advisable to ask their permission before setting foot in any such
water. If a man enters the water and
stirs up the mud of the stream-bed, the
Aguane may come forth and attack
him. While they have been known to
eat human beings who trespass in their
waters, they are also known to be fond
of children, whom they carry on their
shoulders across rivers.

AHI

Represented as either a dragon or a
vast cosmic serpent in the Vedic
myths of ancient India, the Ahi was so
huge that in some versions of the
myth it is described as drinking all the
waters of the Earth, after which it
curled itself around the peaks of a
great mountain range. The god Indra
found it there and slew it, causing the
waters to run free again. It is probable
that this story reflects the period in
winter when the waters are frozen, to
be released again with the coming of
spring.

AHUIZOTL

The Ahuizotl appears in the folklore and
legends of Mexico. So terrifying was
this creature that even to see it was to
invite death. It is usually seen as a flesh-
eating creature that takes the form of a
dog, but with the feet of a monkey and a
human hand growing at the end of its
prehensile tail. Its name means 'water
opossum', and it lies in wait for fishermen in the waters and along the banks
of rivers. It has a number of tricks by
which it catches people, including making small fish and frogs leap about in the
water to attract the attention of would-
be fishermen. The Ahuizotl then reaches
out with the hand at the end of its tail,
and drags its victim beneath the water.
Within three days, bodies are found
floating, and are recognized as victims of
the Ahuizotl by the fact that their eyes,
teeth and nails are missing – these being
delicacies to the monster.

AI APAEC

The supreme deity of the Mochicr people of southern coastal Peru. He takes
the form of an ancient man with long
pointed fangs and the whiskers of a cat.
An anthropomorphized feline god once
worshipped in the north of the country,
Ai Apaec is one of those gods who are
known as the teachers of mankind,
bringing the skills of farming, fishing,
hunting, music and medicine to the
people. He also presides over birth and
his court included a lizard and a dog.

Ai Tojon

A giant two-headed eagle that perches on the top of a mountain and sheds light over the world in the folklore of the Yakut peoples of Siberia.

Aiatar

A creature resembling a giant serpent or snake found in Finnish folklore. Known as the 'Devil of the Woods', this creature is said to suckle small snakes. These snakes can cause sickness in the person who sees them. In some areas of Finland, especially along the edge of the Arctic tundra, the Aiatar is seen as a destructive female force that brings bad luck to all who encounter it.

Aicha Kandida

A predatory water demon or Afrit of Moroccan folklore which lurks along the banks of the River Sebu, around the Aquadel at Marrakesh, and even in the grounds of the Sultan's palace in the same city. She appears as a beautiful young woman who lures lonely men to their death. Once her victim is within reach, she transforms into a gigantic monster and drags her victim away to consume him beneath the water. The only way to escape her is to find another human being or an inhabited dwelling, since the Aicha Kandida is apparently able only to attack one person at a time. Occasionally she will relinquish her prey if bribed by a sufficiently generous gift.

Aida Hwedo

The great Rainbow Serpent of Dahomy mythology.

Aida Hwedo carried the creator Mawu from place to place as she went about creating the Earth. Whenever they stopped for the night, in the morning there were mountains – the piles of excrement left by Aida Hwedo. When the creation was completed, Mawu realized that there were too many large objects on the surface of the Earth and that it was likely to break apart as a result. So she brought Aida Hwedo and commanded him to coil around the inside of the earth's crust. To prevent the serpent from being overcome by the heat, Mawu placed the sea around him to cool his skin. However, if he gets too hot and shifts in his place, he causes earthquakes.

Belief in the rainbow serpent survives in both Surinam and Haitian Voodun belief, and great efforts are made by these people to ensure that the creature is never angered. Thus, before young people marry, if either of them is devoted to Aida Hwedo, they make special offerings to prevent jealousy or resentment in the god.

AIGAMUXA

In the mythology and folklore and of the Khosian people of South Africa, the Aigamuxa are man-eating ogres who inhabit the dunes of the Kalahari desert. Though human in appearance, they have eyes in their instep or in the heels of their feet, so that they are constantly forced to stop and lift a foot in order to see where they are going. Despite the fact that they appear human, they are huge in stature with gigantic hands and feet and enormous sharpened teeth. Whenever they catch human prey, they tear them in pieces and devour them. However, like most ogres, there are very stupid and easily tricked.

AILLEN TRECHENN

A three-headed monster that emerged every Samhain (Hallowe'en) from a mound at Cruachan in County Roscommon to ravage Ireland. It hated all human beings, especially the heroes of Emain Macha and the ancient stronghold of Tara. It was eventually killed by the poet and warrior Amairgen.

AION

The lion-headed god of time in classical Greek and Gnostic traditions. Sometimes shown with four wings or arms (representing the fourfold division of time) or standing on a globe encircled with the signs of the zodiac (representing his reign over the year and the ages). He carries two keys, which unlock the two solsticial gates – a silver key opens the Gate of Cancer and a golden one of the Gate of Capricorn. These gates lead beyond the circle of ordinary time into the infinite realm of the soul.

AIRAVATA/AIRAVANA

In the Hindu mythology of India, Airavata is one of sixteen giant white cosmic elephants who support the Earth on their backs. Airavata stands at the eastern quarter of the world with the god Indra upon his back. The name Airavata comes from the word *iravat* meaning 'Child of the Water'. According to Hindu mythology, this wondrous beast was created from the churning of the waters at the beginning of time. He takes the form of a milk-white elephant with wings and was so beautiful that Indra chose him as a personal war elephant. As Airavata flew through the air, he sucked up all the waters from the Earth and sprayed them over the surface to bring the gift of rain to the human race.

Airavata is also seen as the father of all elephants and initially his many children were also winged; they subsequently lost the ability to fly after interrupting a class being taught by a sage after landing in a tree above him. The sage decreed that henceforward they would serve mankind in whatever way they were required. To this day, white elephants, which are extremely rare, are considered to be descendants of Airavata and as such are reserved for the use of royalty, often being given as gifts between kings.

In the great Hindu mythological epic *Mahabharata*, a different origin is described for Airavata. Here we are told how the god Brahma took a cosmic egg and opened it, holding one half in each hand while chanting seven mantras over them. From the right-hand shell came eight pure white male elephants, each with four tusks; the chief among these was Airavata. From the left-hand shell emerged eight pure white female elephants. Together these sixteen cosmic creatures stood at the eight cardinal compass points to support the Earth. This idea almost certainly influenced the writer Terry Pratchett, who describes four elephants holding up the Discworld in his series of novels of that name.

AITVARAS

In Lithuanian folklore, the Aitvaras is a creature whose natural form is that of a dragon, but which also takes on other forms including those of a black cockerel or a black cat. It is a type of luck-bringer, of which there are numerous instances in European folklore. Often, a person will bring it home unknowingly, and once there it takes up habitation and begins to work on behalf of its new owner. The Aitvaras' one objective is to bring well-being and plenty to the house in which it lives, but it usually does this by robbing neighbouring houses. In return, it demands only the sustenance of an omelette every day, but the household suffers the worst side of the bargain since in time it will take the souls of everyone there.

AKER

The god of the Earth in Egyptian mythology. Aker is represented as a narrow strip of land with a human or lion's head at either end, or sometimes as two lions back to back and joined in the centre. One lion faces the west where the sun rises, the other faces east where the sun sets. The two lions or lion-headed beings are almost certainly the same as those who guard the entrance and exit to the underworld in this tradition.

AKHEKHU

A strange beast described by medieval travellers to the Middle East, the Akhekhu resembled a serpent, but had four powerful legs and clawed feet. It almost certainly derives from the folklore of Egypt.

AKHLUT

A gigantic killer whale mentioned in the folklore of the Inuit, especially those who live along the Bering Sea coastline of Alaska. While its home is the sea, it takes on the form of a giant white wolf in order to prey on humans. Inuit who see large wolf tracks ending suddenly at the edge of an ice floe refer to these as the 'tracks of the Akhlut'.

The Element Encyclopedia of Magical Creatures

Akupara

In Hindu mythology, this is the name of a giant cosmic tortoise that supports the entire Earth on its back.

Al

Al is a terrible fire-eyed demon from Armenian mythology. Originally a demon which carried diseases, the Al is now associated with ill-luck in childbirth. It is said to blind unborn children in the womb and cause miscarriages. It also steals seven-month-old children. As well as its fiery eyes, it has snake-like hair, fingernails of brass, iron teeth and it carries a pair of iron scissors with which it cuts the umbilical cord of its chosen victim, inflicting poison on both mother and child. To shield themselves from its evil influence, pregnant women surround themselves with iron weapons that keep it at bay. The Al have a king who is chained in a hidden abyss, from which he can be heard shrieking constantly. In Afghanistan, the creature is represented as a young woman with long teeth and nails. Her feet are reversed.

Alan

A species of bird-like humanoids with wings, long teeth and hands and feet facing backwards. In the folklore of the Tinguian people of the Philippine Islands, they inhabit the jungles. At night they nest in trees, hanging upside down from the topmost branches like bats. They are also said to have homes beneath the ground that are lined with gold. They are most often represented as helping spirits who give aid to the heroes of the islands; however, at times they can be both mischievous and malicious.

Albastor

A gigantic creature from the folklore of the Cheremis people of eastern Russia. On the ground, it can take the shape of any animal, but it is most often described as a giant, white-skinned man with long flowing hair. It can also fly through the air, at which time it takes on the appearance of a shooting star with a comet-tail of light behind it. Its origin is said to be the souls of baptized and illegitimate children. It punishes people who overindulge in sexual intercourse by providing them with such voracious sexual appetites that they eventually die of exhaustion. It often mates with humans and signs of this may be betrayed by the presence of a sore on the victim's lips. The human lover of a woman who has lain with an Albastor will also become ill.

Alberich

The king of the dwarves in Teutonic and Scandinavian mythology, Alberich lives in a magnificent underground palace, the walls and ceiling of which are covered with gemstones. He guards

The Element Encyclopedia of Magical Creatures

a great amount of treasure, including a magic ring, the mighty sword Balmung, a belt which confers strength upon its wearer, and a cloak of invisibility. In common with most dwarves in this tradition, he is a famous smith and artificer, responsible for many of the great objects of power possessed by the gods – among them Freya's necklace. He is an essential character of the 'Volsunga Saga' and 'Nibelungenlied', which describe the theft of this great treasure and the retribution that followed. Alberich is a major figure in Richard Wagner's operatic 'Ring Cycle', which retells the Teutonic myths with psychological overtones.

ALECTO

One of the Furies from Greek and Roman mythology, this hideous creature is shaped like a human with bat wings and the head of a dog. Like her sisters, she was born from drops of blood that fell on the earth when the great Titan Uranus was castrated by his son, Zeus. Her name means 'the Unceasing' and she is said to be responsible for war, pestilence and revenge.

ALFA

In Scandinavian and Teutonic mythology, the Alfa, or elves, are divided into two tribes: the Svartalfar (dark elves) and the Liosalfar (light elves). The Liosalfar are bringers of light and are extremely beautiful, being tall, with skins whiter than the sun. They live in a realm between the Earth and Heavens known as Alfhime. The Svartalfar, on the other hand, live beneath the earth and their skins are blacker than a night without stars. They are famous smiths and responsible for many fabulous weapons and magical armour. Despite their evil reputation, they are associated with fertility and had a strong following among the Norse peoples. Both races are said to have originated from the maggots that ate the flesh of the cosmic giant Ymir. J.R.R. Tolkien drew heavily on their history in the creation of the elvish races which play such an important part in *The Hobbit* and *The Lord of the Rings*.

ALICANTO

This creature from the folklore of Chile emerges at night, shedding a golden or silvery light from its great wings. The Alicanto is a strange bird-like monster which likes to eat gold and silver, and if it discovers a rich vein of ore, will continue to eat until it is too heavy to fly. Gold prospectors in the Chilean foothills are always on the lookout for the Alicanto in the hope that it will lead them to golden riches.

Alicorn

An alternative name for the European Unicorn.

Alklha/Alicha

A great cosmic dragon from the mythology of the Buryat people of ancient Siberia. Its wings were black and so large that when spread they covered the entire sky – overcast days were said to indicate that the Alklha had opened its wings. The creature appears to have lived in a region high above the Earth, because from here it made periodic attacks on the sun and moon. To this day, the marks on the surface of the moon are said to be the claw or teeth marks of the Alklha. Anyone among the Buryat people, seeing a section of the sun or moon obscured – such as might happen during an eclipse – believed that the Alklha was active and would throw stones into the sky to discourage it. The gods finally found a solution to this troublesome creature by cutting it in half. One half remained in the heavens, the other on the Earth; that way, whenever the Alklha attempted to consume either sun or the moon, the heavenly sphere would fall straight through the monster and resume its place in the sky.

Alkonost

A Russian version of the Siren, this being is half woman and half bird. She lives in the magical land of the dead with her counterpart the Sirin. Her role is to torment the souls of the damned by singing terrible songs to them in her harsh voice and tormenting them with vile punishments.

Alma

A creature originating in Siberia and living in the northern forest and wastelands. The Alma has also been seen in Kazakstan and the Caucasus. The name means 'Wild Man' in Mongolian. It is a fur-covered humanoid like the Bigfoot or Sasquatch found in the United States. Gigantic and humanoid in shape, it is covered in shaggy brown, black or red fur. Sightings of Almas have been reported since the 17th century, the most recent being in 1948 by the Russian scientist, Alexander G. Pronin, who said it looked very like a man but with much longer arms.

In the mid-19th century, a female Alma with reddish-black hair and with a deeply sloped forehead was captured in Abkhazia in the western Caucasus. It was named Zanya. She reportedly mothered six children by different men of which four survived. These offspring looked like normal humans except for being of much darker complexion and immensely stronger than men. Descendants of these Alma children are said to survive to this day and were investigated by Russian historian, Boris Porshney. He was struck by their Negroid features and powerful jaw muscles. He attempted to unearth the remains of Zanya, but they only succeeded in finding the remains of her original descendants whose skeletal structure was nearer to that of a Neanderthal than a modern human.

ALOES

One of a number of strange beasts reported by early explorers of the New World, the Aloes appears in a 16th-century work by the antiquary Ambroise Pare, *On Monsters and Marvels*, in which it is described as a sea creature which had the head of a goose, a very long neck and four large flippers. It may have been a partial memory of the seal with a bird standing on its back.

ALOJA

In Catalan tradition in Spain, the Aloja are the fairies who guard the fate of human beings. They oversee the process of birth and are responsible for the provision of plenty. They are similar in nature to the Fates (Moirae).

ALPHYN

This heraldic beast looks like a tiger. It derives from an Arabic chess piece, the equivalent of the European knight of the chessboard. The Arabic name for this piece is '*al-fil*' and it is usually depicted as an elephant.

ALSVID/ALSWIDER

The name of one of the two great horses (the other was Arvak) that pull the Chariot of the Sun in Norse mythology. Alsvid means 'all swift'. The gods are said to have fixed a pair of bellows beneath the shoulders of the horse to cool it down.

ALTAMAHA-HA

This water monster inhabits the Altamaha River and the marshes around Darien in Georgia, USA. The creature has not been sighted since the early 1960s, but it is said to be 10–40 ft long with a body 1–2 ft wide. It resembles a giant eel although it is much bigger than the largest recorded eel.

Amarok

A giant wolf in the mythology and folklore of the Inuit people of the United States and Canada. Its name is curiously similar to that of Ragnarok, the Norse name for the day of doom when the whole world will be swallowed by the giant wolf Fenris. The Amarok is said to be responsible for the deaths of many hunters on the lonely Arctic tundra.

Ambize

Another of the strange creatures reported by 16th-century travellers, this beast was said to inhabit the seas around the West African coast, especially the Congo delta. It was described as having the body of an enormous fish, but with the head of a pig or ox. It had human hands instead of fins and a round flat tail like a beaver. Though considered a delicacy by local fishermen, it was extremely difficult to catch due to its great size.

Amemait / Am-mit / Ammit / Ammut

A giant flesh-eating monster from Egyptian mythology, the Amemait was responsible for consuming the hearts of souls condemned for earthly crimes and misdemeanours. Its name can be translated as 'Corpse Eater', 'Bone Eater' or simply 'Devourer'. The Amemait is described as being part hippopotamus, part lion, and part crocodile, and is often depicted as accompanying the god Osiris or as a guardian to the gateway of temples.

Amgwusnasomtaka

Amgwusnasomtaka is the name of the crow-mother of the Hopi Indians of the North American south-west. She has a sharp beak and two warrior sons called Hu who have bull's horns and tails. They are represented in the purificatory dances of the Hopi with whips made of yucca plants. Each child who is part of these rites is beaten by dancers representing the Hu *katchinas* (spirits). Amgwusnasomtaka holds the whips of her sons and replaces them from her supply when they wear out. When each child has been beaten in these initiatory rites, she then submits to the same treatment, receiving the lashes upon her back. According to this mystery, Crow-Mother sympathizes with the children in this ritual, which teaches them respect for all the katchinas.

A-Mi-Kuk

A monster reported by the Inuit people of the Bering Strait and Alaska. Described as a huge, heavy creature with a moist and slimy skin, the A-Mi-Kuk lives in the sea but is also capable of burrowing under the earth to emerge in inland lakes. Instead of legs, it has four unnaturally long human arms and hands, which it uses both to walk upon and to capture its prey.

The Element Encyclopedia of Magical Creatures

AMMUT

A goddess of the Underworld in Egyptian mythology, her name means 'Devourer of the Dead', and she is described as consuming the hearts of those who have led evil lives on Earth. Ammut is often shown in the Hall of the Two Truths, where the hearts of dead people are weighed against a feather to discover whether they have done good or evil in their lives. The head of Ammut is that of a crocodile, her front legs and torso belong to a lion or leopard, and her back legs are those of a hippopotamus.

AMPHIPTERE

Although this is one of the many strange creatures found in European heraldry, the Amphiptere also seems to have been known about more widely. In its heraldic form, the Amphiptere is shown with the body of a winged serpent, razor sharp claws and fanged mouth.

AMPHISBAENA

The classical Greek writer Lucan, who described the Amphisbaena as a winged reptile with an extra head on the end of its long prehensile tail, first mentions this creature in his book *Pharsalia*. The creature's name means 'to go both ways'. It became a favourite device of the compilers and embellishers of medieval bestiaries, who often showed this creature in the margins of their books. It is generally shown with its tail curved above its back, grasping its extra head in the jaws of its normal mouth. In this position, it was able to travel by rolling along the ground like a wheel. It must have been a formidable adversary to encounter, since it could run in either direction, possessed the legs of an eagle with claws to grip its victims, and eyes that gave forth beams of light in the darkness. Wounds inflicted by the Amphisbaena generally failed to heal and brought death to the person who had been bitten. Yet, despite its evil nature, it was much sought-after during the Middle Ages for its medical properties. According to Lucan and his fellow-writer Pliny the Elder, its dried skin was an excellent cure for rheumatism. It is described as living in the deserts of Libya and may possibly be based on an actual reptile that is capable of running in both directions, and that raises its tail like a scorpion when threatened.

AMPHISIEN

A variant of the Cockatrice, often found in heraldry. Unlike the ordinary Cockatrice – but like the Amphisbaena – it had an additional head at the end of its tail. Its glance turned anyone who saw it to stone.

AMUN

One of the primal creator gods of Egyptian mythology, Amun is sometimes portrayed as a goose. He is also associated with the ram, which is regarded as a sacred animal and is a reflection of Amun's role as a fertility god. He is also sometimes seen as a snake in which form he is called Kemetaf ('He Who Has Completed His Time'). Beginning as a god of Thebes, Amun eventually became a supreme state god in the new kingdom of Egypt.

ANALOPOS

This antelope-like creature was reportedly found near the Euphrates river in Mesopotamia. It could only be captured by being lured into a thicket where its horns became entangled. A magnificent statue of a beast answering this description was found during the excavations of the ancient Chaldean city of Ur.

ANAMAGQKIU

In Algonquian myths, the Anamagqkiu are the underworld spirits whose chieftains are bears. They dragged Moqwaoi, the wolf-brother of the Great Hare, Manabusch under a frozen lake to his death. Manabusch revenged his brother by killing the bear-chiefs, but the other Anamagqkiu caused a great inundation that flooded the world.

ANAMTABOGA

A great dragon in the myths and legends of Java and Indonesia. It rules over the kingdom of the dead with its wife, Dewi Nagagini.

ANANSI

The spider god and trickster of West African folklore and mythology. Originally a creator god, Anansi has become most widely known as a crafty and cunning trickster who uses his wits to dupe other animals and humans. Early tales describe him stealing the sun and playing jokes on everyone. Stories are told of him along the Gold Coast, the Ivory Coast, in Sierra Leone, Togo, Youruba, Warri, the Cameroons, the Congo and Angola. He is also known everywhere in the West Indies and other parts of the New World and is probably one of the most popular folklore characters among the African-American population of America. He has many names: among the Hausa he is called Gizo, while the Alkan-speaking peoples call him Kwaku Anansa; in South Carolina in the Sea Island folktales he has become Miss Nancy and Gulla Aunt Nancy; in Haiti he is known as Ti Malice. But it is as Anansi that he is best known, from Trinidad to the Congo. It is unclear whether his original form is human or spider, but he is always represented as taking spider form when in trouble, enabling him to scuttle away and hide from the consequences of his japes. His character is similar to that of Hare and Tortoise in the stories of the Bantu peoples, and to Brer Rabbit in southern USA. Yet there is an ambiguity in the way he is perceived: 'Woe to he who would put his faith in Anansi' and 'The wisdom of the spider is greater than that of all the world put together' are two sayings heard widely among

The Element Encyclopedia of Magical Creatures

West African people. The Ashanti and Yoruba people tell how Anansi's children discovered a pot always full of food and broke it, causing widespread famine.

A story from Ghana tells how, during a bush fire, an antelope allowed the spider to hide in her ear and guide her to safety. When the fire was behind them, the spider ran down to the ground and thanked the antelope for her kindness. Soon after, the antelope gave birth to a baby, which spent its first days hiding in the bushes where its mother was grazing. One unlucky day, hunters arrived and spotted the mother. The little one crouched under the shrubs and the mother leapt up to catch the hunters' attention, staying just out of range. After an hour, the hunters gave up and went back to search for the young antelope. But they searched in vain and left the forest empty handed. Later, the mother came back but could not find her baby either. Then she heard a familiar voice. It was Anansi, who had surrounded the baby with a dense screen of spider webs as a way of thanking the antelope for her help.

ANANTA/ANANTA SESHA

The thousand-headed serpent of Hindu mythology, Ananta's name means 'Endless' or 'Infinity', from which one may guess at its size. Its creation occurred when Balarama, the brother of the sun god, fell asleep by the seashore; out of his mouth crawled the great serpent, consuming his body as it came, until only the head remained. The movement of the vast creature caused the churning of the primal waters, from which the sacred drink of immortality was formed. Like many great mythological serpents, the Ananta will destroy creation at the end of each age. Its mouths spew forth fire and its bite is poisonous, bringing instant death. Yet, at times, it will coil itself in such a way that the sun god Vishnu may sleep in the shade of seven of its mighty heads.

ANAYE

The Anaye or Alien gods of the Navaho Indians of south-west North America were of a monstrous and titanic nature. They included the headless Thelgeth, the feather-backed Tsenahale and the Binaye Ahani – twins without legs and arms who killed with their eyes. All the Anaye were killed except for Old Age, Poverty, Cold and Famine who were allowed to continue living so that men would not grow complacent but continue to pray to the gods against the evils that the Anaye brought upon humanity.

Ancient Serpent

An honorific given by the Piute Indians of North America to a huge creature that dwelt in Lake Pyramid, Nevada. Whenever the lake bubbled and formed whirlpools, the Piute believed the ancient serpent was seeking a victim.

Androsphinx

The proper name for the Sphinx in Egyptian mythology. The endless Sphinx was a guardian of the cosmos and an important symbolic aspect of the astrological beliefs of the ancient Egyptians. Only referred to as the Androsphinx when depicted with a human head, it is also known as Hor-em-Asken, a name which may be translated as 'Horus of the Horizon', signifying the rising of the astrological planets. The statue of the Androsphinx which lies in the shadow of the Great Pyramid at Giza is the most famous representation of this creature, there represented with the body of a lion and the head of a woman wearing a Pharaonic headdress.

Angont

A giant and venomous serpent in the traditions of the Huron people of United States. It lived in lonely and desolate places such as lakes, rivers, ancient forests and in great dark caverns beneath the earth. The Angont was said to stretch forth from within its hiding-place to overwhelm unwary travellers, inflicting disease and death upon all who came within its range.

Animal Mounts

Gods and goddesses in many mythologies are closely associated with the animal which becomes their mount, taking them across land and sea, and into otherworldly regions. The powers of the animals are frequently imparted to – or in the service of – the gods, thus emphasizing their nature or deeds.

The magical horse Aonbarr that bore Manannan mac Lír, the Irish god of the Otherworld and the sea, could gallop across land or sea. Aonbarr's name means 'unique supremacy' or 'singular foam'. The white sea horses of every incoming wave belong to Manannan.

In Scandinavian mythology Freya, the goddess of lovers, rides in a chariot pulled by cats, a wonderful image of how love yokes even the most unruly. In Hindu mythology, there are many gods who ride upon animals; these are commonly called 'the vehicle' of the god. Brahma, the creator god who is the source of space and time, rides upon the swan or goose of knowledge which is called the Hamsa. The great and terrible mother Durgha rides on a lion to overcome the great buffalo demon, Mahisha, having no more mercy on him than a lion would show. Shiva, the Dionysian but ascetic god who breaks things in pieces, has the bull, Nandi as his mount, because he has triumphed over the lower nature of man, as all good yogis must do. Nandi is the joyful wanderer who is the embodiment of justice and virtue, which are the qualities which make the strong gentle. Nandi is shown as a bull lying down in many Hindu temples, where worshippers touch his genitals, which are a source of life. He is one of the teachers of music and dancing. The Garuda, half man, half vulture, is ridden by Vishnu, the god who preserves all things. Garuda imparts courage and represents the utterances of the sacred teachings or Vedas, for those who read them are transported upon the wings of wisdom and with the force of lightning.

ANIWYE

This huge and fearsome creature, resembling a giant skunk, is found in the folklore of the Ojibwe people of the United States. Armed with the characteristic pungent spray of its normal-sized brethren, the Aniwye hunts human prey and sprays them to death. It is able to understand and communicate with human beings.

The Aniwye approached a certain village and, having seen it coming, all the inhabitants fled, leaving behind one old woman who was too infirm to travel. When the Aniwye arrived in the village, it tore off the roof of her house and demanded to know where the rest of the tribe had gone. When the woman refused to speak, the Aniwye declared that it would cure her of her infirmities for good: it did so by spraying her to death.

ANJANA

One of the sacred white elephants of the Hindu mythology of India. Anjana, also known as Saumanasa, is the guardian of the Western quadrant of the world with the god Varuna standing on his back. (*See also* Airavata.)

ANJING AJAK

The name of a giant werewolf in the folklore of the people of Java. Like its Western counterpart, it is considered a human being whose evil nature transforms it into the shape of a great wolf with a taste for human flesh.

ANT

Ants are considered sacred among numerous cultures, and are especially prized for their industry, thrift, providence and forethought. In Chinese lore, the ant is considered a righteous creature and represents orderliness, patriotism and subordination to authority. However, since white ants can damage the rice crops, the god of war is sometimes invoked against them.

Among the Hindu, the ant is an example of the transience of existence, and is associated with the cult of the dead. In Zoroastrianism, the ant belongs to the dark forces of Ahriman and is the enemy of agriculture. In classical Greek tradition, the formidable Myrmidon warriors were said to be descended from ants or, according to Strabo, they were men transformed into ants after a plague had decimated the island where they lived. Among the Native American people, ants are respected for their patience, planning, building skills and aggression coupled with stamina. Quetzalcoatl, the Central American god of the elements, turned himself into an ant to steal

King Solomon once came with many men on a flying carpet to the Valley of the Ants, and they discovered to their horror that these insects were as large as wolves. However, the ants were equally terrified by the sight of the king's flying carpet and the people on it, for they had never before seen human beings. A queen governed these ants, and when she discovered the exalted status of her visitor, she ordered her subjects to pay their respects to the king. When King Solomon landed and stepped from his carpet, all the ants sang out in unison: 'Long live the king of all the animals and insects. Praise the Lord!' Then the King of the humans and the Queen of the ants greeted one another cautiously. Solomon asked if there was anything they feared. 'I fear only God,' replied the Queen, 'In case of danger my soldier ants would gladly sacrifice their lives on my behalf.' On another occasion, Solomon heard how the ants had dug a pit so that an elephant fell into it, where it was consumed. They did this because the elephants had boasted that it was the duty of the ants to avoid their feet. Solomon admonished the elephants, telling them henceforward to respect the insects.

maize, which the insects had hidden in a mountain, in order to bring it as a gift to humanity. The Pima tribe of South Arizona divides itself into three groups: Red Ants, White Ants and Black Ants, each of which has its own laws and customs, venerating the respective insect. Among the tribes of West Africa, ants are messengers of the serpent god, while for the Ibo of Nigeria the white ant or termite is sometimes represented as a spiritual ally that can be invoked to destroy the crops of personal enemies. Among the people of China, Persia, India and Greece, ants are also the guardians of treasure.

ANTELOPE

In Sumerian and Semitic mythology, the antelope is a shape adopted by the gods Ea and Marduk while Ea-Oannes is considered to be 'the antelope of Apsu' – 'the antelope of creation'. The antelope is also sacred to Astarte, the goddess of the moon. In ancient Egypt, the antelope was sacred to the goddess Isis and at times represented both Osiris and Horus. As a desert animal it was also sacrificed to Set. Throughout Asia Minor, the antelope was associated with the moon and the Great Mother. In Hinduism, it is an emblem of Shiva, and the gods Soma and Chandra have chariots drawn by antelopes. The Hopi tribe have a yearly ceremony in which societies representing Antelope and Snake enact a ritual in which antelope boys greet snake

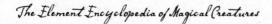

maidens. A mystical marriage is then enacted between these representatives of the animals. Antelopes running are said to stimulate thunder and rain-bearing clouds and, for this reason, they are considered symbols of fertility. The fast-running Antelope was one of the animals that helped Coyote steal fire from the Fire People in a story from British Columbia in Canada.

Several tribes in Africa regard the antelope as a significant animal as it is known to be a form taken by gods and only the creature itself knows where these gods are to be found. The bush-men of the Kalahari desert tell how Mantis created the antelope known as the Eland.

ANUBIS

The great jackal-headed god of ancient Egyptian mythology. He was the guardian of tombs and patron of embalming, and shared with the god Thoth the task of conducting the dead into the judgment halls of Amenti. There he weighed the hearts of the dead against the father of truth. Anubis was originally seen as a god of the Underworld but was replaced later by Osiris, becoming, with his brother Upuaut, a son or attendant of the newer god. He is generally por-trayed in canine form, though the species, whether dog or jackal, has yet to be accurately identified. He is always shown with a jet-black coat, which represents the discoloration of the body after it is soaked in a solution of the carbonate salt natron during the process of mummification. Black also suggests the fertility of the soil and is the colour of the alluvial Nile silt, which produces the rich harvests of the area.

Anubis sometimes appears anthropo-morphically in the form of a man with an animal's head. One Egyptian papyrus derives his name from the verb 'to putrefy'; whether this is accurate or not, Anubis' role probably began with an observation of desert dogs scavenging for bodies in the shallow graves dating from the pre-dynastic period. Anubis was seen as guarding the mummies of recently deceased people from evil forces, enabling them to make the journey to the Otherworld in safety, and his image is often found painted on the doors of tombs or the lids of sarcophagi. Priests responsible for the rituals of embalming often wore an Anubis mask and acted as the god's earthly representative. In the oldest strata of Egyptian mythology, Anubis is a child of Nephthys, or, in later texts, of Isis and Osiris. In the story of the death and resurrection of Osiris, Anubis was responsible for embalming the body until Isis brings it back to life.

Anubis' many titles not only indicate his importance in Egyptian religious traditions but also his function. He is known as *Khenty-imentiu* ('The fore-most of the Westerners'), suggesting his rulership over those buried in the cemeteries along the west bank of the Nile. One ancient text shows Anubis in the act of burying a body in a heap of sand facing west. He is also known as *Khenty-seh-Netjer* ('One who presides over the gods' pavilion'). The effigy of

Anubis discovered in Tutankhamun's tomb represents him crouching on a shrine or pavilion decorated with symbols representing the god. Another title is *Tepy-dju-ef*, meaning 'One who is upon his mountain'. This suggests Anubis watching over the dead from the heights of the cliffs overlooking the cemeteries where they were buried. He is also known as the 'Lord of the Sacred Land', emphasizing again his connection to the landscape. Papyri from the Graeco-Roman period show that Anubis was eventually transformed into a cosmic deity ruling over the sky and Earth. He is even seen as bringing light to the human race, and latterly as manufacturing effective love potions. On the walls of the catacombs of Alexandria, Anubis is dressed in armour as a warrior and acts as a guardian to Osiris. The Greeks identified Anubis, with Hermes, as the being who represented wisdom.

ANZU

The Anzu or Imdugud was the Mesopotamian giant bird with the head of a lion and a saw-like beak. It stole the tablet of destinies from Ea and was eventually killed by Nunurta. Gudea, the ruler of Lagas, dreamt that Ningirsu, an early form of the god Nunurta, commanded him to rebuild a temple E-ninnu ('House of the Fifty Mes' – a *me* is a power). But Ningirsu appeared in the form of the Anzu bird. This seems to be an early legend told before the theft of the tablet of destinies.

AO CHIN

One of four great Dragon Kings described in Chinese mythology. Together they control the rain and the sea. They are under the command of the August Person of Jade. They live in great crystal palaces at the bottom of the ocean, and are tended by crayfish, lobsters and crabs as guards and by the fish as courtiers. Whenever there is a drought in China, the Dragon Kings are petitioned for aid.

AO KUANG

The third of the four great Dragon Kings of Chinese mythology, who control the rain and the waters of the sea. The others are Ao Chin, Ao Shun and Ao Ping.

AO PING

The fourth of the four great Dragon Kings of Chinese mythology, who together control the rain and the sea. The others are Ao Chin, Ao Kuang and Ao Shun.

AO SHUN

One of the four great Dragon Kings of Chinese mythology, who together control the rain and the waters of the sea.

The Element Encyclopedia of Magical Creatures

AONBARR/ENBARR

In Irish mythology, the magical horse belonging to Manannan mac Lír, the god of the sea and the Otherworld. Aonbarr could gallop across land or sea and its name means 'unique supremacy'. Its alternative name is Enbarr, meaning 'froth' or 'singular foam' – from which one may imagine it was connected to the breakers which strike the shores along the coastline of Ireland.

APALALA

A terrifying water monster from Buddhist mythology in the state of Pashawa in India. Apalala both inhabited and controlled the river Swat in the Highlands of Pashawa, which are now in Pakistan.

APER CALYDONIUS

An alternative name for the Calydonian Boar of classical Greek mythology.

APIS

The bull god of Ancient Egyptian mythology. Apis is sometimes called the Son of Ptah and he acts as an intermediary between mankind and the creator god of Memphis. Oracles are also received through his priests. The sacred bull is black with a small white diamond patch on its forehead; between its horns it carries the emblem of the Sun Disc and the Uraeus, though at other times these may be replaced by the Moon. On its back it has the protective wings of a vulture, and the hairs of its tail are divided into two strands, representing the original two kingdoms of ancient Egypt.

Real bulls were culled from a special herd and treated as sacred. In Memphis, these bulls lived in palatial quarters close to the temple of Ptah, where there were also many statues of the bull god, represented as human in shape with a bull's head. The pharaohs of Egypt were identified closely with Apis and bull imagery, with its inherent notion of strength and fertility, was a characteristic of the stories of the god-king who was often known by epithets such as 'Victorious Bull'.

During the funerary rites of the pharaohs, the link with Apis are further emphasized when the king is seen ascending to the sun god protected by a bull. The lifespan of a bull was approximately 14 years, during which period festivals would be held at Memphis honouring it. At its death, all Egypt mourned as for the loss of the king himself. The bull was mummified and its funeral was celebrated with great pomp. Men dragged the sledge on which the embalmed and bejewelled animal had been placed. Its burial place was in the northern quarter of a desert plateau overlooking Memphis. Vast underground catacombs, hollowed out of the rock, contained successive bull burials. Discovered in the 19th century, in some instances huge sarcophagi of granite weighing over 70 tons had been placed to protect the remains of the animals.

APOATAMKIN

A strange, malicious creature, found in the folklore of the Maliseet-Pasamaquaddy people of the north-east coastal area of the United States. Apoatamkin is generally described as human in shape but covered with long hair and possessing enormous teeth. It acts as a means of frightening children, ensuring that they do not wander away from adult supervision. Bogeys of this kind are known all over the world.

APOPHIS

In Egyptian mythology, Apophis is the name of the great cosmic moon serpent that coils around the heavens. It emerged from the great abyss at the time of the creation, omitting a great roar that still echoes across the universe. Every night it tries to deny light to the world by capturing the sun god as he journeys in his celestial boat across the sky. With the help of the guardian serpent Mehen, Ra always escapes – and in the struggle that follows, Apophis' blood stains the sky red. Occasionally Ra may be captured briefly, resulting in an eclipse of the sun.

Tomb paintings from the earliest period of Egyptian history depict the god sailing in his sun boat through a gap in the Western mountains, behind which Apophis lurks, its vast mouth open wide. Apophis is represented in a number of different ways, each more terrifying than the last. Sometimes he is a serpent with the head of a man, and sometimes he is a crocodile, his body strangely twisted and contorted. So terrible is Apophis' nature that he is said to represent darkness, storms and death. He is also an ally of Set, the god of evil. Eventually, Apophis is captured and bound by the god Horus. The god Osiris then chopped him into small pieces, which were allowed to float away on the Nile. (*See also* Mehen, Nagas, Rahu and Tiamat.)

The Element Encyclopedia of Magical Creatures

Apocalyptic Beasts

The idea of the Apocalypse, the end of the world, has been associated in many cultures with the appearance of great beasts that consume the whole of creation and bring an end to time. The best known in the West are undoubtedly the four Beasts of the Apocalypse described by St John. The implication is that there are many of these, but only three are described in detail. The first beast rises from the sea and has the body of a leopard, the feet of a bears and seven heads like those of the hydra, each with lion's jaws. Each head has ten horns, bearing ten crowns. The second beast comes from the earth, and is described as having a similar appearance to the first but with a single head. Its horns are shorter and it has the voice of a dragon. The third creature is called the 'Scarlet Beast', and shares its appearance with that of the beasts from the sea and the land, except that it is red.

Other apocalyptic creatures described in the Bible include the Tetramorphs, an ox, a man, a lion and an eagle, who together surround the throne of Christ; later they were to be seen as symbols of the four evangelists: Mark (the lion) representing Christ's dignity, Luke (the winged ox) signifying sacrifice, Matthew (the man) representing the priesthood of Christ, and John (the eagle) symbolizing the Ascension and divinity of Christ. There are also four great horses: the white horse (conquest), the red horse (war), the black horse (famine) and the pale horse (death). Together these represent divine wrath and retribution and are ridden by the Horsemen of the Apocalypse.

The Old Testament mentions such mythical creatures as Leviathan, Behemoth and the Hayoth, all of which have apocalyptic aspects. In Greek mythology, the Titans, and in Hindu myths, the Asuras, are creatures that seem to represent the forces of creation out of control and rising up to overwhelm humanity.

In Islamic tradition, it is the heavenly cockerel, whose feet are upon the first sphere of heaven and whose head is in the seventh heaven just below the throne of Allah, who announces the world's end. On the final day, the heavenly cockerel will crow for the last time and that will be the signal for the announcing angel to command that the dead rise up.

Apotharni

An estranged race of centaur-like beings, referred to in a work published in the 16th century, that are half human, half horse, like the centaurs of classical Greek and Roman mythology. Unlike centaurs the Apotharni are both male and female (centaurs are only male).

Apsaras

The Apsaras are beautiful water nymphs in Hindu mythology, who made their appearance at the time of the Churning of the Water of creation and now dance in heaven before the throne of Indra. They are particularly associated with the fig and banana trees, and passers by may hear them playing lutes and cymbals. They are companions to the Gandhavas, spirits of air and music. Tradition describes them as the consorts given as reward to the heroic dead at the time of their arrival in Paradise. Perhaps because of this, no single group of beings would take them as wives, and this gave rise to a belief in their promiscuous behaviour. Their other attributes include bestowing good fortune in games of chance and causing madness or derangement in those who hear their music. They live in the water with plants and trees, or, if on land, with peacocks and arjuna trees.

Aptaleon

In Babylonian myth, the Aptaleon was a beast with a goat's body and two serrated horns with which it felled trees, sawing away at the wood. This work raised a great thirst which was only quenched by the waters of the Euphrates river. If the Aptaleon wandered into the desert and found an erechire bush, its horns would become locked fast in the branches. (*See* Analopos.)

Aranda

One of the names of the great cosmic serpent in the traditions of the native Australians. The Aranda inhabited the depths of the deepest billabongs and rivers, where the currents run so deep they cannot be perceived on the surface. Humans unwise enough to draw water or fish in these spots are often caught unawares; the Aranda rises and takes its victim below in one gulp, leaving no sign that it has even been there.

Arassas

A bizarre creature from French folklore, which occupies caves in the French Alps. It has the body and legs of a lizard and the head of a cat. It preys on unsuspecting travellers.

Arcadian Hind

An alternative name for the Cerynian Hind in classical Greek and Roman mythology. Hercules sought it for the third of his twelve Labours.

Arctophonos

One of two giant hunting dogs belonging to the giant Orion in classical mythology. Its fellow was named Ptoophagos.

Areop-Enap

In the creation myths of the Nauru people of the South Pacific, the Areop-Enap was the Ancient Spider who created the Earth and Heavens by prising apart mollusc shells with the help of two snails and a worm. The two snails became the sun and moon, while the worm, Rigi, was the one who forced the molluscs apart. His efforts were such that his sweat became the salt of the sea as he heaved them open. In other stories, Rigi was a butterfly who flew between earth and sea to separate them.

Areyiai

An alternative name for the Harpies of Greek mythology, said to derive from the cries they made. Areyiai translates as 'Slicer' or 'Tearer', giving a clear indication of the kind of creature this was. Originally, they were goddesses of the wind, as the meaning of the word Harpy – 'to transport' or 'to snatch' – suggests. Certainly they are unpleasant creatures, with hag-like faces, pendulous breasts, bear's ears and bat wings.

Argos/Argus

In Greek and Roman mythology, Argos was a giant with a thousand eyes. Sometimes called Panopes ('he who sees everything'), the giant almost never slept, since at all times, when some of his eyes were closed, others would be open. When Zeus, the father of the gods, had an affair with the nymph Io, his jealous wife Hera kidnapped Io and had her imprisoned under the watchful eyes of Argos. Discovering this, Zeus sent Hermes to rescue her. Hermes lulled the giant to sleep with his lyre, and then killed him and cut off his head. Later, when Hera heard this, she collected Argos' eyes and set them in the tail of the peacock, a bird that was sacred to her.

Aria

A variety of malevolent spirit in the folklore and beliefs of the Maori people of New Zealand. Seen as vehicles for the Atua, or spirits, the Aria were responsible for inflicting disease and misfortune, and even the sight of one could bring disaster. The fearsome form taken by this creature was that of the green gecko.

Aries

A giant winged ram from the mythology of Greece and Rome. It was known as Chrysomallus, 'The Ram with the Golden Fleece', and this was its most famous attribute. Its fate is inextricably bound up with that of the Prince Phryxus, son of King Athamus of Thesaly. When the young man was accused by his stepmother of causing a famine in his father's land, he fled, mounted on the ram's back. Having reached safety at Colchis, he gave thanks to Zeus, the king of the gods, by sacrificing the ram. Its miraculous fleece was hung in the temple of the god. It later became the object of the quest for the Golden Fleece undertaken by the hero Jason and his famed Argonauts. Zeus, pleased with the sacrifice, later placed the ram in the heavens as the constellation of Aries, which rules over the astrological period 21 March to 21 April.

Arion

The name of a mighty horse in classical Greek and Roman mythology. Homer calls this beast 'the swift horse, divine in origin'. Arion was said to be the offspring of the sea god Poseidon, who mated with the goddess Demeter, while both were in the form of horses. Arion was said to be partly human, its hooves resembling human feet, while from its back grew eagle wings. It also possessed the gift of speech, and could prophesy events

to come. Among its many riders were the semi-divine heroes Hercules, Copreus and Andrastus.

Armouchiquois

Among the strange beings reported by the first Western explorers of North America, the Armouchiquois were some of the most curious. Their heads were very small and their bodies were very large, and their arms and legs as lean as skeletons yet straight and strong. When they sat on their heels, their knees were more than half a foot over their heads. They were very powerful, strong and determined and much feared by the Native American tribes.

Arusha and Arushi

Two of the great horses of the sun in the Hindu mythology of India. The stallion Arusha and the mare Arushi are the lead horses, pulling the chariot of the sun god Suraya across the heavens.

Arvak

One of the horses of the sun in Norse, Scandinavian and Icelandic legends. Arvak, whose name in Old Icelandic means 'Early Awake', was one of two horses that pulled the chariot of the sun god Sol/Sunna across the sky, the other horse of the pair being called Alsvid or 'All Swift'.

The Element Encyclopedia of Magical Creatures

ARZSHENK

A gigantic humanoid with the head of a bull in the Zoroastrian religion of ancient Persia. Arzshenk is the king of the Devs, demons and servants of the supreme evil being, Ahriman. They are involved in perpetual battle against the Izeds, who represent goodness. The monster was finally killed by the hero Rustram after a battle lasting several days. (*See also* Minotaur.)

ASDEEV

A great white dragon from ancient Persian tradition. The hero Rustram, who has much in common with the classical Greek Hercules, fights and defeats this creature as one of a number of battles undertaken in order to prove himself the hero of his people.

ASHUAPS

Similar to the Loch Ness Monster, this lake-dwelling beast, described as 50–60 ft long, able to lift itself some 3 ft above the water, and either black or deep blue in colour, was first recorded in 1950 in Lac Saint-Jean in Canada. Subsequent sightings, in 1977 and 1978, have confirmed the presence of something large in the water. In 1978, several members of a Native American family from the local reservation were thrown from their canoe by something that rose up from beneath them. Not long after, two other groups saw what they believed

to be the monster, thrashing the waters into foam in the nearby Ashuapmouchouan river. The presence of this curious creature, much like that of the Loch Ness monster in Scotland, has created a considerable amount of media interest, and in recent years a number of investigative teams have frequented the area in the hope of catching sight of the elusive Ashuaps.

ASIN

A female cannibal monster from the folklore of the Native American Alsea people of the north-west coast of America. Asin lives in the forest and takes her victims from unsuspecting wanderers who come near to the edge of the woodland. She is especially fond of children, and uses her sweet singing voice to lure them into her clutches. Once there, they are never seen again. For this reason, the Asin is often seen as a nursery-frightener, intended to keep unwary children from wandering into dangerous territory.

ASP TURTLE

An alternative name for the Aspidochelone, frequently referred to in early European travellers' tales.

ASPIDOCHELONE

A gigantic sea turtle frequently cited in sailors' yarns from earliest times. In classical Greece it was known as Aspidochelon or Aspidodelone or as the Asp Turtle, though the *Physiologus* refers to it as the Fastitocalon. This dates it to at least as early as the 2nd century BC, in Alexandria, where the Physiologus was compiled. Medieval bestiaries named it as Aspidoicholon or Apsodo-Toroise, while Middle Eastern sources, probably deriving from Alexandrian writings, knew it as Zaratan. It was said to be so vast that it resembled an island floating in the sea. Mud and soil accumulated on its back and bushes and shrubs grew there, giving it the appearance of a floating island. There are numerous sailors' tales which described ships anchoring off what they thought was an island, going ashore for the night and lighting a fire. Only at this point did the creature awaken, and sink beneath the water, carrying the unfortunate mariners with it. One of the earliest accounts is in the medieval *Voyage of St Brendan*, when the saint and his companions encounter the great beast and come very close to being destroyed by it – only escaping because of the holiness of their leader. In this source, it is known as Jasconius. Yet the Aspidochelone seems to have lived exclusively on a diet of fish, which swam into its open jaws, attracted by the surprisingly sweet smell that issued from it. J.R.R. Tolkien has a poem about the Fastitocalon, based on the medieval accounts of the Aspidochelone, in his collection *The Adventures of Tom Bombadil*.

Aspis

According to the legend and folklore of medieval Europe, the Aspis was a small dragon with two feet rather than the usual four. While its touch was poisonous and even to come close to it was to invite death, its bite was instantaneously fatal. It had one weakness however – its susceptibility to music, which could make it docile. The name Aspis actually means 'serpent', suggesting confusion in the minds of medieval writers between this creature and the more familiar dragon.

Ass

The most frequently described symbolism for the ass, or its lowlier brother the donkey, focuses on its stupidity, stubbornness, inferiority and fertility, as well as its lasciviousness. An ass in a lion's skin is said to suggest a blustering coward, or a fool pretending to be wise. The earliest depictions of the ass come from Egyptian and Syrian monuments, and these represent not the humble donkey, but the wild ass – the onagar – a much larger animal which is more ancient than the horses described in Semitic traditions. This beast was used like a horse to draw the heavy chariots of the Sumerians and as a baggage animal for their armies. As a desert animal, the ass was associated with the Egyptian god of evil, Set, to whom it was sacrificed, and in later Egyptian symbolism Set himself was sometimes personified as a donkey.

The Element Encyclopedia of Magical Creatures

For the classical Greeks, the ass represented sloth and infatuation; it was sacred to Dionysus and Priapus and the god Typhon was sometimes depicted with the head of an ass. It was also sacred to Cronos, and Silenus, the god of wine, is sometimes shown riding an ass. During the Roman holiday of Vestalia, donkeys were garlanded and given sweet honey cakes to eat. In China, the Taoist immortal Chang Kuo-lao, a bringer of fertility to childless mothers, rides on a magical donkey which, when not required, becomes a drawing of a donkey on a sheet of paper, and can be folded up and put away. In Hindu mythology, asses drew the chariot of the underworld god Ravana when he abducted the beautiful maiden Sita, and is thus seen as an inauspicious animal by the Hindus. For Buddhists, the ass is a symbol of simplicity and asceticism and is portrayed as sleeping by the roadside on a bed of leaves.

Plutarch, the Roman writer, says the ass was revered by the Jews, because it found springs in the desert during the flight from Egypt. The biblical wild ass was symbolic of wildness and desolation. People of wealth drank asses' milk and, like Cleopatra, occasionally bathed in it. During the medieval era, on 14 January every year, the Festival of Fools was celebrated, and the Feast of the Ass was an important part of this. Sacred individuals and royalty were caricatured at this event with impunity, and the biblical stories of Baalam's Ass and the Flight into Egypt were burlesqued. More seriously, in Christian tradition, the ass or donkey

symbolized Christ's entry into Jerusalem. In later Christianity, however, it came to represent the devil, as it brayed in the night and was said to bring bad luck. This notion was shared by the followers of Islam, who held the ass to be an accursed creature that desired to bring misfortune to its owner and brayed to call up evil things.

In the ancient Persian religion of Zoroastrianism, the three-legged ass is often equated with the Unicorn because it has a single horn of gold growing from its forehead. In the *Bundahish*, a 9th-century commentary on the works of Zoroaster, the three-legged ass is described as pure white with eyes in the usual place and a further two in both the forehead and the crown of its head. It has three mouths, each the size of a house, a further three in its forehead and three more on its body. It is thus able to know whatever evil is being plotted or any attempt that might be made to harm it. The creature is so vast that the hooves of its three legs as it stands in the ocean cover an area large enough for a thousand sheep, while a similar number of horsemen could hide beneath a single spur of its hoof. It is considered to be a symbol of righteousness, a servant of the divine Lord Ahuramazda in the fight against evil. It purifies the putrid oceans with its urine, and the amber that washes up on the shore is believed to be its dung. Its white body is considered a symbol of purity and it is known as a champion of the oppressed.

The great sacred novel of the classical world, *The Golden Ass* by Lucius Apuleus, tells the story of a man turned into an ass for mocking the gods. His subsequent adventures teach him a great deal about the sacred mysteries and, in the end, he receives a vision of the goddess Isis who restores him to human form.

ASTERION

The name of the Minotaur in classical Greek mythology.

ASTROPE

One of the horses responsible for pulling the chariot of the sun god in classical Greek mythology. Like its fellows, Astrope was described as pure white, with fire-breathing nostrils. Each morning the nymphs of Time harnessed the great steeds to the chariot of Helios, which they drew across the heavens throughout the day. At night they were stabled in the Blessed Isles, where they fed on magical herbs. (*See* Horses of the Sun.)

ATARGATIS

In Semitic and Syrian myth, Atargatis was the moon goddess who became a mermaid after having given birth to Semiramis. Her shame was so great that Atargatis killed her lover Hadad, and assumed the tail of a fish. The Syrians would not eat fish out of respect for their goddess.

ATRAOIMEN

A monstrous fish-like creature from Caribbean tradition.

Atraoimen became the host for the soul of the hero Kalinago who, tiring of life on the mainland, set sail in search of new lands, eventually arriving at the island of Santa Domingo. There he settled, married and sired many sons. But the sons grew jealous of their father and administered poison to him, at which point his soul passed into the Atraoimen and in this form he pursued his murderers. The sons fled in all directions and were dispersed across a number of islands. In each case, the sons killed the men of the islands, married their women and set up the heads of the slain warriors in caves so that, in time, their own sons could see them and would honour their fathers' strength. Eventually Kalinago, in the form of the Atraoimen, caught up with his sons and slew them. In the process of this pursuit, the Carib people spread across the islands, where they remain to this day.

ATTERCROPPE

A curious and malicious fairy creature from Saxon folklore. Its name means 'Little Poison Head', and it resembles a small snake with human arms and legs.

ATUA

A name for elemental spirits in the folklore of the Maori people of New Zealand. They inhabit the bodies of other monstrous creatures, such as the Aria or, on occasion, animals such as the gecko. They are extremely venomous. The Atua have many different names and attributes, among which are the Mokotiti, who cause diseases of the lungs; the Korokiorwek, who cause birth defects; the Tarakiki, who inflict swelling to the ankles and toes; the Makawe, whose favourite trick is to drive people into hot pools where they are scalded; and the Titihal, who cause pains in the feet.

They are also known among the Polynesian tribes where they are called Nukir Mai Tore or 'People of the Otherworld'. Here they have a less fearsome aspect and are akin to Western fairies.

ATUNKAI

A strange creature from the folklore of the Native American people of Oregon, Atunkai is said to resemble a gigantic beaver, though it is believed at one time to have been a bear which fell into one of the Wells of Ahuluk.

These wells, which contained a number of great water serpents, are said to have the power of transforming anything that falls into them into a monstrous shape.

AUDUMLA

The primeval cow in Norse and Teutonic mythology, who was created out of the melting of the primeval hoarfrost in the vast darkness of Niflheim, the ancient Underworld. Her name means the 'Horned Cow with Plenty of Milk'. Great streams flowed from her udders and fed the giant Ymir, whose body was later used to form the Earth, while at the same time Audumla licked Buri, the progenitor of the gods, free from the salty ice.

AUFHOCKER

A gigantic demon dog in the folklore of Germany. The name Aufhocker may be translated as 'Leap Upon' – and the creature is often seen to do this to its victims. Once it has leapt upon the back of its prey, it grows heavier and heavier until the person is virtually crushed to death. At other times, it will come upon an unwary traveller and walk for a time by his side, then suddenly rise up upon its hind legs until it is tall enough to tear out his throat. These characteristics are similar to that of the Black Dog in British folklore and the Kludde in Belgian tradition.

Though generally portrayed as a dog, the Aufhocker may occasionally appear as a wild black horse, which invites weary travellers to ride on its back. Once mounted, they find that they cannot dismount, while the horse gallops faster and faster, usually ending by throwing them from its back into deep water or swamp.

Aunyaina

According to the Pare natives of Brazil, the Aunyaina was an enormous humanoid creature with tusks projecting from its face like those of a wild boar. It hunted humans for its food and chased anyone foolish enough to wander into the forest. Once it had caught them, it ripped them to pieces with its tusks and consumed them entirely, crunching their bones.

One day, some children who were being chased by the Aunyaina climbed into the trees to escape. The children began to swing from tree to tree on the vines which grew there, but the Aunyaina still followed them. Seeing their plight, a parrot flew into the tree and bit through the vine, causing the monster to crash to the ground. From its broken body came the reptiles and lizards which now inhabit the Earth. The children were too afraid to come down from the tree, and eventually became the monkeys which live there to this day.

Avagrah

In Burmese mythology, Avagrah is one of the names of a great Nyan or Graha, a giant serpent.

Axehandle Hound

One of a number of bizarre creatures from the folklore and tall tales of American lumberjacks. The Axehandle Hound is one of a group of beings, often called Fearsome Critters, which originated in the minds of men enduring the isolation and wildness of the landscape around Wisconsin and Minnesota during the 19th century. The Axehandle Hound is described as having a long thin body in the shape of an axe handle with small squat legs, and a head resembling the head of an axe. It is said to consume the handles of any axes left unattended!

AYIDA

An alternative name for the great Rainbow Serpent in the folklore of the people of Haiti in the Caribbean. Also known as Aida Hwedo, among the people of Benin in Africa. He is the partner of the Vodun cosmic serpent, Damballah, god of rivers and springs.

AZEMAN

A type of vampire described by the people of Surinam on the north coast of South America. The Azeman is in fact a female, who every night dresses herself in the skin of an animal, and travels around the villages and through the forests attacking and killing anyone she encounters. As with many such creatures, there are ways of defeating or capturing her. In this case, she may be prevented from entering your home by the simple method of placing a broom across the doorstep. Another way of defeating the Azeman is to lay several brooms on the floor of your house – for some reason the Azeman becomes obsessed with counting every bristle in each of the brooms, and is often caught when the sun rises, still counting, and turns to ash.

AZI DAHAKA

The name of a great cosmic serpent or dragon in the Zoroastrian mythology of ancient Persia. Originally, its name was translated as 'snake'; however, the modern translation in the Farsi language is 'dragon'. Ultimately, the Azi Dahaka seems to combine something of each of these beings, being portrayed as a winged dragon-snake with three heads, said to represent pain, anguish and death respectively. Each head has six eyes and three pairs of fangs, and the wings of the Azi Dahaka are so huge that when spread they blot out the sun. The great Zoroastrian mystical text *Shanamah* describes the Azi Dahaka as roughly human in shape save for the two serpents growing out of its neck. Zoroastrian mythology describes the creature as the son of a female demon or as the descendant of Angra Mainu, the original spirit of evil. The myths also say that Azu Dahaka began by eating only cattle, but soon acquired a taste for human flesh. He conspired to overthrow the first human being, Yima, and as a punishment for this, was chained under Mount Demavand by the hero Atta. This is not the end of the story, however, as it is said that at the end of time Azu Dahaka will break free and destroy the greater part of humanity, until itself being defeated by the god Keresaspa.

AZ-I-WU-GUM-KI-MUKH-TI

A bizarre and frightening monster from the traditions of the Inuit people of Greenland. It resembled a giant walrus with the head of a dog, dog's legs, gleaming black scales, and a huge fish's tail. One blow from this tail could dispatch a human being, and the Az-I-Wu-Gum-Ki-Mukh-Ti was much feared among the Inuit. The 19th-century explorer E.W. Nelson heard much of this creature from the native people and dubbed it the 'Walrus-Dog'.

AZIZA

Small nature spirits in the folklore of the Dahomey people of West Africa, the Aziza live in the depths of the forest and are very shy, but the Dahomey have encountered them many times and learned from them. They are considered as luck-bringers and as such are frequently invoked by the native people.

BABA YAGA

Throughout Russian and East European folk legend, Baba Yaga is famed as a hag who rides through the air in a mortar propelled by the pestle, or in a great iron kettle with her sweeping fiery broom. She lives in a moveable house which has chicken's legs, in a forest clearing fenced by a palisade made of bones with skulls on top of them, from whose sockets spectral light is emitted. She has teeth of stone or knife-blades. Her mouth can become so huge that passing travellers may mistake it for a cave and so are drawn in and devoured. She is sometimes said to travel with Death and eats the souls of his victims.

Although Baba Yaga has become the archetypal bogey-woman with which to frighten children, she is actually a primal goddess whose knowledge of the world is unequalled. Baba Yaga can also appear as an old peasant woman of kindly disposition. To those who go to her for help, she lends her mirror, her ring, balls of yarn or a self-cutting sword – objects that enable heroes and heroines to achieve their quests. She is helpful to women and a guardian of good order and behaviour, punishing those who outrage it. Her broom shows that she cleanses and cleans, while her pestle and mortar are emblems of creation and destruction. In the earliest legends, she is the keeper of herds, horses and of farming, and is a primal divinity of life and death. In her hands are the reins of nature and its seasons. She controls the flow of milk from the cow, the fall of rain, the growth of crops and she can devour the sun or moon.

Baba Yaga confers upon Koshei, the dragon in human shape, his immortality. She also controls the fire-breathing dragon Chudo-Yudo, who guards the Water of Life and Death. Baba Yaga's house sits between the world of everyday and the Otherworld, where it acts as a guardian to the land of the dead. The food that Baba Yaga brews in her cauldron is often made up of body parts, which makes a soup of new life to those who understand her true function, but which appears evil and repellent to those who fear her.

An elderly couple had a daughter but could not find a godmother for her. Baba Yaga, in the shape of an old woman, offered to be godmother and took the girl to live with her. When the girl offended her by breaking one of her rules, Baba Yaga exiled her to a dark forest alone. There a prince found the girl wandering. He married her and they had three sons who bore the moon and stars upon their foreheads. Baba Yaga demanded these three children in expiation of the girl's crime, taking them and their mother away with her. The prince followed on and found them standing at the centre of a clearing, near a great fire, surrounded by animals. Baba Yaga allowed the prince to take his sons away but withheld her goddaughter to serve her.

The Element Encyclopedia of Magical Creatures

Babi

This aggressive baboon god of the Egyptians lives on human entrails. In the Afterlife, when the deceased's heart is being weighed in the heart ceremony in the Hall of Two Truths, and when it is decided that wherever the deceased will be able to enter paradise, it is necessary to invoke spells to ward off the attentions of Babi. However, in this life, Babi will help defend against snakes and control turbulent waters.

Baboon

The male baboon with its colourful behind and facial mobility gives rise to myths which stress its supposed aggressive and lascivious qualities. The baboon god Babi's phallus becomes the bolt of the door of heaven and is also the mast of the ferryman's boat in the Underworld that conveys the dead towards their judgement. However, it is the baboon's reverence of the rising sun, when it stands up and chitters as the first rays fall that cause him to be associated with Thoth, god of wisdom.

Bacchis

Bacchis was the bull god worshipped by the Egyptians at Hermonthus, one of many shrines to bovine deities.

Backahast

A Scandinavian water horse that lives in rivers and freshwater lakes, the Backahast often conceals itself by appearing like a floating log or overturned boat. Those who are tempted to approach the seemingly useful piece of wood are pulled under the water and eaten.

Badb

One of the triad of Irish goddesses collectively called the Morrigna, Badb along with her sisters Nemain and Morrigan, is responsible for cleansing the battlefield of carrion. She incites armies to battle-frenzy. Badb may appear as a woman but she is most commonly seen in the form of a crow. Badb's Gaulish counterpart is the goddess Bodua or Catubodua.

Badger

Among the Navajo people of south-west North America, Badger was one of the first inhabitants who travelled down through the worlds with Coyote. While Coyote remained with the Navajo, Badger continued down into the yellow world of the Grasshopper people. It was Badger who enabled the Navajo people to escape from the reed in which they were trapped by enlarging a hole that Locust had made in the sky, enabling them to arrive upon the Earth in a little island in the middle of a lake. Badger was also one of the foremost medicine spirits in the south-west, for he is always digging in the ground for roots and plants. A badger paw is worn by women in childbirth for a swift delivery, in imitation of the badger who comes out of his hole quickly.

In China, the badger is considered to be a yin animal, because it retires to its den and comes out at night. In Japan, the wind badger is Tanuki, who looks after the rice crop. He is depicted as carrying a great bell. In Celtic myth, the game of 'badger-in-the-bag' is played at the order of the horse goddess, Rhiannon. She helps her intended husband Pwyll defeat one of her former suitors, Gwawl, by tricking him into entering a bottomless bag. Once inside it, Gwawl is beaten with sticks by Pwyll's men. He begs to be let out and Rhiannon lets him go only after he has promised to bother her no more.

Kenneth Grahame's children's book, *The Wind in the Willows*, has given many their lasting love of the badger from the depiction of wise old Badger who lives like a hermit in the Wild Wood but who is implacable against the foes of Toad.

BAGALA

In Hindu tradition, the crane-headed goddess, Bagala, presides over poisons, black magic and deceitful forms of death. She incites people to torment each other, and has the tongues of enemies in her right hand while in her left she has instruments of torture. Sometimes she has a mace and is dressed in yellow.

BAHAMUT

A great creature whose duty, in Islamic mythology, is to support the Earth. Bahamut takes the form of a bright fish with the head of an elephant or hippopotamus. On Bahamut's back is a layer of sand on which stands a giant bull called Kujata; on the bull's forehead is a mountain of rock which is a vessel for all the waters of the globe. In these waters, the Earth itself grew. Beneath Bahumut was a serpent of even greater size called Falak who held all the fires of hell. In another story, there was a ruby on the bull's back on which stood an angel who held the six hells, the Earth and the seven heavens.

BAKBAKWAKANOOKSIEWAE

Among the Kwakiutl of north-west Canada lives a great bird called Bakbakwakanooksiewae ('the Cannibal at the North End of the World'). His other name is Hokhoku. With his wife Galokwudzuwis, he pursues human beings, smashing in their skulls and devouring the exposed brains. The Kwakiutl enact a dance in which a youth is captured and transformed into Bakbakwakanooksiewae, wearing a beaked mask.

Bakru

Bakru are the South American fairies that are created by magic to be familiars. They can be bought from magicians by the pair, and have the appearance of human children, though they are partially made of wood. It is not considered worth the trouble using them, since they are so troublesome. Only a powerful magician can keep them under control.

Baku

In Japan, Baku is a great tapir with the body of a horse, the head of a lion, and the legs and paws of a tiger. His duty is to devour the nightmares that human beings have, so dreamers call on him to scavenge their bad dreams. Baku ensures that the day can then begin in peace and without the shadow of nightmarish fear. All you have to do is invoke him with 'Devour them, O Baku'.

Bali

In Hindu myth, Bali was the name of a giant prince of apes and monkeys. He had his birth from the hair of his mother, and resembled a hairy man with a long tail. He attempted to overthrow the rule of his stepbrother, Sugriva. This usurpation was punished by the gods who sent Rama to shoot him.

Balor

Balor was the leader of the Primaeval Fomorian people, an Irish giant of such hideous aspect that he is known as 'Balor of the Evil Eye'. He acquired the ability to petrify and disempower people when he was a child. He peered into a forbidden room when his father's druids were creating a powerful potion in the cauldron. As the potion bubbled to the boil, drops spurted out into his eye, which forever afterwards had the ability to bring fear and havoc to all who looked upon it. It was so baleful that Balor kept it lidded. When he needed to look with that eye, four men were required to lift up the lid.

Balor was the lord of Tory Island off the western coast of Ireland. Here he kept his beautiful daughter confined, safe from the society of men, because of a prophecy that his own grandchild would kill him. Cian swam out to the island and slept with the giant's daughter, making her pregnant with triplets. She put the infants into a boat to save them from the wrath of Balor, but two of them drowned. The surviving child became Lugh Lamhfada. One day, the giant saw the young boy Lugh perform an athletic feat with his spear and gave him his nickname 'Lamhfada' (Long-Arm), not knowing him to be his own grandson. When the boy grew up, he defeated Balor in battle. Just as he was about to strike off his grandfather's head, Balor begged Lugh to place the severed head above his own and he would become all-powerful. Fortunately, Lugh didn't listen to his blandishments, for the severed head of Balor would have grafted itself onto Lugh's own body. Lugh flung the head into the depths of the sea so that Balor could quell no more people with his evil glance.

BANEBDJEDET

The Egyptian ram god has a name meaning 'the Soul Lord of Mendes'. Mendes, in present-day Tell-el-Ruba in Egypt, had its own cemetery for the burial of sacred rams. Banebdjedet was the god to whom god-judges appealed when Horus and Set struggled for possession of the throne. He was partial to Set who he felt should win since he was the elder brother of Horus. Banebdjedet is the consort of Hatmehyt.

BANNIK

The fairy or spirit that looks after saunas, bathhouses and freshwater ponds in Russia. He despises Christian symbols and will not enter any building where they are displayed. It is customary to offer him a pail of water and to vacate the sauna on the third firing of the heater, so that the Bannik may have his own bath. Banniks creep under the sauna bench, hissing and giggling. If he scratches your back, it is bad luck, but if he caresses you while you steam, it is a good omen. Sometimes Banniks can be seen if you peer into the steam of the sauna, taking the shape of a known family member. Children were often delivered in the bathhouse, but they were never left there unattended in case they were abducted by fairies. Many people chose not to go to the bathhouse alone for fear of encountering the Bannik who tends to stay out of sight if you bathe in company.

BANSHEE/BEANSIDHE

It is the duty of the banshee or 'woman of the fairies' to foretell the death of an individual. Banshees are attached to particular families and their cry is only

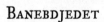

The Element Encyclopedia of Magical Creatures

heard when a family member is about to die. Banshees are reported either to be young women of mournful aspect, or else to take the form of hags. With eyes red from weeping, she continually combs her hair with a gold or silver comb. The very first being to set up a keening cry was the Irish goddess, Brighid, one of the Tuatha de Danaan; she wailed for the death of her only son, Rúadán, and that was the first keening ever heard in Ireland.

There is an account by Lady Fanshawe who stayed in the family house of the O'Briens during the 17th century. Lady Fanshawe was in bed when late at night she was aware of a woman with red hair and ghastly white face who mysteriously said, 'A horse', three times in a loud voice. In the early hours of the next morning, the lady of the house came in to see Lady Fanshawe, telling her that she had been attending to one of her O'Brien cousins who had died a few hours earlier, at the time the apparition had appeared. It is not clear what the banshee meant by her utterance, perhaps only that a mount was ready for the deceased to pass with the banshee into the Otherworld. (*See* Cyhyraeth.)

BAR YACHRE

In ancient Jewish myth, Bar Yachre took the form of a giant eagle-like bird. In a similar fashion to the Roc, it consumed herds of cattle and sometimes human beings.

BARGUEST

The Barguest is a native of Yorkshire, Northumberland and Durham. It takes a variety of forms, predominantly as a black mastiff with fiery eyes, horns and fangs, but also as a bear with glowing eyes and huge claws. Reports state that it drags a chain, or that it is wrapped in chains like Marley's ghost in Dickens' *A Christmas Carol*, symbolic of the chains of sin. Specific Barguests appear around their own locality; for example, the one in Leeds causes all the dogs of the city to bark when it makes its appearance. It has been suggested that the name has been derived from the German *bahrgeist* or 'spirit of the bier'.

BARNACLE GOOSE

The Barnacle goose that migrates from the Arctic down into southern regions of Europe was a great mystery to medieval people. The most common legend relates that the bird was hatched from pieces of driftwood on which barnacles clustered. These barnacles were believed to be eggs from which they hatched. Another story says that they should really be called Tree Geese, because they hatch from trees that grow near the sea. As the fruit-like growths hang heavily, so the goose swims away into the sea. If they fall upon land, then they die. The Barnacle goose was the subject of many theological debates when it came to deciding whether it was fit to eat during Lent – the period when no meat is eaten. The Barnacle goose was also called Ephemerus.

The Element Encyclopedia of Magical Creatures

Barometz

In medieval Europe, the Barometz was thought to be a kind of animal-vegetable being, a native of far eastern parts. Sir John Mandeville's *Travels* described it like this:

There grows a kind of fruit like gourds; when they are ripe, men cut them into two and find within them a little beast with flesh, bone and blood, like a new-born lamb without wool.

Legend held that the Barometz was a beast with long roots that allows it to graze in its immediate vicinity, but when its pasture was exhausted, it would die. Then the Barometz would be scavenged by wolves or harvested by men. It was said to taste like crab meat. The fleece was used to weave clothing and its hooves, which were made of hair, could also be woven. Sir Thomas Brown, in his *Pseudodoxia Epidemica* of 1646, wrote that:

Much wonder is made of the Boramex, that strange plant-animal … which wolves delight to feed on, which hath the shape of a Lamb, affordeth a bloody juyce upon breaking and liveth while the plant be consumed about it.

Other names of the Barometz are Chinese Lycopodium, Jeduah, Scythian Lamb and Vegetable Lamb of Tartary. Various suggestions have been made about the Barometz's possible origins: some say it may have been a description of the cotton-plant or the woolly fern (*Cibotium barometz*) that grows in the Middle East and has been used to stop bleeding.

Barong

In Balinese legend, Barong is a great dragon with protruding eyes. It opposes the plague goddess, Ranga, and keeps disease from the land.

Barushka Matushka

This beautiful horse was the mount of the Russian hero, Ilya Muromets. It is also known as Sivushko or Kosmatushka.

Basadae

It was said that the tribe of Basadae lived in India. They were men, some with heads of dogs, some with one leg or just one eye, with skins so thick that arrows could not penetrate them. They could speak the language of the animals if they ate the heart and liver of a dragon, and could become invisible at will.

Basajuan

Among the Basque people of north-west Spain, the Basajuan is a trickster spirit in the form of a faun who teaches humans agriculture and the smithing of metals. Living high up in the Pyrenean mountains, he protects flocks of grazing goats and sheep.

BASILIC

In French folklore, Basilic was a dragon that haunted the area round the city of Vienne, taking cattle and people. It had a stare that petrified all it looked upon. This state of affairs continued until the brave knight Fretard overcame it, confining it to a well. However, Basilic was said to emerge every 10 years and could only be overcome if someone saw it before it could gaze upon the onlooker.

BASILISK

The original Basilisk of classical tradition was a small venomous serpent whose throat never touched the ground, with a crest upon its head that gave it its name. *Basileus* is the Greek for king, and this ensured that the snake was remembered as the king of all serpents. Everything about the Basilisk was poisonous. Its bite, glance, saliva and smell were all fatal. In addition, it could spit venom at flying birds. The venom of the Basilisk could rot the fruit on trees and pollute water. It was considered to be the cause of the Libyan and Middle Eastern deserts. Pliny described the Basilisk as a snake with white spots or stripes with fiery breath and a death-dealing cry, that had the ability to drive people mad with its poison. The Basilisk shares with Medusa the ability to strike onlookers dead by its glance alone. There were certain strategies that helped protect the traveller during encounters with it: you might carry a crystal globe to reflect back the petrifying stare, you could carry a weasel which can give as good as it gets by way of venomous biting, or you could take a cockerel with you, since its crowing would send the Basilisk into fits.

The magical property of the Basilisk is primarily the power to protect whatever you want kept safe from theft or attack. Many Gnostic seals of the late classical era carry the image of the basilisk in order to ward off evil, in much the same way that military breastplates carry a gorgonian (an image of the Medusa's head). Because one of the main antidotes to the Basilisk was to carry a cockerel, the creature changed its shape in medieval legend, becoming a serpent with a cockerel's head, neck and legs, but retaining its serpent tail. For Christians, the Basilisk was an ultimate symbol of the devil in his form as the one who tempted our first parents, Adam and Eve: beautiful in form and colour but deadly to the human race.

A serpentine Basilisk appears in J.K. Rowling's *Harry Potter and the Chamber of Secrets*, where Harry finally defeats it with the sword brought to him by Fawkes, the Phoenix that lives in Professor Dumbledore's study. He pierces the Basilisk in the eye, depriving him of his petrifying stare.

BASTET

The Egyptian Bastet was a cat-headed goddess who was worshipped at Bubastis. Her name means 'the tearer' or 'the renderer'. Despite these harsh epithets, Bast or Bastet became less savage and more benign in later belief, transferring her more destructive qualities to Sekhmet with whom she was closely alllied. It was held that Bastet was the spark of rage in the eye of her father, Ra, and the instrument of his vengeance. It was forbidden to hunt lions on her festival day, which was held, according to the lunar calendar, in April or May. Bastet was the mother of Miysis, the lion god known as the 'Lord of Slaughter', and also mother of Khensu, the moon god and Mihos, the lion-headed god. Bastet's myth is connected with the eye of the moon, and her temple, which became the focus for the cat, as it was where many mummified cats were buried in special cemeteries.

BAT

The nocturnal appearance of bats after twilight, combined with their many-folded faces, long ears, uncanny upside-down sleeping and seemingly erratic flying have made them associated with evil spirits and beings who haunt the darkness. The bat was demonized in biblical tradition, where it was called 'the devil's bird', even becoming one of the shapes of the devil himself with bat wings. German peasants would nail bats to doors to ward off the devil. In South America, bats were thought of as the 'devourers of the sun' who flocked around the Aztec lord of the under-world, Mictlantecuhtli, carrying human heads in their claws. European natural-ists furthered the evil reputation of the bat by calling the Central and South American *Desmodus* family, vampire bats, thus making an association between bats and vampiric activity.

In Africa, bats are believed to be the spirits of the dead. They hover around the body of the deceased until doomsday. The Rom (gypsy) women of Egypt use bat's blood to anoint the private parts of newborn girl babies in the hope that no hair will grow around her pudenda, thus making her attractive to her husband when she grows up. Such girls are called *muwatwata* or 'visited by bats'. Bats in Egypt are considered to be the guar-dians of pure water, since the sultan of the bats lives in a deep well-shaft.

In Greece and parts of Africa, the bat was a symbol of vigilance. In the pre-Colombian and later Kogi mythology, the bat was considered to be one of the first animals ever created – the offspring of the sun's love for his son. The bat subsequently acquired an association with sorcery. In China, *fu*, the word for 'bat', sounds the same as the word for 'happiness' and so it stands for good luck. Gifts are accom-panied by a card with a pair of bats on it, to convey health, wealth, longevity and an easy death. Among the Ainu of northern Japan, the bat is said to be the one animal that did not come from heaven but was made by the creator in this world. They see the bat as wise and courageous, and able to combat the demons who bring disease.

BATTLESWINE

The ferocious boar who battle the heroes Hildisvini and Sachrimnir in Scandinavian myth.

The Element Encyclopedia of Magical Creatures

BAYARD

Bayard was the legendary horse given by the four sons of Aymon to Charlemagne in early medieval France. Originally, all four sons could ride the horse which elongated to accommodate all the brothers. Bayard was immortal and could gallop faster than any other horse.

BEAN NIGHE

The Bean Nighe or washing woman of the Scottish Highlands is a fairy who is seen washing the bloodstained linen of those doomed to die. If the linen is that of the one who observes the Bean Nighe at her bloody laundry, then he will not have long to live. She was particularly busy during the Jacobite Rebellion of 1745 when she was observed by many. It is said that those who approach the Bean Nighe carefully may ask of her three requests, but she will only grant these if the questioner first answers three questions to her satisfaction. The more daring adventurer might seize on one of her breasts by approaching her from behind. If any is successful in sucking from her breast, then he or she becomes the Bean Nighe's foster child and, as such, is qualified to receive second sight. Some believe the Bean Nighe to be the ghost of a woman who has died in childbirth. When such a death was likely, the family would help wash all the woman's clothes to prevent her having to wash them in the next life forever. (*See* Washer at the Ford.)

BEAR

The bear is an important guardian animal in many regions of the northern hemisphere where it is one of the largest land mammals. The connections between bears and humans have long been noted, for bears are omnivores who can stand upright, their paws having five digits and with an intelligence that seems almost human. This likeness is part of the Korean legend, that tells of how two animals desired to become human, the tiger and the bear. They prayed daily to Hwanung, the son of heaven, Hwanin, and he told both animals to retire to a cave for a hundred days, eating only mugwort and garlic. The tiger was impatient and could not keep to this regime, but the bear continued, eventually becoming a beautiful woman who married Hwanung; their offspring founded the first Korean dynasty of kings.

The behaviour of the bear has given rise to a widespread belief in which the bear is seen as the one who helps renew the world every spring, for in the species which hibernate, the bear seems to die every winter and is reborn in the springtime. In Switzerland and central Europe, the bear is a seasonal herald of the coming of spring.

Throughout the world, bears are commonly seen as symbols of creation. In Hindu star lore, the constellation of Ursa Major (the Great Bear) was regarded as the source of all universal energy and the beginner of the seasons. They called the constellation the Seven Bears or Rishis (Wise Men.) The symbol for the Great

Bear is the clockwise swastika, symbol of good luck and of the four revolving seasons. The Great Bear revolves around the Pole Star so that people can always 'find their *bear*ings'. In Greek myth, Callisto, the bear goddess, is chased by her own son, Arcas, who failed to recognize her; to prevent matricide, Zeus elevated mother and son respectively as the Great and Little Bear constellations.

Among the Ostyaks of western Siberia, the myth is told that bears originated in heaven. One day when Father Bear went out to hunt, Little Bear broke the lock of their house and entered the courtyard of heaven. His paw sank through the floor and through the hole he observed people. When his father returned, he begged to be allowed to visit the world below. He was lowered on a golden cradle with silver chains into the honey-blossom that grew below, and was instructed to leave good people alone but to oppress the evildoers. At the time of the bear ceremony, when he is sent home again, Little Bear filled his knapsack with silver as a present for his father who then raised him up again.

A ceremony based on this story is widely performed over the circumpolar regions of Asia. The most famous example of this was found among the hunter-gatherer Ainu people of Hokkaido and Sakhalin of Japan, where the bear is central to one of their most important rites. They regarded the bear as a divine animal. Up until 1930, they practiced the *Iyomande* or 'sending home' ceremony. Bear cubs were raised for several winters as adopted godchildren who would speak for the people to the mountain bear spirit. They were lovingly fed and tended until their ritual sacrifice when they were slain or 'sent home', a ritual where they were feasted and sent back with gifts to the divine bear parents.

For the Inuit, the bear is both ancestor and way-shower in the hunt. They imitate the polar bear's posture when they stalk the seal, going against the wind, crouching below the horizon and moving only when the prey move away. For the ancient Chinese, the bear was one of the creatures who could cast out evil. Fian-Sian-Che was the bear who was represented the leader of the 'Dance of the Twelve Animals' in the New Year celebration called the Ta-No. For the native peoples of North America, the bear is a central teacher.

Respect for the bear at the point of death is shown across the world. The Koyukon of Alaska never pull a bear out of its den by ropes or chains and they keep dogs away from him. They slit his eyes so that he cannot witness his own death. It is widely believed among all bear hunters that if they do not observe this ancestral respect for grandfather bear, as he is invariably called, he will not show himself again.

Bear is the supreme physician and herbalist, because he digs in the woods for herbs and plants and because he has the ability to heal his own wounds,

The Element Encyclopedia of Magical Creatures

as many hunters who have wounded bears have testified. A Hupa Indian story tells how Bear discovered medicine for pregnant women.

Bear is also the giver of tools. A Siberian story relates how Bear tried to cross a river. As the waters engulfed him from foot to head, he said, 'My heels shall be whetstones, my knees grinders, my shoulder-blades palettes for grinding out colours, my blood will give the colour red and my excrement will be the colour black.' This miraculously recalls the first cave-painters who ground pigment upon bears' scapulars to create the very first art.

Bear fell pregnant and found herself growing too big to walk. She wondered whether she would be the same if she visited the Indian world. As she had that thought, a voice cried, 'Put me in your mouth. You are in this condition for the sake the Indians.' She saw a redwood sorrel growing and put it in her mouth, thinking that this medicine would also help the Indian. She gave it to the Indian nations and every time it is used in childbirth, they are able to talk to her through it.

From the Norwegian folk story *East of the Sun, West of the Moon* in which a white bear marries a young woman, to the armoured bears of Philip Pullman's modern masterpiece, *His Dark Materials*,

the bear fulfils its mysterious guardianship over our world. Today the bear is one of the most protective toys of children. The teddy bear which is given to young children derives from the beginning of the 20th century when President Theodore Roosevelt refused to shoot a bear cub while on a hunt in 1902. From that time onwards, stuffed toy bears were manufactured. Literary bears, such as Winnie the Pooh, Paddington and the bears of the Goldilocks story continue to enchant us.

BEAST OF GEVAUDIN

During 1764–7, the Beast of Gevaudin terrorized parts of south-eastern France. A wolf-like beast, it drove off cattle and preyed upon people, tearing out their entrails. It was said to have red fur and a black-coloured back. A Paris newspaper speculated that it might be a cross between a wolf and a hyena. Despite having been shot at, it continued its predations. King Louis XV sent out soldiers to kill the beast but even after they had thought the beast dead, it killed again. In June 1767, the beast was finally killed by Jean Chastel; he fired two silver bullets into it, believing it to be a vampire. A film was made of this story, *Brotherhood of the Wolf* (2001).

BEAST OF LEETIR DALLAN

This ancient Irish monster had the head of a man and the body of a vast creature, which swelled up like a

The Element Encyclopedia of Magical Creatures

smith's bellows. It was the son of a priest's daughter who was seduced by an Each Uisge.

BEAVER

In North American Algonquian legend, Beaver was one of four sacred animals that were dispatched to bring back a single granule of soil with which Manabusch, the Great Hare, could recreate the world after the flood caused by the Anamagqkiu which destroyed the world. Beaver died trying, along with Otter. Mink failed in the attempt but Muskrat found a grain of sand so that Manabusch could work his magic.

In European lore, the beaver was the byword for industry – 'to be as busy as a beaver'. Beavers had the reputation for being the source of a substance that cured all diseases; this was held in their testicles which it would bite off if pursued and cornered, so as to deprive the hunter of his prize. For the Zoroastrians of Persia, the beaver was believed to be the Luck of the Rivers. To kill a beaver would bring drought to the area as well as terrible misfortune to the hunter.

BEDIARDARI

In Malaysia, Bediadari is the name of the fairies. They are also spoken of as 'the good folk' in the same euphemistic way as people in Britain and Ireland have always done.

BEE

Throughout the world, the bee has been revered as the bringer of sweetness and light, as people have always collected the honeycomb to sweeten their palate and used the wax from beehives and nests to make candles. In Spain, 8,000 year-old cave paintings at Cueva de la Araña show scenes of people collecting honey from a sheer rock face with the help of ropes. Bees are seen as idealized emblems of civilization, with their organized colonies. Respect for the bee has been shown because it was believed the bee was the only creature to have come from paradise completely unchanged by this world. Their industry and the manner in which they build their own intricate hive has impressed many cultures. It was not understood until modern times that the chief officer of the hive is the Queen Bee, early writers speaking of the King of the Bees instead.

Among the Maya of South America, bees were under the patronage of the god Ah Mucan Cab. Among the Chiriguane tribe of South America, the star constellation of the Pleiades is called the bees. Among the Aztecs, the god Quetzalcoatl goes on a journey into the Land of the Dead during which he is said to become a bee. In India, Vishnu, Krishna and Indra are termed 'the nectar-born' ones. Vishnu often appears as a blue bee perched upon a lotus, while Krishna is depicted with a blue bee on his forehead.

In Egyptian myth, the sun god Ra's tears turned into bees as they fell upon the earth. Egyptians saw the bee as the giver of life, and so they used the bee to represent birth, death and resurrection, as well as a symbol of chastity, balanced living and royalty. The king of Lower Egypt was called 'he who belongs to the bee' and the temple of the goddess Neith at Sais was called 'house of the bee'.

In Greece, a similar connection was made between hives of bees and colonies of temple servants. The priestesses of Demeter were called *melissae* or 'bees', and the priestess of the oracle at Delphi was called the Delphic Bee. The word for a full-grown bee larva is 'nymph' and the Greek nymph Melissa was the first to discover honey as foodstuff. Greeks mixed honey with water to create hydromel, a celebratory drink. They associated honey with eloquence after the tuneful buzzing of bees, and many poets and orators have the nickname Chrysostom or 'golden-mouthed'. It is said that the bees of Hymettus dropped honey upon the lips of Plato as he slept when a child, and that the poet Pindar was fed with finest nectar while he was a baby in his cradle. A similar epithet is used of poets among the Celtic peoples for whom mead was the sublime drink that was offered to heroes, imparting intoxication and ecstasy.

The same respect for honey was found among the Mazdeans of Persia, who saw it as the essential ingredient in the divine drink of soma. The Romans held that collectors of honey must be chaste or abstain from sexual intercourse or they might drive the swarms away. They also believed that sudden swarms of bees alighting in a place were bringers of bad luck: a headless bee was a symbol set up to ward against the evil eye. Among the Merovingian kings of early France, the bee was the ultimate emblem of kingship, and honey bees made of garnet and set with gold have been found in their hundreds in the burial of such kings as Childeric in the 5th century.

In Middle Eastern lore, the bee and the lion are frequently connected. This may have been because it was thought that bees were born from the carcasses of lion or oxen: this erroneous belief was based on the false observation that maggots in carcases become bees not flies. We find this belief echoed in the biblical story of Samson, where a dead lion yields bees and the saying 'out of the strong came forth sweetness'.

BEETLE

Many species of beetle have legends and beliefs told about them.

In the North American southwest, Beetle was the animal to whom Utset, the creatrix of the Sia people, entrusted the bag containing all the heavenly stars. Beetle's curiosity got the better of him. As he peered inside, the stars began to tumble out of the bag and could not be restrained or recaptured. But Utset was upset with Beetle and struck him blind which is why beetles have no eyes. The accidental manner of their escape is why stars seem to be set in the heavens in no particular order. However, there were a few stars left in the bag, and Utset placed these in the sky as the Great Bear, Orion and the Pleiades, so that people do not become entirely lost.

The Lengua of South America believe that the giant Beetle created the Earth. Man and woman were created from the grains of earth that were discarded and they were joined together until Beetle separated them. (*See* Scarab.)

BEFANA

In Italy, Befana is the old grandmother who neglected to offer hospitality to the Magi when they called on their way to Bethlehem. She was too busy with her housework when they called and so she followed them. Every Twelfth Night (6 January), on the Feast of Epiphany, she prepares a welcome for them. Because she could not give her own gift to the Christ Child, she now fills the shoes of children with gifts. She has the status of a gift-bestowing fairy in Italian tradition.

BEHEMOTH

Behemoth is a monstrous creature said to be the male mate of Leviathan in the biblical books of Enoch and Job. So large is it, the bones of its upper body are the full extent of the Dendain desert. In one gulp it can swallow acres of land and the river Jordan itself. On the Day of Judgement, in Jewish tradition, the coming of the Messiah would herald the combat of Behemoth and Leviathan to the death. The flesh of their corpses would become the food for the righteous after the judgement. In medieval Christian tradition, Behemoth was understood to be in the form of an elephant who was under the command of the devil; he tempted humans into the sin of greed. In Muslim tradition, Behemoth is cognate with Bahamut, the monster that supports the Earth.

BEIGAD

In Icelandic myth, Beigad was a wild boar which attempted to master the sows of Ingimund. After a long and exhausting hunt, the hunters drove him to the edge of the sea, whereupon Beigad leapt into waves and swam towards a nearby hill. His great feat exhausted him and the hunters speared him to death.

BEITHIR

According to Scots Highland tradition, the Beithir was a huge monster, very like a wingless dragon or serpent, with a long thick tail. It haunts the corries and mighty mountains of Glen Coe.

BELI

This Norse Hrimthursar or Frost Giant will fight with the god Freyr on the day of Ragnarok when the world ends. Freyr has to fight him without any weapon save an antler and will afterwards be given the title, Beli's Killer.

BEN VARREY

This is the name for the mermaid in the Manx language of the Isle of Man. Her male counterpart is the Dinny-Mara or merman. Tales speak of the two natures of the Ben Varrey who can enchant fishermen into dangerous waters with her singing, or can help them find lost treasure.

A young man called Evan was tending his croft while his brothers set out fishing. He heard a melodious voice calling him and saw a Ben Varrey seated upon the rocks with her fish-tail a-swishing. She asked kindly after his old father who had recently fallen sick. Evan ran home to ask his father how he came to know a mermaid. His father related that he had met her many years ago and that she was fond of apples, a bag of which he always took to give to her. Since he had fallen sick, he had not given her any and this was why their prosperity was waning. He told Evan to take some apples to the Ben Varrey who was delighted to receive again what she called 'sweet-land eggs'. Things began to look up for the family and Evan spent more time with the Ben Varrey, delighting in her conversation. He planted an apple tree on the cliff above her bay where the apples could drop right into the sea.

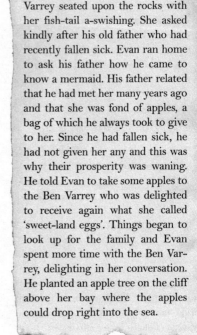

BENDITH Y MAMAU

Literally 'the Blessing of the Mothers', the Bendith y Mamau is the name given to the fairies in Glamorganshire, South Wales. This euphemistic title was used to prevent the fairies stealing children away, but it also connects them back to earlier Celtic beliefs. From the Romano-British era onwards, in the depiction of native deities, we find the Triple

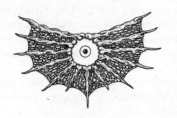

The Element Encyclopedia of Magical Creatures

Mothers, goddesses who are frequently accompanied by smaller beings attired in a hooded cloak, usually called *genii cucullati* ('hooded spirits'). These are the Bendith y Mamau who come and go at the bidding of the Triple Mothers, whose blessing they bear. It is as well to be careful when speaking of them, for they cannot tolerate any disrespect. Instead of bringing a blessing, they may actively remove those things and people we love.

BENNU

The Egyptian Bennu is a bird. In the age of the pyramids, it was represented as a yellow wagtail, but it later became very like a heron with red legs and two long feathers growing from its head. Its name comes from the verb *weben* meaning 'to shine' or 'to rise brilliantly'. A papyrus of the 21st dynasty says of the Bennu that it is 'the one who came into being by itself'. It symbolizes the anticipated rebirth of the soul in the Underworld and was carved onto the backs of scarab amulets buried with mummified bodies. This ensures that the heart does not fail the test of the deceased's past deeds in the Judgement Hall of the Two Truths. It is also a symbol of the sun god Ra, celebrating the sun's rebirth every dawn. According to legend, the Bennu arises from a burning tree, singing such a melodious song that the gods are transported by its sound. Its legend informs the legend of the Phoenix, as related by Herodotus who visited Egypt in the 5th century BC. He wrote of the sacred bird of Heliopolis which, every 500 years, carries its dead predecessor from Arabia to the sun god's temple.

BERCHT/PERCHT

Throughout Germany, Austria and Switzerland, Bercht is the old hag with the distaff who lives in the mountains. She has always been interested in the needs of children. Like Berfana, she leaves gifts for them at Christmas, but she is also the one to whom the souls of miscarried or unbaptized children go. She rides upon the winds of Twelfth Night (6 January), gathering up their souls as she goes. As a young woman, she heralds the growing season, but she also acts as a punisher of those who do not tend their yards, fields or spinning, visiting plagues on those who are disorderly or neglectful.

BERGFOLK

In Norse myth, the Bergfolk were those who fell out of heaven in the wake of angels led by Lucifer but who never entered hell. Some of these peoples became Fairies, Brownies or Nisse, while the other displaced peoples became Bergfolk, inhabiting mounds and banks. They were largely invisible and could change shape. They rode upon three-legged horses and were auxiliary troops in battle but would only fire their arrows when a Christian had done so first. Bergfolk had long noses with which they stirred their morning porridge. Like Trolls, they could steal corn and ale and borrow clothing.

The Element Encyclopedia of Magical Creatures

Bes

This dwarf is an Egyptian god whose chief function is to act as a protector during childbirth. He wears a lion's mane and ears and carries a lion's tail or wears a panther skin, and wields a sword over his head. Clay tablets bearing his image were placed on the crown of the labouring mother if she encountered difficulties. Bes brought good luck to married people and their families, and his image was commonly incorporated into the household where his flourished sword defended all within from attack or threat of scorpions and snakes.

Bhainsasura

In Hindu myth, Bhainsasura is a great elephantine creature with the head of a water buffalo. It spends its time destroying crops and terrorizing villages and can only be appeased with the offering of a pig. It makes its appearance during the rice harvest, expecting to be properly propitiated with sacrifice.

Bhima

In Hindu myth, Bhima was a giant with a great appetite. His given title is Vrikodara ('Wolf's Belly'). As the son of the wind god Vayu he was a strong and implacable warrior. His cousin tried to poison him and dispose of his body in the Ganges, but the serpents of the sacred river recognized and rescued him. Subsequently, he himself rescued the Pandava brothers and killed those responsible for the attempted rape of Draupadi. His primary function in Hindu myth is the suppression of demons.

Biast Bheulach

According to Scottish Hebridean legend, the Biast Bheulach haunted the Ordail Pass on the Isle of Skye. It could appear as a man with only one leg but its howling cries were like those of a great greyhound. Those who had to travel through the pass hurried through it hoping not to meet the beast. A sign that the Biast Bheulach had been abroad was when a man was found dead at the roadside with two mysterious wounds upon his body.

Biast Na Srognig

This water horse or Each Uisge with ungainly legs haunted the waters around the Hebridean islands of Scotland. It was distinguished by a single horn that rose from its head, which is where its name derives 'the beast with the single horn'. It is the only form of water-borne Unicorn in Britain.

Bida

Bida is an African dragon, which appears in the West African *Epic of the Dausa*.

Big Owl

Among the Apache of North America, the Big Owl is a cannibalistic monster who, like the Basilisk, petrifies victims with his glance. Among the Lipan Indians, Big Owl is a giant, a son of the Sun, who tries to marry the daughter of a hero in order to kill him. According to the White Mountain Apache, Big Owl tried to kill all the created people but was in turn slain by his own brother.

Bigfoot

Also known as Sasquatch, Bigfoot is the humanoid creature 7–8 ft tall which haunts parts of the forested and mountainous regions of North America. He is known from both Native American legend as well as the folklore of settlers and hunters. Covered with long black or brown hair, with huge hands and feet, he walks at the angled incline of a skier. Intensely shy and very strong, able to snap great trees in two, Bigfoot has received over 3,000 sightings since 1967 when three men filmed a few minutes' footage of a supposed female Bigfoot. Her arms were about 30 ins long, much longer in proportion to the body than in a human, falling to well below her hips.

The Coeur d'Alene tribes around Spokane speak of Bigfoot as Tree Men with black faces and skin like bear's fur. They emitted a strong odour not unlike burning horn and stood higher than a tepee. They stole fish out of traps and could transform themselves into trees when required. This is not unlike the report made in the 1930s in New Hampshire, where Bigfoot were referred to as Wood Devils, humanoid, grey-haired beings in the deep woodland who can run fast but camouflage themselves by hiding against a tree if anyone approaches.

Biliku

Among the Andamanese Islanders in the Bay of Bengal, where the weather is a predominant concern, Biliku is a female spider who represents the ferocious north-west monsoon. Biliku is married to the mild south-west monsoon, Taria.

The animal ancestors of the Andamanese were the descendants of Biliku, brought into being one stormy night when Lizard decided to hold a dancing party. He became so wild and strong that everyone grew frightened. Whenever anyone tried to catch him, Lizard threw them into the sea, turning them into all kinds of fish and turtles. The one who stopped him was Berep, a crab. Biliku's son was the great hunting spider, Da Tengat, who brought the first cooking and who caused the first darkness.

BILLDAD

In North American lumberjack lore, the Billdad is a beaver-sized creature with large hind-legs like a kangaroo or hare, webbed feet and a hawk-like bill. It lives on fish by lurking in the reeds and leaping down on them, slapping its tail up and down until the fish is stunned. Mature Billdads could leap up to 60 ft.

BILOKO

Among the people of central Zaire in Africa, Biloko are giants with snouts like crocodiles, adapted to eat human flesh, preferring female flesh. Some prefer the eyes, others the liver or heart. There are also dwarf Biloko (sometimes called Eloko) with hands like those of the gorilla.

BIRD-MAN

This creature wearing traditional Japanese dress, has the basic appearance of a human being but has a bird-shaped head, human ears, a cockerel's comb, beak and wattles, with human hands at the ends of its thin wings. He plays tricks on people but is not malicious in nature.

BISAN

Among the Malay people, the Bisan is a cicada spirit who guards the camphor tree. No camphor can be taken without her permission. Those who come to harvest the camphor have to approach the tree speaking in *bahasa kapor* (camphor tongue.) A white cockerel is offered to Bisan that she may reveal where the camphor tree may be found.

BISHOP FISH

According to medieval European legend, this great fish had claws rather than pectoral fins. It had flipper-like feet and legs, and its head was like a bishop's mitre. It was first described by the 16th-century Swiss naturalist Konrad von Gesner, who may have been describing a squid. However, the many legends of fish-men and the fact that the bishop's mitre actually copies the ritual headgear of Mesopotamian fish-priests, may also inform this creature's legend.

BISON

The ancient bison of the cave paintings of Lascaux in southern France is the same animal that is misleadingly called the 'American buffalo'. (The buffalo is a completely different bovine animal.) The bison is an immense, heavy animal which yielded much meat, a tough skin and warm hide to help our ancestors survive the rigours of the Ice Age. Immense herds of buffalo used to roam the North American Plains, amply supporting the Plains Indians in the same way. When food was short for the Mandan Indians, their warriors performed a bison dance designed to change the direction of the herds' wanderings and bring them near to their village.

The legend of how the American buffalo were first released upon Earth tells how a powerful being called Humpback owned all the buffalo, keeping them in a corral in the mountains north of San Juan. Humpback refused to share any of the beasts, so Coyote called a council in which their release was planned. Scouts went out to see how this might be accomplished, but the stronghold seemed impregnable. Coyote then noticed that Humpback's young son had no pet. Coyote turned himself into the bird that the tribes call the kill-deer. Pretending to have a broken wing, he loitered by a spring where Humpback's son took pity upon him and led him into the stronghold. Coyote planned to fly over the corral, causing the buffalo to stampede; however Humpback said the bird was good for nothing and ordered his son to cast it out. The next morning, Coyote turned into a little dog and the boy brought him home. Humpback tested the dog to see that it was what it claimed to be, by holding a coal from the fire near the dog's eyes. As the fire drew close, Coyote gave three barks. Satisfied, Humpback allowed his son to retain the dog, but as soon as dark fell, the dog ran among the buffalo nipping at their heels until they stampeded right into Humpback's house, smashing it down. As they cleaned up the damage, the boy wept for his dog, whom he assumed had been killed in the stampede. 'That was no dog, but Coyote the trickster,' growled Humpback, and that is how buffalo were released into the world. The tribe were growing increasingly cold and hungry, but whenever the bison were driven towards the cliff, they merely swerved right and left. One young woman looked at the escaping herd and cried out in despair, 'If only one of you will jump into the corral, I will marry you.' Immediately, animals began to fall over the cliff but one leapt over the corral wall and took her at her word, taking her away. After cutting up the newly-killed bison, the girl's father missed her and went searching for her. He got the help of Magpie, who showed her where his daughter lay. The bison-husband killed his father-in-law by trampling him to pieces. As his wife mourned, the bison remarked, 'Now you see what it is like when our people are stampeded and killed. But if you can succeed in bringing your father back to life I will let him return to his people.' The women asked Magpie for help, who searched and found a piece of her father's backbone. She covered it with a robe and sang until the robe was covering a whole body which began to breathe again. The bison was impressed by the holy skill of human beings to bring the dead back to life again, and he bade his wife to return with her father and teach their people how to dance and sing like the buffalo. Ever since that time, the Blackfoot have danced the Buffalo Dance, wearing the head and skin of the buffalo.

The Blackfoot Indians tell a story that takes us back to our ancient ancestors who stampeded bison (or buffalo as they are in this story) over cliffs. (*See* previous page.)

BISTERN DRAGON

According to a 16th-century manuscript held by the Berkeley family of Bistern in Hampshire, England, Sir Moris Berkeley fought and slew a dragon which had been killing whoever it encountered. He also died in the fight, together with all his dogs.

BLACK DOGS

Black dogs appear throughout British folklore as supernatural creatures who are met on the road by unwary travellers. The calf-sized dog is generally described as being covered with black shaggy hair and having red glowing eyes. Most accounts describe it as ferocious and menacing, although others speak of the dog as the guardian of the place that it haunts. In the days before metalled roads, most wayfarers used lonely tracks and drover's roads which were kept open by the driving of cattle and other beasts. It is widely assumed that Roman roads were the first roads in Britain, but this is not so. Well-marked causeways were present from the Neolithic and Bronze Age when agriculture required causeways with high embankments as ways of leading animals from field to field. Black dogs often make their appearance upon these ancient roads, near to burial mounds, such as Wambarrows in Somerset. Some of the black dogs are said to guide lost travellers along the way, although others can turn vicious, biting and mauling if attacked. It would appear that a black dog is generally a spectral or spirit animal that demarks the boundaries as a guardian and challenges travellers at certain points upon the road.

The most famous literary dog in this genre is the fearsome 'Hound of the Baskervilles', invented by Sir Arthur Conan Doyle for the Sherlock Holmes' story of that title. Interestingly, the term 'to have the black dog' is a colloquial expression for someone who is feeling depressed.

BLACK SHUCK

Old Shuck or the Shuck Dog is a one-eyed dog, the size of a donkey, who haunts East Anglia in England. Sparks of green or red fire shower out from his eye. Black Shuck, whose name probably derives from the Saxon word *scucca* or demon, haunts the salt marshes of this lonely coastline, patrolling the lanes, river banks and dunes that lead to it. Travellers on the road describe feeling the beast's icy breath and shaggy pelt as it comes alongside them. In Suffolk and Norfolk, Black Shuck's companionship on the road augers sickness or death, especially for those who have the temerity to challenge it. The Essex Shuck, however, is more of a guardian of travellers, guiding them and protecting them if they are attacked upon the road.

The Element Encyclopedia of Magical Creatures

It is generally seen near the gallows or in cemeteries.

BLACK TAMANOUS

Among the peoples of the North Pacific coast of America, Black Tamanous was the cannibal spirit who was overlooked when the Great Transformer rid the Earth of all the gigantic primordial beings which were responsible for bringing evil. Black Tamanous continued to stalk the Earth, bringing terror as it sought to gobble up people. He was the leader of the Cannibal Society among the Kwakiutl tribe. They met every year during the winter season to observe the ceremonial eating of human flesh.

BLATANT BEAST

This creature was created by Sir Edmund Spenser (1552–99) in his long poem, *The Faerie Queene*. The Blatant Beast is clearly modelled upon the Questing Beast of Arthurian legend. It was the offspring of Cerberus and Chimaera, having assorted parts of both creatures, with hundreds of venomous tongues which gave a terrific cry as it wandered in the woods. It was finally muzzled by Sir Calidore and dragged in chains to the land of fairy where it escaped, creating havoc.

BLEMYAHS

According to Pliny the Elder, the Blemyahs or Blemmyes were a race of humanoid beings who lived in Ethiopia. They had eyes and a mouth in their chests, but no heads at all. These extraordinary folk appeared again in the medieval *Romance of Alexander* in which they became golden giants whose lower limbs were so covered with profuse hair that they appeared like torsos arising from undergrowth! Sir John Mandeville said that Blemyahs still existed in the Libyan desert. The children's writer William Mayne gave them a new lease of life in his *Blemyah Tales*.

BOAR

The wild boar is a most ferocious and dangerous animal, standing 4 ft at the shoulder, with curling tusks that can break legs and tear open entrails. Throughout the world, this wild pig has been granted a special place among animals of power. Common themes in myths associated with the boar include the pursuit of the end to tyranny, the test of great courage, the elimination of evil customs, the overthrow of old cycles and the gaining of valour.

In Melanesia, the tusks of the boar are the proper adornments of chieftains and elders. They are seen as representing the crescent moon and the continuance of life after death. In Vedic and Hindu tradition, there are many boars. Ruda is the boar of the sky, while Varahi is one of the many forms that Vishnu takes when he saves the Earth from the chaotic waters; he also is the first one to plough the soil.

Among the Celts, the meat of the boar furnished 'the hero's portion' – the joint of meat that could only be awarded to the most valorous. Many stories relate how quarrels arose from disputes over its apportioning.

The trouble-making Irish satirist, Bricrui, calls the Ulster heroes to a feast at his house. At the distribution of the hero's portion, three heroes rise up to claim it. The story relates how otherworldly challenges were placed upon the claimants in order that they might be eliminated one by one. Cu Chulainn is the clear winner, having submitted to a beheading game from which the other claimants slink away. Having beheaded a mysterious grey giant, Cu Chulainn learns he must surrender his own head in return. Before the axe falls upon the hero's neck, the grey giant wielding it resumes his customary form as the clever chieftain, Cu Roi mac Daire and acclaims Cu Chulainn as the rightful winner of the now cold hero's portion.

King Arthur and his nephew, the Welsh hero Culhwch, seek the ravening boar, Twrch Trwyth because it carries talismans of great magical strength. With warriors from Arthur's court and the assistance of otherworldly heroes,

Culhwch pursues the huge creature across half of Britain in search of the magical comb and scissors that it carries in its hairy crest so that he might finally marry the giant's daughter. In another tale, from the Irish Fionn cycle, the hero Diarmuid is killed by his foster brother who takes on the shape of a great boar.

In general, the boar is associated with warfare, as its fierce and aggressive nature would suggest. Thus we find many boar-headed trumpets and boar-crested helms among the armour discovered in grave mounds all over the Celtic world. Norse heroes decorated their helmets with boar tusks to boast their valour. The god Freyr's mount is Gullinbursti, whose golden bristles make the sun's rays, and in Zoroastrian tradition, the shining boar is a symbol of the sun. People swore oaths by this mighty boar, who was the discoverer of secrets and the detector of lies.

In both Norse and Celtic myth, boars who can be repeatedly hunted, killed, cooked and eaten (as long as their bones remain unbroken), to be hunted the next day are a feature of the Otherworld and its sustenance. Saerhimnir was the diet of the heroes of Valhalla, while the renewable boar is part of the otherworldly feasting of the Irish god Goibniu. This sacrificial cycle of birth and death shows how closely the boar is associated to the cycle of the seasons. The boar was sacrificed to Freyr at Yuletide when it is still traditional to feast on boar's head.

In Greek myth, Adonis, the beautiful youth who represents the spirit of growth, is gored to death by a boar.

The Element Encyclopedia of Magical Creatures

This myth is almost exactly the same as that of the Middle Eastern god, Tammuz, who was also slain by the boar while out hunting. The coming of the spring was the time when women mourned for his falling with great lamentation. The boar was sacrificed to Aphrodite, goddess of love; and it was also sacred to Ishtar, the Mesopotamian goddess of love. Together with the stag, the boar was created by the upholder of good, Ormuzd, to help kill all serpents which, with the dragon, were seen to be the animals of the upholder of evil, Ahriman.

BOAR OF BEN BULBAIN

This Irish boar began its life as the foster-son of Angus mac Og. The Fenian hero Duibhne quarrelled with Angus mac Og and killed the boy, refusing to pay the *eric* or compensatory fine for his death because Duibhne had learned the boy was the offspring of his own wife by a mere shepherd. The shepherd picked up the crushed body of his son, reviving him by the touch of a hazel wand and changed him into a boar. At the same time, the shepherd imprinted into the boar the instruction that he must forever pursue Diarmuid, Duibhne's true-born son. The fortunate Diarmuid lived a life of great heroism and joy until he finally succumbed to the beauty of Grainne. The lovers eloped, bringing on themselves the vengeance of Fionn mac Cumhail who in his old age had become betrothed to Grainne. While they were hiding from Fionn, Diarmuid went out

hunting a mysterious boar that had been spotted near the height of Ben Bulbain, despite Grainne's warnings. He was fatally gored by the boar but Grainne begged Fionn to use his magical powers and heal her lover. Filled with jealousy, Fionn allowed the healing waters to trickle through his fingers three times before they could touch Diarmuid's venomous wound. As Diarmuid died, so the slain son of the shepherd had his final vengeance.

BOBBI-BOBBI

In the Australian Aborigine story of the Dreamtime, Bobbi-Bobbi was a serpent who lived in the heavens. At that time, people had only water to live upon and so the serpent created game animals. The Earth was teeming with creatures that could provide food, but people had no idea how to catch them, so Bobbi-Bobbi took one of his own ribs to make the first boomerang. This throwing stick was an incredibly powerful weapon, and they could not lose it, since it always came back to them. The hunters were so delighted with the boomerang that they used it to make a hole in the clouds. But Bobbi-Bobbi was angered with this violent ingratitude and he withdrew all his help from the people.

BOGGART

Boggarts, who occur all over Britain, are mischievous brownies who misplace and upset things. They follow their chosen victims around and make life as difficult as possible – which is perhaps why on certain days, nothing seems to go right.

A Yorkshire farmer called George Gilbertson got on the wrong side of a boggart which attached itself to his household. The boggart spread mischief all over the house, snatching food from the children's mouths, throwing porridge into cupboards – all invisibly. One day, one of the children discovered an elf-bore or knot-hole in the wood of a cupboard. He started to play with it, thrusting the point of a shoe-horn into the hole. Immediately, the shoe-horn popped out and struck him on the forehead. The boy had discovered the boggart's hiding place. Daily the children played this game with their new friend, but the adults found the disorder and upset that the boggart caused about the place too much to bear, so they decided to move. As they were loading up a neighbour came along to ask why they were moving. 'I'm forced to because of that damned boggart. It's worried my good wife nearly to death and that's why we're flitting.' From the depths of a churn upon the cart came an echoing voice, 'And that's why we're flitting!' It was the boggart.

BONITO MAIDENS

Among the Sa'a people of the Solomon Islands, there is the tradition of the Bonito Maidens. These beings live in pools with the bonito fish and are responsible for the going forth of the shoals. These beautiful maidens have necklaces of porpoise teeth, shell money and other ornaments. They warn the shaman when the shoals are about to appear by leaving some areca nuts nearby while he is sleeping. The first bonito to be caught must be washed ceremonially and placed on an altar to be eaten only by the shaman.

BONNACHON

Pliny the Elder described the Bonnachon in his 1st-century *Natural History* as a cow-like creature with a horse's mane and inturned horns. Its habitat was the deserts and grasslands of Asia. If a passing traveller should encounter one, it was not the Bonnachon's horns that were the most terrifying, but the animal's propensity for ejecting such a great load of dung from its rear end that the ground would be littered for more than two acres. The dung was acrid and would burn any trees, plants, people and animals that were in its vicinity.

BOQS

The Salish people of the north-west Pacific coast of America speak of the Boqs as a humanoid being that walks with a stoop on its hind legs while its arms swing to below its knees. The whole body is covered with thick long hair, but its most striking feature is the male of the species, which has a penis so long that it must be rolled up and carried in its arms. This rolled-up penis can become a weapon of attack in its own right, lashing out at tree trunks and breaking branches to terrify assailants. The Boqs has a distinctive whistling cry, though it can roar and thrash about in the forest.

BORAK, AL

This wondrous creature with a human head, the face of a woman, the ears of a donkey, the neck, mane and body of a horse, the wings of an eagle and the tail of a peacock was the magnificent mount on which Mohammed made his Night Journey from Mecca to Jerusalem and back again. So speedy was the journey that the water jar which the Prophet had overturned when he left had not spilt one drop of water or reached the ground when he returned. It is said that the same creature came to bear Mohammed to Heaven at his death. Al Borak was also the mount of the angel, Jibriol (Gabriel), travelling faster than the eye could see. Al Borak is pure white, though its mane, wings and tail sparkle with jewels and pearls. The breath of his body is like perfume.

BORBYTINGARNA

In Norse legends, Borbytingarna is one of the names of the Trolls. In ancient times, they lived in the forests and mountains, and deep in the fissures of the rocks.

BRAN THE BLESSED

Bendigeidfran or Bran the Blessed was a giant, one of the sons of Llyr, god of the sea. His name means 'Raven'. He lived in North Wales with his brothers and sister, Branwen, whom he allowed to be married to the abusive King of Ireland. When he heard of how she had been treated, he set out to rescue her, taking with him a great fleet. Bran's body was so huge that he was able to use it as a bridge for his troops. During the grievous battle that ensued, Bran's life-giving cauldron was used to help the dead soldiers come alive again, although the reborn warriors were without the power of speech. Bran succumbed to a poisoned spear during the battle. As he felt the poison stream through his body, he gave order that his head should be severed and brought to the White Mount in London, where it should be buried as a safeguard against invasion. His men did as he asked, but before they made the final journey with the head of their lord, they remained sequestered in an otherworldly hall for 87 years during which time the head of Bran maintained conversation with his followers. But after one of their number opened a forbidden door, the men, who had been out of time, felt the flow of time once again and they remembered all that had befallen them. They buried Bran's head at the White Mount, which is the site of the Tower of London where ravens are still venerated as birds who maintain the sovereignty of Britain and keep it free of invasion. Bran's guardianship of the land was questioned by the Dark Age battle-lord, Arthur, who believed that no man should keep the land safe save he alone, so he dug up the head. Bran became part of the Grail legends as King Brons, one of the wounded Grail kings who is also known as the Fisher King.

BRER RABBIT

Brer or Brother Rabbit is one of the heroes of a cycle of tales told by African Americans. Like Anansi and Coyote, Brer Rabbit is a clever trickster who always comes out on top. These stories were a means by which slaves could empower themselves by cheering on the downfall of Brer Rabbit's enemies and opponents, and laughing at the clever antics of the trickster. The Brer Rabbit tales were retold by Joel Chandler Harris in his *Nights with Uncle Remus.*

A South Carolina story tells how Brer Rabbit and Brer Wolf both courted the same girl. Brer Rabbit told the girl that Brer Wolf couldn't go out with her because Brer Wolf was his riding horse. Brer Wolf was incensed and demanded that Brer Rabbit immediately tell the girl the truth. Feigning sickness, Brer Rabbit inveigled Brer Wolf into carrying him to the girl on his back, and saying that Wolf must wear a saddle. This convinced the girl that Brer Rabbit was telling the truth.

BRIAREUS

In Greek mythology, Briareus was one of the 100-armed, 50-headed Hacatoncheires who were born to Gaia and Ouranos. He aided Zeus in the overthrow of the Titans. Briareus, along with his brothers Gyes and Kottos, was set to guard the fallen Titans who were chained down in Tartarus.

BROLLACHAN

This shapeless, unformed monster is a fearsome creature living in the Western Highlands of Scotland. Its very shapelessness strikes terror into the heart, and the Brollachan assume whatever shape you most fear in your imagination.

The Element Encyclopedia of Magical Creatures

It happened that a poor crippled man called Ally Murray who lived on the charity of the miller had an encounter with a Brollachan. One dark night, as he lay beside the fire, a Brollachan who lived in the millstream entered, drawn by the warmth of the fire. It was the child of a Fuath. The Brollachan had eyes and a mouth but could only say two words, 'Mi-phrein' and 'Tu-phrein', or 'myself' and 'thyself'. It cast itself down by the fire just as Ally was throwing on another log as it had begun to burn low. Sparks flew out and burnt the Brollachan who cried out. The Fuath from the millstream rushed in shrieking, 'Who's burnt my Brollachan?' It replied to its mother, 'Me and thee.' Giving Ally a hard stare, the Fuath grumbled, 'Well if it had been anyone else, I'd be revenged on them.' Ally slipped away with a sack over his head and lay down in the machinery of the mill, hoping he would survive until the morning. He was fortunate because the Fuath had disgustedly gone to seek her revenge elsewhere, chasing a poor woman who had been out that night.

BRONTE

In Greek legend, Bronte was one of the horses of the sun who pulled the chariot of Helios. Bronte was harnessed by the Horae, the nymphs who govern time, for the morning circuit of the sun chariot. At twilight, the horses cropped the herbs of the Island of the Blessed all night until the next dawning.

BROWNIE

The brownie (pronounced 'broony') is one of the small folk who generally act as house spirits. The brownie is a friendly being, about 3 ft tall, with brown shaggy hair and brown clothes who comes out at night to attend to the unfinished tasks of the housewife and servants. Brownies become associated with households in a very responsible way, attending to the daily running of the place, seeing to the animals, tending the land and giving good advice. In any household, the brownie will attach itself to one particular person and be their confidante. In return for all these duties, the brownie expects a small reward which must not be omitted unless you wish to offend him. A bowl of cream, a glass of milk or a bannock of oats or cake will ensure that your relationship with the brownie is secure. Brownies do not much like being addressed directly, so it is best just to leave your offering where it can be found and enjoyed. If you have cares and worries, then you mention these as you perform some ordinary task in such a way that the brownie can overhear you.

The Element Encyclopedia of Magical Creatures

There was a brownie who worked in the house of Maxwell, Laird of Dalswinton. He was particularly close to the old laird's daughter. He had helped her arrange her marriage and oversaw everything about her welfare. So when she was seized with the pangs of childbirth, it was the brownie who helped that night, which was just as well as the river Nith was in spate and the midwife lived over the opposite bank. Taking his mistress's fur coat and the best horse from the stable, he rode through the raging waters to the midwife who, in the murk of the night, merely thought that the servant was particularly small. As they rode, she cried, 'Don't go by the old pool in case we meet the brownie there.' 'Have no fear, good wife,' cried the brownie in response, 'you've met all the brownies you're likely to meet.' The midwife arrived in time to ease the brownie's mistress. So glad was the old laird that he wanted to reward the brownie with the eternal salvation of baptism. Hiding in the stable with a stoup of holy water, the laird poured it over the brownie as he was about to unsaddle a horse. As soon as the holy water touched him, the brownie disappeared forever.

The sure way to get rid of a brownie is to offer him clothing, as we learn in J.K. Rowling's Harry Potter books where Dobby the House Elf escapes his servile employment in the home of the unpleasant Lucius Malfoy when Harry Potter slips a sock into the book which Dobby then takes from his master. If you offend a brownie, you may find that you have suddenly got a boggart in the house, for that is what they become if you are not careful. Brownies do not like any kind of meanness, lying or sneaking.

BUATA

Among the people of New Britain, New Guinea, the Buata is a huge boar with curving tusks, immensely stronger and more intelligent than the average pig. The Buata speaks and understands human speech, which is useful, since it likes to eat humans.

BUCCA

The bucca is a form of Cornish spirit or hobgoblin from the south-west of England. Buccas kept very much to themselves and need to be respected properly since they are spirits of the land and sea. Fishermen would always leave a fish for the bucca after they had a catch, and at harvest it was essential to leave a piece of bread and some beer when the harvesters had their lunch. From such respect, the bucca rapidly descended in people's opinions to a mere bucca-boo (from which we get the term bugga-boo or bogeyman).

The Element Encyclopedia of Magical Creatures

BUCHIS

In Egypt, this giant bull had hair that grew in the opposite direction of a normal animal. Its skin was like that of a chameleon, changing colour many times a day. Buchis was the animal of the god Menthu at Hermonthis.

BUCKLAND SHAG

Buckland Shag is the name for a water horse in Devon, England. It emerges from the water to trample its victims to death in a horrible manner. The red-stained rocks of that part of Devon are said to be the bloodstains of its victims. Its depredations ended when the Vicar of Buckland exorcized the beast with bell, book and candle, after which it troubled travellers no more.

BUFFALO

The buffalo is a bovine species most commonly found in warmer latitudes. What people call 'buffalo' in North America are really bison. Buffalo, in common with other cows and bulls, share qualities of life-sustaining fertility and gentleness as well as of virile power and wildness. Among the Zulus of Southern Africa, the buffalo is believed to be able to possess the soul of a human. The young men who tend the buffalo herds frequently draw blood from the vein of a living creature in order to partake of the animal's strength and endurance. In many parts of Africa, it is only the male buffalo that

is sacrificed and eaten, and sometimes only once a year. Among the Baule people of the Ivory Coast, Goli is name of the water buffalo, the protector of the village. Among the Senufo of the Ivory Coast, the buffalo Nasolo is an initiator. In Asia, black buffalo were sacrificed to the god of the chase, while the buffalo was one of the forms in which the Buddha chose to appear. In Hindu iconography, the god of the dead, Vana, rides upon a buffalo; in Hindu tradition, the great goddess, Durgha, slays the mighty buffalo, Mahisha. In Chinese lore, the buffalo is seen as a symbol of man's unregenerate nature, which is why the sage Confucius is shown riding a buffalo, symbolizing his triumph over his animal nature.

BUGGANE

The buggane is a kind of goblin which hales from the Isle of Man in the Irish Sea. It is a swift shapeshifter and has a dangerous and often vicious turn to it. The one that lived in Spooty Wooar, the Big Waterfall, had the reputation of appearing like a great black calf which crossed the road and leapt into the pool making a sound like dragging chains. The story is told of how a buggane came in humanoid form to a house in Glen Rushen. He abducted a girl who had been working there, and put her over his back with the intention of dragging her down into the hollow where the waters fell. But, seeing how she would soon be drowned if she didn't act quickly, the girl reached into her pocket for her turnip knife, cut the string of her apron and slipped away before the buggane was any wiser.

BUJANGA

Among the peoples of West Malaysia and Java, the Bujanga is a winged creature, often described as a dragon, that protects the jungles and forests.

BULCHIN

The Bulchin has the appearance of a plump panther with a human face and a grin not unlike Lewis Carroll's Cheshire Cat in *Alice in Wonderland*. The Bulchin was known to medieval Europe also as the Bicorne.

BULL

The domestication of cattle helped our ancestors move from being nomadic hunter-gatherers dependant upon following migratory herds of animals to becoming settled farmers. Cows might give their milk and oxen their gentle but powerful strength to pull carts and ploughs, but people still retained respect for the bull because of its limitless virile power. One of the earliest ritual implements, said to mimic the sound of the bellowing call of the bull, the bull-roarer, is universally used to summon spirits. Domestic cattle descend from the oriental aurochs, a creature so powerful that the Babylonians and Assyrians thought it impossible to tame without divine assistance. The chariot of the Hittite sun god Samas was pulled by bulls. They also pull the chariot of the Roman Jupiter, Dolichenus, who was responsible for the weather.

The Israelites set up their golden calf when Moses retired to commune with God and receive the Ten Commandments. This idolatry, perhaps retained from their time in Egypt, caused Moses to lose his temper, but it appears that the Israelites were searching their ancestral memory for a divinity that was strong and dependable in a time of great stress and uncertainty. In Sumerian myth, the creator Anu made the Bull of Heaven, Gudanna; the celestial bull was the one who ploughed the furrow of the heavens. The insatiable virility of the bull was one of the qualities worshipped in the Sumerian god, Dumuzi, who was responsible for crops and herds. As the consort of Inanna, the Queen of Heaven, he needed to satisfy her desires. This is reminiscent of the insatiable desire of Queen Pasiphae for the sacred bull in Cretan myth.

The Bull of Minos was the sacred bull from the sea, sacred to Poseidon, sent to Minos as a suitable sacrifice to the sea god. Instead of sacrificing it, Minos chose to keep it. Poseidon's punishment for this act of impiety fell upon the whole Cretan royal family. Such was Pasiphae's desire for the sacred bull, that the artificer Daedelus had to create a wooden cow within which she might lie, so that she could satisfy her desires and not be crushed by the bull's great weight when it coupled with her. The outcome of this union was the Minotaur, as the bull-leaping dances and games depicted upon the walls of King Minos' palace at Knossos, Crete, remind us. After these terrible events, the bull went mad and became the object of Hercules' eighth labour. He was able to lasso it with a rope and then stunned it with his club before bringing it alive to Mycenae. The bull wandered along the coast of the Peloponnese before it came to Marathon where Theseus caught it, sacrificing it to Apollo. In this way, Theseus killed both the bull-headed Minotaur and the bull that fathered the half-human monster. These wild games remain a potent feature of Mediterranean life in the bull-running festival of Pamplona in Spain and the many bullfights which retain the mystique of the ancient bull mysteries.

In the Hindu culture of southern India, the bull is one of the animals which was once the guardian of marriageable young people. Young men showed their preparedness to marry by engaging in a ritual contest called 'embracing the bull'. The best bulls were driven in a stockade where the youths would leap on to the bull's back, so demonstrating their courage. This display of machismo was not exclusively a male prerequisite, for young Hindu girls were once expected to tend a bull for a whole year to demonstrate that they were ready to take on the task of tending a demanding husband.

The Egyptian cult of the bull is seen in the rites of Apis, who is described by Herodotus as a ' black bull with a triangular white blaze upon his forehead, with the shadow-shape of a falcon upon his back, and a beetle upon his tongue'.

Apis was regarded as the conception of his cow-mother from a ray of the moon. He was seen as the avatar of Osiris, and 'the second life and servant' of Ptah, the creating god. The Roman poet Virgil describes the contemporary sacrifice of a bull in Canopus, Egypt, which was pole-axed and laid enclosed in a temple with four windows open to the four winds:

Soon the flesh of the animal's body begins to heat and to ferment … A cloud of insects emerges from it, crawling, vibrating their wings and launching into the air with a great noise.

This sacrifice was made before the coming of the swallows every year. The bull god Menwer was worshipped at Heliopolis while the bull god Bacchis was venerated at Hermonthus.

In Mithraic mythology, the central liberating act of the Persian god Mithras is his slaying of the bull, as a symbol of his supremacy over his animal nature. Mithraic candidates to his cult were initiated by standing in the *taurobolium*, a pit over which is laid a grating, through which trickled down the blood of the bull, so that they might partake of the mystery of Mithras's liberation.

BUNYIP

According to Australian aboriginal legend, the Bunyip (or Bunyee Bunyee) appear in many different forms. The most common features of all kinds are a horse-like tail, and flippers and tusks like those of a walrus. It inhabits swamps, creeks, lakes and billabongs. Like many Dreamtime animals, the Bunyip is fiercely antagonistic to human beings, and defends its home from invasion by devouring people at night. Its loud bellowing cry warns aboriginal people to avoid a water source if a Bunyip has his *gunyah* (home) within it.

Aboriginal legend tells how the Bunyip was created a man first of all but Biami, one of the wisest men created by Rainbow Serpent, had him banished from the tribe after he had eaten his own totem animal. Exiled and angry, Bunyip decided to make life unhappy for the tribes. Lurking in the gloom by day and hiding in deep water-holes, he emerged at night to bring terror to sleeping people, creeping up and devouring them. Some of the younger tribal women decided to test Bunyip's alleged evil nature after being warned to avoid him, and they were trapped into becoming his slaves in the shape of water spirits, who helped lure people into the black waters of Bunyip's gunyah. Like the Sirens, these water spirits had beautiful voices and would sing enticing songs to bring fresh prey to their master.

The hunter Goondah went fishing and landed a Bunyip cub. His fellow hunters bade him throw the cub back as they could hear the mother Bunyip bellowing and rising out of the water. But Goondah had promised meat for his girlfriend. He ran with the cub until he reached his sweetheart, but he was being followed by rising water drawn up by the mother Bunyip. Dropping the cub, he headed for a red gum tree, which he climbed with his girlfriend. As the water swirled higher, he looked down at his feet to see that they were feet no longer and that he, his sweetheart and friends had been turned into black swans.

The elders of a tribe wondered what had become of their young hunters, as they had not returned from hunting. On investigation, the elders found that the hunters' tracks stopped at the edge of a lagoon. One elder dreamed that the missing men were held in a cave near the lagoon and a rescue was mounted. As he reached the far side of the lagoon, the elder discovered a cave entrance, but then two Bunyee Bunyee arose from the waters: four times the size of large dogs, covered with grey hair, with stumpy tails, four hooved legs, large teeth and tusks like a wild boar. The elder followed a line of footprints into the dark cave, stepping over many bones and there he found the missing hunters. They were grieved that he had

been caught as well, but the elder had left instructions behind him, telling the rest of the rescue party to follow at a distance and listen well. With his yam-stick he struck the ceiling of the cave until an answering sound of digging could be heard from above. A fishing net was passed down from above enabling the young men and their rescuer to be drawn up and escape from the devouring Bunyee Bunyees.

The white settlers of Australia perceived the Bunyip more as a herbivorous grazing animal, with a dog-like face and long shaggy coat, although some have been reported with a long-maned neck. Sightings of dog-faced Bunyips come largely from Victoria and Australian Capital Territory, as well as a few off Tasmania. One report of 1852 described the dog-faced Bunyip as about 4 ft long with a bulldog-like head and black shaggy fur, while another report describes it as being the size of a full-grown sheepdog but with two wing-like flippers. A long-necked Bunyip was seen in 1847 by settler George Hobler. He said that it was about the size of a six-month-old calf, brown with a long pointed head set on a long neck.

The Bunyip is believed by some to be a form of extinct Australian marsupial, the diprotodon (*Diprotodon australis*), of rhinoceros size, that lived up until about 10,000 years ago and which may have survived as a kind of marsupial hippopotamus. Palaeontologists conjecture that the diprotodon may have had a dog-like face and a shaggy coat, both features of the Bunyip. A recent Australian stamp was issued depicting the shaggy-coated, dog-faced Bunyip with scales on the upper part of its body, claws and a large tail.

BURACH BHADI

On the Western Isles of Scotland, Burach Bhadi was a serpentine leech or worm with nine eyes on the top of its head. Living in the shallow water inlets and lochs, it could make its way inland up streams and ditches. Whoever was riding beside these waters had to take care that the horse's scent did not bring the Burach Bhadi to the surface. If it did, the great leech would attach itself to the horse's legs pulling horse and rider under to be consumed at leisure. The Burach Bhadi is also known as the Wizard's Shackle, from the way that its sucking mouth grapples on to the limbs of horses.

BURU

The Buru is a reptilian monster that walks the swampy valleys of the Himalayas. In 1947, it was reported by the Apu Tani people to Professor Christopher van Funer-Haimendorf. They said that the monster was about 15 ft long from head to tail. It has a triangular head with flattened teeth, except for the four fangs in its upper and lower jaws. It has armour-plates along its back and tail, and stumpy legs with strong clawed feet. Its skin is a bluish-black, mottled all over, with a pale underbelly.

The Element Encyclopedia of Magical Creatures

BUSSE

In medieval European lore, the Busse was a creature whose body was like that of a bull, though it had the antlers and head of a stag. This hybrid creature could change colour when it was being pursued, skilfully camouflaging its whereabouts to confuse the hunter.

BUTO

This Egyptian snake goddess was worshipped in the Lower Egyptian delta at Buto. She was the nurse of Horus. Arising from the front of every Pharaonic crown, Buto is shown as the protective snake, the cobra in the rearing-up pose of the uraeus.

BUTTERFLY

The butterfly's extraordinary metamorphosis has been a symbol in almost every culture of transformation and rebirth. For the Aztecs, the butterfly was especially associated with women who had died in childbirth. The Aztec goddess of sacrifice Itzpapalotl was herself a butterfly goddess. Butterflies were also regarded as symbols of fire, because of the dance they do when many are swarming together, like the flames of a conflagration of colour. Among the Hopi in North America, the butterfly is one of the animals of the creator and so they perform Butterfly Dances in honour of the butterfly Kachina, with this prayer:

Now for cornblossoms we wrestle,
Now for bean-blossoms we wrestle.
We are Youths, in the corn
Chasing each other in sport.
Playing with butterfly-Maidens.
Come here!
Thunder will move here,
We shall summon the thunder here,
That the maiden plants
May help one another grow up.

This song shows the close relationship between the butterfly and the process of pollination so important to the peoples of the south-western United States. Among the aborigines of Australia, butterflies are considered to be the returning souls of the dead. For the Maori however, the butterfly is a symbol of longevity and immortality. For the Greeks, the butterfly was the symbol of the soul or psyche. The story of the soul's transformation from human to immortal status is told in the tale of Eros and Psyche. In Christian iconography, the butterfly is sometimes shown on the hand of the Christ Child as a symbol of his resurrection. For the Chinese, the butterfly is the emblem of immortality, joy and leisure. When it is shown with the plum, it signifies longevity. When it is depicted with the chrysanthemum it portrays beauty in old age.

The Element Encyclopedia of Magical Creatures

Bwbach

The Bwbachod (plural) are the Welsh equivalent of the brownie. The Bwbach shares the same friendly temperament in keeping house and good order. They clearly have a vested interest in preserving the old pagan ways, for they have a particular hatred of teetotallers and dissenting ministers. A story tells how a Bwbach pulled away the stool against which a Baptist minister was praying so that he sprawled to the ground. When he returned to his prayers, the Bwbach began clattering the fire irons and gurning through the window. The minister persisted at his prayers, whereat the Bwbach shapeshifted into the minister's double – a fearful sign of impending death, whereat the minister took himself speedily elsewhere from that parish.

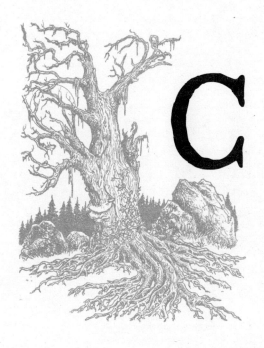

Cabyll-Uisge

In the Isle of Man in the Irish Sea, the Cabyll-Uisge is the water horse that lurks in pools, lakes and rivers. It takes livestock, dragging cattle and sheep down into the depths of the water where they are devoured. Sometimes, it can take the shape of a young man who then lures unwary maidens away from the path onto uncertain ground where it then turns back into its animal form and tears them in pieces.

Cacus

In Greek myth, Cacus was the half human, half spider, three-headed, fire-breathing son of Volcanus, daughter of Medusa. He lived on the Aventine plain in the land of the Etruscans where corpses were burned. Casus' name means 'wicked'. He stole four bulls and four cows, cattle from the herd of Gery-oneus, that Hercules was driving on his tenth labour. Cacus captured them by pulling them by their tails into a dark cave. But Hercules unroofed the cave by tearing the rocks from the hillside, rescuing his beasts. Although Cacus spewed fire at the hero, he was throttled to death with his famous wrestler's grip, 'the knot of Hercules'.

Cailleach Beare/Bheur

The Cailleach Beare is the tutulary (guardian) goddess of the Beare peninsula in the south-west of Ireland. Her counterpart, the Cailleach Bheur, is the name she is given in Scotland where she is regarded to be a primordial goddess, the keeper of deer which she milks. The word *cailleach* means 'grandmother' or 'veiled one', and is still used as a respectful term when referring to an old woman in the Gaelic language.

Cailleach Beare (sometimes known as 'Cally Berry') is a form of the goddess of sovereignty who bestows the land of Ireland upon a suitable candidate who can kiss her aged and ugly form without repugnance. As soon as she is kissed, she turns into a young maiden. She is the goddess Buí, the Yellow One, whose hair is the colour of ripened grain, the consort of the mercurial god, Lugh Lamhfada, (*see* Balor). The ability to renew her youth through seven periods of time is the Cailleach's most wondrous gift. She outlives all her husbands and from her, races of people are born. A medieval Irish poem has her narrating her deeds and lamenting her fate, as a nun retired from her famous and lengthy existence, waiting for the ebb of the tide before she leaves the Earth.

The Cailleach Bheur is her Scottish-Gaelic counterpart. As a blue-faced hag she is the personification of winter. Once she has banged her staff upon the ground, ice begins to form and snow starts to fall. The Cailleach is in charge from Samhain (Hallowe'en) and Imbolc (Candlemas). She enters into a combat with her servant and successor, the goddess Brighid, who finally sends gentle showers of rain to melt the Cailleach's ice and snow. The Cailleach Bheur has a pool in the mountains in

The Element Encyclopedia of Magical Creatures

which she renews herself, like her Irish counterpart. Legend holds that the Cailleach once had several sisters who renewed themselves in its water; however, over time, they lost their virtue and one by one the sisters sacrificed themselves so that one of their number might live on.

CALLICANTZARI

In the folk traditions of modern Greece, Callicantzari is the name given to the beings we know from ancient myth as satyrs. These beings are still said to inhabit the upland slopes of forested mountains. Some, such as the Irish leprechauns, can be quite small while other Callicantzari are giant in stature but have the contorted features of monstrous goats. Every year towards Christmas and during the twelve intercalary days between the Old and New Year, they are free to roam about, but while they are absent, the world tree grows sufficiently to make good their damage. During their days of freedom, they whirl about the Earth at night, creating chaos, carrying off women, dancing with strangers, but any home from which fire can be seen is safe from their depredations. On the island of Chios, it is believed that any child born during the twelve days of Christmas may become a Callicantzaros (singular) and has to be branded upon the heel to avoid this occurrence.

CALLITRICE

In the lore of medieval Europe, the Callitrice was a kind of satyr with a great beard and long, thick tail. According to a 12th-century bestiary, the Callitrice was believed to live in the remote regions of Ethiopia, where it may exist to this day, so steep and secluded are the mountains of that land.

CALOPUS

In the folklore of medieval Europe, the Calopus was the name given to a beast with the body of a horned wolf whose head and body sported spines like a porcupine. Because of these copious spines, it frequently became caught in undergrowth, thus enabling the unwary traveller to run off before it could kill or maim with its horns.

CALYDONIAN BOAR

Also known as the Aetolian Boar in Greek mythology, the Calydonian boar was sent as a punishment to the king of Calydon for having neglected to make sacrifice to Artemis. The boar made a wasteland of the countryside, destroying crops and human habitations. It was finally overcome when the king's son, Meleager, called upon all Greek heroes to hunt it. It was finally shot by Atalanta and killed by Meleager himself. After its death, it continued to make trouble for each of the heroes wanted a trophy from its body to distinguish the feat of its heroic death.

Calygreyhound

This animal is most often found in the books of heralds as a fantastic animal that supports the armorial bearings of titled individuals. It has the head and body of an antelope, with eagle's talons upon its front legs and the hooves of an ox upon its rear legs. The Calygreyhound is often chosen for a heraldic supporter because it represents swift motion.

Camaheuto

Off the coast of Chile, the people of the Chiloé Islands speak of a sea monster in the form of a sea horse or sea bull that is born in the upper estuaries and inlets and makes its way down to the open sea as it matures. It leaves little wildlife left in its wake, voraciously consuming all the birds and animals on its way to the sea. The Camaheuto has clawed feet with which it gouges out gullies and coves in the cliffs. Here it lurks, ready to consume any human beings who are shipwrecked or cast overboard while out fishing.

Camazotl

In Mayan mythology, the bat god Camazotl was defeated after the creation of human beings. He was one of the four great winged beings who attacked the wooden bodies created by Gucumatz and Tepeu that were intended to become the first living humans. They each attacked a different part of the body to prevent the pollution of the primordial world.

Cameleopard

In Sumerian and Egyptian myths, the Cameleopard was a composite creature with the skin of a leopard and the appearance of a giraffe, with two long horns that curved backwards. It was believed that the giraffe, which this description seems to fit, was the offspring of a camel and a leopard.

Camoodi

Among the people of Guiana in South America, the Camoodi is a gigantic serpent which lives deep in the jungle. Its presence might have been unknown to any outside this region, but in 1896 a hunting party came across a great fallen tree crossing their path. While they were thinking how to by-pass this obstacle, the hunters were appalled to see that the tree was actually a serpent too vast to comprehend, as it began to slither off. The scouts with the hunters told them that they had been privileged and very lucky to escape the Camoodi, protector of the jungle.

The Element Encyclopedia of Magical Creatures

CAMPHURCII

According to a 16th-century document, the Camphurcii was an amphibious creature with the body and forelegs of a deer while its rear legs were those of a goose. It had a 3-ft horn sticking from its forehead like the Unicorn. The Camphurcii lived only on the Island of Molucca, where it blamelessly fed on fish.

CANOPIC ANIMALS

The Canopic Animals are the guardians of the dead in the mummification process of Egypt, where the internal organs of the deceased were placed in canopic jars, each of which was stoppered by one human and three animal-headed deities. These animals were called the Sons of Horus and the 'Friends of the King'. They help the monarch ascend into the eastern skies by means of ropes and wooden ladders. In the Old Kingdom, the canopic guardians were regarded as the souls of Horus. Imsety is the human guardian, under the protection of the goddess Isis, who guards the liver; Hapy is the baboon, under the protection of the goddess Nephthys, who guards the lungs; Duamutef is the jackal, under the protection of the goddess Neith, who guards the stomach; and Qebehsenuef is the hawk, under the protection of the goddess Serket, who guards the intestines.

CAOINTEACH

In Scots Gaelic tradition, the Caoin-teach is a small, white-capped woman with a green shawl who wails when there is to be a death in the Western Highlands of Argyle. Her name merely means 'the keener' or 'the mourner'. The practice of keening or wailing the dead was a professional task in ancient Gaelic tradition. A chorus of keeners would attend the corpse of the deceased and set up a wailing and singing of the attributes of the dead person in such a way that enabled the bereaved to mourn properly. (*See* Banshee and Cyhyraeth.)

CAPRICORNUS

According to Greek myth, Amalthea was a nymph or the goat of that name who suckled Zeus. The horns of the goat flowed with nectar and ambrosia. Ovid tells how one of the horns broke off and that nymphs filled it with fruit for Zeus, which is the origin of the term 'cornucopia' or 'a horn of plenty' (*see* Achelous). Amalthea was turned into the constellation Capricorn (Latin for 'goat's horn') immortalized in the stars for her nurture of the baby Zeus.

CARNEROS, LOS

In the legends of the Canary Islands, Los Carneros is the name for the great horned ram with which parents threaten their children when they are misbehaved. Los Carneros appears in an annual fiesta where he is borne in huge effigy, just to remind children to be good.

CARP

Throughout China and Japan, the carp is the fish that represents the qualities of courage and perseverance through struggles. When the carp swims upstream to spawn, it is believed to 'leap to the Dragon's Gate' and become a dragon. This process is applied to the examinations of scholars who are called 'carps who have leapt the Dragon Gate' when they succeed, thus making the carp the symbol of literary or scholarly prowess. The carp is also shown as a pair of fish with one set of eyes, an emblem for all lovers, as well as for marital fidelity, a happy household and many children. In Japan, the carp is the emblem of the Samurai, who are believed to share the carp's stirling qualities of courage, endurance, good luck, dignity and resignation to fate.

CAT

Cats have walked among us and lived around us for millennia. The relationship between cats and humans is often seen as both opportunistic and helpful, enabling the cat generally to be the one who benefits most.

Cats have been central to myth and legend. The Egyptian cat cult based at Bubastis, where Bastet's shrine was to be found, derives from the myth of the great jungle cat which cuts off the head of the serpent Apophis that tried to strangle the sacred persea tree. It was death to kill a cat in such a culture of cat reverence, for they were regarded as being the living exemplars of Bastet. If the cat of the household died, it was customary for the householder to shave off his eyebrows and to mummify the cat's body with the same care and respect as would be shown to a human body.

Cats also had divine duties in ancient Thailand where Siamese cats were the traditional guardians of temples and palaces. Further east, in China, the cat is seen as a shapeshifter. It is understood to be under a curse for not having wept when Buddha died. For the Japanese, the cat, together with the fox and badger, is associated with shapeshifting, trickery and the power to subdue ghosts and vampires. Japanese sailors keep one on board to protect them from sea monsters and ghosts. The Ainu of northern Japan believe that cats bring misfortune because they came from the ashes of a demon who was defeated by the mole god. Other Ainu stories tell how the cat was created to chase the rats who bit off the devil's tongue. Both legends give reason why people should be careful around cats, since they had demonic origin.

This demonic connection is also found among the Zoroastrians who take the perceived division between cats and dogs into a wholly more serious area of debate. They believe that dogs are the animals belonging to Ormuzd, defender of all good, while cats are the animals beloved of Ahriman, the prosecutor of all evil. In Persian tradition, nearly all the false gods are depicted with a cat's head. But in Muslim belief, it is the dog that is outcast and cursed, and the cat that is respected for it received a blessing from the prophet Mohammed.

Among the Romans, the cat was the companion of the goddess of liberty and, as a creature which can exhibit both complete relaxation and lascivious freedom, a symbol for the throwing off of all restraint. In Scandinavian tradition, cats pulled the chariot of the Norse goddess, Freya. In Celtic tradition, the cat often shows its troubling and punitive nature. In the Irish *Voyage of Maelduin*, the sailors enter a great treasury which is guarded by a cat leaping from pillar to pillar. The gold and jewels prove too great a temptation for one of Maelduin's sailors, who puts a piece of jewellery under his shirt intending to steal it, but before he is able to step over the threshold and escape, the cat transforms itself into an avenging bolt of flame that instantly incinerates the thief.

In American Indian myth, the younger brother of Coyote is Wild Cat who is the patron of stealth and scouting. But the Tiger Cat or Cat-a-Mountain is a symbol of fierceness and ingratitude. In Peru, the cat Ccoa is the spirit of the storm; hail rains from the eyes and ears of its huge head. Also in South America, in Chile, lives Guirivulu, a cat-monster who has a tail that ends with a claw. It lives in deep pools and uses its claw to drag prey into the water.

Under Christian influence, the cat became increasingly associated with lack of restraint and eventually with the devil. The cat became the primary animal familiar of the witch, a sign that the cat's owner was up to no good. Cat superstitions are widespread. For instance: Sailors take care not to use the word cat when they are at sea; what you say in front of a cat will not necessary remain a secret; a black cat that crosses your path will bring you luck.

Rudyard Kipling's story of *The Cat Who Walked By Itself*, reminds us of the ironic independent dependence of the domestic cat upon its chosen family, whereas Lewis Carroll's Cheshire Cat in *Alice in Wonderland*, depicts the enigmatic wisdom and seemingly random nature of cat affection.

CAT FISH

The Cat Fish is a Chinese fish monster which causes earthquakes. It lives at the base of a volcano and its upheavals bring all kinds of disturbance. It appears in the legend of Monkey King or Sun Wu Kung, when Monkey and his friends are accompanying the monk Tripitaka on his way to receive the scriptures from Buddha. His friend Sandy is swallowed up by the Cat Fish and when Monkey goes to rescue him, he too is devoured. While the monk prays to stop another earthquake, Monkey finds Sandy making up to a fairy spirit in the Cat Fish's stomach. Along with Pigsy, the third friend who is also consumed, the heroes decide against getting out of Cat Fish by the back door and try to go out the way they came down. Sandy tickles the Cat

Fish in the throat until the monster starts to laugh and spits them out.

CATAZONON

According to the 2nd-century BC writer Aelian, the Catazonon was a Unicorn who inhabited the land of India. It had a yellow-red coat with a black horn and mane. It lived in the mountains, preying upon the lion, which was its enemy.

CATERPILLAR

According to Australian aboriginal myth, the caterpillars were the ones who volunteered to go to the skies to find out what happened after death. They made their return as butterflies.

CATH PALUG

This giant cat features in several early Welsh poems. Cath Palug's name means 'the cat with the sharp claws'. It is described as one of the offspring of the sow Henwen, which having been chased to the edge of the sea dropped a litter of kittens which took to the water and swam away. Henwen resembles the many monstrous Murchata or sea cats of Irish tradition. Cath Palug itself was no stranger to the sea, having swam the Menai Strait between North Wales and the island of Anglesey where it was said to continue its marauding. It was successfully slain on that island by Cei (the Sir Kay of later medieval Arthurian legend) who went against it with a shield that looked 'a mere fragment' next to the gigantic cat. A medieval French story tradition tells how a cat called Chapalu or Chatloup (a corruption of Cath Palug) pushed King Arthur into a bog and then overcame him in war, passing through Britain to conquer it, wearing the crown of Britain. This tale may relate to the early medieval stories of the conflict between King Arthur and Mordred (or Medrawt), in which Mordred's symbol is the cat.

CATH SITH

In the Highlands of Scotland, the Cath Sith or Fairy Cat is a great black cat the size of a large dog. It has a white blaze upon its chest and its hair sticks up all over its arched back. The Cath Sith bears all the hallmarks of the existing Scottish wild cat, being both fierce and highly secretive. The Cath Sith appears as the blazon of many Highland clans which show a cat ready to strike with outstretched claws. The legend 'touch not the cat bot [except with] a glove/targe [a small round shield]', is the cap badge motto of the Mackintoshes, the MacPhersons and the MacBains.

CATOBLEPAS

According to the Roman naturalist, Pliny the Elder, this creature lived in the highland wastes of Ethiopia and the deserts of southern Egypt. It was described as a beast with an enormous head on a thin scrawny neck, making it droop its head downwards all the time, which was just as well since one glance from the Catoblepas meant instant death. This description seems very much to echo that of the wildebeest or gnu. Gustave Flaubert made it one of the hellish animals that assailed poor St Anthony in his *Tentation de St Antoine* of 1874.

CATTLE OF GERYONEUS

In Greek mythology, the Cattle of Geryoneus were the purple-red cows owned by Geryoneus, a son of Chrysaor who sprang, with Pegasus, from the neck of Medusa when she was beheaded by Perseus. Hercules' tenth labour was to capture the oxen of Geryon. He had to journey through Libya and Egypt before coming to Mount Abas where the cattle were stabled, receiving the help of the sun god Helios, who lent his golden cup, the barque in which he normally sailed each evening to reach the east in time to rise at dawn. The cattle were guarded by the dog Orthos, backed up by the centaur Eurytion. A fellow herdsman tipped off Geryoneus about the imminent theft of his herd and he fought fiercely with his six arms and three bodies, but Hercules killed him and drove the herd into the barque of the golden cup. Hercules had his work cut out trying to keep the herd together, fending off raiders all the way back. His most serious opponent was the half-human, fire-breathing Cacus

who stole four bulls and four cows, pulling them by their tails into a dark cave. Hercules unroofed the cave by tearing the rocks from the hillside, rescuing his beasts and throttling Cacus to death with his famous wrestler's grip, 'the knot of Hercules'. The cattle were eventually driven safely to the shores of Mycenae where they were sacrificed to the goddess Hera.

CCOA

Among the myths of the Quechua tribes of Peru Ccoa is a cat who is the spirit of storms. It has a grey coat with darker stripes about its body. Perpetual hail streams from its eyes and ears whenever it is abroad. To avert storms, Ccoa is the subject of many offerings, especially in the time before harvest when his attentions could ruin the crops.

CECROPS

In Greek mythology, the Cecrops was human from the waist up but a serpent from the waist down. He came into being when his father King Erechtheus spilled a drop of sperm upon the Earth. He is credited with founding the city of Athens, dedicating it in honour of Athena. After Erechtheus died, Cecrops instituted many different customs including marriage, monogamy, burial rather than cremation of the dead, writing and bloodless sacrifices.

Ceffyl Dwr

This water horse lives in the mountain pools and waterfalls of north Wales. Its grey body has a spectral glow that illuminates the mist around it. Its method of attack is to leap from the waters when someone is near, hooking its forelegs over the shoulders of the unfortunate wanderer. If the grip of its forelegs does not strangle him, then the Ceffyl Dwr will trample and kick the stranger to death. In south Wales, the Ceffyl Dwr is said to have wings, but these are lacking in the water horse of the north. The insubstantial nature of the Ceffyl Dwr, which looks solid enough when you encounter it, changes rapidly should anyone try to ride it, for it evaporates into the swirling mists from which it emerged.

Celaeno

In Greek mythology, Celaeno is one of the Harpies, monsters with the bodies of birds and faces of women. She has the reputation that accompanies her name, which means 'black'. Like all her sisters, Celaeno was fleet of foot and wing but her terrible claws made her a raptor or 'snatcher' of prey. She was the mother of two human sons by the god Poseidon, Eurypylus who fought in the Trojan Wars and accompanied Jason on his quest for the Golden Fleece, and Lycus who became the king of the Fortunate Islands.

Celestial Stag

In Chinese myth, the Celestial Stag is a deer capable of human speech and understanding. It lived both in the heavens and in the underworld where it wandered in mines and caverns, offering to show lost miners where rich gems were if only they would help it to the surface. The surface of the Earth was not its proper place, however, and should the Celestial Stag set foot upon it, it would become an amorphous blob of diseased jelly.

Celestial Creatures

In world astronomy, the patterns that the constellations make in the heavens have most commonly been those of animals. In Sumerian mythology, the three-headed dragon, Mushussu, was the constellation of Hydra. Greek mythology provided the horse Pegasus while the Egyptians described Sirius the dog star. Half-animal and half-human fusions are represented by the centaur Cheiron who is the archer of Sagittarius.

In the southern hemisphere, the Southern Cross forms the toes of a great ostrich in South American star-lore, while in Brazil it is seen as a huge ray fish. The Milky Way is the Ostrich Way for the Australian Aborigines while for the Hopi of North America it is the stream of stars that Coyote let out of the pot. The Polynesians see it as the Long-Blue-Cloud-Eating shark. Legends of the Pleiades are very vivid. The Ibos of Africa, like the Dyaks of Polynesia, see them as the hen with chickens, while to the Greeks they were a roost of doves. An Onandaga Indian story from North America tells us how dancing children became animals who formed the Pleiades.

While their elders set up camp around Bear Lake, the children amused themselves by making up dances that imitated animals, especially the birds like Hawk, Eagle and Falcon. One day, an old silver-haired man attired in white feathers came to warn them to stop, but they ignored him. The next day the children begged their parents for food while they were out dancing, but their elders told them they must come home to eat like everyone else. After several days of going without their dinners, the children grew light-headed from lack of food. As they danced, so their dancing feet began to leave the ground. They felt strange, as if something was happening to them, but they realized that they must not look down if they were to keep dancing.

An old woman gathering firewood saw the children rising like smoke and called after them to come back, but they kept circling into the sky. She rushed to their parents who piteously begged the children to return. Only one of the children looked down and fell through the sky like a falling star. The rest of the children reached the stars and became the constellation we call the Pleiades, though the Onandaga call it the Ootkwatah.

Centaur

The centaurs had the upper body of a man and the lower body of a horse. They were the offspring of Centaurus, a son of Apollo and Stilbe, one of the Mares of Magnesium. The *cento* part of their name means 'to prick', 'to goad' or 'to wound', and they were certainly known as wild, brutal and untameable creatures, all except the wise and gentle Cheiron; *tauro* refers to the 'bull', although centaurs were really half equine in nature and appearance. Centauros was the offspring of Ixion who visited Juno in the form of a cloud. But instead of giving birth to something divine, she bore 'the most unblest of the Graces'. Centaurs frequented the mountains of Thessaly, where they retained an orgiastic, sensuous and unruly reputation, especially when they descended upon the wedding party of Lapiths, Greeks from the north of Thessaly, who had gathered to celebrate the marriage of Pirithous. 'The Rape of the Lapiths' showing centaurs killing, raping and overcoming the Lapiths was a famous subject depicted in many tapestries and paintings in later Renaissance times. Their passionate and untamed nature made them suitable associates for the Bacchic or Dionysian revels, and centaurs were depicted on tombs and funerary monuments as underworld guardians.

Xenophon called centaurs Hippocentaurs. The centaur with the bow and arrow remains the emblem of the zodiacal sign of Sagittarius. Some have seen similarities between centaurs and the Gandhavas, the cloud-horses of

When Hercules was upon his fourth labour, he was welcomed by the centaur Pholos who was the guardian of a great jar, a gift intended for Hercules' refreshment, which had been given by Dionysus. Pholos did not know that it was wine in the jar, having never tasted it. Once the jar was opened, all the centaurs from miles around were drawn by its intoxicating and alluring scent. The centaurs fell into a drinking bout, growing wilder and more intoxicated on the wine, becoming combative and dangerous. Hercules had to defend himself and so he drew out one of the arrows, poisoned by the blood of the Hydra. Aiming at an unruly centaur, Hercules accidentally struck gentle Cheiron. He tried in vain to save the wise centaur with healing herbs but Cheiron was pierced in the knee and could neither recover nor die, and so he retired with his incurable wound to his dark cave. He suffered for many years until he offered himself to Zeus as a substitute for the tormented Prometheus who had been sentenced to have his liver torn out daily for the sin of stealing fire from heaven. As Pholos was trying to pull out a poisoned arrow from a fellow's corpse, the bolt pierced his foot and killed him too. Hercules buried Pholos and continued on his way to Mount Erymanthos.

The Element Encyclopedia of Magical Creatures

Vedic tradition. Christian iconography used centaurs to depict the devil aiming fiery arrows at the ungodly, attempting to stimulate man's animal nature and rouse his passions to commit acts of lewd indecency and harbour heretical thoughts. But other theologians saw centaurs as symbols of Christ's mortal sufferings who were allowed to take revenge upon those who had betrayed him to his death. In C.S. Lewis's Christian allegories, the Narnia books, such as *The Lion, the Witch and the Wardrobe*, centaurs are part of the train of Aslan, the great lion king, the most notable of which, Glenstorm, acts as the herald of Prince Caspian in the book of the same name.

The magical powers of centaurs enable human beings to unlock repressed desires and thoughts.

CENTICORE

This is the name that the French give to the creature known elsewhere in European heraldic tradition as the Yale. It has the breast and thighs of a lion, the ears, mouth and hooves of a horse, the muzzle of a bear and the voice of a man. The classical historian, Solinus, wrote that it came from the plains of India.

CENTIMANES

In Roman mythology, this is the alternative name given to the Hecatoncheires, the hundred-headed giants, Kottus, Gyges and Briareus. The Centimanes helped the Olympian gods conquer the Titans, becoming their jailors lest they escape and let loose chaos upon the world once again.

CENTIPEDE

In Japanese legend, the giant centipede was a monstrous insect which lived upon cattle and humans in the northern mountains. The people of that locality sent messengers to help rid them of its terrible depredations. The hero Hidesato hunted it, successfully shooting an arrow through the centipede's head. In return for his services, the Dragon King of Lake Biwa gave him an eternally-renewing bag of rice.

CERASTES

The two-horned desert snake of Egypt. The name *cerastes* was used by Greeks for the African snake which has a horny protuberance over each eye. Pliny wrote that the Cerastes buried itself in the sand and moved its horns to attract birds. Like many other snakes, it was believed to be a detector of poison in food and drink, and to protect people from the evil eye.

The Element Encyclopedia of Magical Creatures

CERBERUS

Cerberus was the three-headed (sometimes fifty-headed) dog with a serpent's mane found in classical Greek tradition who guarded the entrance to Hades. His task was to prevent the living from entering the underworld – a task he fulfilled except in the cases of Orpheus, Aeneas and Odysseus, each of whom tricked their way into the land of the dead and out again on their own particular errands. Aeneas had the help of a sibyl who drugged Cerberus with honeyed opiate while Orpheus sent the dog into a charmed sleep with the sound of his lyre. Cerberus barked whenever he was exposed to light and his saliva was the source of the poisonous plant, aconite.

It was appointed to Hercules as his twelfth labour to bring Cerberus from the underworld – a feat which was nothing short of overcoming death itself. In order to prepare himself for this labour, and so as not to violate the sanctity of the underworld divinities, he had himself initiated into the rites of Eleusis. But Hercules had been responsible for the spilling of much blood, including the slaying of centaurs. To regain his purity, he underwent special secret rites. He persuaded Charon, ferryman of the dead, to ferry him over where Cerberus was waiting. The Hydra was said to be Cerberus' sister, and since Hercules had already overcome her, when the hero approached, the guard-dog fled to the god of the underworld, Hades, and hid under his throne. Assailed by ghosts and by a vision of the Gorgon,

Hercules offered the flesh of one of the underworld cattle to them to propitiate the god. Hades allowed Hercules to take Cerberus with him but only if he could catch him without weapons, armed only with a breastplate and lion-skin. Hercules crept up behind Cerberus and choked him until he gave in, and permitted himself to be led out on a chain. One version of the story has Hercules returning the dog himself, but another tells how Cerberus broke away from him at the fountain near Mycenae and the temple of Hera which was known afterwards as 'the water of freedom'.

Cerberus is clearly the inspiration for J.K. Rowling's Fluffy, the giant three-headed dog which guards the attic of Hogwarts School in *Harry Potter and the Philosopher's Stone*.

CERCROPES

In classical mythology, the Cercropes were a race of humanoids who lived in the wilderness of Asia Minor around Ephesus. They preyed upon travellers until the hero Hercules defeated them and brought them to the judgement of Zeus who transformed them into apes.

CERNUNNOS

Cernunnos is the deer-antlered god with a humanoid body in Celtic myth. There is no one particular myth concerning him, for only his image remains. The *cer* part of his name, relating to his antlers, means 'horned'. He is found primarily in sculpted statues and reliefs from ancient Gaul (modern France), but the clearest image is found on the silver votive cauldron, the Gundestrup Cauldron, discovered in Denmark which shows him seated, wearing a stripy close-fitting tunic and trousers, with a royal torc or neck-ring about his neck. In one hand he holds up another torc while in the other he holds a ram-headed snake, as if to show that he combines the animal instincts of the beasts and the cultured wisdom of humans.

In Welsh myth, such a figure is shown as the guardian of animals, a threshold guardian between our world and the other. Visitors to the Otherworld have to answer his challenges before they are allowed in. Like Herne, leader of the wild hunt, Cernunnos may admonish and punish those who injure those under his protection. He is a Lord of the Animals. Julius Caesar speculated that Cernunnos was the same as the Roman Dis Pater, god of the departed spirits of the underworld. Traces of his cult remain in the legends surrounding the Breton saint, Korneli, who is a patron of horned beasts.

CERYNEAN HIND

In Greek mythology, the Cerynean Hind was a wild female deer with golden antlers. She began life as the Titan Taygete, the companion of Artemis who was Mistress of the Animals (*see* Lords and Ladies of the Animals). Taygete succumbed to the attentions of Zeus and Artemis punished her friend by turning her into an antlered hind. The Cerynean Hind ranged through the countryside of Arkadia and into the mountains of Argos, laying waste to farms and fields. The quality of the hind that made it deadly was not its wildness but its effect upon potential hunters who became totally obsessed by the thought of their prey, finding it impossible to stop, even though the hind led them into unknown countries. Most hunters died of sheer exhaustion. Thus, the magical property of the Cerynean Hind is the dangerous compulsion to follow desires to their end whatever the cost.

Hercules undertook to hunt the Cerynean Hind as his third labour. He followed it for a whole year, throughout Arkadia and beyond, into Hyperborea, the land beyond the north wind, and on into the Otherworld itself. He finally came to the Garden of the Hesperides where he found the hind beneath the tree of the golden apples where the apple-guarding serpent Ladon dwelt. In some versions, Hercules took the hind's golden antlers, but others tell how he tied the hind's legs together and carried her back into Arkadia where he was met by Apollo and his sister Artemis, who was exceedingly annoyed at the capture of her sacred animal. Hercules excused himself by saying that he was only carrying the hind into Mycenae alive, and Artemis forgave him.

The Element Encyclopedia of Magical Creatures

CETUS

In Greek mythology, Cetus was a sea monster that had the head of a greyhound, the body of a whale and a two-part tail. This monster was created by Zeus solely for the purpose of destroying Andromeda, the daughter of Queen Cassiopaea. The Queen had boasted that Andromeda was more beautiful than the goddesses and sea nymphs – a statement that so offended the gods that the queen was forced to chain her daughter to a rock in the sea in order to make restitution to the gods. While Andromeda turned and pulled against her chains, Cetus made ready to devour the maiden. Fortunately, the hero Perseus arrived just in time with the freshly-severed head of the Gorgon, Medusa. As Cetus emerged from the waters, it saw Medusa and was turned to stone. Andromeda was rescued, becoming the wife of Perseus. The rock where Andromeda was chained is still visible at the port of Joppa (Jaffa), the old part of the modern city of Tel Aviv in Israel.

CHAMELEON

The ability of the chameleon to change colour has fascinated people for centuries. Throughout Africa, myths about the wise Chameleon abound. In Zaire, people look upon Chameleon as a shapeshifting god who can appear in many forms.

Since the creator was pleased with the outcome of his efforts, as an after-thought he sent Chameleon down to Earth to tell them that they were not to die for ever but would come back to life like the moon. Chameleon set out but he was very slow. Since no response had come back, the creator sent Hare with the same message. He travelled much faster on his long leaping legs, but he could not remember the words properly, telling people that they would all die for ever. By the time Chameleon arrived it was too late, since the creator's message cannot be altered after it has been delivered. The moral of the story is that it is best to make haste slowly

CHAMP

According to North American folk tradition, Champ is the monster that lives in the depths of Lake Champlain, which lies between Quebec in Canada and Vermont in the United States. The Abenaki Iroquois people call this creature Tatoskok and see it as a horned serpent. It has been sighted many times: its thick serpentine body is about 30-ft long with humps along its back, and some have reported a horse-like head. For the local communities around the lake, Champ is regarded as the Loch Ness Monster of their lake, drawing a vast tourist industry. Scientists have explored the possibilities of Champ, suggesting that he might be a plesiosaur, zeuglodon or basilosaurus – a prehistoric snake-like whale, remains of which have been unearthed near Charlotte, Vermont, only a stone's throw from the lake itself.

CH'ANG O

In Chinese mythology, Ch'ang O was the king of the snakes. He had the ability to change in size from tiny to enormous in order to match his enemies. He was finally defeated at the celestial battle of Mu which was fought between the gods and immortals.

CHANG LUNG

In Chinese folklore, Chang Lung was originally a magistrate during the reign of Chung Tsung in the 7th century. Through his practice of pious meditation in the local temple, he began to metamorphose into a dragon protector. His son became anxious about his father's long absences and finally discovered what was happening. Chang Lung confessed to his son that he was being challenged by another dragon and required the help of all his sons to overcome him. His sons made Chang Lung wear a red ribbon about his arm so that they might tell which dragon was which. The

rival dragon was finally shot and killed by the arrows of Chang Lung's sons. From that time onwards, Chang Lung remained in dragon form as a protector of the temple and his community.

CHAPALU

In medieval French legend, Chapalu was the name of an enormous and insatiable cat which preyed upon the unwary. In French Arthurian legend, Chapalu was overcome by Sir Kay.

CHARADRIUS

The Charadrius is a bird, a kind of white, unspotted plover. According to the *Physiologus*, it symbolizes the sinless incarnation of Christ. If one were brought to the bed of an invalid, it was able to predict life or death. It had the ability to look into the face of the sick and draw out illness by flying up to the sun with the residue of the disease so that it might be melted by the solar flames. In missals and Psalters, the Charadrius was often depicted as the bird that cures spiritual blindness or indifference, such as in the case of Saul, who was smitten with temporary physical blindness and spiritual illumination on the Damascus road, after which he changed his name to Paul, later becoming St Paul.

The Element Encyclopedia of Magical Creatures

Charun

In Etruscan myth, Charun was an animal-headed god with tusks and flaming eyes who presided over death and torment. He took particular delight in the writhings of those in pain or in the grip of their death-agony. Later Roman belief took his name for the ferryman over the river to Hades, calling him Charon.

Charybdis

In Greek mythology, Charybdis was the daughter of the Earth goddess Gaia and the sea god Poseidon. She stole the cattle of Hercules, offending Zeus who punished her by sending a thunderbolt. She became turned into a monstrous, formless sea entity like a whirlpool who three times a day sucked the sea into herself and three times spat it out again. She was never seen, but remained in the deep sea. In the *Odyssey*, Odysseus had to pass between the twin terrors of Charybdis and Scylla.

Chaturdanta

In Indian tradition, Chaturdanta is the name of the elephant who led his herd to the only source of water in the middle of drought. As the elephants came to the lake, they trampled many animals including the hares. Silimukha, the king of the hares, sent his eloquent hare messenger, Vijaya, to persuade the elephants to seek some other place. Vijaya climbed up onto a rock and spoke to Chaturdanta saying, 'I am the ambassador of Silimukha, the moon, who says to you that you have defiled the cool waters of my lake and killed my people. If you do this again, you shall receive my punishment.' Chaturdanta swore never to do this again, so Vijaya took him to visit Silimukha but instead led the great elephant to the still lake.

Cheeroonear

Among the Aboriginal peoples of Australia, Cheeroonear is a dog-faced man with arms so long that his hands trail upon the ground. From chin to belly he has a drooping dewlap of many folds. He is accompanied by a pack of dogs.

A legend from the Nullabor Plain tells how Cheeroonear turned up at a waterhole in the middle of a severe drought. He drained the very last drops of the billabong, drinking so heavily that his stomach ballooned out and he began to vomit out human bones and remains. The people gathered at the billabong were horrified to recognize the remains as those of their relatives. Cheeroonear told them that they would not live long enough to report this to others. That night the people consulted their medicine men, the Winjarning brothers. They directed them to make two lines of brushwood leading to and converging on the billabong. At dawn, Cheeroonear's hounds approached the waterhole, they followed the line of the brushwood road, but as each leant forward to drink, one of the Winjarning brothers' boomerangs severed its head. Finally, Cheeroonear himself came to see what was happening. As he followed the brushwood road, he too was clubbed upon the head by the waiting warriors. When he did not come home, his wife came to the billabong. Before she was chopped to pieces by the waiting warriors, her unborn child leapt from her body and slithered off into the undergrowth in the shape of a snake so that the line of Cheeroonear might continue.

CHEIRON

Also known as Chiron, he was the gentle centaur who acted as mentor to many heroes. Cheiron was the offspring of Cronos who visited the Oceanid nymph Philyra in the form of a stallion. Cheiron lived in a cave on the slopes of Mount Pelion. He is frequently shown draped with a robe of stars, with an uprooted tree over his shoulder on which are the spoils of the hunt, and a dog by his side. He was looked to as the arbiter and bringer of education, law, medicine and prophecy, so that many of the Greek heroes were sent to be trained by him, including Aesculapius, Jason, Peleus and Theseus.

The gods did not disdain to consult Cheiron also. When Apollo was out hunting, he saw the virgin Kyrene guarding her father's beasts and how she wrestled with a lion to protect them. Apollo asked Cheiron what he should do and the centaur counselled him to take her as his wife. On a swan-chariot, he bore her to Libya. Cheiron prophesied that her son would be divine. He would be raised by Hermes, the Horae and the goddess Gaia and become an immortal and perfect child who would love men. This child was the immortal Apollo made new, Apollo Aristaios or 'the best Apollo'. His father took his namesake to Cheiron to be raised by wise centaurs. He was the first to snare wolves and bears. The son of Apollo Aristaios was Aesculapius the great physician. Apollo took Aesculapius from his mother, Koronis' womb, when the pregnant mother lay dead on her pyre and brought him to Cheiron, who taught him the art of healing.

Cheiron was accidentally wounded by one of Hercules' poisoned arrows which had the venom of the Hydra upon them. Hercules tried in vain to save the wise centaur with healing herbs but Cheiron was pierced in the knee and could neither recover nor die, and so he retired with his incurable wound to his dark cave.

Finally, when Hercules was attempting to liberate Prometheus, who had stolen fire from heaven, from his eternal punishment, it was Cheiron who agreed to take Prometheus' place, since he had been set there to suffer for the sake of all humanity who enjoyed the gifts of the gods. Prometheus had been bound to have his ever-regenerating liver pecked away daily by an eagle for eternity. Cheiron suffered this fate gladly since he could not die. But Zeus relented and set him in the sky as the constellation Centaurus, or Sagittarius, according to some sources.

CHERUFE

Among the Araucanian peoples of Argentina and Chile, the Cherufe is a monster who preys upon young women in the high Andes mountains. The sun god sent two of his warrior daughters to stand watch on the Cherufe and freeze it with their magical swords. However, the Cherufe is a crafty beast and it often escapes their watchful guardianship, sliding off to create more volcanic eruptions and chase more young women.

CH'I LIN

This is the alternative spelling of the creature from Chinese mythology that has a deer's body and an ox's tail, with a single horn on its head, and the legs and hooves of a horse.

CHI LUNG WANG

In Chinese folklore, Chi Lung Wang is the protector of domestic water supplies and is the one who is in charge of the pumps when it comes to putting out fires. His name means 'Fire-Engine King Dragon', and he is a dragon who is under obedience to the Dragon King, Lung Wang, who is the provider of water to the whole Earth.

CHIAI TUNG

This is an alternative spelling of the Chinese Unicorn, which is called Hai Chiai.

CHICHELVACHE

In medieval European folklore, the Chichelvache is the wife of Bicorne. Chichelvache takes the form of an undernourished cow who has a miserable expression on her human face. She is supposed to live on a diet of wives who were both obedient and tyrannized by their husbands. Chichelvache and Bicorne were frequently represented in allegorical sculptures and misericords in churches to represent the lot of wives and husbands. Sometimes Chichelvache ('Scrawny Cow') is called by the alternative Chichifache ('Thin-Face'), which is how Chaucer spelled it in his 'Clerk's Tale' in *The Canterbury Tales*.

CHICKEN

See Cockerel.

CHIMAERA

The Chimaera or Chimera was the creature with body of a goat, the fore-parts of a lion, the hind-parts of a serpent and, sometimes, is shown with the heads of all three animals ranged along its back. Chimaera was one of the many children of Echidna and Typhon. It spat fire and was responsible for killing everyone in the city of Lycia in Asia Minor. It was finally dispatched by the hero Bellerophon, who rode upon the back of Pegasus, and killed it by thrusting his spear into its mouth. As the metal of the spear melted in the heat of its gullet, the Chimaera choked to death.

CHIO-TUAN

In Chinese mythology, Chio-Tuan is the Unicorn who appeared to Genghis Khan in the 13th century, warning him to stop his wars. He is the same as Ki-Lin and Ch'i Lin.

CHITRA-RATHA

Chitra-Ratha is the king of the Gandarvas in Hindu mythology, the centaur-like beings who are in charge of the divine soma of the gods. As well as brewing medicines, Chitra-Ratha is also the divine musician who provides music at the banquets of the gods. He is sometimes discovered in woodland clearings making music and dancing with the Apsaras. It was in such a place that the yogi Medhavi was seduced from his ascetic practices by the dancing girl, Manjughosha, as she danced to the divine music of Chitra-Ratha.

CHIVATO

Among the Araucanian people of Chile, Chivato was a cannibalistic monster. He had been a child who was abducted by witches. Over the years, he changed into a monster who had a taste for flesh. Several Chivatos were believed to live in the caverns beneath the towns of Ancud and Chiloc. The caverns were accessible by a tunnel leading from an islanded lake. They preyed upon young women who came to draw water from the lake.

CHO'OS SHYON

Cho'os Shyon is one of the eight giants of Buddhist Tibet who are known in India as the Dharmapalas or protectors of the dharma (teachings.) They are inimical to all enemies of Buddhism and protect the faithful.

CHORTI

In Guatamalan folklore, the Chorti is a gigantic wild man whose metal-clawed feet are backwards-pointing. The Yaqui of Mexico know of a similar giant

The Element Encyclopedia of Magical Creatures

creature who roams the uninhabited wastelands.

CHRYSOMALLUS

In Greek mythology, this is the name given to the flying ram with the Golden Fleece.

CHUDO-YUDO

In Russian folklore, Chudo-Yudo was the many-headed, fire-breathing dragon who is a child of Baba Yaga. Its brother was Koshchei the Deathless. It controlled the Waters of Life and Death.

CHUPACABRAS

This vampire animal, also known as the Goatsucker, has been reported since the mid-1990s throughout Latin America, especially round Mexico and on the island of Puerto Rico. There are a variety of reported descriptions: one is that of a lizard-like being with greenish skin and dorsal spines, standing 3–4-ft high, with a long nose and forked tongue, that hops like a kangaroo; another says that it hops like a kangaroo but has coarse grey fur and facial hair, and the head of a dog with long teeth; a third description is that of a hairless wild dog with a high dorsal ridge, deep eye sockets, long teeth and claws. They move remarkably quickly and some say that it has basilisk-like eyes that paralyse its prey.

The Chupacabras sucks the blood of livestock such as goats, horses, fowl and cattle. Sudden animal deaths are laid at its door, especially if two puncture wounds are found on their necks. In July 2004, a Texas rancher killed a hairless, dog-like creature that was attacking his livestock. Skeletal analysis of the creature is proceeding at the University of California. The Chupacabras may originate from Central American aboriginal myths concerning the 'mosquito-man' who sucks blood from animals through his long nose, just like a mosquito. (*See* Cryptozoology.)

CICADA

The cicada has been symbolic in many cultures. In Greek mythology, it is sacred to Apollo because of the way it pours out its song. The cicada came into being from the man Tithonous who obtained immortality – but forgot to ask for eternal youth to accompany it. Out of pity, he was changed into a cicada. Because they are so often associated with immortality, it was bad luck to kill one. It was also believed that cicadas lived on dew alone and were bloodless. In China, cicadas were kept in cages as pets. They were symbols of temperance, immortality and eternal youth, and jade cicadas were put into the mouth of the dead to signify immortality. Among the Polynesian peoples, it was believed that no one should make a noise while the cicada was making its song.

The Element Encyclopedia of Magical Creatures

According to the Andamanese Islanders in the Bay of Bengal, the Cicada was killed by the great hunting spider, Da Tengat. As he crushed the Cicada to death its dying shrill cry sounded, and the first darkness fell. All the creatures were terrified and they began to sing in order to make the Cicada sing once again. Da Tengat lit the darkness by showing his people how to make torches from resin. Finally, all their torches caused the dawn to come again.

CINNAMOLOGUS

In Arabia, the Cinnamon Bird built its nests in the tallest stems of the cinnamon tree. Men prized these nests but could not take them because the stems were too fragile, so they aimed at them with arrows loaded with lead and sold the Cinnamologus's nest to those hungry for spice.

CIPACTLI

In Aztec mythology, this fish-like crocodile was the primordial sea monster out of which the gods created the Earth. The god Tezcatlipoca sacrificed his foot to Cipactli in order to help form the Earth itself.

CIREIN CROIN

In Scottish folklore, the Cirein Croin ('Grey Crest') is a massive sea serpent, so huge that it can swallow whales. It is also known as Curtag Mhòr a'Chuain ('the Great Ocean Whirlpool').

CIUDACH

In Scottish tradition, the Ciudach was a cannibalistic monster that inhabited the deep caverns of mountains. It shares a name with a giant from Roscommon in Ireland, who may be the same being. The giant Ciudach came to Scotland following the deep declivity of the Great Glen, as did the Loch Ness Monster.

CIVATATEO

In Mexican folklore, the Civatateo were the deadly white vampires who served the gods. They were once noblewomen who died in childbirth and returned to Earth with all the powers of priestesses. They are recognizable by the death's head which is printed on their clothes or tattooed on their flesh. They

The Element Encyclopedia of Magical Creatures

lurk in churches and holy places, and stalk travellers at crossroads.

CLURICAUNE

In Irish folklore, the Cluricaune is a household fairy. It lives a solitary existence and shares the characteristics of the leprechaun. Cluricaunes have a wizened appearance and are dressed in green. Cluricaune has a purse full of silver and his favourite place is the wine cellar where he will sit in solitary drinking sessions until the casks are dry. He is known to harness sheep and ride them over the fields at his pleasure.

COCKATRICE

In the legends of medieval Europe, the Basilisk transformed into a new creature called the Cockatrice. Instead of having a serpent's body, it had the yellow body and wings of a dragon, a cockerel's head, neck and legs, a human face and the tail of a snake. In some descriptions, it had an additional head at the end of its tail, like the Amphisbaena. It was believed to live in the deserts of North Africa and the only antidote to its poison was to carry a cockerel with you. Like the Basilisk, its look would kill all who gazed upon it, even for an instant.

COCKEREL

The cockerel's distinctive and raucous dawn crowing has made it a symbol throughout the world of regeneration and return. The bird is often portrayed standing upon a drum in temple architecture. It was the cockerel who called the goddess Amaterasu out of her cave, whence she retired as the world lost its light. Cockerels are given the run of Shinto temples as sacred birds because of this.

In Islamic tradition, when Allah was creating the sky, he created a huge cockerel whose feet were upon the first sphere of heaven and whose head was in the seventh heaven where stands the Ultimate Mosque, Masjid al Aqsa, which is just below the throne of Allah. Every night, Allah creates 70,000 new angels to worship him in that mosque. One utters the call to prayer while it is still dark on Earth, and at the same moment the cockerel crows. This crowing is the call to prayer for all cockerels upon Earth who immediately call that the day is dawned. On the last day, the heavenly cockerel will crow for the last time and that will be the signal for the announcing angel to command that the dead rise up.

In Christian iconography, the cockerel is the bird whose cry announces the betrayal of Christ by St Peter when he denied that he knew his Lord. But it has remained a symbol of vigilance against evil and is often found as a weathervane on church towers. In Indonesia, the image of a cock and his hen are found in every home for their presence will stave off marital disputes and ensure faithfulness. A similar tradition is found in Judaism where the cock and hen are emblems of the groom and bride at weddings. In Chinese religion, the cockerel's name was a word signifying luck. The white cockerel protects the innocent against evil spirits and ensures the purity of new life overcoming death, while the red cock is a guardian against fire. In Scandinavian mythology, the gold cock Vithafmir lived at the top of the cosmic world tree Yggdrasil. In the underworld, the red cock Fralar lives in Valhalla ready to waken heroes for the last days of world or Ragnorok.

The cockerel is commonly sacrificed, as in the rites of Rome where they were offered to the *lares*, the spirits of the house. In the rites of voudoun, the blood of the cockerel is used to open the way to the Otherworld in sacrifice. In Buddhism, the cockerel is a symbol of carnality and pride, and with the pig and snake, is depicted upon the mandala of *samsara* (the weary round of existences) as one of the passions that prevents one reaching nirvana or enlightenment. (*See* Sacrificial animals.)

COCQCIGRUES

In the folklore of France, the Cocqcigrues are a family of unspecified monsters who are referred to in the common phrase, '*a la venue des Coquecigrues*' ('when the monsters come'), meaning a time unlikely to come.

COINN IOTAIR

In Irish legend, the Coinn Iotair ('Raging Hounds') are the magical hunting hounds of the legendary chieftain Crom Dubh, the 'Black Crooked One'.

COLUINN GUN CHEANN

In the Highlands of Scotland, you need to walk carefully in case you meet the Coluinn Gun Cheann, the 'Trunk without a Head'. This monster was active around the estate of the Macdonalds of Morar on the Isle of Skye. It was indifferent to women and children, allowing them to pass, but it would attack any man who travelled the 'Smooth Mile' to Morar House at night, killing and mutilating them. It would seem that the Headless Body was primarily following a protective duty to guard the Macdonald's estate from strangers and invaders, but it had little discrimination. The Macleod of Raasay eventually banished him, but we do not know where to, so it is best to beware.

Con Rit

In south-east Asian cryptozoology, this sea beast has been found along the seacoast of Vietnam. Its name means 'centipede' or 'millipede', but it is considerably longer – being about 60 ft. The one found by Tan Van Con in 1883 had a sectioned body, just like an insect. These segments, 3-ft wide and 2-ft long, were hexagonal in shape. The description has been thought to resemble the Chinese Dragon with its tough hide, armoured plates and whiskered face.

Coranyeidd

In the Welsh story of Lludd and Llefelys, we hear how King Lludd (or Lud) of Britain was troubled by Coranyeidd (or Coranians), a kind of intrusive spirit who overheard whatever was said so that no secrets could be kept. He went to sea in the English Channel and tried to talk to his brother King Llefelys of France as their two boats met. Speaking through a talking horn or speaking trumpet, neither brother could understand the other very easily because Coranyeidd kept getting in the horn, so that the brothers heard insulting things about each other. Llefelys poured wine through the speaking horn and ejected the Coranyeidd who were blocking the tube. He advised his brother to take some special insects and crush them up, putting them into the water supply and this would rid Britain of the Coranyeidd.

Cornu

In Irish legend, this is the monstrous black bird which was banished by St Patrick to the waters of Lough Derg to live upon the miserable and penitential island that is known as St Patrick's Purgatory. Hundreds of pilgrims come to this island every year to pray outside in the rain, endure cold winds and undergo a complete fast in order to purge their sins.

Corocotta

In European legend, the Corocotta was reported by travellers as a lion-sized beast with a wolf's head. The creature had an unmoving stare, for its eyes did not swivel in their sockets. Instead of teeth, it had a series of bones that crushed whatever it fed upon, so that it might swallow it whole. It was cunningly able to imitate the calls of other animals so that others of their kind might be lured into its vicinity.

Cottus

One of the Hecatoncheires, or hundred-handed giants who were the offspring of the Earth goddess Gaia and Uranus in Greek mythology. With his brothers, Briareus and Gyges, Cottus helped the Olympian gods in their war against the Titans.

Cotzbalam

In Mayan mythology, Cotzbalam was one of the four great birds who attacked the wooden bodies that were intended to become the first living humans. They each attacked a different part of the body to prevent the pollution of the primordial world. The others were Camazotz, Tecumbalam and Gucumatz.

Cow

The domestication of the cow was a significant development in the history of civilization. The central place of the cow as the sustainer and provider of people is widely acclaimed in world mythology and folk belief.

Marital customs show how central the cow is both as an emblem of fertility and as a unit of wealth – our word 'pecuniary' derives from the Latin *pecu* meaning 'cattle'. In rural cultures, the cow has traditionally been part of a girl's dowry, making her a good marital prospect. In Hindu culture, cattle accompany bride and groom to the bride's village when she returns after the wedding to visit her father's house. On the return journey, back to her new house, the bride's dowry cows are encouraged to dance over an egg which they eventually break in order to mark the bride's change of state from virgin daughter to married woman, and to help her overcome the separation from her family and home village.

In ancient times, the connection between the Milky Way and the cow is reflected throughout world legend. The Gaelic words for the Milky Way, *Na Bó Finne*, translate as 'the cow's run', while the medieval pilgrimage routes to the shrines of St James of Compostella in north-west Spain and to Our Lady of Walsingham in Norfolk, England, are both called 'the Milky Way' (*see* Celestial Creatures).

Among the Dinka of the Sudan in Africa, young women who are eligible to be courted carry cow's horns, while the young men lead the 'song bulls' to them, especially pampered oxen, in a rite that combines human courtship with bovine fertility and virility. In India, the cow is sacred and must never be harmed because the primordial mother of life, Aditi, is the provider of all. Even among those who eat meat, no Hindu will eat beef. The sacred syllable 'Aum' is chanted by the pious – and understood to consist of three colours: the red cow of dawn, the white cow of the day and the black cow of dusk – in a chant which encompasses life from beginning to end.

During the Sung dynasty, a Zen Buddhist teacher called Seikyo drew a series of pictures relating cow-herding to the spiritual path: a lost cow represents the loss of way; finding traces of the cow represent the finding of the teachings which the seeker does not yet fully understand; catching sight of the cow represents the seeker remembering what is most important; catching the cow is the possession of spiritual practice which still needs discipline; herding the cow is a daily process of keeping watch on the self-deceptive and confused mind; and coming home on the cow's back represents a oneness with the spiritual teaching.

The Element Encyclopedia of Magical Creatures

There are more than 100 words relating to the cow in Gaelic which is an indication of the importance of these animals in the Celtic world. Among the Celtic people, the cow was the standard unit of currency, and many famous stories – such as the Tain bo Cuailnge (Cattle Raid of Cooley) are concerned with the theft of famous cattle, which invariably gave rise to a war, with one side or the other fighting for possession of the animals. In the Tain, there is a description of the two semi-mythical bulls; the Brown Bull of Cuailnge was described as follows:

> dark brown dire haughty with young health
> horrific overwhelming ferocious full of craft
> furiousfieryflanksnarrow bravebrutalthickbreasted
> curly browed head cocked highgrowling and eyes glaring
>
> *(trans. Thomas Kinsella)*

Both cows and bulls represented plenty to the Celts and it is not surprising to find accounts of the sacred origin of such beasts. In Ireland, three wondrous cows arose from the sea – a white (bo-finn), a red (bo-ruadh) and a black (bo-dhubh), very similar to the three cow-syllables of the Hindu chant of Aum. The Crodh Sidhe are the cows belonging to the fairies. The cow was also inextricably linked with the goddess Bride or Brighid (later St Bridget) who was the matron of dairy-work and the protector of all dairy animals: she is often depicted milking. Cow's milk – especially that of white cows – was said to possess healing properties. In an ancient story about a battle between the Britons and the Irish, in which the latter were losing many men to the effect of poisoned arrows, a famous Pictish Druid named Trosdane told the Irish leaders to fill a pool with the milk from 150 white cows. The wounded men then bathed in the milk and were cured.

In Estonian legend, the cows of the giant Näkki were stalled at the foot of a great whirlpool and grazed along its ripples. Like all otherworldly cattle, they gave the most wonderful milk, but only the bravest heroes were ever able to catch one and introduce it into his own herd where it improved the stock to the envy of his neighbours.

In Egyptian mythology, the horns of the cow became part of the crowns of both Isis and Hathor, and also Nuit but the primordial Mehet-Weret is the cow goddess of the sky. She is believed to be the mother of Ra. Her name means 'great flood' and she represents the waters of the heavens along which the sun boat passes. She is shown as a cow, crowned with the triple moon crown, lying down upon a reed-mat with a flail across her shoulders as her badge of office.

COYOTE

Also known as Sedit, Coyote is the divine trickster of the south-western Indians of North America. He is the instigator of many things and customs, in common with many other tricksters whose function is to break through boundaries and conventions so that new things may come into being. He

The Element Encyclopedia of Magical Creatures

creates people and brings fire, as well as being the bringer of death. His shape is both human and that of a coyote.

As the bringer of death, he also had to experience its pain.

A story from the Thompson River Indians of British Columbia tells how Coyote determined to steal fire from the Fire People, supernatural beings who alone had the secret of making fire. With Antelope, Fox and Wolf, he gatecrashed a party they were having and made himself a headdress from yellow pine shavings. The Fire People danced first and then Coyote and friends performed an answering dance, but Coyote complained that he could hardly see to dance, so that Fire People built up a bigger and bigger fire. As the blaze grew higher, so Coyote's friends began to leave, excusing themselves from the party because they were too hot, but actually to get into position to help fulfil Coyote's plan. Coyote danced alone getting nearer and nearer to the fire until his headdress caught alight. Then he ran out, passing his blazing headdress to Antelope who passed it onto Fox and Wolf. Each of the animals was killed by the Fire People until only Coyote was left. As they drew near to kill him, Coyote threw his headdress into a tree which burst into flames. From that time to this, men have been able to make fire by using wooden fire-sticks. This was Coyote's gift to humans.

A legend of the Pomo Indians of California tells how one day Coyote saw a rattlesnake going down a hole and called people to look, for he wanted people to know death. He got everyone to dance around it until the chief's daughter was bitten on the ankle by the rattlesnake. She cried out in pain but Coyote got them to dance on. A few hours later the girl died and the chief demanded that Coyote resurrect her. He said, 'If people live forever there will be too many people and not enough food.' So the girl was laid on the pyre and cremated. A few days later Coyote awoke to find that his own daughter had died, for the chief had poisoned her in revenge for his own girl's death. Coyote mourned all night and went to the chief and said, 'My daughter must live again.' 'That's not fair!' said the chief. 'You said it was wise to let people die when my daughter died.' Coyote accepted that his words must also apply to himself and put his daughter on the pyre to cremate her. He mourned all that night and every night afterwards, which is why the coyote always howls at night.

The Element Encyclopedia of Magical Creatures

CRAB

The constellation of Cancer the Crab was created by the Greek goddess, Hera, who raised up the crab that had tormented Hercules when he was attempting to kill the Hydra. Among the Andamanese Islanders in the Bay of Bengal, Lizard decided to hold a dancing party. He became so wild and strong that everyone grew frightened. Whenever anyone tried to catch him, Lizard threw them into the sea, turning them into all kinds of fish and turtles. The one who stopped them was the crab, Berep.

CRANE

The extraordinary mating dance of the different species of cranes about the world is often reflected in folk customs. This courting dance is seen in the long-necked crane, which pairs off with one mate. The male rubs his wings together in a rhythmic and erotic way against the female. This dance is part of the initiation of pubescent girls among the Watusi tribes of Zaire. Young, unmarried girls dance in a quadrille in pairs, bare-breasted, with their outstretched arms like wings, the hands are raised to caress the cheek of the opposite girl just like the crane's dance; as they dance they utter a ululating and hypnotic cry. Those who have undergone this dance are then marriageable. Among the Bushmen of the Kalahari, the Blue Crane is the sister to Mantis, the great trickster and provider.

In Hindu tradition, the crane-headed goddess, Bagala, presides over poisons, black magic and deceitful forms of death. She has the tongues of enemies in her right hand while in her left she has instruments of torture. Sometimes she has a mace and is dressed in yellow.

The stories of the Irish hero Fionn Mac Cumhail tell how Aoife, daughter of Dealbhaoth, was transformed into a crane by a jealous rival for the affections of Ilbrec. After her death, the god of the Otherworld, Manannan Mac Lir, had a bag made from her skin in which he kept a number of mysterious treasures. Later, Fionn won the Corrbolg (Crane Bag) for himself. As a child, Fionn is rescued from enemies determined to kill him by his grandmother, who turns herself into a crane and carries him away to safety. Later, he is connected with four cranes, 'The Children of the Cailleach of the Temple', which bring death in their wake. In the 'Excuse of Guile's Daughter', the house of the poet Guile is guarded by cranes who repel visitors by their calling 'Shun this Place', 'Avoid this Fence' and 'Don't Come In'.

In classical folklore, the crane is supposed to be a weather forecaster who gives the go-ahead for farmers to plant their fields. The crane is sacred to Apollo as the bird of Spring who comes with the returning light of the sun. The crane dance was annually performed for this reason. In Chinese mythology, the crane is a messenger of the gods who flies between Heaven and Earth. Its role is to carry the souls of the deceased to the Western Paradise. It represents immortality, vigilance, happiness, luck and high office.

Christian tradition accords the crane with the status of a cleric or monk because of the way it stands unmoving, and the crane thus represents the watchfulness, obedience and loyalty of a good monk. The bestiaries often show the crane taking a bone out of the throat of a fox, which becomes an emblem for saving lost souls, since the fox is often seen as a representative of the devil. In heraldic lore, the crane's foot or *'pied de grue'* is the symbol for the branching lines of the family tree and thus it forms the basis for the word 'pedigree'.

CRAYFISH

Among the Ainu people of North Japan, the Crayfish is the god of the rivers or 'the god who walks backwards'. It was Crayfish who, in North American myth, dived to the bottom of the waters for the mud from which the Great Spirit recreated the Earth after the deluge.

CREATING CREATURES

Animals are often the ones who create the world and the first human beings. In the Finnish epic of the *Kalevala*, the world is formed from a huge egg which is laid by a giant bird, just as it is in Greek Orphic cosmology where Eros leaps out of the egg of Nyx. In Hindu tradition, the world is created by being churned out of the milk of Aditi, the primordial cow.

In the Solomon Islands of Melanesia, the creators of life were the Figonas. Hatuibwari was a winged serpent with a human head, four eyes and four breasts with which he suckled all creation. The greatest Figona was Agunua who created a male child, but he was so helpless that Agunua made a woman to make fire, cook and weed the garden.

As with Australian aboriginal Rainbow Serpent, sometimes the movements of the primal animal creator create the form of the land features, lakes or hills. In most cases, animals help men after the first creation to acquire gifts, skills and foodstuffs. This is the case with Coyote and Raven. However, among the Inuit, Raven is first to be born from the darkness and comes to create the Earth. Finding a giant pea-pod one day, he pecks it open and out comes the first man. Raven continues to support this creature by creating caribou and musk ox, before creating a woman and all the supplies to make food, clothes and shelter.

The first creation is not always successful and a secondary creation often becomes necessary. The first creator and his demiurge are often at odds. Among the Kiwaian people of Papua New Guinea, the creator was a crocodile called Ipila who carved a man out of wood and brought him to life with sago milk, calling him Nugu. Ipila then made three other men but two refused to do as Nugu asked and they became meat-eaters – and finally crocodiles. Nugu and his male companion could not make any more men between them. Ipila kept interfering in their every scheme, changing their handiwork, like an older brother who cannot stop interfering with the play of his younger brothers. Finally, Ipila grew angry with his first creation and condemned Nugu to hold up the world forever, like the giant Atlas in Greek myth.

CRETAN BULL

In Greek mythology, the bull from the sea came ashore on the island of Crete, sent by the sea god Poseidon as a gift to Minos. It was intended as a sacrificial animal that Minos might offer back to Poseidon, but Minos, having set his eyes on the magnificent white bull, decided that he would keep it to improve his own herds. Substituting a lesser bull in sacrifice, Minos roused Poseiden's anger and he set a dreadful curse upon Minos and his family. Minos' wife, Pasiphae, became enamoured of the bull and the great artificer Daedelus had to make a wooden cow in which Pasiphae might lie to be mounted by the animal. Later she gave birth to the Minotaur. Its father, the Cretan bull, then ran madly about the island until Hercules captured it while on his seventh labour. No longer in its first youth, the bull was finally set free to roam the plains of Marathon.

CRIOSPHINX

In Egyptian mythology, the Criosphinx is a lion-bodied sphinx with the head of a horned ram. It is normally shown sitting down in the posture of a guardian outside temples. The Criosphinx was one of the animals of the creator god Amun, as a guardian of souls.

CROCODILE

The crocodile is feared all over the world as an unpredictable carnivore that lies in wait for all unwary mammals, human or animal. It is strongly associated with the underworld in Egyptian and Christian traditions, and with the seduction of young women in both Africa and Australia. In other parts of the world, it is associated with dance and song.

A origin of dance story is told in ancient Chinese mythology, where K'ouei the crocodile is called the inventor of dance songs. He banged his tail upon his stomach and the noise that he created made him laugh. The laughter was like thunder, but when he beat and sang together, everyone could dance.

In Egyptian mythology, the crocodile was a divinity called Sebek, the child of Neith. The crocodile was also the animal associated with the god Set. In this shape, he hid in the reeds lying in wait for the corpse of his brother Osiris who he rent into many pieces. It was only the ingenuity of Osiris's wife, Isis, who brought back the pieces together and resurrected her husband, that overturned Set's plans of domination. The Earth god Geb turned Set into the form of a crocodile and from this time onwards, Set became one who punishes wrongdoers. He is also associated with the Greek Typhon during the Ptolemaic period. In the Book of the Dead, there was a crocodile-headed monster which devoured the sinful hearts of those who were unworthy of the afterlife. The crocodile's wide gaping mouth was seen as a symbol of the abyss. Four crocodiles who lived at the four corners of the Earth laid in wait to threaten the newly deceased who had to possess the correct magical words to pass them and enter into the afterlife process.

The voracious nature of the crocodile is famed throughout Africa. Among the A Bakongo peoples, there is a tale of an elderly lecher who delighted in watching the girls bathing. He obtained a crocodile fetish from a medicine man and ordered his wife to make him porridge. The next morning after he ate this, he turned into a crocodile so that he might eat the girls. But the village elders were aware of the predatory old man's intentions and they asked the medicine man to sprinkle some magical powder upon the waters so that the old man turned back into his harmless human shape again.

For the Aboriginal peoples of Australia, the crocodile is an ancestor who lives in Alcheringa, the Dreamtime. But one crocodile called Pikuwa is a seducer of women just like the man in the Bakongo legend. The Caribs of the Orinoco Basin in South America call themselves 'crocodile people', believing that the first beings were caymans (a kind of alligator). The females were all beautiful, but some of the men were so ugly that they were exiled. The ugly ones remained in crocodile form. Among the Kiwaian people of Papua New Guinea, the creator was a crocodile called Ipila who carved a man out of wood and brought him to life with sago milk, calling him Nugu. Ipila then made three other men but two refused to do as Nugu asked and they became meat-eaters and finally crocodiles.

The medieval bestiaries gave it further associations of deceit by reporting that the crocodile pretended to cry, thus luring travellers to lean over the water so that it could devour them. From this, we get the expression 'to weep crocodile tears', meaning that the grief is merely a pretence. Leonardo Da Vinci wrote, 'The crocodile first catches and kills a man; after his death it weeps over him with mournful voice and many tears. Only then does it cruelly devour him.' The most famous crocodile to enter modern literary tradition is the crocodile who swallowed the alarm clock of Captain Hook in J.M. Barrie's play, *Peter Pan*. The alarm clock enabled Hook, who feared the crocodile above all other foes, to know when it was in the vicinity. It finally devoured the pirate, in the just and time-honoured way of its divine ancestor, Set.

The Element Encyclopedia of Magical Creatures

CROW

Like the raven, the crow is a bird which appears in world mythology as a soothsayer, an omen of death and as a creator and cleanser, taking away all that was decayed. Full of intelligence, cunning and playfulness, the crow was seen as a guardian of the sacred law among the tribes of North America, a creature whose far-seeing eye saw past, present and future all at once. For the Algonquin peoples, Crow was the bringer of grains and beans. In the Ghost Dances, which are danced to solicit the help of their ancestors, Crow is a primary spirit messenger.

In Australian aboriginal legend, Crow, along with Tortoise and Frog, dissented in the corroboree (gathering) that suggested that Kangaroo and Emu, and Dingo and Goanna should mate. The animals fell to fighting but when they grew hungry, pelicans dived for fish to feed them and a fire was started to cook them. Crow warned them that to cook fish away from where they had been caught was illegal and the animals began to argue. Frog threw his voice to make it sound as if Crow was insulting Kangaroo, so confusing the other animals that they fell out even more and decided for ever after to have their own languages.

Crows and ravens have an intricate and detailed history in Celtic lore and legend. The Irish battle goddesses, Morrigan and Badbh, regularly took the shape of crows, and both crows and ravens were their allies and companions. In Scottish folklore, the crow is said to have 27 different cries (a magical three times nine), each of which relates to a different event. These oracular cries can foretell the coming of important guests, an impending loss or death, or the coming of good fortune, and a complete body of lore was built up from listening to the varied calls of the crow, which has the ability to mimic many kinds of sounds as well as to communicate with its own kind. When there is a *molmacha* (flock of crows), all crying together, it is said that no one can understand their words but the most wise seer in the land.

In Greece, the crow was an unlucky sign. Although they were sacred to the goddess Athene, she would not allow them to perch upon the roof of the Acropolis in Athens, for most people believed crows to be an omen of death if they landed upon a roof. However, this did not stop Apollo shapeshifting into the form of a crow when he was fleeing from Typhon.

The medieval bestiaries looked upon the crow as a bird of parental devotion. It was also believed that crows led the migration of the storks. Confusingly, medieval Christian belief held that the crow was both a sign of the devil because of its scavenging behaviour *and* a symbol of fidelity, since it was believed that crows did not seek a new mate if their own partner died. The magical properties of the crow include an ability to divine the future and to dismantle the past, as well as to teach human beings how to mix love, humour and playfulness.

CRYPTOZOOLOGY

New and previously unknown creatures are frequently reported. Some, like the Chupacabras (Goatsucker), Ropen and Mothman are so recent that people have poured scorn on their very existence, suggesting they are inventions or beasts of urban legend. The study of such creatures is called cryptozoology, since naturalists and scientists seldom bother to investigate them. But if we look at the interest in magical creatures from the earliest recorded times, it is clear that very many beings would fall under this category. The term 'cryptozoology' was coined by Bernard Heuvelman, but really he may stand alongside classical writers such as Pliny the Elder and medieval travellers such as Sir John Mandeville.

Certain reports of creatures are believed to be the product of mass hysteria, scapegoats to explain events of mysterious or unknown origin. Some creatures are so fantastic that they are clearly composites of other animals, like the Jackalope, but unfortunately this can lead to all cryptozoological creatures being placed in the same category. In many instances, the deeper people delve for answers, the clearer it is that some creatures have had a long existence within native legends. This is certainly true of the Australian Bunyip and the Canadian Champ, both of which appear in native legend and whose prehistoric remains have now been found in the vicinity. One thing is clear. Naturalists continually have been amazed to discover new species or hybrids, or to discover that species previously thought to be extinct are still living, such as the prehistoric fish the coelocanth which was first seen again in 1938 and is now regarded as a true 'living fossil'.

CTEATUS

In Greek mythology, Cteatus was one of the monstrous twins of the Molionids. With Eurytus, his brother, they were the sons of Poseidon and were hatched from a silver egg.

CUCKOO

The first calling of the cuckoo announces spring and early summer to Europe, where it acts as a signal to sow crops. In Hindu tradition, the cuckoo is eternally wise, a bird who knows the past, present and future. In Japan, the cuckoo is a sign of unrequited love, possibly because of its continuous cuckooing. In Finland, the 18th May is St Eric's day when St Eric is supposed to arrive with the migratory birds. He carries a cuckoo under one arm and a swallow in his hand. This was the traditional sign that the sowing of oats must be completed and the barley sowing begun. In medieval scholastic tradition, students calling 'cuckoo' was the signal that the scholastic term had begun, much to the disgust of the citizens of collegiate towns, who would have to put up with yet more wild student behaviour. In medieval English folklore, the adult cuckoo's habit of laying its eggs in the nests of other birds made it the symbol of a cuckold.

CURUPIRA

In Brazil, Curupira acts as a kind of Pan-like figure. He is a bald, one-eyed dwarf with great ears and a hairy body who rides a pig. His feet are double-jointed to his legs and so he can move in whichever direction he pleases. He is benevolent to all creatures, even hunters, as long as they kill and do not just wound their prey. For a gift of tobacco, he would help find stray cattle.

CWN ANNWFN

The Cwn Annwfn ('Hounds of the In-World') are the white, red-eared fairy hounds who live in the Welsh Underworld. They are controlled by their master, Arawn, Lord of Annfwn. They follow the scent of souls who have offended or abused others and they are heard howling and belowing over the mountains at night. They are part of the Wild Hunt which pursues wrongdoers and hunts them into the ground until they can run no more, in much the same way that the wrongdoers did to their own innocent prey.

CYCLOPS

The three Cyclops were the children of Gaia by Ouranos. They were gigantic beings with a single round eye in the middle of their forehead. Their names, Steropes, Brontes and Arges, refer to the action of thunder and lightning. They were thrown into the underworld of Tartarus by the Titans but they were rescued from there by the Olympian gods who persuaded the giants to fight on their side. For this service, the Cyclops were given forges under Mount Etna where they forged the weapons of the gods. The Cyclops were killed by the avenging arrows of the god Apollo because their smithcraft had fashioned the arrows that killed the healer Aesculapius.

CYHYRAETH

In Welsh tradition, the Cyhyraeth is a spectral woman who weeps and groans before a death, or to herald an epidemic or disaster. No one sees her, but her presence is known by the wailing that she makes. She is primarily active in South Wales. She is like the Caointeach of Scottish tradition or the Banshee of Irish tradition.

CYLLARUS

In Greek mythology, Cyllarus was one of the centaurs who came to the marriage of Perithous the Lapith. Unused to drinking wine, which caused centaurs to become uncontrolled and lecherous, Cyllarus entered into fighting with the wedding guests and was killed.

CYNOCEPHALI

In early medieval legend, the dog-headed Cynocephali were a species of missing links who looked like dog-headed humans with black hair all over their bodies. Marco Polo said that they lived in the Andamanese Islands of the Indian Ocean, while Sir John Mandeville said they lived on the island of Macumeran. They have been described right back in time to the Greek historian Ctesias who flourished in Persia around 500 BC, and wrote that the Cynocephali also had horse's necks. In the usual storyteller's way, Herodotus embroidered their qualities even more by suggesting that they lived in Ethiopia and both breathed and barked fire.

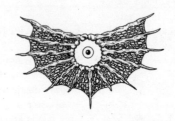

DA

Whenever the Dahomey people of West Africa catch sight of a rainbow or a certain iridescent sparkle on the surface of the sea, they believe they may have seen a glimpse of the great Rainbow Serpent, Da, after whom they are named. This mighty cosmic creature is both male and female, and its colours reflect this, beginning with a blue, masculine head, then ranging through all the colours of the rainbow to its red, female tail. According to the Dahomey creation myth, the world was created when the god Mawu was carried in Da's mouth across the heavens. When the great serpent rested in the evening its excrement formed both the earth and the mountains, its 7,000 glistening coils shaping the terrain. Within its coils are held the ocean, and the movements of the great serpent's body create the tides and currents of the air. Until the end of time, Da rests, supporting the universe on four great pillars at each of the points of the compass.

Da is one of many Rainbow Serpents in the traditions of the Southern Hemisphere. They are found throughout Australasia, the South Seas and the Far East. He may also reoccur in the Vodun traditions of Haiti as Dambhalla, having been carried there in the 16th or 17th centuries by the Fon peoples.

DABBAT

According to Islamic tradition, Dabbat is a monstrous serpent, destined to arise from the earth on the Day of Judgment, along with the Antichrist named Daggiel. The Dabbat will accuse mankind of not believing in the divine revelations and will bring about the destruction of everything. The Dabbat is therefore identified as one of the many Apocalyptic Creatures found in religion and mythology worldwide.

DADHIKRA

According to the Hindu mythology of India, the Dadhikra is a winged white horse, bearing a striking resemblance to Pegasus in Greek mythology. Born from an ocean of milk, it represents the new moon. It has the wings of an eagle and is said to be both beautiful and swift. Its importance to the mythology of the Hindu people is related to the symbolism of the horse sacrifices once practised widely throughout India.

DAGON

Among the Philistines and Phoenicians, Dagon appears to be a fish god. The name *Dagon* is a diminutive derived from the Semitic root *dag*, meaning, 'little fish'. Coins discovered in Philistine or Phoenician cities show Dagon as a composite figure, human in the upper part of the body, fish-like in the lower. He seems to have been worshipped in maritime cities such as Azotus, Gaza, Ascalon and Arvad.

The classical writer Philo tells us that 'Dagon, after he had discovered corn and the plough, was called Zeus of the plough.' He adds that, according to an old Phoenician legend, Dagon was one of the four sons born of the marriage of Anu, the lord of heaven, with his sister, the Earth, which seems to point to a watery being. It may be that a dual understanding of Dagon developed along the shore of the Mediterranean in the course of time as a result of the different derivations of his name. Most scholars agree that the name and worship of Dagon were imported from Babylon, and the Tell-el-Amarna letters (c. 1480–50 BC), mention the names Yamir-Dagan and Dagan-Takala as rulers of Ascalon, suggesting that worship of the god among the inhabitants of Palestine is genuinely ancient, since kings often took the names of their deities. Unlike Baal who, among the Canaanites, was essentially a local deity, Dagon seems to have been considered by the Philistines to be a national god.

'To him they attributed their success in war; him they thanked by great sacrifices, before him they rejoiced over the capture of Samson' (Judges, 16:23).

DAHAK

According to the mythology of the ancient Persian religion of Zoroastrianism, the Dahak, also known as Azi Dahaka, is a vast winged, three-headed dragon, each with a mouth that exudes fire, and a body made up of scorpions and lizards. The creature was born from the evil will of Ahuramazda, the personification of evil in the Zoroastrian system. The sole purpose of the Dahak was to destroy all goodness in the world. The hero Thraotona or, in some versions of the myth, Atar, who fought for several weeks before finally subduing it, bound it in mighty chains beneath a mountain. It is prophesied that at the end of time the Dahak will rise to destroy all of humanity; however, the same prophecy says that another hero, Keresaspa, will finally defeat the creature. Dahak recently became known to a whole new generation of cult television enthusiasts in the mythology created by the writers of the TV series *Xena, Warrior Princess* (1995–2003) and *Hercules: The Legendary Journeys* (1994–2002). Here, the Dahak is once again a symbol of evil that cannot be destroyed and which takes on a human form on occasion.

DALHAM

A well-known and much-feared djinn mentioned in Islamic mythology. The Dalham usually materializes in the form of a man riding a camel, though apparently these are of one piece and together make up a kind of composite creature. The Dalham is most often found on isolated islands along the North African coast and along the shores of the Arabian Peninsular, where he is known to cause wrecks by luring ships onto sharp rocks. Once the forces of nature have completed their task, the Dalham consumes the bodies of the drowned sailors.

Damballah / Damballah Wedo

In the Haitian Vodun traditions, Damballah is the eldest and chief of the Loas or Rada, the great pantheon of this religion. He is perceived as a primordial serpent deity who created the world and the gods. Valleys and mountains were caused by his passage across the newly formed Earth. Along with his wife, Aida Hwedo, who is also a Rainbow Serpent, he is sometimes likened to the Kundalini serpent of Hindu mysticism. Damballah has many aspects, including one in which he appears as St Patrick. He is also called by the name Damballa la Flambeau (Damballah the Torch) and it is said that the rainbow is his sign of dalliance with his wife. Damballah is of such great age and antiquity that he does not speak; instead, when possessing a follower during a ritual, he manifests by making the inspired initiate crawl on the floor like a serpent. Another sign by which Damballah is known are the ripples on the ocean, which are said to be caused by the motion of his coiled body. Some scholars believe that Damballah derives from the cult of Da, which was brought to the Caribbean by the Fon people during the 16th and 17th centuries.

Dan Ayido Hwedo

An alternative name for the Rainbow Serpent, Aida Hwedo, worshipped by the Dahomy people of West Africa and by the Haitian followers of Voudon as the spouse of Damballah.

Ddraig Goch

The Welsh name for the Red Dragon (*Y Ddraig Goch*) widely used in heraldry and on flags representing the land of Wales. The source of this dragon can be traced back to a story told by the 12th-century medieval writer, Geoffrey of Monmouth, though the association may well have originated in its use by the Romans as a standard. They in turn are believed to have borrowed it from the Dacians, whom they defeated in the 2nd century.

Dancing the Animals

As far back as the 2nd century, when the scholar Pollux wrote of the *morphasmos* ('imitation of creatures') or dances by which people suggest different animals by their movements, we have been 'Dancing the Animals'. Such imitative dances form the basis for dance ceremonies worldwide, especially in those cultures where people depend on the bounty or timely migration of animals to keep alive. There are early examples of this depicted in prehistoric cave paintings in France and Spain, where our ancestors painted animals and the ceremonies and dances that would help lure the animals to the hunting grounds. Among the ibex, bison, horses and aurochs are found humanoid figures, sporting the animal heads of their desired prey.

For those who see the animal as a divinity, the dancer does not merely imitate the animal but becomes the animal god whose help he desires. In this way, from earliest times shamans, medicine-people, hunters, initiating elders and others have literally become the inspirited gods embodied in the tribal circle, often lit by the mysterious flickering firelight in the depths of night when such mysteries are enacted.

Throughout parts of civilized northern Europe, the remnants of prehistoric animal dances and ceremonies are still embodied in seasonal folk custom, especially about the time of the year when winter is hardest and food traditionally least abundant: from the accounts of Saxon penitentiaries, which penalized those who went attired as wild horned beasts at the calends (end) of the year, to the winter guizers or disguisers who still go out across the snow portraying the Winter Goat or Schiepercht, or the Hobby Horse, Mari Lwyd or Grey Mary, who still demand poetical dialogues at every door. These creatures still walk among us, creatures known to our prehistoric forebears who had to dance these animals in order to obtain the food that would help them survive the winter and to help drive away sickness and pain.

According to Geoffrey of Monmouth, the tyrant Vortigern, having usurped the kingdom of Britain, and now seeking to flee from the rightful heirs to the throne, attempted to build a secure stronghold in the mountains of Snowdonia. However, each night, the work of his builders was undone, and was discovered in ruins by morning. Consulting his Druidic advisers, Vortigern was told that he must sacrifice a fatherless child, whose blood would ensure that the building of the tower would proceed without further trouble. Vortigern's soldiers went in search of such a child, and soon returned with a boy said to be the offspring of a local princess and an otherworldly demon – hence, no (human) father. Vortigern gave orders for the child to be killed, but before this could happen the boy spoke up, declaring that he knew the real reason why the tower would not stand.

Beneath the foundations was a pool of water, and in the pool a stone chest, and in the chest two dragons that fought eternally. It was the tremors made by their battle which caused the tower to fall each night. Vortigern ordered his builders to dig deep down, and, sure enough, all was revealed to be as the child had said. When the stone chest was opened the two dragons flew into the air and began to fight. Eventually the Red Dragon destroyed the White. The child now explained the significance of the two dragons: the White Dragon represented the Saxons, who were soon to invade Britain; the Red Dragon represented the Welsh people, who would defeat them for a time. The child went on to prophesy Vortigern's death, and the coming of a greater king – no less a figure than Arthur. The child then revealed his name as Merlin, who was to become the most famous prophet and enchanter of the mighty cycle of stories that evolved around the figure of King Arthur who also bore a dragon on the crest of his helmet. Since that time, the Red Dragon has been the emblem of Wales.

DEER

The shy deer who walks unknown in the deep woodlands appears in myths from all over the world. Representations of deer appear in sacred and magical contexts in ancient Egypt where they were sacred to Isis, although the animals themselves had died out in that area before the 1st century AD, after which they no longer featured in Egyptian art or religion. Among the Greeks, the deer was sacred to the moon goddesses Artemis, Aphrodite and Athena, and was also sacred to Apollo at Delphi. Writers from the classical world described how a deer wounded by an arrow would go in search of the herb dittany (*Origanum dictamus*), which would cure it of the wound by ejecting the arrow from its body.

In the Vedic religion of ancient India, Vayu, god of the winds, is often portrayed riding on a deer. The animal is particularly significant to Buddhism as it is associated with the first sermon preached by Buddha in a deer park at Sarnath. Deer are depicted on either side of the Wheel of the Law in Buddhist tradition and are described as representing mediation, gentleness and meekness. However, in Chinese Buddhism, the deer is listed as one of 'the three senseless creatures' representing love sickness, just as the tiger represents anger, and the monkey greed.

In Celtic tradition, the deer is a form often taken by otherworldly women, such as the woman Sadbh in the cycle of stories relating to the hero Fionn. Having mated with Fionn in human form, Sadbh resumed her deer shape, but later gave birth to the hero Oisin, whose name means 'Little Fawn'. There are several deities connected with deer among the traditions of the Celts. These include Flidais, the goddess of venery or sexual gratification, who is driven in a chariot drawn by deer. In general, deer appear as guides and enticers into the Fairy Realm. Salbuide, a son of the king of Munster, died while chasing an otherworldly deer, together with 30 warriors, 30 attendants, and 30 deer hounds.

There are also a number of stories in which humans take on the form of deer; notably the story of the magician Mongan, and in the saga of Tuan Mac Caraill who in order to extend his life lived for many years as a deer before metamorphosing into the shapes of other creatures. Nor was the significance of the deer limited to pre-Christian stories. In one of the early tales relating to St Patrick, we are told that he wrote his famous hymn 'The Deer's Cry' (also known as St Patrick's Breastplate) as a memorial to having escaped from his enemies by taking on the form of the deer. St Patrick was merely using a form of pagan invocation called the Fith-Fath ('Deer's Shape') which was uttered when people wished to become invisible to observation.

The deer is also important among the Native American peoples, where it appears as a totem animal. There are a number of deer tribes and clans, and in the animal myths of the people of the south-east woodlands the deer is the leader of the four-footed clans. Among the south-western tribes of the Yaqui peoples, the Deer dance is enacted to encourage food and fraternity among people and animals. The deer is believed to be a rain bringer, with the ability to dispense thunder and lightning which fertilizes the Earth. The Lakota tell a story of the deer in which a friendly spirit gave to each animal the means of protecting itself. To the deer it gave speed, but one day a doe passed the spirit, accompanied by its ungainly young, and the spirit realized that in giving speed to deer it had forgotten the awkwardness of its young, so it gave spots to help the new-born be camouflaged in the woodland

The Element Encyclopedia of Magical Creatures

undergrowth until it was able to run more swiftly.

For the South American Indians, sometimes deer have the less pleasant task of carrying the soul of a sorcerer or sorceress. Ancestors can also reincarnate as deer. Mixcoatl, the Aztec god of hunting, has as his companion a two-headed deer, while in Mayan tradition the double-headed dragon sometimes appears with deer hooves. In the symbolic art of the Mayans, the deer appears at the base of supporting pillars, suggesting that the animal was a foundation upon which both society and religion were founded. Human forms with deer's heads are also a common feature of Mayan art.

Among the Ainu people of Japan, the deer is said to have been created to provide food for the people; however, originally they were the hunted animals used by the gods, at which time they were white. The bones and hair of deer consumed in a heavenly feast by the gods were distributed over the mountains and changed into living deer. The magical properties of the deer are invisibility, swiftness, and the ability to move between the worlds of everyday and the Otherworld.

DELGETH

The Navajo people of North America describe this creature as a carnivorous antelope, one of a number of evil creatures known by the general name of Anaye. According to tribal belief, during the time when the first people emerged from the earth, men and women lived apart for a time. The

Delgeth also emerged at this time, and terrorized the people until two of their greatest heroes, Nezgani and Thobadzistshini, finally destroyed all of these primordial monsters.

DELPHYNE

In the mythology of classical Greece and Rome, Delphyne is the name of the sister of the Titan named Typhon. She is described as having the body of a woman with a serpent's tail not unlike Melusine. According to the myth, Zeus, the king of the gods of Olympus, was captured by Typhon and imprisoned in a cave. Typhon removed the sinews from the god's legs so that he could not escape and placed Delphyne to keep watch over him. Later, Zeus was rescued by Hermes and Aegipan, who either stole the sinews back or took some from Typhon himself. Once released, the god struck Typhon down with a thunderbolt and placed him in the underworld region of Tartarus. There Delphyne later joined her brother, and the two remain imprisoned to this day. Jointly, they are considered to be the originators of bad weather conditions, especially typhoons, which are named after Typhon himself.

DERKETO

A monstrous creature, half whale, half dragon, from the mythology of Mesopotamia and Babylon. The goddess Inanna (Ishtar) gave birth to this mighty creature after consorting with one of her

The Element Encyclopedia of Magical Creatures

many lovers. Her birth pangs caused a great tidal inundation that covered much of the Earth. According to other authorities, Derketo was the first mermaid.

Atargatis, the mother of the legendary Assyrian queen Semiramis, was a goddess who loved a mortal shepherd, thereby causing his death. Ashamed of her actions, she tried to hide herself in the form of a fish. But the waters of the lake into which she jumped could not or would not conceal her divine nature and so she took upon her the form of a human woman above the waist, a fish below.

The 2nd-century Greek writer Lucian of Samothrace wrote in his book *De Dea Syria*:

I saw the likeness of Derketo in Phoenicia, a strange marvel. It is woman for half its length, but the other half, from thighs to feet, stretched out in a fish's tail ... [The People of the area] consider fishes to be sacred, and they never eat them; and though they eat all other fowls, they do not eat the dove, for she is holy so they believe. And these things are done, they believe, because of Derketo and Semiramis, the first because Derketo has the shape of a fish, and the other because ultimately Semiramis turned into a dove.

Despite Lucian's account, the apparent confusion between these two creatures probably arises from his misreading of carved images on the temples of an earlier time than his own.

DESANA

In the myths of the Amazonian Indians, Desana is the Master of Animals and Fish (*see* Lords and Ladies of the Animals). He appears as a dwarf, covered in the juices of magical plants. He can take the shape of a lizard, jaguar, squirrel or fish. Before any hunter goes in search of game, he must go first to the shaman to negotiate with Desana because a deal must be struck. If game animals are taken, there must be a due exchange that human souls after death must reincarnate as game animals themselves in order to keep the balance of life.

DEV

A race of primordial giants found in the traditions and folklore of Armenia. Described as enormous beings with seven heads, each head having a single enormous eye in the centre of its forehead. Prodigiously strong, they have been observed tossing huge boulders at each other as if in play. They also have the ability to turn into serpents, which suggests they may have originated at a much earlier time than recent records suggest.

DEVIL FISH

In Samoan tradition, the Devil Fish takes the form of an octopus. Originally coming from Fiji, he made his home in a deep inland cave in Apia, furnishing it with red and white coral and using rocks to make the rafters.

The Element Encyclopedia of Magical Creatures

Destroying Creatures

Just as there are animals that help create the world and bring it into being, so there are also creatures that help destroy it. From a human perspective, we tend to see all creation as good and positive and all destruction as evil and negative, but this is not always the case. Just as in the animal world itself there are scavengers who clear away decay and help keep the Earth clean by feeding upon what no one else wants, so in mythology we need the creatures who will dismantle and close down what has been made, so that there are no loose ends.

The end of all things has different names: the Day of Judgment for Christians; the kabbalistic Jewish Tikkun or 'mending' of the world; for Gnostics it is the Apoctastasis or the 'End of the Ages'; for the Zoroastrian Persians it is the Fraskart or 'rehabilitation of creation'; for the Norse it is Ragnorok, 'twilight of the gods'. The destroying creatures often have a fearsome appearance and are animals that already have a reputation for predation or scavenging, such as the wolves Fenrir and Mangamyr who eat the sun and moon in Norse mythology. Sometimes the destroying creatures help in the judgement of the world, as in Islamic tradition where Dabbat is a monstrous serpent, destined to arise from the earth on the Day of Judgment to accuse mankind of not believing in the divine revelations. Dabbat will help bring about the destruction of everything. Many Apocalyptic Beasts stand ready to bring things to the end. In the Book of Revelation there is the lamb with seven horns and seven eyes which depicts the spirits of God. The four horsemen of the Apocalypse ride four great horses: the white horse of conquest, the red horse of war, the black horse of famine, and the pale horse of death. Creatures such as Leviathan, Behemoth, the Hayoth, and Gog and Magog all have apocalyptic aspects.

The Vaimauga tribe made the Devil Fish their god of war because, if they were preparing to fight and heard him pounding on the landward side of the island, they were filled with fear, but if they heard him to seaward, then they felt confident of victory. The Samoan hero, Tiitii-a-Talaga, was said to have beheaded a Devil Fish that was always dragging passers-by off the path and eating them.

DEVIL'S DANDY DOGS

In the folklore of western Britain, especially around the area of Dartmoor, many stories are told of the Devil's Dandy Dogs – a pack of fire-breathing, fire-eyed hounds led by the Devil himself over the moorland on stormy nights. Anyone unlucky enough to get in their way will be torn to pieces, though prayer can turn them aside. They are similar to the Whist Hounds, who hunt on wild nights and are considered to be a sign of imminent death to anyone who sees them. They are said to be the souls of unbaptized children, though others say that they steal such souls.

DHAUL/DHOL

In the folktales and beliefs of rural India, this is the name of the great sacred white cow that supports the universe on its horns. Cows have been sacred in India from very distant times, and continue to be revered to this day. Dhaul is related to the cosmic cow.

DHEEYABERY

Among the legends and folklore of the Kamilaroi people of Western Australia, the wonderful story is told of a young man named Yooneeara, who one day decided to walk all the way to where the sun sets. His journey took him to some very strange places, and on the way he met many bizarre creatures – none more so than the Dheeyabery who, though they looked like human beings from the front, from behind were simply huge masses of unformed flesh.

DHINNABARRADA

In the legends and folklore or the Kamilaroi people of Western Australia, the story is told of how a young man named Yooneeara decided to travel to where the sun sets. On his journey, he met many bizarre creatures, including the Dhinnabarrada. This family of monsters had the bodies of human beings but the feet of emu. They were very swift and Yooneeara feared that he would be unable to escape them. However, foresight had caused him to carry a live bandicoot in his dilly bag, and at this point he set it free.

Dhrana

A mighty serpent in the Hindu mythology of India, Dhrana is described as a seven-headed king of snakes. Like the Naga Muchalinda, he is also the guardian of a god, in this case Parsva. This god maintains a constant war with the evil Meghamalin, and Dhrana is frequently called upon to protect his master.

Dhumavarna

In the mythology and folklore of the Indian sub-continent, the Dhumavarna is described as a composite being, part human and part serpent. The story is told of how the monster kidnapped the young and handsome prince Yadu, whom it spotted walking one day by the seashore and decided that he would make a perfect husband for his daughters. The Dhumavarna took the prince to his underwater kingdom, and there married him to his five mermaid daughters.

Diff Errebi

The polite name of a giant Djinn in the folk traditions of the Moroccan people. As in many other cultures it was considered unlucky to address any other-worldly being by its true name, hence Diff Errebi, which means 'Noble One', was used as a way of currying favour with this volatile being, who could be both unpleasant and savage if one got on the wrong side of him.

Djieien

A vast and hideous spider monster from the traditions of the Native American Seneca people. Generally, it was indestructible, keeping its heart buried under its lodge, much like the giants of later fairy tales whose hearts were often hidden in a separate place. The story is told of the hero Otheigwendha, who encountered the Djieien and, in his struggle with it, ripped a branch from a nearby tree and struck at the monster in an attempt to kill it. His stroke missed the loathsome creature but went into the earth and pierced its heart, killing it instantly.

The Element Encyclopedia of Magical Creatures

Directional Guardians

Many peoples worldwide see the everyday world as part of a greater spiritual cosmos. This belief is often demonstrated by the location of four magical animals at the four main directions of the compass, so that there is a protective animal which oversees the north, south, east and west of the world.

In Mayan tradition, four great forest jaguars, the Balam, guard the directions with ferocious teeth and sharp claws. For the Winnebego Indians of Wisconsin, with its severe winters, it is four bears who stand at each point of the compass – white, red, grey and black for the east, south, west and north, respectively. In Hindu tradition, there are the eight Lokapala (guardian) elephants with their female consorts who stand at the eight points of the compass, each with a Hindu deity upon its back. As the strong animal, the elephant holds the cosmos stable. In China, it is the Ssu Ling who are the four

spiritual creatures: in the west, stands the Ch'i-Lin (or Ki'Lin), the Unicorn; in the south is the Feng-Huang, the phoenix; in the north is Gui Xian, the tortoise; and in the east stands Lung, the dragon.

In rites, prayers and rituals, these directional guardian animals are invoked and remembered before any magical or transformatory work can begin, for they hold the four corners of the cosmos in their safe-keeping. In Navajo sand paintings, the *hatali* (medicine person), creates mandalas on the ground in coloured sand for the healing and balance of individuals and the community. These invariably depict four sacred beings, sometimes in animal shape. The person who is feeling ill, displaced or out of balance is encouraged to sit in the middle of this sacred picture in order to feel their spiritual connection with the magical animals who keep the world safe. *See also* Supporters of the Earth and Sky.

DJINN

These are the primary species of demons in Arabic tradition and are widely known throughout most of the Islamic world, especially in the Sahara and parts of the northern and eastern Mediterranean. There are many variations to their names including Dgen, Dschin, Genie, Ginn, Jann, Jinn and Junun. There are actually several classes of Djinn, including the powerful Marid, the Afreet, the Shaytans and the Jann. Not all are evil and some can be helpful – like the Genie of the Lamp in the story of Aladdin. However, the majority are very ugly and savage in nature. They can take numerous shapes and have been known to appear as human beings, monsters, cats, ostriches, dogs and snakes. When they do take human form, it is often that of a beautiful woman, who may only be detected by the fact that the pupils of her eyes have vertical slits. The evil Djinn cause sandstorms and water spouts, and for this reason when the *Zoba'ah*, a whirlwind that forms itself into a pillar of sand stretching to enormous heights, sweeps across the desert the Arabs believe it to be caused by the flight of one of these evil demons. Almost the only defence against the Djinn is iron, and as in the traditions of European fairies, any iron object can bind them.

According to Koranic tradition the Djinn were created from fire, or have fire in their veins instead of blood. Their first leader was called Taranushi, but in time he was overthrown and they have since possessed many chieftains.

Other traditions say that the Djinn are composed of air and were created 2,000 years before man, who they will not outlive, since it is prophesied that they will be destroyed at the Last Judgment. Some traditions say that the Djinn are governed by 40 (or 72) kings named Suleyman. One particular tradition describes a battle between Djinn and angels in which the Djinn were the losers, being driven from the mainland to the islands in the Arabian Gulf. One young Djinn, named Azazel, was taken prisoner and brought up among the angels. In time, he became their leader and took the name Iblis. When Adam was created, God commanded the angels to worship him; the only one who refused to do so was Iblis, and for this disobedience he was turned into a devil and became the leader of a race of Djinn called Shaytan, from which the Western name for the devil, Satan, derives.

Earth Djinns dwell in drains, toilets, cemeteries and dark damp ruins. Water Djinns inhabit any water source, be it river, fountain or well. They are deemed particularly malevolent and like nothing more than to entice humans into the water so that they can drown them. Tree Djinns inhabit the trees and are the most benign of the species, with the exception of the Djinn that inhabits the fig tree, who causes humans to quarrel with each other if they chance to rest beneath the shade of its branches. Stories are told of humans and Djinn marrying but while a human man may marry a female Djinn, a human female may not marry a male Djinn. The offspring of such marriages

The Element Encyclopedia of Magical Creatures

will appear human but have the magical abilities of the Djinn, including the power of flight, the ability to walk through walls, and extreme longevity. In general, Djinn are very hard to kill and are extremely long-lived, but men have found ways to kill them, and in their own wars the Djinn can destroy each other.

DOBHARCHU

The name of the father of all otters in Ireland. The Dobharchu is so powerful that it can break through rocks and tunnel at incredible speeds beneath the earth. It is of a great size, being about 6–8 ft from head to tail, with short white fur and a dark-brown cross marking its back. The otter was a sacred animal among the Celts, probably because it was equally at home on land or in water (the margins of watery places were considered as gateways to the Otherworld). The Dobharchu, also known as the Dorraghow, is sometimes called the 'King of the Lakes'. The native people of Ireland, who described him as both ferocious and terrifying, held him in the highest respect.

DOBIE/DOBBY

A British house fairy, known mostly in the north of England, and as others of its kind, it likes to help human beings. They particularly like to join in with the kind of tasks undertaken by labourers, and are sometimes given the job of guarding treasure. However, the Dobie is not known for its wisdom, and often makes ridiculous mistakes or is easily confused. In parts of West Yorkshire, the name Dobby is applied to an evil fairy who leaps on the backs of unsuspecting travellers on horseback and garrottes them. Today, the Dobie is probably best known from its appearance in the Harry Potter books by J.K. Rowling, where it generally assumes the role of a helpful but not very bright companion to the young wizard.

DOG

The dog was probably domesticated as long ago as 7500 BC, and it has been with us ever since. Although seen by most societies as a friend and companion, a guardian and defender, some have regarded it, especially in sacred or mythological terms, in a less friendly light. This ambiguous history is reflected in that dogs can be either solar or lunar creature. Solar dogs chase away winter, bring fire and destroy enemies. Luna dogs, such as those associated with Artemis, goddess of the moon and hunt, act as intermediaries between various deities of the moon. The 2nd-century Roman writer Apuleius says that 'the dog ... his face alternately black and golden, denotes the messenger going hither and thither between the higher and the infernal powers.' The dog is also a guardian of the underworld, as is the case of the three-headed dog Cerberus. The Roman author Plutarch says that dogs symbolize 'the conservative, watchful, philosophical principle of life'.

The Element Encyclopedia of Magical Creatures

Throughout the ancient world, the importance of the dog varies hugely. In ancient Babylon it was revered. In Phoenician traditions, the dog is associated with the sun, and became an emblem of the great physician Gala, giving rise to a class of priests called 'Dogs'. The Arcadian goddess Belit-ili is represented either with a dog sitting by her side or on a throne supported by four dogs. Hittite ritual records how a small figurine of a dog was made of tallow and placed on the threshold of a building. The following invocation was then spoken aloud: 'You are a little dog of the table of the royal pair. Just as by day you do not allow other men into the courtyard, so do not let any evil thing in during the night.'

In the Semitic lands, the dog is a companion of lizards and scorpions and had a far less favourable position; this habitual dislike was carried over into Judaism where the dog was held in contempt and is considered unclean and a scavenger. According to the Book of Revelation, it was said to be the companion of sorcerers, fornicators and blasphemers. This idea was shared in Islamic tradition, where the dog is regarded as unclean and driven away from inhabited places, though greyhounds were occasionally used for hunting.

Dogs were venerated in Egypt and were considered sacred to Anubis the Jackal god, and to Hermes as messenger of the gods. In the classical world in general, the view of the dog is ambivalent. The term 'cynic' – meaning dog-like – implies an impudent form of flattery. Homer calls the dog shameless but associates it with Aesculapius the physician and healer. Sirius, the dog star, was a faithful companion of the hunter Orion. Hecate has a pack of dogs that signify her warlike aspect, and dogs were sacrificed to her at the roadside.

In ancient Indian tradition, the Vedic god of the dead, Yama, has two ferocious dogs as companions, each with four eyes, who act as his messengers and scout the world looking for souls of those about to die. Indra, chief of the Vedic gods, has a hunting dog as his attribute and constant companion. In China, the celestial dog T'ien Kou symbolized both creation and destruction. The reason behind this may lie in an ancient association of the dog with comets, meteors and eclipses, which were seen to have both detrimental and beneficial effects. At his most destructive, the celestial dog is known to carry off newborn children if they are left unguarded, while the spirit of the dog star is the ruler of the astrological house of each particular family.

There are numerous famous dogs in Celtic tradition, reflecting the importance ascribed to the animal. The hero Arthur's great hound Cafall left its footprint on a stone, called to this day Carn Cafall, which if moved in the evening was back in its original place next day. Fionn possessed a great dog named Bran, which is extolled in stories and poems alike.

Yellow paws that are on Bran,
Belly whitish-grey, heath coloured,
Eye like sloe, crooked claws,
And two sharp pointed ears, keenly active,
Two ears alike, so red ...

The Element Encyclopedia of Magical Creatures

In Celtic folklore tradition, there is a reference to three green dogs (certainly fairy animals) named Fios, Luaths and Tron – that is Knowledge, Swiftness and Heaviness. Frequent references are found to the Cwn Annwfn (Hounds of the In-World or Underworld), a pack of red-eared, white-bodied hounds that hunt across the lands of mortals as well as in the Otherworld. They are said to be the same as the Wild Hunt, references to which abound in Celtic and Teutonic mythology, as a pack led by Gwyn ap Nudd, the lord of the Otherworld, or sometimes by Arawn himself, in pursuit of the souls of evil or unworthy people.

The dog was also associated by the Celts with healing, its saliva being believed to have curative properties. A shrine exists at Nettleton Shrub in Wiltshire dedicated to a Romano-British deity named Apollo-Cunomaglus ('Hound Lord'), which shows that in this area, and therefore probably elsewhere, there was an established association between hunting and healing, qualities known to have been combined in the figure of Apollo.

In Norse and Teutonic mythology, Odin is accompanied by two dogs, Geri and Freki, and two ravens that act as both counsellors and messengers. A monstrous dog named Garmr is the guardian of the underworld. Among Native Americans, the dog has long been recognized as a faithful companion, guardian and protector. It is seen as a hero and messenger, also bringing rain and discovering fire. The Iroquois tribes sacrificed a white dog at the New Year

festival in the belief that it would carry their prayers to the next world. The Huichol Indians of Central America describe themselves as descended from the dogs who survived the Great Flood. The Aztec god Quetzalcoatl takes on the form of a dog before entering the Land of the Dead – again suggesting the dog's ability to open the ways between the worlds. There is also a dog god named Xolotl, who is said to be the twin brother of Quetzalcoatl.

Among the Ainu of Japan, dogs are stationed along the road to the other world and act as guides to passing souls, directing them on their way to their proper destination. Among the aborigines of Australia, to whom Dog is a totem animal, wild dogs or dingoes are to be found around the campsites of the native people, who protect them as valuable members of the tribe. Wherever we look in the culture and mythology of the world, we find the dog portrayed as a constant companion, guardian and guide to humanity.

DOGS OF FO

The Dogs of Fo, which are found in Chinese tradition, are no ordinary dogs. They are hybrid creatures, described as having the body of a lion, the wings of an eagle, the head of a dog – sometimes with a single horn like that of the Unicorn – and a bushy or feathered tail. Representations of these creatures usually show the male with one front paw resting on a globe, while a puppy usually accompanies the female.

The Element Encyclopedia of Magical Creatures

DOLPHIN

Dolphins have been considered sacred from the earliest times and were known in Egypt as well as the classical world of the Mediterranean. In some cultures, they are known as the King of the Fishes and represent the power of the sea itself. The Roman writer Pliny wrote that 'the dolphin is the swiftest of all other living creatures whatsoever, and not of the sea fish only ... it is quicker than any fowl, swifter than the arrow from the bow.' The dolphin is also seen as a saviour and a guide to souls in the underworld and as a psychopomp who conducts the dead to the Isles of the Blessed.

In the classical world, the sun god Apollo is closely associated with the dolphin, which is found carved in relief on the walls of his temple at Delphi. In his aspect as Apollo Delphinos, founder of the Delphic oracle, Apollo is said to assume that the form of that creature. Symbolically, the Greeks associated the dolphin with the marriage between the masculine sun god and the feminine power of the Earth mother, Gaia. The Greek words for dolphin, *deiphis*, and for womb, *delphys*, were seen to reflect this deeper symbolism. The dolphin's long-standing association with music, which it makes with its song and appears to enjoy hearing, also dates back to classical times when 'the music-loving dolphin' is written about. In several stories from Greek myth, the dolphin saves people who would otherwise have drowned at sea: both the immortal hunter Orion and Telemachus, the son of Odysseus, being among them. One tradition says that the Isthmean Games were founded in honour of Melicantes, whose dead body was brought ashore by a dolphin. In both Greek and Roman traditions, the sea gods – Poseidon and Neptune – have the symbol of the dolphin as their emblem. The dolphin is also said to represent Aphrodite, the Woman of the Sea, and both nymphs and nereids are generally depicted riding on dolphins.

A Greek story from the 2nd century BC tells how a dolphin fell in love with a beautiful boy from the gymnasium of Iassos, on the borders of the sea. Whenever the boy paddled, the dolphin would come closer. At first fearful, the boy soon learned how to ride the dolphin out into the deep whenever school was finished. But one day, the boy forgot where he was and he flung himself belly-down onto the dolphin's back, catching himself on the dorsal spike which ruptured his flesh. The dolphin felt how heavy the boy was riding and how the sea was turning purple with his blood. The dolphin then ran itself upon the shore with the boy upon his back. They lay lifeless on the beach and died to the great compassion of all who saw them. Iassos built a mausoleum for them both, showing the two lovers together. On the beach, they still honour Eros as the god who had led boy and dolphin to that place.

Among the Native American people, the dolphin is seen as a messenger between this world and the next. It is also said to represent the Great Spirit, the essence of everything. Christian symbolism sometimes replaces the more usual fish, said to represent Christ, with the dolphin, and in religious symbolism a dolphin with a ship or anchor can represent the Great Ship of the Christian Church. A dolphin pierced by a trident, or hung upon an anchor, is said to symbolize the Crucifixion. The Christian churchman and historian Bede attributed the dolphin with the power to forecast the weather when he wrote: 'When dolphins leap more often from the waves, the wind shall rise from a quarter towards which they leap.'

DOMOVOI

In Slavic tradition, the Domovoi are protective house spirits like the brownie. They help with household chores and are treated as one of the family. It is important to put down a saucer of milk or some bread near the stove, which is where the Domovoi go to rest. If the Domovoi are disturbed, then so is the household. If they take a dislike to someone, you can be sure that everyone will know, for they will torment them, misplace their possessions and play tricks. A piece of salt bread wrapped in a white cloth is an offering that will placate the Domovoi if you get on their wrong side. Normally quiet and invisible, Domovoi often make noises to warn the household of

impending death or trouble. If they play on a comb, making music, then a wedding is likely. If a Domovoi is very angry, it can sneak into the bedroom and sit upon a sleeper and suffocate him to death.

DONESTRE

A race of strange semi-humanoid creatures originating in the legends surrounding Alexander the Great. Though basically human in shape, they had the head of a lion, huge eyes, furry ears, and a long mane that extended over the shoulders and almost to the waist. The Donestre were said to know all the languages of the human race, and would greet lone travellers in their own tongue, thus reassuring them and enabling the Donestre to lure their victims to their deaths. A Donestre kill would usually be known by the fact that the only thing left behind was the head; even more strange was the fact that after it had killed, the creature would sit by the head of its victim and weep.

DONN OF CUALGNE

A great bull from the ancient traditions of Ireland, the Donn was so vast that a whole army could stand in its shadow and its back was so wide that games could be played there by as many as 50 people. The Donn was also known as Donn Tarbh (the Brown Bull), and it was said that it had only to low to sire calves by every cow that heard its voice in Ireland. Such a prize was the Donn that he became a source strife between the tribes of Ulster and Connaught, each of whom desired to possess it. Though little remains of the original epic tale, it is likely that at some point the story of the Donn formed part of a primal creation myth among the Celtic peoples. The Donn was originally a pig-keeper named Friuch (Boar's Bristle) who contended with Ruach (Boar's Grunt) the pig-keeper of Ochall. Their conflict continued for some time, during which they shifted shape into ravens, water beasts, stags, warriors, phantoms, dragons, and water worms. Finally, they transformed into the Brown Bull of Cuailnge and the White Bull of Connacht – in which form they remained thereafter. In the great Irish epic *Tain bó Cuailgne* (The Cattle Raid of Cooley), Queen Maeve of Connacht provoked war with Ulster by attempting to steal the bull. At the end of the conflict, the Donn met and killed the hero Finnbennach but was itself mortally wounded.

DOVE

The dove is considered sacred and magical wherever in the world it is known. In general, it symbolizes the soul, and is also seen as a messenger between God and Man. Among the primal traditions of the world it is described as representing peace, innocence, gentleness, timidity and chastity – although in some areas it can represent lustfulness. In virtually every tradition that knows of the dove

it is considered sacred to the creating Great Mother or to the Queens of Heaven. Thus in Babylonian and Mesopotamian traditions it is the symbol of the goddess Ishtar and in Christian belief the symbol of the Virgin Mary. The Phoenicians saw the dove as a companion to the moon goddess Astarte, while the Syrian goddess Atargatis bore a sceptre with a golden dove on its tip.

In the mythology of ancient Egypt, the dove is associated with the Tree of Life, and is portrayed sitting in its branches or carrying the fruit of the tree in its beak. It also has a special affinity with the olive and to this day the image of a dove carrying an olive branch is almost universally recognized as a symbol of peace. Only in Japan, where an ancient legend describes the dove as a messenger of war and sacred to the god of war is this symbolism reversed.

In a classical Greek myth, during the time that Zeus was hidden from his father Cronos by his mother Rhea, doves kept him alive by feeding him ambrosia. The dove is also sacred to Adonis, Bacchus and Aphrodite, who is often shown in a chariot drawn by doves. The Roman writer Aelian stated that white turtledoves were sacred not only to Aphrodite and Demeter, but also to the Fates and the Furies, showing that even the peaceful dove could be considered dangerous when it served such destructive forces. A dove that lived in the sacred oak of Dodona gave the oldest oracle of the god Zeus. It apparently spoke with a human voice, and the priestesses of the sacred site were known as 'doves'. Other sources say that the oracular answers were conveyed not by the voice of the bird but in its flight, which could be read according to the circumstances. Yet another version attributes the oracle to the sound of the rustling of leaves caused by doves sitting among the branches of the sacred oak.

The turtledove was domesticated by the Hebrew people and these were the only creatures that could be appropriately sacrificed according to the Law of Moses. Doves are the most mentioned birds in the Bible and were considered to be particularly sacred. In Old Testament tradition, the dove represents freedom, escape from tyranny, simplicity, harmlessness, innocence, meekness and constancy. In the New Testament, it represents the Holy Spirit, and in later medieval tradition is perceived as bringing the sacred wafer into the vessel of the Holy Grail.

In Babylonian, Chaldean, Greek and Hebrew traditions, the dove is associated with the story of the Great Flood, in which its appearance symbolized an end to the inundation and a return to normal life. As Christianity developed, it adopted the dove as a symbol of the Annunciation, and it is frequently portrayed in medieval and Renaissance art as bringing the news of the imminent birth of the Christ child to the Virgin Mary. In Christian symbolism, the dove is placed opposite the black raven which represents sin and evil.

The ancient book of natural (and fantastic) history, the *Physiologus*, says that the turtledove, which dwells in solitude, typifies sadness and loneliness.

If she loses her mate, it is said that the female will not take another and in this way she represents chastity and continence.

Draco

Draco is the version of the dragon found in Graeco-Roman myths and traditions. Descriptions of the creature found in early classical writings suggest a kind of winged serpent rather then the more traditional shape of the dragon. However, by the 12th century, when the dragon had developed into a familiar heraldic device, it had become modified. Bestiaries of the period described the Draco as a great serpent with a crest on its head and a very small mouth.

Draconcopedes

In versions of the myth of the Garden of Eden in which the serpent is described as a dragon, it is usually referred to as a Draconcopedes. Medieval folklore often portrays these beings as vast serpentine creatures with the head, face and breasts of a woman.

Dracontides

According to the classical Greek writer Aristophanes, this is the name given by the gods to the great king Cecrops after he had been changed into a dragon. In some versions of the myth, he is a type of hero, described as the first king of Athens, who brought the benefits of civilization to the country.

DRAGON

Of all mythological creatures, the dragon is surely the best known. Virtually every culture in the world has its dragon myths, and countless stories have been told of its origins, history and of its defeat at the hands of dragon slayers. The dragon slain by St George is perhaps the most typical and consistent in its imagery, and dragons found in the bestiaries of heraldry echo it very closely. In each instance, it has bat wings, a barbed and often poisonous tail, and it breathes fire. It is depicted thus in numerous English folktales, and it is often portrayed in Christian churches, or in the many paintings that describe St George in the act of slaying the creature. In most of these, the dragon is usually represented as a far smaller creature than its more ancient forbears.

Most British dragons are really worms, a name that comes from Scandinavian tradition. These creatures are wingless, generally have lengthy bodies, and a poisonous rather than fiery breath. Dragons and worms have several traits in common – they tend to be scaly, haunt wells or pools, and have a deep attraction to maidens and princesses. Both creatures are known to hoard treasure, which they have either gathered for themselves or inherited, becoming guardians by chance. All are extremely hard to kill.

It is generally accepted that the myth of the dragon grew out of the remains of extinct dinosaurs discovered in ancient times and believed to belong to magical or unearthly creatures. Details such as their fiery breath and wily nature were added afterwards. Artefacts depicting dragons of one kind or another have been found as early as the 4th millennium BC. Excavations in Pakistan and China have unearthed objects decorated by winged snakes, while a cylinder seal dating to the late 2nd century BC shows a creature which is not far in shape from the traditional idea of the dragon.

The word 'dragon' derives from the ancient Greek *drakonta* or *drakon*, which mean 'to watch' or 'to look at', suggesting that even at that point in time the notion of a dragon as a guardian was already established. In the Greek myth, it is a dragon that guards the Golden Apples of the Hesperides, while in European tradition it is usually crouched upon a vast mountain of treasure. The Latin word for dragon is *draco* and in classical Roman art the Draco is generally depicted as a vast serpent with wings resembling those of a bat, a long tail and fiery breath. Pliny the Elder in his *Historia Naturalis* (AD 77) gives an account of dragons in the land of Ethiopia, describing them as perhaps 60 ft in length and living primarily off the flesh of elephants. The story is told that they twined themselves together to form a huge living raft and then sailed across to the Arabian Peninsula. These dragons were said to possess a stone called the Dracontias, which was lodged in the brain. In medieval times, alchemists sought these with great diligence, as they were believed to be an essential ingredient in the creation of the Elixir of Life.

The most ancient stories relating to the dragon make it a power that must be defeated or bound by a god or hero. These cosmic battles, which date back to the earliest times, include the story of the Egyptian Horus and Typhon, the Babylonian Marduk and Tiamat, the Greek Apollo and the Python, and the Graeco-Roman Hercules and the Hydra, and many more. Slaying the dragon often disguises a deeper struggle between light and darkness with the dragon usually symbolizing the dark, and its slayer light and goodness. Out of this also came the traditions of the dragons as guardians of treasure – a just reward for those brave enough and strong enough to overcome these mighty adversaries.

Early references to dragon-like creatures turn up in Babylonian, Egyptian, Chinese, and Japanese accounts, as well as in classical Greek and Roman sources. In many of these the dragon described is not the evil creature of later mythology, but often a great serpent that represents the primal matter of creation itself, or the life-giving waters of Ocean. In this context, its wings are described as sending forth the air, which is the breath of life. It is also seen as a messenger of the sky gods. Later, this symbolism changes, perhaps with the shift from Paganism to Christianity, which caused beings representing the ancient powers of the gods to become darker and more negative.

The 4th-century BC Greek playwright Euripides was one of the first classical writers to describe a dragon breathing fire; while in the Old Testament, Moses mentions fiery serpents and Isaiah speaks of high-flying fire-breathing creatures which resemble dragons. In Egyptian myth, Apophis is a dragon of darkness who has to be overcome every day by the sun god Ra. In Roman myth, the goddess Ceres flies through the heavens in a chariot drawn by two dragons, and later lends this to the hero Triptolomus to enable him to distribute corn to the human race. Medusa, though not a dragon herself, in one version of the story escapes from Jason in a chariot drawn by a winged dragon. Apollo may be seen as a type of dragon slayer, who kills the Python of Delphi – though the latter is more a serpent than a traditional dragon.

One of the earliest stories featuring a dragon of cosmic proportions is found in the Babylonian *Epic of Creation*, composed during the 2nd century BC. Here we learn of the struggle between the god Abzu, god of the primordial waters beneath the earth, and his consort Tiamat, who was a dragon of the sea, against their son Ea, the all-knowing god of wisdom. Ea fought and killed Abzu and replaced him. He then engendered the hero Marduk on his consort and prepared for war against his mother. To swell the ranks of her forces in the coming war, Tiamat gave birth to a host of dreadful creatures:

Giant snakes, sharp of tooth and
   unsparing of fang.
She filled their bodies with venom
   instead of blood,
She cloaked ferocious dragons with
   fearsome rays
And made them bear mantles of
   radiance, made them god-like …

Biblical tradition takes the idea of the dragon and marries it with ancient images from Middle Eastern belief and tradition. Even the Serpent of the Garden of Eden is sometimes referred to as a dragon, while in the Book of Revelation a red dragon with multiple-crowned heads appears. Its tail is so great that it sweeps a third of the stars from the sky, throwing them upon the Earth. A great war then ensues between the beast and the archangel Michael and his angels, who cast it down upon the Earth. Three unclean spirits like frogs come out from the dragon's mouth, which are said to be devils, working false miracles. Finally, the dragon is thrown into a bottomless pit, where it will remain for at least 1,000 years, imprisoned by an angel with a key and chain.

In Hindu tradition, the dragon represents manifest power and the spoken word, and is a representative of both Aruna and Soma. The great god Indra slew a dragon named Vitra in order to release the primordial waters and make the Earth fruitful.

It is without doubt in China that the dragon achieves its most complex mythological and symbolic status. Here it represents the highest spiritual

power and is emblematic of the representatives of such power on Earth. Dragons are said to influence every aspect of life and in this context are one of the 12 symbolic creatures of the Zodiac. Among its many other attributes, it is known to represent the sun, the heavens and the fertilizing rain. Often dragons are represented as living in elaborate palaces above ground or beneath the sea, and there is evidence that in ancient times offerings were made to them. Oriental dragons are also known as shapeshifters and they can make themselves invisible at will. They have many different characteristics, some good some bad, The celestial dragon, T'ien Lung, is a guardian of the home of the gods and is sometimes represented as holding up the sky. Fu T'sang, the Imperial Dragon, is a guardian of treasure. One very specific description shows that the dragon had become acknowledged as a hybrid being and that every aspect of it had symbolic meaning. It is said that:

The dragon's horns resemble those of a stag, his head is that of a camel, his eyes those of the demon, his neck that of the snake, his belly that of a clam, his scales those of a carp, his claws are those of an eagle, his soles those of a tiger, his ears those of the cow.

In both China and Japan, traditionally the dragon was able to change itself into a bird, and in a monastery in Kyoto there is a painting depicting a composite creature, half dragon, half bird. In Japan, the dragon myth evolved its own pattern. An ancient story tells how a dragon was formed from part of the fire god Kaguzuchi. It produced rain and snow in response to the prayers of men. And, as in both China and India, Japanese river gods took the form of dragons and were believed to bring rain. But it was only with the introduction of Chinese and Indian dragon myths that Japanese rivers became filled with dragons.

An ancient Japanese story tells how the daughter of the sea god happened to notice a beautiful young man looking into a well near the palace gates, and invited him into her father's realm. The sea-king's daughter married the youth, who was also a prince, and after three years in the kingdom of the sea, they returned to earth so that the prince's pregnant bride could give birth – to a son and heir. The prince built her a palace in which she could give birth, but the princess begged him not to watch her. As so often in stories such as this, he could not resist, and saw that she turned into a sea dragon to give birth. Angry and ashamed, the princess deserted her son and husband, and returned to the sea forever.

In British folklore, there are several stories relating to winged, fiery creatures: one being that of the Dragon of Kingston who was eventually choked to death by a giant boulder that rolled down from a ridge into his mouth as he opened it to belch forth flames. The Dragon of Wantley in Lancashire was another dragon of this kind. An account of this creature from *Legends and Traditions of Lancashire* is typical of this kind of story.

The Serpent of Handale in Yorkshire was half dragon and half serpent, since it had fiery breath and a venomous sting. It was a great devourer of maidens until a young man named Skaw killed it when he set out to rescue an earl's daughter. The dragon that haunted Winlatter Rock in Derbyshire was probably the Devil, who had taken this form in order to prey on the local population. The evil creature was finally driven off by a monk who stood upon a rock with his arms outstretched in the shape of a cross. His concentration was apparently so great that his feet sank into the rock and left impressions there that could still be seen in the 19th century. Apparently, the monk did not kill the dragon, but drove it away. It took refuge down a mine in the Derbyshire hills and the waters have been said to taste sulphurous and be slightly warm ever since, evidence of the dragon's presence.

This dragon was the terror of all the countryside. He had forty-four iron teeth, and a long sting in his tail, besides his strong rough hide and fearful wings. He ate trees and cattle, and once he ate three young children at one meal. Fire breathed from his nostrils, and for a long time no man dared come near him. Near the dragon's den there lived a strange knight named More of More Hall, of whom it was said that so great was his strength that he had once seized a horse by its mane and tail, and swung it round and round till it was dead, because it had angered him. Then, said the tale, he had eaten the horse, all except its head. At last, the people of the place came together to More Hall, and with tears implored the knight to free them from the fearful monster which was devouring all their food and making them go in terror of their lives. They offered him all their remaining goods if he would do them this service, but the knight said he wanted nothing except one black-haired maid of sixteen to anoint him for the battle at night, and array him in his armour in the morning.

When this was promised, he went to Sheffield, and found the smiths who made him a suit of armour set all over with iron spikes, each five or six inches in length. Then he hid in a well, where the dragon used to drink, and as it stooped to the water, the knight put up his head with a shout and struck it a great blow in the face. But the dragon was upon him, hardly checked by the blow, and for two days and a night they fought without either inflicting a wound upon the other. At last, as the dragon flung himself at More with the intention of tossing him high into the air, More succeeded in planting a kick in the middle of its back. This was the vital spot: the iron spike drove into the monster so far that it spun round and round in agony, groaning and roaring fiercely, but in a few minutes all was over, it collapsed into a helpless heap, and died.

Dragons are less prevalent in Celtic tradition, despite the importance of the Red Dragon or Ddraig Goch in Welsh lore.

A story is told of a gypsy boy who came to a village within a day of the time when every man save one had been devoured by an especially ferocious creature. The sole survivor pleaded with the gypsy to leave before the dragon came back, but as they spoke a huge shadow fell over the Earth and the dragon landed right in front of them. As the monster approached, the gypsy boy held up his hand and said that if it tried to eat him it would choke. The dragon

The Element Encyclopedia of Magical Creatures

expressed its doubts as to the truth of this and suggested a test. Then it picked up a huge stone and crushed it to dust. The gypsy bowed, and asked the dragon if it could squeeze water out of a stone. Then before the dragon understood what was happening, the gypsy picked up a muslin bag full of cheese and began to squeeze the liquid from it. Impressed, the dragon decided to befriend the gypsy. This kind of trickery continued for some time, and in each case the boy got the better of his adversary. Finally, having pretended friendship with the dragon, the boy invited it back to his camp. There they were met by hoards of naked gypsy children. When the dragon asked who they were, the boy said they were all his children and that they were so hungry he thought the dragon might make a good supper for them. At that, the dragon flew away and was never seen again.

Dragons are particularly popular in the folklore and legends of Russia, and most conform to the classical type. Such natural phenomena as eclipses of the sun and moon are widely accepted to be caused by dragons; though when the heavenly orbs reappeared this was taken as a clear sign that if even such mighty creatures as dragons could not withstand the power of the heavens, then mankind could survive them also. Most of the dragons in Russian legends and folk stories are less intelligent than their counterparts elsewhere in the world.

The appearance of the dragon can vary a great deal according to which part of the world it comes from. In some places it has a head that is reptilian, while in India it sometimes has the head of an elephant, a lion or bird of prey; in the Middle East it is usually serpentine and may have many heads. The colour of the dragon ranges from green, red or black to yellow, blue or white. Dragons seem to love ruins and are often found in ancient castles, palaces or cities that have fallen into ruins. They are also found in swamps, deserts and caverns, on mountains and in the forest. The story of the assault on the dragon's lair is almost as fixed as the form of the dragon itself. In almost every instance, the hero, once he has found a way to kill the dragon, ends by cutting off its head, tongue, feet or tail, often to prove that he has killed the creature, but sometimes because it carries power of its own. Thus, in the Teutonic myth of the hero Siegfried, having defeated the dragon, he cuts out its tongue, getting some of its saliva on his lips in the process. Thereafter he can understand the language of birds and animals.

In Norse and Germanic tradition, we find one of the prime stories of the dragon in the epic poem *Beowulf.* In the oldest traditions of the Norse people, Nidhoggr ('One Full of Hatred') is the Dragon of Death, which drinks the blood of the dead and eats corpses. According to the Norseman Snorri's *Edda*, it is said that Nidhoggr will survive the end of the world and live in the one that will replace it. Elsewhere Nidhoggr is described as living under the roots of the world tree Yggdrasil. A squirrel acts as a messenger between the dragon and a great eagle which sits at the top of the tree, sowing discord in the human race. The Midgard Serpent lives at the centre of the Earth or in the ocean, and was created from the eyebrows of the primal giant Ymir – though some sources describe him as the offspring of the black-hearted trickster god, Loki. Norse mythology describes this creature as living in the primeval ocean that surrounds the world. Later, Thor is said to have used an ox skull as a hook to catch the great serpent, dispatching it with his mighty hammer. In some versions, Thor himself dies as a result of breathing the poisonous breath of the serpent.

The dragon is found on the banners of many different peoples, including the Persians, Romans, Welsh and Norse. This may have contributed to its fierce and warlike nature. The myth of the dragon continues to grow, with the literary works of J.R.R. Tolkien presenting the memorable Smaug the Golden and Anne McCaffrey's 'Pern' series adding an entire new line to the story, in the shape of her Dragonriders.

The magical properties of dragons include the ability to guard treasure and knowledge, to usher in new cycles of time, to shape and sculpt the Earth and to endure to the ending of the world.

DRAGON-HORSE

This hybrid creature, from Chinese mythology, is a messenger of the gods. It had the body of a dragon and the front quarters of a horse. This being bore both the vital essence of Heaven and Earth and it was revealed to the Yellow Emperor as the interpenetrating symbol of the Yin and Yang, the balanced polarity of the female and male energies in the world.

DRAKE/FIRE-DRAKE

The Drake is a dragon in the traditions and folklore of gypsies from the Balkan states of south-eastern Europe. It is described as a vast human with the head and feet of a dragon. Sometimes it is to be seen riding on a giant horse and is said to live in a fantastic palace with a human wife. The name Fire-Drake is an alternative name for the dragons of Norse and Teutonic tradition.

DRYADS

One of two species of guardian tree spirits found in Greek mythic tradition. The others are the Hammadryads, who are permanently attached to their trees, and sometimes die when their trees are cut down. Dryads, on the other hand, are able to leave their trees and wander or dance in the groves of the forest. They are often described as companions to the moon goddess Artemis, and they also sometimes accompany Dionysus, the god of wine. It is considered unlucky to see them or remain in their company. The name dryad comes from the Greek *drys*, meaning oak.

DUAMUTEF

The Canopic Animal that is responsible for guarding the stomach of the deceased in the mummification process. Duamutef has the head of a jackal. He is under the protection of the goddess, Neith, and his name means 'he who praises his mother'. Duamutef was told by Horus to worship the deceased and give him confidence in the afterlife. Duamutef preserves the sense of taste and appetite for enjoyment.

Dun Cow

A gigantic cow found in the folklore of Britain. In many parts of the country, there are stories of giant cows of this kind. All are able to give unlimited quantities of milk if treated well. However, anyone foolish enough to attempt to take more milk than they are entitled to, found themselves facing a terrifying monster. In the medieval tale of Sir Guy Warwick, this happened when a greedy woman attempted to use a sieve to collect the cow's milk. So angry was the cow that it ran amok and had to be chased by Sir Guy. He trapped the creature on Dunsmore Heath and killed it. For some time after this, one of the cow's gigantic horns could be seen exhibited at Warwick Castle, though in all probability this was an elephant's tusk brought back by a Crusader or a medieval traveller.

There was a man called MacKenzie who was one of the tenants of Oonich in Lochaber. It happened that every night his cattle-fold was broken down and the cattle grazed through his cornfields. He was sure that neither the neighbours nor the cattle were responsible, and concluded that it must be the fairies, so he fetched his brother, a one-eyed ferryman – who had the second sight – to watch with him. Late in the night, they heard the sound as of stakes being pulled up, and the one-eyed ferryman, moving quietly towards the far side of the field, saw a dun, polled cow throwing the stakes aside and butting the cattle to their feet. She then drove them through the broken fencing to the cornfield. The ferryman followed her silently, and saw her go up to the Fairy Knoll of Gerry Mac Brandy.

The knoll opened before her and she went in. He hastened after her in time to stick his dirk into the turf at the door, so that it would not shut. The light streamed out of the knoll and he saw everything. In the centre of the knoll sat a circle of big old grey men round the fire on which a cauldron was burning. By this time, the farmer had come up, but could see nothing until he put his foot on his brother's foot and then the whole scene was clear to him, and he was very much alarmed, and wanted to go away. But the ferryman called out in a loud voice: 'If your Dun Cow ever troubles Oonich fold again, I will take everything out of the knoll, and throw it out on Rudha na h'Oitre.' With that he pulled out the dirk and the door shut itself. They went down home, and the dun polled cow never troubled them again.

The Element Encyclopedia of Magical Creatures

Dunnie

A kind of shapeshifting spirit from the traditions and folklore of north-east England. A well-known Dunnie inhabited the area around Hazlerigg in the country of Northumbria and used to materialize in the form of a donkey, or sometimes a plough horse which, when harnessed by an unsuspecting farmer, would toss the harness off at a crucial point and gallop off laughing. Some sources suggest that the Dunnie was originally the ghost of a Border reiver, who was caught and killed robbing a granary. He seems to have had a large amount of plunder hidden in one of the caves nearby, and, having died without revealing its whereabouts, continued to haunt the place. However, the Dunnie's powers of shapeshifting suggest he was more than just a ghost, while his practical jokes suggest that there might be a touch of goblin about him.

Dzu-The

One of three types of giant Yeti described in the traditions and folklore of the people of Tibet. The chief variation appears to be in size, and at least two other creatures are mentioned, known respectively as the Meh-The and the Yeh-The.

Ea

One of the trio of creator gods in Babylonian and Mesopotamian mythology. Together with Anu and Enlil, Ea (or Enki) is the creator of mankind; however, his first concern was for the sea, over which he ruled. Originally, he was portrayed as a human being with a long, flowing beard in which swam fish; later, he developed into a hybrid creature, one half human, the other half fish.

Each Tened

In Irish mythology, the Each Tened ('Fire-Horse') comes to remove evildoers. Like the Each Uisge, it takes the unwary, but to ride upon it is to burn, since it is fiery hot.

Each Uisge

An especially malevolent water horse in Irish and Scottish Gaelic folklore, this creature inhabits areas of saltwater or large inland lakes, a fact that distinguishes it from the Kelpie, which primarily inhabits running water. The Each Uisge is a particularly fearsome creature and its main purpose is to capture and kill humans. As with all water horses, it usually appears as a sleek and handsome horse, which offers itself to be ridden.

A tale was told around the area of Aberfeldy, Perthshire, which described how seven little girls and a small boy were playing in a field near their home. There they encountered what they thought was a beautiful pony. Eagerly they sought to mount it. As each one climbed on its back, the back grew longer to accommodate them. The little boy noticed this and hurried off to hide amid some rocks by the side of a nearby lake. Seeing him, the Each Uisge shouted: 'Come back, little scabby-head!' At which point the little girls began to scream, but found they could not get down. The pony galloped off into the nearby lake. The little girls were never seen again, though next day their livers – apparently the only part inedible to the Each Uisge – were discovered floating in the water.

In most instances, it is said that the water horse is most likely to emerge from the water during the month of November, a period sacred to the Celtic people from early times. In this month, it can often be seen galloping along the seashore or on the slopes of gentle hills, inviting foolish mortals to come for a ride that will undoubtedly be their last.

EAGLE

Of all natural creatures possessing a mythological aspect, the eagle is more widely known and written about than any other. Its natural grace and wild beauty doubtless has much to do with this, and from earliest times the eagle has represented the sun, light and the triumph of good over evil. Some of the earliest references to the eagle in this context come from the mythologies of Babylon and Mesopotamia. In these traditions, the eagle is often double-headed, representing its ability to see in both directions at the same time, and emphasizing its association with wisdom. It is also often an emblem of war gods, particularly of Ninurta who was worshipped in Assyria, Babylon and Canaan, and a symbol of the Assyrian Asshur, who is a storm god and brings both lightning and nourishing rain. The Babylonian sun god Marduk is also sometimes depicted as an eagle.

In Egyptian mythology, the eagle was a symbol of both the Nile river and the Royal House of Thebes. It also represented the sons of Horus, the hawk-headed god of Ancient Egypt. In Greek mythology, the eagle is the only bird said to dwell in the heavens. It signified extreme bravery and is often found carved on the tombs of heroes. It is even found on the tomb of the great philosopher Plato, where it represents his aspiring spirit. In Graeco-Roman myth, the eagle is associated with Zeus and Jupiter, and also with Pan, who later yielded it to the king of the gods. The Roman poet Virgil called it 'the gods' weapon-bearer'.

One of the most famous symbolic uses of the eagle was in the traditions of ancient Rome, where the Emperors and their legions marched under the symbol of the Aquila, the eagle standard. At imperial funerals, an eagle was released to signify the soul of the emperor departing for heaven.

There was a widespread belief throughout the ancient world in the eagle's ability to renew itself every 10 years. In a similar fashion to the Phoenix, it is said to fly into the sun until its feathers are scorched, after which it plunges into the sea, emerging restored. This myth probably informed the story of Icarus and his flight into the sun. The tradition is widely known and used among the Hebraic peoples and the eagle appears in both the Old and New Testaments as a symbol of resurrection. It was later associated with Christ, as a symbol of both resurrection and triumph over the forces of darkness.

The compilers of medieval bestiaries used the eagle as a symbol of human spiritual renewal, baptism and the restoration of grace. Many sources claim that eagles can gaze unblinking into the sun, and that when their young are fledged the parent eagles take them up as close to the heavenly orb as possible and force them to look into it; if any are too weak to do this they fall to the ground and are abandoned by their parents.

In Syrian tradition, the eagle represents the goddess Atargatis, and is believed to have carried souls up to the heavens. This vision of the eagle was probably borrowed from Sumerian tradition, as it appeared in the myth of

The Element Encyclopedia of Magical Creatures

Etana. In this we learn that the eagle lived happily in the same tree as a serpent, until the eagle, for no apparent reason, attacked and devoured the serpent's young. At this, the serpent turned upon the eagle, trapping it in its coils and breaking its foot. At this point, the hero Etana, who needed help to find a herb that would bring fertility to his childless wife appears on the scene. He attacked the serpent and wounded it, freeing the eagle. He was then able to enlist the bird's help in flying up to heaven, where the herb was believed to grow. Although, Etana lost his nerve and fell back to Earth, the Sumerian king lists still include his name, and declare that he lived to a great age and did indeed father a child to rule after him. In time, this myth became associated with the idea of the soul's journey to heaven, and the eagle itself became a psychopomp carrying blessed souls to the celestial realm. In Semitic beliefs, souls came from the sun and had to return to it after death, and the eagle was perceived as an appropriate vehicle to carry them.

In the beliefs of the Phoenician people, the god Melkarth threw himself on to a funeral pyre, at which point he metamorphosed into an eagle and flew into the heavens, having conquered death.

A little-known early Welsh poem, 'Arthur's Dialogue with the Eagle', takes up the themes of transformation (the eagle is Arthur's cousin Ewilod in eagle shape) and of wisdom (the eagle is possessed of great knowledge) in the form of a riddling dialogue:

Arthur: *Eagle clear of speech,*
Will you say to Arthur
What is the greatest evil I might do?

Eagle: *To do evil with premeditation,*
And to abide long in its purpose
Is called sin and failure.

Arthur: *Eagle, rich of speech,*
I will question you on your discourse.
What is the worst that can happen
  to man?

Eagle: *Arthur of elevated wisdom,*
Having experienced everything,
The worst is to be judged without hope.

In Ireland, there remains a tradition that says that Adam and Eve are still living and took the form of eagles to dwell forever on Earth. This is a reflection of the idea that eagles live to a great age – anything from 100 to 150 years. In the Irish text known as 'The Oldest Animals', the eagle's life is shorter only than that of the salmon.

In Norse mythology, the eagle is said to roost in the branches of the world tree Yggdrasil, and to engage in endless conflict with the Midgard Serpent, which lives beneath its root and represents darkness and chaos. The eagle is also connected with the god Odin who, in the form of an eagle, carried off a sacred drink known as the Mead of Poetry. According to this myth, after the war between the rival gods the Aesir and the Vanir, both parties seal their peace by spitting into a vessel. From their mingled saliva was then created a being called Kvasir who was eternally wise. Later, however,

The Element Encyclopedia of Magical Creatures

Kvasir was murdered by two renegade dwarves and his blood drained into a cauldron. This blood was then mixed with honey and then brewed into mead. Anyone who partakes of this becomes a poet. Odin set out to steal this magical brew for the rest of the gods. By this time it has come into the possession of a giant named Suttungr. Odin makes himself indispensable to this being by tricking the giant's servants, who were mowing hay, into killing each other. He then enters into service with the giant and works a whole summer for him, doing as much work as nine people. As his reward he asks for a sip of the mead. To this the giant agrees, but when the moment comes he refuses even a few drops. Once again, Odin resorts to a trick. He bores a hole through the mountain on which the giant lives and crawls up it in the form of a snake and sleeps for three nights with the giant's daughter. At the end of this time, she allows him three sips of the mead, and since these are god-like sips they virtually empty the cauldron in which the mead is kept. Odin then changes himself into the shape of an eagle and returns to his home in Asgard pursued by the giant, also in the shape of an eagle. Odin regurgitates the mead into a series of bowls, accidentally allowing a few drops to fall to earth, where they become accessible to all poets. The giant is then slain and the drink becomes the property of the gods.

In Finland, the North Wind itself is said to take the form of a vast invisible eagle, the flapping of whose wings brings storms and darkness. In the same tradition, the father of the gods manifests as an eagle, and the giant Thjazi takes on an eagle's form when he abducts the goddess Idhun. Further east, the Chinese associate the eagle with warfare. It is perceived as a solar creature, whose power evokes images of carnage. But warriors, especially those who are fearless in the face of all odds, tenacious or keen of vision, invoke the eagle as their totem. In Japan, the Ainu regarded the golden eagle as a manifestation of the Great Spirit, a bird of paradise who dwells in the highest heaven. This eagle never touches the Earth but gazes upon its beauty. He is the guardian and friend of the Ainu, and his specific task is to help them. He is venerated because he is said to have saved them from starvation at some distant point in the past.

Among the Native American people, the eagle is of huge importance and is considered to be the greatest of birds. The eagle-feather headdress worn by the chieftains of many tribes acknowledges the existence of the Thunderbird, who carries messages between Earth and sky. In this tradition, the eagle is the master of the heights and the upper air and its feathers are said to carry the thoughts and prayers of the people to the Great Spirit. The Hopi people say that the eagle holds both this world and the next in its talons; to the Zuni, the White Cap or Bald Eagle is 'passing stout of heart and strong of will' and guards both the upper region (Earth) and the heavens. In Aztec and Mayan culture, the eagle was so important that there were several military orders named after it. For these people, the eagle represented celestial power, the brightness of day, and the rising sun which devoured the serpent of darkness. In Australian aboriginal tradition, the eagle carries the souls of the dead back to the Dreamtime. The magical properties of the eagle are longevity, wisdom and supremacy over all odds.

EALE

The Eale or Yale is a composite animal found in India. Black or tawny in colour, the Eale is the size of a hippopotamus, with an elephant's tail and a boar's jaws. His two horns swivel, enabling him to fight opponents coming from different directions.

ECHENEIS

The first we hear of this creature is in the 1st-century *Historia Naturalis* of the Roman Pliny the Elder in which he describes the existence of a tiny sea serpent, roughly 6 ins long, but able, despite its size, to prevent a ship from moving once it has attached itself to the hull. After this time, the Echeneis became widely known among travellers and sailors of the world's oceans. Also notorious as the Remora or Mora, it inhabited the polar seas and apparently could freeze the air with its breath. Early explorers who found themselves caught and immobilized in icy waters believed this indicated the presence of the Echeneis. Pliny thought that the

great Roman general Mark Antony lost the battle of Actium because one of these creatures attached itself to the hull of his ship, thus preventing him from manoeuvring and commanding his navy as he wished.

ECHIDNA

In Graeco-Roman tradition, this is a hybrid creature, woman to the waist, serpent below. An offspring of the primal gods Gaia and Tartarus, she occupied a cavern close to the land of Scythia, from where she is said to have emerged, showing only her human parts, to attract human males. Once she had captured her prey, she would quickly embrace them in her serpentine coils and consume them. Later, Echidna mated with the monster Typhon and bore a number of horrendous offspring, including the giant dogs Cerberus and Orthos, as well as the Chimera, the dragons of Colchis and Ladon, the Harpies, the many-headed Hydra, the cannibal Scylla, the Nemean Lion, and even the Greek Sphinx. She is also said to be the mother of the eagle which pecked at the liver of Prometheus. In Edmund Spenser's 16th-century poem 'The Faerie Queene', he describes Echidna as the mother of the Blatant Beast. The hundred-eyed monster, Argos, finally killed Echidna.

The Element Encyclopedia of Magical Creatures

Eel

The annual miracle of the eels which return to spawn in the Sargasso Sea and the maiden voyage of the young elvers to a freshwater home baffled people for many centuries, for only immature eels were found in freshwater. Aristotle concluded that they were generated 'from the entrails of the earth', while Pliny thought they grew from fragments of the adult eel's skin.

Eels were deemed sacred by the ancient Greeks, and especially the Phoenicians who had a sanctuary dedicated to the god of war that included a pool filled with eels, which were said to be covered in gold leaf. Eels also had a significant presence in the traditions of Polynesia where they were associated with myths of the flood. In Tahiti, the eel is an animal ancestor, while in China it is said to represent carnal love.

On the Samoan island of Savaii, a young eel called Tuifiti swam to live with the beautiful maiden, Sina. She caught him in her calabash and fed him until he grew so long that he outgrew it, soon overflowing the nearby spring waters. He grew to a tremendous size and never stopped following her. Eventually she cursed him and tried to run away. He entered a gathering of elders, circling them, and spoke of his love for her. 'I have never lost the art of magic making. When I die, cut off my head and bury it before your house. The tree that grows there will be of use to you. When the winds blow, take its leaves and weave fans for yourself, eat the fruit of it when you are thirsty and every time you do this, you will be kissing me.' Tuifiti died of lovesickness, and where Sina buried his head, a long narrow trunk rose up, becoming the first coconut tree.

Efreet/Efrit

Alternative names for the Djinn in Islamic folklore and tradition.

EIGHT-FORKED SERPENT OF KOSHI

An important creature in the mythology of Japan, the Eight-Forked Serpent, as its name suggests, comes armed with eight heads and eight tails on its gigantic body. Its eyes shine bright red, and it is so huge that when it moves, its body creates seven valleys and seven mountains. Trees grow upon its back and necks so that it resembles nothing so much as a huge slab of moving earth.

Every year for seven years the great beast demanded a sacrifice of one of the Emperor's daughters. Failure to provide this would result in the destruction of the entire country. When the eighth year came around, the Emperor's last surviving daughter, Princess Comb-Ricefield, was due to meet the fate of her sisters but the hero god Brave-Swift-Impetuous-Male intervened. He created a huge enclosure with eight enormous towers. Within each of these he placed a vat full of rice beer, then hid and waited for the eight heads of the Serpent of Koshi to appear over the horizon. Anticipation of the promised sacrifice, together with the smell of the alcohol, drew the attention of the creature, which soon had its eight heads in each of the eight vats of beer. After a while, the serpent slept deeply, at which point the hero emerged from hiding and severed the eight heads from the eight necks. Blood from the monster flooded the entire area, but among the wreckage of the creature's body, the hero discovered an enchanted sword, which can be seen to this day in the shrine at Atsuta.

EIKTHYMIR

A giant cosmic stag in Norse and Teutonic mythology. Its name means 'The One with the Oak-Like Antlers'. It stands on the roof of Valhalla, the home of the gods, and grazes upon the leaves of the great world tree Yggdrasil. Drops of water falling from the tips of its antlers fill the spring Hvergelmir, which feeds all the rivers of the world. The cult of the stag was widespread in Norse mythology, and probably represented the power of Odin and the strength of the line of kings.

ELBST

This creature, similar to the Loch Ness Monster, is found in Switzerland. According to most accounts, the Elbst inhabits Lake Selisbergsee in the Canton of Uri near Lucerne. The earliest description of it dates from 1584, and the most recent from 1926. Descriptions vary but most sources suggest that it has a long serpentine body, a large head and four clawed feet. Some have said it resembles a dragon. One description says that its head resembles that of a huge pig. All accounts agree that the monster likes to emerge from its lake at night and dine off sheep grazing in the alpine pastures. A favourite trick of this creature is to surface suddenly beside a boat on the lake, swim alongside it for a while, then disappear beneath the surface with a casual flick of its gigantic tail. Such appearances are believed to precede an imminent storm. Some of the more superstitious inhabitants of the area equated the Elbst with the Beast of the Apocalypse (*see* Apocalyptic Beasts).

ELEPHANT

Naturalists have learned that the old proverb 'an elephant never forgets' is indeed true, for the elephant is able to remember, guide and protect her tribe, ensuring their safety. Led by matriarch elephants, an extended family will live together and care for each other, even attending to wounds by using their trunks to apply styptic clay to staunch blood flow. Pliny the Elder, the 2nd-century Roman collector of animal lore, claimed that they accompanied dying members to the elephant's graveyard. In the Indus Valley, elephants have been domesticated since about 550 BC.

The elephant has always represented strength and wisdom, while the traditions of its long memory and patience have made it a favourite subject of stories and myths, wherever it is known. Pliny denied this but said that the elephant was a spiritual creature which worshipped the sun and stars, and bathed in the river at the time of the New Moon to purify itself.

In Graeco-Roman tradition, both Dionysus and Bacchus are portrayed as riding in a chariot drawn by elephants, and in Roman tradition they were said to symbolize victory over death, including long life and even immortal-

ity. At Pompeii, Venus is shown accompanied by elephants. Since it was believed that they worshipped the sun, they were also said to represent life and light, and in this context carried torches in processions through the streets of Rome.

In Hindu tradition, the elephant is the steed of the god Ganesh who is depicted as elephant-headed. Ganesh represents wisdom and is appealed to in prayers to help shift what seem like immovable burdens. Indra, who guards the eastern quarter of the heavens, rides the white elephant named Airavata, and on his visits to Earth the King of Heaven rides on a great white elephant. The elephant is also sacred to Buddha. A white elephant appeared to his mother to announce the imminent birth of a great one, and in one of his incarnations Buddha is described as the Great Elephant. In China, the Buddha P'u Hsien rides on a white elephant, which signifies sovereignty, sagacity, strength and energy. In Thailand, people whisper secrets to the elephant and ask for help in solving their problems.

In the West, the elephant is the enemy of the great serpent and this relationship was adopted in Christian tradition as symbolic of Christ's triumph over evil. In medieval iconography, two elephants sometimes represent Adam and Eve. In Africa, the elephant is always a wise chief, who settles disputes among forest creatures. Here is a story from Kenya of how elephants originated.

The Element Encyclopedia of Magical Creatures

A very poor man heard of a being that was particularly generous to the poor and decided to visit him. It was a long journey, but when he finally arrived, he saw vast herds of cattle and sheep grazing on green pastures, and there in the centre was the mansion of the one he sought. Guessing his need, the bountiful one ordered his men to give the poor man a hundred sheep and a hundred cows, but the poor man refused. 'Thank you', he said, 'but I do not want charity, I want to know how to become rich.' The kindly one reflected for a while, then produced a flask of ointments and gave it to the poor man. 'Rub this on your wife's eye-teeth,' he said. 'Wait until they have grown, then sell them.' The poor man went home and obeyed the instructions, promising his wife that they would soon be rich. After some weeks, her canines began to grow into tusks as long as the man's arm. Then he persuaded his wife to allow him to extract them, took them to the market and sold them for a herd of goats. But after a few weeks, the woman's canine teeth had grown again and were even longer than before. This time she would not let her husband remove them. Gradually, not only her teeth but her whole body became bigger and bigger, her skin turning thick and grey and wrinkled. Finally, she ran off into the forest, where she lived thereafter. She gave birth to a son who was an elephant. Her husband used to visit her in the forest, but she could not be persuaded to go back, though she did give birth to several more healthy elephant-children.

In Southern Africa, the tale is told of a girl who grew so fat that no man wanted her as a wife. She was even-accused of witchcraft and was finally exiled from the village, wandering off into the wilderness. There she met with an elephant, who spoke to her very politely in her own tongue. She agreed to stay with him and he helped her to find food in the forest. After a while, she gave birth to four human sons, all very tall and strong, who became the ancestors of the Indhhovu clan. In most African tales, the elephant is described as almost too kind for its own good, so that it even feels pity for evil characters and is often tricked by them. The Wachago people in Tanzania say that the elephant was once human, but was cheated out of all his limbs except its right arm, which is now its trunk. The Ashanti of Ghana relate that all elephants were once human chieftains, and if they find an elephant dead in the forest, they give him a chieftain's burial. Among the Tuareg of the Sahara, the elephant is still seen as a great benefactor even though elephants no longer roam that region.

The poem 'The Blind Men and the Elephant' by the 19th-century American John Godfrey Saxe is a children's

The Element Encyclopedia of Magical Creatures

favourite, based upon an Indian fable. As the six blind men feel the unknown creature before them with their questing hand, they try hard to determine what kind of beast it really is. As they each feel the side, tusk, trunk, leg, ear and tail of the elephant, the sages think they have found a wall, a spear, a snake, a tree, a fan and a rope. The last verse and moral of this poem being:

And so these men of Indostan
Disputed loud and long,
Each in his own opinion
Exceeding stiff and strong,
Though each was partly in the right,
And all were in the wrong!

Moral:
So oft in theologic wars,
The disputants, I ween,
Rail on in utter ignorance
Of what each other mean,
And prate about an Elephant
Not one of them has seen!

The magical properties of elephants include strength, memory and deep intelligence to solve problems and shift burdens.

ELLE-FOLK/ELEN

Unlike the great elves of ancient times, these are a diminutive race found in Danish folklore. Elen men appear to be prematurely aged, while the women are tiny, beautiful and young. They can be identified from the fact that their backs are completely hollowed out. It is considered unlucky and dangerous to meet them; the females will enchant young men, especially hunters, by singing so sweetly that no one may resist them. The Elen live in the Elenmounds, many of which are actually burial mounds from an older time. They possess a society like that of human beings, with their own kings, laws and traditions. Local folklore around Store Heddinge in Sjaeland describes an ancient oak forest as the Elen King's army, which comes to life each night and fights against his enemies.

ELOKO

These are a race of dwarves from the folklore of Zaire, in Central Africa. Extremely fierce and cannibalistic, they are considered to be the spirits of ancestors who still have matters to settle with the living. This causes them to act maliciously. They live in the deepest and darkest part of the rain forest and dress in leaves. They guard treasure that consists of the rarest game and fruits of the forest. Only the bravest hunters will enter this area, since in order to be successful they must possess strong magic, without which they would not survive. Many tales are told about wives insisting on joining their husbands in the forest, only to faint when they see an Eloko. The Eloko have no hair, but grass grows on their bodies. They have piercing eyes, snouts with mouths that can be opened wide enough to swallow a human – alive or dead – and extremely long, sharp claws. They carry little bells that can put spells on passers-by unless they happen to possess very strong counter magic. (*See* Biloko.)

A story is told of a hunter who took his wife, at her own insistence, into the forest, where he had a hut with a strong fence around it. Before he went out to inspect his traps, he said to her, 'If you hear a bell, do not move. If you do, you will die!' Not long after he had left, the woman heard the chiming sound of a little bell that came closer and closer. Finally, a gentle voice asked to be let in. It sounded like a child. The woman opened the door and there was an Eloko, looking small and innocent and smelling of the forest. She offered it some food, but it refused saying, 'We eat only human flesh. I have not eaten for a long time. Give me a piece of your arm.' Completely under the spell of the Eloko, the woman agreed. That night the husband found only her bones on the floor of the hut.

ELVES

In the 20th century, due in part to Hollywood accounts of Santa's elves running his workshops at the North Pole, the elf has become associated with a diminutive creature, possessed of little magic, and with almost nothing of its original qualities remaining, save for its skill in making beautiful objects. Yet the old traditions portray elves as very different creatures. Among the Norse, Teutonic and Scandinavian peoples, elves are tall, extremely beautiful, and very powerful. J.R.R. Tolkien, in his *The Lord of the Rings* trilogy, did something to set the record straight, although he borrowed aspects from a number of cultures to create the almost angelic elves who appear in his books. Shakespeare also perceived elves as human-like in appearance, as we may see from the descriptions of the beautiful Oberon and Titania in *A Midsummer Night's Dream*. But Shakespeare, who knew a great deal about English folklore and traditions, made their fairy subjects diminutive, thus combining two strands of belief.

A person may be said to have 'elfin beauty' when they possess fine bones, light and silken hair and large eyes. In Anglo-Saxon, there is an adjective, *aelfsciene*, that means 'as pretty as an elf'. In fact, the importance of elves in earlier Western culture can be inferred from the number of words and phrases of this kind that have survived into recent times. For example, 'elf-shot', which refers to prehistoric arrow heads picked up in ploughed fields and assumed to have been made by elves; 'elf-bore', which is applied to a piece of wood from which the knot has fallen out, leaving a shapely hole behind; 'elf-child' is one who may have been a changeling; 'elf-cup' is a stone with a hollow in it filled with morning dew; 'elf-fire' is another name for the Will-o'-the-Wisp; 'elf-locks' may be either knots in the hair, said to be caused by elves deliberately tangling it during the night, or short springy curls; 'elf-taken' is a phrase used to suggest those who are temporarily mad; 'elf-twisted' is used of a person who has suffered a stroke; and 'elf-bolt' is a disease of farm animals said to be the result of being shot by elf arrows.

In more recent times, there has been a general diminution of the elves. In Scandinavia, they have become associated with the Hulder, a small race with more kinship to dwarves or brownies. They have also acquired a tradition of being mischievousness and spiteful. Anglo-Saxon traditions mention two races of elves, the Liosalfa (Light Elves) and Svartalfa (Dark Elves), each of which possesses the attributes one would expect from their names. In Germanic mythology, the Forest Elves are called Schrat, while Danish folklore has the Elen or Elle-Folk, who have an unfriendly relationship with humanity. In Sweden, the elves are known as Elvor, Grove Folk.

EMPUSA

In the mythology of classical Greece, the Empusa is a terrible female monster described as having one leg of brass, while the other is that of a donkey, but she is human from the waist up. She was sent by the goddess Hekate to torment travellers on dark roads, after which they were themselves often accused of her own crime of grave-robbing. Contemporary Greek folklore still speaks of the Empusa, but she has become a shapeshifting evil spirit who may appear in the form of an ox, a dog, a mule or, more rarely, as a beautiful woman.

EMU

In the traditions of the Australian Aborigines, the emu is a totem bird and an ancestor. Emu is seen as one of the first creatures that rose with the sun from the sacred ocean. Objects sacred to tribes, such as the Chirunga and the Tjuringa, are often carved with the footprints of the bird. At certain times of year, elaborate ceremonies are performed in honour of Emu.

EMUSHA

In the Hindu mythology of ancient India, the Emusha a gigantic black bear. During the creation, when all life was emerging from the churning waters of chaos, the demon Hiranyaksha attempted to prevent the Earth from manifesting. The great bear was sent to use its power to push the earth above the waters and so defeat the powers of evil.

ENDROP

A water monster from the folklore and traditions of Romania. The *Physiologus*, a 2nd-century book of creature lore compiled in the city of Alexandria, describes it as a type of Hippocampus or water horse.

The Element Encyclopedia of Magical Creatures

Engulfer

A stretch of water spoken of by the Cour D'Alene people of British Columbia, Canada. This lake, which is also called Hinqumemen, is said to rise up, and even pursue its victims, following them across the land until it engulfs them and drags them back into the depths.

Eous

One of the four horses of the sun in classical Greek mythology. According to the poet Ovid, the four horses that drew the chariot of the sun were Eous, Acthon, Phlegon and Pyrios. Like Pegasus, they were winged and extremely swift.

Epirotes

According to classical Greek mythology, the god Apollo established a walled garden containing a number of dragons. These dragons were said to be descendants of the Python of Delphi and were thus able to divine the future for those living in that place. Each year a maiden was offered to the dragons, on the understanding that if they refused the offering, the next twelve months would be disastrous; however, should the dragons decide to accept the maiden, the people were ensured of good fortune. Apollo gave the task of guarding the hidden garden to the great serpent Epirotes.

Epona

Among the continental Celts, the cult of the goddess Epona centred around Alesia in eastern France. She was the daughter of a hybrid union, as the story tells it,

A certain Phoulonios Stellos who hated women had intercourse with a mare. In time, she brought forth a beautiful maiden, whom she named Epona, a goddess of horses.

Epona is matron of all horses, and she is portrayed seated side-saddle upon a horse, often accompanied by a bird, dog or foal. Her statues were erected in every stable in the Celto-Roman world, wherever Celtic ostlers and horse-dealers settled. Her cult was spread by the Roman army all over Europe, including Britain where she accords with native mythology of the horse goddess, Rhiannon, and in Ireland with the cult of Macha. Remarkably, Epona is the only Celtic deity to be included in the Roman religious calendar, being worshipped on 18 December as part of the rites of Ops and Consus; on that day, all cloven footed and hoofed beasts were rested. This festival, so near midwinter, suggests that Epona's prehistoric role was originally to bear the sun chariot across the sky.

The Element Encyclopedia of Magical Creatures

ERESHKIGAL

Queen of the Sumerian underworld, Ereshkigal has a strange and horrific appearance. She has a horn on her back and another on her forehead. She has sheep's ears and human hands. Her body is that of a fish and from hips to feet she is a dog. Her body is completely covered with scales like a serpent.

Ereshkigal's title is 'Queen of the Great Below' and she lives in a palace which has seven doors, each guarded by a warden. In the story of the goddess Ishtar's descent into the underworld, Ishtar has to leave some token at each of the doors until she is naked – the earliest origin of the more mundane 'Dance of the Seven Veils'. Ereshkigal denies Ishtar's request to mourn her brother-in-law Dumuzi (sometimes described as her lover) and has the goddess hung upon a hook so that she might suffer and overcome death.

ERICHTHONIUS

According to Graeco-Roman myth, when the god Vulcan attempted to rape the young goddess Athena, some of his seed splashed upon the earth and developed into a child that was one part male infant and the rest serpent. Athena carried him to the Acropolis in the city of Athens and gave him into the care of the daughters of King Cecrops, instructing them, under pain of her greatest displeasure, never to look directly at the child. Inevitably they did so, and were so horrified by what they saw

that they ran screaming to the edge of the Acropolis and threw themselves to their deaths.

ERQIGDLIT

A group of blood-drinking monsters in the legends and traditions of the people of Greenland and Baffin Island. Among the Inuit people of Labrador and the Hudson Bay coastline of Canada they are considered among the most fearsome and terrifying monsters of which they have knowledge. They are also known as the Adlet.

ERYMANTHEAN BOAR

The boar of Erymanthos belonged to the Greek goddess Artemis who had her dance floor on Mount Erymanthos. The wild boar was an enemy of civilized and settled peoples, choosing to live untamed in the forested mountains. When it came down the slopes to the farmers' fields below, it turned its savage attention to uprooting and distroying their husbandry. This boar was the subject of Hercules' fourth labour. Having undertaken to bring back the boar alive to Mycenae, he travelled to the region of Arcadia where he was welcomed by the centaur Pholos. The kindly centaur met an accidental and untimely death following a great drinking bout. Hercules buried Pholos and continued on his way to Mount Erymanthos where he lured the boar from its lair, driving it up into the snowline of the mountain

The Element Encyclopedia of Magical Creatures

where he caught it in a trap. Throwing it across his back, he returned with it to Mycenae.

EURALE

One of the Gorgons of Graeco-Roman mythology. Her name means 'wanderer' and she is sister to Medusa and Athenno. All three Gorgons were originally beautiful women, but they were transformed into their hideous shapes as a punishment for disobeying the gods. Descriptions in classical sources vary in detail, but agree that the Gorgons had snakes for hair, bodies covered in scales, hands of brass and bat-like wings. Their most fearsome and terrible attribute was their ability to turn anyone to stone who met their gaze. The hero Perseus was able to defeat Medusa by looking at her reflection in his polished shield, and then beheading her as she slept. From her blood came the winged horse Pegasus. Though pursued by Medusa's sisters, Perseus escaped and, in the course of his adventures, turned his enemies to stone by showing them Medusa's head.

Gorgon images were popular as the guardians of temple precincts, where they are often found represented with their snake-like hair and open mouthed showing sharpened teeth. The Gorgoneon was an image often represented on the shields of warriors. Some sources claim that the giant Orion was an offspring of Eurale and the god of the sea.

EURYTION

In Greek myth, this centaur was encountered by Hercules during his sixth labour to cleanse the Augean Stables. Eurytion's name means 'the good shot', since all centaurs were considered fine shots. When Hercules was visiting King Dexamenos of Olenos, he arrived at the moment when Eurytion was pressing himself upon the king's daughter as a bridegroom and was about to carry her off. Hercules immediately intervened and killed the centaur before he could ravish the princess.

The Element Encyclopedia of Magical Creatures

F

Fafnir

One of the great dragons of Norse and Teutonic mythology. Originally Fafnir, whose name means 'the Embracer', was one of three sons born to the dwarf Hriedmar – the others being Otr and Regin. According to Norse myth, the trickster god Loki mistook Otr for a real otter and accidentally killed him, for which Hriedman demanded blood money. Loki promised to fill an otter's pelt with gold. However, amongst the treasure he hid a ring that brought its owner not only wealth but also eternal misfortune. From the moment the dwarf received the gift, he also received the curse. Fafnir fell under the spell and craved the gold so greatly that he conspired with his surviving brother Regin to steal it but in the process they killed their father. Fafnir did not wish to share the treasure, even with his brother, and he fled to Gritaheid, where he lay down on the hoard and changed into the most hideous wingless dragon or worm. Meanwhile, Regin approached the mortal hero Sigurd and bribed him to kill Fafnir. Having slain the creature, Sigurd cut out its tongue and cooked it over a fire. In the process, some of the dragon's blood got onto his hand, which he then licked. The blood gave him the understanding of all languages, including those of animals and birds. By this means, he learnt that Regin, who had now fallen victim of the curse of the ring, meant to kill him. Sigurd lay in wait for the dwarf and slew him instead, keeping the gold for himself. He was to get no good from it, however, and he ended his life tragically. The composer Richard Wagner (1813–83) based his Ring cycle on ancient northern myths and renamed Sigurd as Siegfried.

Falak

In Islamic mythology, Falak is the cosmic serpent responsible for building the adamantine walls of the Realm of Fire. Beneath the sea is the Realm of Fire, and here Falak still dwells. He is said to be so hungry that were it not for his fear of Allah, he would consume the whole world.

Falcon

Like eagle and hawk, the falcon is a solar creature, blessed with the powers of ascent, inspiration, freedom and victory. In Egyptian mythology, the falcon and the hawk represent the god Horus who is depicted as either falcon or hawk-headed. In the iconography of Ancient Egypt, the widespread wings of the falcon represent the heavens. As a solar creature, the falcon is also identified with the sun god Ra, and in Thebes the bird is the emblem of the war god Menthu, who is represented as being either falcon- or bull-headed. In Norse myth, the god Odin often took the form of a falcon when he visited Earth; the falcon is also attributed to the goddess Frigg, and sometimes with the trickster god Loki. In China, the attitude to the falcon is ambivalent: it can be either a beneficent or destructive force, being associated with war. Among the Ainu of Japan, it is a helper of humanity; for the Native

Fairies

Fairies are a race of beings between humans and spirits. They live as our neighbours, but because human beings have often failed to look after their part of the Earth's guardianship, we seldom encounter fairies, for they regard us as boastful breakers of promises. If, however, you can establish a good relationship with them, if you leave offerings for them – usually the first fruits of whatever produce you possess, as long as it is not meat – they will be good neighbours to you. Because of the human propensity to act in a superior way – and also because fairies seldom breed – they often take thriving human children and leave a changeling in their place.

The word 'fairy' derives from the Latin *fatum* ('fate'). The theory that the fairies are the ones who bestow individual destiny or specific gifts is found in the widespread European figure of the Fairy Godmother who endows a baby with the gifts it will need for life. This idea is found in the Welsh Bendith y Mamau and the French Bonnes Mères, as well as in the Spanish Fada and Italian Fata.

The origin of fairies is told in a Christian folktale from the Western Highlands of Scotland.

At the creation of the world, God made many beings before mankind. Some of them, like the angels who followed Lucifer, wanted to make their own abode and burst out of heaven leaving the gates ajar. The rush of their going caused many other beings to be sucked out of heaven. God became aware of what was happening and pronounced, 'Let those who are out stay out, and those who are in stay in,' and sealed the gates once more. All the rebellious angels made their home in hell, but the beings who had been involuntarily locked out had to remain on Earth and became the fairies.

Different races of fairy peoples are found all over Britain and Ireland. They are sometimes involved in territorial disputes such as those of the Cornish Piskies who fought the English fairies for possession of all land west of the River Parrett and banished their enemies forever. Some territorial disputes seem more historical, like the long exile to the hollow hills of the Irish Tuatha de Danaan who gave way to the human race of the Milesians. Many otherworldly tribes of beings like dwarves, elves and goblins are generically called 'fairy folk', although they have distinctly different natures.

Throughout the world, people are warned to be respectful of fairy beings, especially of their queens. Fairies, like bees, are ruled over by queens. Remnants of these powerful figures are found in the Italian Befana, the Gaelic Cailleach Beare and the German Percht, all of whom have become attached to midwinter festivities.

Also like bees, fairies can swarm in beneficent or malign ways, which we see in the Scandinavian Alfar and Svartalfar, as well as the Scottish Seelie Court and Unseelie Court (the Blessed Court and the Unholy Court); the Malaysian Bediadari are forms of trooping or swarming fairies.

Wherever we look, we find that a common task of fairy folk is to protect the natural world in all its forms and in this they are nearer to elemental spirits like gnomes. In India, it is the Vidyeshvaras who look after the woods and wild places, while in Greece, we find fauns, centaurs, dryads and nymphs. These beings have leaders who are usually half animal, half humanoid like Puck, or Cheiron or dwarfish like the Indian Kubera.

The gossamer-winged, butterfly fairy of folktales is derived more from the Persian Peri. Our present notions of fairies show a diminishment both of human respect and fairy size, for they are invariably portrayed as tiny, colourful, bewinged creatures full of twinkle and no power. Such depictions are at odds with the vigour of real indigenous fairies who can appear in different sizes and whose actions are robust and even lusty. Fairies hold a trust for the sake of the whole Earth. Their wisdom and guardianship is a reminder to humans of the respect we must give to our environment: vigilant, faithful and loving.

American people, the falcon is the younger brother to the eagle and among the tribes of the south-east woodlands it represents warfare, in which instance the eagle comes to represent peace.

FARASI BAHARI

In the Indian Ocean, lives a species of green horse called Farasi Bahari: these are not sea horses, however. On an island off the coast of East Africa, the Farasi Bahari stallions graze on certain nights of the year. Horse breeders find out which night this is and leave their mares on the island in the hope that they mate with the stallions to produce the prized green horses. But the Farasi Bahari will not emerge from the waves if they even smell a human being. The crossbred horses are prized because they have super-endurance to gallop without tiring, because they have no lungs.

FASTITOCALON

This is a name for one of the many monstrous creatures that float on the oceans of the world, and have the appearance of islands, complete with a hard rocky surface and flora and fauna. Unsuspecting seamen who step on to this seeming island soon find themselves in trouble as it sinks below the water, taking them with it. It is likely that the origins of these creatures are the great whales that follow the ocean currents, their skins often attracting limpets and seaweed, which gives them a land-like appearance. J.R.R. Tolkien, in his collection of poems

and songs from the Red Book of Westmarsh, *The Adventures of Tom Bombadil*, includes the Fastitocalon, which he describes as a kind of giant turtle.

FAUN

A hybrid creature from Graeco-Roman mythology, the faun is usually represented as a man above the waist and a goat below, with small horns upon its head. Fauns are said to be the offspring of the god Faunus, known as 'the kindly one', a god of the Forest and a protector of the creatures who lived there. The foundations of the temple dedicated to him still exist on an island in the Tiber. Faunus was sometimes identified with Pan, and in this form appeared in the erotic dreams of women. The Renaissance natural magician and healer Paracelsus (1493–1541) defined fauns as mystical spirits who had control over the elements.

FEARSOME CRITTERS

A large group of bizarre creatures from the folklore of lumberjacks in the United States. Famed for their tall tales, the wild wit and dizzying inventiveness of these tree-fellers gave rise to a world peopled with strange beings. A whole menagerie of odd inventions, alternately of terrifying or hilarious aspect, can be traced to this source. Often their names give a strong clue as the nature of the creature – for example, the Come-at-a-body or the Hidebehind. However, some clearly derive from more classical sources, such as the Flibbertigibbet or the Harpy-Hag. Others are playful spellings of familiar creatures such as Meskitto. From the 18th century onward, stories featuring these critters were collected by enthusiastic storytellers and anthropologists.

Fei Lian

A celestial being who commands the winds in Chinese mythology. Fei Lian, whose name means Wind Lord, is described as having a sparrow's head with bull's horns, the body and legs of a stag, with the markings of a leopard and a serpent's tail.

Fei Lian conspired with Chi-Song-Zi the rain god to overcome the ruling deity Huang Di. However, the attempt failed and Fei Lian was exiled to a cavern high in the mountains. From there he continued to exert a baleful influence, sending forth vicious storms to trouble the world. Eventually, he was defeated by the celestial archer Yi, who punctured the bag in which Fei Lian kept the winds, then hamstrung the creature and forced it to crawl humbly before him in a parade which honoured Huang Di.

Feng Hwang

The name given to the Phoenix in Chinese mythology. It personifies the primordial strength of the heavens and has the head and comb of a pheasant and the tale of a peacock. Its sweet song makes it a messenger between Heaven and Earth, but it will never be glimpsed if the land is at war. The Feng Hwang is drawn to the sound of flute-playing and, once in a blue moon, you may hear it singing along with the tune that is being played. Feng Hwang is one of the Ssu Ling, the four heavenly creatures who keep the world in balance, along with the Tortoise, the Ch'i-Lin and Dragon. Feng Hwang shares the balance of yin and yang within itself, for it represents the solar yang and the lunar yin powers. Feng Hwang represents the Empress, and the qualities of beauty and peace. Not only does it keep these powers in balance, it also represents the five elements, for its head is that of the solar cockerel while its swallow-back represents the lunar crescent, its tail represents the trees and flowers, its wings the wind and its feet the earth.

Fenoderee

Fenoderee (or Phynnodderee) is a type of brownie from the folklore and traditions of the Isle of Man. There are a huge number of stories and traditions focusing on his character, and he often helps mankind with the ploughing, reaping and sowing; though at times can be both difficult and tricky. One story tells how he fell in love with a mortal woman, married her, and lived in the human world until she died. At this point, he tried to return to the fairy world but was refused entrance because when the Fairy King had asked him a favour he refused it, preferring to stay in the world with his human wife.

The following account from Walter Gill's *A Manx Scrapbook* shows what a powerful worker he could be.

He was not too shy to start work at daybreak and let himself be seen and admired in the grey light by the respectful villagers ... The Fenoderee not only mowed for them, he carried for them, reaped, made bands, tied sheaves and built the stack for them, threshed it and stacked the straw again, herded sheep and cattle, and whisked ... stone about the land like a little giant he was. He attacked his jobs like a convulsion of nature, making the hard ground soft and the soft ground water ... When he mowed he flung the grass to the morning star or the paling moon without heed of the cock's kindly word of warning from the nearby farmyard ... The concentrated fury of his threshing resembled a whirlwind, an earthquake, doomsday ... In the zeal and zest of the shepherding he sometimes drove an animal off the cliffs, but he made up for that by folding in wild goats, and hares along with the sheep. For he was a doer not a thinker, mightier in thew than in brain.

FENRIS/FENRIR

In Norse and Teutonic mythology, the mighty wolf who will eventually destroy the world. Fenris is one of the three children of the trickster god Loki and the giantess Angbodr, the others being the Midgard Serpent and the goddess of the Underworld, Hel. The gods brought up the wolf as one of their own, but in time he grew so vast that his upper jaw touched the sky and his lower jaw the Earth. Such was his strength and dark temper that the gods decided to bind him. At first, they tried to do this by using a fetter called Loeding, and when this broke they tried another chain called Dromi. But Fenris broke free from both of them. Finally, the dwarves made the fetter known as Gleipnir, which was light and soft but incredibly strong. According to an ancient Norse riddle, the dwarves made it from the sound of a cat, the beard of a woman, the roots of the mountains, the breath of a fish and the spittle of a bird – all things which may be said not to exist. The gods intended to use this to bind Fenris on the Isle of Lyngvi in the midst of Lake Amsvarmir. However, the great wolf became suspicious, and demanded that one of the gods put his hand into its jaws before he would allow the chains to be put upon him. Tyr agreed to this, and when the wolf realized that he could not break the chain he bit the god's hand off. At this, the gods decided to bind Fenris to a great stone, which they then placed deep beneath the earth. Finally, they propped open his vast jaws with a sword. From that moment on, Fenris has

The Element Encyclopedia of Magical Creatures

howled perpetually, and the foam from his jaws formed a river known as Van.

It is said that on the day of Ragnarok, when the world ends, Fenris will finally break free and consume all of creation, including the gods, before being slain in turn by Odin's son Vidar. A second hound, known as Garm, appears to be identical to Fenris, and is also said to pull free of his chains at the time of Ragnarok. Two other wolves are mentioned as being involved in these events, one of whom, Mangamyr (Moon Eater) sometimes called Hati, will devour the moon, while Fenris will eat the sun.

FIAN-SIAN-CHE

According to ancient Chinese folk tradition, Fian-Sian-Che is the bear spirit who casts out evil. He is the leader of the Dance of the Twelve Animals in the New Year celebration called the Ta-No. Boy dancers attired as different animals whirled about Fian-Sian-Che after hurling menacing gestures at the forces of evil. Then all twelve, led by the bear spirit, ran through the countryside to take their healing powers to cast out evil.

FIRE DRAGON

According to the native Huron and Iroquois people in north-eastern United States, the fire dragon is a celestial being who was active in the creation of the world.

FIREBIRD

According to Russian folklore, the Firebird was a wondrous creature with eyes that sparkled like crystal and golden feathers that shone as bright as the sun. The Firebird was owned by Tsar Vyslav Andronovitch, but it used to steal golden apples from the nearby garden of Tsar Dalmet Vyslovovitch. Dalmet was jealous of his neighbour's bird and he sent his three sons Dimitri, Vasili and Ivan to find and bring it back. Helped by a magical shapeshifting wolf, Ivan succeeded in the quest by performing a difficult task for Tsar Dalmet, claiming the Firebird as his reward. But on his way home, his two brothers ambushed and killed him, afterwards claiming they had completed the quest while their brother had died on his journey. Their false claim was exposed when Ivan was brought back to life by being sprinkled with the Water of Life and Death by the wolf that had helped him earlier. The brothers were thrown into jail and Ivan kept the Firebird for his own.

According to another tradition, the Tsar of all the Russians was presented with a feather from the tail of the Firebird by a famous *bogatyr* (a heroic knight-errant). The Tsar, being greedy, demanded that the warrior bring the bird itself, but the man was reluctant to do this since, according to this tradition, the Firebird was huge and aggressive. However, he eventually managed to trap it by scattering maize all over a field and hiding in a tree until the bird swooped down to eat. It happened that the *bogatyr* had a magic horse, and as the Firebird pecked at the grain this fabulous creature leapt forward and stood upon the bird's outstretched wings, thus allowing the *bogatyr* to bind it and take it back to the Tsar.

FIRE-DRAKE

The name sometimes applied to dragons in Norse mythology. These follow the traditional shape of the dragon, being serpentine, bat-winged and fire-breathing. Following the Saxon invasion of Britain in the 5th century, a number of dragons in English folklore, including the creature killed by the hero Beowulf, were described as Fire-Drakes. Beowulf kills the Fire-Drake after his spectacular success with the subduing of Grendel and his mother, but the Fire-Drake finally kills him. In Ben Jonson's poem 'The Jackman's Song', this blessing protects against the Fire-Drake:

The Faiery beame upon you,
The starres to glister on you;
A Moone of light
In the Noone of night,
Til the fire-Drake hath o're gone you.

FOX

The fox is one of the many extremely cunning creatures of world mythology, and it is represented as alternatively helpful and hindering of mankind. In the West, the fox is almost universally seen as a trickster, while in the East it also possesses great strength and has the ability to shapeshift and transform one object into another. Such traditions probably originate in Sumerian myth, when the fox was associated with the trickster god Ea. It is claimed that the fox revived this god after he had eaten poisonous plants. According to Zoroastrian myth, the fox has unusual powers, including the ability to frighten off demons. In Graeco-Roman tradition, Dionysus and Bacchus were both associated with the fox as a guardian of vines. Like its cousin the jackal, in Old Testament terms the fox is seen as symbolic of cunning and duplicity: Herod is described as 'the cunning fox'. Christian tradition equates the fox with the devil and this is repeated in the 2nd-century Alexandrian text *Physiologus* which describes how the fox buries itself in the earth as if dead, and then, when ravens and other scavengers come to eat it, it leaps out and catches them. The medieval bestiaries repeat this story and call the fox Vulpis, always representing it as fraudulent and ingenuous. Both these sources influenced the writers of the European epic of the Middle Ages known as 'The Tale of Reynard the Fox', which represents the animal as hypocritical, sanctimonious and guileful. Reynard's chief adversary was the wolf Ysengrim. In the symbolism of the medieval Feast of the Fools, when all levels of society were pilloried and satirized, foxes were often depicted wearing monkish clothing, suggesting the way in which these supposed men of god were perceived by the ordinary people. Foxes in cowls were used to represent the itinerant friars who wandered the land, offering to the gullible pardons which would ensure unfailing entrance into heaven.

The Element Encyclopedia of Magical Creatures

According to the Californian Yurok people, there was once a time when the foxes were angry at the sun. Twelve of their number were chosen to catch the sun and bring him down. They held a council about this and twelve of the bravest foxes were chosen to capture the sun. They made ropes of sinew, and waited until the sun in his descent from the sky touched the top of a certain hill. Then the foxes caught the sun and tied him fast to the top of the hill. But the Yurok people saw this and cut the sinews, setting the sun free again. While it was tied to a mountain the sun burned a great hole in the ground and the truth of this story is known to this day, because the hole can still be seen.

Among the Miwok tribes of North America, Silver Fox and Coyote were the creators of the universe. In the time before time, the world was made up only of water and on the water walked a single fox. Being lonely, it began to sing, and Coyote appeared. The two journeyed on for a while together and finally Fox suggested that they create the world. 'How shall we do that?' asked Coyote. 'We shall sing and dance,' answered Fox. First, however, he thought of a lump of clay, which at once appeared. Throwing it upon the water, the two creatures began to sing and dance. As they did so, mountains, valleys, rivers and streams came into being. When they finished dancing, the world was complete and ready to be filled by animals and people.

In Native American traditions, the fox is again a trickster, although it has greater powers than the northern fox. The fast-running Fox was one of the animals who helped Coyote steal fire from the Fire-People in a story from British Columbia in Canada. Among the Inuit, the fox is an important mystical ally. Brer Fox is a familiar character in early American literature, sharing many of the attitudes of Brer Rabbit.

The fox was one of the primary gods of the Inca of Peru. They named the constellation, known to us as the Pleiades, after the fox. This constellation marked the place in the eastern sky where the sun rose at the winter solstice, and perhaps for this reason the fox is one of the most important characters in the Inca creation myth. As with many other cultures, the Inca had a flood story. In this the fox is found clinging to the top of a mountain as the waters rise. Finally, he is almost jostled from his perch by the other animals, so that his tail touches the water, and it is for this reason that the fox is said to have a black tail.

The Element Encyclopedia of Magical Creatures

In both China and Japan there are many myths of fox spirits appearing in human form, often as beautiful maidens who cause trouble and bring disaster to those who encounter them. The true nature of these spirits can be revealed by looking at their reflection in water or a mirror. Although the fox is an archetypal illusionist, trickster and magician, it is not always malific and may be called upon for help if properly rewarded. In Japanese tradition, the fox is also an aspect of the rice deity Inari, and is the spirit of the rice itself, making it an extremely important creature. Fox spirits are also said to secrete a compound similar to the Elixir of Life, and there are a number of stories of heroes and heroines who go in search of this. In Japan, a black fox is said to bring good luck; a white fox the opposite; two or three foxes together mean imminent disaster. (Strangely, a very similar tradition exists in Wales.) Among the Ainu people of Japan, the fox is admired for its kindness and the shamans of this tradition keep fox skulls for use in divination. In China, the fox symbolizes long life and the spirits of the dead sometimes migrate into the bodies of foxes.

FREKI

One of several monstrous wolves from Norse mythology. Each was predicted to take part in the destruction of the world on the day of Ragnarok.

FROG

From ancient times, the frog has been recognized as a symbol of procreation, fertility, birth and regeneration. In Ancient Egypt, the four male gods, known as the Ogdoad, who were deeply involved in the creation of the world, were all shown as frog-headed. In addition, the frog was sacred to Heqet (or Hequat), the goddess of childbirth who was also the midwife at the birth of the world and known to be a protector of mothers and newborn children. Later still, the frog became an emblem for Isis and Hathor as goddesses of fertility and birth respectively. Amun, the god of creation, is sometimes depicted as a frog-headed man.

Graeco-Roman tradition describes the frog as an emblem of Aphrodite or Venus and as a representative of fertility and harmony between lovers. Frogs are said to croak in the swamps of the Underworld in Greek tradition. In ancient times, they were used as charms as well as being attributed with medicinal qualities. Christianity took on the frog as a symbol for the higher stage of spiritual endeavour, as opposed to the toad which represented evil and negativity.

European folklore and superstition declares that it is unlucky to kill a frog which, like a butterfly, can house the spirits of dead children. Despite this association with death, if a frog enters someone's house it is said to bring good luck. To hear a frog croaking during the day has long been thought of as an omen of rain. Frogs, together with pigs, cats, and crows, are among those frequently attributed to the role of witches' familiar, and, during the Middle Ages, people widely believed that witches could transform themselves into frogs.

In British Columbia, native tribes of the area describe Frog as a symbol of happiness, while further south the Blackfoot tribes described it as a manifestation of Old Man, a spirit which defeats a group of evil underwater beings symbolized by tadpoles. These creatures were believed to be the enemies of mankind. Old Man's victory is repeated when tadpoles emerge as frogs.

As a creature of water, the frog is considered to be sacred to the moon, and is often described as being a rainmaker or rain bringer. In China, the frog spirit Ch'ing Wa Sheng, is venerated as a healer and for the prosperity it can bring to those engaged in business. A frog in a well is said to depict a person of small understanding and less vision. In the Ainu mythology of Japan, the frog was originally a woman who behaved badly, killing husbands and generally displeasing the gods until they turned her into a frog. Afterwards she only gave birth to frogs.

In the Vedic traditions of ancient India, frogs are described as deities, and

One day at the beginning of the dry season, the gazelle challenged the frog to a race. Naturally, the frog lost, and the gazelle claimed a pot of beer as its prize. But the frog said, 'Wait, give me a chance to win the next round! Can you rise from the dead?' Of course, the gazelle did not believe the frog could, but the next day, when the frog and his wife were at home, the gazelle set fire to their home, burning it to the ground. All the other animals in the village mourned the frogs, who were such good neighbours. After six months, the rains came and soon the place where the frog's house had been was underwater. That night when the gazelle came to drink, he saw the frog in the water with his wife surrounded by numerous young frogs, all croaking happily. Irritated by the noise, the gazelle demanded to know what they were doing. 'We are singing,' answered the frogs, 'we are so happy that the rains have come and that we have come back to the earth.' 'Where have you been?' asked the gazelle. 'Why, in the country of the dead, of course, since you killed us in the fire,' answered the frog. 'What is it like down there?' asked the gazelle. 'Very pleasant,' said the frog, 'don't you see how well we are looking. See all our children – they were all born in the land under the earth. The god of the Dead blessed us!' The gazelle, who had no children, was so jealous that he went home to his wife and set his own house on fire. Of course, he was killed, for he did not know that frogs bury themselves in the earth at the beginning of the dry season and sleep there until the rains come!

The Element Encyclopedia of Magical Creatures

their croaking is known as the chanting of Brahmins performing rites and praying for rain during the time of drought. In the Hindu holy book the *Rig Veda*, the Great Frog supports the universe and represents the dark matter from which all creation is formed. But in the Zoroastrian religion, the frog is evil and belongs to the evil force of negativity known as Ahriman. In Africa, in the native traditions of Mozambique, the frog represents resurrection. In the oldest myths, the frog is as revered as a god, as the fable on the previous page illustrates.

The magical properties of the frog include the ability to bring rain, the power to change and come back to life.

FUATH

A tribe of spectral monsters from the folk traditions of the Scottish Highlands. Taking a variety of forms, the Fuath (or Fuathann) live close to lochs, rivers and the open sea, indicating that they are essentially water monsters. They are occasionally known as the Arrachd (or Fuath-arrachd). A Fuath is the mother of the Brollachan, a malevolent creature given to attacking children. The name Fuath translates as 'hatred' or 'aversion' in Scots Gaelic, or as 'hate' or 'likeness' in Old Irish.

FU-HSI

According to the mythology of Ancient China, Fu-Hsi ruled over the great third age of humankind, which stretched from 2852 to 2738 BC. The emperor was

described as half serpent with the head and body of a human, or alternatively with a human torso but the head of a bull with horns emerging from its forehead. He shared the throne with his empress, Nu-Kwa, who was also described as human from the waist up and serpent below. These primal beings brought the gifts of architecture and the arts to humanity, and are often depicted entwined together and holding up symbols of these skills.

FU-TS'ANG

A venerable dragon from the mythology of ancient China, Fu-Ts'ang has a special responsibility for the minerals of the earth and is sometimes known as the Dragon of the Hidden Treasures.

FYLGJA

In Norse mythology, a Fylgja is an animal spirit that accompanies the soul of a person. It might be in the form of an eagle, wolf or it might be a troll. The Fylgja is drawn to a person who has a character with an affinity to the form in question, appearing in dreams and visions to give messages. The name is also used of the 'fetch' or spiritual-double of a person. If this is seen by another, it signifies that they are either out of their body in a dream or else they have left this life.

Gaasyendietha

A type of fire-breathing dragon from the mythology of the Seneca people of the north-western coast of North America. The appearance of a meteor in the sky is said to represent the passing overhead of this creature, which is of enormous size. However, despite its fiery qualities, the Gaasyendietha lives in rivers and lakes.

Gaborchend

According to Celtic tradition, these beings were among the first races to inhabit Ireland in a time before recorded history. They were said to have the bodies of humans but the heads of goats. They perished in the early wars between the monstrous Fir Bolg and the Tuatha de Daanan.

Gabriel Hounds

One of a number of names applied to a pack a spectral hounds that, in the folklore of Britain, hunt the souls of the dead. Described as monstrous dogs with human heads, they travel high up in the air, occasionally hovering above a house, indicating the imminent death of someone within.

Gadhra

In the ancient Irish story of the Siege of Druim Damhgaire, the spell-working druid Mog Ruith calls upon the monstrous Gadhra as the ultimate weapon of mass terror. Gadhra of Druim mac Criadhnaidhi is a giant who has two different appearances depending on which side of his body you see first. During the Siege, Gadhra shows his beautiful appearance towards the Munster side but turns his monstrous side to the enemy.

He was rough and spiny like a pine and as large as a royal castle. Each of his eyes was as large as a king's cauldron, and they jutted out of his head; his knees were turned backwards and his heels turned forwards. He held in his hand an iron trident; he was covered in a brown cloudy mantle, horned and bristling with bones and horns; a billy-goat and a ram followed him. And all were stricken with terror who saw him in this array.

Ga-Gorib

A South African monster, Ga-Gorib, was called 'the thrower down' by the Khoisin people. It sat on the edge of a pit, daring passers-by to throw stones at him. Any persons foolish enough to do so found that their stones flew back and hit them, so that they fell into the pit. This state of affairs ended when the hero, Heitsi-eibib, approached the monster. Distracting Ga-Gorib's attention, he threw a stone which landed under the monster's ear, knocking the predator into his own pit. Another story tells how Heitsi-eibib fell into the pit after slipping while the monster chased him; his miraculous escape from the pit enabled him to wrestle Ga-Gorib into the pit forever.

Gaki

Monstrous creatures from the legends and folklore of Japan, the Gaki are roughly human in shape, but have huge stomachs, and their bodies are bright red or green. They have the heads of horses or oxen, with three eyes each and twisting horns and talons. They suffer constantly from terrible hunger and thirst, which drives them to hunt human beings. Gaki feed off the souls of evil men and women who are about to die and they take them to the torments of the lower world.

Galley-Trot

A creature described in the folklore of Suffolk and northern Britain, it takes the form of a shaggy white dog, about the size of a bullock. Its indistinct outlines make it difficult to see clearly and this adds to its fearsome aspect. The dialect word 'galley' means 'to frighten' or 'to scare'.

Galokwudzuwis

A bizarre and terrifying creature from the folklore of the Kwakiutl people of northern Canada, Galokwudzuwis is represented as a monstrous flesh-eating bird. Her name means 'Crooked Beak of Heaven', and she is often depicted with a strange growth on her massive beak. She hunts human prey with her equally monstrous husband Bakbakwakanooksiwae.

Ganareva

A vast dragon from the Sumerian mythology of ancient Mesopotamia. Ganareva was so large that its head was in the sky while its feet rested on the ocean. It was a destroyer of lands and preyed on humans. The hero Keresapa was sent to destroy this vast creature, which troubled the world greatly. A series of horrific battles followed in which the monster repeatedly seemed to have the upper hand. As many as 15 horses were killed under the hero, who was also blinded, and his family were abducted by servants of the evil monster. But in the end Keresapa succeeded in defeating the monster. One of the horses of the sun that pull the sun chariot in the Sumerian tradition was named after the creature.

Gandarvas

The Gandarvas are Indian beings who have a human torso and a horse's or bird's head. The Gandarvas, whose name means 'the fragrances' or 'celestial harmonies', are celestial beings who live in the sky as aspects of the sun. They wear fragrant garments and feed upon herbs and the scent of water. They guard the place of the life-giving elixir the soma. They have the ability to restore virility, as they did for the god Varuna, giving him a special aphrodisiac plant. The Gandarvas attend weddings and are invoked in nuptial rites. They play wonderful music on the *vina* and teach musical knowledge to people.

The Element Encyclopedia of Magical Creatures

GANDHAVA

One of the great horses of the sun according to the Vedic mythology of ancient India. The name derives from the Sumerian monster known as the Ganareva, a vast dragon defeated by the hero Keresapa.

GANESH

The god of wisdom, learning and prudence in Hindu mythology. He is usually represented as a heavy-bodied man with either red or yellow skin, and with the head of an elephant missing one tusk. His name means literally 'Lord of the Hosts', and he leads a troop of lesser deities. He is the son of the goddess Shiva and the god Parvati, and is sometimes said to be generated from the dead skin of Parvati's body. He often appears riding on a rat or attended by one. The rat and the elephant head symbolize Ganesh's power to vanquish obstacles, either by trampling them underfoot or by entering a granary secretly.

A number of myths describe how Ganesh acquired his head. According to one, his proud mother showed him off to Shiva, whose glance burnt the child's head to ashes. Brahma advised her to replace it with the first and finest head she could find. Her choice was an elephant's head. According to another myth, Shiva struck off Ganesh's head when his son prevented him from entering Parvati's bath. The god then replaced it with that of an elephant to placate his wife. The loss of one tusk is explained by the legend in which Rama went to visit Shiva, but he was sleeping so Ganesh blocked his entrance, at which Rama threw his axe at him. Recognizing the axe as it flew towards him, Ganesh allowed it to strike him, severing one tusk.

GANJ

A huge treasure-guarding dragon from the mythology of ancient Persia and modern-day Iran.

GARGAM

A Breton giant given to roaming the countryside at night in search of prey. The name Gargam may be translated as 'Curved Thigh' which together with its nickname of 'the lame' suggests that he may derive from the Celtic god Bran, who is sometimes referred to as 'Pierced Thigh'. Both these characters may have contributed to the character of the Wounded King in the myths of the Grail. It is also possible that the name Gargam influenced the 16th-century French writer Rabelais (1494–1553) in the creation of the giant Gargantua described in his books *Pantagruel* (1532) and *Gargantua* (1534). Gargam's Welsh equivalent could be the giant Gwrgwent.

GARGOUILLE

In French folklore, Gargouille was the dragon of the river Seine. It was said to have ravaged the city of Rouen and was killed by St Romans sometime in the 7th century. Gargouille was given to spouting water and this is why his name has been given to the monstrous gargoyles through whose mouths the rain runs spouting away from the tops of buildings.

GARM

One of the great mythological dogs of Scandinavian tradition, Garm (or Garmr) guards the mouth of Hel and is described as having four eyes and being permanently spattered with blood. He is said to be particularly savage towards those who did not show kindness to others in life. He will howl loudly at the beginning of Ragnarok, the end of time. At the finish of the day, when only he and the one-handed god Tyr are left standing, they will slay each other.

GARUDA

An important composite creature from the Hindu and Buddhist mythologies of India. Also known as Taraswin, meaning 'Swift One', Garuda is variously described as having the body of an eagle, which may be gold, green or red. He also has four human arms, and wings that are either golden or scarlet coloured. His head is bird-like but with the face of a human – it may be coloured either gold or white. Garuda is described as the son of Kasyapa and Vinata; however, he was hatched from an egg that took 500 years to reach maturity. His father took a second wife, who was a Nagini; she enslaved Vinata and treated her cruelly. In order to ransom her, Garuda took upon himself the task of stealing the drink of immortality, the *amrita*, from the gods. In the process, he had several furious battles with the serpentine Nagas. His defeat of them so impressed the god Vishnu, that Garuda thereafter became his celestial steed.

GENGEN WER

In the Egyptian creation story, the goose Gengen Wer carries the egg from which all life emerges. In order to help Egyptians keep respect for life in mind, believers were urged to think of themselves as being the guardians of the actual egg itself, especially when they made the afterlife journey through the underworld.

GERD/GERDR/GERTHR

One of the giantesses of Norse mythology. The daughter of the giantess Angrbroda and the frost giant Gimir, she bore the appearance of a beautiful woman. The sun god Freyr fell in love with her and sent his servant Skirnir to persuade her to meet with him. The god promised Skirnir his magic sword if he was successful in his errand. Initially, Skirnir used gentle words to win over Gerd, but when rejected he used runes to trick her into agreeing to meet his master.

Geri and Freki

Two gigantic dogs belonging to the Norse god Odin in Scandinavian and Teutonic mythology. Geri means 'Ravener' and Freki means 'Glutton'. Geri was one of the hounds of hell who protected the goddess Hel and her region.

Gerjis

A gigantic monster in the shape of a tiger from the folklore of the people of western Malaysia. According to tradition, the Gerjis preyed upon other animals until those that remained were forced to take action against him. The mouse-deer Kanchil persuaded the monster to get into a deep pit that had been prepared beforehand. Kanchil then kicked earth on top of the monster and the elephant dropped a tree on top, crushing the Gerjis' skull.

Geryon

One of the great giants of Graeco-Roman mythology. Humanoid in appearance, this being had three bodies, three heads and six arms, all of which sprang from a single trunk below the waist. The son of the giants Chrysaor and Callirrhoe, Geryon ruled over a region known as Epirus, now the Iberian Peninsular. Geryon's great pride was a herd of vast red oxen who were guarded night and day by the giant Eurythion and his monstrous dog Orthos. Capturing this herd was one of the twelve labours of the hero Hercules.

Geush Urvan

In ancient Persian mythology Geush Urvan was the name of a gigantic cosmic bull – a celestial being so vast that it contained within it the seeds from which every other animal and plant in creation emerged. It grazed on the empty world for more than 3,000 years before being killed by the god Mithras in an act of creation.

Ghaddar

A species of cruel and ugly djinn in the folk traditions of the Yemen and Upper Egypt. Said to be the offspring of Iblis, a being of infinite evil, they resembled gigantic humanoids and were said to torture and torment their victims before abandoning them in a remote part of the desert.

Giant Dingo

A monstrous man-eating beast from the beliefs of the native people of Western Australia.

During the Dreamtime, the Giant Dingo, accompanied by a monstrous snake, took hundreds of victims, until all of the tribes were too frightened to light a fire in case it attracted the attention of this evil creature. Finally, the heroes Jitta-Jitta the Wagtail Man and his companion Kubin the Robin Man set out to kill these two creatures. Waiting until the wind was blowing from the right direction, they lit a great fire at the entrance to the cave that was the Giant Dingo's home. Jitta-Jitta went inside, attacked and killed the Giant Dingo. When he emerged from the cave, Kubin was hiding in a nearby tree shaking with terror. Spurred on by shame, Kubin found the courage to go into the cave himself and kill the snake. Since this time, both the Wagtail and the Robin have been considered sacred and may not be hunted.

GIRTABLILI

In Babylonian mythology, Girtablili was half man and half scorpion. This is one of the forms taken by the goddess Tiamat in the creation epic of Babylon. (*See* Scorpion Man.)

GIU XIAN

In Chinese mythology, Giu Xian is the Tortoise, one of the four spiritual creatures or Ssu Ling. It is the symbol of long life and righteousness. By the time it was 1,000 years old it was able to speak human language. Giu Xian is also associated with the ability to divine, for the cracks in its shell are related to the ancient divinatory practice of the I Ching.

GLAISTIG

A strange shapeshifting creature from the folklore and traditions of Scotland. Also known as the Maighdean Uaine (Green Maiden), this creature sometimes appears as a giant woman, sometimes as half woman and half goat, or completely in the form of a goat. In each case, she has something about her of the colour green. She will often appear by the side of a stream, begging to be carried across by unsuspecting travellers. The fate of such people varies from being simply led astray to having their throats cut.

However, the Glaistig has another side, and in some stories is described as a benign household familiar similar to the brownie, who undertakes domestic tasks while families are asleep. In this aspect, she is also a protector of children and old people, and as the Green Glaistig she is known to wail for the imminent death of one of her charges much like the more familiar Banshee. A story told in the village of Lochaber,

Inverness, describes how a smith once caught a Glaistig and threatened her into producing a herd of magical cattle and a beautiful house. When she had done this, he allowed her to go, but as she extended her hand in farewell the smith hacked it off. To this day, the vegetation growing in the area is said to be stained red with her blood.

GLAS GHAIBHLANN

A gigantic grey-white cow with green spots from the traditions of Celtic Ireland. This cow, which is probably a distant memory of a cosmic being, gave endless amounts of milk and was the property of the smith god Goibniu, or in some versions of Cian, a mysterious character from the dawn of the Celtic world. As word of this wonderful creature spread, the evil giant Balor stole the cow, taking her back to his home on Tory Island. Cian disguised himself and made his way to the islands where he made himself irresistible to the giant's daughter Eithne, who showed him how to recover Glas Ghaibhlann. Eithne later gave birth to the god Lugh Lamhfada.

GLASHTIN

The Manx version of the water horse, numerous examples of which are found in Celtic tradition and folklore, especially in Scotland and Wales. This particular creature often appears as a dark, splendidly handsome young man, with flashing eyes and curly hair. However, he may be distinguished from a real human being by his ears, which are pointed like a horse's.

Giants

From earliest times, giants have had an important presence in the mythology and folklore of the world. From the ancient Titans of the classical world to the blundering, easily fooled giants of folktale, they may be seen as supporting the world (*see* Supporters of the Earth and Sky) or playing a part in its destruction. Giants can be friendly or unfriendly, clever or stupid; they can be so vast as to be almost beyond our ability to imagine, or just simply larger than life. They seem always to represent a distant time or an older race, perceived as larger than us. Yet the most persistent lore of giants has more to do with the landscape in which they are set than with any distant memory of an immemorial race. Often, where huge boulders are found lying in open country, left behind by the retreating glacial ice, these are seen as evidence of giant activity. Thus we hear of the Cailleach Bheur forming the mountains of Scotland and the Hebridean islands, or of Cormilion, who is said to have been responsible for St Michael's Mount in Cornwall; or there is the Giant's Causeway in Ireland, built by Fionn mac Cumhail to serve him as a bridge,

and the various Giant's Cauldrons to be found in Germany, Norway and Italy. These in turn are echoed in more recent traditions by the American giant Paul Bunyan who is described as having created the Grand Canyon.

There are so many different types of giant that the only thing most of them have in common is their size and strength. Some, such as the mighty Bran the Blessed in Celtic tradition, clearly derive from gods, and in Britain at least the vast chalk hill figures such as the Cerne Abbas giant and the Long Man of Wilmington are almost certainly representations of ancient deities. In the pseudo-history of Britain composed in the 12th century by Geoffrey of Monmouth, the earliest inhabitants of the island were giants whose leader was called Gogmagog – a conflation of the Biblical Gog and Magog, who were themselves giants. According to Geoffrey, this giant was defeated by the Trojan Corrineus, who was equally mighty in stature and wrestled with Gogmagog, ending by throwing him from the top of the cliffs in Cornwall. Even the ancient name for Britain, Albion, is said to derive from an ancestral giant.

The word 'giant' itself derives from the classical mythology of Greece in which there are tales of a race known as the Gigantes, the offspring of the primordial goddess Gaia and her consort Uranus. These are described as part human and part serpent, and were born from the blood of their father, who was castrated by the god Zeus. These beings are truly primordial and were only defeated by the gods of Olympus with the help of the great hero Hercules, who imprisoned them, along with the Titans, in the underworld. In the same tradition, we find the Cyclops.

It is possible, as with the dragon, that the idea of the giant originated with the discovery of huge prehistoric bones. In Biblical terms, the existence of such beings caused a problem, since historical records indicated the presence of giants after the time of the Flood, when all forms of life save those included in Noah's Ark were supposedly wiped out. Some Old Testament scholars got around this by suggesting that Noah himself came from a race of giants and that it was only in the years afterwards that his descendants dwindled to the size of ordinary men and women. The Bible also mentions other giant races, such as the Anakim, the Enim and the Nephalim, who are said to have married into human stock.

The mythology of the Norse and Teutonic peoples is thronged with giants, beginning with the Jotuns, vast beings that ruled over the Earth in ancient times. These derived from an even more primordial giant, Ymir, from whose dismembered body all life was generated. The same tradition also spoke of Frost Giants, Fire Giants, and Earth Giants, all of whom were so immense that they were capable of challenging the gods themselves.

In the East, giants are less familiar, though there are several in the mythology of Thailand and the Vedic mythology of India. Among those described as especially important are Perusha, Madhu Kasitabha and Baliu. In each case these are represented as primordial beings that were partially responsible for the creation of the world. The same is true of China, where we find Pan-gu and Begda San, and in Mongolia the Manzasiri, all of which are held to have been active at the time when the Creation was taking place.

Among the native peoples of North America, there are a number of traditions relating to giants. Mostly they are described as benevolent towards humans, though there are exceptions that seem to originate in memories of natural disasters. Some, such as Chahnameed or Tsavboojok, are positively evil and prey especially on children.

In contrast to the foolish giants of folklore, there are the cruel, bloodthirsty ogres, of the type most often pitted against the wily Jack the Giant Killer. These tended to possess several heads, and are often carnivorous. In more recent times, giants have become an important part of literary history; from the scatological adventures of Gargantua, penned by the 16th-century French writer François Rabelais, through the literary giants of Dante Aligheri and Miguel de Cervantes, to the nursery rhyme creatures endlessly spouting 'Fee, Fi, Fo, Fum!' In our own time, we encounter giants in the world of J.R.R. Tolkien's *The Lord of the Rings* and *The Hobbit*, Roald Dahl's *BFG* and in J.K. Rowling's Harry Potter series, where the larger-than-life character of Hagrid is revealed to have giant's blood running through his veins.

GLYCON

A serpent with a human head in the traditions of the god Mithras in ancient Persia. According to some Mithraicists, he was also the avatar of the Aesculepius, the Greek god of healing, who carries a staff with a serpent coiled around it.

GLYRYVILLU

Opinions vary as to the exact shape and form of this creature, which is found among the traditions of the people of Chile. In some districts it is called the Vulpangue and is described as a serpent with the head of a fox. Elsewhere in the country it is described as either a dragon or a giant fish. One version has it as a flat, circular creature with eyes around the edge of its body – a description which sounds like that of a giant ray. The 18th-century 'Essay on the Natural History of Chile' by Juan-Ignacio Molina (1740–1829), describes local people as terrified to go into the water in case they encountered the Glyryvillu.

GNOME

Gnome is the name that the natural philosopher Paracelsus (1493–1541) created to describe the elemental spirits of the Earth. He also coined the words 'sylph' for an air spirit, 'salamander' for a fire spirit and 'undine' for a water spirit. 'Gnome' derives from a combination of Latin words and is itself a contraction of *genomus* or 'earth-dweller'. The names of these elemental beings are solely used by magical and hermetic practitioners and do not appear in folklore or myth. Gnomes are more properly dwarves or goblins in that they are concerned with the products and treasures of the earth. In Indian belief, it is Kubera who guards the earth's treasures and who allows certain humans to find jewels and precious ores like gold and silver.

The most notably gnome-like divinity of Egyptian mythology was Geb, the earth god, who has the characteristically dwarfish stature and wrinkled old man's face. The Fijian Veli live an existence somewhere between dwarves and fairies. It is more likely that Paracelsus created the category of gnomes after the earth-dwellers of his own land and culture, the mining dwarf. Today, of course, gnomes are more commonly found as garden ornaments, but that is not to say they do not have their own adventures. A spate of gnome thefts from British gardens resulted in one householder receiving occasional postcards from the stray gnome: each card showed his erstwhile garden guardian photographed beside world landmarks such as the Taj Mahal and Sydney Opera House. The gnome in question has not yet come home but continues on his world travels.

Goat

The goat seems to have been associated with fertility and creative energy from the earliest times. It shares many of the attributes of the gazelle and the antelope, while the wild goat of Old Testament times and Arabic lore is the ibex. Apart from the dog, it may have been the earliest domesticated animal.

The Sumerian god Marduk is often accompanied by a goat, while in Greece the creature was sacred to Artemis the huntress, and to Dionysus, who took the form of a goat when fleeing from the giant Typhon. Inevitably, fauns and satyrs, who are considered to be half goat and have goats' horns, have added to its sacred aspect. The god Pan is also represented with goat's legs, horns and beard. Like the deer, the goat is sacred to Faunus, the god and guardian of woods, fields and shepherds. It is also connected with other nature gods such as Sylvanus; while both Dionysus and Bacchus are shown from time to time in a cart drawn by goats.

The sacredness of the goat was widespread throughout Graeco-Roman culture and a she-goat was sacrificed to Artemis during her festival of Munichia in Athens. Herodotus tells us that, in the rights dedicated to her in Libya, the statue of Athene was ritually clad in a goatskin called an *aegis*. Both goats and dogs were sacrificed at the Roman festival of Lupercalia, during which women were whipped with goatskin thongs to invoke fertility.

In Hebrew tradition, the goat is very important as it represents the sacrifice of the Israelites to their god. Known as the Scapegoat, it was chosen from two animals, one of which was dedicated to God and the other sent into the wilderness as a bearer of human sins. In Old Testament tradition, the goat symbolized lewdness, and this tradition was later carried over into medieval Christianity, where the goat came to represent the Devil, lust and the damned, as opposed to the sheep, which symbolized the souls of the righteous.

In Norse and Teutonic mythology, Thor, the god of thunder, has a chariot drawn by goats. The sacred goat Heiddreun supplied the heavenly mead that the gods imbibed daily. Throughout Europe, the Oats Goat is made of the last grain stalks of the harvest to bring blessings to the next year's harvest.

In China, the goat spirit Yang Ching is associated with the star Fan-Yin and is therefore considered transcendent. It is invariably represented with a white face, horns, long beard and special headdress. In the West, the goat also has cosmic significance, and has long been a traditional symbol of wintertime, especially the midwinter period. This is the time governed by the constellation of Capricornus. In a myth of the Tsimshian tribes of the north-west coastal regions of North America, it is the goat that teaches hunters to maintain good relations with those whom they hunt.

The Element Encyclopedia of Magical Creatures

One day, the people of the earthly paradise Temlaham were permitted to hunt the mountain goat as long as the hunters fulfilled the hunting rituals of propitiation and thanks. However, these procedures became neglected over time, and the attitude of the hunters became bullying and opportunistic. The king of the mountain goats invited the hunters to a feast on the mountaintop. When the hunters arrived, they were confused because the goats had disguised themselves as men, although they did find it odd that these men ate grass rather than human food. While they all feasted together, a magical one-horned goat appeared. The hunters thought it was a human costumed dancer at first, but as the creature span and cracked his hooves upon the ground a great earthquake shook the mountain. All the hunters of Temlaham fell into the cracks that opened up – all except for one hunter who had once sheltered a mistreated kid and nursed it carefully back to life.

There are a number of representations of the goat in carvings found across the ancient Celtic world. Deities with goat horns are found in both Gaul and Britain and the Gaulish Mercury sometimes appears with a goat at his side. Many of the more frightening creatures of folklore from Ireland, the Isle of Man and Scotland represent themselves as giant goats or as half goat, half man. The benign Irish Pooka takes its name from the word for he-goat, *poc*. The Goborchend in Irish tradition are a tribe of goat-headed beings who attack human travellers.

GOBLIN

The name 'goblin' may derive from the Greek *kobaloi*, meaning simply 'evil spirit', developing through the Latin form *cobalus* into the French *gobelin* and, finally, the English *goblin*. It is now used as a general name for evil and malicious spirits, usually small and grotesque. Prefixing the word with Hob is considered to make them seem less terrifying since Hobgoblins were believed to be helpful and well-disposed toward men. In general, the term goblin seems to be used for any of the uglier and more malignant spirits such as Boggarts, Bogies, Bogles and Ghouls. Some sources suggest that goblins originally emerged from beneath a rock in the Spanish Pyrenees, from where they spread across Europe. They are also referred to as a group of fairies that live in churchyards, crevices in rocks, or among the roots of ancient trees. In European folklore, goblins are generally described as about knee-high, with grey hair and beards. Like the more kindly Brownie, they are often found in the home and can be propitiated by small gifts that make them better behaved. The best way of getting rid of a goblin is to scatter flax seed all over the floor, so that

The Element Encyclopedia of Magical Creatures

when the creature appears at night to do some mischief he will be obliged to pick up the seed. He will seldom complete this task before dawn and after several attempts he usually gives up and goes away. J.R.R. Tolkien made good use of goblins in *The Hobbit* as adversaries for his heroes; though in time they developed into the more fearsome and terrible Orcs of his *The Lord of the Rings* trilogy. Christina Rossetti's famous poem 'Goblin Market' simply makes them small and malicious.

GOLEM

An artificial human being created from mud in the traditions of Judaism. The word *golem* literally means 'body without soul', clearly separating the artificial creature from a living, breathing human being. The word appears only once in the Hebrew Bible (Psalms 139:16) where the reference is to the creation of Adam; but there have been numerous interpretations of this reference through the centuries. In Jewish literature, the golem is referred to as a stage in the creation of the first man. According to this tradition, God took 12 hours to complete Adam, and in this time made a number of failed attempts, one of which was the Golem.

A later tradition refers to a magical book, the *Sefer Yetzira*, which dates from late antiquity. This book described the letters of the Hebrew alphabet as the building blocks of creation, and taught that they could be manipulated in such a way as to give those who worked with them unlimited power. If, the book

suggested, God created human beings from the power of letters, then it must also be possible for humans to create a being in the same way. The exact formula required could only be learned though years of mystical discipline and study – which is why it is invariably a rabbi who is described as seeking out the answer to this mystery, and thus to being responsible for the golem.

One group in particular, the Pietists, who flourished in Germany throughout the 12th and 13th centuries, were believed to have created more than one golem. The main figures in the movement, Rabbi Samuel and Rabbi Judah, were believed to be especially successful, and the writings of one of their followers, Eleazr of Worms, remains the best source for golem recipes. What is clear from these, however, is not that the rabbis responsible for creating golems were working with magic, but rather that the creatures were brought into being as part of a mystical or ecstatic state of consciousness within the soul of their makers, and that they existed only while this state of being could be maintained.

Golems could be troublesome. A Polish Rabbi named Jaffe created a golem to light fires for him on the Sabbath, but one day the creature went out of control and set fire to everything in sight. A later Rabbi, Elijah of Chelm, a famous 16th-century healer and magician, made a golem to serve him. At first all went well, but gradually the creature grew stronger and harder to control, so that at last Rabbi Elijah had to destroy it. Interestingly, this was done by removing a card on

The Element Encyclopedia of Magical Creatures

Gods, Men and Animals

In world mythology, gods and animals are not always separate species of being. Gods can take on animal form or even the physical attributes of animals while retaining anthropomorphic features as well.

According to the Hindu *Shatapatha Brahmana*, 'No god is without animality, no animal without humanity, no man without a part of divinity.' It sets out the three components which all human beings possess: their divine, animal and human natures. 'Those in whom the *pati* [master] is dominant are the wise, who are close to the gods. Those who are ruled by their animal natures are called the *pashu* [cattle]. Those who understand the connection between gods and animals are those who practise the *pasha* [sacred bond], understanding the laws which maintain the universe.' The Hindu Lord of the Animals is called Pasupati. Shiva looked at the gods and said, 'I am the Pasupati, Lord of the Animals. The courageous Titans, the Asuras, can only be destroyed if each of the gods and other beings assumes his animal nature.' But,

because the gods were reluctant to do so, Shiva said, 'It is no disgrace to recognize your own animal. Only those who practise the rites of the brothers of the animals will be able to overcome their animal nature.' And then the gods and Titans realized that they were all the Lord's cattle.

Human beings are not exempt from having animal natures either. Many beliefs around the world ascribe a spirit animal to each person, a spirit companion who protects their life-power. In some cultures, this spirit animal is embodied by the human being when they pass into dream or take soul-flights into the Otherworld. Elsewhere, the animal becomes manifest during sacred dances which honour the animal spirits where, to the rhythm of drums, singing or percussion, people's spirit animals become apparent from their movements and callings. Among shamans, this animal relationship is strongest and a considerable part of shamanic seances. For many witches worldwide, the ability to pass into animal shape is a feature of working spells or magic.

which was written the sacred word of creation, the *aleph*, which was hung around its neck.

The best-known golem legends originate around the 16th century in the city of Prague. Rabbi Judah Low (*c.* 1525–1609) was the greatest Judaic scholar and mystic of his time, but he was eventually excommunicated because it was thought that he had not only practised forbidden magic but also created a golem according to the ancient methods described in the *Sefer Yetzira*. He did this to protect the ghettos of Prague, which were under great threat of persecution at that time. The golem became a deterrent to all who sought to persecute the Jews of the city, and only when the danger was past did Rabbi Low take the creature to the attic of the Altneuschul, the ancient Synagogue of Prague, where he removed the paper bearing the sacred name, just as Rabbi Elijah had done, at which point the golem fell to dust. This same dust is said to be preserved to this day in the closed attic of the synagogue, though it is many years since the golem last walked the streets of the city. (*See also* Stallo.)

GOLLINKAMBI

Also known as Vithafnir, this is a great golden cockerel that sits at the top of the world tree Yggdrasil in Norse mythology. It keeps watch for signs of the end of all things on the day of Ragnarok.

GONG-GONG

A vast and malignant dragon in Chinese mythology. Black in colour, with a mighty horn on the front of its head, this creature caused great disturbance in the world in the time before recorded history. In particular, Gong-Gong had such hatred for the celestial emperor Yeo that it drove its horn into the side of a mountain named Buzhou and tore it from the earth, setting free the waters imprisoned within it to flood the world. Gong-Gong then drove its horn into the sky and ripped a great tear in the fabric of the cosmos that caused the light of the sun and moon to grow dim. The goddess Nu Kwa later restored the destruction wrought by Gong-Gong, by reorganizing Heaven and Earth to take again their former shape.

GONG-SI

The Gong-Si are zombies of Chinese mythology. Though they have physical bodies, they are not alive and have no will of their own or the ability to think. There are still Chinese alive today who say they have seen Gong-Si and that before the Civil War and the Second World War, the dead regularly walked the roads of rural China, drawn back to their ancestral homes. If a dead Chinese was buried away from home without any of the accompanying rituals, they were likely to take to the zombie form in a desire to return home. In modern Hong Kong cinema, the Gong-Si are the slaves of an evil Taoist priest who sends armies of these animated corpses against kung-fu heroes.

GOOSE

In recent times, the goose has been associated with silliness, so that to call someone 'a silly goose' implies foolishness. This is a comparatively recent development in the mythology of this bird, which from ancient times has been recognized as wise, swift and powerful.

Like the swan, the goose is a solar animal, particularly in India where both creatures are acknowledged as vehicles of Brahma and representatives of the creative principle, learning and eloquence. Despite this solar quality, the wild goose is frequently associated with the moon in Chinese and Japanese tradition. It is known as 'The Bird of Heaven' and is represented as a messenger, generally bringing good tidings. For the Egyptians, the goose, together with the duck, was a primordial bird that carried the cosmic egg from which all life was hatched. The goose was one of the many appearances of the creator god, Amun who had the ability to take many forms. It was also associated with Isis, Osiris and Horus, in each case symbolizing love.

In the Graeco-Roman world, the goose was sacred to the goddess Juno, the goddess of the North Wind, and also to Hera, the Queen of Heaven. For the Greeks especially, it signified love, watchfulness and the qualities of a good housewife. It was also associated with the sun god Apollo, and because of its swiftness, with Hermes the messenger of the gods. The Roman poet Ovid called it 'wiser than the dog' and 'a protector of the house'. Both Greeks and Romans kept tame geese and, on one occasion, when the Gauls attacked Rome, the loud honking of the geese alerted the citizens to their approach and saved the city.

In the *Gallic Wars*, Julius Caesar says that the goose was not eaten by the Britons, being a sacred bird. In Celtic tradition, it was associated with the god of war; while in Gallic iconography, Epona the horse goddess is often depicted riding on a horned goose. In Christian symbolism, the goose represented vigilance and providence and was associated with St Martin; to this day, a goose fair is still held in France on the saint's day, 11 November. Another famous goose fair was held at Nottingham in England at Michaelmas.

For many people, the goose symbolizes swift winds and is considered a weather prophet. It is still considered lucky for sailors to see a goose as it floats rather than sinks. In more modern times, Mother Goose has come to represent motherhood and protection for children, as manifested in the nursery rhymes and children's stories of countless collections.

Gorgon/Gorgos

The original Gorgon was an extremely primitive creature described in the earliest mythology of Greece. Generated by the Earth goddess Gaia to support the Gigantes in their battle against the gods of Olympus, it was killed by Athene, who buried its head beneath the foundations of the *agora* in Athens. Later, the name Gorgon was given to the three daughters of the gods Ceto and Phorcys. Originally beautiful, the women were transformed into hideous monsters by Athene after the god Poseidon seduced one of them, Medusa, in the goddess' temple. They are said to be in the form of women with wings, with huge tusks that protrude from their mouths causing their tongues to protrude from their jaws. They also have snakes for hair, and a single glance from one of them can turn anyone who sees it into stone. Two of the Three Sisters, Eurale and Stheno remained immortal, but the hero Perseus killed Medusa.

Gorynich

One of the most fearsome dragons mentioned in Russian folklore.

Gorynich was the nephew of an evil sorcerer who had abducted the Tsar's daughter and imprisoned her in a dark castle in the mountains, intending her to be the bride. The Tsar offered untold riches to anyone brave enough to recover his daughter. Many tried but all failed, but at last one of the palace guards, a young man named Ivan, said that he would undertake the task. He had heard two crows whispering together, discussing where the princess was hidden. The Tsar equipped Ivan with a magical sword and everything that he needed for his journey. After many adventures, he finally arrived at the fortress of the sorcerer, which was unguarded since its owner believed that no one could the find the place, or would have the courage to enter. Ivan searched the castle until he found the princess, who told him of her betrothal to the dragon. Just as they were about to flee, the sorcerer entered and, growing to the size of a giant, attacked Ivan. Fortunately, the young hero was ready with his magic sword, which flew out of his hand, hacked the head off the giant and then flew off through every part of the fortress, hacking at every being it met, including the dragon Gorynich. When all of the evil beings were dead, they returned to the Tsar and Ivan took the princess for his bride.

The Element Encyclopedia of Magical Creatures

Goryschche

A vast 12-headed she-dragon from Russian folklore. The name Goryschche derives from the word *gora*, meaning 'mountain', giving some idea of the size of the creature.

The story goes that Goryschche the dragon terrorized the Russian people for many years, stealing hundreds of her young men and packing them, still living, into her cavernous den in the Sorychinsk Mountains. Finally, a young hero named Dobrynya Nikitich decided to try his hand at killing her. He set out for the mountains and found a place teeming with the dragon's young. These he dispatched rapidly, and trusting that this would deter the dragon without his having to meet her, he set off for home. Arriving by the side of the stream, Dobrynya took off his clothes and went for a swim. Once he was in the water, he suddenly became aware of clouds of smoke and flames above his head. It was Goryschche swooping down upon him out of the sky. Enraged by the death of her children, the dragon demanded that he surrender his life to her, but instead Dobrynya dived beneath the water and swam ashore, finding that he had come out on the bank furthest from where his armour and weapons were laid. Uncertain what to do next, he saw a priest's hat lying on the ground, and seizing it up he used it to defend himself. In fact, the hat had remarkable powers, because he was able to sever 11 of the dragon's 12 heads with it. At this point, Goryschche begged for mercy and Dobrynya spared her on one condition – that she never attack the Russian people again.

Arriving back in Kiev, Dobrynya discovered that the dragon had already broken her word, and carried off the Tsar's daughter. Mounted on his father's old horse, Dobrynya rode into the mountains. There he once again found the ground teeming with the dragon's young and once again destroyed them. Then he rode on until he reached the dragon's lair. The dragon protested bitterly over the slaying of her offspring, but Dobrynya pointed out that she had broken her word and he demanded the return of the Tsar's daughter at once. When the dragon refused, Dobrynya attacked her, and for three days they battled until finally the hero was triumphant. However, he now found himself stranded in the middle of a vast lake of the dragon's blood. Falling on his knees in prayer, Dobrynya called upon Mother Earth to swallow the dragon's blood, and instantly a chasm appears and the lake drained away. Dobrynya now entered the network of caves in which the dragon had lived. Within he found and released many hundreds of Russian people trapped by the dragon. In the very last chamber, he found the princess. Together they returned triumphantly to Kiev where Dobrynya was rewarded with a vast treasure and the hand of the princess.

Gosh/Gshuurun/ Goshuurvan

Also known as Geush Urvan these are alternative names for the great primordial bull or cow of the Zoroastrian mythology of ancient Persia. This vast creature was created on the same day as the first human being, and was intended to provide all things for humans to survive upon Earth. However, both Gosh and the original man were destroyed by the evil being known as Ahriman, necessitating a second creation.

Gou Mang

One of several cosmic dragons from Chinese mythology, Gou Mang, together with Rou Shou, are messengers of the sky gods and are sometimes represented as a double dragon. Gou Mang brings good fortune with the return of spring, and is said to promote longevity, while Rou Shou represents bad fortune and the coming of autumn.

Gowrow

A huge, wingless, dragon-like creature from the folklore of the Ozark people of North America. Said to be at least 20 ft in length, with twin tusks emerging from the front of its head, it was reported as recently as the 19th century.

Graeae

Like the Gorgons, this monstrous trio are said to be the daughters of the primal beings Phorcys and Ceto in Greek myth. However, while the Gorgons are characterized by their writhing locks, gnashing tusks and the ability to turn people to stone with a single look, the Graeae are feeble hags who were born with long grey hair and have only one eye and one tooth between them. When he set out to destroy the Medusa, the hero Perseus had first to encounter the Graeae, who guarded the way to Medusa's lair. Perseus intercepted the single eye as it was passed between them, and retained it until they promised to help him accomplish his task. The Greek mythographer Hesiod mentions two names for the Graeae: Pemphredo and Enyo; later writers added a third, named Deino.

Grasshopper

For the people of the Graeco-Roman world, a golden grasshopper signified nobility. The Greek author Aristotle said of the grasshopper that it was the only creature that had no mouth but used a tongue-like formation on its nose to feed solely upon dew.

In Chinese myth, Pa Cha is the spirit of grasshoppers, and protects people against other destructive insects. It is depicted as having the head and claws of a bird of prey with ear tufts similar to those of an owl. In Chinese culture, the grasshopper signifies good luck, the abundance of summer, many male offspring and general virtue. In the folklore of Europe, the grasshopper and the ant are often contrasted as representing irresponsibility and improvidence against industry and providence. The ant is seen to work all summer long to lay up stores for the winter, while the grasshopper sings throughout the summer and starves during winter.

In the traditions of the Navajo people of North America, the Grasshopper people were the original inhabitants of the underworld from which the first people travelled on their way to the surface of the Earth. Grasshopper Mother, in the traditions of the Choctaw people, stayed behind in the underworld and was killed by those who had been delayed in reaching the surface. Those who had already succeeded in emerging prayed to the Great Spirit to close the tunnel so that the murderers should remain in the underworld, where they were transformed into ants. Australian Aboriginal lore connects the grasshopper with lightning, and it is said that anthills are often places where lightning strikes. This is an obvious connection between the grasshoppers' ability to leap from place to place and the unpredictability of lightning flashes.

GREAT HORNED SERPENT

Among the Iroquois people of North America, the Great Horned Serpent is a messenger of the monsters that dwell in the Great Lakes. Pictograms have been found carved on rocks in this area that depict the creature as a giant rattlesnake. As a messenger, it was not necessarily seen as a malevolent being and it was invoked before crossing the lakes. It was assumed that the Great Horned Serpent would carry the prayers of those about to embark to its master, who would refrain from swallowing them in its turbulent waters.

GREAT LYNX

Among the Ojibwa people of North America, this is another name for the water monster Mishipizhiw. It is described as a huge cat-like creature with a saw-toothed backbone and an extremely long and flexible tail with which it can catch its victims, dragging them to a watery grave.

GREAT SERPENT OF HELL

Among the Peigan people of Canada, this is a huge creature which preys upon hunters and steals their catches.

A Sioux woman named Onwi-Menocha, which means 'Woman of the Moon', used to disappear from time to time into the forest. Her husband suspected her of meeting the Great Serpent and forced her to tell him by dancing the 'Dance of the Secret Loves', which was intended to reveal the nature of any unlawful relationship. Onwi-Menocha covered herself in green body-paint and then proceeded to dance, her writhing movements suggesting to everyone that her lover was indeed the Great Serpent of Hell. Her husband demanded, as was his right, that she be killed, but she vanished once again and was seen no more in the land of the living. However, she continued to appear to her husband in dreams, assuring him that she was indeed with the Great Serpent, and that together they would protect his hunting trails.

GREMLINS

Gremlins came into being during the First World War, when the Royal Navy found that certain things kept going wrong with equipment. They were first named in 1922 when an RAF pilot called Le Bourget airport for a weather check and was told 'Gremlins sur la Manche' ('Gremlins over the Channel'). At which point his radio died. The word comes from the Old English 'gremian' to vex. During the Second World War, Gremlins grew in strength and cunning, acting in a characteristically annoying way, and affecting just about every thing they could to make trouble. They were believed to be about 12–20 inches high and were a cross between an American jack-rabbit and a bull terrier. They were sometimes seen wearing green trousers, a red jacket, spats and a top hat, although the marine Gremlin always had webbed feet and fins. Since they had no wings, they had to infiltrate whatever was moving. On airfields, they would live in underground burrows ready to hop on board. They drank petrol and could cause havoc during flight by running from wing to wing and causing crews to bail out. They themselves were capable of landing safely by spreading out their great feet, parachuting head first and landing on their top hats which were shock absorbent. They were always interested in the radio air-waves, where their interference caused great problems. In Gremlins, we see a set of new-wave Boggarts who can infiltrate technology of all sorts and who are blamed for problems with electrical transmissions of any kind.

The nautical origins of Gremlins are not without antique mythology for it is told in the Welsh story of Lludd and Llefelys (*see* Coranyeidd). Gremlins, of course, figure in a series of films of the same name, produced by Steven Spielberg, where they appear similar

Green Man

The Green Man is one of the most widely recognized creatures in world mythology. Acknowledged as immemorially ancient, he represents all of nature, combining elements of the animal and the vegetable worlds. Visitors to the churches and cathedrals of Europe will have seen him many times, peering down from the rooftops inside these buildings, squinting from the tops of pillars or carved underneath choir stalls. In most cases, he is represented as a semi-human face, but when one looks closer, this face is made up entirely of leaves. In some later images, he has become more human, but leaves still grow from the corners of his eyes, sprout from his nostrils and pour from his mouth. The oldest representations of the Green Man are found in ancient temples of the Near East, especially in what was once Mesopotamia. From here the image spread into Graeco-Roman symbolism, and is often found carved on fountains or on the walls of temples throughout the classical world.

In ancient Egypt, where water was scarce and the annual rising of the Nile waters was essential to all life, green gods and goddesses played an important part in the spirituality of the two lands. The colour green was honoured above all, and to do 'green things' came to mean doing good, while to do 'red things' meant to do evil. Osiris, perhaps the most important deity in Egyptian life, was both a god of vegetation and resurrection. In the Pyramid Texts, he is known as 'the Great Green' and is depicted as green skinned in acknowledgement of his life-giving energy.

The East, too, knows of the Green Man, and his face is to be seen looking out from the elaborate carvings of Angkor Wat. In India, carvings exist which clearly show this ancient personification of nature. Other aspects of the Green Man include the formidable Green Knight from the 14th-century medieval poem 'Sir Gawain and the Green Knight'; and his character is echoed in the human figure of the outlaw Robin Hood. In more recent times, the Green Man has become something of a symbol for the world-wide ecological movement, as well as being accepted into the pantheon of modern Paganism.

to koala bears with long ears and teeth. These cinematic Gremlins originally came from China where they were called the Mugwai (but *see* Moqwaoi, who are different) and whatever you did, you should never, ever get them wet, since this caused them to multiply.

GRENDEL

A water monster described in the 8th-century poem *Beowulf,* believed to have been written in Britain. In this famous and much-translated poem, Grendel, who appears to be a kind of dragon, lived in the swamps close to the mead-hall of King Hrothgar. The creature could not bear to hear the sounds of people enjoying themselves celebrating in the hall, and would emerge from the swamp at night, killing as many as 30 warriors, dragging them away to be devoured in the swamp. Hearing of this tale, the hero Beowulf sailed to Denmark and offered to rid the land of the monster. He and his men remained in the mead-hall and when the monster appeared Beowulf did battle with it, finally severing one of its arms. In the morning, the severed limb was found hanging from the rafters of the hall, while the waters of the nearby swamp turned red with the creature's blood. While the warriors were still celebrating, Grendel's Mother emerged from the water, seeking vengeance for the death of her son. Beowulf then fought her and, after a protracted battle at the bottom of a lake, slew her. Despite the

familiarity of this tale in Britain, it is scarcely known in Scandinavian mythology.

GRENDEL'S MOTHER

The mother of Grendel in the 8th-century epic poem *Beowulf.* After the eponymous hero had slain her son, the monster emerged from the waters of the swamp, reclaimed her son's severed limb and seized one of the king's men. In the morning, Beowulf entered the watery swamp where the two monsters had lived and swam to the bottom, where he fought a great battle. Beowulf slew the monster and returned to the surface where he was greeted with roars of delight, and a great feast was given in his honour. Many years later, he was to be slain in battle, poisoned by a dragon.

GRIFFIN/GRYPHON/GRIFFON

The griffin is customarily depicted as a lion with an eagle's or raptor's wings, beak and, sometimes, talons, although it can simply have lion's paws. It has prominent, upturned ears that seem to have developed from earlier Egyptian forms, where it is shown with a crest on its head. In addition, the front of the griffin's body is frequently spotted like a leopard. In classical times, all four of its feet were those of a lion, but in later times it had two front lion's legs and two hind eagle's talons. The griffin takes its name from the Greek word *gyphos,*

The Element Encyclopedia of Magical Creatures

meaning 'hooked' or 'curved', an allusion to its sharply curved beak. It is one of the oldest magical creatures, depicted in the Fertile Crescent, the cradle of Western civilization, and remains today as a powerful protector of modern civil institutions such as banks, car plants and breweries.

Griffins were a feature of Egyptian and Mesopotamian art from 3000 BC, spreading into Syria, Anatolia and Cyprus. In Sumerian myth, the griffin is the mount of the weather god, Iskur, where it is depicted vomiting forth streams of water or lightning from its mouth upon the parched land. In Assyrian art, the griffin is frequently shown venerating and protecting the Tree of Life, as well as flanking divine figures to assist the check of evil. One theory of its name's origins suggests the Middle Eastern word *kerub* or cherub – two cherubim adorned and protected the Ark of the Covenant in the Pentateuch. Griffins were shown with the Egyptian sun god, Malakbel, and in the Old Kingdom they were a symbol of the victorious ruler striding across the bodies of enemies wounded or killed in battle.

By 1700 BC, the griffin was depicted in King Minos' palace on Crete, where it is shown fighting with bulls and lions, as well as lining the walls of his throne-room. The Greeks adopted the griffin to adorn vases, mosaics, lyres, gems, seals, coins and reliefs, but they appear primarily to have been carved upon tombs to guard the dead and to act as bearers of the soul. In the 5th century BC, the Greek writer

Herodotus related a story about a one-eyed people known as the Arimaspians who wrested their immense wealth of gold from griffins. He learned this tale from a mysterious traveller, Aristeas of Proconnesus, who told how the griffins guard the gold of the northern lands of Scythia. In Aeschylus' tragedy, *Prometheus Bound*, Prometheus warns Io to beware of 'the sharp-beaked, unbarking hounds of Zeus' and the one-eyed Arimaspians who live on the gold-streamed plains of Ploutos. From this account, which precedes that of Herodotus, it would appear that griffins do not inhabit the lands north of Greece, but the celestial regions where Zeus dwells, and that the griffins are drawn to the realms of Pluto, the god of wealth and of the underworld.

The griffin became closely associated with many Greek divinities, including Nemesis, the goddess of justice, whose chariot was drawn by avenging griffins. Because her task was to protect the good and punish the proud by rolling them down from their vaunting and lofty position to a more humble posture on the ground with her wheel, the griffin is often depicted with a paw resting upon the wheel. This emblem was adopted by the Roman Empire to symbolize universal justice.

In the medieval legends surrounding the figure of Alexander the Great, who had conquered the known world in the 4th century BC, Alexander attempted to fly on a griffin to the edge of the horizon. He built a flying machine with poles spiked with food and chained griffins behind these

The Element Encyclopedia of Magical Creatures

poles. As they attempted to eat the food, so they flew up into the air, but he was ultimately forced to descend. This caused medieval authors to see the griffin as a symbol of *superbia* or over-reaching pride. A poem said to be the epitaph inscribed upon the tomb of Alexander draws upon this myth of his flying griffins:

> O, mankind, who will die,
> Why do you desire to be lifted on high?
> Why, the more you gain,
> The more do you desire to possess?
> Everything passes away,
> And the flower of life also comes to
> an end.
> The higher you climb,
> The greater your fall from the heights to
> the depths.

Griffins were the birds of Apollo, pulling his sun chariot across the heavens, and so they are also depicted upon the lyre, the musical instrument of Apollo. His sister, Artemis, who is the goddess of the wild beasts, inherited the role of Mistress of Griffins. Following the Greek manner of carving griffins upon tombs, the Romans went further by showing the griffin holding a cloaked figure on its back as psychopomp or bearer of souls between life and death.

The 2nd-century classical author Aelian told of the Indian griffin, which dug up gold with its beak in order to build a nest with it, and was strong enough to overcome elephants and tigers. Its eyes were like fire. The griffin, which was merely trying to protect its young, would attack Indian hunters who attempted to steal the gold. This description seems to relate the nature of the griffin to that of the Roc (or Rukh).

The Gundestrup Cauldron, a Celtic votive cauldron made sometime between 300 BC and 300 AD, possibly in Thrace and customized for a Celtic chieftain, was found in a Danish bog in 1880. It bears one of the earliest northern depictions of the griffin. Together with a pair of elephants and a lone feline animal, a pair of griffins attend the Goddess of the Cart who appears to be some kind of Mistress of the Beasts. This image is unique, portraying the only known depiction of the northern Goddess of the Cart, whose peripatetic rites required ritual sacrifices at bogs and sacred sites.

The Roman great mosaic in the Villa Romana del Casale in Sicily depicts animals of many kinds being hunted from all over the known world and shipped ready for use in the Colosseum and the Circus Maximus in Rome. The only mythic animal in the mosaic – the only animal in the whole great mosaic that will survive the beast-hunts of the circus – is the griffin, shown in a predatory position on top of a cage in which a human being is trapped. This image marks the last pagan understanding of the griffin as an untameable creature which cannot live beside human beings, although a 10th-century lexicon, the *Suda*, speaks of the Avars, an eastern tribe, being forced to migrate due to the appearance of many griffins in their lands who would not stop until they had devoured the whole human race.

The classical lore of griffins was transmitted solely through Roman literature until the fall of Constantinople in the 15th century when ancient Greek works once again began to be available in Western Christendom. The griffin survived into Christian myth by virtue of an accident of translation because the Vulgate Bible had rendered a Hebrew word into the Greek – and so into Latin – as griffin, which is how the creature appears in the list of Moses' unclean animals that are unfit to eat. If an animal was in the Bible, it was thought that it must exist. According to the 2nd-century AD Greek *Physiologus*, the griffin catches the rays of the rising sun upon its wings, carrying them across the sky with the help of another griffin, while St Michael and the Blessed Virgin pray for all Christians. In the *Etymologies* of St Isidore of Seville, the griffin was said to be hostile to horses, which it would tear to pieces as soon as they were sighted. He placed their home in Hyperborea, the land beyond the North Wind.

The griffin became primarily a kingly emblem of power and might. Robert the Pious, who was king of France at the turn of the first millennium, made all his people swear upon a griffin's egg that he had encased in a silver reliquary box, in order to be sure of their faithful oath. So it was that the griffin's reputation safeguarded Robert's reign more readily than any holy relic, so feared was its retaliation against perjury. As it had once adorned temples and sanctuaries throughout the Fertile Crescent, now the griffin appeared as a gargoyle on cathedral roofs and church buildings, and on book covers to ward off would-be desecrators.

The appetite for griffin stories did not diminish in the middle ages. The 12th-century letter supposedly sent by the mythical Prester John, the Christian king of the Far East, to the Greek emperor Manuel, described how there was a valley of jewels in his kingdom. Men threw down sheep carcases there and the jewels adhered to them. As griffins flew down to fly away with the carcases, the jewels would fall to the ground, making an easy harvest for all jewel merchants. This story is similar to that told of the Roc – Marco Polo's travels relate that he heard that in Madagascar griffins pick up elephants to a great height and then dash them to pieces upon the ground in order to feed upon them.

The natural history of the griffin, believed in the Middle Ages to live somewhere in the East, was related by many writers. The 12th-century mystic St Hildegard of Bingen wrote of the griffin's egg-laying, describing how the griffin must first find a narrow cave into which it can barely fit, wherein its eggs will be safe from lions who will trample them to pieces if they get the scent of them, and safe from sunlight and gusts of wind. Sir John Mandeville, whose *Travels* are full of wild tales, relates that a single griffin is stronger than eight lions and a hundred eagles, and that their feathers make strong bows and arrows. The 9th-century Irish theologian John Scotus thought that the griffin was a model of chastity since it remained celibate when its mate died. The fabled ability of griffins to find gold made it both a suitable emblem to ward off greed and rapacity,

The Element Encyclopedia of Magical Creatures

as well as becoming a Christian by-word for greed. The griffin's reputation for living far in the north made theologians declare it to be faithless, uncharitable and lacking in any goodness. Its medieval standing fell mostly due to its inclusion in the Pentateuch as an unclean beast, and so the griffin became seen as a symbol of avarice, tyranny, cruelty and even the devil.

Dante rescued the griffin from such infamy in his *Divine Comedy* where he meets a griffin on the borders of Purgatory and the Garden of Eden where Dante encounters his first love, Beatrice, in the triumphal procession of love. Here, the griffin is restored to its original Middle Eastern role as the adorer and protector of the Tree of Life, preserving the seeds of justice. Writing three centuries later, a fellow Italian, Ariosto, gave the griffin a new lease of life by inventing the Hippogriff, the offspring of a horse and a griffin. This unlikely creature can only be tamed by a hero and it flies up to the earthly paradise to help Orlando regain his lovelorn wits. It was a Roman, Virgil, writing in the 1st-century BC, who held that one of the most unexpected things would be to find griffins mating with horses: it took another 17 centuries to bring this occurrence to another readership!

The debunking of the griffin's existence was aided by many detractors, including the 16th-century Polish writer Mathias Michovius and the 17th-century British writer Sir Thomas Browne. But the griffin found a supporter in Alexander Ross who refuted Browne by saying, 'If any man say that now such animals are not to be seen; I answer, it may be so, and yet they have not perished; for they may be removed to places of more remoteness and security, inaccessible to men.'

The most familiar griffin known to children worldwide is that of Lewis Carroll's Gryphon in *Alice in Wonderland*, whom Alice finds sleeping in the sun. When Alice awakes from her adventures, she knows that 'all would change to dull reality' in which 'the shriek of the Griffin ... would change to the confused clamour of the busy farmyard.'

The magical properties of the griffin include vigilant protection against evil, a strong grip to guard and protect precious objects, and to frighten away anyone rash enough to contemplate the desecration of a holy place. Its untameable nature remains its best defence.

GRIFFIN VULTURE

A monstrous bird from Graeco-Roman mythology, the Griffin Vulture is the offspring of two monsters: Echidna and Typhon. Its main purpose was to torture the giant Prometheus, who was doomed to suffer eternal torment for stealing fire from the gods to give to humanity. Every day, the Griffin Vulture pecked at the giant's liver who, being immortal, could not die and grew a new liver each night. In the end this agonizing fate was halted by the hero Hercules, who killed the vulture by shooting it with an arrow as it flew overhead.

The Element Encyclopedia of Magical Creatures

Groundhog

The curious celebration of recent times known as 'Groundhog Day' takes place in the United States on 2 February, Candlemas. On this day the groundhog, a small mammal, is said to come out of his burrow. If he catches sight of his own shadow he retreats back into his hole for six more weeks, expecting further cold weather or the late coming of spring. If, however, he stays above ground, then spring will come early and it will be a good year for farmers. The origin of this custom is somewhat obscure. Candlemas has been celebrated in the Christian calendar for many hundreds of years, and in Scotland it is celebrated as one of the quarter days; however Groundhog Day seems to be a combination of natural observance and superstition. It is celebrated widely throughout North America, and the film *Groundhog Day* starring Bill Murray, made much of the mystical qualities of the day by having its Scrooge-like hero relive the same day again and again until he learns the lessons of care and humility.

Grugach

There are two distinct traditions concerning the Grugach. The name comes from an old Irish word which can mean hairy or long-haired, but it is also applied to goblins, enchanters, wizards and fairies. However, it is most often described as a helpful spirit similar in some ways to the brownie, both in the Highlands of Scotland and in Ulster (Northern Ireland) where it is known as the Grogan. Described as low in stature, hairy, with broad shoulders and possessing great strength, it is famed as a hard worker.

In Ballycastle, Ireland, the story is told of how a particular farmer used to lay out a number of sheaves of corn in the granary every night for the Grugach to thresh by morning. One day he left the flail on top of the corn stack, and forgot to set out the usual number of sheaves. The Grugach thought that this meant he was to thresh the whole stack, and in the morning was found dead on top of the grain, having worn himself out with the work. The farmer gave the Grugach an honourable burial, and mourned him long after.

The Ulster Grogan generally appear as naked, hairy little men about 4 ft in height; another description says that the Grugachs have large heads and soft bodies and appear to have no bones when they roll down the hillsides. In the Highlands, the Grugachs may be richly dressed and watch over cattle. Some Highland stories describe the Grugach as a fairy woman dressed in green with long golden hair, who may appear as either beautiful or as worn and haggard. She would sometimes enter houses dripping with water and ask to dry herself by the fire. There were also male Grugachs in the Scottish Highlands, some of whom were handsome youths who wore red and green clothing. But for the most part they were naked and shaggy. One account describes how a farmer's daughter, pitying the nakedness of their particular Grugach, made him a shirt, but since to give clothing to any of the fairy people was considered a way of getting rid of them, the Grugach fled the farm immediately, weeping. (This is a detail made good use of in J.K. Rowling's Harry Potter books where the house elf, Dobby, can only be released from service by being given clothes.) Elsewhere in Scottish tradition, the Grugach is a more fearsome and frightening individual, playing all kinds of tricks on the mortals he encounters, and even displaying magical powers.

GRUGYN SILVER BRISTLE

One of several giant boars described in Celtic mythology. The most famous of these was Twrch Trwyth who, together with his sons Grugyn Silver Bristle and Llwydwg the Hewer and many other porcine offspring rampaged across Britain during the time of the great warrior Arthur. Apparently, all three had once been kings, whose evil deeds caused them to be transformed into the shape of pigs. The story is told in the great Welsh epic tale of 'Culhwch and Olwen' from *The Mabinogion*.

One of a number of tasks given to the Culhwch to enable him to win the hand of a giant's daughter is to take a comb and scissors that lie hidden among the bristles of the great boar's neck. Together with Arthur and his host, a great chase begins in which they follow the three rampaging boars across south Wales to the rivers Wye and Severn by a route so closely delineated that it may still be followed this day. When the great pigs are caught, a running battle ensues and many of the hunters are killed, until finally only Twrch Trwyth and his sons are left alive. Finally, Grugyn Silver Bristle is surrounded by a ring of hunters and after a great fight is slain; to this day, the spot is marked in the name Garth Grugyn.

GRYLLUS

This monstrous creature, usually described as part beast and part human, with a second face where its stomach should be, first appears in the mythology of the Graeco-Roman world. Pliny the Elder (AD *c.* 77) mentioned several artists who specialized in portraying the Gryllus (or Grillus); while the Greek historian Plutarch (AD *c.* 46–120) tells an alternative version of the famous encounter between Odysseus and the sorceress Circe in which she turns his

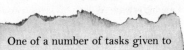
The Element Encyclopedia of Magical Creatures

men into swine. When Odysseus tries to disenchant his men, one of them gives a carefully reasoned explanation of why they would prefer to stay in their porcine state. The name of this man is given as Gryllus. Homer himself had used the word *sus* for swine, but Plutarch adapted this, marrying it with the word *gryl* 'to grunt'. Later, during the Middle Ages, the Gryllus became a familiar image in the serio-comic images which decorated elaborate Psalters or prayer books and was also found carved on the walls or pillars of medieval cathedrals, representing human folly or vice.

GUCUMATZ

The great Quiché Mayan serpent, also known as Cucumatz, was the bringer of civilization and agriculture. In Guatemalan tradition, he appears as a feathered bird-serpent. A wind and rain god, he had three manifestations: lightning, lightning bolt and thunder. He was also a creator and fertilizer of the earth, living alone in the darkness and stillness, and visiting the underworld known as Xibalba. Among his titles are 'Bowels of Earth', 'Bowels of Heaven', 'Four Ends of Earth' and 'Heart of Heaven'. His emblems were a black or green stone (probably jadeite) or flint.

GUDANNA

A gigantic bull found in the mythology of ancient Sumer. This creature had such poisonous breath that it was able to kill 200 warriors at a time simply by breathing on them. According to the great epic poem *Gilgamesh*, the oldest surviving piece of literature in the world, the Gudanna was originally created by the god Anu at the behest of the goddess Ishtar, who sought to wreak vengeance on the hero after he had refused her advances. With the help of his hugely strong companion Enkidu, Gilgamesh managed to slay the bull, but this so enraged Ishtar that she slew Enkidu in revenge.

GUITA

The Guita is a kind of dragon found in the folklore of Spain. It is often to be seen as an effigy paraded through the streets of small towns in Catalonia. Its name apparently means 'Kicking Mule' but despite this curious title the Guita's effigy represents a huge serpent-like green dragon with a long neck, a black face and huge jaws with fangs. Fireworks are frequently set off within its mouth to simulate fiery breath. It is a popular symbol of fear and delight among the people of the townships.

GULLFAXI

Gullfaxi means either 'Golden Mane' or 'Golden Horse'. He belonged to the giant Hrungnir, who challenged the god Odin to a race against his own magical steed, Sleipnir. The giant's mount proved to be slower than the god's, but Gullfaxi ran so fast that he was only brought to a halt when they reached

Asgard, the home of the gods. As a consequence of this trespass, the thunder god Thor killed Hrungnir in single combat. Thor then gave the giant's horse to his three-year-old son. This displeased Odin, since he thought that he should have been given the prize. He reprimanded Thor, but the god's son was permitted to keep the mighty beast. Elsewhere, Gullfaxi is listed among the horses of the gods. His name may have influenced J.R.R. Tolkien in the creation of the great mount Shadowfax, ridden by the wizard Gandalf in *The Lord of the Rings*.

GULLINBORSTI

Gullinborsti is a giant boar that draws the chariots driven by the god Freyr in Norse mythology. His name means 'The One with the Golden Bristles' and he can run faster through the air and across water than any horse, both by day and night, since his bristles shine so brightly. From the almost metallic description that Snorri Sturluson gives of Gullinborsti in *Gylfaginning*, with his shining bristles, it is possible that the boar, also called Slidrugtanni, is actually a kind of mechanical automaton. This idea is reinforced by the fact that Gullinborsti was made by the blacksmith dwarf Brokkr whose name implies 'one who works with metal fragments'.

GULON

A monster with rather disgusting habits found in the folklore of Sweden. Though it may have been around for much longer, it is first mentioned by the 16th-century traveller Olaus Magnus, who describes it as somewhere between a lion and a hyena with a fox's tail and long, razor-sharp claws. It was usually seen amid the northern snowfields where it lived on carrion. Its practice was to gulp down anything it could find, living or dead, eating ravenously until its body was swollen and distended. It would then seek out a narrow gap between two trees and squeeze itself between them, thus forcing out a build up of gases from its body and enabling it to feed again. It is said that this was the only point at which it was vulnerable to attack, and though its flesh was never eaten, its blood was said to have aphrodisiac properties and was sometimes served, mixed with honey, at weddings.

GURANGATCH

A water monster from the Dreamtime mythology of the native Australian people of New South Wales. Described as a kind of lizard-fish of immense size, this creature preyed upon human beings for many years.

The hero, Mirragen the Cat-Man, sought to win the position as the best fisherman in the village. So he went to a certain pool which he knew to be inhabited by Gurangatch and, with the help of spells and charms, drew the monster to the surface. Despite his every effort, he was unable to catch it, so he obtained some poison bark to place in the pool to drug the monster. While Cat-Man was doing this, the Gurangatch burrowed through solid rock and escaped. But Cat-Man did not give up and he pursued the monster for many more days. Finally, the Gurangatch tunnelled through to the village of Cat-Man and caused it to be flooded. Exhausted, Mirragen begged help from the Bird People, one of whom dived beneath the surface of the pool where the Gurangatch had made a temporary resting place, and seized a scale from its body. With this prize, the Cat-Man had to be content, but to this day when rivers overflow their banks this is still ascribed to the activities of the Gurangatch.

GUYASCUTUS

One of the strange and unlikely creatures jointly known as the Fearsome Critters, described by the lumberjacks of 19th- and early 20th-century North America. The Guyascutus was initially described as a kind of dragon but there are a number of variants – typical of these bizarre inventions – that describe it as a 10-ft alligator with a covering of overlapping scales similar to those of an armadillo and a dorsal ridge of bone-like protuberances. Elsewhere it is said to resemble a white-tailed deer, but with the ears of a rabbit and ferocious fangs. In each instance, its most notable feature is that its legs are shorter on one side than the other, and are apparently able to telescope, enabling it to stand upright even on a sloping hillside. If this was not enough, it also possessed a prehensile tail that enabled it to swing from the trees or hang on to sharp rocky escarpments.

One of the tales told of the Guyascutus speaks of a travelling Wild Animal Show which listed the creature among its attractions. Not surprisingly, when the show arrived in a small Midwestern town, it was a sell-out. However, before proceedings could begin, a man arrived at the entrance to the tent shouting that the Guyascutus had escaped. Needless to say, all the patrons of the event fled in terror – thus enabling the show people to depart with all their takings.

GWAGWAKHWALANOOKSIWEY

Images of this terrifying creature, a flesh-eating bird from the traditions of the Kwakiutl people of Canada, are often found carved on the elaborate masks which feature in Kwakiutl ceremonies. In appearance, it looks like a gigantic raven, and is also known by the name Hokhoku. It is said to be

The Element Encyclopedia of Magical Creatures

related to the Bakbakwakanooksiewae, 'The Cannibal-at-the-North-End-of-the-World', which together with his equally monstrous and unpronounceable wife Galokwudzuwis, preys upon humans, breaking open their skulls with its long beak and eating their eyes and brains, which it regards as delicacies.

GWIBER

The name sometimes given to the white dragon in an early story of the prophet and enchanter Merlin.

GWILLION

The name of a hag-like fairy in the folklore of Wales. Sometimes called the Old Woman of the Mountains, the Gwillion looks like a poor old woman wearing a four-cornered hat, ash-coloured clothes, and a cooking pot on her head. She leaps out in front of unwary travellers crying, 'Wwb!' (You can try saying this yourself by standing up suddenly and wobbling your lips in a menacing way while shaking your head sidewise.) Anyone who hears her is likely to end up drowned in one of the bottomless mountain lakes. The Gwillion roams the hills caring for her herds of goats, whose long beards she combs every Wednesday, which is the Sabbath of the Welsh fairies. The Gwillion herself is also sometimes said to take the form of a goat.

The Gwithin, as this race of fairies is called, have a great dislike for human beings and are prone to lead them into swamps. They are afraid of storms and will sometimes seek out lonely houses on the mountains for shelter. Like most European fairies, they are also afraid of iron or steel, and anyone able to corner a Gwithin with a knife made of either of these metals must have a wish granted. However, the negative aspect of this is that the entire tribe of Gwithin will then hate you forever, making it impossible to travel in the mountains in safety. In the 19th century, a man named Evan Thomas described how he found himself surrounded by Gwithin as he rode through the mountains, but when he drew out his knife they promptly vanished.

GYTRASH

A kind of sinister fairy from the folklore of northern Britain. At night, it can take the form of a large horse, donkey or sometimes a shaggy black dog with webbed feet. It has huge saucer-shaped eyes and walks with a splashing sound. It is generally described as lurking silently by the side of the road waiting for unwary travellers; however, some stories speak of it in a more positive light as helping to lead lost travellers to safety. There is a memorable description of the Gytrash in Charlotte Brontë's novel *Jane Eyre*. (*See also* Padfoot.)

H

Habaek

In Korean mythology, the Habaek was a water god who lived in the Yalu river.

Habergeiss

The Habergeiss is a nocturnal bird with three legs whose moans and screams announce death in Austria. Every 5 January, the Habergeiss is represented at the annual Perchtenlauf festival where horned beings hit the legs of spectators with birch twigs. Habergeiss becomes a horned goat hobby-horse with a snapping mouth, and is represented by two men, one wearing the horned mask and the other playing the back-quarters of the beast. It gambols about, snapping at passers-by.

Haferbock

In German folk tradition, the Haferbock is the straw or Oats Goat who lives in the fields. He is associated with the fertility of the fields and his likeness is brought into the house, made from grain of the last harvest. He figures in winter festivals and is similar to the Krampus (Winter Goat).

When his eldest daughter was taken to be the wife of the sun god Haemosu, Habaek was affronted that no official arrangements or negotiations were made. He summoned Haemosu to a test of skill in which they shapeshifted. Habaek became a carp, while Haemosu became an otter and caught his father-in-law. Habaek then became a deer but Haemosu became a wolf and chased him. Lastly, Habaek became a quail, but Haemosu caught him when he became a falcon. By this means, Habaek had to acknowledge his son-in-law's supremacy in the air, on the land and in the water.

Finally, an official wedding ceremony was made and Habaek made ready to send his daughter Yuhwa to heaven in Haemosu's chariot. But the girl decided to return to her father. Incensed at this turn-around and all the trouble and loss of status that he had been involved in on her behalf, Habaek ordered that his daughter's lips be stretched out and that she be put into a stream, where she became a fish. Later, the king's fisherman netted her, but her mouth had been so elongated that she was unable to speak until she had cut her lips three times. The king brought her into his household but Yuhwa finally fell pregnant by the sunbeam which Haemosu sent through her window.

The Element Encyclopedia of Magical Creatures

Hai Ho Shang

In Chinese mythology, Hai Ho Shang is the fish which has a monk's tonsure and a scaly hood over its head. It has a long monk's robe which lengthens into a tail. It is of huge size and attacks sea-going junks, overturning them so that the crew drown. Attacks can be averted if the crew do a ritual dance and burn feathers, which Hai Ho Shang cannot abide. Some sources have said that he is like a merman.

Hai Riyo

Hai Riyo is a creature from Japanese folklore. It has the head of a dragon and the body, wings and claws of a bird. Sometimes called the Tobi Tatsu or Schachi Hoko, it is found in the decorations of Chinese temples. It may derive from the Ying Lung.

Haiit

The Haiit was believed to live in the forests of central Africa. This large creature had a humanoid appearance covered with shaggy fur. It had a small tail and three-toed feet, which it used to climb in the jungle. Its human-like face and ability to climb makes it almost certain that the Haiit was an early description of a monkey. It was first reported in the era of maritime exploration and colonial expansion in the 16th century by André Thevet in his *Cosmography*.

Haizum

In the Islamic traditions of the Koran, Haizum is the heavenly horse upon which the archangel Gabriel delivered direct communication to the prophet Mohammed.

Halcyon

The Halycon bird is found in Greek mythology. It was originally the woman Alcyone, wife of Ceryx, who went on a voyage to consult the oracle of Apollo. Zeus had been offended by Alcyone and he sent a storm to drown Ceryx. However, Alcyone's mourning was so profound that she drowned herself when she saw her husband's dead body. The gods turned her into a bird and, as she continued her mourning, so Ceryx's body was also changed into a Halcyon. It has a long neck and is bright blue with white and purple markings. Although some have equated it with the kingfisher, it is not a bird that appears often – usually only at midsummer or midwinter. When the Halcyon is on its nest by the seashore, the weather becomes calm while the eggs are preparing to hatch and for seven days after they have emerged. These periods of calm are known as the 'halcyon days' and were times when the sea was navigable. The Halcyon is still a harbinger of mourning as well as of calm.

Half Chick

According to European folk tradition, Half Chick is the name of a folk hero who is called Mediopollo in Spain and Demi Coq in France. Stories about Half Chick are known throughout Europe from Estonia and Finland through to the Mediterranean, and from Britain to Russia and the Czech Republic.

Half Chick was the partially grown runt of a chicken's clutch of eggs. Having found some money under a dung pile, he set off to buy grain from the king. Half Chick confided his task to the river who decided to accompany him by hiding in the hero's anus. At the king's palace, Half Chick was sent to stay with the king's chickens whom the king believed would overwhelm and kill the miserable runt, although the king was quick enough to take his money. But Half Chick let the fox out and it killed the king's chickens. The next night, Half Chick was stabled with the king's horses and let the wolf out, so they were killed. On the last night, Half Chick was thrown into an oven but he released the river which not only put out the fire but also flooded the palace. In order to get rid of the nuisance, the king sent Half Chick off with both the grain and his money returned.

A similar story is told in a Cochiti Indian tale from New Mexico, where the hero is called Half Rooster. This story probably entered the Americas through the tales of the Spanish colonists. Half Chick is the unquenchable folk hero of the weak and the underdog, whose cunning is overlooked by the opportunist because of his puny size.

Hamadryads

In Greek mythology, the Hamadryads are tree nymphs or dryads whose life is bound to the tree whose life they share. When it is cut down, so they also die. The upper half of their bodies is female while the lower halves are the trunks and roots of the tree.

Hamsa

In Hindu mythology, Hamsa is the divine goose upon whom the creator Brahma rides. Hamsa is seen as the guardian of creativity. Those ascetics and yogis who have gained release from the cycle of rebirths through their practice are said to be like Hamsa. The yogic principles of breathing are governed by the in-breath or 'ham' and the out-breath of 'sa'. Hamsa represents the divine essence which every person possesses.

Hanuman

In Hindu mythology, Hanuman is the monkey god of speed and strength. He was the son of Vayu, the wind god, and

the monkey nymph Anjana. He is depicted with a yellow skin and an endless tail. He helped Rama retrieve his wife Sita from the abduction of the demon Ravana. While he was fighting, his enemies greased his tail but he merely swung it around so that their city burned down. He also gathered medicinal herbs to heal the wounded. For his great service, Rama awarded him the gift of eternal life and youth. His statue is displayed in every Indian gymnasium for he is the presiding deity of all forms of exercise and combat. Hindus also worship him as the god of the village and as the patron of women who desire children. Apes are regarded as sacred because of Hanuman, and they are often allowed to roam in temples.

HAP

In Egyptian mythology, Hap was the sacred bull of Memphis, and regarded as a symbol and incarnation of Ptah-Osiris. Hap was the offspring of a virgin cow who had been impregnated by lightning or a moonbeam. Also known as Apis, Hap became Serapis in the afterlife, where he was seen as a fusion of Osiris and Apis. Actual bulls were selected by their markings to serve as a living avatar of Hap. After it had been installed as the living god, the bull had the power to impart prophecy on its breath which was inhaled by its worshippers. When the Serapeum of Memphis was excavated in the 19th century, 64 mummified bulls were discovered. It has been suggested that the Golden Calf set up by the Israelites when Moses was receiving the Ten Commandments, was a likeness of Hap.

HAPY

One of the Canopic Animals which is responsible for guarding the lungs of the deceased in the mummification process, Hapy has the head of a baboon. He is under the protection of Nephthys, the goddess of the underworld. Hapy was considered to be one of the souls of Horus.

HARE

The hare has a complex mythology from the Americas to Japan. Many myths make a connection between the hare, the moon, the dawn resurrection and immortality.

A Hottentot myth from Africa tells how the moon sent an insect to Earth with the message, 'As I die, and dying live, so you shall also die, and dying live.' The insect was overtaken by Hare who asked it what the message was and offered to run faster and deliver it. Hare came to men and said, 'The Moon says to you, "As I die and dying perish, so you shall die and dying perish."' Then Hare returned to the Moon and told her what he had said. She was so angry that she struck him with a piece of wood on the nose and, since that day, the Hare's nose is split. This is similar to the story told of the chameleon.

The Element Encyclopedia of Magical Creatures

In the hare, we find the origins of the 'Easter Bunny' which is found in the United States. In Europe, especially in Austria, the Czech Republic and Hungary, coloured eggs are placed in hidden nests for children to find on Easter morning, but the Hare that laid the eggs is honoured that afternoon when children must visit their grandmothers or an older female relation. Children used to dress in a cape with head and ears like a hare carrying a small waterbutt filled with dyed eggs. Elsewhere in Europe, there is the custom of the hunting of the hare. These customs derive from an early European tradition of honouring the goddess Ostara or Eostre (the name from which Easter is derived) whose creature was the hare. In Buddhist tradition, Buddha himself was reborn as a hare who instructed his friends how to observe the holy days.

In Indian tradition, Vijaya is the ambassador of the hare moon-god, Silimukha. In China, the hare lives in the moon eternally creating the elixir of immortality. He was once a courtier who accompanied his emperor to the spirit of a holy mountain to learn the secrets of immortality. When the emperor had been initiated, the spirit of the mountain begged him to leave the courtier behind. Every day this man went and gathered flowering plants to feed the mountain spirit. After a while he ate some himself and became so spiritualized he turned into a hare. In Japan, the Ainu believed that hares came down from heaven as the hair of god's deer. They thought the hare was a bearer of the evil eye and that any hare tracks in snow must be scooped out and turned over to avert evil.

Seeing that the moon was ripe for a holy day, Hare told his friends Monkey, Jackal and Otter to obtain food to offer to a beggar and not to eat until they had offered him the food. Each of the animals stole food from humans but the Buddha in the form of a hare decided to offer himself. The king of the gods, Sakka, decided to test the hare and appeared in the form of a beggar. The hare told him to fetch wood and when the fire was burning to call him for he would leap into the fire. The beggar must then eat him. But when Buddha leapt into the fire, it was as cold as snow. He asked the beggar the meaning of this, at which Sakka had to admit who he really was. In order to celebrate the hare's virtue, Sakka squeezed the nearby mountain and with the extracted essence he painted the hare's image on the moon's disk. This image is what in Europe is called 'the Man in the Moon'.

Among the Algonquin natives of North America, the Great Hare, Manabusch is the great creator and trickster. As Michabo Ovisaketchak, 'The Great Hare Who Created the Earth', he is the original hunter whose footsteps measured eight leagues. He was so big that the Great Lakes that border Canada and United States were the beaver dams he made. By watching the spider spin her web to catch flies, he invented the art of netting so that fish could be caught. He bequeathed many signs and charms that help in the hunt. In the autumn, he settles down to his winter hibernation by smoking a great pipe, the smoke of which becomes the clouds and mist that fill that season. His brother is the snow and his house was in the east, which is why the doors of medicine lodges are sited in that direction. In Mayan myth, the hare was the inventor of writing. Throughout South and Central America, the hare is associated with the moon.

Queen Boudicca of the Iceni, who fought against the Romans in the 1st century in Britain, used the hare as an instrument of divination. Since hares notoriously run zig-zag and not in straight lines, possibly to put off any pursuer, by observing the way the hare that she released from a fold in her robe ran, she was able to tell the course of her next battle. She gave thanks to the goddess Andraste, the goddess who gives victory.

Hares are frequently seen as shapeshifters or the form in which witches choose to go. In the Isle of Man, old May Day was the signal for setting the gorse on fire in order to 'burn out the witches who are hiding in the shape of hares'. A familiar method of despatching any such shapeshifting witch was to shoot at a suspect hare with a bullet made from a silver sixpence. If she was a witch, the hare would disappear and someone in the village would be found in bed bleeding from a wound caused by a silver bullet. The lucky rabbit-foot amulets that some people carry are related to the hare which has the ability to bring fertility and wealth, as well as to avert harm.

HARIVAMSA

Harivamsa is the name of the boar, an emanation of the Hindu god, Vishnu. Harivamsa is the embodiment of the sacrifice according to the sacred teachings of the Vedas where all the parts of his body represent every virtue of the sacrifice. His body is said to be like the steps that lead to the altar. His pathways are the most secret teachings of the *Upanishads*, his speed is the offering to gods and ancestors.

HARPY

In Greek mythology, the Harpies were the sisters who were the personifications of the storm-winds. They had the shape of birds with hideously hag-like faces, drooping breasts, bear's ears and clawed talons. Poseidon is described as being their father or their lover. But their parentage is much disputed and too tangled in Greek myth to give an unambiguous certainty. Hesiod says that they are born of Thaumas, grandson of the Earth goddess, Gaia, and the Oceanid Electra. Homer speaks of Pordarge 'the racer' who was raped by Zephyros, the Western Wind. She then became the mother of two immortal horses, Xanthos and Balios. Hesiod speaks of Aello 'the wind-footed one', and Okypete 'she who is swift in flight' and Okythoe 'the swift footed'. The two other named Harpies are Kelaino 'she who is dark,' and Mapsaura 'a blast of wind'.

The Harpies are fleet-footed and winged, but their claws are made for snatching, which is what the name 'Harpy' means – a 'Snatcher'. They interfere in the lives of human beings and intervene to their detriment. Whatever they touch is said to become contaminated. If people were lost at sea, it would be said that 'the Harpies snatched them away'. The enemies of the Harpies were the sons of Boreas, the North Wind who finally overcame them. The Harpies used to descend upon the food of the blind seer Phineus whenever he sat down to eat. To assist Phineus, the sons of Boreas banished the Harpies to the depths of the Earth under the island of Crete. They are sometimes confused with the Erinyes (or Furies) as well as with the Sirens.

HATHOR

In Egyptian mythology, Hathor is the universal cow goddess who is called the Mother of Ra, the sun god. She represented the female power of nature that was perpetually conceiving, creating, bringing-forth, rearing and maintaining all things with her milk. The part of the *Egyptian Book of the Dead* that relates to the retention of heat in the body of the deceased so that the body might be resurrected is said to have been transmitted by the Cow of Heaven herself. The *Book of the Dead* also depicts 'the seven Hathors' who are shown as seven cows with a bull:

these are the equivalent to the Moirae (or Fates) who determine the destiny of a child at birth. They are called 'Universal Lady', 'Sky-Storm', 'She from the Land of Silence', 'She from Khemmis', 'Red-Hair', 'Bright-Red' and 'She Whose Name Lives Through Skill'. Invoking the seven Hathors protects the body from evil and harm.

HATI

Hati or 'Despiser' was the wolf who would devour the moon at the time of Ragnarok, the world's ending, in Norse mythology. He was assisted in bringing the world to an end by Skoll, who pursues the sun in the same way.

HATUIBWARI

In the Solomon Islands of Melanesia, the creators of life were the Figonas, great winged serpents. Hatuibwari was a Figona with a human head, four eyes and four breasts with which she suckled all creation. The greatest Figona was Agunua who created a male child, but he was so helpless, Agunua made a woman to make fire, cook and weed the garden.

HAUG-BUI

In Anglo-Saxon lore, the Haug-Bui were the barrow-wights or spirits who lived in the ancient turf-covered graves of forgotten ancestors. It was said they were especially adept at guarding treasure. St Guthlac of Cambridge actually lived in such a hollowed-out barrow and was continually having to defend himself against the attentions of the Haug-Bui, who kept up a running assault upon him. These bedraggled, alarming creatures with their thin faces, long teeth and flaming eyes had their knee joints backwards. They could only be killed if they were beheaded and then their skulls placed between their knees. A number of early burials have been excavated from prehistoric barrow burials showing this singular form of exorcism of evil spirits or witchcraft. Frodo Baggins is rescued from the attentions of the Haug-Bui or Barrow Wights by Tom Bombadil in Tolkien's *The Lord of the Rings*.

HAVFRUE

In Danish folk legend, the Havfrue was the mermaid who combs her long golden hair. Like the Havfine of Norway, the Havfrue herds the waves to shore as her cattle, trying to get them to graze upon the dunes. The birth of Christian IV of Denmark was said to have been prophesied by a Havfrue, who have the ability to see into the future. Her male counterpart is the Havmand. A statue of a Havfrue can be found in Copenhagen, based upon the 'The Little Mermaid' who features in the Hans Christian Andersen story. The Little Mermaid's duty was that of a typical Havfrue – to bring the prince and his crew to the bottom of the sea – but she chose not to let him die.

HAVMAND

In Danish folk tradition, Havmand is the merman who lives along the shores. He is handsome, bearded and friendly to those whom he meets, although his female counterpart, the Havfrue, is often seductive and predatory. The Havmand sometimes has blue skin and green hair. It is not clear whether the creature that was reported to the Bishop of Bergen in Norway was indeed a Havmand, but the finders said they saw a beached creature with the front paws of a seal calf and the face of a man. It was about 28 ft long.

HAWK OF ACHILL

According to ancient Irish myth, the Hawk of Achill is one of the oldest creatures. His story comes to us in the form of a dialogue between himself and Fintan mac Bochra, one of the first men to colonize Ireland. Fintan himself has lived through several animal incarnations of his own, having become an eagle, a falcon and a salmon. The hawk is a staggering 6,515 years old and discusses with Fintan the whole history of Ireland from the time of the great flood. Fintan tells the hawk that when he was in the form of a salmon, he experienced the coldest winter's night at the waterfall of Assaroe encased in the ice, and that while he was there a bird came and pecked out one of his eyes. The hawk admits that it was himself who did that. Fintan then requests compensation for this theft. Then the hawk tells him about battles he has witnessed and feasted upon, including the conflict in which Fintan's twelve sons fell at the Battle of Moytura Cong. The hawk stripped the flesh and took a juicy gobbet from each of the fallen sons. He also boasts of having eaten up the hand of the High King of Ireland, Nuadu, who afterwards had made a prosthetic silver hand. The magical property of the Hawk of Achill is length of life and memory through the changes of time.

HAYAGRIVA

In Tibet, Hayagriva is one of the Dharmapalas who protect the teachings of Buddhism and the land of Tibet. His name means 'horse-necked'. He has a stocky human body and a horse's head, although sometimes he is shown with a smaller horse's head above his own human one. Other drawings show him with three horses' heads, which is when he takes the form of Krodha Atigyhya, the 'Angry Highest Secret'. In this form, he also has six hands which carry a goad, a noose, a club and sword, together with the lotus emblem and a skull cap. Hayagriva or Tamdrin as he is also called, is the protector of the Padma family of Buddhas and Bodhisattvas (those who refuse to enter Nirvana until all are enlightened). He is seen as an emanation of Amitabha Buddha and is understood to embody the speech of all the Buddhas. His essence resides in the chanting of the syllable '*hri*' which, like the stallion's whinny, is the sound that cuts through illusion and reveals the nature of reality. Hayagriva also protects horses.

In Hinduism, Hayagriva is a Daitya (opponent of the gods). He stole the sacred teaching of the Vedas as they slipped from Brahma's mouth while he slept. But in later tradition, Vishnu took the form of Hayagriva to recover the Vedas. Vishnu will come again in the form of a horse-headed being called Kalki to re-establish a golden age before he destroys the world.

HAYASIRSA

Hayasirsa is the horse-headed protector of scripture, an incarnation of the Hindu god, Vishnu. He rescued the sacred teachings of the Vedas from the bottom of the ocean at the request of Brahma, for two spirits had abducted and hidden them there.

HAYMEHYT

Haymehyt is the sheep consort of the ram god, Banebdjedet, to whom the god-judges appealed when Horus and Set struggled for possession of the throne. He was partial to Set, whom he felt should win since he was the elder brother of Horus.

HAYOTH

The Hayoth is the Jewish name given to the Four Holy Creatures (Tetramorphs) of Ezekiel 1 and Revelations 4. Each of the Hayoth have human forms with four faces and four wings, with brazen ox's hooves. They had human arms and

The Element Encyclopedia of Magical Creatures

hands. Each had a four-fold face: a lion's face to the right, a bull's face to the left, a human face ahead and an eagle's face behind. Each had two wings that touched behind their bodies and two wings that covered the body in the front. Fire flashed between them and they ran to and fro like thunderbolts. The Hayoth were part of the Ofanim or Wheels of Ezekiel's vision, which appeared like a very complex fiery chariot. Over the vault above their heads was a sapphire throne with a fiery man seated upon it. This vision is studied in detail and meditated upon with awe by kabbalists who study the mystical and esoteric teachings of Judaism, for it reveals the nature of the godhead. The Hayoth appear again in the vision of St John the Divine in Revelations 4 where they have been modified to four separate animals: a lion, a bull, a man and an eagle, each of which have six wings and who sing the *Sanctus* acclaiming God as almighty forever. (*See* Apocalyptic Beasts.)

HEA-BANI

Hea-Bani or Ea-Bani is the Mesopotamian version of the centaur. Hea-Bani, like Cheiron of Greek myth, was a wise hermit. He had the head, arms and upper body of a man but the lower body and hooves of a bull. The son of Ea (or Enki), he acted as a counsellor of the hero Gizdhubar, who had a dream of stars falling upon him. He journeys into the marshes to find Hea-Bani, who interprets it for him and helps him overcome his enemies. Hea-Bani died in a similar accident to that which caused the death of Cheiron. When the goddess Ishtar was spurned by Gizdhubar, she flew to heaven to ask Anu to avenge the insult to her vanity. Anu created the Bull of Heaven to punish her errant lover. This being took the form of Humbaba (or Khumbaba) but Gizdhubar overcame the heavenly avenger with the help of Hea-Bani.

HECATONCHEIRES

In Greek mythology, the primordial goddess Gaia gave birth to these three giants, each of whom has a hundred arms and fifty heads; their father was Ouranos. The Hecatoncheires were Kottos 'the Striker', Briareus 'the Strong' and Gyges 'the Many-Limbed'.

HEIDDREUN

In Norse mythology, Heiddreun is the goat that stands eating the leaves of the tree Laerathr. Her udders give clear mead, which flows into the beakers of the Einherjar, the courageous warriors slain in battle who live immortally. In one story, the giantess Hyndla accuses the goddess Freya of being as lascivious as Heiddreun.

HELIODROMUS

According to medieval European folk tradition, Heliodromos is a composite creature formed of a vulture with a mammalian body, somewhat like a griffin.

The Element Encyclopedia of Magical Creatures

Henwen

In the Welsh Triads, a great sow called Henwen is pursued by King Arthur because of a prophecy that she will be the ruin of Britain. In different parts of the land she gives birth to a grain of wheat, a bee and a grain of barley before giving birth to a wolf cub and a young eagle, as well as the giant cat Cath Palug, whose depredations harmed Britain until it was overcome by Arthur's warrior, Cei (*see* Cath Palug). Henwen's name means 'the Old White One'.

Heqet

In Egyptian mythology, the frog-headed goddess Heqet is the consort of Khnum. She is associated with the processes of death, resurrection and birth. The Egyptians held that the frogs that jumped out of the silt left by the annual Nile inundation were born from this mud, which is why the frog is associated with the rebirth of the body and soul. Women wore amulets of Heqet to help them carry their babies to term and for a safe delivery. Households often possessed an ivory knife bearing an image of Heqet as a magical protection to keep everyone safe. As the divine midwife, she helped all midwives in their work.

Herne the Hunter

Herne the Hunter is the leader of the Wild Hunt in English tradition. His legend places him in Windsor Great Park near the Great Oak. In Shakespeare's play *The Merry Wives of Windsor*, the bibulous and lascivious Falstaff gets mixed up in the country revels and dresses up as Herne. The name 'Herne' is similar to that of Cernunnos and is the root of 'horn'. Herne the Hunter was given a recent resurrection in a British TV series, *Robin of Sherwood*, where he appears as a shaman who embodies the beneficent and sometimes challenging powers of Herne upon the fertility of the land and the keeping of order.

Herren-Surge

In Basque folklore, the Herren-Surge is a snake with seven heads that can fly through the air even though it has no wings. It lives underground and has the habits of a dragon. It eats any unattended herds of animals.

Hieracosphinx

In Egyptian mythology, the Hieracosphinx is a sphinx which has the body of a lion and the head of a falcon. Sphinxes in this form are generally representative of the god Horus.

Hiintcabiit

In the legends of the Arapaho peoples of North American, Hiintcabiit is a great horned serpent that lives in rivers and mountain lakes. When Hiintcabiit took two human wives and his second, younger wife River Woman bore a child, the jealous first wife drowned her. River Woman's brother, Beaver Foot, took the child in his arms and went searching for his sister's body along the river. Hiintcabiit came up to the surface with River Woman so that she could feed her hungry baby, but the displacement of water was so great that the village was nearly swamped. Beaver Foot held back the flood but as Hinncabiit brought River Woman to the surface, a hunter shot him.

HILDISVINI

Hildisvini is the boar on which the goddess Freya rides. He is also called Gullinborsti 'the one with golden bristles'.

HIMAPANDARA

In Hindu belief, Himapandara ('Snow Palace') is one of the Lokapala elephants who is the guardian of the North quarter of the world. On his back rides the god Kubera.

HIPPOCAMPUS

The Hippocampus or Hippocamp is a sea creature from classical mythology, which had the front parts of a horse and the back parts of a fish or dragon. The sea god Poseidon's chariot was drawn by Hippocampi.

HIPPOCENTAUR

Hippocentaur is the full name for the centaur, having the head and upper body of a man with arms, and the lower body and four-hoofed legs of a horse.

HIPPOGRIFF/HIPPOGRYPH

A hippogriff is the hybrid result of crossing a griffin with a horse. This creature should never have been possible since it was held in classical times that the griffin loved nothing better than a nice meal of horse flesh. Indeed, 'I'll do it when horses and griffins mate' became a saying meaning 'sometime never'. However, nothing deterred, the Italian poet Ariosto decided to make a Hippogriff as the uncontrollable mount of his wizard Atlantis in the epic poem 'Orlando Furioso'. Hippogriffs sprang up in medieval times, fusing the horse's body with the wings, beak and claws of the griffin with its half-eagle and half-lion features.

HIPPOPOTAMUS

The hippopotamus is a very powerful creature whose uncertain mood can be very dangerous to those near or on the waters where it lives. Throughout Africa, the hippopotamus has a mixed reputation for being both predatory to the unwary but also protective to those who are pregnant or mothers.

The hippopotamus was the form taken by the Egyptian goddess, Taweret, wife of Set. She is shown standing upright with a hippopotamus's body and with human arms and legs. She carries an emblem called a *'sa'* – a rolled up papyrus shelter for herdsmen who are out tending flocks. She also carries the life-giving *ankh* (torch) symbol with which she expels typhonic forces. She was the matron of women in childbirth. Another Egyptian goddess, Rerat, was also shown as a hippopotamus. The deceased had to know the names of the door guardians to the gates that led to the afterlife, one of which was guarded by Rerat. Traces of this goddess hippopotamus are still found in Mozambique where the Ronga people speak of Mpfuvu, who lives in the lush water meadows surrounded by a happy throng of babies who are her protégés.

The strongest associations are to be found between the hippopotamus and Set, who takes this form in his long contest with Horus. It is believed that the hippopotamus is the origin for the stories about Behemoth in the Old Testament, from its fearsome capacity to swim underwater and to suddenly emerge with destructive results.

HLGHAN XHIILA AND HLGHAN GHAGING

Among the Haida peoples of the northern Pacific coast of Canada, Hlghan Xhiila ('Pierced Fin') and Hlghan Ghaging ('Floppy Fin') are the killer whales who lead the Qqatsgha Llaanas, a pod of killer whale gods who look after the strait between the island and the mainland of the Haida. They are frequently depicted on totem poles and house doors as protective divinities who bring plenty.

HOB

The helpful Hob is a brownie-like spirit who looks after the health of children, notably curing them of whooping cough, according to North Country traditions in Britain. If your child had this cough, the way of summoning Hob was to say this rhyme, as you put your child into a cave on Runswick Bay, near Hartlepool:

Hobhole Hob! Hobhole Hob!
Ma bairn's gotten t'kink cough,
Tak't off, tak't off! (take it off)

Hob and Puck have a lot in common. Like many brownies, Hob must never be given clothing, or he will take offence and cease helping you with your domestic tasks. A nastier kind of Hob used to haunt the road between Hurworth and Neasham near Darlington. Eventually, he was exorcized and conjured under a large stone on that roadside for 99 years. It was said that if anyone ever sat on the stone, Hob would never be able to escape from under it. It has been said that Hob's name comes from an Old English name 'Hob Thurse' meaning 'the Hob Giant'.

Hobgoblin

Hobgoblin is a being who is nothing like as pleasant as a Hob and perhaps not as nasty as a goblin, but this is a matter of opinion. Hobgoblin is the kind of name that English people have used to miscall the honest Hob when they are impatient, or an insulting way that Puritans have of addressing goblins whom they associate with demons and other tricksy spirits. Shakespeare was aware that if you call someone a bad name, they will begin to take on that nature, for in his *A Midsummer Night's Dream*, a fairy addresses Puck with:

> *'Those that Hobgoblin call you, and*
> *sweet Puck,*
> *You do their work, and they shall have*
> *good luck,*
> *Are you not he?'*

Hobyah

The Hobyah is a Scottish goblin who ate people and kidnapped children. Earliest mention of Hobyahs comes from a single Perthshire story in which they are eaten up by a black dog. Recently, more stories about Hobyahs have been written by the children's writer, William Mayne, so this is not the end of their existence.

Hoenir

Hoenir is the bird in Norse mythology that laid the egg from which the whole world came. He is also called 'the Lord of the Mud' and 'Long-legged', because he brings life out of the primeval ooze and is often understood to be a stork. This may be the origin of the European notion of the stork as the one who brings new babies. He was the silent companion of Odin and Lodurr, and appears in human shape in the myth of the creation of men. His silence betokens the primordial state of life before manifestation. He was the silent companion of Odin and Loki.

Hoh

In Mayan tradition, Hoh the crow was one of the four creatures that brought maize to the gods so that they could make humanity. The other animals who helped in this creation were the parrot Quel, Utiu the coyote and Yac the forest cat.

Hokhoku

In the legends of the Kwakiutl people of the north-west Pacific coast of Canada, Hokhoku is one of the names of a cannibalistic bird also known as Bakbakwakanooksiwae. It opens the brains of its victims before dipping in its long thin beak to pluck out the contents.

Hoopoe

The Hoopoe is a long-billed, thrush-like bird with an erectile crest. According to Islamic tradition, it gained its crest from King Solomon, who awarded the bird a golden crown for its wisdom in refusing to pay homage to women, or according to another tradition, the crown was given because the hoopoe shielded him from the sun with his wings. However, after a time, many hoopoes were being killed for their golden crowns by greedy hunters so they asked Solomon to remove the crowns that were causing so much envy. Instead, Solomon gave them colourful crest feathers in their place. Other traditions surround the hoopoe and Solomon. The hoopoe is a curious bird, always eavesdropping upon people, and it reported to Solomon as a spy. One day it told the king of the most beautiful woman it had ever seen. This was Bilqis, Queen of Saba, who we know as the Queen of Sheba. While spying upon her palace, the hoopoe discovered that the queen wanted it to visit her. In the Koran, it is said that Solomon's letter to Bilqis was an invitation to embrace Islam.

Because of its downward-looking glance and inquiring demeanour, the Arabs believed it to be looking for wells and springs, calling it '*Al Hudhud*' ('Doctor-bird'). In the Persian poem, 'The Conference of the Birds', by the 12th-century poet Attar, the hoopoe is the messenger of the invisible world because of its breast-markings which read '*Bismillah*' ('In the name of Allah'), showing that it has entered into the way of spiritual knowledge. A Romanian story tells how the hoopoe was not satisfied with the food that God supplied and demanded better. Eventually, God punished it by making it a scavenger

that has to scour dunghills and other places. This legend is associated with the habits of the hoopoe, which eats insects that feed upon decaying substances. It emanates a bad odour, which keeps predators at bay. Some have said that the Garuda from the Hindu and Buddhist mythologies of India was originally a hoopoe.

HORAE

The Horae are the nymphs of the seasons who keep the order of nature and who are the guardians of the appropriate moment. They were born of Themis and Zeus. They are called Eunomia (Lawful Order), Dike (Just Retribution) and Irene (Peace). They were also in charge of good order, right use and peace, while Irene was the mother of Plautus or 'wealth', which can only accumulate in times in peace. They were the ones who swathe the goddess Aphrodite as she arises from the sea. From their name we derive the word 'hour'. For those whose sense of timing is unfortunately askew, and who are covered by embarrassment at their own wrong-footedness, the Horae can help give them a sense of rhythm and a sense of rightness.

HORDSHYRDE

The dragon Hordshyrde is found in both Norse and British tradition as the great dragon that guarded the treasure horde found by Beowulf. Beowulf killed Hordshyrde with the help of Wiglaf, but Beowulf had already been poisoned by the dragon and subsequently died. Hordshyrde is also described as a Fire-Drake.

HOR-EM-AKHEN

Egyptian mythology informs us that Hor-em-Akhen ('Horus of the Horizon') is the name given to the Androsphinx. The Greeks called it Harmachis.

HORNBILL

The hornbill is one of the important birds of African tradition. Pliny the Elder noted that it is a faithful bird that mates for life. When the African species of female hornbill is sitting on eggs, the male walls her up in a tree hole with mud and spittle, bringing his wife food, water and even flowers. According to Senufo mythology of the Ivory Coast of Mali, the hornbill was one of the first five creatures to appear upon the Earth. It was the first animal to be killed as food and it was the bird chosen to carry the souls of the dead to the underworld. Among the tribes of Melanesian New Ireland, the rhinoceros bird, a form of hornbill, is worshipped as a totem. She is the butt of jokes, representing human vanity and weakness.

HORNED SERPENT

The Horned Serpent is a creature whose myths are widespread through-out North America. Menacing and

magical, these immense serpents have two horns upon their heads. The powdered blood of the Horned Serpent had magical properties, but few ever succeeded in obtaining any. The power of the Horned Serpent had the ability to work against those who tried to ally themselves with it, as is told in the Mandan story where the killing and eating of the Horned Serpent results in the one who eats becoming a water serpent himself. The Hurons tell how Tijaiha went so far as to sacrifice his mother-in-law to the Horned Serpent in order to have its power, but his own people out-lawed and finally killed him, for Tijaiha's actions showed that he had aligned himself with the serpent. The Shawnee held that pubescent girls were desirable to the Horned Serpent and great care was taken that they might not go near the waters where he lived.

HOROMATANGI

In Maori legend, Horomatangi or Ihu-Maataotao was one of the monstrous race of Taniwha. It had the form of a giant lizard. He created the great Karapiti blowhole where a great geyser gushes out. He has the reputation of overturning boats.

HORSE

All horses descend from the prehistoric toed-horses that our Palaeolithic ancestors first stampeded over cliffs as food, and later tamed as mounts. The two surviving breeds of horse nearest to these early horse-ancestors are the Tarpan of Mongolia and the Przewalski horse of the Central Asian steppe. The domestication of horses happened some time during the transition to agriculture. In early Celtic tradition, wherever a people's horses moved, that was the area of land that they owned. To turn your horses loose was therefore a symbol of conquest, although in medieval legend, the unbridling and turning loose of horses to their wild state was the act of a warrior whose wounds or infirmities stopped him pursuing the art of chivalry or knighthood.

In mythology, the horse frequently appears in connection with the sun as the animal that draws it across the sky: this is found in early Bronze Age remains in northern Europe, and in the Greek myths of Helios and his sun chariot pulled by his team of four horses (*see* horses of the sun). Erichthonios, the legendary King of Troy, had a herd of 3,000 horses that were desired by the North Wind, Boreas. He turned into a stallion to mate with the mares, who produced 12 fillies swifter than any other horse.

The horse was always sacred to the Celts and is in many ways the totem animal of Britain and Ireland. Evidence for the widespread existence of horse-cults has been found all over the country and may be linked with the worship of the horse goddess Epona. The Uffington White Horse, carved out of the chalk on the Wiltshire downs, has been a focus for ritual for longer than any one remembers.

Recent archaeological investigation has pushed back its date to the Iron Age and beyond. The European Celtic horse goddess, Epona, was the only Celtic divinity to have a feast day, 18 December, of her own in the Roman calendar, when it was usual to rest all cloven-footed and hooved animals for the midwinter rites preceding Saturnalia. This resting of the beasts came down into the Christian tradition of the kneeling animals who acclaim the newly-born Christ in the stable, and possibly to the folk tradition that all the animals speak on Christmas Eve.

The long tradition about horses speaking is retained in the expression 'the horse's mouth' whereby the truth is discovered, and it can be traced back to India where the sacrificial horse was the source of all speech. Wise, speaking horses who help their riders are found across the world.

Magical steeds abound in Celtic tradition, ranging from the horses of Manannan Mac Lir which can carry people across the wave-tops to the otherworld kingdom of the sea, to the favoured mounts of such heroes as Arthur, whose famous grey mare, Llamrai, is listed in the Triads along with:

Three bestowed horses of the Island of
  Britain:
Slender Grey, horse of Caswallawn son
  of Beli,
Pale Yellow of the Stud, horse of Lleu
  Skilfull-Hand,
and Host-Splitter, horse of Caradawg
  Strong-Arm.

The Element Encyclopedia of Magical Creatures

Cuchulainn possessed two famous horses: Dubh-sron-gheal ('black-white-nose') and Dubh-srannal ('black-snorter'). Fionn's steeds were Dubh-saoileann ('black eyes') and Liath Macha ('grey mist'). The ideal of horse flesh is described in the Irish Brehon Laws:

A big horse, sound, young, noble, high-headed, load-carrying, lively-hearted, broad-breasted, haughty, easy-bearing, sleek, slender-legged, well-descended, free from spear-thrusts, free from sword-cuts, his form well-set, tractable to the hand, without lumps or flags on his back, not broken-backed, not rough-stepping, not too low, not too high, not shy, not starting, not big-mouthed, not ill-stepping, not lazy, not lame, not kicking, not dusty-haired, not puffing, not drop-eared, not shaky … perfectly sound, easy-ridden, obedient. If he be not such, he is rejected.

Tradition speaks also of the Kelpie, the water horse, which would appear near a lakeside seemingly a gentle and biddable horse, but as soon as anyone mounted it, it would gallop unstoppably into the depths of the water, drowning its victim.

In European folk tradition, the hobby-horse dances are connected to the encouragement of the growing season. Most hobby-horse dances are done around the midwinter period or at May-time, when winter and summer begin. In Wales and Ireland, the hobby-horse known as the Mari Lwyd and Lair Bhean, or the The Grey/White Mare, goes about knocking at doors and entering into riddling dialogues with the householder before barging into the house to bring its wild energy.

In Hindu tradition, the horse figured in sacrificial rites called the Asvamedha. The Vedas describe the horse as an embodiment of the cosmos: the dawn as his head, fire in his mouth, the year in his soul, the heavens are his back, his belly is the whole of space, his flanks are the earth, his limbs the seasons, his joints are the lunar months, his bones the constellations, his yawns are lightning and his movement thunder, while his urine is the rain. Hayasirsa is the horse-headed protector of the scriptures.

In Tibetan tradition, horses are associated with power, wealth and spiritual wisdom. When a fine riding horse dies, it is accorded a simplified sky-burial such as humans have. Its skull is split open to enable the horse's consciousness to be reborn. The horse-headed Dharmapala called Hayagriva or Tamdrin is one of the emanations of the Amitabha Buddha.

Although it is now hard to think of North America without horses, the horse was unknown to the New World and when the Spanish conquistadors arrived on horseback, the native peoples believed man and horse to be a single being like a centaur. The North American natives were immensely taken with the horse and it soon became a central part of Indian life, lore and warfare. The Dakota Indians, having no name for the animal, called it 'a mysterious dog'. Their legends told how the horse had originated from the foundations of the Otherworld that were covered with fire, water, wind and waves.

The ancient European games, where the racing of the sacred horses replicated the track of the sun across

The Element Encyclopedia of Magical Creatures

the sky, are now more mundanely continued at every racetrack across the world where the horses run for money and prizes. Yet the original sacred riding is still continued in many parts of the world where horse-back processions go out seasonally to demark the territory and ensure the well-being of the land.

HORSE KING

This is the English translation of the name of the Buddhist Tamdrin or Valaha, also known as Hayagriva. The Bodhisattva, Chenresi, took on the form of the Horse King, Valaha, in order to come to the rescue of a group of shipwrecked merchants who had landed upon an island of demons and had subsequently taken to their way of life. As a giant horse upon whose back many could ride, he tried to rescue them all, but only one was strong enough to close his eyes and not be tempted to return to the demonic way of life. To this one, the Horse King taught the Four Noble Truths that he might console the relatives of the lost ones, and show them how to live useful lives of virtue.

HORSES OF DIOMEDES

In Greek mythology, the Horses of Diomedes were the objects of Hercules' seventh labour. These four man-eating horses are sometimes shown as winged on vase-paintings and seals. They were related to the Harpies, Gorgons and Erinyes, and lived in Thrace in the land of Boreas, the god of the North Wind, who mated with mares. The owner of the horses was Diomedes, son of the war god, Ares. Diomedes was one of the gods of death and he kept the horses chained to a bronze manger in which he placed the bodies of unfortunate strangers. The horses had already torn apart Glaukos, son of Sisyphos, at the funeral games of Pelias, and their reputation ensured that no one wished to encounter them. In order to tame the horses, Hercules cunningly captured Diomedes and put his body in their manger. He drove the four horses back to Mycenae where they were dedicated to Hera. Their pure-blooded descendants were said to have survived until the time of Alexander the Great.

HORSES OF THE SUN

In classical mythology, the horses of the sun drew the chariot of the sun god Helios across the sky. After pasturing in the Isles of the Blessed in the far west, the horses were harnessed to the chariot each morning by the Horae and began their daily journey from dawn to dusk. The horses were Actaeon, Aethiops, Ameethea, Astrope, Bronte, Erytheros, Lampon, Phaethon, Phlegon, Purocis, Pyroieis and Sterope. In Scandinavian myth, the horses are Alsvid, Arvak, Hrimfaxi and Skinfaxi. In Indian belief, they are the Gandarvas.

HORUS

In Egyptian mythology, Horus was the falcon-headed god who was the lord of the skies and the patron of divine kingship. Both king and sun were associated with the falcon-winged disc that is the sign of Horus. There are many different and complex myths surrounding Horus from the earliest Egyptian times onwards, as different areas of Egypt worshipped him in his different aspects. In early times, he was the god of Lower Egypt and in rivalry with Set, who was god of Upper Egypt. In the battle between them, Horus lost an eye. Later myth saw him as the child born to Isis and Osiris.

Horus was born to Isis after an extraordinary happening. Osiris had been lured into a chest by his brother Set and his body was thrown into the Nile in many fragments. Isis mourned her loss, assuming the form of a kite and eventually retrieving her husband's body-parts in one place ready for magical resurrection. She had congress with her dead husband and conceived Horus, whom she hid in the marshes.

Just as Christians have a devotion to Jesus as the Christ Child in statues such as the Infant of Prague or the Child of the Nativity, so Egyptians worshipped Horus as Harpocrates (Horus as a Child). Harpocrates is shown in the form of a young boy who has a finger upon his lips. Just as Mary had to hide Jesus as a child, so Isis had to hide Horus in case his uncle Set found him. As Harpocrates, Horus protects against evil forces and dangerous creatures. Amulets show him standing upon the back of a crocodile, holding snakes, scorpions, lions and antelopes in his hands.

On gaining his maturity, Horus determined to seize power from Set. A court case was brought before the god, Geb. Set and Horus contend as hippopotami to see who can stay under water the longest. It is during this contest that Set cuts out one of Horus's eyes, which is later restored by Hathor using gazelle milk. Eighty years pass in which the two dispute in more and more complex trials of strength until the court awards the throne of Egypt to Horus. This triumph is depicted in symbolic ways in many Egyptian reliefs and can be seen in the gilded wooden statuette of Tutankhamun, who stands on a papyrus boat with a lasso and harpoon in his hands spearing a hippopotamus.

One of Horus's main symbols is the *udjat* (Eye of Horus), which he lost and then had restored. It shows a human eye with a long spiral tail that mimics the markings of a falcon. The *udjat* represented the king's strength, protection against Set and all his doings, an emblem of purification, wine and the offering given to the waxing moon. It was placed in the mummy wrappings of the deceased as a talisman or worn as a necklace. Horus was married to Hathor and their son was Harsomtus.

HRAESVELGR

Hraesvelgr was the eagle who created the winds in Norse tradition. He sits in the north of the world, beating his wings. His name means 'corpse-eater', not because he is a demonic or evil being, but because for many of the frozen northern lands, the burial of corpses is impossible because the ground is too hard. In many cultures, the excarnation or exposing of the body to the winds and scavengers of the air is the quickest way to de-flesh a corpse.

HRIMTHURSAR

Hrimthursar are the hoar-frost giants of Norse tradition. The chief of their number is Ymir, the hermaphroditic first being who was born of the ice, and gave birth to sons from his leg. The Hrimthursar hold back the cold north from encroaching upon fertile land, at least until Ragnarok, the ending of the world.

HSI WANG MU

Hsi Wang Mu (or Xi Wang Mu) has a variety of appearances, one of which is a monster with the teeth of a tiger, the tail of a leopard and a human face. She was originally the goddess of epidemics, but she changed into the revered Queen Mother of the West in Chinese tradition, where she is seen as the source of Yin or female energy. She rules over the western paradise of the immortals in the Kunlun Mountains, where she was attended by the Jade Girls, who were three-legged birds. She tends the peaches of immortality and when they are ripe –

every 3,000 years – she invites all the gods to a feast. All who eat of them are released from death.

HSING-T'IEN

In Chinese legend, Hsing-T'ien is the great monster who has a giant human shape but has a mouth in his navel and eyes in his chest, like Acephali in Greek tradition. He wanders looking everywhere for his head, for he was beheaded during the battle of Mu, which was fought between the gods and monsters. He wields an axe and shield with which he confronts people.

HUA-HU-TIAO

In Chinese Buddhist tradition, Hua-Hu-Tiao is the otherworldly white-winged elephant which was kept in a bag of panther skin by the Diamond King. When the Diamond King felt it was time for men to learn the error of their ways, he would release Hua-Hu-Tiao to create havoc and chaos on the Earth, killing many people. It once swallowed the warrior Yang Ching, which was a big mistake, for the hero continued to fight inside the elephant's belly and he ripped it open from within.

HUALLEPEN

In the folklore of Chile, the Huallepen is a composite animal with the head of a calf and the body of a sheep with twisted legs. It lives in pools and occasionally mates with the sheep or cattle that graze nearby.

HUANG FEI-HU

In Chinese mythology, Huang Fei-Hu is the Earth god who takes the form of a one-eyed bull with a snake's tail. He became the mountain god who guards the holy mountain of Tai Shan in eastern China where the dead come for judgement. From here, he acts as a judge to the souls of those who have recently died.

HUGINN

Huginn ('thought') is one of the two ravens that accompany Odin; his brother is Muninn ('memory'). They sit on Odin's shoulders and whisper all the news that they gather from their flights about the world. He sends them out in the morning and they return by breakfast of the next day.

HU-HSIEN

Hu-Hsien are the spirit foxes of Chinese folk tales. These shapeshifting creatures can assume human form, usually of a handsome youth or beautiful maiden. Hu-Hsien can act like an incubus or succubus, a male or female spirit that visits members of the opposite sex and steals their vital sexual energy from those who fall in love with them.

However, they are normally betrayed by their love of wine, for when they become drunk they lose their human form and are unmasked for what they really are. Because scholars are considered virtuous and venerable, Hu-Hsien often appeal to them when they need to hide from the wrath of the Thunder God who sends thunderbolts to punish them for their misdeeds. In return for protection, Hu Hsien grant favours to scholars, promising to lead them to high office.

HUITZILOPOCHTLI

In Aztec mythology, Huitzilopochtli was the god of war. He takes the form of a hummingbird, but when he chooses a human shape, he has a black face with hummingbird feathers upon his head and left leg, and he holds a mirror and a snake. He was the primary deity of the city of Tenochtitian and was the son of Coatlicue. He killed his sister Coyolxauhqui and threw her head into the heavens where it became the moon. As the sun, Huitzilopochtli arises as a young warrior who has just won a great victory over the night stars. He is carried to his zenith by dead warriors and as he falls in the sky he is conveyed by the souls of women who died in childbirth, who take him to the west where he will fall and die to be reborn again the next morning. Aztecs sacrificed prisoners to Huitzilopochtli in order to help the sun rise each dawn, for no other food but blood would lift him into the sky.

HULDRA

Huldra is a Norse fairy or wood nymph. She has a beautiful appearance but conceals a long tail beneath her robe. She lives in a mountain where she guards her cattle.

HUMBABA/HUWAWA

In the Sumerian *Epic of Gilgamesh*, Humbaba was the dangerous giant who lived in the cedar forests of the Zagros Mountains. When Gilgamesh and his companion Enkidu came to the forest, they saw the many paths tracking through the forest and grew afraid of the huge creature who had made them. Humbaba took the shape of a fire-breathing dragon and mocked the tiny companions who looked like tortoises crawling on the earth. Humbaba had the legs of a lion with vulture's feet, bull's horns and a tail with a snake's head at its end. The gods took pity on Gilgamesh and joined in the combat against Humbaba, who was protected by seven veils of terrifying radiance. They darkened his face and trapped him so that he could not escape. But Gilgamesh and Enkidu were implacable despite his pleadings. They severed his head and floated down the river on a raft.

HUMMINGBIRD

The Hummingbird has a strong association with the sun and also with great joy. In Mayan tradition, Hummingbird comes from the Black Sun and the Fifth World of mythic creation; it carries the secrets of duality in its breast.

Hummingbird is a character in the legends of the Paiute Indians of North America. He once filled his trousers with seeds and set out on a journey to discover what lay beyond the sun. He ate one seed a day but his journey was so long he had to return since there were no more seeds left in his store. This legend seems to relate to the hummingbird's habit of eating upon the wing. For the Anasazi Indians, Hummingbird was a messenger. In Venezuelan folklore, the hummingbird stood upon a crow and brought the first tobacco seeds from Trinidad.

HURU-KAREAO

In Maori legend, Huru-Kareao was one of the Taniwha and kin to Horomatangi. He lived in a lake near Tongariro in the form of a reptile or lizard as the guardian of this region. If people mistreated each other, Huru-Kareao would cause a disaster to remind them to behave better. When the European settlers reached this region, they took the sacred log that floated upon the lake – a piece of wood that was inviolate and symbolic of Huru-Kareao – and incorporated it into the building of a church, despite warnings to the contrary. The wood rotted preternaturally soon and those who had cut the log into planks died of no known cause, showing that Huru-Kareao was still active.

Hvcko Capko

In the stories of the Seminole Indians of Oklahoma, Hvcko Capko ('Long Ears') was a composite creature with the head of a large-eyed wolf, a grey body and a horse-like tail. It lived in rocky places and had a terrible smell – which is how you knew it was near. Hvcko Capko was believed to be the carrier of disease, which ensured that contact with it was avoided at all costs.

Hwang

In Chinese tradition, the Hwang is an alternative name given to the Feng Hwang or Phoenix. It cannot appear unless the land is at peace.

Hybris

Hybris is the mother of Pan, according to one version of his birth in Greek mythology. The name is the same as the word *hubris* which today tends to mean 'overweening pride', but which, in early Greek, implied 'shamelessness' or 'violent disorder'.

Hydra

In Greek mythology, Hydra was a monstrous water serpent with a shapeless body, the offspring of Echidna. Like her brother, Cerberus, the murderous Hydra had many heads and was nicknamed 'bitch of Lerna'.

Hydra was born in the middle of a swamp and lived twined about the roots of a gigantic plane tree which grew beside the triple spring of Amymone. From there it ravaged the herds of the surrounding countryside. If anyone succeeded in severing one of Hydra's heads, another two grew from the neck, thus making her overthrow a hopeless task for any hero. Hercules undertook to kill the Hydra as the second of his twelve labours. He brought some help with him in his chariot in the shape of the young hero Iolaos. They located Hydra at the triple spring and shot fire-arrows into her lair to force her out. Hydra then coiled herself around Hercules' foot. As if that wasn't enough, a gigantic crab emerged from the lair and bit his foot. He continued his struggle, finding that every time he cut off one Hydra head, two more indeed did grow, so he called upon Iolaos to assist him. Iolaos uprooted virtually a whole forest in making fiery brands with which to cauterize the severed necks of the Hydra so that she could grow no more heads. When Hercules had struck off the final head, he dipped his arrows in the poison that welled from Hydra's body and buried the remains. In order to honour her hero, the goddess Hera raised to the celestial vault the figure of the Crab that had so tormented Hercules, thus creating the constellation of Cancern.

Hydrus

In classical tradition, Hydrus (or Idrus) was the water snake that lived along the river Nile, although Pliny thought it was an otter. Its enemy was considered to be the crocodile, who would roll the Hydrus in the mud before swallowing it down. But once down in the stomach of the crocodile, Hydrus would burst through the stomach wall. In medieval Christian tradition, Hydrus became the emblem of Christ's resurrection, breaking through the bounds of death after the Harrowing of Hell, to emerge resurrected on Easter Day. This is a mythic reprise of the Egyptian story of Osiris, and of Horus overcoming Set.

Hyena

Many spurious tales are told of the hyena, whose appearance has confused many observers. Diodorus Siculus thought it was a cross between a dog and a wolf, while Sir Walter Raleigh suggested that it was the hybrid of a dog and a cat. It was held that hyenas had the ability to change sex, as well as doing many other duplicitous things, such as imitating the human voice in order to lure men to their deaths. Arabic lore states that hyenas are the reincarnations of sorcerers who return to steal their enemies' flocks. Throughout Africa, the hyena is seen as a trickster or shapeshifter, and because it is a scavenger, eating up corpses of decaying animals, it often has stories about its unclean habits and is seen as evil, treacherous and lascivious. In East Africa, people believe that the glowing spirits of the dead can be discerned inside the eyes of the hyena who has devoured their flesh. In this way, it is believed that the ancestors can return to their old haunts by using the hyena to ride out at night as ghosts.

Hyena Men

In Mali, the Hyena Men are spirits who take the forms of men and of hyenas whenever they like. They have an insatiable appetite for meat and will do anything to obtain a massive blow-out meal. Hyena Men can be made by magical spells, which are obtained from one who has eaten human flesh. This magic helps them become hyenas at night. They have been known to dig in cemeteries and feast on corpses.

HYLAEUS

Hylaeus was the centaur whose love for Atalanta was spurned and when he pursued her she killed him, although another story tells how Hylaeus died in the battle of the centaurs against Hercules.

HYRCINIAN BIRDS

According to the classical writer Pliny, the Hyrcinian Birds live in the Hyrcinian forest of Germany. They have feathers that light up and reveal the way even in the darkest night. For the Romans, the forests of Germany were terrifying places, the haunt of unknown monsters that might do horrific things.

Some Hyena Men grew tired of dead, grey, maggot-strewn flesh and fancied something more succulent. They found a sleeping shepherd and devoured him raw before helping themselves to the juiciest sheep, which they roasted. With their huge carving knife, which is called ala jugu ('god's enemy'), they entered a village in hyena form and each stole a child from a nursery. Still hungry, they had a sheep as dessert, singing a song, 'There's no god today, we can please ourselves.' Then one Hyena Man jumped over the fence of what had once been his own home and caught his mother, devouring her, while his companion, in human form, stole away the chief's wife and raped her before eating her.

IBIS

The ibis was a bird particularly sacred to the ancient Egyptians. Being heart-shaped, it represented the heart under the protection of Thoth/Hermes, the god of wisdom, learning and writing. When fleeing from the giant Typhon, Hermes changed himself into an ibis. The bird is also sacred to Isis, symbolizing the moon as the hawk symbolizes the sun. The moon god Aah is also sometimes portrayed with the head of an ibis. The white ibis appears in Lower Egypt at the time when the inundation of the Nile takes place, making it especially sacred.

ICHNEUMON

Also referred to as the Egyptian rat, the Ichneumon was said to be a carnivorous creature similar to the Indian mongoose or weasel. In Egyptian hieroglyphics, it represents strength in unity, an idea that possibly derives from its habit of combining with others of its kind to attack its most frequent enemy, the crocodile. According to the Roman naturalist Pliny, it was the deadly rival of both the asp and the crocodile. Strabo, the Greek geographer, historian and philosopher, listed it among the beings worshipped at the ancient city of Herakleopolis as a destroyer of crocodiles. When it wished to take on one of these creatures, the Ichneumon used to wallow in mud and allow it to harden in the sun, forming a hard protective crust. It would then dart into the open mouth of the crocodile, devour its insides, and emerge again after the creature was dead. It was also said to attack the asp in this manner, though some maintained that it only destroyed its eggs. Pliny and Plutarch both relate this heroic feat, which is also told of the otter and Hydrus.

ICHTHYOCENTAUR

A hybrid creature, part horse, part fish, the Ichthyocentaur is sacred to the god Pan in Graeco-Roman tradition as a symbol of fertility. Later, the 2nd-century work of natural history known as the *Physiologus* describes the Ichthyocentaur as possessing the head and torso of a man, the forelegs of a horse or lion, but with a hind part formed of the tail of a dolphin.

IGPUPIARA

A strange version of the mermaid found in the local traditions of Brazil. The name derives from the word *Hipupiara*, which means 'Dweller in the Water'. It differs from other mermaids in that its lower part is formed of a single mass of flesh which takes the shape of a fish. Its head is non-human, bearing a resemblance to a seal, and it has very long arms with five webbed fingers. It is most feared for attacking its victims in the water, consuming only their extremities. Early travellers to the area in the 16th century report a number of sightings along the coast of San Vincente.

Ihu-Maataotao

One of several names for a class of lizard-like monsters, sometimes described as similar to dragons, from the folklore of the Maori people of New Zealand. Legend says that if one of these monsters is caught and killed, and its gut opened, the undigested remains of its victims will fall out.

Ikaki

A minor water spirit in the shape of a tortoise with a mischievous nature. Ikaki loves to dance and to eat humans, and plays a leading role in the ritual dances performed by the Kalabari people of Nigeria.

Ikaki is a supernatural tortoise who lives behind the ancient village of Olomo, rarely allowing himself to be seen. He made forays to the edge of the forest to dance, but whenever he did so, people came to watch him. He always sang a warning song to them: 'Remember my words. Don't anyone touch me. I am Chief Tortoise, Chief Grey Hair.' But the people enjoyed his dances so much that they kept calling him back. Eventually, he danced and sang, 'Amegage. Human meat, yum-yum. Amegage. Human bones, yum-yum.' Then, as he raised his right legs, all the people in the east died; as he raised his left legs, all the people in the west died. Ikaki went back into his shelter of the deep forest never to be seen again. However, the few survivors left on Earth came together in order to imitate the great tortoise's dancing. They were uneasy about the part where they must lift their legs, though, and so they consulted the oracle of Chuku that told them to modify their movements to avoid further deaths.

Ikuutayuuq

Throughout the region of the Arctic Circle inhabited by the Inuit people, hundreds of carefully arranged piles of rocks known as *inuksuut* are to be found. Though these have other ritual significance, around the Hudson Bay area they are said to cover the bodies of victims destroyed by two monsters. The Ikuutayuuq, the name of which means 'One Who Drills', together with her equally terrifying brother (who is not named), sought human prey. They then dispatched their terrified victims by holding them down and drilling holes through their bodies until they died. This murderous pair was eventually hunted down by a hero of the First People of the area, who succeeded in killing Ikuutayuuq. After this her brother fled, never to be seen again.

Illuyankas

A primal dragon in Hittite mythology of ancient Mesopotamia, Illuyankas was a gigantic serpentine monster with several heads. Two versions tell of its death. In the first, the goddess Innaras prepared a great feast for the dragon. At the feast, the dragon became so bloated and drunk that Innaras and her lover were able to bind it in chains, after which the wind god Taru slew the monster and scattered the parts of its body over the Earth. The other version tells how Illuyankas encircled the gods in its vast coils and plucked out their eyes and hearts, swallowing them so that they were rendered powerless.

However, the son of Taru took the dragon's daughter as his love and persuaded her to return the eyes and hearts as a gift. Once sight and breath was restored to the gods, they rose up as one and destroyed the monster.

Ilomba

A spirit that takes the form of a water snake in the beliefs of the native people of Zambia and Zaire in Africa. The creature resembles a normal snake but is actually the creation of a sorcerer, which carries out attacks on his enemies. It has a human head that may resemble the person who has created it. To everyone else it looks like a normal snake, but to its designated victim it looks like its creator so that he is warned of its evil intent, although usually paralysed with fright. Once it has identified its prey, the Ilomba will bite swiftly and suck its victim's blood. In order to create one of these spirits, the sorcerer takes blood from his enemy's back, chest and forehead and, together with his nail parings, mixes them with roots from the forest, placing all these ingredients into a snakeskin. This operation will take many weeks until the false snake is more than a yard in length, after which it will begin to eat eggs and milk in infancy. This is insufficient to satisfy it and, after five years, it begins to demand blood and kill people if its owner does not give it any victims – usually starting with a foetus, then a grown baby, and finally an adult. After each killing, the Ilomba will feast on the spirit of its victim and increase its size by doing so. Some say it grows an extra head after each meal of this kind. The sorcerer who creates this monster is also given the power of exhuming its victims, who can be revivified and become zombie slaves. The Ilomba is so closely linked with its owner that if it is destroyed the owner will die soon afterwards. Once a sorcerer has created an Ilomba he can never get rid of it, for if he does not give it human blood regularly it will expire and he will die at the same time. Invariably, one day it will be killed and the sorcerer too will die suddenly and unexpectedly.

IMDUGUD

In the mythology of ancient Mesopotamia, this creature is described as a winged lion with the head of an eagle or even a double eagle's head. It was associated with thunder and for this reason was considered benign as thunder indicated the coming of rain to the dry desert lands. His wing flaps caused whirlwinds and sandstorms, and his name may derive from the word for 'mist' or 'fog'. In Mesopotamian myth, the Imdugud steals the tablet of destinies from the god Ea. This tablet was one of the emblems of Ea's sovereignty, giving him supreme powers in Heaven and Earth: it is a mandate of authority which he is shown holding in reliefs. Imdugud was killed by the god Ninurta who restored the tablet. When the Sumerian hero Lugalbanda is wandering in the Zagros mountains he comes upon the fledging Imdugud in

its nest. In the *Gilgamesh* epic, it is said the Imdugud makes its nest in the sacred hlaub tree planted by Innana in Uruk. It is also known as the Anzu bird when it appears in heraldic inscriptions and reliefs.

I-MU KUO YAN

A race of one-eyed giants in the traditions of ancient China. They are included in the many volumes of the *Great Imperial Encyclopaedia*, which set out to list every creature and spirit, god and goddess in the country.

INCUBUS

In medieval clerical belief, an incubus is a male spirit who lies with women at night, provoking their lust. According to British legend, Merlin is the offspring of such a union. His mother refused to tell who lay with her and stories circulated that her night-visitor was a demon. After this, Merlin is known as 'the boy who has no father'. The female counterpart to the Incubus is the Succubus.

INUGPASUGSSUK

A friendly giant from the traditions of the Inuit people of Canada. Inugpasugssuk was so enormous that even the lice on his body were the size of Arctic lemmings. He lived on a diet of fish, whale and seal, but was kindly disposed towards humans, whom he helped with

The Element Encyclopedia of Magical Creatures

their fishing. When his passing threatened one of the villages, he was known to move the houses to one side to save the people.

IQI-BALAM

The Moon Jaguar in the traditions of the Quiche people of Mexico, Iqi-Balam is one of four beings, known collectively as the Balam, who guard the four directions and are considered fearsome and terrible monsters.

IRUSAN

According to medieval saints' lives of Ireland, Irusan is the gigantic King of the Cats, which grew to be the size of an ox and inhabited a cave in the mountains of Knowth, Northern Ireland. Irusan was blessed with extraordinarily acute hearing, and when he overheard the great bard Senchan Torpeist uttering a satire about cats, he came to take revenge. Appearing suddenly, the giant creature tossed the poet across his back and made off with him. Fortunately, St Ciaran heard the unfortunate poet crying for help,

and seizing a red-hot poker from the fire, slew Irusan as it passed by the monastery at Clonmacnoise.

ITZPAPALOTL

An Aztec deity, which normally takes the form of a butterfly. In this form she is seen as a representative of the soul which all life forms share. She sometimes takes the form of a deer and is associated with agriculture. Her male counterpart is Itzlacoliohqui ('Carved Obsidian Knife') who represents matter in its lifeless state. With Tezcatlipoca who is responsible for the spark of life, these Aztec divinities form a trinity who guard the different states of life.

IWANCI

According to the Jivaro people of the Amazon region of Ecuador, the Iwanci are huge serpentine monsters that may appear either in the shape of the frightening Macanci, a type of water snake, or as the all-embracing Pani or Anaconda. Whatever form they take, these monsters are inimical to humanity and devour whoever they encounter.

The Element Encyclopedia of Magical Creatures

J

JACKAL

The jackal is a wild dog commonly found in Africa. The Egyptian god Anubis has a jackal's head and in this guise is the essential psychopomp who leads the deceased through the trials of the afterlife. This probably springs from the fact that the jackal is a scavenger that spends a lot of its time in burial grounds, attempting to find food. In the Old Testament, the jackal came to represent desolation – as in 'a dwelling place of jackals, the desolation for ever' (Jeremiah 9:11). In Buddhist tradition, the jackal represents a person deeply rooted in evil and wrongdoing, incapable of following the light. In Hindu belief, jackals and ravens are both scavengers who accompany the Black Kali in her aspect as the destroyer. In Zoroastrian religion, the jackal is closely associated with Ahriman, the principle of evil. Among the Dogon people of Africa, Yurugu is the jackal-fox who brings dissention and divination. He acts as the adversary and solution-finder to God's difficulties.

JACKALOPE

A fictitious creature from the folklore of North America, the Jackalope is said to be a cross between a jack rabbit and an antelope, and is usually portrayed as a rabbit with antlers. Some legends report that the Jackalope can convincingly imitate any sound, including the human voice, and it uses this ability to elude pursuers. Certainly, Jackalopes are so shy that none have ever been captured. Those who have taken the existence of this creature seriously have suggested that it may be a hybrid of the pygmy deer and a species of killer rabbit! The origin of the Jackalope legend is attributed to the writer Douglas Herrick (1920–2003) of Douglas, Wyoming, who seems to have invented it for the amusement of his family.

JACULUS

The Jaculus is a creature described in classical Roman and European folklore – particularly during the Middle Ages. Its name means 'javelin', which probably derives from its habit of launching itself on its victims from a high tree and sinking its fangs into their neck. Described as a vast winged serpent with two forelegs, it is mentioned by the Latin poet Lucan (AD 39–65) in his work *Pharsalia*. It is probably related to the Wyvern.

JAGUAR

As one of the most dangerous members of the cat family, the jaguar is greatly feared as both a magical animal and one whose bite can transform its victim into a were-beast. For this reason, the roar of a jaguar heard in the night is said to signal the return of a dead person. Many Aztec and South American deities take the form of jaguars, including Tepeyollotl, the monstrous jaguar that devours the setting sun each night, and Tezcatlipoca ('smoking mirror')

The Element Encyclopedia of Magical Creatures

the Aztec god of the wind who in the shape of the jaguar shines down from the constellation we know as Ursa Major. It is said that he was knocked from the sky by the Feathered Serpent and became a great jaguar when he fell into the sea.

The Kenaima is the name given to the man-eating were-jaguar of South America. The ability for men to become jaguars and jaguars men is so widespread in South America that it is sometimes very difficult to tell which is which. When the Taupinambi tribe in Brazil imprisoned a German anthropologist, Hans Staden, in the late 19th century, he was offered a basket of human flesh. When he refused it, his captors asked why. He responded by saying, 'There are almost no animals that will eat the flesh of their own kind, so how can I eat human flesh?' To which his captor replied, 'Well, I am a jaguar and I find it good!' This gives us some idea of the prevalence of the were-jaguar in that part of the world.

JARAPIRI

A hybrid monster, man from the waist up, serpent below, who inhabits an area named Wimbaraka, north-west of Alice Springs in Australia. It seems to be associated particularly with this place, and may be a form of *genius loci* or spirit of place.

JASCONIUS

The mighty whale-like creature on which the Irish St Brendan and his monks landed, thinking that it was an island. The brothers prepared a cauldron of food, but as it boiled, the island began to undulate. St Brendan and his crew barely had time to scramble back to their boat before it sank beneath the water. God told Brendan that the beast is called Jasconius and that it is always trying to bring its head to its tail, but can never do so because of its length. Later, the travellers celebrated the Mass of Easter upon the back of the monster, which was almost certainly a whale.

The religious significance of Jasconius is pointed out in the 2nd-century Alexandrian natural history book known as the *Physiologus* in which the whale is called Aspidoceleone. The text likens the whale's plunging into the sea to the plunge of the sinner into hell-fire. Brendan's successful celebration of a mass upon the whale's back represents the triumph of Christ over the tomb.

JATAYA

One of two offspring of the Garuda, the bird-steed of the god Vishnu in the Hindu mythology of India. Together with its sibling Sampati, it is described as of enormous size with a human head. According to the myth, Jataya was killed by Ravanna, the demon king of Sri Lanka, after which his brother avenged him.

JIDRA

The Jidra grows up out of the earth like a plant, and remains permanently attached to the soil by a single root. Like the Barametz it partook of both animal and vegetable form, but looked harmlessly plantlike to those who approached it. It has a voracious appetite and consumes everything and anything that comes within reach, be it plant, animal or human. It is mentioned a number of times in the travellers' tales of the Middle Ages, and is well known in the folk traditions of the Middle East. Its bones were highly prized for their aphrodisiac effect when ground to powder and added to wine. The only way to kill the Jidra was to sever its root, at which point, like the Mandrake, it was said to scream.

JINSHIN-UWO

In Japanese mythology, this is the name for the Earthquake Fish that is believed to be responsible for the disturbances which shake the Earth so frequently in this part of the world. It is described as an eel 700 miles in length that holds the islands of Japan on its back. It is said to stretch from north to south, its head lying beneath Kyoto in the south, and its tail beneath Awomori in the north. Some authorities have suggested that these locations should be reversed, since it is in the south that earthquakes are more frequent and it is easier to equate this with the lashing of the eel's tail.

JOGAH

Jogah is the generic name given to three tribes of diminutive nature spirits in the folklore of the Iroquois nation of North America. The three tribes are the Gahonga ('Stone Throwers') who inhabit rocks and rivers; the Gandayah who maintain the fertility of the Earth; and the Ohdows, who live in the Underworld and control the monsters who live there, preventing them from reaching the Earth's surface in search of the sun's warmth.

JORMUNGANDR

One of the oldest surviving names for the Midgard Serpent in Norse and Teutonic mythology. The word *jormun* is linked linguistically with 'immense' and 'the earth' and was sometimes used in early poetry.

JULUNGGUL

An alternative name for the Rainbow Serpent of native Australian mythology, so-called by the natives of Arnhem Land.

K

Ka-en-Ankh Nereru

The great cosmic snake described in the mythology of ancient Egypt. So vast is the body of this creature that it stretches from horizon to horizon across the arch of the night sky. In a daily enactment of the sun's rising and setting, the god Ra reaches the horizon in his sun boat and enters the body of the serpent through its tail; in the morning, he emerges renewed from its mouth and begins his daily journey across the skies once more.

Kaia

In the beliefs of the people of the Gazelle peninsula of New Britain, Melanesia, the Kaia are spirits whose power was at one time much greater but who have been demoted to the status of demons. They make their home in the depths of the Earth, occasionally emerging from the mouths of volcanoes to bring terror and destruction to human beings. They most often take the form of snakes, eels or pigs, sometimes combining all three to form terrifying hybrid monsters.

Kaliya

In the Hindu mythology of India, Kaliya is a bejewelled serpent with five heads that inhabits the deepest parts of the river Yamuna. This creature was the one-time king of the serpents, emerging at night from deep holes in the ground with his hordes of follow-ers to lay waste to the surrounding countryside. When they had finished rampaging across the country, they would retire to a certain tree that grew beside a deep lake. One day the god Krishna climbed this tree in order to dive from its topmost branches into the water beneath. The burning light and heat of the deity caused a great wave of superheated water to consume the tree. This so enraged Kaliya that he ordered a host of serpents to encircle the god, intending to destroy him. But Krishna escaped easily and danced on the head of the serpent, causing it to lose all its powers. This so terrified Kaliya's followers that they elected to depart at once and live in the deepest part of the ocean. In response, Krishna promised that the Garuda bird, which liked to eat snakes, would never trouble them again.

Kallicantzari/Kalkes

A tribe of hairy, dwarfish, semi-humanoid beings with long tails described in the contemporary folklore of Greece. The Kallicantzari probably derive from the more ancient satyrs of classical Greek mythology. A second group are much larger with heads resembling that of a goat or dog, complete with long straggling beards and rough shaggy hair all over their bodies. They also have cloven hooves and walk on their hind legs, and are sometimes as much as 20 ft tall. They live beneath the earth where they are said to occupy their time gnawing at the roots of the World Tree (a concept not

The Element Encyclopedia of Magical Creatures

unlike that of the Norse Yggdrasil). However, since they are nocturnal, as the winter nights grow shorter they have less and less time to pursue this evil course.

During the Twelve Days of Christmas, between Christmas Day and Epiphany (6 January), the Kallicantzari emerge above ground, creating havoc by abducting women, destroying crops and olive groves, demolishing houses, killing livestock and making unsuspecting travellers dance with them until they are exhausted and fall to the ground, where the Kallicantzari devour them. However, these creatures are terrified of sunlight and if they can be detained above ground until cockcrow they are destroyed by the sun. Any children born at this time were considered unlucky, and there was a practice in certain parts of the country of branding the child on the heel to make sure it would not turn into a Kallicantzari. When they returned beneath the ground at the end of the period of festivities and as the days began to grow in length again, this was the cause of much rejoicing among human beings, knowing that the World Tree had grown strong again. Unfortunately, the Kallicantzari would soon begin gnawing at its roots again, the whole cycle repeating itself throughout the year.

KALKI/KALKIN

The tenth and final incarnation of the god Vishnu in Hindu mythology. The name Kalki literally means 'the White Horse' and, according to Hindu belief, Vishnu will destroy the wicked and restore purity to the world at the end of the period known as *Kali Yuga*.

KAMA-DHENU

According to Hindu myth, Kama-Dhenu is the cosmic cow of plenty, born during the Churning of the Ocean, which brought about the creation of the world. Her udder produced an eternally flowing fountain of milk that nourished all beings and granted her possessor, the sage Vasishta, everything he desired. She was also capable of granting wishes. On one occasion, she produced an entire army of warriors to defeat the god Arjuna. Kama-Dhenu was also said to be an offspring of the sun goddess Rohini.

KAMI

According to the mythology of ancient Japan, the Kami is a kind of giant catfish responsible for causing the earthquakes that occur frequently in that part of the world. According to one tale, the Great Deity of Deer Island stopped this by thrusting his sword into the earth, transfixing the Kami's head. From this time onward, whenever the earth shakes, the god has only to lay his hand on the hilt of the sword to quieten it. The hilt of this vast sword, carved in granite, may be seen emerging from the earth near the shrine of Kashima. The story is told that in the 17th century a certain great lord dug for six days in an attempt to acquire the sword. At the end of the sixth day, he had still not reached the point and gave up. Elsewhere in Japanese tradition the Earthquake Fish, Jinshin-Uwo and the Earthquake Beetle, Jinshin-Mushi are said to be related to the Kami. Elsewhere in Japan, *kami* is the name given to the spirits of nature.

KANGAROO

Among the Aboriginal Australians, the kangaroo is one of the most important animals, both as a totem and spiritual supporter, as well as a provider of food. For many it is the ancestor-kangaroo Krantjirinja who is honoured in dances and initiatory rites. In one of the most remarkable ceremonies, the leader of the rites imitates the legend of Krantjirinja in vigorous dances before lying down, echoing the long sleep of the ancestor from the Alcheringa or Dreamtime. Wearing a red conical hood that symbolizes the kangaroo's penis, he slowly awakens and grazes, then approaches the gully where the blood of boy initiates has

been shed before sleeping again. After 15 days of dances, the initiated boys imitate these dances, passing the kangaroo penis back between their legs to each other, before it is thrust into the bloody gully, symbolizing the insemination of the kangaroo ancestors.

KAPPA

In the Shinto religion of Japan, the Kappa are water spirits who pull children into the water and drown them, and who also attack travellers. They are unable to survive for long on land since they must keep their heads wet. They are described as having long hair, the body of a tortoise, scaly limbs, and an ape-like face. They live on a diet of cucumber and blood and they fly on enchanted cucumbers which sprout wings like dragonflies.

KARASA TENGU

A huge bird-like creature large enough to carry a man through the air, the Karasa Tengu consumes human prey in the folklore and traditions of Japan. Equipped with enormous talons, animal ears and a huge red beak, it invokes great fear whenever it is mentioned.

KAR-FISH

In the Zoroastrian mythology of ancient Persia, the Kar-Fish encircles the Tree of Life and keeps at bay the lizards faithful to the evil power of Ahriman. Described as having the keenest eyesight of all living beings, the watchfulness of the Kar-Fish will continue to the end of time.

KARINA

A demonic being from the mythology of Islamic Africa. She often appears as a bird, particularly an owl, and is feared throughout the Islamic countries, and among the Hausa, Swahili and Nana peoples. In Indonesia, she is known as Kuntianak and may possibly be identified with the Sheerree of Berber tradition, a bird of the High Atlas Mountains, which is said to have breasts with which it suckles new-born babies at night.

KARKADANN

Karkadann is a type of Unicorn from the traditions of Persia, India and North Africa. The name Karkadann comes from the Sanskrit *kartajan*, meaning 'Lord of the Desert'. Described as white in body, as large as a rhinoceros and with a tail like a lion, the Karkadann has two or even three hooves on each foot. Unlike the white or silvery horn sported by most unicorns, the Karkadann has a black spiralling horn in the centre of its forehead. It is extremely fierce and known to hunt creatures as large as the elephant. Only the song of the ringdove can calm it: so fond is the Karkadann of the sound of this song that it will go to great lengths to protect a nest of ringdoves.

KARORA

In the myths and legends of the Aboriginal people of Australia, the Karora is a distant ancestor of the bandicoot and one of the Creating Creatures of the Aborigines.

At the beginning of time, Karora lay at the bottom of a deep hole that would one day be filled with water. Above this dry water-hole towered a gigantic pole that reached up into the clouds. But this was no ordinary pole – it had skin like a man's and was alive. It had grown out of Karora's head as he lay sleeping. Now, after endless aeons of darkness, the time had come for the beginning of life. From the belly and the armpits of Karora there tumbled an endless stream of bandicoots, which scrambled out of the hole and scattered across the plain in search of water, food and light. Slowly light appeared and the pole that grew from Karora's head was bathed in light. With the light came heat that penetrated deep into the hole where Karora was lying. He woke from his long sleep, turning his head and breaking the roots of the living pole.

He stood up and watched the gambling bandicoots who were his children. Throughout the day Karora watched the creatures at play or scurrying in search of insects. The sun climbed out of the sky and began its descent to the west. As it sank from sight, Karora descended to the shelter of the hole and fell asleep again. During the night, a new creature emerged from his armpit, changing shape until it took on the form of the first mortal man. In the morning, Karora was pleased to see a copy of himself lying by his side. He instructed his son to kill two bandicoots and cook them. They then shared the food together. That night two more sons were born to Karora, and the following night four more appeared and so on, night after night. The bandicoots began to dwindle in number as they were killed for food, and soon began to prove more difficult to catch so that the hunters were forced to roam further afield on the plains. One day, there were no more bandicoots anywhere near the water-hole where they had been born. The hunters spread out across the land to form the first human race. Karora returned to the water-hole and now sleeps peacefully below the water. But at any time he might arouse himself and come to the surface; therefore his spirit is still appeased by gifts of branches and leaves from all who come there.

KARZELEK

In the folklore of Poland, the Karzelek are spirits that live in mines and underground workings and protect miners from danger, leading them back to the surface if they become lost or helping them to discover rich veins of ore. Their name means 'treasurer' and they are the guardians of gems, crystals and precious metals. While they are generally friendly, if anyone insults them they can be deadly, bringing tunnels crashing down upon their enemies. It is considered bad luck to cover one's head, whistle or throw rocks while in the presence of the Karzelek.

KASAI REX

A mysterious creature believed to live in the jungles of Central Africa and said to resemble a large dinosaur. Numerous sightings of this creature have occurred over the years, the best-known dating from 1932. According to this, a Swedish plantation owner named Johnson and his African servant were travelling through the Kasai Valley (hence the name of the creature) when they came across a grazing rhinoceros. They were being careful not to disturb this animal when suddenly a 40 ft long, lizard-like creature erupted from the bushes and attacked the rhino. At this point, Johnson passed out, while his servant ran away in terror. When Johnson came to, the creature was still feeding on the carcass of the rhinoceros. He described it as having long, sharp teeth, big jaws, a long thick tail, and legs that he later said reminded him of a lion. The colour of the creature was predominantly dark red, with dark vertical stripes running down its neck, back and tail. After a while, the creature finished his meal and returned to the jungle. Suggestions as to the identity of this creature include Tyrannosaurus Rex, Allosaurus, Megalosaurus and Gigantasaurus.

KASHI

An evil spirit from African tradition, particularly in Angola, the Kashi has two faces, one human looking, the other, which is on the back of its head, that of a hyena. It hides its second face behind a long, thick swathe of hair that is usually dressed in a very ornate fashion.

KASWA, AL

Al-Kaswa was the name of the camel that bore the prophet Mohammed in his flight from Mecca. Where the camel knelt was where the prophet built the Kaaba, the sacred shrine to which all Moslems kneel to pray worldwide.

KAUKAS

Described as a dragon or a kind of goblin in the folklore of Lithuania, the Kaukas is similar to the Aitvara, and manifests as a winged dragon with a fiery tail. It attaches itself to families and may bring them good fortune in

The Element Encyclopedia of Magical Creatures

the form of riches and stolen goods. Like many dragons or dragon-like creatures, it is often described as a guardian of treasure.

KEELUT

A type of monstrous dog similar to the Black Dog of European tradition, it is described in the folklore and mythology of the Inuit people of Canada and the Alaska. In this instance, it is referred to as being hairless and, as is generally the case for such creatures, the Keelut follows unwary travellers at night, attacking and killing them whenever possible.

KELPIE

The classic water horse in Celtic, and especially Scottish, tradition. The Kelpie haunted rivers rather than lochs or the sea. When a storm was due, the Kelpie could sometimes be heard howling and wailing. He could also assume human form when he needed to, appearing as a rough shaggy man. In this shape, he would sometimes leap up behind solitary riders, gripping them in his strong arms or frightening them to death. However, his most usual shape was that of a young horse and in common with others of his kind his favourite trick was to lure travellers onto his back and then rush with them into a deep pool, where he struck the water with his tail, causing a sound like thunder, and then vanished in a flash of light. He was also suspected of sometimes tearing people to pieces and devouring them.

A brave member of the MacGregor clan once found a Kelpie with a magical bridle and took it off. The Kelpie begged him to put it back, but the man kept it and used it to work magic. On the other hand, anyone who could put the human bridle on the Kelpie could subdue him to his will. A man of the Graham clan from Morphie once caught a Kelpie in this way and used it to drag stones to build a new castle. When the castle was finished he took off the bridle and the poor exhausted Kelpie ran in to the nearest river, where he paused and said:

> Sad back and sad bones
> Driving the Laird o' Morphie's stones.
> The Laird of Morphie will never thrive,
> So long as the Kelpie's alive!

From then on, misfortune dogged the Grahams of Morphie to the end of their line.

KENEUN

In the Iroquois myth of North America, Keneun was the golden eagle who was chief of the Thunderbirds. He is never seen, but we know of his presence whenever lightning strikes from the skies, which is the light from his eyes, or when we hear thunder that is the beating of his wings. He guards the sacred fire that the Great Hare, Manabusch stole.

KESHI

In the Hindu mythology of ancient India, the Keshi, a name meaning 'long-haired', is described as a huge, long-maned, vicious horse that attacks humans without warning. It eventually met its end when the god Vishnu put his hand and arm into its mouth and down its throat, choking it.

KETO

A particularly hideous sea monster in the Graeco-Roman tradition. She was the wife of the sea god Phorcys. Their offspring were the even more monstrous Gorgons and their guardian sisters the Graeae.

KEYEME

According to the folklore of the Taulipang people of the Amazon Basin in South America, this creature, which is normally an extremely large humanoid in form and known as the Lord of the Animals, can transform itself into a gigantic water serpent by donning a rainbow-coloured skin.

KHEGLEN

A shadowy, though widespread, belief found throughout the tribal lands of Siberia, concerns the ancestral spirit of the cosmic elk, Kheglen, who stole the sun and was pursued across the sky by the female bear spirit, Main-Mangi.

Eventually, Main-Mangi caught up with Kheglen and slew her, releasing the sun, whose guardian she then became. This is clearly part of an ancient astronomical myth that is still re-enacted by the native peoples of the area. Kheglen and her calf, represented by the constellation of Ursa Minor, hid among the stars during the day, only emerging at night when they are hunted by Main-Mangi, whose ski tracks are the Milky Way. The cosmic Elk is eventually overtaken at the end of winter, and slain by the hunter. With her death comes new life as the ice breaks up, the snows end, and calving takes place in the pastures. New life springs from the parts of the elk's body butchered by the hunter bear. Among the Siberian natives, these early spring ceremonies of the sun's return are re-enacted in the form of a great hunt. The dissection of the earthly elk is ritualized to echo the idea of new life emerging from death. To some groups, the whole constellation of the Milky Way is the Elk, Ursa Minor its Calf, and the constellation Bootes the hunter-bear.

KHEPRA/KHEPRI

In the earliest creation myths, Khepra is seen as the creator of the gods. By uttering his name aloud, Khepra made a solid place on which to stand, then he copulated with his own shadow and ejaculated Shu, the god of air, and Tefnut, the god of water. From these two emerged all the rest of the panoply of Egyptian deities. The

The Element Encyclopedia of Magical Creatures

choice of this insect to represent one of the forms of the sun god shows how keen the Egyptian eye was in observing the natural world and extrapolating mystical ideas from it. Kephra represents the sun god at dawn on the eastern horizon and is invariably depicted pushing the disc of the sun upward from the underworld on its journey across the sky. The Egyptians would have seen scarab beetles rolling balls of dung across the ground and from this emerged an image of the sun's crossing of the heavens. Nor did the analogy end here, since they also observed that scarabs appeared to emerge spontaneously out of the dung balls. They thus came to represent the idea of reincarnation, as the god coming into being, self-created without any of the natural cycle of reproduction. The creator god therefore manifested in the form of the *Scarabaeus sacer*, better known as the dung beetle.

KHNUM

The ram god of ancient Egyptian mythology, Khnum was called 'High of Plumes, Sharp of Horns'. His main task was the control of the annual inundation of the Nile river which began in the caverns of the god Hapy, who personified the flood itself. He was assisted in this supervision by the goddesses Satis and Anukis, and in this aspect he was regarded as the soul of the sun god and was known as Khnum-Ra. Another of his titles was 'Lord of the Crocodiles', again emphasizing his connection with the river.

But it was through his powers of procreation, clearly an echo of the ram's notorious fertility, that he became known as a creator god. He is represented as seated before a potter's wheel on which stands a being that he has just moulded into existence. Khnum normally performs this creative task at the behest of other gods, breathing the life force into the created being. At one point, he may have been associated as the war-champion of the sun god. A number of mummified ram's skulls, decorated with gilded headpieces and buried in stone sarcophagi have been discovered, especially on Elephantine Island where a cult of Khnum was established.

KHYUNG

In the legends and folklore of Tibet, the Khyung is the eagle of space. Originally an important protective spirit in the shamanic, pre-Buddhist Bon religion of Tibet, when it was a clan and mountain spirit, it is now considered to be the tutulary guardian of lamas and mediums. The Khyung flies higher than any other bird. It was born full grown from its egg, signifying to the Dzogchen traditions of Tibetan Buddhism that it represents the unborn nature which yet harbours the self-existent maturity of enlightenment potentially within it. Like the Garuda bird of Indian and Indonesian myth, the Khyung acts as a mount to the gods and enlightened ones.

The Element Encyclopedia of Magical Creatures

Kiau

Kiau is a type of serpent or marsh dragon from the medieval traditions of China. One of these creatures was killed in 1129 by a local hero, having plagued the fishermen along the Chien-Tang River for many years.

Kichiknebik

A great horned serpent from the beliefs and traditions of the Native American people. Also known as the Great Serpent or Manitou Knebik, it was large enough to swallow a buffalo in one gulp, but despite its size could move swiftly on both land and water.

Kikimora

A female house-spirit in the mythology of the Slavic people of Russia, Kikimora is variously described as having a head as small as a thimble and a body as thin as a straw, though she can also look like an ordinary woman. Like many other such creatures, the Kikimora looks after farm animals and does the housework. However, if the housewife is slovenly, the Kikimora will keep everyone awake at night, whining or whistling in their ears, or tickling them. She often comes out at night to spin cloth, and it is said that if anyone sees her when she is doing this they will die soon after. The only way to appease an angry Kikimora is to wash all the pots and pans in a special tea made from ferns.

Kingfisher

A number of myths surround the kingfisher, which is also known as the Halcyon. According to early writers, the kingfisher was reputed to make its nest either on the seashore or actually on the sea itself. It was claimed that from the moment the eggs were laid until the young flew free of the waters, the sea remain calm. From this came the idea of the Halcyon Days, a period before and after the winter solstice when the winds were calm for a period of two weeks. According to the 4th-century Greek writer St Basil,

… [the halcyon] breeds along the shores depositing its eggs on the sand itself. And it builds about the middle of winter when the sea is dashed upon the land by many violent winds. But, nevertheless, all winds are lulled and the ocean wave is calm when the Halcyon broods during the seven days, for only in so many days does it hatch its young. And since these have need of sustenance, Providence, bountiful to the smallest thing, provides seven more days for the development of the young ones.

Other writers claim different lengths of time, some claiming eleven, others nine, but most agree on seven days. In Greek mythology, Alcyone, daughter of the wind god Aeolus, discovered her husband drowned and threw herself into the sea in sorrow. But the gods, to reward her deep love, turned her into a kingfisher. Aeolus then commanded the winds not to blow during the period when the eggs were laid and the young in the nest. This connection with the wind god appears to be the reason for the custom of using the mummified body of a kingfisher, with outstretched wings, as a weather vane. This practice was maintained until the 18th century.

Medieval myth claims that the kingfisher was originally grey in colour, but that during the Biblical Flood it flew up to heaven to overlook the waters and in the process flew so close to the sun that its breast was burned red and its back took on the colour of the sky. In Chinese myth, the bird symbolized calmness, beauty and a gentle nature.

KINNARAS

In Hindu belief, Kinnaras are horse-headed musicians who make music at the court of Kubera, the king of the Yakshas. They are considered to be celestial humans who have the *rajas* tendency, meaning that they are motivated by intellectual motion, and they are under the protection of the creator Brahma. Kinnaras seem to be associated with centaurs, even though they have horse-heads rather than the centaurs' horse bodies. It is worth noting the Indian word *kinnara* comes from the same root as Greek *kentauros*.

KIRIN

Kirin is the Japanese version of the Unicorn. Described as a multi-coloured creature with a single horn protruding from its forehead, it is considered to be an agent of the gods, dispensing goodness and justice to those who deserve it, and punishing in an appropriate fashion those who do evil deeds.

KIRNI

According to the folklore of old Japan, the Kirni is similar to the medieval griffin, having the body of a lion with the head, torso, and legs of an eagle and an extremely wide wingspan. In common with its European cousin, the Kirni is said to protect hoards of treasure.

KIRTIMUKHA

In Hindu mythology, this creature is depicted as the disembodied head of a lion with protruding eyes, thick eyebrows that resemble horns, and a halo-like flame of bushy hair extending above its head. From its mouth spews forth pearls and flowers. According to the myth, the Kirtimukha is the result of a momentary flash of anger on the part of the god Shiva when he was informed that he was unworthy to marry his beloved Parvati. His rage took on the form of a man-lion monster that sprang from his forehead and then turned on its progenitor demanding food. Shiva suggested to the beast that it eat itself, which it did, leaving only its face and a string of pearls that were once its entrails. The god appointed Kirtimukha to be the guardian of doorways and commanded that ever after he should be offered sacrifices of meat.

Kitzinackas

A great water serpent from the traditions and beliefs of the Lenape and Algonquin people of North America. Unlike many such creatures, which were regarded as dangerous and fearful, the Kitzinackas was sacred to these people, and the shamans would invoke them through the medium of ritual dance.

Kiyo

A particularly fierce fire-breathing dragon from the medieval traditions of Japan.

> Once upon a time a novice monk fell in love with a serving girl in his local tea house. For some time he courted her, then remembering his vows left her and returned to his monastery. So angry was the girl that she set out to learn magic, and when she had done so took upon her the form of the dragon. She then went to the monastery where her former suitor was now a monk, but when he saw her he hid beneath a great bronze bell. Kiyo belched forth a great spurt of flame that melted the bell, killing the cowardly monk.

Kkuuxuginaagits

In the Haida myths of the north-west Pacific coast of America, Kkuuxuginaagits is the martin or 'Plain Old Marten' who has a contest with Taadlat Ghaadala, the swallow. They run a race from the depths of the Earth to the apex of Heaven, creating a link between the two. This line and the totem pole that is associated with it can both provoke as well as measure earthquakes.

Kludde

A monster from the folk traditions of Belgium which preyed upon travellers at night on lonely roads. It has much in common with the Black Dog, and with the Kelpie of Celtic tradition, but unlike these it had the ability to change its shape. It could appear as a giant dog, or as a cat, frog, bat or horse. However, a telltale blue flame that flickered around its head would identify it. It was reported that if the Kludde jumped on the back of an unsuspecting traveller, it would then grow heavier and heavier, finally forcing its victim to the ground, at which point it savaged them to death.

Knockers

Also known as Sprigguns and Buccas, these are small spirits that live in the Cornish tin mines. They are similar to the German Kobbold but are friendly rather than evil, for they knock in the mines to indicate where a rich vein of ore is to be found. At one time, it was believed that they were the ghosts of Jews who had worked in the mines, and local tradition claimed that Jews who took part in the Crucifixion were sent to work in the Cornish mines as a punishment. Miners frequently reported seeing small demons or imps in the mines, sitting on pieces of timber or lying about in curious attitudes. They were not afraid of these strange beings as their presence often indicated where a good lode of ore would be found. Strange knocking sounds coming from within the mines at night were considered to be made by these creatures, who continued to work long after the miners had left.

KNUD-GOAT

In Finland, the Knud-Goat (or Yule Goat) is one of the magical animals that is processed on St Knud's Day, 13 January. The Knud-Goat is the same goat that heralds the winter solstice, when a goat would have been slaughtered at the time of Yule, a word that means 'goat'. The Knud-Goat goes about after the midwinter festivities have passed, when people have to return to work again. The one who represents the Knud-Goat wears a mask with large horns and a calf's hide over his back with a tail of leaves. This is traditionally when the last of the Christmas beer is drunk and on this day, people processed

In a certain mine, the Knockers were always active in their subterranean operations. In one particular place they seemed more busy than at any other and this was believed to indicate that great wealth must exist at this part of the lode. Yet, notwithstanding the inducements of very high pay, no miner could be found who was brave enough to venture into that shaft. Then an old man and his son went out one Midsummer's Eve, and saw the small people bringing up baskets of shining ore. They told the little miners that they would save them all the trouble of breaking down the ore, and that they would share one tenth of the rich yield they extracted and leave it by for the Knockers. An agreement was reached and the old man and his son were soon very wealthy. The old man never failed to keep his side of the bargain, but his son was greedy and selfish and sought to cheat the Knockers. No good came of this, for the lode soon failed, the young man took to drink, squandered all the money his father had made, and died a beggar.

from house to house to help drink up the last drops! Men and women exchange clothes, wear masks or blacken their faces, tying straw sheaves to their backs. As they approached each house, the Knud-Scribe knocked on the door, demanding beer for the Knud-Goat, which was poured into the barrel they pulled behind them on a sledge. Those who refused to contribute beer knew they would not receive help during the harvest later on in the year. At harvest, a straw goat or *raiskollispukki* was made and would process from house to house once more with its cross-dressed supporters. (*See* Oats Goat.)

KOALA

An Aboriginal myth tells how the animals wanted to cross the waters to Australia. They got Starfish to distract Whale, the creator, so that they might take his canoe. When Whale learned what had happened, he tore Starfish into pieces and pursued the canoe. The other animals kept paddling wildly as Whale chased them, but it was due to Koala that they reached land successfully because of his great paddling arms. As they came ashore, their many feet broke the canoe and they struggled to shore to become animals and animal-men, from whom all beings are made.

KOBOLD

In Germanic folklore, the Kobold is a gnome-like spirit that lives in the mines and is skilled in the working of metal. The name is also given to a household brownie-like creature who helps households with unfinished tasks in return for hospitality and the sharing of the family supper.

KOGUHPUK

This creature, from the legends and folklore of the Inuit people of the Bering Straits in Alaska, appears as an enormous subterranean beast that lives beneath the earth and burrows for its food. It is sensitive to light and emerges only once in the depths of winter for one night only. Huge bleached bones, almost certainly those of long-dead mammoths, are said to be the remains of Koguhpuk who were caught on the surface at dawn.

KOJIN

A gigantic female ogre from the legends of Japan. The Kojin had thousands of arms, which she used to crush her victims to death. She was especially fond of killing and eating children, but in more recent times was turned back to goodness, becoming a protectress of children instead of their hunter.

KOLOWISI

Among the Zuni people of the southwest United States, the Kolowisi is a vast horned serpent, with a razor-toothed maw and numerous sharp fins on its body. Zuni legend tells of a young girl going to a spring to bathe and finding there a small baby, which she took home with her. But she failed to tell her parents of this, and that night, as the baby slept by her side, it transformed into the Kolowisi, which took away the girl to become its wife.

KOMOKWA

The god of the sea in the Haida and Kwakiutl myths from the north-west coast of America, Komokwa rules over the killer whales and sometimes takes on their form. At the highest tides, he has been known to come ashore accompanied by a great host of his subjects. He lives in a vast underwater palace supported on the backs of sea lions, and it is said that any mortal able to make, and survive, the journey to Komokwa's home would receive the right to wear a mask representing him and learn the secret dances and songs which ritually invoked him during sacred feasts.

KONGAMATO

A strange flying reptile, possibly a descendant of a pterosaur, a close relative of the more familiar pterodactyl, which are said to have been seen in the Jiundu swamps in the Mwinilunga district of western Zambia, near the border of Congo and Angola. In 1923, a traveller reported this creature to be smooth skinned, with a wing span of 4–7 ft and a beak full of teeth. Local people knew these creatures well, calling them Kongamato ('Overwhelmer of Boats'). They are usually described as either black or red in colour and they had a reputation for capsizing canoes. When shown a drawing of a pterosaur, every native present immediately and unhesitatingly identified it as a Kongamato. Further reports appeared in 1925, when a distinguished English newspaper correspondent reported a sighting of a winged creature in Rhodesia in a place widely known as the abode of demons. In 1942, another traveller reported stories the natives had told him of a large bat-like creature that lived in northern Rhodesia (now Zambia) in a dense swampy region. Even to look upon it meant death.

KOSHEI THE DEATHLESS

One of the most popular tales in the folklore and mythology of Russia is that of Koshei the Deathless, who is sometimes described as a **dragon**, while at other times is considered to be the male aspect of the demon Baba Yaga. His name derives from the word *kost*, meaning 'bone'. He could not be killed because his soul was hidden outside his body. Stories differ as to where the soul was kept, but most suggest that it was inside an egg, which was, in turn, inside a duck or other bird, which was then hidden inside a rabbit. All three creatures were in a remote and inaccessible place, such as beneath a large oak tree on an island in the middle of a huge ocean. Many stories tell how Koshei finally met his death when he

The Element Encyclopedia of Magical Creatures

One story tells how Koshei lived in a great golden palace where he kept an unnamed princess captive. Her suitor continuously circled the walls of the palace but he was unable to find a way in. The princess, deciding that she liked her would-be lover, decided to kill Koshei and made an effort to find out where his soul was hidden by being nice to him. At first, Koshei said that his soul was in a broom in the kitchen, but when the princess threw the broom onto the fire her captor remained unharmed. She tried again several times and Koshei told her that his soul was in a worm that lived beneath the largest of three oak trees at the top of a hill. Finally, Koshei told her that his soul was really inside an egg and that the egg was inside a duck and the duck within a hare – all three being hidden within a basket which was inside a steel chest that lay beneath a great oak that grew by itself on a small island far out at sea. The princess got word of this to her suitor; he set off, found the egg, and came back to the palace, where he confronted Koshei. Horrified to see the egg in the young man's hand, Koshei reached for a sword, but as he did so the young man squeezed the egg, at which Koshei let out a piercing scream. Knowing this was at last the right hiding place, the young man crushed the egg, killing the monster outright.

kidnapped the beautiful princess Vasilissa. The hero Bulat the Brave came in search of her and persuaded her to find out where her captor had hidden his soul. Having recovered the egg from his hiding place, Bulat returned to the forest home of the dragon and broke the egg on its forehead, killing it at once.

KRAKEN

The terrifying sea monster from the legends of Scandinavia. Also known as the Krabben and Skykraken, the Kraken is described as being of great length and breadth with a number of fins and tentacles extending from the side of its body. The monster's favourite trick was to encircle passing ships with its enormous body and drag them beneath the water. This action created a whirlpool, so that anything that escaped from its initial attack was sucked under. The Kraken has a taste for human flesh and was so vast that it could consume an entire fishing fleet – boats and men – at one time. The amber washed up around the shores of the North Sea was said to be its excrement. When not attacking its prey, the Kraken lay on the surface of the sea and like the Fastitocalon and Aspidochelone of seafaring lore, it was often mistaken for a floating island. Unwary mariners who attempted to land on its back, and to light cooking-fires, soon learnt the error of their ways. Despite their fear of it, fishermen noted that large schools of smaller fish always seemed to swim before it, so that those brave enough to risk the Kraken's jaws were able to secure a notable catch. In the 1680s, a Kraken was reported stranded on the coast of Norway; while a local tradition at Rousay, in the Kyles of Bute, Scotland, claims that a Kraken was washed ashore in 1775. The description in an 18th-century book, *The Natural History of Norway*, includes mention of how the Kraken turned the sea dark with a discharge of liquid, suggesting that what the author of this book may have been describing was either an octopus or a cuttlefish of unusual size. The English poet Alfred, Lord Tennyson, while still a young man, wrote of the Kraken:

Below the thunders of the upper deep,
Far, far beneath the abysmal sea,
His ancient, dreamless, and uninvaded
* sleep*
The Kraken sleepeth: faintest sunlights
* flee*
About his shadowy sides; above him swell
Huge sponges of millennial growth and
* height;*
And far away into the sickly light,
From many a wondrous grot and secret
* cell*
Unnumber'd and enormous polypi
Winnow with giant arms the
* slumbering green.*
There hath he lain for ages, and will lie
Battening upon huge sea worms in his
* sleep,*
Until the latter fire shall heat the deep;

Then once by man and angels to be seen,
In roaring he shall rise and on the
* surface die.*

KRAMPUS

The Krampus is the Winter Goat who goes about in the days between winter solstice and Epiphany (6 January) in the Austrian Perchtenlauf Festival. Elsewhere, the Krampus is known as the companion of St Nicholas. Throughout the Austrian Tyrol, into Bavaria and parts of Italy, the Krampus is a fertility demon, with a long tail and fur, who carries a chain, a birch branch and a big black bag. He acts as a foil to St Nicholas, for as the saint gives gifts at Christmas, so the Krampus punishes those who have been bad. Really bad children may even get carried off in his black sack.

KTING VOAR

One of many strange creatures listed among the findings of cryptozoologists. The Kting Voar ('jungle-sheep') is found in Cambodia and Vietnam, where it is known as Ling Dong ('mountain goat'). Its most significant feature is its peculiarly long and twisting horns that measure up to 20 inches in length. There is virtually no evidence for the existence of this animal, though the biologist Wolfgang Peter bought a set of horns apparently belonging to this creature in a market in Ho Chi Min City. Some believe that the horns are simply cow's horns that have grown to peculiar length and shape; however, other zoologists believe in its existence.

sought as a means of discovering events that were to come.

KUBERA

In Hindu belief, Kubera is the king of the Yakshas, the genii who guard treasures. He guards all the precious stones and metals of the earth, along with 'the nine treasures', which are the sacred ores and jewels of the earth. He takes the form of a fat, white dwarf who has three legs, eight teeth and one eye. His body is covered with ornaments. He holds a mace and sits in the hall at the centre of his kingdom in the north Himalayas. He is entertained by Kinnaras or faun musicians. The *Vijayanaanda Tripathi* text says of him:

Whatever treasures are in the earth, they all belong to Kubera. Only through his kindness do men obtain precious metals and stones from the entrails of the earth. The nidhi vidya ('Science of Treasures') teaches that mineral wealth is alive and moves of itself from place to place. According to the merits of men, Kubera brings out his treasures or hides them. During the rule of a deserving kind, precious stones and jewels come near to the surface of the earth and are easily found.

KUDAN

A creature from Japanese legend depicted as a bull with a man's head, three eyes on each flank and horns along its back. It is said that the Kudan always told the truth and so it was often

KUJATA

A cosmic bull in Islamic mythology, the Kujata has 4,000 eyes in its head, 4,000 ears, 4,000 mouths and 4,000 nostrils; its body also has 4,000 legs and feet. In the great cosmic hierarchy, the Kujata stands upon the back of the cosmic fish Baharmut, which in turn stands upon the surface of the cosmic sea, which is situated above an abyss, which is in turn above a vast sea of fire – all of which are above the back of the cosmic serpent. An enormous glowing ruby sits upon Kujata's back, and upon this is an angel who supports the weight of the world on his shoulders.

KULSHEDRA/KUCEDRE

An Albanian fire-breathing dragon with nine tongues, the Kulshedra is what the Bolla evolves into at the end of its cycle. It sometimes appears as a woman with pendulous breasts, covered with hair. The Kulshedra causes water shortages. In such times, it requires a sacrifice to propitiate it.

KUMIHO

An otherworldly fox with nine tails described in the folklore and traditions of Korea. It is able to transform itself into a beautiful girl, and in this form seeks to seduce men and kill them. An ordinary fox, which is able to live a 1,000 years, automatically becomes a Kumiho. A number of stories appear in collections of oral traditions from Korea including one where the Kumiho transforms itself into the look-alike of a bride at a wedding. No one, not even the bride's mother, can tell them apart until the creature's clothes are removed. Several tales describe encounters between hunters and beautiful girls who live alone in the woods and possess certain fox-like qualities. These stories suggest that while the Kumiho is able to change its appearance to that of a human being, it still has a fox-like aspect to it – something which enables it to be recognized by hunting dogs.

Unlike the fox of Japanese tradition, which sometimes changes into a woman in order to marry a man who has been kind to it, the Kumiho never appears as a benevolent figure and is invariably cruel and likes to play tricks on humans. In one story, a hunter comes upon a fox scratching at a human skull in the woods. Before his eyes, the creature changes into an old woman and goes down to a nearby village. The hunter follows her and sees her reunited with her children, who believed her to be dead. The hunter then warns the children that the Kumiho had actually killed their mother and that it intended to make them its next victims. The children kill the Kumiho, which assumes its own form again in death.

KUNDRAV

In Sumerian mythology, this dragon-like monster of the abyss had its body in the waters and its head in the sky. Kundrav was always trying to destroy the land and all upon it, but it was in fact set there to guard an evil dragon, its opponent, who wished to destroy the whole universe. Kundrav was slain by Keresaspa, who fought with it for many days and nights. Keresaspa did not know of the other more dangerous dragon. He first had to get a toothpick to prise out the dead men from its teeth. Despite being flayed, the monster ate the hero's 15 horses, blinded him and pushed him into a thicket, carrying off his family.

KURMA

The great cosmic tortoise of Hindu mythology. A gigantic creature whose upper shell forms the outer limits of the heaven, and whose lower shell is the basis of the Earth, Kurma was created from a cosmic egg by the god Prajapatii. The first Indian mapmakers represented the sub-continent as resting on the surface of the tortoise's shell, with all other lands separate from and surrounding it. Kurma is one of the avatars or animal manifestations of the preserving god Vishnu. After the deluge, Vishnu took the form of Kurma in order to recover those things of value lost during the great inundation. When the gods churned the ocean of milk using the serpent Sesha-Naga as a rope, they could only do so by asking Kurma to go to the bottom of the sea to act as a support for the mountain with which they churned the waters. From this churning came forth the ambrosia of life, Laksmi the goddess of good luck, the wine

The Element Encyclopedia of Magical Creatures

goddess Varuni, the sacrificial elixir of soma, the nymphs the Apsaras, the divine horse Uccaihshravas, the wish-cow Surabhi, the royal elephant Aira-vata and many other things and beings. Kurma the tortoise is believed to be the one who keeps the Indian continent safe upon his back, thus manifesting the virtue of the preserving Vishnu.

Kw'en

A gigantic fish, several miles in length, that was said to occupy the Great Northern Sea of China according to the myths and legends of that country. Remarkably, the Kw'en could transform itself into a massive bird called the P'eng.

Ky-Lin

A variant of the Unicorn from the mythology and traditions of China. The Ky-Lin has the head of a dragon, with a single horn, the mane of a lion, the body of a stag, and the tail of an ox. This is taken to indicate that the Ky-Lin represents the five elements and the five virtues. It is also said to embody the yin–yang balance between masculine and feminine: 'Ky' being male and 'Lin' female. Its single horn stands for the unity of the world under one great ruler and the Ky-Lin, which normally lives in Paradise, only visits the world at the birth of wise philoso-phers or during the reign of especially virtuous monarchs. Like its Western cousin, the Ky-Lin is always repre-sented as extremely gentle and it never uses its horn to defend itself. In Chinese art, it appears in the company of sages and immortals, and anyone shown mounted on a Ky-Lin must be a person of great fame or virtue. The term 'To ride a Ky-Lin' indicates a person of outstanding luck and ability. It personifies all that is good, pure and peaceful in the world.

LABUNA

In Islamic tradition, Labuna is the great fish that swims in the lower ocean. On its head is the Earth bull holding up the globe between his horns. Labuna eats 70,000 specially-created fish each day which gives it the ability to swim for three days and is served by an angel who is deputed to provide it with food.

LADON

In Greek mythology, Ladon was the many-headed vigilant, dragonish serpent that guarded the sacred golden apples of the Hesperides. Ladon was the brother of Echidna, and uncle to Cerberus, Orthos and Hydra. Ladon's eyes never closed in sleep but watched perpetually. The Hesperides, nymphs who would have taken the apples for themselves without the watchful guardianship of Ladon, assisted Hercules in his eleventh labour, by singing so sweetly that the serpent fell into a doze, enabling him to steal the golden apples.

LAIDLEY WORM

In English folk tradition, the Laidley or Loathly Worm is a dragon, who is really the Lady Maisry or Margaret, enchanted by her stepmother.

In the Child Border Ballad of the same name, the Laidley Worm is the enchanted form of the King's son and his daughter is turned into a 'mackrel [sic] of the sea'. The enchanted children look after each other and live upon any who come against them until the king himself comes to see what has befallen seven of his knights whom they have vanquished. The Laidley Worm replies,

> *'Seven knights have I slain,*
> *Since I lay at the foot of the tree,*
> *And were you not my own father,*
> *The eighth one you should be.'*

The king sends for his second wife, the sorceress and makes her take off the spell. She strikes the Laidley Worm with a silver wand and blows a horn to restore the Mackrel of the Sea back into Lady Margaret. The king sends for firewood and burns his wife so that she can no longer wreak her magic upon his family.

Northumbrian legend tells how King Ida of Bamburgh Keep had two children: his heir, the Childe of the Wynd, and his daughter, Margaret. After the children's mother died, King Ida remarried a sorceress who cursed the girl into the shape of a serpentine dragon so that her maiden bower became a serpent's den. This happened while the Childe of the Wynd was in foreign lands. The Laidley Worm devastated the country all around, blighting crops despite offerings of cattle brought to propitiate it. Finally, the Childe of the Wynd returned home in a ship made of rowan wood. When the queen sighted it, she attempted to send her spirits against it to prevent the ship landing, but because the ship was made of the magical rowan wood – traditionally the tree that bends enchantment – she was unable. The curse was so strong upon Lady Margaret that, as the Laidley Worm, she lashed the waves to create a storm. But the ship skilfully drew to shore and the Childe of the Wynd leapt ashore to face the worm who opened its jaws to send fire against him – but nothing came out. Undaunted, the Childe of the Wynd caressed his enchanted sister and kissed her scaly brow. Withdrawing into her cave, she re-emerged as a human woman once more.

The Childe of the Wynd then took his vengeance upon his stepmother, for he had magical powers of his own. He cast his spell upon her, 'Squat, hiss, spit, in likeness of an ugly toad.' She immediately shrank and shrivelled into the shape of a toad, spitting at any maidens she met with jealousy and frustration and was driven out of court.

LAIR BHEAN

In Irish folk tradition, the Lair Bhean or Grey Mare is a hobbyhorse who goes about on Samhain night (Hallowe'en) led by a band of revellers who accompany her. She is represented by someone wearing a white sheet and a horse's skull and she attempts to come into each house with songs and a riddling contest. The Lair Bhean sometimes goes out again on St Stephen's Day (26 December) with the Wren boys. The custom used to be observed in many parts of Ireland and now seems confined to the south-east. It is remarkably similar to the Mari Lwyd, with whom the Lair Bhean shares many characteristics.

Lakhmu

In Mesopotamian legend, Lakhmu is one of the primordial titans created when the god Abzu lay with the goddess Tiamat, mother of chaos. All of Lakhmu's children, Igigi, Anu and the Anunnaki, rose up against their grandparents, rather as the Olympian gods overthrew the Titans in Greek mythology. Lakhmu and its progeny were all destroyed by Marduk, the sun god.

Lakin Chan

In Mayan tradition, Lakin Chan is the Serpent of the East. He is the creator of mankind and of all life on Earth. He invented writing and is the guardian of herb-lore, medicine and books. He is the son of Hunab-Ku, the 'god behind the gods'.

Lama

The Lama is a protective female deity in Sumerian mythology. These beneficent Lamassu (plural) are like the nymphs of Sumerian tradition who are shown conducting the faithful into the precincts of the temples where gods are installed.

Lamastu

In Babylonian myth, Lamastu is a goddess, the daughter of Anu who is the mistress of demons. She preys upon unborn and newly born babies and causes pregnant women to miscarry or lie on their babies. Lamastu has the head of a lion, donkey's teeth, naked breasts and a hairy body. She has blood-stained hands, long fingers and nails and the feet of the Imdugud bird. She is sometimes shown suckling a piglet and a whelp, while holding snakes in her hands. Pregnant women would fend off her attentions by wearing the bronze head of Pazuzu. On many amulets, Lamastu is shown being conducted to the underworld by Pazuzu. She often appears with her boat with which she sails along the underworld river. Lamastu was also the bringer of disease, as plaques portraying her also show a man lying on a bed of agony. In respect of both her disease-spreading and stealing of young children, as well as her bird-like feet, Lamastu is the forerunner of Lilith.

Lambton Worm

In the Northumbrian folk legend from the north-east of England, the Lambton Worm is a serpentine monster.

The heir of Lambton fished a small worm out of the water. At first, he thought it to be of great size because of the fight the fish put up, but he was so disgusted by its puny ugliness that he threw it into a well. A passing stranger looked down the well and said that it looked like a newt, only it had nine holes either side of its mouth, and that this betokened no good. Shortly afterwards, Lord Lambton went to the Crusades, but the worm in the well grew until it was so large it had to seek elsewhere to live. It crawled out and wound itself nine times around a hill, squeezing it with its coils. Thereafter, it began devouring livestock and devastating the land. The old Lord Lambton's steward poured milk into the trough in the courtyard to propitiate it, but finding a source of food it liked, it returned daily until the milk of nine cows was needed to fuel its appetite. Many knights came to subdue it and were overthrown or killed.

Seven years later, the heir of Lambton returned and resolved to finish the creature off. He consulted a witch who advised he wore a suit of mail studded with razor blades. She said that if he stood on a certain peak, he would be victorious but that he must swear to kill the first thing he met after killing the worm but, if he failed to do so, the next nine generations of Lambtons would not die in their beds. He advised his father that, when he had killed the worm, he would sound three blasts on his horn and that this was a signal for his father to let loose the knight's favourite greyhound who would become the necessary sacrifice. Young Lambton fought courageously against the worm that twined around him, trying to squeeze him to death until, eventually, Lambton cut him in two. He blew three blasts triumphantly, but his old father, hearing the welcome sound, forgot his instructions and rushed to congratulate his son. Not wishing to commit parricide, Young Lambton blew his horn again, which brought his greyhound to his side which he promptly slew. In this way, he hoped that the curse would be avoided, but legend tells how the Lambtons for the next nine generations died troubled and violent deaths. Genealogical searches through the Lambton family line show that from the 15th century onwards, the heirs died in battle, and one was even hung for recusancy during the Catholic persecutions under Elizabeth I. The curse seemed to abate during the 18th century when the first Lambton heir for many generations died at the age of 64 in his bed.

Lamia

In classical legend, the Lamia had the shape of a woman to the waist and that of a serpent below, but she was able to assume the shape of an ordinary woman. Legend tells how she was originally a Libyan queen whom Zeus took as his mistress. He hid Lamia from his jealous wife, Hera, by placing her in a cave in Africa, bidding her leave her eyes outside on watch while she slept each night. But Hera found the cave and turned Lamia into her half-serpentine shape and took away her children by Zeus, destroying them. From then onwards, Lamia has had an implacable hatred that she takes out upon the human race by enticing men and children into close proximity with her before killing them.

From classical times onwards, Lamia has taken other roles. She has been associated with the Empusa as a kind of vampire. Since then, the story and role of Lamia has developed in two distinct ways. She has become an evil fairy or nursery bogey of some antiquity – Aristotle relates his grandmother telling him that Lamiae lay in wait in the wilderness preying on little boys; but she has also become a Succubus, helped by Burton's *Anatomie of Melancholy* where he retells a story in which a philosopher named Menippus was seduced by a phantom woman with whom he became besotted. At their wedding feast, the magician Apollonius of Tyana realized that the woman was none other than a Lamia, a serpent-woman. The Lamia begged him to be silent, but when he revealed her true nature, the Lamia and all her goods vanished into the air. In Topsell's *Historie of Foure-Footed Beasts* (1607), the Lamia is shown in a woodcut as a scaly, four-footed creature with paws on her front limbs and hooves on her back limbs. She has a woman's face and breasts but also a phallus. John Keats's famous poem on the Lamia sees her as a Succubus, thus bequeathing an undying legend of the seductive, vampiric female.

Lampon

In classical legend, Lampon was one of the horses of the sun. It pulled the golden chariot of Helios. Every morning, the Horae harnessed the horses of the sun ready to make the journey across the sky. They finally landed again on the Isles of the Blessed at dusk, where they grazed until the next morning.

Landvaettir

In Norse mythology, the Landvaettir are beings from the lowerworld. These elf-like creatures were the guardians of the land. It was out of respect for them that, in Icelandic lore, the dragon-headed prows upon the bow of the ship had to be removed when approaching land so that the Landvaettir would not be driven, or frightened, away.

LEI CHEN-TZU

In Chinese mythology, Lei Chen-Tzu is a hero who became a great winged, green dragon, with a boar's tusks. He was hatched from an egg that resulted when his father Lei, the Thunder Dragon, sent a thunderclap to Earth. He was adopted by the god of literature, Wen Wang, whom he loved so much that he rescued him from imprisonment by shapeshifting from a man into a dragon. While still in human form, Lei Chen-Tzu ate two apricots given him by his father, Lei; these had the effect of making him become a green, boar-faced dragon. He was so implacable in this form that he was easily able to rescue his foster-father.

LEI GONG

In Chinese mythology, Lei Gong (or Lei Kung) is the god of thunder. He has the beak, wings and claws of an owl but a human body; and he is blue. He wears a loin cloth and is shown carrying his emblems of hammer and drum with which to produce thunder. In the bureaucratic way of Confucian deities, Lei Gong is an official in the Ministry of Thunder, helping to keep celestial administration going. Lei Gong pursues all who are guilty of undetected crimes.

LEOPARD

The leopard appears throughout African myth and folklore as a sure killer. Among Africans, it is the leopard and not the lion who is the royal beast of kings. In Zaire, the leopard skin covers the royal seat and a cap of leopard skin is the equivalent of a crown. The leopard has the reputation of being a lascivious and unpredictable lover.

LEPRECHAUN

The leprechaun has become the standard image of Irish kitsch, a being with a rosy face, boozy demeanour and green attire, the stuff of St Patrick's Day parades the world over, but leprechauns have a far more ancient lineage and are a race far removed from the popular images of cheery, wish-bestowing fairies. The name comes from the Middle Irish word, *luchorpán* ('little body'). The first recorded reference to leprechauns comes in the 8th-century story of 'The Death of Fergus mac Leiti' where the original *luchorpán* are water spirits. The luchorpán seize upon Fergus while he lies sleeping on the seashore. When he wakes, he finds he is hovering over the water held in their grip. He traps three of them and makes them promise to share their swimming skills with him in return for their release. They grant him waterproof powers and the ability to swim underwater, but bar him from Lake Rudraige. Unfortunately, Fergus goes there and finds himself in a deep-lake dive with a terrible monster (Muirdris) which causes a facial disfigurement which disqualifies him from his rulership. A later 13th-century version of this story introduces a comedic element giving the leprechaun king Iubdan and his queen Bebo and their poet Eisirt wonderful witty exchanges with Fergus.

A confusion arose between *luchorpán* and the solitary fairy being of Ireland known as the Cluricaune who is a cunning spirit who haunts cellars, drinks, smokes and plays tricks. This came about possibly due to the publication of Crofton Croker's *Fairy Legends* (1825). Since that time, leprechauns seem to be entirely male and solitary. One long-established tradition makes the leprechaun a cobbler who is found and seized by a human and made to show the way to the crock of gold. Leprechauns were not originally toadstool sitters, with red Galway beards and green hats, but that is how they survive in the imaginations of today – a mixture of Cluricaune, brownie and European fairy. Their reputation as cobblers is perhaps the oldest thing about them, for it has been suggested that their original name derives from the Irish god, Lugh, and that they should be known as *lu-chorpan* ('Lugh-bodies'). The Welsh variant of Lugh, Lleu, is known as one of the 'Three Golden Shoemakers'. Lady Wilde's collection of tales, *Ancient Legends of Ireland*, relates the most familiar traditions about the leprechaun.

LEVIATHAN

In Biblical tradition, Leviathan lies in a circle surrounding the world like Ouroboros but with the intention of overcoming it, not preserving it. It cannot live in the Mediterranean Sea because it is too big, preferring the Indian Ocean. According to the 2nd-century Slavonic *Apocalypse of Abraham*, Leviathan is a danger to the world's existence:

'And I saw there the sea and its islands, and its cattle and its fish, and Leviathan and his realm and his bed and his lairs, and the world which lay upon him, and his motions and the destruction he caused the world.'

The mindfulness of the pious was an active restraint upon Leviathan's perpetual attempt to meet head to tail. 'Let it be on your mind and it will not move from its place,' says the 8th-century Irish *Epistil Isu*. The Hebrew word *liwiathan* is translated as crocodile, but its *liwya* (writhings) are more like those of a great serpent than any crocodile.

LIGHTNING SERPENT

The Lightning Serpent is a feature of Aboriginal Australian lore. It is a great serpent that lives in the heavens and descends to Earth when it is stormy. The energy released from its striking and rebounding from the Earth is the lightning which heralds the welcome rains.

LILITH

In Hebrew tradition, Lilith was the first woman who was created. God punished her for tempting Eve in the

The Element Encyclopedia of Magical Creatures

form of a serpent and causing the Fall of Man. Another story tells how she wanted to join the ranks of the cherubim but was forced to go to Earth instead. There she saw that Adam already had a partner and so she found herself an outcast in the desert. Lilith appears as a beautiful woman with wings, reptilian or bird-like feet and, in one relief, is shown flanked by lions and owls, the traditional beasts of the wilderness and the night.

In Talmudic tradition, Lilith was made at the same time as Adam but, believing herself to be his equal, she flew away into the desert where she consorted with demons insatiably until she had created a race of demons. God sent three angels to bring her back but when she refused, they threatened to drown her. Her chief power is to kill helpless children but she agreed not to harm any protected by talismans against her. She roams the world for unprotected children. As a Jewish demon, Lilith is much feared and orthodox Jews still make talismans against her to protect their children. In Mesopotamian lore, Lilith derives from the demons known as Lilitu who haunt open country and who are dangerous to pregnant women and children. These Lilitu are sometimes shown as scorpion-tailed she-wolves. The traditional Lilitu or *ardat-lili* ('maiden lilu') appears exactly as Lilith is described in Isaiah 34:14:

She is neither wife or mother, nor has she known happiness; she has not unclothed herself for her husband, nor is there milk in her breasts.

LION

The lion's roar reminds us of just who is King of the Beasts. This title should perhaps be reserved for the lioness who is much busier about the business of the kill than the male lion, which sleeps up to 18 hours a day in a truly regal torpor. The strength of the lion is one that human beings are continually trying to gain for themselves from the exploits of Hercules and the Nemean Lion onwards, when he took the lion's skin as his emblem of victory. Lions have the reputation for not putting up with evil, as we see from the mount of the Hindu goddess, Durga, who defeats the buffalo demon, riding upon a lion that attacks the buffalo while she engages the demon with her many-armed weaponry.

From Mesopotamian tradition onwards, the lion was regarded as truly representative of kingly prowess and power. To reinforce this comparison between the king of the animal kingdom and the sovereign himself, medieval kings began to keep lions in their menageries to impress ambassadors and act as a visible emblem of power. The lion-hunt reliefs from the Assyrian period in the British Museum are an impressive testimony to the respect placed upon the lion in Mesopotamian culture, where a prince had to slay his first lion in order to ascend to the throne. But the attributes of the lion were not seen exclusively as masculine prerogatives. Divinities such as the Mesopotamian Innana and, later, Ishtar, were compared to lions in their ferocity and warlike nature, while the

Egyptian goddess Sekhmet whirls out of the desert in the form of a lioness, killing and rending whoever falls in her path.

In Africa, the lion is revered as a god and, like in the Thai story, is believed to be the founder of many dynasties. Magical lion forebears taught the arts of hunting, bush-lore and the spellcraft that brings game to their human descendants. In Sudan, there are stories of women who are the offspring of lions and humans, but they can be easily discerned for they will eat only meat – no grains or vegetables – and it is good to notice this before you marry one, unless you wish to become the next meal!

According to Islamic tradition, God created the lion from the blood of the prophet Noah (or Nuh). While Noah had been nailing the planks of the Ark together, Satan came in the shape of a wild boar and dislodged a plank that had been nailed down. Noah hammered it back into place three times, but on the third attempt he hit his thumb in his haste to finish before the rains started. The blood that flowed into the sand was changed into the lion which then chased away the boar.

LION AND UNICORN

The lion and the unicorn appear together in British folk tradition as the emblematic animals who represent the Scottish and British thrones, for they appear as the heraldic shield supporters of the monarchs of Great Britain. Lion and Unicorn have a traditional antipathy and are often said to be fighting against each other. The origins of this myth appear in a story by the 14th-century writer John de Scheppey:

A lion met a unicorn and pretended to be at death's door. Seeing the lion so weak, the unicorn overlooked their usual enmity and talked to him. The lion begged the use of the unicorn's horn as a crutch to help him visit his wife for the very last time, saying it would be returned. But without its horn, the unicorn had no means of defence. Thinking the lion was hobbling off on his last journey, the unicorn was shocked when the lion made a sneaky ambush, running at the unicorn with its own horn. The wounded unicorn berated the lion for his treachery but the lion mocked the unicorn for his trustful weakness in aiding an enemy.

The conflict between the lion and the unicorn is a mythic representation of the difficult relationship between the Scottish and English thrones which were not incorporated until the Act of Union in 1705. From this fight, the famous nursery rhyme derives, which is quoted and re-enacted in Lewis Carroll's *Through the Looking Glass*:

The Lion and the Unicorn
Were fighting for the crown:
The Lion beat the Unicorn
All round about the town.

Some gave them white bread,
Some gave them brown;
Some gave them plum cake,
And drummed them out of town.

LION GRIFFIN

The Lion Griffin or Lion-dragon is commonly featured in Mesopotamian wall reliefs. With a lion's foreparts and a bird's hind legs, tail and wings, it is very like a Griffin. The Lion Griffin appears in the temple of the warlike god Ninurta, whose animal this appears to be, although the storm god Ishkur (or Adad) rides a similar beast which is an Umu Na-Iru ('Roaring Weather Beast').

LITTLE MANITOU

Little Manitou is a water serpent native to the Otsitsot peoples of North America. A scamp called Carcajou ('Glutton') sacrilegiously visited the tribe's sacred tree, with a view to mocking tribal beliefs. Suddenly, he was transfixed by a great light, which emanated from a great horned serpent calling itself Little Manitou ('Little Spirit').

LIZARD

Lizards have the amazing ability to shed their skin and renew themselves, giving rise to a series of myths about transformation. The Polynesian god Tangaroa changed into a green lizard when fine weather was due. In Graeco-Egyptian myth, the lizard was an animal associated with Hermes and Serapis, gods of the Hermetic mystery cults, which are to do with the mystical transformation of the soul.

Around the Mediterranean, house lizards are fed as guardians spirits. Among the Amazonian Indians, the lizard is a manifestation of Desana, Master of Animals and Fish, who is normally in the form of a dwarf (*see* Lords and Ladies of the Animals). In the Pacific, Moko, king of lizards is a god who protects fishing, while the Aboriginal people of Australian regard the lizard Tarrotarro as an ancestor who separated the sexes and taught the people tattooing.

LOCAPALA ELEPHANTS

The Locapalas or Guardian Kings are the Hindu equivalents to the Tibetan Dharmapalas. These eight guardians superintend a direction (*locapala*) of the universe. A pair of colossal elephants — a male and his consort — stand facing the eight directions with the whole world upon their backs. In the north, the god Kubera, Lord of Riches, is with the elephant Himapandara. In the north-east is Soma, the Lord of the Moon, with the elephant

Supratika. In the east is Indra, King of Heaven with the elephant Airavata. In the south-east is Agni, god of fire, with the elephant Pundarika. In the south is Yama, King of the Ancestors and Lord of the Dead, with the elephant Vamana. In the south-west is Surya, god of the sun, with the elephant Kumuda. In the west is Varuna, Lord of Waters, Knowledge and Destiny, with the elephant Anja. In the north-west is Vayu, Lord of the Wind, with the elephant Pushadanta. The Locapala Elephants themselves stand upon the tortoise, Akupara, while the whole universe is bounded and encompassed by the World Serpent.

LOCH NESS MONSTER

The famous Scottish water monster, affectionately known as Nessie, had its first recorded appearance in the Life of St Columba, the 6th-century saint from Ireland who founded the monastery of Iona. The Life calls the monster *aquatilis bestia* which seems to be the Latin translation of the Gaelic all-purpose term Piast.

Today the monster excites a great deal of attention, with coach-loads of visitors disembarking in the hope of seeing the distinctive V-wave that heralds Nessie's appearance. The many sightings speak of a 30-ft body with humps that undulate beneath the surface of the water and occasionally the eel-like or serpentine head of the creature can be seen peering up. Several teams of scientists, naturalists and cryptozoologists have monitored the loch, keeping watch using radar and ultra-sound to detect any motion. Prehistoric survival arguments cite the plesiosaur as a possible origin for the monster. Nessie may be the only aquatic monster to have her own website. Many films have been made featuring Nessie, including *The Private Life of Sherlock Holmes* and the more recent *Loch Ness*.

St Columba encounters the monster at the mouth of the River Ness that flows out of Loch Ness into the Moray Firth and the North Sea. Columba sees a Pictish man burying one of his friends on the banks of the river and asks to know the cause of death. The man had been swimming in the river, he was told, and his strokes had disturbed the water and the water monster in the depths below rose and savagely bit him. Despite this danger, Columba asks one of his brothers, Lugne, to swim across for a boat. Lugne is pursued by the disturbed monster but Columba makes the sign of the cross and forbids it to touch the swimmer.

LOCUSTS

In Islamic tradition, locusts were the first animals to be created. They took pity on Adam when he was expelled with Eve from the Garden of Eden

The Element Encyclopedia of Magical Creatures

because the locusts were made out of the left-over clay that had formed the first man. Their king is eagle-sized and receives his orders directly from God. The patterns on locusts' backs are understood to be old Arabic writing which states 'God is One.' They are in the service of God and can be sent out against those who offend the Creator, such as when the Pharaoh refused to let the Children of Israel go out of Egypt.

In the Hopi legend of Spider Woman and the migration of the clans, the Blue Flute clan created the locust, a hump-backed flute player, to bring tropical warmth with his flute playing and help melt the snow that blocked the Back Door to the Fourth World. Forever after, the art of flute playing has been under the locust's protection.

LORDS AND LADIES OF THE ANIMALS

Throughout the world, the creatures are under the protection of gods and goddesses as well as divine herdsmen and shepherdesses who guard the safety and soul of all animals. In the presence of the Lords and Ladies of the Animals, all creatures come together unafraid, surrounding their divine protector. Many species of animals who would normally be antagonistic to each other, cease their predations when they gather in the presence of these figures. In early East Mediterranean mythologies, we find the Mother of the Mountain, who is called Rhea, Diktynna and Artemis; while in Asia Minor there is Cybele,

whose mountain throne is guarded by two lions. These ancient goddesses reveal themselves as the Lady of the Beasts. In Hindu mythology, this role is taken by Parvati who, with her husband, Shiva, make up a partnership of the Lord and Lady of the Animals. Among the Bushmen of Africa, it is the goddess Ko who is the matron of the hunt. She is a tall, luminescent goddess who dances with the hunters and communicates with them about the location of game, telling them which animals they may or may not take. She breathes upon those whom she favours. A painting from Ehorongue in Central Africa shows her with her nymphs, who have the spotted skins of antelope. In Mesopotamian myth, it is Sakkan who is the god of the animals, responsible for their fertility, while in the Amazon it is the dwarf, Desana who guards the life of animals. Shamans negotiate with him so that hunters may take game animals but human souls must agree to reincarnate as animals of the hunt.

The Celtic god, Cernunnos, with his stag's antlers, is a primal herdsman around whom all the animals flock for security. His role is found in the Wild Herdsman of the Welsh medieval story of Owein, in *The Lady of the Fountain*, which is itself based on pre-Christian myths. The Wild Herdsman sits under a tree and when he bangs his club upon the tree and brays aloud, all the animals come:

… as numerous as the stars in the sky, so that it was difficult to stand in the glade among them. There were serpents, dragons, and many animals whom he bade go and

The Element Encyclopedia of Magical Creatures

feed. Then they bowed their heads and did homage to him as their lord.

LOTAN

In Mesopotamian legend, the seven-headed dragon Lotan is the adversary of the god Baal, who finally kills it. Lotan represents the primordial chaos from which order is created. Like Leviathan and Tiamat, it surrounds the world.

LOU CARCOLH

In French folklore, Lou Carcolh is a giant mollusc-serpent that has hairy tentacles, a huge shell and leaves a slimy trail behind it. It lived under the town of Hastingue in the region of Les Landes in south-west France. Whoever went near Lou Carcolh became sucked into its cavern and eaten.

LUNG

The Lung (or Lung Wang) are the dragon kings of Chinese mythology who are the servants of the Yuanshi Tian Zong (the 'Celestial Ancient of the Primordial Beginnings'). In Taoist belief, there are many Lung who guard the five cardinal points, as well as celestial Lung who guard the heavens and those who patrol the four oceans of the world. Sometimes, the Lung have the body of carp, tiger's legs, eagle's talons, stag's horns. Each Lung has a pearl of wisdom in its mouth, while the fire and smoke issuing from its mouth are the power to release rain clouds.

LYRE BIRD

In Australian Aboriginal legend, the lyre bird with its beautiful tail feathers is the one who stood aloof from the battle between the animals at a great corroboree (gathering). The corroboree had been assembled to discuss the laws of marriage between animals, but they all fell out from one another. The result of this argument was a tremendous battle in which nobody won. It was decided that each species of animals would have its own language. Because the lyre bird tried to offer words of reconciliation and bring peace, it alone of all animals is able to imitate all the animals in its songs and dances.

The Element Encyclopedia of Magical Creatures

M

Mafdet

Mafdet appears in both Egyptian and Mesopotamian mythology. In Egyptian tradition, she is a panther goddess who is inimical to snakes and scorpions. A single scratch from her claws will kill a snake, and in tomb paintings the barbs of the king's harpoon are known as Mafdet's Claws. In one description, she is described as wearing braided locks, which probably refers to displaying the bodies of the creatures that she has killed.

Magaera

In Graeco-Roman tradition, Magaera is one of the Furies, monstrous beings who exact retribution from those who have perpetrated certain crimes, such as matricide or patricide, which remain unpunished by human laws. Her name means 'Envious Fury'.

Magpie

In the East, the magpie is known as the bird of joy and it brings good fortune to those who hear it; in the West, the same chattering is said to mean trouble between husband and wife, and the bird generally signifies ill omen and can bring disaster upon those who encounter it. Even to have a magpie landing on one's house is a sign of imminent death. In Europe, ancient folk traditions describe how the sight of a single magpie brings sorrow, while two together bring joy. In medieval bestiaries, the bird is said to represent the unseemly chatter of those who do not pay sufficient attention in Church, and is used as a symbol of the devil, its handsome black and white feathers representing vanity. In Norse mythology, the magpie is associated with witchcraft and is one of the forms believed to be taken by witches when they attend the Sabbat.

In the time before time began, when there was neither sun nor moon nor stars, the sky was fastened tightly to the Earth. But the Magpies grew tired of their cramped conditions and of the darkness in which they lived, so they decided that if they worked together and thrust at the roof they might be able to raise it above the Earth. Each bird found a stick, holding it firmly in beak or claw, and at a given signal all pressed their sticks against the firmament. At first, there was no movement, but as they strained their feet on the ground and pushed their sticks against the mass above them, there came a creaking and groaning and a crack of light showed on the near horizon. Finally, the sky began to move. The Magpies' feet left the ground, the air between earth and sky was filled with the beatings of thousands of wings. The higher it went the easier it became for the birds to move the sky. Once again, they made a concerted effort. No longer did the sky press upon them. It was floating in the air like a great cloud. Again they pressed upward and suddenly the sky split apart from end to end and light flooded into the world. The sky floated loose and became a pathway for the goddess of the sun and the god of the moon and all the starry beings that would one day live within it. The Magpies never forgot that moment when the sun first shone upon the world, and in memory of the event, each day they greet the new morning with their chattering song.

In Native American tradition, the magpie is a trickster, although in the Blackfoot story about how the Buffalo (*see* Bison) dances were to be danced, the magpie was the one who enabled the human wife of the buffalo to resurrect her father by finding a piece of his vertebrae, so that she might cover it with a bison-skin and sing her father back to life. In Australian aboriginal myth, the noisy Magpies were responsible for bringing light to the world.

Makara

The name Makara is given to more than one composite creature in the traditions of India, Indonesia and Thailand. The word itself simply means 'sea monster', but it has more than one incarnation in a variety of different forms. Some see it as a huge crab, others as part crocodile and part bird, or even more strangely as a deer with a fish's tail. On Hindu temples, it is found carved around doors and acts as a guardian to these sacred places. The gods Ganga and Varuna have both been depicted riding upon its back, as has Vishnu.

MALXAS

The name of the gemsbok who is represented in the Kalahari bushmen's gemsbok play, a hunting ceremony. Malxas is a playful gemsbok, sometimes peacefully grazing, sometimes wild and alert. He keeps hunting dogs at bay by stabbing his antlers towards them.

MAMALAMBO

The goddess of the rivers of Natal in south-east Africa, Mamalambo's name means 'The River Mother' and at times she appeared in the form of a snake. She was particularly helpful to those who brewed beer. In the old days, this was a job mainly undertaken by women; the following story, told to Jan Knappert and recorded in his book *African Mythology*, illustrates this.

One day a woman who ran the local beer shop decided she lacked customers, so she went to the bank of the river Umgeni, near Durban, and performed a ceremony to call upon the River Mother to bless her beer. She watched carefully and after a time found a piece of wood no bigger than a matchstick floating on the water. This she knew to be the River Mother. She took the piece of wood home and placed it in the bottom of the barrel in which she kept her beer. Then she made a fresh brew and poured it into the barrel. From that time onward, her shop was always full of customers and the legendary fame of her beer spread far and wide. This attracted the attention of the police, and since brewing beer without a licence was illegal, the police invaded the premises to search for the illicit brew. They found the barrel and opened it, but all they found was a long snake that hissed at them. It was Mamalambo, protecting the woman and her customers. When everyone returned after the police had left, the beer barrel was found to be full again and the drink even better than before.

MANABUSCH

Manabusch is the Great Hare in the Menominee Indian tradition of North

America. Manabusch was originally one of a pair of twins but the other died at birth, so his grandmother Nokomis put a wooden bowl over the surviving twin to protect it. When she looked under it later, it had become a white hare that she called Manabusch. His early adventures include the theft of fire that he stole to keep himself and his grandmother warm. He paddled eastward in his canoe until he came to a wigwam where an old man and his daughters gave him shelter. While they were busy, Manabusch stole a glowing brand from the fire and jumped into his canoe. They gave chase, but Manabusch came home running. The wind blew the brand into flame as he ran. Nokomis then gave the sacred flame in trust to Keneun, chief of the Thunderbirds. Manabusch's wolf brother, Moqwaoi, was pulled under a frozen lake and killed by the underworld spirits, the Anamagqkiu. In attempting to avenge him, the spirits raised the waters causing a great inundation from which the hare escaped only by making the tree he was hiding in grow larger. After the waters subsided, Manabusch asked the surviving animals to help him recreate the world, which he could do only if he had a grain of soil. Otter, Beaver and Mink all looked for one but perished in the attempt. Finally, it was Muskrat who brought the speck of earth to the Hare.

MANEKI NEKO

In Japanese folklore, this is a good-luck symbol that takes the form of a cat sitting on its haunches with one paw raised in a beckoning gesture. Japanese shopkeepers use it to lure customers into their shops.

MANIBOZHO

This is the name the Algonquin Indians of North America give to the Great Hare, who is both creator and trickster. (*See* Michabo *and* Manabusch.)

MANIPOGO

One of the many lake monsters similar to the famous Loch Ness Monster. This creature is described in the folklore of the native people living around Lake Manitoba, Canada. On 12 August 1962, two men who were fishing in this lake took a photograph of what they believe to be the Manipogo.

MANTA

A vicious sea monster from the folklore of the people of Chile. Described as a huge flat extent of skin, not unlike a flayed cow's hide, with eyes around its edge, four more eyes on top where a head would have been, tentacles and a tail with claws, the Manta lives in the ocean off the coast line of Chaloc, though it has been known occasionally to bask in the sun on the sands of the shoreline. So vast

The Element Encyclopedia of Magical Creatures

is it that when it returns to the water it may cause a storm. The Manta is almost certainly related to the Cuero, the name of which means 'hide' in Spanish. This creature was said to have originated from the folded skin of a donkey that fell into a river, opened out and began to consume anything and everything that came its way. Its favourite trick is to lure unsuspecting swimmers into the shallows then enfold them with its massive hide, sucking all the vitality and goodness from their bodies.

MANTICORE/MANTICORA

A hybrid monster referred to in the myths of Mesopotamia, Ethiopia and India. Also known as Martikhora, Mantiserra Memecoleous, Mancomorion and the Satyral, it was a favourite creature in the menagerie of beasts included in the bestiaries of medieval Europe. Its name comes from the Persian *mardkhora*, which means 'man-slayer', and has led some writers to suppose it may have been a man-eating tiger. Mentioned by a number of early classical writers, the earliest description is believed to have come from the writings of the Greek physician to Artaterxes Mnemon (404–359 BC), which was later transcribed by the Roman author Aelian in his book on animals. Pliny the Elder referred to this in his *Historia Naturalis* of AD 77; the description is worth quoting in full:

There is in India a wild beast, powerful, daring, as great as the largest lion, of a red colour like cinnabar, shaggy like a dog ...

Its face however is not that of a wild beast but of a man, and it has three rows of teeth set in its upper jaw and three in the lower; these are exceedingly sharp and larger than the fangs of a hound. Its ears also resemble a man's, except that they are larger and shaggy; its eyes are blue grey and they too are like a man's, but its feet and claws, you must know, are those of a lion. To the end of its tail is attached the sting of the Scorpion, and this might be over a cubit [18 inches] in length; and the tail has stings at intervals on either side. But the tip of the tail gives a fatal sting to anyone who encounters it, and death is immediate. If one pursues the beast it lets fly its stings, like arrows, sideways, and it can shoot a great distance; and when it discharges its stings straight ahead it bends its tail back; if however it shoots in a backwards direction, then it stretches its tail to its full extent. Any creature that the missile hits it kills; the Elephant alone it does not kill. These stings, which it shoots, are a foot long and the thickness of a bulrush. One writer asserts (and he says that the people of [Ancient] India confirm his words) that in the places where those things have been let fly others spring up, so that this evil produces a crop. According to the same writer, the Manticore devours human beings; indeed it will slaughter a great number; and it lies in wait not for a single man but would set upon two or even three men, and overcomes even that number. The Indians [of Asia] hunt the young of these animals while they are still without stings in their tails, which they then crush with a stone to prevent them from growing stings. The sound of their voice is as near as possible that of a trumpet.

The Element Encyclopedia of Magical Creatures

A recent, even more startling description comes from the French poet and novelist Gustave Flaubert, who spent time in the desert of Africa and heard of the Manticore there. In his *The Temptation of St Anthony*, the Manticore says of itself:

'The gleam of my scarlet hair mingles with the reflection of the great sands. I breathe through my nostrils the terror of solitudes. I spit forth plague. I devour armies when they venture into the desert. My claws are twisted like screws, my teeth shaped like saws, and my curving tail bristles with darts, that I broadcast right and left, before and behind.'

In the Middle Ages, the Manticore was frequently described in the bestiaries, most of which retained the description given by Aelian and Pliny more than 1,000 years earlier.

MANTIS

Among the bushmen of the Kalahari, Mantis is the provider of food and protector of human beings' material goods. He is a trickster figure, with a mantis's head and a man's body. He is married to the rock hyrax Dassie, and has an adopted daughter who is Porcupine. Mantis's sister is Blue Crane. He stole fire from Ostrich by making the bird stretch its neck to take some delicious plums from the treetop. As Ostrich stretched, it raised its wings to balance itself and that was when Mantis darted in and stole the fire that was hidden under the bird's wing. This was the first fire that helped bushmen cook food and make light in their shelters. Mantis also created the Eland.

MARI LWYD

The Mari Lwyd is a horse's skull decorated with ribbons and bells, which lies at the heart of an ancient ritual that the people of Glamorgan and Gwent in Wales still use to mark the passing of the dark days of midwinter. At this time of year, which was always a time of fire festivals, many ceremonies were performed throughout the world to encourage the return of the sun, when it dipped below the horizon for the longest period of time, causing many to believe it might never return. The Mari Lwyd was part of such a ceremony. Essentially, the parading of the skull around villages, with a variety of accompanying games, was intended to remind the sun that people were still alive and still awaiting its return. Although customs involving animal skulls in this way are widely known across the world, the Mari Lwyd, which is unique to Wales, is highly appropriate to a people who long ago declared the horse to be sacred. The processing of the Mari (which may still be seen at Llangynwyd, near Maesteg, every New Year's Day), carried by a group of chosen people, involves the arrival of the horse at the door of either a house or a pub, where they sing several verses of an ancient song. Then comes a battle of wits in which the people on one side of the door and those on the other exchange a series of challenges, insults and riddles, all of them in rhyme. At the end of this battle of wits and skill, which can last as long as the creativity of the two parties, the Mari enters with another song and is made welcome in the house. Towards the middle of the 19th century, the custom almost died out, being considered too pagan for the chapel-going Welsh, but it was revived in the 1920s and continues to this day.

Masalai

In Melanesian mythology, this is a term for animal spirits that occasionally become demons and can also take on the form of human beings. Some Masalai appear as men, some as women and some as children. Some are kind and help people, while others are vicious and do harm – and can even be cannibals. Masalai do not have a spirit world of their own; they just live in the bush or in old houses. Masalai men may appear to women in the form of hounds and mate with them, while the women may take on attractive physical shapes to seduce human men, whom they marry, and produce unusual or special children; some Masalai women appear in the form of cassowaries, and in that shape manage to attract men.

In the Manus Islands, they tell the tale of the popular hero Pokop who came across a fire on the path where he was walking, and decided to roast the fish he had just caught. Not knowing that the fire came from an invisible Masalai, who can produce flames from their behinds, when he finished, he threw the bones back into the fire. Suddenly the fire exploded, for the Masalai did not appreciate the fish bones. Pokop fled and the Masalai pursued him, wishing to devour him, but the hero was too smart and made good his escape.

Mat Chinoi

The titular leader of a tribe of nature spirits in the traditions of the Semang people of Malaysia. Similar to European fairies, they are small and inhabit flowers and trees in the forests of the area. Mat Chinoi looks like a huge snake, and within his enormous body are contained the female Chinoi – complete with fine headdresses and elaborate costumes. On the outside of his body is a male Chinoi called Halak Gihmal, who acts as guardian of the females.

Matangi

In Hindu tradition, Matangi is the ninth of the ten powers of transcendent knowledge that the Great Mother possesses. As Matangi, the goddess appears as an elephant who destroys all evil. After periods of evil, war and need, Matangi re-establishes the rule of peace, calm and prosperity. In her human form, Matangi takes the iconic form of a woman with three lotus eyes and a white crescent upon her garland. She shines like a blue lotus, representing a forest fire that consumes the habitations of demons. In her hands are a noose, a sword, a shield and an elephant hook.

MATSYA

Matsya is the first avatar or manifestation of the Hindu god, Vishnu. Matsya is the fish that saved the seventh lawgiver, Manu Satyavrata, the progenitor of the humans born since the flood. When Manu was brought water with which to make his ablutions, he found a fish in the bowl that asked for his protection, promising to rescue him from the coming flood. Matsya grew so great that he had to be kept in larger and larger vessels until only the sea would hold him. He was recognized by Manu as an incarnation of Vishnu so that when Matsya told the lawgiver to build a ship in which to store the plants, animals and sages who were to escape the flood, Manu did as he was told. The Hindu ark was then fastened to a rope attached to the great serpent Sesa-Naga who kept it safe while the inundating waters flowed unrestrained over the Earth. This serpent fought with the demon Hayagriva for the possession of the Vedas, which he had stolen from Brahma. The sacred scriptures were then given to Manu Satyavrata who then taught them to the human race that they might guide successive ages.

MAUTHE DHOOG

An infamous Black Dog said to haunt Peel Castle on the Isle of Man, England. It is variously described as the size of a calf with eyes like pewter plates, or as a spaniel with shaggy hair, and there are numerous accounts of people who have encountered this creature. One such tale speaks of a time in the 17th century when Peel Castle was occupied by military forces. A bored soldier on guard duty, having had a few drinks, bragged that he would search for the Mauthe Dhoog. His terrified cries brought his fellows to a corridor, where he was found lying face down, gibbering about the Dhoog. Soon afterwards he died. A similar fate befell a Methodist minister brought in to exorcize the creature. The 18th-century novelist Sir Walter Scott referred memorably to this incident in his poem 'The Lay of the Last Minstrel':

For he was speechless, ghastly, wan,
Like him of whom the story ran,
Who spoke the spectre-hound in Man.

MEDUSA

One of the Gorgons, three sisters from classical Greek mythology who were transformed into monsters by the goddess Athena after the sea god Poseidon had raped Medusa in a temple sacred to the goddess. They are described as looking like women but with leathery, bat-like wings, great tusks sticking out from a gaping mouth and snakes for hair; Medusa also has clawed hands made of brass. Any mortal who looked into her face was instantly turned to stone. The three were the children of Ceto and Phorcrys, the Old Man of the Sea, but unlike her sisters Euryale and Atheno, Medusa was a mortal and met her end at the hands of the hero Perseus, who beheaded her while she slept. From her spilled blood sprang the monstrous Chrysaor and the winged horse Pegasus. Though pursued by Medusa's sisters, Perseus escaped and eventually used the severed head to turn his enemies to stone.

Medusa's name means 'ruler' or 'queen', and the appearance of both her and her sisters as hideously ugly women probably derives from a similar monster, the Lamastu, found in Mesopotamian myth. Images of the Gorgons were especially popular as the guardians of temples and are found carved on pediments above the entrance to such buildings. During the 16th-century, it was still widely believed that Gorgons inhabited North Africa, where they had hidden, guarded by the Graeae.

Mehen

A cosmic serpent in the mythology of ancient Egypt, Mehen guards the boat in which the sun god Ra travels through the underworld. Ra was constantly under threat from the serpent Aapep as he journeyed in his sun boat through the night. Mehen set himself to protect Ra against this adversary.

Meh-The

A name for a type of Yeti mentioned in the beliefs of the Nepalese people from the Himalayas. There were three different kinds of Yeti, categorized according to height. The Yeh-The is the smallest, the Meh-The is the medium-sized one, and the Dzu-The is the largest.

Mehet-Weret

In Egyptian mythology, Mehet-Weret is the primordial cow goddess of the sky who is believed to be the mother of the sun god Ra. Her name means 'great flood' and she represents the waters of the heavens along which the sun boat passes. She is shown as a cow, adorned with the triple moon crown, lying down upon a reed mat with a flail across her shoulders as her badge of office. The scribe, Nebseni, makes this prayer to her: 'Strengthen me just as you have strengthened yourself and show yourself upon Earth, you who return and withdraw yourself and may your will be done.'

Mehturt

A great cosmic cow also identified with the goddess Hathor from Egyptian mythology. A sky goddess, Mehturt is

The Element Encyclopedia of Magical Creatures

sometimes depicted with the boat of the sun god Ra travelling along her belly as she straddles the Earth.

MELIAN NYMPHS

The Meliae or Melian Nymphs were the Ash Nymphs who were born from the blood that spurted when Uranus was castrated by Cronos in Greek mythology.

MELUSINE/MELISANDE

The origin of Melusine (also known as Melisande) is probably from the classical Greek Lamia. Both are described as having the body of a woman from the waist up, but that of a serpent below. Stories of Melusine began to appear in the folk traditions of medieval Europe from an early date. They were collected in the

King Elinus of Albany (an early name for Scotland), had recently lost his wife and sought relief from his sorrows in solitary hunting. One day he went to quench his thirst at a certain fountain, and as he approached it, he heard the sound of singing and found a most beautiful woman sitting beside the well. She was in fact a fairy woman named Pressina, and King Elinus at once fell deeply in love with her. She consented to marry him on the condition that he would not visit her during her confinement with any children that he begot upon her. In time, Pressina gave birth to three-daughters: Melusine, Melior and Palatina. Overjoyed by the news of the birth, the king forgot his promise and rushed to see his wife and children, finding her bathing them. She cried out that he had broken his word and, snatching up the babies, she vanished. She took refuge on a hidden island off the coast of France that could only be found by accident.

From the heights of this place, she could see the shores of Albany, and she showed it to her children every day, telling them that it was only because of their father's treachery that they were living in exile.

The children, naturally enough, became embittered against their father and resolved to revenge themselves upon him. Melusine took her two sisters and together they used magic to capture their father and all his wealth inside Mount Brandelois, or in a cave in Northumbria in England. Having done this they returned in triumph to their mother, who was much displeased, for she actually still loved Elinus deeply. She punished Melusine by turning her into a serpent from the waist down. This affliction was not constant, but came upon her from time to time, and would continue to do so until she met a man who would marry her on the condition that he never see her on a Saturday, and would keep that promise for ever.

The Element Encyclopedia of Magical Creatures

For years, Melusine wandered through France in search of such a man, until one day in the Forest of Colombiers near Poitiers she met the ruler of the area, Count Raymond of Lusignan, who agreed to marry her and honour the condition stipulated by her mother. They would have been completely happy but for the fact that every child born to them was deformed in some way. Raymond still loved his wife deeply but one of his cousins poisoned his mind with suggestions that these children were the offspring of another man, who Melusine visited on Saturdays when her husband was forbidden to see her. At length, Raymond could bear the suspicion no longer, and one Saturday night he hid and observed his wife emerging from her bath and saw that below the waist she was a serpent. He still loved her so much that he resolved to keep the secret and say nothing of what he had seen, even to her. But the secret could not be kept.

Some of their children were not only monstrous in appearance but also in character. One of them, Geoffrey, who was born with tusks, was particularly evil. One day, he quarrelled with his brother, and when the brother took refuge in the abbey of Melliers, he set fire to it and burnt it to the ground, along with his brother and 100 monks. When the dreadful news came to Melusine, she went to comfort her desolate husband, but in his grief he burst out: 'Get from my sight you pernicious snake! You have contaminated my children!' Melusine fainted at this; but when she revived she said: 'A curse is now upon me. I am condemned to leave this place and to fly through the air until the Day of Judgment. Until this castle falls I shall appear before the death of each lord of Lusignan, wailing and lamenting for the sorrows of the house.' She leapt from the window, where a print of her foot remained as long as the castle stood, and vanished from the sight of Count Raymond forever. After this she became the Banshee of the Lusignan family, and after the castle had fallen into ruin and the lands returned to the royal ownership, she appeared before the death of every King of France, until at last the castle of Lusignan was destroyed by fire, after which she was seen no more. Her descendants were a troubled tribe and the family died out in the 17th century.

14th-century *Chronicle of Melusine* by Jean D'Aras. Unusually, she is considered to have been one of the founders of the Lusignan family, one of the great noble families of medieval France. The story appears in an account written by the Dominican friar Stephen, who was himself of the House of Lusignan.

The Element Encyclopedia of Magical Creatures

MERMAID

Perhaps the most famous of the many magical creatures of the sea, the general character of a mermaid is well defined. According to these traditions, mermaids are like beautiful maidens from the waist up, with the tail of a fish below. They carry a comb and a mirror and are often to be seen combing their long, beautiful hair and singing with irresistible sweetness on a rock beside a sea. Shakespeare describes this perfectly, when Oberon in *A Midsummer Night's Dream*, says:

> *Once I sat upon a promontory*
> *And heard a Mermaid on a dolphin's back*
> *Uttering such dulcet and harmonious breath*
> *That the rude sea grew civil at her song*
> *And certain stars shot madly from their spheres*
> *To hear the sea maid's music*

But mermaids have a darker side. They lure young men to their death and their appearance presages storms and disasters. According to such beliefs, mermaids not only bring misfortunes but also provoke them, and they avidly seek human lives, either drowning men or devouring them. They are said to be born without souls, and the only way they may obtain one is by marrying a human. In some of the earliest Celtic descriptions, they are sometimes monstrous in size, such as the one recorded in the medieval Irish Annals of the Four Masters, who was 160 ft in length, with hair 18 ft long, fingers 3 ft long and a 7-ft nose! She was believed to have been cast ashore in AD 87.

Several stories exist describing mermaids who were caught and held to ransom for the sake of the wishes they could grant and the knowledge they could impart. None ever failed to remain true to their bargains, though the wishes granted by mermaids are often tricky and dangerous. In Scotland and Ireland the question of whether mermaids, like fairies, could ever find salvation was often raised. It was considered unlikely, but in Ireland there was one mermaid, named Liban, who is described as having died and entered heaven – though it should be said that she was not born a mermaid but was transformed into that form.

In general, mermaids are said to live in an undersea world of great splendour and richness, but they may assume human form, especially to visit markets and fairs. They often lure mariners to their destruction, and are said to gather the souls of the drowned in cages. There are many different explanations of the origin of the mermaid. In early Irish tradition, they are said to be pagan women transformed into that shape by St Patrick. One middle European folktale says they are Pharaoh's children, drowned in the Red Sea when Moses parted the waters. But the most usual and widely accepted tradition concerns their evolution from gods and goddesses of the early religions of the world, who were themselves represented as half fish, half human in form. Among these are the Chaedean Oannes and Philistine Dagon as well

The Element Encyclopedia of Magical Creatures

as the Syrian Atargatis, all of whom are represented as half fish. The mythographer Robert Graves in his seminal book *The White Goddess* associated the mermaid with the love goddesses Marian and Aphrodite, both born of the sea.

Medieval belief in the mermaid was widespread and substantial, as a story from Holland dating from about 1430 shows. It tells how, when the dikes near Edam broke during a storm, some young girls found a mermaid floundering in shallow water. They got her into the boat, took her home, dressed her in women's clothes and allowed her to live with them. She was said to be able to weave and spin with extraordinary skill, but never learned to speak. In 1560, some fishermen in deep water off the coast of Ceylon caught several mermaids in their nets, which were afterwards dissected by a learned physician. He reported that internally and externally they were constructed like human beings.

In Japanese tradition, Ningyo is the name given to the mermaid who wards off bad luck and protects the land with peace. However, mermaids have often been known to lead people astray, but getting hold of the cap or belt of a mermaid gives one power over her. The marriage of a mortal man to a mermaid is widely reported in folklore, and the descendants of such unions are still believed to live in remote parts of the world. Such people are usually considered to be under some kind of curse, which may prevent them from sleeping since they constantly hear the sound of the sea in their ears. One of the most famous stories about mermaids is Hans Christian Andersen's *The Little Mermaid*, in which a mermaid falls in love with a handsome prince, voluntarily assumes human shape in order to gain an immortal soul and to be near him for ever, but is doomed never to speak. When the prince finally marries a human princess, her heart breaks. Her statue is to be seen in the harbour at Copenhagen.

Belief in mermaids was still widespread in the coastal areas of Britain in the 19th century. As recently as 1947, an 80-year-old fisherman from the Isle of Muck in the Inner Hebrides claimed to have seen a mermaid near the shore, combing her hair. The word mermaid may derive from the French for sea, or be a corruption of the Saxon *merrymaid*. In the British Isles, where mermaids have always been common, she has many different regional variations in her name. She is known as Ben Varrey, Clytie, Gwyndwy, Mari Morgan, Roane and Selkie. Despite their widespread appearance in folklore the world over, their description and character varies very little, suggesting that belief in these extraordinary creatures has been present for a very long time. (*See also* Merrow.)

MERMEN

Mermen are, on the whole, less attractive than their female counterparts, not only in appearance but also by nature. Generally speaking, they do not come ashore or court mortal women and father their children. They often seem to personify stormy seas, and it is they who raise storms and wreck ships if one of their kind is hurt in any way. They were considered rough husbands and even capable of eating their own young if they were hungry enough. The Scandinavian merman or Havmand is described as a handsome creature with a green or black beard, living on cliffs as well as in the sea.

'The Tale of Abdullah and Abdullah' in the *Arabian Nights* tells the story of a poor fisherman, Abdullah, and his benefactor, a merman who bears the same name. Abdullah the fisherman becomes rich through his association with Abdullah the merman and visits the undersea realm, where he is an object of some amusement because he has a bottom instead of a tail! A Syrian story tells of a merman married to a human wife, whose son knows both the language of the earth and the sea. But probably the best-known motif in folktale and ballad tells of the merman abandoned by his human wife, popularized in Matthew Arnold's poem 'The Forsaken Merman'.

Like the mermaid, the origin of the merman goes back a very long way. Figures with the head, arms and torso of a man and the lower body and tail of a fish are found in most periods of Mesopotamian and Babylonian history. To the Syrians, the creature was known simply as *kulullu* ('Fish-man'), and together with Lion-man and Scorpion-man forms a group of human-animal hybrids common to this tradition. A possible origin of the merman is said to be the bull walrus, whose appearance was widely reported by fishermen in the northern oceanic waters.

Another theory of their origin comes from the people of the Pacific Rim, in whose myth, the sea god Tangaroa is often represented as a giant fish giving birth to all the creatures of the sea, including mermen and mermaids. In this tradition, it is from these beings that humanity sprang, and people are really fish who have lost their fish-like appearance and qualities.

The medieval historian Gervais of Tilbury (1211) reported that there were many mermen in the waters around the coast of Britain. In Scotland and throughout Scandinavia they may appear as horses, while in the Mediterranean world they are specifically half-man, half-fish. In 1723, a Royal Commission was set up in Denmark to disprove the existence of mermen and mermaids, but, to their surprise, they encountered a merman near the Faroe Isles with deep-set eyes and a black beard. Among the Norse people, the Margygr were horrible to look upon, with squat features and piercing eyes, and in Greenland they were associated with the Kraken.

The Samish people of north-western America tell the story of Ko-kwal-alwoot, who was gathering shellfish from the sea when a hand emerged from the waters and clasped hers. At first, she was afraid and ran away, but when the same thing happened several more times she began to speak with the unseen owner of the hand, whose gentle voice she learned to love. After a time, the owner of the hand, who was a merman, asked her to marry him. He described the wonders of his kingdom beneath the waves and Ko-kwal-alwoot told him she was happy to become his wife. To begin with, her father would not give his consent, but the merman told him that until he agreed his tribe would get neither food nor water from the sea. And, sure enough, the salmon stopped coming into waters where the Samish fished, and the river became salt and undrinkable. Finally, Ko-kwal-alwoot's father consented to allow his daughter to marry, but he asked that she be allowed to return every year for one day to see her family. The merman agreed to this and Ko-kwal-alwoot went into the sea that very day. Each year thereafter, she returned to the land, but each time she looked less and less human. Barnacles began to grow upon her hands and face and she seemed less happy on land. At last, her father released her husband from his promise and Ko-kwal-alwoot came no more. But it is said that she still watches over the lands of the Samish and ensures that there is always plenty of good salmon to catch.

MERROW

The Irish equivalent of the mermaid, and like them they are beautiful, though they have fish tails and are webbed between their fingers. They are greatly feared because they announce the coming of storms, but are considered gentler than most mermaids and often fall in love with mortal men. The offspring of these marriages are sometimes said to be covered with scales, just as the descendants of the Seal People are said to have webbed fingers. Sometimes they come ashore in the form of small hornless cattle but, in their proper shape, they wear red, feathered caps, by means of which they are able to travel underwater. If these are stolen, they cannot return to the sea again in much the same way as Selkies cannot if their skins are stolen. Although the female merrow is beautiful, the males are very ugly, with green faces and bodies, sharp red noses and piggy eyes. They seem, however, to be generally pleasant in character.

The Element Encyclopedia of Magical Creatures

MERWER

A giant sacred bull from the mythology of ancient Egypt. Also known by the Greek name Meroe, this mighty being, sacred to the sun god Ra, was represented as either black or white in colour. Like many such sacred animals, it was represented in the sphere of Earth by a real animal, which was mummified and kept in the precincts of a temple, such as the one that could once have been seen at Heliopolis.

MESHKENABEC

Also known as Misikinebek or Mashenomak, Meshkenabec is a vast lake serpent, with plate-sized scales, a scarlet head and eyes that radiated red light. This creature was greatly feared and respected by the Woodlands Indians of North America. It lived in a deep lake with many smaller serpentine attendants, and was eventually defeated and killed by the hero Manabozho who stopped it swallowing people by becoming its victim himself. While inside the serpent, he danced a war-dance and stabbed it in the heart before hacking his way out, allowing other victims to escape with him.

MICHABO

Among the Algonquin Indians of North America, the Great Hare, Manibozho or Michabo, is the great creator and trickster. As Michabo Ovisaketchak, 'the Great Hare Who Created the Earth', he is the original hunter whose footsteps measured eight leagues. He was so big that the Great Lakes that border Canada and United States were the beaver dams he made. By watching the spider spin her web to catch flies, he invented the art of netting so that fish could be caught. He bequeathed many signs and charms that help in the hunt. In the autumn, he settles down to his winter hibernation by smoking a great pipe, the smoke of which becomes the clouds and mist that fill that season.

MIDGARDSORMR/ MIDGARD SERPENT

A monstrous serpent from Norse and Teutonic Mythology that lives in the primeval ocean surrounding the world, and that winds itself around the world. The name can be translated to mean either 'Midgard Serpent' or 'World Serpent'. It is described as the offspring of a union between the trickster god Loki and the giantess Angrboda. Its siblings are Hel, the goddess of the underworld, and the gigantic wolf Fenris, who was bound in chains by the gods until the last battle of Ragnarok. When the Midgard Serpent was born, the gods were so horrified by its appearance that they threw it into the ocean, where it grew until it was large enough to encircle the whole of Middle Earth, and the arches of its coils, when it lifted them above the ocean, were seen as rainbows. Many of the gods feared the World Serpent and had encounters with it, particularly the thunder god Thor. One day, the god

The Element Encyclopedia of Magical Creatures

accepted the challenge to a fishing contest from the giant Hymir. The agreement was that whoever caught the largest fish would be the winner. The giant caught two whales, but Thor, who had determined to use the heads of two of his prize bulls as bait, caught the Midgard Serpent. According to some versions of the story, when Hymir saw the terrible head emerging from the water he threw himself from the boat and was drowned; in others, the giant cut Thor's fishing line and the two of them made good their escape and returned to land to enjoy a feast of whale meat. In another story, Thor was challenged by one of the Frost Giants to prove his strength by picking up a certain cat. To his astonishment, he found that he could not do so, and at that Loki revealed that he had cast a glamour over the Midgard Serpent so that it appeared in the shape of a cat. Thor had been trying to lift the giant serpent, which was beyond even his strength. In the myth of Ragnarok, the end of the world, it is said that the Midgard Serpent will rise up from the ocean, bringing devastation in its wake. At this time, Thor will meet the monster in battle and the two will slay each other.

MIHOS

The lion god from ancient Egyptian mythology. Described as the son of the cat goddess Bastet. His chief centre of worship was at Leontopolis (modern Tell el-Muqdam) in Lower Egypt on the Eastern delta. A temple dedicated to him was erected at Bubastis, a place sacred to his mother. To the ancient Greeks, he was known as Miysis.

MILCHAM

Jewish legend speaks of the Phoenix as the Milcham. When Eve had eaten of the forbidden fruit of the Tree of Knowledge, she conceived an envy of the animals' sinless nature and she enticed all to eat of the tree. Every animal except the Milcham obeyed her and it was rewarded by the gift of immortality. It was allowed to live in a walled city in an inviolate condition for 1,000 years. When they pass away, a fire consumes the Milcham, which then expires, leaving only an egg. This is the start of another generation, which also lives for a cycle of 1,000 years.

MINHOCAO

During the late 19th century, a number of sightings were recorded in numerous parts of South America of a creature resembling a giant earthworm. One account, dating from the 1840s near the Rio dos Papaganaios in the Parana State, described a woman who went to draw water from a well one morning. She saw, a short distance off, an animal that she described as being as large as a house moving along the ground. In the same district, a young man later saw a huge pine suddenly overturn, the surrounding earth begin to move, and an enormous, black worm-like animal appear, about 80 ft long with two horns on its head. A report in the *American Journal of Science* from the period mentions instances where livestock had been captured by one of these creatures and dragged under the water, suggesting that it was actually a type of water serpent. The name Minhocao comes from the Portuguese word *minhocar* (earthworm). There is also a similar creature from the folklore of Nicaragua called Sterpe, which was described as being similar to a huge snake. Various suggestions have been put forward by cryptozoologists, including the suggestion that the Minhocao was a surviving Glyptodont (a prehistoric South American animal which resembled an armadillo); while others have suggested a giant Caecilian, a worm-like amphibian native to Mexico and South America. No sightings have been reported since 1870.

MINK

In the myths of the Menominee Indians of North America, the Anamagqkiu spirits caused a great flood, destroying the world. After the waters subsided, Manabusch the Great Hare asked the surviving animals to help him recreate the world, which he could do only if he had a grain of soil. Mink, Otter and Beaver all looked for one but perished. Although Mink did his best, it was Muskrat who finally brought the speck of earth to the Hare.

MINOTAUR

According to the myth, Pasiphae, the wife of King Minos of Crete, evinced an unnatural desire to mate with a great white bull sacred to Poseidon, the god of the sea, or possibly the god in this form. She employed the Greek craftsman Daedalus to create an artificial cow's body into which she climbed, thus enabling herself to be enjoyed by the bull. The result of this coupling was that she brought forth a bull-headed child, who was named Asterion, but who is best known today as the Minotaur. The second part of the myth describes how Daedalus built a great maze beneath the court of Minos in which the monster was placed. Because he had within him the blood of a god, he was not killed but rather placated with human sacrifices, which were sent into the maze to be consumed by the monster.

At this time, Crete exercised enormous power in the Mediterranean world, and received tribute from the city-state of Athens. This tribute took the form of seven young boys and girls who were sent to the island every seventh year to be sacrificed to the Minotaur. This continued for a number of years, until the Athenian hero Theseus substituted himself for one of the tributes. Once in Crete, he was befriended by the King's daughter, Ariadne, who undertook to help him destroy the Minotaur. She gave him a ball of red twine that he could unwind behind him as he threaded the passageways of the maze beneath the court, and use it to find his way out again. In the maze, Theseus encountered the

Minotaur and slew him. He then escaped from Crete with the Princess Ariadne, who he later abandoned on the island of Naxos.

Behind this myth lie threads of history. Bulls seem to have been worshipped in Crete from an early time, and young men and women learnt the difficult and dangerous art of bull leaping, which entailed grasping the horns of the animal and somersaulting over its back. Minos himself seems to have been a legendary figure, the son of Zeus and Europa, whom Zeus carried to Crete from Tyr or Sidon in the shape of a bull. He is described as living three generations before the war with Troy and the island's Bronze Age civilization was named Minoan after him. Underlying the whole myth is the suggestion of a Bronze Age cult of Zeus as bull or perhaps the worship of Poseidon in that shape. In recent years, the artist Michael Ayrton immortalized the Minotaur in a series of astonishing bronze sculptures, paintings and etchings; and explored the myth unforgettably in his novel *The Maze Maker*. The novelist Mary Renault wrote two bestselling novels, *The King Must Die* and *The Bull From the Sea*, which explore the story of Theseus and the minotaur in great depth and detail.

MISHIPIZHIW

This water monster, from the traditions of the Ojibwa and Algonquin peoples of North America, has the body of a great cat with a saw-toothed ridge along its back extending to a long and sinuous tail with which it captures its victims. It is also said to raise fierce storms on the surface of the water by churning them with its tail. Accounts of the Mishipizhiw – also known as the Mitchipissy – survive from as early as the 17th century, and an early photograph of Lake Superior, dating from 1850, shows an unexplained bow wave streaking through the water that has been attributed to the Mishipizhiw.

MISIGANABIC

This vast serpent, described by the Algonquin people of North America, is at least 30 ft in length and shines in a multitude of colours when it rises to the surface. It has a head that resembles that of a horse and for this reason is sometimes called the Horse-Head Serpent. Not based in any one place, it has been sighted in the waters of the Blue Sea Lakes, the Cedar Lakes, Lake Bitobi, Lake Deschenes, Lake Desert, Lake Pocknock and Lake Trente-et-un-Milles. Although it is considered bad luck and to presage death if one looks upon Misiganabic, the creature is also greatly respected since it cleans the waters of the lakes.

MNEVIS

A great bull associated with the cult of the Sun in the mythology of ancient Egypt. Originally an autonomous bull god, Mnevis (or Merwer) became associated with the cult of Ra. The bull's hide is always white or black and he wears the Sun Disc between his horns. At Heliopolis, where his cult was most powerfully established, the cow goddess Hesat was known as his mother. The sacred bull was seen as an earthly representative of the sun god, acting as a herald for divine communications between the god and the priests who served him. Mnevis was also an intermediary for the interpretation of oracles, a phenomenon of Egyptian religion that was particularly apparent in later dynasties. The Heliopolitan solar bull was one of the few gods to survive the wholesale reinvention of religion by the pharaoh Akhenaten. According to an inscription at Heliopolis, the pharaoh prepared a special burial place, which has as yet to be discovered, and a bull was kept at this site as a living representative of the god.

Taiowa, the Creator, formed his representative Sotuknang and ordered him to make the universe. Sotuknang made water, land and air, and then the First World. Into this world he placed Kokyangwuti, Spider Woman, who created the twins Poqanghoya and Palongawhoya. These two made the earth, the mountains, the rivers and the seas and helped to keep them in good order. Then Kokyangwuti made all living things, including mankind. But, after a time, men grew disobedient and listened to the trickster Mochni and to Kato-Ya the Snake. As a result, the First World was destroyed by fire along with the men who had been disobedient, although some were permitted to survive beneath the earth, from where they made a long and arduous journey back to the surface many ages later to begin the Fourth World.

MOCHNI

Mochni was the Mockingbird who plays a part in the creation myths of the Hopi people of Arizona in North America.

MOEHAU

A large hairy humanoid creature with bony fingers, similar to Bigfoot and the Yeti but native to New Zealand. According to the Maori people, these creatures arrived at a time before recorded history. They lived on the South Island in the mountain regions where they were known as the Moeroero, while those that lived in the interior of the island were known as Maero. The combination of these two names produced Moehau and this gave rise to a spate of legends. Sightings of the creature were reported from the 1850s onwards, but belief in the creature seems to have diminished after reports of an escaped gorilla from a ship moored off the coast in the 1920s. In more recent times, the story has become complicated by the addition of rumours of a red-haired people living in a cave on Mount Moehau, known locally as the Coromandel Man, though actual bones or traces of this creature have not as yet been produced. As with the Yeti and Bigfoot, evidence to support the existence of this creature remains speculative.

MOHIRIIKKWCHEP

Japanese mythology describes this creature as a gigantic fish whose name may be translated as 'World Backbone Trout'. It was one of the first beings to be created and it still supports the world upon its back. However, it is so vast that when it moves it sends shock waves through the earth above it. For this reason, it has to be kept secure in the mud beneath the oceans. Two sea gods usually perform this task but every now and then it wriggles free, and causes earthquakes and tsunamis until it is brought back under control.

MOKO

The Great Lizard or Lizard King in the mythology of the Mangarian peoples of the South Pacific. Moko was half man, half lizard in appearance, but had many human descendants, including the great hero Ngaru, who was his grandson and who he constantly protected with his magic.

MOLE

In the West, the mole is synonymous with blindness and can also represent misanthropy. As an underground dweller, it is considered to be in touch with the powers of the underworld. Among the native people of North America, the mole is regarded as a guardian and master of the lower regions and is known as 'stout of heart and strong of will'. For the Ainu people of Japan, the mole was originally a deity who came from heaven and defeated the Great Demon, finally rolling it into a fire where the demon was burnt to ashes. However, since these ashes were the remains of supernatural beings, they still had life in them and from them came the fox and the cat, who are said to be of the same family and both to have demonic natures.

The Element Encyclopedia of Magical Creatures

MOLIONIDS

In Graeco-Roman mythology, these monstrous twins were the children of the nymph Molione by the sea god Poseidon/Neptune. They were hatched from a silver egg. The earliest form of their legend describes them as separate beings named Cteatus and Eurytus. Later myths describe them with a single body with two heads, four arms and four legs. They fought on the side of their uncle Augeas in his war with the hero Hercules and were finally killed by him at Cleonae.

MONKEY

Perhaps because of its semi-human form and wild nature, the monkey is one of the most widely featured animals in the mythologies of those countries that form its natural habitat. Monkeys have a reputation for cleverness because they resemble wise old men; this is why, in myth, the monkey always beats the crocodile. However, the turtle is wiser than the monkey, because he is older, so he always wins when they contend.

According to the myths of the Tagalog people in the Phillipines, the god Bathala was the only living being in the world. Feeling lonely, he decided to make some friends. He went down to Earth to fetch some clay, but the ground was bone dry, so he ordered the rain to fall. Then Bathala created mountains, rivers, plants, trees, animals and birds. Finally, he decided to make man, but when he had almost finished shaping the clay, the lump slipped from his hand. He held on to it by the lowest end of its back but this part stretched into a rope of clay. The lump fell into a tree and stayed there. Bathala said: 'You will become a monkey and live in the trees forever.' The rope of clay became the monkey's tail. Bathala then made man.

In the mythology of the Cameroons in Africa, the story is told that there was once a man who lived in the forest with his wife and baby daughter. He made a large banana garden so they had plenty of food. One day, thirteen hungry monkeys who lived in the forest came to the house to beg for some bananas. The man gave them willingly, so the monkeys came back every day. When they saw the lovely young girl, they stole her as well, rushing into the trees with her. The man saw what happened but he was too late to stop them. He went to consult a great diviner, who said, 'The monkeys are all females and childless, so they long for a baby. That is why they took yours. There is only one way to get your daughter back and that is by becoming a monkey yourself and winning their confidence. It will take you at least a year.' And he gave the man a bag containing the medicine to turn him into a monkey and back again.

The man took the first medicine, became a monkey, climbed a tree and joined the female monkeys, one of whom was nursing his daughter. He soon won their confidence and brought them bananas from his own garden since they no longer dared to go near it. The man learned the language of the monkeys and heard them say that all they wanted was to marry him. So he married them, and in due course all thirteen gave birth. Now they were all busy nursing and trusted him to feed his own daughter. One hot afternoon when they were dozing, he ran away home with his daughter, and resumed his normal shape and his old life. A year later, his wife gave him a son. The monkeys then reappeared and threatened to steal his son unless he returned to the trees with them. This he did – and soon all the monkeys had babies again. This happened several times until a new race was born – the chimpanzee.

Hanuman is the Hindu monkey god whose statue appears in Indian gymnasiums as the patron of speed, agility and strength. A similar connection is made in China where the monkey bodyguard of the Buddhist monk, Hsuen Tsang, used many subtle movements to defend his master. These motions developed into the Kung Fu martial arts technique of the Ta Sheng Man School.

In Thai mythology, the Buddha was a monkey in a previous existence, helping fellow animals or poor, misguided people on their way to salvation. The three wise monkeys are often depicted in Japanese art and are well known in the West. What is not so widely known is that each of them has a name. Mizaru has his hands over his eyes, Kikazaru covers his ears and Iwazaru has his hands on his mouth. In Western culture, they appear as fools, since Westerners want to know everything – especially if it is dangerous or bad. Buddhists, however, are neither afraid nor interested in gossip or any other news. They hope to keep their minds pure, free from slander, seduction and desire.

In Borneo, there is an island of monkeys, who are believed to be the souls of people lost in the jungle. The Bahau people in central Borneo believe that the souls of the dead migrate into grey monkeys, and therefore they eat these creatures only in times of great necessity. In Mali, the monkey's propensity for tricks and naughtiness is seen as evidence that the chimpanzee spirit Ngofariman holds sway. In Mayan culture in South America, the god of the North Star is portrayed with a monkey's head, and there were monkey deities depicted in ancient Peruvian art, sometimes with human heads and limbs. In Christian symbolism, the monkey represents trickery, vanity and luxury; it can also be associated with the devil and is represented as such in the medieval bestiaries, where it typifies cunning and hypocrisy, deviousness and conceit.

MOON BIRD

A Japanese fisherman once found a robe of white feathers on the beach. No sooner had he picked it up than a beautiful shining girl emerged from the sea, begging him to restore her property. For, she said, 'Without my plumage, I cannot go back to my home in the sky. If you give it back to me, I will sing and dance for you.' The fishermen took pity on her and returned her lovely robe of feathers. She put them on, took up her lute, and sang a hymn to the moon, where she had her palace. Gradually, as she danced, she rose up into the sky, where she unfolded her white wings and flew away towards the moon.

MOQWAOI

In Menominee Indian legend, Moqwaoi is the Wolf brother of the Great Hare, Manabusch. One day he walked out onto a frozen lake and was pulled under the ice by Anamakiu, an underworld spirit. Manabusch mourned for his brother for four days, but on the fifth, Moqwaoi's ghost visited him and told him to make a great fire that would guide the dead to their new home, and to keep them warm on their journey. Manabusch's attempt to revenge the death of his brother led to a great inundation that flooded the world.

Monsters

What exactly constitutes a monster differs according to who is making the definition. Many of the creatures described in this book could be called monstrous, but this may simply mean that they are large, whereas the implication of the word 'monster' is that the subject in question is hideously deformed. Certainly, fascination with such creatures has been with us for a long time, as witnessed by the number of descriptions of strange beasts that are to be found dating back to the earliest times. Most of these descriptions revolve around the idea that these creatures are aberrations of nature, malformed beings that have no place in creation. In ancient mythologies, there were many composite creatures, part humanoid, part animal or bird. In Babylonian mythology, for example, the eagle represented the goodness of nature, while other winged creatures such as the dragon, the Griffin, the Hippogriff and the Chimaera represented the forces of evil and destruction. In classical mythology, creatures such as the centaurs, satyrs and the Minotaur could be perceived as either good or evil.

In earlier times, freakish combinations of creatures, the kind of hybrids listed in bestiaries – including such strange monsters as Hydra, Fastitocalon, Sphinx and Ichneumon – were accepted as part of Creation. Monsters were everywhere – on land, in the waters and in the air – embodying all facets of the natural world. In some instances such creatures were regarded as signs from the Creator, sometimes of natural disasters to come. The Babylonian priest Berosus wrote:

There was a time they say when all was water and darkness, and these gave birth and habitation to monstrous animals of mixed form and species. For there were men with two wings, others with four, and some again with double faces. Some had the horns of goats, some their legs, and some the legs of horses and the fore-parts of men, like the Hippocentaurs. There were bulls with human heads, dogs with four bodies ending in fishes, horses with dogs' heads, and men and other creatures with the heads and bodies of horses and the tails of fishes, and a number of animals whose bodies were a monstrous compound of the dissimilar parts of beasts of various kinds.

Together with these were fishes, reptiles, serpents and other creatures, which by reciprocal translation of the parts of one another, became all portentously deformed.

Among the native peoples of North America, these creatures tended towards cannibalistic ogres, flying heads or giants, or else they were representations of the ordinary world seen through a darkened glass. For example, Burr Woman, an old woman who sits on the hero's back and cannot be dislodged; Sucking Monster, a giant who ingests his victims; Pot Tilter, an old woman who has a pot attached to her back that sucks people in; and the Cliff Ogre, a giantess who kicks people over a cliff to be eaten by her young.

Wherever one looks throughout the world, there are creatures of this kind – perhaps dreams, perhaps arising from our deepest levels of unconsciousness, or representations of our most profound fears. Among the most popular stories nowadays are those which deal with such monsters as Dracula, Frankenstein's Monster, the Werewolf and King Kong, all of whom are modern examples of monsters that have seized our imagination and continue to fascinate us.

MORAG

A creature similar in type to the Loch Ness Monster, which inhabits Scotland's Loch Morar. The name Morag comes from the Gaelic word *mhorag*, meaning 'spirit of the lake'. The Morag is described as 25–30 ft in length, reptilian or serpentine in appearance, brown in colour, with three humps. A number of sightings have been reported since 1887, one of the most famous being that of two men, Duncan McDonnell and William Simpson, who were fishing in the loch in August 1969. Duncan McDonnell said afterwards, 'I heard a splashing or disturbance in the water astern of us. I looked up, and about 20 yards behind us this creature was coming directly after us in our wake. It took only a matter of seconds to catch up on us. It grazed the side of the boat.' Simpson then grabbed his rifle and fired at the creature, which sank from view.

MORGENS

Also known as Mari Morgens, Mary Morgens, Sea Morgens or Morganezed, these are Breton water fairies or mermaids which lure sailors to join them in their underwater palaces. One particular Sea Morgen, called Dahut, was responsible for the destruction of the city of Ys, which sank beneath the sea after she raised a great storm. The Morgen is ever young and seductive. She sleeps by day in an under-water grotto, rising at night to sit on the rocks along the shoreline. Sitting in the

The English folklorist Ruth Tongue was told a story in Cornwall in 1916 about a fisherman who heard singing coming from St Audrie's Bay and went to investigate. Though he tried to be quiet, the Morgens heard him coming and fled back to the sea. In their haste, they left behind a baby, and the fisherman who had recently lost a child took her home and adopted it. The man's wife found that she could never get the baby's hair dry, even in the sun. All went well for a time, and the girl grew up, but she spent a great deal of time paddling in every pond and stream in the area. Then one day a nosy neighbour told her that girls should dry their hair like good Christians. At that moment a strange song was heard coming from the distance. 'Whatever is that?' asked the neighbour. 'That is my song,' replied the girl. 'It calls to me. There will be a storm tonight.' Of course, the neighbour cried out that the girl must be a witch and ran to rouse the people to drive her away. The girl ran away from them, laughing because they could not keep up with her. She ran down to the sea and out onto the rocks. A great wave swept her into the water and she was never seen again.

moonlight, she combs her hair with a golden comb, singing a song whose charm is irresistible. Any sailor who hears it is doomed, for if she touches him the man will die – the frustrated Morgen is left clutching a corpse, her passionate nature unfulfilled, while the touch of her hand condemns the man's soul to wander eternally through the sea without comfort.

MORRIGAN

The Morrigan, whose name means 'Great Queen', was the chief goddess of war, magic and shapeshifting. As a goddess of victory, she was a great ally of the Tuatha de Danaan during their struggle against the Fomorians. She sealed this pact by making love with the great god Dagda at the feast of Samhain (Hallowe'en) over the river Uinnius, with one foot on either bank of the river. When the Fomorians were finally overcome, it was she who proclaimed the victory and prophesied the future, as well as announcing the peace:

'Peace up to heaven,
Heaven over earth,
Earth under heaven.
Peace in everyone!'

The Morrigan was said to live in a cave at Cruachan in Co. Roscommon. She was an inveterate shapeshifter. Drawn by the Ulster hero's great valour, she attempted to seduce Cuchulainn, coming to him in the form of a lovely young woman, but he told her that he had no time for a dalliance. During his time of greatest peril, the Morrigan then returned to him in the forms of an eel, a wolf and red heifer. Cuchulainn fought these beasts, breaking the eel's ribs, putting out the wolf's eye and breaking the heifer's leg. Then the Morrigan returned to him in the form of an old woman with all these injuries upon her and tricked him into healing her by begging three blessings from him. Bound by his warrior's oath and his many geis (taboos), Cuchulainn gave the old woman his blessings. But he did not fend her off forever. When he came to his death, Cuchulainn bound himself to a pillar stone determined to deny his enemies to the last. As he expired, the Morrigan came down to feed upon him in the form of a raven.

MORRIGNA

The Morrigna are a triad of Irish goddesses who physically cleanse the battlefield of carrion but they also, like the Valkyries, are interested in the valorous souls of those who have been slain in battle. They are called Badb, Morrigan and Nemain, and they often take the form of crows or ravens. They were all born of the great Earth goddess Ernmas.

MOTHMAN

A bizarre creature reported in the area of West Virginia around Point Pleasant and Salem. Described as looking like a brown-skinned man with wings, it was apparently first sighted on 12 November

The Element Encyclopedia of Magical Creatures

1966 near to the town of Clendenin. Five men digging a grave in the local cemetery saw the creature take off from some nearby trees. A few days later a couple driving along the road near Point Pleasant saw what appeared to be a man, maybe 6 ft tall, with deep wings folded against its back; months later they saw the same creature on a hillside above the road: it spread its wings and rose into the air and followed them, keeping pace with their car for some miles. Another sighting, took place some weeks after this outside a house in Salem. The owner was watching TV when he heard a loud whining sound outside, followed by the howling of his dog. He went outside to find out what was going on, only to see two huge red circles that looked like eyes or bicycle reflectors. Returning to the house for his gun, he emerged to find that his dog had vanished together with the creature. The dog was never seen again. As word of these reports spread, so the creature was named Mothman from a character in the popular *Batman* television series. Rumours of UFOs and Men in Black became attached to the creature and, in 2002, a popular film starring Kevin Costner appeared called *The Mothman Prophecies*.

Mouse

The humble mouse has many fascinating associations in world mythology. In classical Greece, it seems to have been worshipped because, since it was a creature that lived below ground, it was therefore in touch with the powers of the underworld. Both Zeus and Apollo were connected with the mouse, possibly because mice were used as food for the snakes sacred to these gods. It was also believed that the mouse was a soul animal – a form likely to be adopted by the soul as it left the body. In the Old Testament, mice are considered unclean and are equated with the Devil as devourer. Some early Christian art depicts the mouse gnawing at the roots of the Tree of Life. In the fables of Aesop, the Mouse and the Lion symbolize strength in weakness and weakness in strength, and this symbolism is found also among the Native American people, where the mouse can represent both great power and great weakness. Among the native people of Dakota, North America, the waning moon is said to be nibbled away by mice. In Japan, the Ainu people say that the mouse and the rat are of one family and were the first beings to be created together. Providing they are honoured they do no harm, but if ignored they can wreck havoc and destruction.

Mpfuvu

In Mozambique, the Ronga people worship a goddess in the form of a hippopotamus called Mpfuvu. Once a young mother had a rival who wanted to kill her child. The young mother gave her baby to be fostered by Mpfuvu who already protected many babies in this way in her lush green water meadows. The mother would come every night to the riverbank and sing over the waters, 'Manan Mpfuvu!

Mother Hippopotamus, strong and big!' At this song, Mpfuvu would surge out of the waters with the baby and give him to his mother to be suckled. In this way, he grew up to be a brave warrior.

MUCHALINDA

In the traditions of Buddhist India, the Muchalinda is a giant cobra, the king of the Nagas, although Hindus recognize Vasuki, not Muchalinda. When he saw that Buddha, unaware of an approaching storm, was meditating under the Bo tree, the Muchalinda transformed himself into the form of a gigantic snake and wound himself around both the tree and the seated master seven times, finally spreading his hood to bring shelter. After the storm passed, the Muchalinda reappeared in the guise of a young man who then did honour Buddha.

MUIRBECH

This Irish water serpent's name translates as 'sea bee'. It has green skin, an eye that quells the onlooker and eats quantities of men and their tame beasts. It is encountered by the Irish hero, Fionn Mac Cumhail, who learns that the beast originated as a worm or serpent that swallowed a quarter of the brain of Mes Gegra, a hero whose brains had been turned into a massive slingshot pellet. There the pellet swelled up, making the serpent a monstrous size. Muirbech rose from its swamp home and swallowed 100 of Fionn's men complete with their dogs. But Fionn cannot avenge his men because a prophecy says that Tailchenn or Adze-head – the nickname of St Patrick – will come and subdue the Muirbech, tying it up with a single rush where it will be bound until Judgement Day.

MUIRDRIS/SMIRDRIS

The Irish Muirdris is a sea serpent or sea dragon set with spikes about its body. It has the ability to swell itself up and contract again like a smith's bellows. Huge, terrifying and implacable, with its belly covered with numerous teats, it lives in Loch Rudraige. Its terrible appearance causes onlookers to succumb to terror or death on one sighting.

In one tale, the maiden Scathderc (or Mirror) drowns in a spring while she is looking at the Smirdris. The spring then swelled up to become Loch Lurgan, briefly engulfing the province of Leinster.

MUIRSELCHE

The Irish name means 'sea snail' but the Muirselche is probably a giant octopus or cuttlefish. Its chief ability is to suck things and people into its huge maw that was like a treasure bag or repository. It could even suck in an armoured man. It was finally overcome by the Dagda, the good god, with his club of tempest, who chanted a spell against the Muirselche causing it to ebb away: 'Turn your hollow head, turn your greedy treasure-seeking body, turn your crest, turn your death-dealing darkness, turn!'

MULJEWANG

A water monster from the mythology of the Australian Aborigines, the Muljewang was said to inhabit the Murray River and Lake Alexandrina. There is disagreement as to whether the Muljewang is a single creature or whether there are many of them. They are sometimes described as a number of evil creatures, half man, half fish, and at other times as a single gigantic monster. One legend tells of an attack on a riverboat owned by European settlers. The captain of the boat saw two huge hands grasping the edge of the boat's hull and immediately went for his gun. Aboriginal elders who were on board warned the captain not to shoot but he ignored then. Not long after, he began to suffer from weeping red blisters that broke out all over his body. He took six months to die. Large clumps of

---

The Irish hero Fergus Mac Leiti had the magical ability to swim underwater by stopping his ears with herbs. The only prohibition on this gift was that he was not supposed to go to a forbidden loch. Needless to say, Fergus was irresistibly drawn there to prove his heroic powers. He dived under the lake and saw the Muirdris inflating and contracting itself like a bellows. So terrifying was the monster that Fergus's mouth became permanently sunken back into his head − a fact that he did not realize. The deformity was so terrible that his friends ensured that Fergus retreated to a house where no one would taunt him and where he must always have his hair washed by lying on his back so that he never saw his face mirrored in the water. For seven years, he lived in obscurity until he berated the slave washing his hair for her slowness; immediately the woman taunts him with his deformity. Fergus realized how hideous he looked and returned to fight the Muirdris. For a whole day and night he wrestled with it, the lake seething with the struggle. Finally, as Fergus plunged his sword into the beast, the Muirdris takes him down to the bottom of the loch and the water turned red with both their blood.

floating seaweed are said to hide the Muljewang, which should be avoided at any cost.

MUNINN

One of two ravens that sat on the shoulders of the god Odin in Norse and Teutonic mythology. Muninn's name meant 'memory'; that of his brother Huginn, 'thought'. Every day these birds flew across the world, noting everything that was happening; they left in the morning and returned to the god by breakfast of the next day to report all they had seen.

MURCAT/MURCHATA

The Murcat (singular) is one of many sea cats who are found in Irish tradition. St Brendan encounters one on his voyage to the Island of Promise. It was the size of a three-year-old horse, grown huge by gorging upon fish. It chased St Brendan's skin boat: 'Bigger than a brazen cauldron was each of his eyes; a boar's tusks had he; furry hair was upon him; and he had the maw of a leopard with the strength of a lion, and the voracity of a hound.' In the humorous tales of the modern Irish writer, Myles na Gopaleen, the map of Ireland, when turned on its side, is itself a depiction of a Murcat!

MURGHI-I-ADAMI

Not one but two fabulous birds from the mythology of the Islamic world share this name. They are said to resemble peacocks but with human faces and the ability of speech. Should anyone sitting near by chance to overhear them, they would hear many secrets and possibly much that would influence their own lives. During the Middle Ages, European travellers returned with stories of these creatures, which became part of the mythology of the bestiaries. They are said to have originated in the Garden of Eden, being exiled at the time of the expulsion of Adam and Eve, bringing with them secrets they had overheard in Paradise.

MUSKRAT

In the myths of the Menominee Indians of North America, the Amamagqkiu spirits caused a great flood, destroying the world. After the waters subsided, Manabusch the Great Hare asked the surviving animals to help him recreate the world, which he could do only if he had a grain of soil. Beaver, Otter, and Mink all looked for one but perished. It was Muskrat who successfully brought the speck of earth to Hare.

Musmahhu

In Sumerian myth, Musmahhu is a seven-headed monster depicted as a dragon with seven heads on snake-like necks. It is killed by the god Ningirsu (or Ninurta).

Musussu

The great cosmic dragon in the mythology of Babylon and Mesopotamia. Also known as Sirrush, this monster had the body of a vast dragon, but with the tail of a serpent on which was a poisonous sting. Its hind legs had the appearance of an eagle's, while its forelegs were those of a lion. Its head resembled that of a huge snake. Horns projected from the top of its head and down its neck, and it was covered from head to tail in thick scales. It was the guardian of the Ishtar Gate of the city of Babylon and was considered to be an emanation of the god Marduk.

N

Naga Pahoda

In Indonesian belief, Naga Pahoda is the king of the serpents who lives as a vast primordial snake in the ocean depths. When the daughter of the god Batara Guru fell out of heaven towards the oceans, Naga Pahoda lay ready to swallow her up, but Batara Guru scattered dust that formed the land so that she might have a place to live. Naga Pahoda rose up and squeezed the newly formed land into many islands, scattering them throughout the ocean.

Nagas

In Indian tradition, Nagas are snakes, most like cobras in form, but all Nagas are serpentine in nature, beings who inhabit the primordial oceans. Nagas are all believed to have been generated by the sage Kasyapa who had twelve wives. Their offspring include not only the Nagas but other creatures, including birds. They all live in the underworld city of Bhogavati. In Tibetan Buddhist belief, Nagas live in waterways and other places underground. They are susceptible to careless actions of humanity when nature and the environment are ignored or polluted, so Nagas may reflect to humans the suffering of the Earth by causing unwanted manifestations such as skin diseases.

But Nagas also bestow blessings, including fertility of crops and other wealth, which underlies their connection with dragons as keepers of treasure.

Many of the festivals in Kashmir relate to ancient Naga worship because the whole Kashmiri valley was once a great expanse of water walled in by high mountains. When the valley was uplifted by the Earth's movements, it was put under the care of the Nagas, according to the earliest known text of Kashmir, the *Nilamatapurana*. Nagas are closely associated with rivers and their courses; indeed every spring, river and watercourse has its own guardian Naga. Among the Hindus, the king of the Nagas is Vasuki; he bears the Nagamani, a jewel that bestows healing and good fortune on those who view it. His sister is Manasa Devi, the cobra goddess who cures snakebites. Indian Buddhists recognize Muchalinda as the king of the Nagas.

The reason that snakes are able to renew themselves is traced back to the myth that tells how Kadru, the ancestor of the Nagas, enslaved Vinata, mother of the birds. In order to ransom her, the Garuda stole the elixir of immortality, the *amrita*, from the gods. But before the serpents could taste it, Indra retrieved it. As he fled with the amrita, some drops fell to earth and the serpents slid through it, coating their skins with the renewing liquor. The Nagas raised their cobra hoods to protect Buddha and are frequently shown sheltering other sages and yogis, such as the great Nagarjuna, the champion of Buddhism in India who is depicted with a halo of a multi-hooded Naga. Nagas are found as far afield as Cambodia, where they are carved on the great temple of Ankhor Wat.

The Element Encyclopedia of Magical Creatures

Nakki

In Finnish and Estonian folk tradition, the Nakki is the water god who lives beneath the sea in his palace. Estonian stories associate him with the whirlpools that suck down fishing craft; these are said to be caused by the Nakki who causes the eddies which rock the boats. Sometimes the Nakki is described as a water horse who entices people into the many lakes of those lands, particularly at dawn and dusk.

Namtar

In Egyptian myth, Namtar is the guardian serpent of the entrance to the underworld. He also allows the sun god Ra to issue from the underworld when he takes his flight across the night sky back to the point where his daily voyage begins.

Nanabozho

Nanabozho is the name given to the trickster Manabusch among the central Woodlands Indians of North America. Among the Potawatomi, Nanabozho was the eldest of quadruplets. The youngest child killed his mother at his birth. The second brother was drowned by the immortals and became the overseer of the dead, but Nanabozho initiated people into the Midiwinwin or Great Medicine Society in reaction to this event, that proper ceremonial procedures might be kept around death, disease and calamity. He takes the form of a hare.

Nandi

Nandi is the bull mount of Shiva, the Dionysian bull god who breaks things in pieces. Shiva rides him because he has triumphed over the lower nature of man, as all good yogis must do. Nandi is the joyful wanderer who is the embodiment of justice and virtue, which are the qualities which make the strong gentle. Nandi is shown as a bull lying down in many Hindu temples, where worshippers touch his genitals for they are a source of life. He is one of the teachers of music and dancing.

Nara

The Nara are a race of winged horses in Hindu belief. The god Kubera, Lord of Riches, journeys across the heavens on the backs of his chosen Nara.

Neckhbet

Neckhbet is the Egyptian vulture goddess who is local to the east bank of the Nile. She is the protector of the pharaoh and appears on royal collars and pectorals with the outspread wings of the vulture, while queens wore the vulture-headdress, the wings of which curve about the wearer's head. Her hieroglyphic sign means 'to encircle'.

Neckhbet also attended royal births and she was associated by the Graeco-Egyptian rulers of Ptolemaic Egypt with the Greek goddess Eileithya: 'she who comes to aid birthing women'.

Nehebu-Kau

Nehebu-Kau is an Egyptian snake god, whose name means 'the one who harnesses spirits'. Like his mother, Serket, he is an invincible protector who is able to restore health to those who have been bitten by poisonous serpents, insects or scorpions. No magic, spell or enchantment can overcome him. He received these powers after swallowing seven cobras; the only way in which his power can be controlled is when the sun god Atum presses his fingernail on Nehebu-Kau's spine. When the deceased person is about to proceed to the Halls of Judgement, he prays to all the gods to obtain the favour of this snake god, for it is Nehebu-Kau who gives hospitality to the pharaoh when he first enters the afterlife, welcoming him and giving him his first food. Nehebu-Kau was originally born human but he devoured some of the coils of the world-serpent Apophis, after which he grew a serpentine head and the tail of a scorpion.

Nemain

One of the triad of Irish goddesses collectively called the Morrigna, Nemain, along with her sisters Badb and Morrigan, is responsible for inciting men to battle and cleansing the battlefield of carrion. Nemain is the wife of the Fomorian war god Neit.

Nemean Lion

In Greek mythology, the Nemean Lion was a savage beast that could not be killed by any weapon. It was the offspring of the serpent goddess Echidna who conceived it from congress with her own son, the hound Orthos. The Nemean Lion was thus the brother of the Theban Sphinx. According to another legend, the beast originally lived with the moon goddess Selene, but she shook him off the moon's surface and he fell down upon Mount Apesas. The Nemean Lion was overcome by Hercules in the first of his twelve labours.

Hercules was staying with a poor man, Molorchos, whose son had been killed by the lion. In order to honour his guest, Molorchos wished to kill his only ram but Hercules told him to wait for 30 days; if he did not return within that time, then the ram should be sacrificed to him as a hero, but if he did return, then the ram must be offered to Zeus. Molorchos taught Hercules how to approach the lion's den by blocking up one of its two openings. He must attack the lion by means of a wrestling match and not by using his club or sword. Hercules wrestled with the beast and finally strangled it to death. But he was so weary from his labour that he fell into a deep slumber. At length, he awoke on the last of the 30 days and made his way back to Molorchos's house where his host was on the point of sacrificing the ram to Hercules to honour the dead hero, but the ram was instead offered to Zeus Soter (Zeus who Rescues). Hercules skinned the lion and cut off the creature's claws. In order to honour his semi-divine son, Zeus transported the lion to the heavens where it became the constellation Leo in the zodiac.

NEREIDS

The Nereids or 'wet ones' are the spirits of the sea. They are mermaids who attend upon the sea goddess Thetis, and daughters of the nymph Doris by Nereus, the Old Man of the Sea who has the power of changing into many shapes. There were 50 Nereids and they are cousins to the Harpies, and the Phorcids who include the Gorgons, Ladon, Echidna and the Graeae. Hesiod believed that the Nereids were formed from the union of the seas and rivers. At the wedding of Peleus and Thetis, the Nereids performed a spiral dance upon the sand in their honour. They also helped guide Jason and the Argonauts safely past the Wandering Rocks and the flame-spouting Planctae. The Nereids attended the funeral of Achilles during the siege of Troy and mourned his death along with the Muses.

NESSUS

In classical mythology, Nessus was a centaur, the son of Ixion and Nephele. He was a companion to Hercules and was jealous of his wife, Deianira, who he attempted to abduct. Nessus was one of the centaurs who Hercules shot with his arrows that were poisoned by the blood of the Hydra at the battle between the drunken centaurs and the Lapith wedding guests. As he lay dying, Nessus told Deianira to bottle some of his blood because it would ensure the safe return of her husband if he were to be unfaithful. Later, when it seemed that he had strayed from the path of fidelity, Deianira smeared Hercules' shirt with Nessus's blood. When the hero put it on, its poison permeated his skin and he died in agony.

NGANI-VATU

In Fijian folk tales, Ngani-Vatu is a great bird, so large that it blots out the sun from the sky. Its wings when spread and in flight are the cause of storms.

When the hero Okova was out fishing with his wife, Ngani-Vatu flew down and snatched her away. Okova searched anxiously, finally coming to the island of Sawailau where the bird was said to live. He found only a cavern full of bones, and recognizing a finger of his wife among the bone pile, he swore to be avenged. With the help of his brother, Kokoua, he waited by the cavern until Ngani-Vatu returned with new prey. While it fed, the two men thrust their spears into the bird's underbelly. The bird's death caused an avalanche of rocks but they managed to steal a wing feather to act as a replacement for the sail that they had lost for their return voyage to the island. They tumbled the carcass off the cliffs into the sea, causing a great tidal wave.

NGARARA

In Maori legend, the Ngarara was an *atua* or divine being. She was a beautiful woman with a long tail, rather like a mermaid. When she wished, she could retract her tail and assume legs and feet. She may have been a water-lizard woman with amphibious tendencies, if the story about her encounter with a young man called Ruru is anything to go by.

Ngarara lived on an island with her two servants until a young man called Ruru landed and saw her fire smoking. He was invited to share Ngarara's meal, but he forbore to eat when he realized the food had Ngarara's scales in it and – had he eaten – he himself would have taken on serpent's scales. The two servants tried to prevent his escape but he made it back to his boat and told his brothers. Taking advantage of the mist, the brothers fashioned a statue in the likeness of Ruru upon the beach under the shelter of a reed hut. When the mist rose, Ngarara came and wound herself about the statue. The brothers set fire to the hut so that Ngarara was only able to escape by leaving her tail behind. Purified by the fire, she lost her malice for ever after.

NHANG

In Armenian folklore, Nhang is a water spirit in female or seal form who drags men under the water and sucks their blood after having seduced their victims. The same word in Persian means crocodile.

NIDHOGGR

Nidhoggr is the dragon of death in the Voluspa, that drinks blood and eats the flesh of corpses. After Ragnarok at the ending of the world, it will live in Nidavellir. It gnaws endlessly upon the roots of the world tree Yggdrasil. The messenger who goes between the top of the tree where sits the eagle and the bottom of the tree where Nidhoggr coils is Ratatosk. In later Christian times, Nidhoggr was not forsaken, becoming the dragon that tormented the dead in the bowels of hell at the spring of Hvergelmir.

NIFOLOA

A Samoan insect with one sharp tooth the size of a man's finger, the Nifoloa's bite results in death unless medicine is given immediately. No puncture wound is visible but the victim suffers greatly. After medicine is given, the tooth indentation will show up. The Nifoloa follows lone people walking home. If a wayfarer returns with the shivers and the healer is sent for, the medicine is never referred to by name, but called 'the medicine on the chief's tooth'.

Nifoloa is cunning, however, and if he hears that a healer is searching for the right medicine, he will immediately strip the herbs from the ground that grow nearby.

NIXI

In the myths of Scandinavia, Germany and Switzerland, the Nixi is a freshwater being who haunts lakes and rivers. Female Nixis are like mermaids who entice humans into the water. But unlike mermaids, they are seldom good looking, having a wizened appearance, with green hair and skin. Male Nixis are like old men from the neck up, with the body and brush of a fox and the hooves of a horse.

NKOMBE

In the myths of Zaire, Nkombe is the 'sun bird' or falcon who accompanies the hero Lianja. When the Earth seems too dark for people to do their work, Lianja calls together a Parliament of Animals to do something about it. The fish, bats, owls and the animals of the dark forest absent themselves, being uninterested in more light, but the insects and birds crave its warmth. The leader of the parliament is Nkombe who flies into the heavens with Lontsingo the Fly to find the sun and to speak to the divine Yemekonji. Yemekonji offers them three parcels, two of which are brightly painted. Nkombe counsels that they take the plain grey parcel. As they reach the place where earth and sky meet, he unwraps it and the sun breaks through the clouds.

NOBLE THE LION

In Merovingian times, in early medieval Gaul, it was believed that animals assembled about their animal king, Noble the Lion, every Whitsun. This council laid out proceedings for the year ahead and also acted as a tribunal at which cases could be heard and judged. At such an assembly, Reynard the fox was tried for his misdemeanours. (*See* Parliament of Animals.)

NOHOCH CEH

Among the Maya of Yucatan, the Nohoch Ceh or 'the Renowned Deer' is one of the *yumilekax* (spirit owners) of the forest who become visible only at night. This is the time that hunters go forth. They have to be alert to supernatural dangers and trickery from the *yumilekax*. Nohoch Ceh is one of the largest of these creatures, having a bees' nest in its antlers. Normally it ignores deer hunters, but it might intervene and speak to one who was killing too many deer.

A certain hunter recklessly killed many deer, far more than he could gainfully eat or share with others. From the belly of the first deer he shot fell a stone which he took with him. After a while, he heard many deer coming and he hid ready to shoot them, but not one of them died. The spirit deer came closer and grew more numerous and, seeing his bullets had no effect, he took to a tree. But there he was not safe, for they began digging with their feet, destabilizing the tree. Now he felt like the hunted, fearful that he would be eaten by the animals. While he wondered what his fate would be, one of the deer spoke to him. It was Nohoch Ceh, who reminded him about the stone: 'Give me the stone and you'll be free.' He threw it down and the deer picked it up and went away. Many hours later, he climbed down the tree shaking, resolving never to shoot deer again.

The Element Encyclopedia of Magical Creatures

Norns

In Norse mythology, the Norns are the guardians of fate. They live in a hall under the great world tree, Yggdrasil. They are called Urd, Verdandi and Skuld, their names meaning 'Past', 'Present' and 'Future' or 'Became', 'Become', 'Becoming' respectively. The Norse poet and statesman Snorri said that there are other Norns who are attached to each living child and oversee their term of life. Some of the Norns are of divine origin while others are descended from the elves and dwarves. (Urd is also the name given to the well of destiny.)

Nr-Simha

Nr-Simha is an avatar or manifestation of the Hindu god, Vishnu. Nr-Simha is a man-lion, entering this form for the purpose of overcoming the spirit Hiranya-kaspiru who tried to kill his own son Prahlada. Prahlada had a great devotion to Vishnu and despite Hiranya-kaspiru's tortures, the boy was protected from harm. Hiranya-kaspiru's life was assured because Brahma had sworn he could not be killed by day or night, by god, man nor beast, neither inside nor outside his palace. In order to save Prahlada and destroy his evil father, Vishnu appeared at twilight when it was neither night nor day, as a lion-headed man being neither man, beast nor god, within a pillar being neither inside nor out. With his claws, Nr-Simha tore out Hiranya-kaspiru's entrails.

Nu Kwa

In Chinese mythology, Nu Kwa is human from the waist up but has the lower half of a serpent. She is inseparable from the serpent-bodied Emperor Fu-His, with whom she is eternally entwined. She is the creator of humanity and is responsible for keeping the world in order. After making humans, Nu Kwa put down a rebellion against her order. When the rebel chieftain pulled down the pillars of the sky, she remade it by melting turquoise. She used the toes of Kashyapu, the cosmic tortoise, as direction markers. After the great flood, she restored the earth by using ash from burnt reeds. She established the custom of marriage and is the embodiment of creativity and cosmic order.

Nuit

Nuit (or Nut) is the Egyptian sky goddess who was the daughter of the air god Shu and the goddess of moisture, Tefnut. Although she is sometimes seen as woman whose curved body is the support of the sky, stretching herself away from the raised phallus of her partner Geb, she was visualized mainly as the Sky Cow. When the sun god Ra decided he had had enough of ruling the Egyptian people, he mounted the back of the cow, Nuit, whose four legs are the four quarters of the world and the pillars of heaven.

The Element Encyclopedia of Magical Creatures

Nummo

These divine twins in semi-human, semi-serpent form, were made by the creator Amma, according to the Dogon of Mali. Their father taught them speech and shared the essence of their father's seed, for the twins were water beings, capable of spreading life through their flow. When the Nummo saw the nakedness of Mother Earth they were still speechless and came down to Earth by pulling fibres from the heavens. These fibres formed the first clothing, but they also fell as coils of tornados, torrents, eddies and whirlwinds. They made the earth moist so that plants grew. As the Nummo plaited garments from the fibres, they raised them to their lips and speech was imparted to the plaits and coils. These fibres covered the genitalia of their Mother Earth, making a plaited skirt in which water and words would always be present. It was Yurugu who sought to uncover this skirt. Nummo was also said to have swallowed the skull of the first serpent ancestor. The contractions of its body as he swallowed it echoed the contractions of labour and to this day, the serpent pair are seen as the guardians of the birth process.

Nyarvirazi

According to Rwandan legend, Nyarvirazi was a chieftain's daughter who liked going into the wilderness alone. She drank from a pool of what she thought was water, but in fact was lion's urine. On the way back, she began to crave her father's calves, which were grazing in the bush. Suddenly, she found she had tawny hair all over her body and had become a lioness. After her meal, she resumed her human shape. This continued to happen until the missing livestock caused her brother to be suspicious. He discovered what was happening to her and bade her be careful never to tell her secret to her husband. After she was married, Nyarvirazi had a daughter, Nyavirungu. But when Vigara, her husband, heard the midwives say, 'At least it doesn't have claws and teeth,' he demanded to know what they meant and he thrust at her with a spear, grazing her side. Just the sight of blood caused her to shapeshift into a lioness and she devoured Vigara, and then went home to her father.

Nymphs

Nymphs are female spirits or semi-divinities who all originate from the great goddess, Gaia, in Greek mythology. Gaia created the mountains in whose valleys the nymphs love to range. From the Meliae or ash Nymphs, who came into being from the drops of blood shed when Uranus was castrated, a race of strong men descended. Nymphs tend to live in natural habitats and become associated with their locality, which they guard. As young and beautiful women, they associated with gods such as Pan, Hermes, Apollo, Dionysus and Artemis – all divinities who resort to wild, secret places. They are often seen with satyrs and Sileni (*see* Silen). According to where nymphs are found, they are divided into orders such as Dryads, Hamadryads, Meliae, Naiads, Nereids, Oceanids and Oreads. The word *nymph* means 'bride' or a marriageable woman.

Nyx

In primordial Greek myth, Nyx is the goddess of night. She took the form of a great bird with black wings. The wind impregnated her and she gave birth to a silver egg that lay in the lap of darkness. From the egg was born Eros, the winged god of love whom no one can withstand. According to the Orphic mysteries, the offspring of the silver egg was Protogonos ('the first-born god') whose name was Phanes. When he broke through the shell, he revealed and brought Light into existence.

O

O Goncho

A gigantic white winged dragon from the traditions of Japan. The O Goncho inhabited a particular stretch of water near Yamahiro. Every 50 years, it transformed into a golden bird with a cry resembling the howl of a wolf. This metamorphosis and the cry of the O Goncho were believed to presage imminent disaster.

Oannes

A fertility deity from the mythology of Babylon, Chaldea and Phoenicia. Part man, part fish, he lived among humans during the day and at night vanished into the depths of the sea. A god of wisdom, he was credited with the revelation of the arts of agriculture, healing and writing. Every night and each year at the winter solstice he was swallowed by the monster Tiamat, but reappeared each morning and each spring.

Oats Goat

In the folklore of Eastern Europe, this is the name of the spirit of the growing oats and also the name given to the figure made from the last sheaf cut from the field of growing grain. In Prussia especially, the Oats Goat is a prominent field spirit, of whom children are warned, and reapers hurry with the work to keep ahead of the Oats Goat who pushes laggards from behind. In some parts of Germany, there are two such goats, a he-goat and a she-goat.

In the Grenoble region of France, a live goat is decked with flowers and ribbons and turned loose in the field: when the reaping is over it is caught and killed, and roasted for the harvest supper. Its skin is then made into a cloak, which is usually worn by the farmer during the threshing of the oats, but it can be transferred to any reaper who gets a backache.

Oberon

The king of the fairies in medieval romance literature. Oberon's origins are unclear, but he seems to have first appeared in the medieval French romance *Huon of Bordeaux*, were he is called Oberon and is described as a dwarf king and either the brother of Morgan le Fay or her son by the Roman Emperor Julius Caesar. According to another late Italian romance, he is said to be the King of Avalon, and in this version, when King Arthur is mortally wounded in his last battle, he is taken to Oberon's kingdom and becomes his heir. Other sources say that he is the son of Cephalonia, Queen of the Hidden Isle, and that at his christening fairy women bestowed many gifts upon him, although an evil fairy cursed him with shortness of stature. But it is in literature that he is best known. The poet Edmund Spenser describes him as the father of Gloriana in his great poem *The Faerie Queene*, and Shakespeare immortalized him in *A Midsummer Night's Dream*, where he is tall and beautiful rather than dwarfish. Wanderers in the unfrequented byways of the forests of northern Europe may encounter him on the road. Oberon will try to engage them in conversation and lead them astray. If they respond they are lost forever; if they remain silent, Oberon causes it to rain and hail and a great black river to appear. However, this is no more than an illusion and it may be escaped if the traveller has the courage to walk through it.

OCEANIDS

The Oceanids are sea nymphs, the 3,000 daughters of Oceanus and Tethys. One of their number, Doris, married Nereus, the Old Man of the Sea, and bore the Nereids. Another was Styx, the guardian of the river that divides the living from the dead.

OCTOPUS

One of the most feared inhabitants of the sea is the octopus, whose name derives from the Greek *octo* (eight) and *pous* (foot). A medium to large member of the cuttlefish family, its soft sack-like body, large head and beaked mouth made it seem most bizarre and terrifying to ancient seagoing peoples. Its eight tentacles, each armed with suckers, can reach a span of 14 ft and many a tale has been told about giant octopuses attacking and pulling whole ships and their crews to a watery grave. All the major naturalist writers of the ancient Mediterranean world, including Aristotle, Pliny and Aelian, refer to this creature, and they all agree that it

possessed the ability to disguise itself in order to deceive its prey.

In Polynesian myth, the octopus rose from the primordial waters and gave birth to two children, Fire and Water, who began a conflict that ended in the destruction of the world by flood. The octopus then became sacred as the sole survivor of this earlier world. It is sacred in Samoa but in Hawaii it is described as a false creator who made an attempt to create man and then lead a revolt against the gods. More recent stories, such as Jules Verne's *Twenty Thousand Leagues Under the Sea*, have continued to cast the octopus as a frightening and malevolent creature.

ODONTOTYRANNUS

A monster mentioned in the writings of the classical world, particularly in Greece between 400 and 300 BC. Described as an enormous black beast with three horns protruding from its forehead, it was said to inhabit the area of the River Ganges in northern India. Among the wilder tales associated with Alexander the Great is one which describes an attack by Odontotyrannus on the Macedonian army. Apparently, the monster was large enough to consume whole elephants.

OGOPOGO

There were a number of sightings of this monster during the period from 1952 to 1975 around the area of Lake

Okanagan in British Columbia, Canada. Each description differs from the other, with some versions describing the monster as having the appearance of a huge log with a horse's head; others describing an undulating serpent with several humps or sharp ridges along its back; while still others have claimed it as a 70-ft serpentine creature with many fins. Whenever the waters of the lake become especially disturbed, local people say that this is Ogopogo. The same local traditions suggest that the creature lives either in the lake or on the tiny Rattlesnake Island.

OGRE

The generic term 'ogre' is given to many of the cannibalistic giants of world culture when mythology is beginning to lapse into folklore and fairytale. It was first used by the French storyteller Perrault in his *Contes* (1697), and more bizarrely by George Macdonald in his *Phantastes* where he uses the word ogre to describe a sinister, pointy-toothed woman who tempts the hero into looking into a certain cupboard by warning him against such action. This reverse psychology succeeds in making him look within. Ogre is a name loosely given to any bugbear or bogeyman. The most recent cinematic appearance of an ogre is that of the foul-breathed *Shrek* who, against the odds, wins the hand of the princess.

OLDEST ANIMALS

An important aspect of the ancient awareness of animals was their ability to provide inspiration, or to possess knowledge of the past that far outstripped that of a human – the reason given being that they lived far longer than us. The average lifespan of a bird or beast was probably unknown at this time, which may account for such a belief. Some creatures were believed to live to a very great age, or were seen as of otherworldly origin and thus possessed of wisdom more deep than that of mortals. In Celtic tradition there is an ancient theme known as 'The Oldest Animals', in which a number of creatures are consulted about various things and refer the questioner to successively more ancient beings. The joint memory of the Oldest Animals stretches back to the beginning of time, allowing them to access ancient memories of things forgotten by others. In many cultures, a list of the most ancient animals becomes a virtual calendar of life on Earth.

In the Welsh saga of 'Culhwch and Olwen', various animals – the blackbird, stag, owl, eagle and salmon – are consulted as to the whereabouts of the lost god Mabon, who is finally discovered, and rescued, by the warriors of Arthur, helped by the animals themselves. In a remarkable Irish poem known as 'The Hawk of Achill', Fintan, who represents a lineage of wisdom-holders dating back to a proto-Celtic demi-god named Vindos, dialogues with the hawk, each learning from the other. Fintan and the Hawk swap stories and traditions through the ages until they finally reach their own time and, having apparently nothing further to say to each other, die on the same day. This is a very ancient theme that flows throughout Celtic tradition. Behind it lies the age-old theme of the Quest for Knowledge, in which the shaman-poet or priest sought out the deep places of the inner realms and returned with riches beyond the dreams of mere men.

Olgoi-Khorkhol

Also known as the Mongolian Death Worm, this creature is said to live in the Gobi Desert. Sightings have been reported that described it as roughly 4 ft in length, dark red in colour and able to spit a highly corrosive poison at its attacker, which is said to kill almost instantly. In addition, the Olgoi-Khorkhol can deliver an electric shock capable of killing animals as large as a camel. It lives beneath the sands of the desert, only emerging to hunt at night. Various speculations have been put forward that it may be an undiscovered amphibian, a unique burrowing reptile, or possibly even an unknown form of spitting cobra. Its ability to deliver an electric shock make it particularly unusual for a land-based creature, as this is something normally only associated with seaborne creatures.

Olitiau

A cryptozoological creature originating in West Africa. Described as the equivalent of the East African Kongamoto and the Indonesian Abool, it appears to be a giant bat with a wingspan of 10–15 ft. Numerous sightings have been reported, one of which was in the Assumbu mountains of the Cameroon in 1932 by the famous hunter Ivan Sanderson. Sanderson said: 'Its lower jaw hung down and ... I could have counted the huge white teeth if I'd had time – they were a good two inches long ... the whole animal was coal black ... and did not appear to be hairy.' It has been suggested that the Olitiau is a surviving prehistoric creature, possibly a pterodactyl.

Oni

In Japanese tradition, these evil spirits cause disasters such as famine, disease or earthquake. They appear human but have three eyes, enormous mouths, horns and very sharp nails. They are also winged and fly around, seizing the souls of dying wrongdoers. A ceremony known as the *Oni-yarahi* is performed every year to expel these spirits from villages and towns across the country.

Oniares

A race of huge-antlered water demons found in the traditions of the Caughnawaga Mohawk people of Montreal, Canada.

A man named Da-Ra-Sa-Kwa, which means 'Moss Collector of the River', went one day to the lake in search of wood. He saw a log that looked right, and waded out to get it; but as soon as he stood upon it he found himself trapped by his feet. The log took the struggling man to the edge of nearby rapids and dragged him over. In the depths of the waters below, he met a race of humanoids that gave him a serpent skin to wear. As soon as he put it on, all of them, including Da-Ra-Sa-Kwa, transformed into Oniares. Ever after, the man and his companions preyed upon his own people.

OPHION

In the traditions of the ancient Greek Orphic religion, Ophion is a cosmic serpent that emerged from a vast egg at the bidding of the goddess Eurynome. According to one version of the myth, Ophion became the consort of the goddess and gradually grew in pride until he assumed the right to rule over all of Creation. This infuriated the goddess so much that she fought a battle with the serpent and banished it to caverns beneath the earth for the rest of time. Another version describes Ophion as the offspring of the primal gods Euranus and Gaia

and the mate of Eurynome. When the Olympian gods overthrew the Titans, both Ophion and Eurynome were banished to the centre of the Earth or thrown into the ocean.

OPHOIS

The wolf god of the ancient Egyptian World, worshipped at the temple at Lykopolis (now Assiut). Its aggressive nature made it an appropriate god of war.

ORC

It may surprise many people to know that Orcs did not originate in J.R.R. Tolkien's *The Lord of the Rings*. Prior to this they were mentioned by the prophetic poet William Blake who described them as servants of the devil. However, they have an even earlier incarnation in the classical world, where they are discussed by the Roman naturalist Pliny the Elder, who says that the Orc is a natural enemy of the whale, and he describes them as an enormous mass of flesh, armed with teeth. One of these creatures was seen at Ostia during the reign of the Emperor Claudius, when it gorged itself on a cargo of hides that had fallen overboard from one of the Emperor's ships. Later, the Saxons refer to Orcs as powerful spirits of the Earth. They appear again in Ariosto's epic medieval poem 'Orlando Furioso' as the Beast, in an episode which

The Element Encyclopedia of Magical Creatures

follows the story of Perseus and Andromeda; here, the hero Rogero saves the fair Angelica from certain death at the mercy of an Orc:

> *Yet with his spear in hand, though not in rest,*
> *The ugly Orke upon the brow he strake,*
> *(I call him Orke, because I know no beast,*
> *Nor fish from whence comparison to take)*
> *His head and teeth were like a boar, the rest*
> *A mass, of which I know not what to make.*

OREADS

The Oreads are the mountain nymphs, daughters of Gaia, the great Greek mountain mother. They are some of the wildest and least tameable nymphs.

ORTHOS

The dog that guarded the desirable, red-purple cattle of Geryoneus that were stabled in hidden barns on Mount Abas in Greek myth. It gave tongue when Hercules came to steal the cattle in his tenth labour, and was assisted by the centaur Eurytion, but the hero clubbed the dog to death.

OSCHAERT

One of the many fearsome Black Dogs mentioned in the folklore of Europe. This particular creature, which originates in the area around the town of Hamme, near Duendemonde in Belgium, shares the characteristics of the rest of its kind, and has been described as the size of a horse with fiery eyes. In common with most of these creatures, it preys upon travellers at night, leaping onto their backs and growing heavier until it crushes its victim beneath it. The Oschaert is known especially to seek out those troubled by guilty conscience. A local priest is said to have exorcized the monster a number of years ago and banished it across the sea for a period of 99 years.

OSTRICH

According to a South African Bushman story, it was Ostrich who originally possessed the gift of fire, but told no one else about it.

At one time all food was eaten raw and people had no fires to brighten their shelters at night. One day Mantis noticed that when Ostrich ate, the food smelt different and more appetizing. He followed to see what was happening. When Ostrich went apart to eat, he lifted his wing furtively and took fire from beneath it, then dipped his food into the fire. When he was done, he tucked the fire back under his wing again. Mantis decided to steal this fire, since Ostrich would obviously not share it. He came and called to Ostrich to see a wonderful tree with yellow plums, telling him that the best plums were on the topmost branches. As the Ostrich craned his neck to reach them, he lifted his wings to balance himself. At that moment, Mantis snatched some of the fire and brought it to the Bushmen tribes. Forever afterwards, Ostrich has never flown and holds his wings pressed tightly to his sides to keep secret the rest of the fire that he still retains. Some think that preoccupation with this theft is what makes the ostrich lay its clutch of eggs and cover them with sand while leaving one egg uncovered. The ostrich is so busy brooding about the theft that it makes her forgetful and she lays an egg to one side in order to remember where the nest is.

OTTER

Perhaps because it is equally at home on sea or land, the otter has had an interesting career in terms of its magical and mythological associations. The Roman writers Pliny and Aelian both call the otter *Enhydris*, which means simply 'aquatic', but helps to distinguish it from the Hydra or water snake. They also apply the belief that the otter is the enemy of the crocodile, though in myth it is actually the Ichneumon that is responsible for the death of this creature.

The otter was an important cult animal in the traditions of ancient Peru and was associated with the ocelot because it lived near streams and water. For the Native American people it represented feminine energy and the power of the Earth. It is also known as a trickster in North America. Native stories tell that, when caught, the otter pleads not to be thrown into the water and drowned, but when this plea is ignored it swims away laughing. Otter is the buffoon among the Cree people. Assisted by the Loon he helps the dead across the water to the next world. In the myths of the Menominee Indians of North America, the Amamagqkiu spirits caused a great flood, destroying the world. After the waters subsided, Manabusch the Great Hare asked the surviving animals to help him recreate the world, which he could do only if he had a grain of soil. Otter, Beaver and Mink all looked for one but perished. It was Muskrat who brought the speck of earth to Hare.

In Gaelic, the name of the otter is either *dobran* (water-one) or *dobhar-chu* (water-dog) and the animal is considered sacred and magical to the Celts for a number of reasons – the most prominent being that it is vulnerable only in a spot beneath its chin and under its forearm but is otherwise inviolable. For this reason, otter skins were considered lucky and possessed the ability to preserve life – as in the tale of the King of the Otters who was eventually slain by the hero Muiredach, who afterwards wore its skin as a mantle to protect him. The spot on the otter's skin that gave it its vulnerability, curiously, became attached to the lucky moles that appeared on the skin of humans, which were called *ball dobhrain*.

The otter is one of the shapes taken by the 6th-century Welsh shaman-poet Taliesin and is said to represent faithfulness and the harbouring of essential abilities and inner world skills. It is often depicted in pursuit of an eel, which is itself a symbol of wisdom and power. The otter, which catches and eats these eels, thus becomes imbued with knowledge.

Among the Ainu people of Japan, the otter god is not listed amongst the most important of deities. This is because he was told by the Creator to make foxes and to colour them red, but he forgot and made them white instead. The foxes complained, so the otter rubbed them all over with salmon roe to change their colour. The otter is generally forgetful and wastes time and resources, taking a bite out of a fish and then forgetting to finish it. A forgetful person is known as an 'otter head'.

Anyone who eats otter flesh, or even a fish killed by an otter, must tie a band around his or her head to prevent the spirit of the creature entering the brain and causing loss of memory.

OUROBOROS

A vast serpent-dragon of ancient Egyptian mythology, which represents eternity and is depicted as devouring its own tail. At the same time, it constantly renews itself, a process which will bring about the end of time if it is ever interrupted. The Ouroborus became a famous symbol in the traditions of ancient magic and sorcery, and is often to be found on talismans once used by magicians.

OWL

In the ancient world, the owl was associated not only with wisdom but also with darkness and death. It was sacred to the goddesses Athena and Demeter, and in most places its hooting presaged death or misfortune. In ancient Chinese mythology, the owl was a one-footed dancer with a human face who had originally been in the form of a drum. The raven-nosed emperor Yu forced Owl to perform a dance of submission for opposing him and made the owl the emblem of smiths. To this day the owl is not afraid of thunder because it was his dance that invented thunder and lightening.

In the lore of the Ainu people of Japan, the owl is generally considered to be evil and to bring misfortune. However, the eagle owl is trusted as it warns people of approaching evil. Such owls were kept in cages and venerated, though they were eventually sacrificed so that their spirits would take messages to the gods. The screech owl was said to warn against danger and to confer success in hunting, but the horned owl was a carrier of ill omen. It is considered unfortunate to have an owl fly in front of one, but total disaster to see it fly across the face of the moon. In the first instance, evil consequences could be avoided by spitting, but in the second the situation is so serious that the only remedy is to change one's name and leave town!

According to the Cree people of North America, the presence of owls can make speaking very difficult. Owls are believed to cause stuttering and that, in turn, causes the owls much mirth. If someone stutters inadvertently, this is said to attract owls. However, if any of the Cree believe owls to be causing supernatural difficulties in the village, someone will go and purposely begin to stutter in the woods. This will summon an owl that can then be confronted with the problem and made to resolve it.

Throughout much of Africa, the owl is considered to bring bad luck. In East Africa, to hear its hooting at night can be disastrous for a newborn baby. If the child already suffers from an illness, people say in Swahili that this child has been hooted over. In Ghana, it is believed that witches have owls as familiars or can change themselves into the shape of these birds. In this form,

they enter people's houses at night and attack their victims on the astral plane. The Yoruba of Nigeria relate that witches or sorcerers can leave their bodies at night, and that when they do so they take on the shape of owls. In daytime, they sit dozing harmlessly in the shade, but at night they enter their victims' houses through a hole in the roof and suck their blood.

Traditionally a bird of ill omen, the owl is strongly associated with a figure from Welsh tradition known as Blodeuwedd. She is a woman created from flowers by the enchanters Math and Gwydion for their nephew Llew. Her name, which means 'flower-face', seems to have foreseen her destiny, which was to be turned into an owl as a punishment for her betrayal and connivance in the death of her husband. In *The Mabinogion* story of 'Culhwch and Olwen' one of the significant animal helpers is the Owl of Cwm Cawlwyd, who along with his fellows is of great age and wisdom. Elsewhere, in Gaelic tradition, an early Scottish song, 'Oran na Comhachaig' preserves the following dialogue:

Oh wailing owl of Srona,
Mournful is thy bed this night,
If thou hast lived in the days of
  Donegal,
No wonder thy spirit is heavy.
I am coeval with the ancient oak,
Whose roots spread wide in yonder
  moss,
Many a race has past before me,
And still I am the lonely owl of Srona.

The Element Encyclopedia of Magical Creatures

Ox

The ox has always symbolized strength, toil, wealth and sacrifice and in some traditions it is symbolically interchangeable with the bull, though as it is castrated, it does not share the fertility significance of the bull. According to the Roman writer Varro, it was a capital offence to kill an ox throughout Attica and the Pelopennese. Only in dire emergencies could it be sacrificed, and even then this was seen as murder and a scapegoat had to be found. Alternatively, the knife used in the killing could be destroyed or thrown away.

Niu Wang, the Chinese god of oxen, protects the creatures against epidemics and is associated with the spirit of the star T'ien-wen. Hadhayosh is the great ox of Zoroastrian mythology. It carried the first human beings across the ever-pure sea, Vourukasha. When the Frashkart or ending of all things comes, it will provide the fat that will help make the immortal drink of haoma.

OXEN OF GERYON

These cattle had three bodies each, and were guarded by the giant Eurytion and the dog Orthos on the island of Erytheia. One of the twelve tasks of the hero Hercules was to capture these oxen and to slay the dogs that guarded them. This he successfully achieved.

P

Padfoot

According to Yorkshire folklore, the Padfoot was an inhabitant of the moorlands around the city of Leeds. It was reported to be in many different shapes: either a great sheep with shaggy fleece and red eyes or a black donkey or great white dog. The first that a traveller knows of its appearance is the sound of its footsteps padding behind them in the dark, sometimes accompanied by the clanking of chains.

Pai Lung

Pai Lung is a white dragon of Chinese mythology, one of the Lung (Dragon Kings). It came into being after a family sheltered an old man from a storm. After he had left, the young girl who had opened the door was found to be pregnant, so her family threw her out of the house. When she was delivered, her baby was nothing but a ball of white flesh that the midwife subsequently threw into water. It turned into the dragon, but Pai Lung's mother never recovered from the shock of having given birth to a dragon and she died. Her grave became a shrine. Pai Lung's own temple is on Mount Yang Suchow in Kiangsu.

Pal-Rai-Yuk

In Inuit tradition, the Pal-Rai-Yuk is a water creature that lives in the estuary swamps and rivers of Alaska. It has two heads, two tails, six legs, three stomachs and a sharp ridge running along its spine. Inuit hunters would paint the image of Pal-Rai-Yuk upon their canoes before fishing in order to avoid its attentions.

Palulukon

In Hopi traditions of the American south-west, the Palulukon is a water serpent. Like the Nagas of Asian tradition, it is necessary to behave in tune with the environment otherwise Palulukons will cause the earth to move or stop springs flowing. In Hopi belief, the whole world floats upon the backs of two Palulukons in the primordial ocean.

Pan

In Greek mythology, the god Pan is the son of Hermes and the nymph Dryope. His name has been said to mean 'All' but the root is the same as found in the words 'pasture' and the Latin *panis* (bread). He is essentially a pastoral guardian of flocks. From the waist up he has the appearance of a man with horns on his head but below he has a hairy goat's body, legs and hooves. He lived largely in Arcadia where he guarded flocks, beehives and herds and took part in the revels of the Oreads. He seduced various nymphs including Echo and

The Element Encyclopedia of Magical Creatures

Eupheme, and was familiar, he said, with all of Dionysus's Maenads. The unwary traveller can be overtaken by panic in the presence of Pan, but this only happens to those who have relinquished their animal instincts and sold out to civilization.

Despite Pan's wild nature, he was a patron of the arts, teaching Apollo the art of prophecy and Hermes the art of playing the pipes. According to a story reported by Plutarch in his 'On the Silence of the Oracles', a sailor called Thamus was bound for Italy when he heard a divine voice calling to him: 'When you reach home, proclaim to all that great god Pan is dead.' When he disembarked and shared these tidings, there was general lamentation for the loss of a god so good. This story, however, may be due to a mishearing of the lamentations around the eastern Mediterranean coast for the annual death of the god Tammuz, lover of Ishtar/Inanna, for whom the lament *Thamus Pan-megas Tethnece* ('the all-great Tammuz is dead') was annually chanted.

PAN-GU

In Chinese mythology, Pan-gu is a giant who hatched from the cosmic egg from which the sky and Earth were formed. The upper part of the egg was the heavens and the principle of Yang, while the lower part of the egg was the Earth or the principle of Yin. His exertions to be born from the egg caused him to fashion the mountains and the earth and, as he grew at the rate of ten feet a day, he soon became enormous. After emerging, he burst apart and died, and his whole body formed the universe, giving his breath to the winds, his voice to the thunder, his body to the Earth, his eyes to the sun and moon, his sweat the waters and his hair became the vegetation. The fleas upon his body became the first humans.

PANTHER

According to the classical speculative lore of writers such as Aristotle, Pliny and Aelian, the panther was believed to sleep for three days after it has fed before awaking with a roar. It was thought to emit a wonderful fragrance which made it attractive to all animals except the dragon. This wonderful scent was also thought to overcome its prey gently. In North American Indian traditions, however, the panther was considered by the Algonquins and Ojibwas to live in the underworld and have a less savoury reputation, although among the Cherokee, the panther was a sacred animal, able to see in the dark.

Parliament of Animals

Animals have their own assemblies, councils and parliaments in which they order the world and put things to rights. Assemblies of birds were a common theme in poetry and folk tale. The 12th-century Persian poet, Farid-ud-Din Attar's *Conference of the Birds* and Chaucer's *Parliament of Fowls* have a similar origin.

In Australian Aboriginal legend, all the animals gathered for a great corroboree (gathering) to discuss the laws of marriage. It was suggested that kangaroos should mate with emus and dingos with goannas. The majority of species wanted this, but tortoise, frog and crow dissented, causing a tremendous battle in which nobody won. Finally, it was decided that each species of animals would have their own language. Because the lyre bird offered words of reconciliation and tried to bring peace, it alone of all animals is able to imitate them all in its songs and dances.

In the legends of Zaire, when the Earth seemed too dark for people to do their work, the hero Lianja called together an assembly to do something about this. The fish, bats, owls and the animals of the dark forest absented themselves, being uninterested in more light, but the insects and birds craved its warmth. The leader of the parliament was Nkombe who flew into the heavens with Lontsingo the Fly to find the sun and to speak to the divine Yemekonji who gave them light. In Merovingian times, in early medieval Gaul, it was believed that animals assembled about their animal king, Noble the Lion, every Whitsun. This council laid out proceedings for the year ahead and also acted as a tribunal at which cases could be heard and judged. At such an assembly, Reynard the Fox was tried for his misdemeanours.

Although such animal councils remained part of folk tradition, the animal-assembly stories of early traditions, with their respect for animal wisdom, began to melt away and be replaced by more anthropomorphic tales. Increasingly, it was believed by the whole of Christendom that man was the master of all animals, and, as Adam had named the beasts in the Garden of Eden, so human beings were seen as the most wise of all God's creation. By the Middle Ages, other forms of animal assemblies began to abound. It became the custom for monarchs to assemble their own menageries that animals of many different and unusual kinds might reflect the power of the king. To amuse and impress visiting dignitaries, these animals, frequently brought from far-distant shores, pined in the captivity of cold northern climes, bereft of habitat, isolated from fellow and like creatures. Animals such as the king of beasts, the lion, were popular captives, overseeing a court of randomly picked and wholly disaffected animals that heralds were fond of depicting upon armorial bearings.

Pasupati

In Hindu tradition, especially in Shiavite belief, Pasupati is an aspect of the god Shiva who is the divine herdsman, the ruler of the Earth, the friend of life and the guide of each species in its development. He lives in the forests and mountains, wandering naked, teaching his secret wisdom of the art of life to all. He is responsible for bringing to Earth the arts of music, dance and drama by which wisdom can be imparted to the crowd. He oversees the rhythms of the universe and is their boundary keeper. All living beings are understood to be his 'cattle' while he is the keeper of the reins that bind them.

He can take the form of an animal if he wishes, and every time someone encounters an animal by chance and there is some understanding between them, it is said to be Pasupati who they meet in that animal. Whenever you see a hunter on the trail, or the constellation of Rohini (Taurus) in the sky, you have also seen Pasupati. His wisdom is said to be the very highest, since no one can be more wise than the spirit or totem animal that informs their soul. Pasupati is the lord of the Vidyeshvaras, the forest spirits who protect the natural world. 'All the divinities are called Pashupatas or brothers of the beasts since they belong to the flock of Pasupati. All those who consider the Lord of the Animals as their god become brothers of the beasts.' (Alain Daniélou, *Gods of Love and Ecstasy: The Traditions of Shiva and Dionysus.*) When they are part of his flock, then they can receive his teachings. This practice is considered to be Pashupata Yoga whereby the practitioner becomes a brother of the animals and realizes the unity of all living things.

Pazuzu

In Assyrian and Babylonian mythology, Pazuzu was the underworld spirit who had a predominantly humanoid shape, but a canine face with bulging eyes, a scaly body, a snake-headed penis, and the talons and wings of a bird. He protected people against pestilential winds and against the depredations of the demon Lamastu. Pregnant women wore emblems of Pazuzu to enable them to carry their child to term. Pazuzu made a more recent appearance in the film of *The Exorcist.*

Peacock

The peacock has always taken a central place in Asian folklore, only coming into European tradition much later, since it is a bird native to India and Sri Lanka. The peacock's extraordinary plumage has today made it a favourite display bird for public parks and gardens, though its penetrative screeching cry makes it less popular with the neighbours. Peahens have a much duller plumage and leave it to the males to display their tails in their courtship competitions. The Hindu saying 'a peacock has the feathers of an angel, the voice of the devil and the walk of a thief,' sums up the many ways in which it is generally viewed.

The Element Encyclopedia of Magical Creatures

The peacock has been long associated with Paradise. In the 12th-century Persian poet Attar's epic poem *Conference of the Birds*, the Peacock describes itself as an original inhabitant of Paradise, created by the 'Painter of the World' (God), his glorious plumage a remembrance of the delights of Paradise. But he became friends with the serpent and let down his instincts and so suffered the same exile as Adam and Eve from the Garden of Eden. For the Muslims of Java, peacocks still guard the gates to Paradise.

The possession of a peacock's feather is considered auspicious in Asia but bad luck within Europe, possibly due to the eye on each feather and its perceived connection with the evil eye or envy that overlooks and brings misfortune to others. The peacock was the bird associated with the Middle Eastern god, Tammuz, while in Greece it was sacred to the Greek goddess, Hera, whose chariot was pulled by two peacocks. In Buddhist tradition, the peacock is the vehicle of Mahamayuri-Vidyarajni (Mother of all the Buddhas) who in Japan is called Kujaku, while in Hindu belief, it is the vehicle of Sarasvati, goddess of the arts.

Within Persian tradition, the motif of the two peacocks who adore the Tree of Life connects back into early Sumerian mythology and forward into Christian tradition where the same motif represents resurrection. The image of two peacocks drinking is also a symbol of spiritual renewal, since it was believed that peacocks' feathers did not spoil, and the bird's spring moulting coincided with the Easter festival. In Hindu lore, its flesh was considered to be poisonous because, at the time of the Churning of the Ocean that created the divine *amrita* drink of immortality, the peacock absorbed the negative energies of this process. In early Christian Europe, the peacock was also seen as an emblem for *superbia* (pride and boasting), which led in the Middle Ages to the naming of a pair dance called the *paduana* or *pavane*, in which each partner of the pair could 'show off' their steps in an individual measure like a peacock. In alchemical lore, the *cauda pavonis* (peacock's tail) is the name given to the part of the alchemical process where the material becomes iridescent.

The Element Encyclopedia of Magical Creatures

A Buddhist tale tells how Princess Peerless, wife of King Brahmadutta, ruler of Benares, heard the call of Goldenglow, or Suvarnaprabhasa, the King of the Peacocks who lived on the sacred mountain Kailash. She begged her husband to bring her the bird so he sent his huntsmen to find him. They set out but were unable to trap him and soon they began to starve. Goldenglow appeared to them and out of pity agreed to come to Benares if the city was suitably cleaned and decorated in his honour. The king did as he was bidden and soon Suvarnaprabhasa arrived in a chariot decorated by seven kinds of precious jewels. Offerings were made to the Peacock King, but the King of Benares wanted these offerings done precisely, so he asked Princess Peerless to make them. Unfortunately, this close proximity to Goldenglow meant that the Princess's secret would soon be made known, for she had become pregnant from an adulterous affair, so she determined to kill the Peacock King. She kept offering him poisons, but instead of fading away he got stronger and his plumage more resplendent. Eventually, Goldenglow spoke to her, telling the Princess that he knew of her deception. Realizing that the Peacock King was invulnerable, she fainted away, losing a great deal of blood. She died shortly afterwards and was reborn in hell for her evil intentions. The King of Benares was renamed Shariputra and the peacock Goldenglow had been none other than Buddha himself.

Pegasus

When the Greek god, Poseidon lay with Medusa, Athene turned her into a terrible monster whose very glance could petrify the onlooker. Only Pegasus was able to defeat her and, as he decapitated her, the seeds of her union with Poseidon were released from her body, becoming the warrior Chrysaor and the winged horse, Pegasus. Pegasus became a favourite of the Muses of Mount Helicon and created the sacred well, Hippocrene, by stamping his hoof upon the ground. Pegasus became the helper of the hero Bellerophon who sought him out and tamed him by throwing a golden bridle over his neck, the gift of the goddess Athene. Flying upon the horse's back, Bellerophon destroyed the Chimaera.

Later in his story, and after much praise, Bellerophon got above himself and began to think of himself as a god. He undertook a flight to Mount Olympus, home of the gods, but Zeus sent a gadfly to sting Pegasus under the tail, that caused him to rear and unseat his rider. Bellerophon fell to earth into a thorn bush and wandered the land blind, lame and accursed for his presumption until he died. Pegasus remained on Olympus as the pack beast for Zeus' thunderbolts.

PELICAN

In classical and early European tradition, the pelican with its huge beak was believed to lay eggs whose young were almost lifeless when they hatched. In order to keep them alive, the parent bird was supposed to pluck at its own breast to produce life-giving blood that revived the chicks. The pelican became a central part of Christian symbology as an emblem for Christ who so loved the peoples of the world that he gave his very blood for their salvation. Christ was addressed as '*Pie Pelicani, Jesu domine*' ('Merciful Pelican, Our Lord Jesus'). The bird became an alchemical symbol for purification and also an emblem within Masonry, whose initiatory dialogue included this interchange:

The Wisest One asks the Most Respectable candidate:

'*Do you know the Pelican?*'
'*Yes, Wise One.*'
'*What does it mean?*'
'*It is the symbol for us of the Redeemer of the World and of perfect humanity.*'

P'ENG

The P'Eng is a great bird that in Chinese mythology began life as a fish called Kw'en. After it became a bird, it was so huge that its wings blotted out the heavens. In the typhoon season, the P'Eng flew south from its northern home.

PERI

The Peri are the fairy people of Persia where they represent the beings of forest and river, predating the Zoroastrian and Islamic religions. During the Zoroastrian period, the small but beautiful Peri were believed to emanate from the demon Parikas, but in effect they were seen to be on the side of the virtuous, engaged in avoiding the evil Deevs who tried to abduct and imprison them in cages like little birds. Such imprisoned Peri were kept alive by their companions who brought them the nourishment of sustaining perfumes.

PHAETHON

One of the horses of the sun, in Greek mythology Phaethon is the 'Shining One' who pulls the sun chariot driven by the god Helios.

PHEASANT

In Chinese legend, Song-Sseu is the name of the mythical bird with a human head and the body of a female pheasant. This divine pheasant was traditionally embroidered on the ceremonial dance robe of a marriageable princess, for the first calling of the pheasant was a signal to young people that it was time to come out and dance. According to legend, the raven-nosed emperor Yu collects the feathers of the divine pheasant, which is like a Bird of Paradise with eight wings, from the place where his father's body lies buried, for that is where she roosts.

PHLEGON

In Roman myth, Phlegon is one of the four winged horses of the sun. The poet Ovid lists Achton, Eous and Pyrios as the other horses. These four were harnessed daily to the chariot of the sun and driven across the heavens by the charioteer Phaethon.

PHOENIX

The origins of the golden-plumed Greek Phoenix lie with the Egyptian Bennu that was a heron said to be the first creature to emerge from the primordial mud. The Bennu is the bird sacred to Ra. Venerated as the manifestation of the sun god of Heliopolis, it was said to appear only once every 500 years. It lived upon dew and flew to other lands, gathering a ball of fragrant myrrh to make a pyre on which it burned itself to death. After three days it rose from the ashes. Pliny relates that the Phoenix gathers a nest of cassia and frankincense in which to die and incubate itself. Under the Imperial Roman dispensation, the Phoenix became the emblem for the undying Empire, and was depicted upon coins and mosaics. In Persia, the Phoenix was known as Al-Salmandra, which can be a four-footed beast or a bird which lives in fire. A similar story about fiery death is told about the Simurgh. Both birds appear to be related to the Roc and the Garuda of Hindu belief.

Jewish legend speaks of the Phoenix as the Milcham. When Eve had eaten of the forbidden fruit of the Tree of Knowledge, she conceived an envy of the animals' sinless nature and she enticed all to eat of the tree like herself. All except the Milcham obeyed her and he alone was rewarded by the gift of immortality. It was allowed to live in a walled city in an inviolate condition for 1,000 years. When they pass away, a fire consumes the Milcham leaving only an egg that lives for another cycle of 1,000 years. The length of time that a Phoenix lives is given in this Greek saying from Hesiod that measures the generations:

> The croaking cormorant lives nine
>   generations of ageing men,
> The stag lives four times the cormorant,
> The crow outlives three stags,
> But the Phoenix outlives nine crows,
> And we, the fair-haired nymphs,
> Daughters of Aegis-bearing Zeus,
> Outlive ten phoenixes.

In Chinese mythology, the Phoenix is called the Feng Hwang, which is one of the Ssu-Ling, the four sacred creatures of the directions. Feng Hwang shares the balance of Yin and Yang within itself for it represents the solar Yang and the lunar Yin powers. Feng Hwang represents the Empress, and the qualities of beauty and peace. Not only does it keep these powers in balance, it also represents the five elements, for its head is that of the solar cockerel while its swallow-back represents the lunar crescent, its tail represents the trees and flowers, its wings the wind and its feet the earth. In Japanese mythology, the Phoenix is known as the Ho-O, which comes to Earth in successive ages to herald a new era before returning to heaven. The Ho-O represents the sun, as well as justice, fidelity and obedience.

In Christian iconography, the phoenix's three-day rebirth was seen as a perfect figure for Christ's resurrection on the third day after his crucifixion. In China, as the Feng Hwang, it is seen as an emblem of conjugal union. In J.K. Rowling's *Harry Potter and the Chamber of Secrets*, Harry Potter is assisted in overcoming the Basilisk by Fawkes, Professor Dumbledore's Phoenix.

PHOLOS

In the fourth labour of Hercules in Greek myth, when he was looking for the Erymanthean Boar, Hercules journeyed into the region of Arcadia where he was welcomed by the centaur Pholos. The centaur was the guardian of a great jar which had been given by Dionysus, a gift intended for Hercules' refreshment. Pholos did not know that it was wine in the jar, having never tasted it. Once the jar was opened, all the centaurs from miles around were drawn by its intoxicating and alluring scent. The centaurs fell into a drinking bout, growing wilder and more intoxicated, and becoming combative and dangerous.

Hercules had to defend himself and so he drew out one of the arrows, poisoned by the blood of the Hydra. As Pholos was trying to pull out a poisoned arrow from his fellow's corpse, the bolt fell upon his foot and killed him too. Hercules buried Pholos and continued on his way to Mount Erymanthos.

PHORCIDS

In Greek mythology, the Phorcids are the children of Ceto, daughter of the Earth mother Gaea, by Phorcys, a wise man of the sea. Strangely fair and foul, they include the serpentine Ladon, the monstrous Echidna, and the sisterhoods of the Gorgons and the Graeae.

PIG

The domesticated pig stands aside from the wild boar and sow. Themes of celestial association are found whenever we consider pigs. In Egyptian myth, the sky goddess, Nuit, suckles her many piglets, who are the stars. In Breton legend, the sow with her farrow are the phases of the moon who wax and wane.

Among many parts of the world, the pig is an unclean animal because of its habit of scavenging; for instance the story of the expulsion of evil spirits from the possessed man into the Gaderene Swine in the Gospels. Sacrificial pigs are frequently given to the underworld, especially in the rites of Eleusis, where they are given to Demeter in return for a good harvest.

The Element Encyclopedia of Magical Creatures

The high status of the boar and sow in Celtic myth is contrasted by the low status of those who herded domestic pigs. However, because pigs are seen throughout British legend as the uncoverers of healing properties, and of the acclamation of kings, they frequently appear in the origin myths of royal palaces in both Ireland and Britain. Both Sir Tristan from the Arthurian legends and the early Welsh hero, Culhwch, are born in a pig sty.

King Bladud of the city of Bath in south-west England, tells of the legendary founding of the city. Outcast and ailing because of a blemishing skin complaint, Bladud watched how pigs dug in the mud and healed their own blemishes. Following suit, Bladud found his skin was clear once again. He founded a sacred temple over the muddy swamp where he had been healed, which became the hot springs of Bath. His legend further relates how he attempted to make wings and fly, perhaps focusing for us the origin of the saying 'pigs might fly'.

In Buddhist tradition, the pig is the symbol of ignorance and greed; it is one of the three animals upon the Buddhist Wheel of Life, which represents the sensual desires binding humanity to the wheel of *samsara*, the endless cycle of existence.

PIKUWA

In the Aboriginal legends of Queensland, Australia, Pikuwa is the saltwater crocodile who is a seducer of women.

Pikuwa was once conducting two young women and their parents across a river when they saw some beehives. The parents left the girls to fetch the honey as they had smaller hands. When they were far away, Pikuwa tunnelled into the banks of the river and climbed up inside the tree where the beehive was. As the girls poked sticks into the hole, Pikuwa cried out, identifying himself to the girls who were very frightened. He made an assignation with them and they arrived trembling, expecting to be killed. But he scratched out a hollow in the ground and lay with them both all night. The next morning, as he lay in the sleep of ecstasy, the girls piled logs on top of Pikuwa who lay in the hollow. The girls' parents returned and heard how their daughters had been deflowered. The father bade them call to him and pretend to want him once more. As Pikuwa arose, the father clubbed him over the head to death. The women hacked his body to pieces, removing any edible parts.

PISKY

In the West Country traditions of Devon and Cornwall, and in Somerset where they are called Pigsies, Pisky is a name given to the fairy people. Piskies vary in size, but have red hair, pointed ears and noses that turn up at the end. They customarily wear green. There is a widespread tradition in the West Country that piskies are the souls of unbaptized children or the souls of the ancestors who died before Christ's coming. Since they were unable to be baptized, they remained on Earth, being unfit for heaven, but not wicked enough for hell.

The most common tale told about piskies is that they mislead travellers who afterwards say they have been 'pisky-led'. Piskies are said to be very territorial and they fought a battle with the other race of fairies whom they defeated and banished to beyond the River Parrett, so that everything to the west of the river is Piskyland. They are reputed to steal horses, which they ride round and round in circles or 'gallitraps' – this is the cause of fairy rings. To step into such a gallitrap is fraught with danger, for it is said that you will enter into the power of the piskies. It was a common belief that if a criminal set even one foot into a gallitrap then he would be hung; this accords with the well-known hatred of all fairy folk for human deceit and dishonesty. In the film *Harry Potter and the Chamber of Secrets*, the vain, self-aggrandizing teacher Gilderoy Lockhart unleashes a cage full of Cornish piskies for his unfortunate pupils to capture.

PIXIE

Pixie is an Anglicization of the folk more properly entitled Piskies. It should be realized that the Cornish term 'to be pixilated' has little to do with piskies and much more to do with strong drink.

POLEWIKI

In Polish mythology, Polewiki are field spirits who have the appearance of dwarves with different coloured eyes and grass instead of hair. They are usually seen at noon or at dusk, for they are vigilant to ensure that everyone is working hard, tending the fields. They are dressed in white or black, with no colours about their person. They have the reputation of leading people astray, making them lose their sense of direction, and they are given to ride over sleeping people with their horses. If anyone drinks while at work and falls asleep in the fields, the Polewiki are incensed by such laziness and may even kill the sleeper. The proper propitiatory gifts to Polewiki are two eggs, a cockerel, a toad and a crow placed unseen in a ditch.

POLYPHEMUS

In Greek myth, Polyphemus was the giant son of the sea god Poseidon and the nymph Thoosa who ate human flesh. Polyphemus was one of the Cyclops, having only a single eye in his forehead. Odysseus and his men had the misfortune to land on the island where Polyphemus grazed his livestock. Every evening the giant drove them into the back of a cavern and placed a huge stone in the entrance to keep them safe. Having killed some of Odysseus' men after the crew had taken shelter and eaten a kid, he imprisoned the rest, intending to eat them at his leisure. Odysseus fashioned a stake of olive wood in the fire and offered the Cyclops wine to drink. Being unused to strong drink, he drank deeply and asked the man his name, to which Odysseus replied '*Oudeis*' (nobody). Promising to eat him last of all, Polyphemus slept and Odysseus drilled into the Cyclops' only eye. Wakening in agony, Polyphemus blamed Oudeis, but the sailors responded, 'If nobody is to blame then you must be delirious.' Feeling his way to the entrance, the Cyclops stood guard, but the canny sailors tied themselves each to the underside of a sheep and so escaped into the outside world, as Polyphemus felt each of his animals as they left the cavern. Untying themselves, they ran to their ship and rowed off, shouting goodbye. Polyphemus threw rocks at them, but they mocked him, telling him who had been responsible for his blinding. This unwise admission led to Poseidon listening to the complaints of Polyphemus and he made the rest of Odysseus' voyage fraught with problems, delaying his long-awaited homecoming.

Pooka

In Irish tradition, the Pooka or Puca is a mischievous spirit in half-animal form who can transform at will. Pookas punish graverobbing and ingratitude, and have been known to help rescue beasts that founder in bogs. He sometimes helps in household tasks and tidies up after people. Irish children call snails 'pookas' and bid them put out their horns in a nursery rhyme. Before Hallowe'en it is safe to eat the wayside blackberry, but not afterwards when the Pooka smites the fruit, making it inedible by dirtying it.

Poqhiraj

In Hindu belief, Poqhiraj is the heavenly flying horse of Bengal.

Porcupine

In Australian Aboriginal legend, Porcupine was the brother of Turtle. But one day, Turtle and his friends ganged up against Porcupine and thrust their spears into him. Which is why the porcupine has a spiky coat and why the turtle and his kind are forced to swim underwater, having no power when on land. Among the bushmen of the Kalahari, Porcupine is the daughter of a monster who is called the All-Devourer. Her father was so fearsome that Porcupine went to live with gentle Mantis. She married Kwamang-a, the rainbow god, by whom she had Ichneumon, a bossy young mongoose who is continually trying to upset his adoptive grandfather, Mantis.

Ptesan-Wi

Among the Lakota tribes of North America, Ptesan-Wi is the name given to White Buffalo Calf Woman, one of their greatest teachers, the messenger who passes between the Buffalo (*see* Bison) and people. Ptesan-Wi appeared in the times before the Sioux had horses (before the first Spanish invaders).

Two young men saw a young woman walking towards them floating over the ground, so they knew she was holy. The man who stretched out his hand to her was immediately burnt by lightning into a blackened heap of bones, but the other ran back into camp to acclaim her coming. Carrying a bundle, she entered the medicine lodge erected in her honour, showing how the sacred altar must be set up made of red earth and a buffalo skull. Opening her bundle, she instructed the chief in the use of the sacred pipe and how it must be circulated sun-wise, revealing how the smoke of the prayers rising heavenwards was the living breath of the Grandfather Mystery. She showed how the pipe stem was the bridge between the sacred world above and the sacred world below, how the stone of the pipe bowl represented the buffalo. The buffalo himself represented the universe and the four directions, each leg of the buffalo representing the four ages of man. She also gave the women precious things from her bag including corn, pemmican, wild turnip, the skill of keeping the fire and the way to cook food by dropping a hot stone into a buffalo stomach filled with water. She spoke of herself as the four ages of the world, promising to return in every cycle. As she stepped into the distance towards the setting sun, the people all saw that she turned into a black buffalo, a brown one, a red one and lastly a white buffalo calf. The White Buffalo Calf is considered to be the most holy thing anyone could ever see. As soon as she vanished, the buffalo herds appeared, enabling people to live entirely from their great bounty.

PUCK

In English folk tradition, Puck is a household spirit, a kind of brownie, most famous from his appearance in William Shakespeare's play *A Midsummer Night's Dream* where he is the assistant of the fairy king, Oberon.

PUKIS

Among the Latvians, Estonians and Lithuanians of the Baltic states, Pukis, Pukys or Puuk is the name given to the household dragon. A Pukis takes the form of a cat when it is upon the ground but becomes a dragon when it flies through the air. All Pukis have a tendency to be tricksters and guard treasure in a fiercely exclusive way. This works to the advantage of the householder but against his neighbours.

PWCA

The Welsh Pwca is related to the Irish Pooka, the Cornish Bucca and the Manx Buggane. It lives by itself and can act like a brownie or house spirit, although it can also choose to behave as it pleases if it is not respected.

Pyrios

Pyrios is one of the four winged horses of the sun in Roman myth. The poet Ovid lists the others as Achton, Eous and Phlegon. These four were harnessed daily to the chariot of the sun and driven across the heavens by the charioteer Phaethon.

Python

There are many species of pythons, some of which grow over 20 ft in length and which can swallow whole animals and digest them in their stomachs over many days and weeks. In Greek mythology, Python is the name given to the female dragon who lives in the chasm of the oracle of Delphi. Apollo came to Delphi and tried to remove Python, killing it. He then governed the oracle where the resident priestess sat over the cracks of the chasm to give oracular answers to the questions of supplicants. However, Python was not forgotten, for she seemed to become embodied in the priestess or Pythoness who was the mouthpiece of the oracle.

In Zulu lore, there was a queen who did not give birth but who swelled up until she was enormous. She finally gave birth to a Python over the space of many hours. Both her women and her husband avoided her, forcing her to live alone. But after a few months her offspring began to shed its skin and then it began to give birth to five boys and five girls. The oldest boy was called Uthlathu Yesiziba (Python of the Pool). Finally, the king returned, delighted to find that he had ten lovely children. He made Uthlathu Yesiziba his successor.

QAILERTETANG

Among the Inuit peoples of Baffin Island, Canada, Qailertetang is the seal servant of the goddess Sedna. Qailertetang's role is to journey from the depths of the freezing seas of the underworld where Sedna has her realm to the land of humans to report on the misdemeanours of men. Sedna already knows that wrongdoing has occurred because her finger-stumps ache. At the annual festival that honours Sedna, a dancer is attired as Qailertetang, complete with seal flippers, and she inspects the paired dancers. Weaving in between them, she rearranges the pairs until she is satisfied, after which those pairs must go off and be husband and wife for a day and a night. This practice is believed to enhance both human and seal populations. The rest of the festival includes a frank public appraisal of tribal misconduct that year, to show to Qailertetang that the tribe is aware of its responsibilities, for they know that she will report back to Sedna who may punish them if they hide their misdemeanours. These sins endanger everyone, for Sedna will cease to send the seals on which they rely for food and clothing.

QEBEHSENUEF

Qebehsenuef is one of the Canopic Animals who is responsible for guarding the intestines of the deceased in the mummification process. Qebehsenuef has the head of a hawk. He is under the protection of the goddess, Serket, and his name means 'he who cools his brother'. Qebehsenuef was told by Horus to refresh the deceased after his struggles to attain the afterlife.

QUAIL

The mythology of the quail is widely spread about the world. In China, the quail is associated with the Phoenix or Feng Hwang as the Scarlet Bird of the Astronomers. In Taoist belief, the quail is the essence of Yang, representing the element of fire and summer. Among the Ainu people of Japan, the quail was the only bird to be created upon Earth, the others having emanated from heaven. It is regarded as the essence of good living, since it is well covered with feathers and well nourished. In Hindu belief, the quail heralds the return of the sun, as the myth in which the divine twins, the Asvins, who are representatives of the day and night help revive a quail that has been swallowed by the wolf of darkness.

In Russia, the quail is paired with the hare as the creatures of the sun and moon respectively. It was one of the birds sent to feed the starving Israelites in the desert after the Exodus from Egypt, although it was forbidden food to those who worshipped the Middle Eastern god, Baal, to whom quails were sacrificed. Leto, the mother of Apollo and Artemis in Greek myth, was turned into a quail by the jealous Hera. In this form, Leto flew safely to Delos to give birth to her children. In Roman folklore, the

The Element Encyclopedia of Magical Creatures

quail was the gift of a lover to his beloved, since the bird was considered to be amorous.

QUEL

In Mayan tradition, the parrot Quel was one of the four creatures that brought maize to the gods so that they could make humanity. The other animals who helped in this creation were Hoh the crow, Utiu the coyote and Yac the forest cat.

QUESTING BEAST

In Arthurian legend, the Questing Beast, also known as Glatisant, is a hybrid creature with the head of a snake, the body of a leopard, the hindquarters of a lion and the feet of a hart (stag). Its origin comes from a dark tale of incest in which a woman who sleeps with her brother, gives birth to this strange creature and is afterwards torn apart by dogs. The pursuit of the Questing Beast properly belonged to the knight Sir Pellinore, although it is later taken up by the Arabic knight Palamedes after the death of Pellinore in Sir Thomas Malory's *Le Morte D'Arthur*.

QUETZALCOATL

In Central American myth, Quetzalcoatl is the Great Feathered Serpent of Toltec and Aztec traditions. He is the god of the wind who represents spirit freed from matter. He is a regenerator and shaman, a god of fertility and the bringer of the arts of civilization. He takes the shape of a plumed serpent, with the colourful feathers of the quetzal bird instead of scales. He is often seen in the company of hummingbirds, for they represent the *nahua* (disembodied soul). Quetzalcoatl is understood to range over the world like a wind, presiding over spiritual matters. He is the son of Mixcoatl, the Cloud Serpent; his brothers are Camaxtli the red, Tezcatlipoca the black god of night, and Huitzilopochtli. The four brothers guarded the four directions. Quetzalcoatl's symbol was the morning star, Venus, which was one of his four temples. The others were the moon, the medicine temple and the temple of Xipe Toltec, which only those of pure Toltec descent might enter. In his human shape, Quetzalcoatl wore a red conical hat like a conch shell, symbol of his power as a wind deity, a wind mask, a priestly feather-fringed shirt and he carried a spear-thrower and arrow. Quetzalcoatl can take many forms and has appeared, like Vishnu, in many incarnations.

Quetzalcoatl came to Earth down a knotted ladder that resembled a scourge, although he himself desired no sacrifice. Two other gods came to Earth to assist him in the ordering of civilization. During the first age of the sun, Quetzalcoatl struck down the ruler Tezcatlipoca, turning him into a jaguar, which ate the giants that were taking over the Earth, before throwing the ruler into the sea, an action which is repeated every time the constellation Ursa Major descends into the sea. In the second age of the sun, Tlaloc the wind god struck Quetzalcoatl, creating a great hurricane, but in the fourth age of the sun, four men were created who assisted Tezcatlipoca and Quetzalcoatl, who then became the rulers of the skies. The act of throwing his son Nanautzin, who was conceived by the goddess Chalchiuhtlicue, into the fire, caused the fifth age of the sun to be born. Tlaloc did the same with his son who became the moon. During this phase, Quetzalcoatl became an eagle traversing the sky in the day and emerging into the underworld as an ocelot. There are many tales concerning Quetzalcoatl's combat with Tezcatlipoca. In legend, Quetzalcoatl was a white-skinned man, a belief that caused the Aztecs to falter when confronted with the Spanish invaders led by Cortes, because they were sure he was an incarnation of the god. In Mayan myth, he is called Kukulcan.

QUIKINNA'QU

Quikinna'qu is the Big Raven of Koyrak Indian myth in North America. Quikinna'qu is also known as Big Grandfather or Creator who puts on his raven-coat to fetch reindeer for the people. It is also said that he was made when the creator was sharpening his knife in the sky; a whetstone chip fell to Earth and became Quikinna'qu. His wife is Miti'. He is simultaneously a shaman, the first man and the culture hero who fetches the essential components and tools for basic living. When Koyrak shamans treat their patients, they address them in the name of Quikinna'qu, saying, 'Big Raven is working for you here, Big Raven is healing you.'

R

Rahu

In Hindu tradition, Rahu is the monster that takes the form of a man with a dragon's head and a long tail. Rahu gate-crashed the festival at which the gods were drinking the sacred liquor, *amrita*, after the Churning of the Ocean. The sun and moon reported his presence to Vishnu who threw one of his discuses and beheaded Rahu. However, Rahu had drunk sufficiently of the *amrita* to partake of immortality. As his head flew into the heavens, it pursued the moon, devouring some of its light every month and occasionally swallowing the sun in vengeance for their spying upon him. He is thus associated with the lunar cycle as well as eclipses of sun and moon.

Raiju

In Japanese mythology, Raiju is the spirit of lightning who takes the form of a cat, badger or weasel. When a tree has been marked by lightning, people say that it has been scratched by Raiju. During thunderstorms, it becomes agitated and leaps from tree to tree, just like a cat. Raiju likes to hide in human navels, so it is advisable for people to sleep on their fronts during a thunderstorm unless they want to harbour this busy spirit.

Rainbow Serpent

The Rainbow Serpent is one of the most important creating spirits of the Australian Aboriginal Dreamtime (Alcheringa). This huge, multi-coloured python-like serpent lives in the deep-water channels, rivers and billabongs, and was responsible for the formation of all such gullies and creeks where water can flow. During the dry season, he sleeps in the mud but when the wet season comes, he rises into the sky, glistening with rain, bringing colour to everything that has been hard-baked by the dry season. Iridescent objects such as pearls and shells are pleasing to him. In the north-west he is called Kalseru and brings rain and fertility. Originally, he held inside himself all creatures and green plants because he wanted to be part of everything, but humans needed to get the Rainbow Serpent to give forth the nurture of green things and waters. A shaman turned himself into a colourful kookaburra and flew about the serpent, causing him to release all the creatures that were inside him. Nearly every part of Australia has its own local myth about the Rainbow Serpent who is held in considerable awe and respect.

However, the Rainbow Serpent is not found exclusively in Australian myth, but also in Africa and parts of Melanesia and Polynesia. In the Dahomey culture of West Africa and in the corresponding folklore of Voudon in Haiti, the Rainbow Serpent is Aida Hwedo, the first one to be created. He carried the creator Mawu on his back so that the creator could fill the world. His track through the earth caused river channels and chasms, and his dung created mountains. The Rainbow Serpent of the Congo basin lives in lakes and his reflection is seen in the waterfall. In Nigeria, the serpent is called Oshumare.

The Element Encyclopedia of Magical Creatures

Raja Naga

Among the Malay peoples, Raja Naga is the king of the serpents who lives at the bottom of the sea in a wonderful palace called Pusat Tasik. Raja Naga is the largest of the Nagas.

Raksa

A Raksa is a titanic spirit of Hindu belief who wanders about at night devouring human beings, disturbing sacrifices, bothering pious sages and upsetting people. Rakasas can take the form of humans or animals but they always have a monstrous appearance with flaming eyes, sharp teeth and a super-long tongue. When the monkey Hanuman entered the city of Lanka in the epic story of the *Ramayana*, he observed many Rakasas. Some of them affronted the eye, while others seemed beautiful. Some had long arms and terrible shapes, some were fat, others lean. Some were dwarves or giants, some had only one eye or ear. They had huge bellies and pendulous breasts, crooked legs, projecting teeth. Some were serpent-headed, or had the heads of donkeys, horses or elephants. The Rakasas were born from the foot of Brahma and a daughter of Daksa the Skilful.

Ram

The virile and assertive ram has been seen as a personification of the masculine and procreative power the world over. The ram is the one of the most common sacrificial animals. When Ur of the Chaldees was first excavated, one of the most remarkable finds was a statue of the Ram in the Thicket, a ram on its hind legs peering through a golden-leaved bush. This image is remarkably similar to that found by the relieved Abraham who, in the Book of Genesis, is directed by God to sacrifice the ram and not his son Isaac.

Rams' horns were a feature of sovereignty and were assumed as symbols by gods and kings alike. The Phoenician god, Baal, wears these horns, but they are also sported by many Egyptian deities. The ram was the symbol sacred to the Egyptian god Amun who was known as 'the lord of two horns'. Its gilded head and horns were set at the prow of his festival boat. Herodotus tells how the hero Hercules was impatient to see the true form of Zeus/Amun. In order to conceal his mystery and to preserve Hercules from the sudden shock of his divinity, Zeus/Amun covered himself with a ram's fleece, which is why Amun remains a ram-headed god. The creating god Khnum wears the flattened horns of the now extinct species of ram called *Ovis longipes palaeoaegyptiaca*, which was not found anywhere after 2000 BC, attesting to the antiquity of this divinity. The sacred Ram of Mendes embodied the souls of the gods Ra, Osiris, Khepra and Shu.

The Element Encyclopedia of Magical Creatures

Among the Khoi peoples of Namibia, there is a Sun Ram called Sore-Gus who was found by a hunter called Giri and he was amazed to see this glimmering golden ram. He shot it with his arrow and cut off some of the meat immediately. On the way home, he suffered a terrible thirst, but whenever he found water, it immediately dried up. A wise man deduced that Giri had slain the Sun Ram. He instructed Giri to return to the ram's body and to replace the meat he cut from it, praying that the Sun Ram stand up and be restored. As soon as Giri uttered the prayer, Sore-Gus stood up, began to shine and all the waters flowed back into their pools again.

In Greece, the ram was sacrificed to Zeus/Sabazios and to Dionysus, while the devotees of Attis bathed in its blood. The Golden Fleece sought by Jason and the Argonauts once adorned the back of a great ram. In Hebrew ritual lore, the ram's horn or *shofar* is blown to announce the New Year, clearly showing the pastoral antecedents of the Jewish race, which also used red-dyed ram's skins to house the Ark of the Covenant in the Tabernacle. In Hinduism, the ram is sacred to Agni, the god of Fire.

In Derbyshire, England, the Derby Ram is a major character celebrated in a Mummer's play still performed at the New Year in the streets of the town. The ram is impersonated by a person who holds the pole and hides under the blanket that make his costume. He is then ceremonially killed and resurrected. The song that commemorates the ram speaks of his great size and the resourceful use of his body parts to furnish an eagle's nest from his horns, wool that clothes the whole navy, blood that turns a waterwheel, eyes that make footballs, hide to make shoes, a tail that becomes a bell rope and a head that becomes an oven.

It took all the men of Derby to take
away his bones,
And all the women of Derby to roll
away his stones. [testicles]

A version of this song was popular with George Washington and his troops. The Ram song passed into southern US tradition as the New Orleans jazzman's processional funeral song as the mourners return home from the cemetery, 'Didn't he ramble'.

Ratatosk

In Norse mythology, Ratatosk is the squirrel who runs up and down the world tree Yggdrasil and brings the messages of the eagle who sits at the top of the tree down to the dragon Nidhoggr who lives in the roots. Unfortunately, Ratatosk does not report the messages clearly and sows discord between the two.

The Element Encyclopedia of Magical Creatures

RAVEN

The myths of the clever raven are found worldwide. This extraordinary bird makes a frequent appearance as a trickster spirit, both in raven and human form. Their throaty, almost human, calls have been the subject of divinatory speculation and their movements and obvious intelligence have led to many stories about ravens being messengers between gods and humans. In Norse myth, Odin's ravens Huginn and Muninn, 'Thought' and 'Memory', fly about the world bringing him all the news, alluding to the raven's notoriously nosy nature. As a bird of wisdom it is unparalleled, but because it is a scavenger, it sometimes acquires an evil reputation for attending the field of slaughter.

In the Irish stories of the Ultonian hero, Cu Chulainn, the hero is much at odds with the raven goddess the Morrigan because he rejects her amorous intentions. She then pursues him mercilessly throughout his short but vividly bloody career. Finally, Cu Chulainn is unable to fight any longer and he ties himself to a pillar to die standing up as a warrior should. As life leaves his body, the Morrighan perches upon the pillar to be the first to peck out his eyes. The Morrighan's sisters Badh and Nemain form the triple Morrigna of ravens who can take human form. In Welsh myth, the god of wisdom in ancestral memory is Bran the Blessed whose association with ravens is due to the fact that his name means 'Raven'. After a fruitless battle with the Irish, he ordered that his few surviving followers cut off his head and bear it to the White Mount, there to be buried to repel invasion. His legend lives on in the tradition of the Tower of London, the site of the White Mount, that if the resident ravens that are still kept in Bran's memory leave the Tower, then Britain will suffer invasion. In the story the 'Dream of Rhonabwy' in *The Mabinogion* there is a famous scene in which Arthur and Owein play a board game in which the playing pieces mirror real life: Owein's ravens (perhaps warriors in raven dress) fight with Arthur's soldiers, killing endless numbers of them until Arthur finally calls halt.

To the Roman followers of the Persian god Mithras, the raven was a symbol of initiation into the grade of the sun. As such, it is the remover of pollution, as in the Zoroastrian tradition. This solar symbolism is reflected in Greek legend where the raven was the companion of the sun god Apollo. In China, it was believed that a three-legged raven lived in the sun. Each leg represented the rising, midday and setting of the sun respectively.

The Element Encyclopedia of Magical Creatures

Among the Inuit, Raven is the hero who brings life. Once Raven was born out of darkness. As he was walking about, he felt trees, plants and grasses. The more he pondered their meaning, the sooner he realized that he himself was the Raven Father who created everything. He flew out of the darkness and found the Earth, causing plants to grow upon it. Then while he was overflying the land, he found a giant pea pod from which the first man emerged. Raven made caribou and musk-oxen for them to eat, teaching man how to respect his fellow creatures. Then he created a female companion for the man, and showed them how to make clothes, shelters and canoes.

In Biblical lore, the raven is the bird Noah first sends out to seek for dry land although it is the dove that returns first. The prophet Elijah was kept alive in the wilderness by the care of ravens, which brought him bread and meat. It is likewise the emblem of St Benedict, the wise and practical founder of Western monasticism, and the helper of St Bernard, founder of the Dominicans, who was stopped from eating poison by a percipient raven as well as being the companion of St Cuthbert, who lived a hermetic existence surrounded by wild creatures. The raven also makes a sinister appearance in Edgar Allan Poe's poem, *The Raven*.

REMORA

Remora is an alternative name for the Echeneis, the great fish of Roman report. It is only about one foot long and four inches thick, but it wraps itself around a rock with its sucking mouth and attaches itself to vessels by its horn. The Remora was said to be the cause for the slow progress of Mark Antony's flagship at the Battle of Actium, where one is supposed to have attached itself to the ship in order to draw up sunken gold from the sea bed. As it says in Joshura Sylvester's poem, 'Du Bastas his divine weekes and Workes':

> *The Remora, fixing her feeble horn*
> *Into the tempest-beaket Vessels stern,*
> *Stayes her stone-still, while all her stout*
>   *Consorts*
> *Saile thence at pleasure to their wished*
>   *Ports.*

REYNARD

Reynard the Fox is one of the most popular figures of medieval European legend, the trickster hero who has a whole fox-epic to himself in the 12th-century French poem '*Roman de Renart*'. Reynard tries to catch the cockerel Chantecler, but since the cock exhorts the fox to refute various insults hurled after him by his pursuers, Reynard has to open his mouth and inadvertently lets Chantecler go. He offers the titmouse the kiss of peace telling her that Noble the Lion, King of

The Element Encyclopedia of Magical Creatures

Beasts, has proclaimed peace, but the bird is not convinced and makes him kiss her with his eyes closed. She merely touches a piece of moss to his mouth and escapes, just before some hunting dogs come along and Reynard himself is forced to run off. In one adventure, he finds himself in the den of Ysengrin the wolf and is accused of being Ysengrin's wife's lover. He rapes Hersent, Ysengrin's wife and is hauled off to court where he protests it was out of love. Before judgement can be given, Reynard makes good his escape. The Reynard stories were very popular and they passed into Germany and Holland. These stories are particularly insulting about the mendicant orders of monks who wandered about Europe begging and preaching, and some were obviously used to make social comment through the more acceptable and oblique medium of animal stories. This tradition continued right through into the 19th century where Wilhelm von Kaulbach's pictures both illustrate Reynard's tale and poke fun at and satirize the Establishment. Reynard the Fox ducks and dives like any hustler or n'er-do-well, always trying to come out on top. His stories appeared in English during the 17th century and he has remained a favourite children's story character ever since.

RIGI

In the creation myths of the Nauru people of the South Pacific, the worm Rigi, helped Areop-Enap, the Ancient Spider, create the Earth and heavens by prising apart mollusc shells. His efforts were such that his sweat became the salt of the sea as he heaved them open. In other stories, Rigi was a butterfly who flew between earth and sea to separate them.

Road Predators

For many magical or monstrous creatures on the borders of our world, it is the other way round, for it is they who seek for unwary human wayfarers on the lonely road, people out late and alone whom they may pursue, molest or devour. Salutary travellers' tales speak of such lurking companions of the lonesome path, on desolate moorland, over trackless desert or in eerie mountain passes. Tales from the time before gasoline took us from A to B, when the traveller went on foot, or with a single donkey or horse, come from all over the world, telling us to be careful how we tread in certain places.

These haunters of the lonely road are often location-specific, patrolling a particular road or region, like the Black Dog, Padfoot or Barguest. In many cases, it is what is not seen but felt that causes the traveller alarm, a sense of being watched or followed, of which the only evidence is the prickling between the shoulder blades, as Coleridge's Ancient Mariner experiences:

> *Like one, that on some lonesome*
> *   road*
> *Doth walk in fear and dread,*
> *And having once turned round*
> *   walks on,*
> *And turns no more his head:*
> *Because he knows, a frightful*
> *   fiend*
> *Doth close behind him tread.*

Whether the traveller is about to be pounced upon from a tree by a Jaculus or is followed by the Ki Du whose eyes glow in the dark, he certainly knows that, though man may be top of the food chain, there are creatures who have other ideas.

ROBIN GOODFELLOW

Robin Goodfellow is the English hob-goblin or fairy whom William Shake-speare associates with Puck in his *A Midsummer Night's Dream*. The name has a euphemistic air to it as if those who dealt with Robin had to propitiate him with a title that makes him sound more neighbourly than he can be. While Robin Goodfellow may sometimes enable housewives to finish their tasks as would a brownie, most often he plays the trickster. An early 17th-century pamphlet, *Robin Goodfellow, His Mad Pranks and Merry Jests*, speaks of him as the son of Oberon and a country maid. He acquires the gift of shapeshifting and uses this to his own benefit. Robin meets wayfarers out late on the road and leads them a merry dance, causing them to lose themselves in woods, lakes, bogs and thickets:

Sometimes I meet them like a man,
Sometimes an ox, sometimes a hound;
And to a horse I turn me can
To trip and trot about them round.

In Shakespeare's portrayal, Robin Goodfellow or Puck is a conniver with Oberon to confuse the Athenian lovers in the wood and to play the trick of making Oberon's mistress, Titania, fall in love with an ass – all tricks that Robin much enjoys.

ROC

The Roc (or Rukh) is the great bird of Middle Eastern legend. It looks like an eagle or vulture, with horns upon its head and a wingspan of astounding width. It can pick up and carry an ele-phant if it pleases. Marco Polo stated that he had seen one of its great feath-ers while at the court of Kublai Khan. He also reported that a Roc had car-ried off a bride. In *The Thousand and One Nights* tales of Arabia, the sailor Sinbad is shipwrecked on an island entirely made of brushwood enclosing a dome. It isn't until the sky grows dark above him that he realizes that the whole island is a nest and that the dome is an egg. He clings to the talon of the Roc and drops from its grasp without the bird noticing. It is thought that the giant Aepyornis of Madagascar, which was 8–9 ft high and laid 13-in eggs was believed to have been the basis for many stories about the Roc.

ROPEN

In the stories of New Guinea, the Ropen is a pteranadon-like creature with a leathery wingspan of about 3–4 ft. When Western missionaries first started to penetrate Papua New Guinea in the 1950s, they began to hear tales of the Ropen, which people said lived in the caves along the islands of New Britain and Umboi on the Bismarck Archipelago. People said it flew by night and had a long tail ending in a diamond-shaped tip, a beak with teeth and razor-sharp claws. When the English missionary Tyson Hughes was helping the Moluccan tribes of Ceram Island in

The Element Encyclopedia of Magical Creatures

the 1980s, he was told about the Orang-bati ('men with wings') who lived in the caves of an extinct volcano, Mount Kairatu, in the centre of the island. The Ropen has a taste for decaying flesh and is said to harass any funeral gatherings, swooping down upon the corpse.

ROSHWALR

In Norwegian folklore, the Roshwalr is a horse-whale, a vast whale with the head of a horse. A severed head of a Roshwalr was sent to Pope Leo X in 1520 and drawn by the naturalist Ambroise Paré. It is realized now that the Roshwalr was none other than a walrus.

ROU SHOU

In Chinese mythology, Rou Shou is the counterpart dragon to Gou Mang. Together they go as the messengers of the sky god. Rou Shou is associated with the western direction and is the herald of autumn, just as Gou Mang heralds the spring in the east.

RUSALKI

Rusalki are the water nymphs of Slavic mythology. They live in the waters of lakes and rivers and frequently sun themselves on rocks or along the branch of an overhanging tree. Rusalki look like human women except for their translucent skins and the tails that they sometimes have. They have

the ability to transform into water creatures at will, and also into horses. As nymphs of the seasons, Rusalki spin the cycle of each season. The tradition says that they are the spirits of drowned girls, like the Lorelei, but in common with the Sirens, they sing to attract young men with a view to making them enter the water, at which point they are pulled under.

A Russian story tells how young Ivan Savelevich, a seal hunter, spent one winter in the Arctic Circle playing his balalaika. As he played, his oil lamp ran out but he played on and was aware of a sound of dancing inside his hut. Relighting the lamp, he found no one at all. This kept on happening, so he hid behind a curtain with the lamp shaded and peered out to see a Rusalka dancing. Ivan fell in love with her, becoming so obsessed that he dived into the water to live with her. After a long while, he yearned for home but could find no way back until he remembered that Rusalki could be rendered harmless if one made the sign of the cross. He did so and was able to swim to the surface. However, having blessed himself, he might no longer return to his darling Rusalka any more.

RYUJIN

In Japanese mythology, the Ryujin is a sea-dragon god who lives at the bottom of the sea. He is a controller of the tides, with a huge mouth into which he sucks the water, letting it all out in one rush as he breathes slowly in and out. His messengers are turtles.

When Empress Jingo tried to invade Korea, she prayed to Ryujin, sending her messenger to collect the Tide Jewels for her fleet. Throwing the Low Tide Jewels into the sea, the tide receded and beached the Korean fleet. As the sailors jumped out onto the mud-flats, Jingo threw the High Tide Jewels and they were all drowned. A tidal wave then carried the Japanese fleet onto the Korean coast, giving them victory. Ryujin then presented the Tide Jewels on a pink shell platter to the Empress' son, Ojin.

S

SABGARIFYA

In Egyptian tradition, Sabgarifya are a form of Hippocampus. The sea stallions come to graze off a certain island at a particular time of the year and horse breeders bring their mares in season so that they might be mated with the Sabgarifya. The foals are believed to be able to run without ever tiring because they are thought to have no lungs.

SADHUZAG

In medieval European lore, the Sadhuzag was a creature with the head of a goat and the body of a deer but which was like a great bull in size. On its head and body it had 74 horns to ensure that it was given a wide berth.

SAEHRIMNIR

In Norse mythology, Saehrimnir was the wild boar that was roasted and eaten every night by the Aesir and the warriors of Valhalla. The next morning it was again on the hoof, ready to be hunted and cooked once again that night. The ever-renewing pig is found also in Irish myth, where the Feast of Goibniu the smith-god offers a similar opportunity for the worthy warrior to feast perpetually in the hollow hills of the Blessed Otherworld. Saehrimnir is cooked, prepared and jointed by Andhrimnir, the cook in Valhalla, in the great sooty cauldron Eldhrimnir.

Sacrificial Animals

Animals have always been the links between human beings and the gods. Throughout the world, people have sacrificed animals as offerings to the gods. The reasons for sacrifice vary: sometimes it is so that the gods might wish to join in and enjoy a feast, but it can also be to appease them in order to avert punishment, or to obtain some request or prayer. Animals thus sacrificed or ritually set apart to be shared with the gods or spirits invariably involve the primary domesticated animals that are kept for meat such as the bull, cow, cockerel, goat and sheep.

In many parts of Africa, it is believed that the only way to make a connection between the gods, ancestors and spirits, and ourselves is through sacrifice. Without sacrifice, the lineage will wither. In cases of familial or tribal disputes, the medicine that binds people back into good relations requires the sacrifice of an animal. According to the Dogon of Mali, it is believed that all living beings have souls (*kikinu*) and the vital power of life (*nyama*). At the moment of sacrifice, the celebrant alerts the gods to the aim of the sacrifice by means of prayer, then the blood of the animal victim flows upon the altar carrying its nyama. The altar is believed to be a living being, drinking the blood like a baby at the breast of its mother. The sacrificial act restores connection between beings living in the everyday world with those in the Otherworld. In this case, sacrifice is a means of revolving the circuit of energy between the worlds. Sacrifices also remove impurity. In Norse mythology, the boar Sonargoltr was sacrificed in a *sonarblot* (blood sacrifice) to ensure a good harvest, while in Middle Eastern tradition, it is a different kind of sacrifice – a ritual setting aside – that is the reason for the scapegoat. The Laws of Manu, which were transmitted by Manu Vaivasvata in ancient Vedic times in India, say:

He who injures animals that are not harmful, from a wish to give himself pleasure, adds nothing to his own happiness, living or dead, while he who gives no creatures willingly the pain of confinement or death, but seeks the good of all, enjoys bliss without end … The slaughter of animals obstructs the way to heaven.

In one of the collection of Buddhist stories known as the Jataka tales, Buddha denounces the sacrificers of cows, noting that:

We see no cattle asking to be slain
That they might have a new and
    better life.
Rather they go unwillingly to their
    death,
Struggling vainly with their last
    breath.

All hunters in traditional societies maintain a respectful view of their prey. Initiation into the adult role of the hunter involves the learning of prayers or propitiation that leads the animal's soul to the rightful place in the Otherworld, as well as understanding the hunter's code of 'take only what you need; spare the females with young'. The taking of a large meat animal from one's livestock to feed the community invariably involves a sharing in nurture and a thanksgiving.

SALAMANDER

According to classical accounts, the Salamander was a great lizard whose bite was exceedingly poisonous. People believed that it lived in volcanoes or could be found in the hottest part of a fire. Salamanders were thought to poison fruit trees, according to medieval bestiaries. In an Anglo-Saxon bestiary, the salamander is said to stop the mouths of lions as an illustration of how the faithful will be freed from the fires of Judgment.

SALMON

The salmon's extraordinary journey between the sea and the freshwater rivers where its parents spawned and back again is a yearly miracle from which many cultures have benefited and been inspired. In north-west California, the beliefs of the Karok people centred upon the laws laid down by the Ikxareyavs, the First People, who had special powers. The most important of these was Coyote, who ordained that people would eat salmon and acorns, but that life would not be easy; death would continue to come in order to keep the world from overcrowding. Their celebration of the salmon revolved around the cycle of the fishes' annual upriver spawning, which was marked by the Jump Dance – part of a ritual cycle that makes the world new every year – and by the use of a sacred obsidian knife, which was used to cut open the first salmon.

In Celtic tradition, the Salmon of Wisdom is one of the most important magical creatures. It is one of the oldest animals with a proverbial memory, going back to the roots of creation itself. All that has ever happened is retained in the Salmon's memory. In the British story of 'Culhwch and Olwen', it is imperative that the Divine Youth, Mabon, is liberated from his place of imprisonment, yet no one knows where, when or why Mabon was imprisoned. The seekers inquire of many animals, each of which sends them on to another beast or bird: the blackbird, the stag, the owl, the eagle. Last in line is the salmon, the oldest, who has heard rumour of Mabon's anguish behind the walls of the fortress at Caer Loyw (Gloucester). The salmon bears the seekers on its back and helps them bring Mabon out.

The early Celts depended upon an oral culture in which all information, mystical empowerment and lore was retained by the mind of the shamanic bard or poet. Tradition was handed down by oral recitation, through the transmission of a teacher to a pupil, in the seeding embers of ancient firesides and within the collective shamanic journey-experience, which all poets enacted as part of their bardic incubation. The central myth of primal inspiration among the *filidh* (vision poets) of Ireland concerns the well of Segais in which the Salmon of Wisdom swam, fed by the hazelnuts that dropped into the pool from overhanging trees. It was believed that hazelnuts conferred knowledge. The Irish god of the Otherworld and the Sea, Manannan, explained to King Cormac that the five streams that flow out of the central pool of the Salmon of Wisdom are the five streams of the senses by which inspiration flows down from the Otherworld into our own. The salmon's mysterious powers were observable by all who watched its spectacular yearly return to its birthplace to mate and spawn. The rainbow-speckled fish teeming in great abundance would make a great impression as they sought their source. The Celts too were a people who returned to their source and kept faith with it. The oral transmission of lore was strictly upheld that the tradition be faithfully remembered word for word. The true tradition was the quarry of all shamans and the quest for the Salmon of Wisdom became one of the prime shamanic stories.

The Irish hero Fionn Mac Cumhail came to Finn Eces, the druid, to be taught. Finn Eces had just caught the Salmon of Wisdom and was about to roast it over a fire. He set Fionn to tend the fish and make sure it did not burn, and in so doing lost his chance of All Wisdom, because hot liquor splashed from the fish on to Fionn's finger so that he put it in his mouth to cool. In aftertimes, Fionn had only to put that finger in his mouth to know whatever he needed about anything.

The abundance of salmon during their annual return to source is lauded in cultures as distant as the north-west Pacific coast of America where the first salmon is praised as 'the Chieftain', and the eastern Pacific coasts of Japan where the Ainu people venerate the salmon as 'the Great Thing'.

SAMAS

The Mesopotamian Lion Man, shown as a man above the waist and a lion below, stands upright and carries a staff. He is also called Uridimmus or 'Mad Lion'. He may represent the Sumerian god Utu who brings the beneficent light of the sun to Earth. Samas is the god of truth, justice and rectitude, a destroyer of evil and a protector of kings. He enables the king Etana to free an eagle that has been trapped in a pit by a serpent. Samas brings the plant of life to Etana and enables him to fly to heaven on the eagle's back.

SAMEBITO

In Japanese myth, the Samebito is half shark and half human with a black skin, a beard and green eyes. This being was encountered by the hero Totaro when he was crossing the Long Bridge. Instead of attacking him, Samebito asked for food and shelter, for it had been exiled from the ocean. Totaro gave Samebito hospitality in the lake of his own palace grounds. Later, when Tataro fell in love with the lovely Tamana, Tamana's father tried to prevent the union by asking for a bride price of 10,000 precious stones. This price was far too high for him and Totaro fell into a decline. Samebito was alarmed and distressed by his rescuer's predicament. It shed tears of such sadness that each of them turned into precious stones, which Totaro was then able to exchange for Tamana's hand in marriage.

SAMPATI

According to Hindu tradition, Sampati is a human-headed bird, the son of Garuda. His brother is Jayaya, a similarly human-headed bird who was destroyed by Ravana, the demon king of Sri Lanka. When Hanuman was searching for Sita, it was Sampati who overflew Ravana's city and discovered that she was held prisoner. When Hanuman returned with his armies to rescue Sita and overthrow Ravana, Sampati's brother was also avenged.

SASQUATCH

Sasquatch is the Canadian name for Bigfoot. Native American legends call this shy, hairy, ape-like biped 'Hairy Giant'. Standing 7–9 ft and weighing in at 600–900 lbs, he is a beast that you would remember seeing. The first sighting by a white man was in 1811 in the town of Jasper, Alberta, when a trader came across footprints that were 14 in long and 8 in wide in the snow. He might have overlooked them as the print of snowshoes or boots that had melted wider than the step of a man except that there were clearly four toes to each footprint. There was another sighting in 1884 when a train crew stopped the train to give chase to a Sasquatch that they captured and called Jacko. Their prisoner seemed to fit the description of a gorilla or chimpanzee. When some miners were found with their heads cut off in 1910, blame fell upon Sasquatch. But another story in 1924 contradicts the idea of Sasquatch as being a carnivore, for a Canadian lumberjack reported being captured by a family of Sasquatch that fed exclusively upon roots, grasses and spruce tips. Several sightings have been in the region of Mount St Helens. But the supreme prize of cryptozoology must go to Roger Patterson and Bob Gunlin who, in 1967, at Bluff Creek Riverbed in northern California, managed to capture the first ever footage of a Bigfoot, which showed a few seconds of a large, long-armed female Sasquatch moving across a clearing. This much-analysed footage shows a bulky creature covered with ape-like fur and with a slight conical crest of hair upraised on top of its head.

SATYR

In Greek mythology, satyrs are beings who are human above the waist with goat's legs and cloven hooves below the waist. They bear small horns upon their head. They are members of the Silvani or Forest Peoples and their leader is Silenus. Satyrs have a particularly lascivious nature, pursuing the nymphs with rampantly sexual intentions, and often getting drunk or playing pranks. In Greek drama, especially after tragedies, actors attired as satyrs enacted performances that were humorous and satiric, which is where the word 'satire' comes from. In medieval lore, the satyr became the main depiction of the devil, who acquires their goat-like ears, cloven hooves and tail. The devil inherited the satyr's taste for music-making. Interestingly, the devil was believed to be the only one who was able (or indeed permitted) to dance.

SCAPEGOAT

The custom of selecting by lot and sending out a male goat into the wilderness once a year was common to ancient Israel, as well as to parts of Asia and Africa. The selected goat stands in the presence of the community or village while the people ritually put upon it the burden of their sins. It was taken out into the desert or left at a crossroads where travellers passed in the hope that a stranger would consider it 'lost' and steal it away, thus bearing away any sins with it or becoming infected with them. Formally, the ceremony was founded by Moses, where two goats were led to the altar and the high priest cast lots to see which goat was to be the Lord's and so could be sacrificed in the temple. The goat that failed the lottery was presumed to be the goat of the demon Azazel, to be cast out into the wilderness (*see* Leviticus 16.)

SCARAB

The Scarab or Dung Beetle became a powerful symbol to the Egyptians of the path of the sun, for the beetle rolls its dung-ball along the earth just as the globe of the sun passes across the sky. It was associated with Khepra the God of Creation, 'He Who Comes Out of the Earth'. Emblems of scarabs made of earthenware or soapstone were buried in the mummy wrappings of the dead in order to help them to revive in the afterlife. Among the Basuto peoples of African Transvaal, the Scarab Beetle or Copri is believed to be the form in which the soul leaves the body.

SCORPION

The scorpion is a creature that lives in dry desert regions. Its ability to sting and go on stinging has given it an ambiguous symbology. In Zoroastrian tradition, the scorpion is seen as an animal of the dark spirit of evil Ahriman, who fights continually against the light. The cult of Mithras assigns the scorpion to one of the Dadophori, the light-bearing twins who light the way above and below: needless to say, the twin carrying the downward-pointing torch is assigned the scorpion. However, in

Mesopotamian tradition, the carved rounded stones recording grants of land often bear the scorpion, perhaps as spiritual boundary guardians. The scorpion was sacred to the goddess Ishtar.

The Egyptians believed that dead crocodiles might turn into scorpions and that is why Set takes the form of a scorpion as a punishment for trying to murder Horus. Isis prayed to Ra who sent Thoth to cure the child. The goddess Serkhet is also a scorpion goddess. Among the Amazonian people, it is believed that the scorpion was sent by the creator to punish men for impregnating those women whom he himself desired.

One version of the myth of the constellation Scorpio derives from the story of how the hunter Orion boasted to Artemis that he could rid the land of dangerous wild beasts. Apollo was suspicious of Orion's intentions towards his virgin sister, and sent a monstrous scorpion to pursue him. None of his weapons were able to overcome the scorpion and he dived into the sea. Apollo then raised the alarm and told Artemis that the creature bobbing about in the waves was the rapist of one of her Hyperborean priestesses. Artemis aimed and shot her friend Orion dead, without having intended to harm him. Her grief was so great that she demanded Aesculapius revive him. Zeus' thunderbolt stopped the healer in his tracks and Artemis set Orion's image in the stars where he is perpetually pursued by the scorpion.

SCORPION MAN

In Mesopotamian myth, the Scorpion Men or Girtablili are the attendants of the god Samas or Utu. They are shown with a horned cap of divinity, a human bearded head, the hindquarters and talons of a bird, a snake-headed penis and a scorpion's tail, raised to sting. A Scorpion Man was also attendant upon Tiamat, the great Babylonian goddess of Creation. Scorpion men and women guard the gate of Mount Masu where the sun arises. Scorpion people frequently appear on Assyrian instructions against psychic attack.

SCYLLA

In classical tradition, Scylla was a water nymph, the daughter of Typhon and Echidne. She takes the form of a beautiful woman from the waist up but beneath her waist she has the heads of six fierce dogs mounted upon the twelve dog's legs. Sometimes this appearance varies and she has twelve tentacloid legs and three sets of teeth mounted in six heads. Once she had been entirely beautiful, the beloved of Glaucus but when he caught the attentions of the sorceress Circe, the enchantress caused Scylla to change to her present shape. Another story tells how Circe cast poison into her bathwater. Hercules killed Scylla. A later version of her story told how her father was Phorcys who tried to restore her through fire and ashes, but she became lodged in her monstrous form and in order to hide her terrible condition, she threw herself into the sea and hid in the caves of southern Italy. This tradition is the most commonly accepted one for she became associated with the Straits of Messina and ate six of Odysseus' sailors before she was transformed into a dangerous rock of the same name. In medieval depictions, Scylla is shown with the tail of a dolphin, the body of a wolf and the upper body and head of a woman.

SEA HORSE

The Sea Horse is the name usually given in European tradition to a creature with the head of a horse, the flippers of a seal and a sinuous dolphin's tail, although it can sometimes have cloven hooves. The connection between the sea and the horse is long established in many traditions worldwide. The cresting waves of the sea are commonly seen to resemble lines of horses. The Greek god of the sea, Poseidon, takes the form of a black stallion who mounts Demeter, who is hiding from him in the shape of a black mare. In her distress, Demeter retires to the mountains to give birth to twin foal-children. Poseidon's common depiction is of riding a chariot pulled by sea horses.

SEAL

For the peoples of the northern seas, the seal has long been a creature of magic. It not only preserves life with its flesh, oil and hide, it has a spiritual life of its own that is well attested. Many seals have the ability to take human form and Selkies and Roane have frequently come to the shore and begun human relationships and borne children before returning to the sea again. These relationships begin when the human partner steals and hides away the creature's seal skin. It is when the seal rediscovers the skin that they return to the sea again. On the Faroe Islands of the North Atlantic, people believe that seals cast off their coats every ninth night and come onto land to dance until dawn.

The Inuit of the Arctic Circle are dependent on the seal. They have developed many secret ways of hunting it, but they maintain their special relationship between people and seal by acknowledging it as a living spirit. When they hunt, they entice it with a song:

> Orphan, little Orphan over the far side
>   of the sea,
> From the fair far side of the beautiful
>   sea,
> Creep carefully from the water in the
>   shape of a seal.

SEDIT

Among the south-west coastal peoples of North America, Sedit is the name given to Coyote the Trickster.

When the Hus, the two Creating brothers, began to build a ladder between Heaven and Earth in order to prepare the Earth for Creation, they were interrupted by Sedit who inquired why they were doing such a stupid thing. If they left the ladder where they intended then when men became old, they would only have to climb into Heaven to become young once again; men would not bother to have children and life would have no direction. The brothers saw his point and pulled the ladder down, but the younger brother told Sedit he would now have to suffer death himself. Sedit realized he had talked himself into a terrible predicament and he tried to make wings out of the sunflowers so that he might fly up to heaven, but his flight was short-lived. He crash-landed on Earth and died. Since this time, every living being upon Earth is subject to a fixed term of life.

SEDNA

In the Inuit legend from Baffin Island in the Arctic Circle, Sedna is the mistress of the underworld who created all the fish and sea animals. Sometimes Sedna appears in the guise of a seal.

Originally in the form of a woman, Sedna ('The One Down There') was the daughter of a malign chief called Savirqong ('The Man with the Knife'). Refusing to marry all the suitors whom he put forward, she married a bird instead. The chief killed her husband and took Sedna out on a boat. As the sea swelled in a storm, Sedna fell overboard. Clinging to the edge of the boat in the freezing water, she begged her father to pull her back in, but he believed she had been punished for making an unnatural match with a bird and he took out his knife and sliced off her fingers one by one. As these fell into the sea, so each part of her flesh became a fish or sea mammal.

For the Inuit, Sedna is the Sea Mother in whose keeping are all the animals of the sea. Every autumn when animals mate, the Inuit hold a dance festival in her honour, where couples make an elaborate dance to thank the goddess for her bounty, for Sedna regulates the supply of seals on which the Inuit rely. Part of the festival includes a frank appraisal of what is not right in tribal affairs, for Sedna is believed to know about misdeeds because her severed finger-stumps still cause her pain whenever humans do wrong. Her servant Qailertetang regularly visits the land and reports back to her about the behaviour of people so that Sedna can punish them. Shamans consult and propitiate Sedna when the people seek to go hunting.

SEGA

The Sega is a small parakeet sacred to Samoan tradition. It originated as a blood clot that was born of Sinainofoa, who later gave birth to daughter Sinaaleia who was married to the King of Fiji. He saw the bird and asked his wife to get it but she declined, saying it was her brother, so he stole it anyway.

One story tells how Taeotagaloa, a brother of Sinaaleia, came down from heaven to find the Sega. His canoe led him to Fiji where there was a terrible famine and people were practising cannibalism. In pity, Taeotagaloa gave his sister's people breadfruit branches and coconut stalks to replenish the land. On his way, while returning to Samoa with the Sega, he encountered Luu Uafato with whom he swapped possessions. The Sega then came into Luu Uafato's hands until his death when he wished the Sega to be buried with him, but the Sega devoured his dead body and kept watch over his grave before it started to eat people. It is said that the Sega supplies victims to the demon Savea Siuleo for his cannibalistic feasts.

The Element Encyclopedia of Magical Creatures

SEKHMET

SELKIE

Sekhmet is the lioness-headed goddess of war in Egyptian mythology. Sekhmet is one of the three gods of Memphis, along with her husband Ptah and her son Nefertem. Her name means 'the Powerful One', and she is the daughter of the sun god Ra. Many of her statues show her standing fiercely protective, or else seated holding the symbol of the *ankh* of life in her hand. The rage of Sekhmet is meted out against the enemies of the pharaoh and she is seen as a warrior with arrows that pierce hearts and is surrounded by a fiery glow. The hot desert winds are considered to be her breath. In an ancient myth in which Ra fears that mankind is plotting against him, Sehkmet goes forth to avenge him, leaving pools of blood in the desert where men flee to avoid her. Ra realizes that Sekhmet's bloodlust is unstoppable and so he causes red ochre to be mixed with vats of beer and cast upon the land so that it looks as though she has completed her tasks of wiping out mankind and she desists from her slaughter. Sekhmet's other aspect is that of healer, for she can ward off pestilence. Prayers were addressed to her by the priests of Sekhmet who were charged with healing. She is also greatly skilled in the arts of magic.

In the traditions of Orkney and Shetland, Selkies are the seal beings that have the ability to take human shape when they come to land. The common seal is exempt from this magical ability, which is conferred only upon the larger seals such as the Grey Seal and the Crested Seal. Selkies live in the sea and bask upon the rocky skerries, but they can slip off their skins, which they usually hide behind a rock, in order to come ashore. They sometimes make marriages with ordinary humans, usually forced to such a relationship when the partner has hidden their Selkie skin. In most traditions, the Selkie eventually discovers the hidden skin in a chest and puts it on again with some expedition and dives back into the waters, sometimes taking the fruit of their union back with them, to the chagrin of the human partner. The reason for Selkies being in this condition is hotly contested. Did they merit such a strange state because they were once angels driven out of heaven? Or were they sinful humans living out their term of purgation or purification in the shape of seals? Some ministers held that Selkies were capable of salvation. Selkies are not considered to be the same as the Roane who have a much more gentle and forgiving nature.

The chief Selkie, called the Great Selkie of Sule Skerry, comes as a lover to a mortal woman upon the Shetland islands and sleeps with her. According to the great ballad of the Selkie,

The Element Encyclopedia of Magical Creatures

when he returns to collect his son, the Great Selkie is rejected by his earthly mistress whom he pays off with money for 'her nurse's fee'. The Great Selkie takes his son and teaches him 'how to swim the foam', but he already prophesies the death of himself and his son at the hands of a seal-hunter, the husband of his old mistress. This ballad has its roots in a much older tradition concerning the hero Mongan and his father, the Irish sea god, Manannan, who visits the bed of a woman called Kentigerna. Mongan is born of their union and Manannan comes to collect his son from Kentigerna to give him an Otherworldly education. He prophesies to the mother a similar short life for the prodigious hero as the Great Selkie prophesies for his son. Manannan says that Mongan will be shot by a 'dragon-stone' and come to an untimely end.

Traditions about seal-folk abound round the coastal waters of Britain and Ireland. Traces of Selkie legends recur in the Welsh story of Math, son of Mathonwy. When the goddess Arianrhod pretends to be a virgin in order to obtain the post of virgin footholder at the court of her uncle, King Math, she is made to step over his druidic staff in order to demonstrate her fitness. No sooner has she done so than she immediately gives birth to a child, Dylan. Math oversees his upbringing but Dylan cannot remain upon the land. He makes his way to the waters and dives into the ocean. It would seem that his mother Arianrhod had had relations with one of the Selkies some time prior to her test.

SENMURV

The Senmurv is a winged monster found in Persian and Mesopotamian myth. It has the head and wings of a bird, and the body of a dog. Alternatively, it can be seen with the head and paws of a dog, the body of a bird or even with the head of a dog, the body of a musk ox and the wings of an eagle, with the ability to roost like a bat. It lived in the soma tree from which all plants and trees derived. When the Senmurv flew from or landed in the tree, its motion caused seeds to drop from the soma tree, which fell to Earth to fructify it. These seeds were gathered by the winged dog, the Chamrosh. In a later Persian tradition, the Senmurv and Simurgh became gradually merged into one.

SERKET

The Egyptian scorpion goddess, sometimes called Selkis or Selket. Her full name is Serket Hetyt or 'she who makes the throat breathe', because her scorpion sting had the power of life or death. Her main duties are concerned with the embalming process, where she is called 'the lady of the beautiful house', a name for the embalmer's tent. Serket was the protecting goddess of one of the Canopic Animals, Qebehsenuef, who guarded the intestines of the deceased. She was also the overseer of the difficult pathway that the soul takes in the afterlife, watching over the place where the path twisted dangerously. Legend says she was responsible for binding the serpent,

Apophis. Sometimes she is depicted with a female body and lioness's head, with a crocodile head projecting behind. At other times, she is shown as a rearing serpent, but sometimes she is a woman with a scorpion upon her head with its sting ready to strike. She guarded against the sting of scorpions and was invoked for the venomous bites of snakes as a healer and protector. She was the mother of Nehebu-Kau.

SERPENT

The most common magical creature across world mythology is undoubtedly the serpent. Serpents and snakes have the capacity to transform and renew themselves by shedding their skins, a factor which has established them in the mythology of the world's beginnings. Their ability to remain still for long periods, patiently digesting their prey or just sleeping in a torpid condition until their metabolism enables them to move again has also accorded them the power of patience, which endures through many ages.

Primordial, cosmic serpents are frequently part of the creative beginnings of the world, like the Australian Aboriginal Rainbow Serpent from whom all life comes. Such great serpents require human beings to keep their oaths and agreements to maintain the Earth with respect, as we find in the North American Horned Serpent, which is capable of turning upon those who disrespect the Earth. Cosmic serpents are responsible for moulding mountains and creating channels for rivers by the serpentine coils of their body, using their immense strength to shape the Earth itself.

Serpents are associated with more than one element, but their chief element is water. Everywhere on Earth, the Serpent is found as a oceanic water serpent or as a river spirit or Naga. The association between serpents and water is quite striking. Part of their Earth-guardianship concerns the drying up of waters as a punishment, as well as sending inundations on those who transgress.

Serpents are often associated with the mythology of dragons and in languages such as Norse, where 'worm' is the word for any serpentine or dragonish creature, we see a strong symbology of flight, fire and treasure-keeping. These treasure-guarding serpents are often winged. The ability of venomous serpents to kill has created an aura of either respect or fear. Medicine people the world over have learned that small amounts of venom may have curative properties if used judiciously but large amounts can kill. In the Armenian story of Shah-Mar, this ability to strike someone instantly dead or raise them up is fully exploited by the hero Purto. This two-sided property of giving or taking life continues to surround the serpent.

The serpent, like the spider, retains a horrid fascination or repulsion for many people and is a sure provoker of phobic behaviour. Those who cannot even look at snakes believe them to be slimy and find serpentine motion eerie

The Element Encyclopedia of Magical Creatures

and unsettling, even though they rationally understand the serpent's skin to be smooth and the animal to be non-venomous or threatening to humans.

Serpents and snakes have retained their fascination and magical properties into our own world. One of the strangest survivals of the myths of this ecstatic and magical animal is that of snake-handling, which still takes place in the south-east of the USA, where backwoods Christians fearlessly pick up poisonous snakes as a charism or special gift that is written about in the New Testament. This snake-handling goes right back into ancient times, and was possibly part of Orphic and Gnostic cults from the early centuries of Christianity and before. In parts of southern Italy, ecstatic dances associated with the Tarantella are still danced to throw off the venom of snakes. Many communal dances, like the modern conga or the Aboriginal snake dances of the corroboree or the medieval line dances where people link hands and move in a single line, following their leader, are based upon the spiralling and serpentine movements of the snake. The magical powers of the serpent are undoubtedly the power to transform, the ability to grant ecstatic trances and dances, the ability to withstand the ages and to endure to the end of all things. Serpents bring or dry up waters. The serpent embraces the whole world, like the Midgardsormr or Ouroborus, surrounding the globe in its coils.

SERRA

In medieval European lore, the Serra is a winged sea monster. It has the head of a lion, the body and tail of a fish, and the wings of a bat. It was thought to chase ships although most often it would just fold its wings and disappear upon the waters again. In Anglo-Saxon bestiaries, the Serra is said to be symbolic of all who renege on their good intentions by becoming distracted by frivolous amusements.

SESHA-NAGA

Sesha-Naga is a Hindu world serpent with over 1,000 heads. It wears a purple robe and has a plough in its coils – a reference to its ability to shape the Earth. Sesha-Naga lives in the primordial ocean, where its yawns cause earthquakes. It is the traditional protector of the Hindu god Vishnu. At the end of time, Sesha-Naga's many mouths will flow with poison to dissolve the Earth. When the fish Matsya instructed the sage Manu to create the Hindu ark, it was fastened to a rope attached to the great serpent who kept it safe while the inundating waters flowed unrestrained over the Earth. This serpent fought with the demon Hayagriva for the possession of the Vedas, which he had stolen from Brahma. The sacred scriptures were then given to Manu Satyavrata, who then taught them to the human race that they might guide successive ages.

SET

The god Set (or Seth) is the Egyptian lord of the desert. Through Set's breath, worms emerge from within the Earth. All metallic ores are said to be 'the bones of Set' for he is considered to be the lord of metallurgy. The earliest representations of Set show him in different animal forms ranging from the aardvark to the okapi antelope the most common one shows him with the ears and head of the ass. Sometimes called 'the Seth Beast' this indeterminate form actually betrays elements of both canine and equine origin. This suggests that either Set's animal form is mythical, as is the griffin's, or else it represents a form of animal now extinct and unknown to us. Many other animals are associated with him, including the hippopotamus, crocodile and fish.

Osiris brought great and enduring civilization to the people of Egypt and married the beautiful Isis, whom he made regent in his absences, thus causing Set to grow resentful and jealous. With the help of 72 allies, Set created a banquet to honour Osiris who he invited to view the beautiful chest of cedar wood, inlaid with ivory and ebony. Everyone was amazed at its craftsmanship and Set offered to give it to the one who fitted therein. The guests each tried, Cinderella-slipper fashion, to accommodate themselves into the chest but only Osiris found that it fitted perfectly. As soon as Osiris was inside, Set and his henchmen closed it up and sealed it with molten lead, tossing it into the Nile. The chest floated up to the coast of Lebanon where it was enclosed by a tamarisk tree that grew up tall. Eventually, the King of Byblos ordered the tree cut down to make a pillar in his hall. Isis by her magic discovered that Osiris' body was encased in the pillar and she persuaded the king to give it to her, and she took it back to Egypt.

Hiding the body of Osiris in a papyrus thicket, Isis hurried off to Chemmis in the Delta where it is said that she gave birth to the posthumous son of Osiris, Horus. Set, however, found the body and cut it up into 14 pieces, scattering them up and down the country. With her sister Nephthys, Isis sought the parts of her dead husband's dismembered body. Where each part was found, Isis made a wax effigy of that part and gave order to the priests that they enshrine and worship it, serving it with sacrifices of an animal. Each facsimile was treated as if it were the actual body part. This ensured the widespread cult of Osiris, rather like, as in later Christian myth, the parts of the True Cross were distributed throughout Christendom. Nephthys and Isis recovered all the parts of Osiris except the phallus, which had been eaten by Oxythynchus fish. The body was embalmed with the help of Anubis and Thoth, while Isis turned herself into a hawk and used her wings to fan the breath of life back into Osiris. He revived sufficiently to become the King of the Underworld. Osiris' role in the Upperworld was taken by his son, Horus, who also resumed the familial feud with Set.

At the order of Ra, Set and Horus lay down in one bed. During the drowsy hours of midnight, Horus laid hand upon what he thought was his own penis, but which was in fact that of Set, who had put his erect penis between Horus' thighs. Horus realized what was happening when semen appeared in his hand but no answering pleasure came from his own flesh. He called upon his mother and showed his polluted hand to Isis who cut it off, making him a new hand. She then got Horus to fill a jar with his own semen and went to anoint Set's favourite food – lettuce – with Horus's seed.

Set went to the Tribunal of the Gods to unmask Horus as a degenerate, but all did not go well. Horus said that he was innocent of offence, and Thoth called forth the semen of Set to make answer, which it did from the waters. Then Thoth called forth the semen of Horus which it did, emerging from Set's forehead as a golden disk. Thoth removed this disk and placed it upon his own head, stating that Horus was in the right. The pair had a contest upon the Nile waters in boats; when Set's sank, he turned into a hippopotamus and capsized Horus' boat. But the gods finally accorded the kingship to Horus. Set was then banished to making thunder and causing fear in men's hearts.

Set was primarily a god of Upper Egypt who was venerated as a god of nomadic hunters, but to the farming peoples of Lower Egypt around the Nile Delta, he seemed both sinister and alien. In the period following Egypt's conquest by Assyria, Set became entirely associated with the national enemy and as a source of evil, largely because the word 'desert' implied 'foreign land' and because the Assyrians associated Set with their own god Sutekh, a form of Baal. Set's major temple was at Nebet, 30 km north of Luxor, near modern Tukh. Early legend states that Egypt was divided into two by the dwarf Earth god Geb, who gave the northern Lower Egypt to Horus and southern Upper Egypt to Set. Set was called the 'Red God' after the name of the desert lands of Upper Egypt. Set's turbulent nature was clear from the outset, for he burst from the side of his mother Nuit. In most versions of his myth, he is antagonistic to his brother Osiris, as the story of Isis and Osiris detailed by Plutarch reports.

Horus and Set had a long antagonistic relationship: Horus was the sun god and Set his antithesis, the god of night. Earlier stories about Set as the guardian of the sun barque of Ra became subsumed in the myth that Set was himself the same as the Apophis Serpent that menaced the sun boat. The terrible contentions between Horus and Set led to more and more outrageous contests between the antagonists, including the attempt by Set to rape Horus.

Under the Greek Ptolemaic dynasty of Egypt, Set became associated with the Greek Typhon, the monstrous, ass-headed creature who attacked the Olympian gods. Zeus finally threw Mount Etna on top of Typhon, which to this day still hurls molten rocks and fire from its volcanic crown. This story is believed by some to be a remembrance of the volcanic eruptions that inundated the Eastern Mediterranean during the 15th century BC when the island of Thera (modern Santorini) became a great caldera. This event destroyed the Minoan civilization. Set continued to be associated with evil into the Christian era when he was seen to be a mighty demon.

SHAH-MAR

In Armenian legend, Shah-Mar is the giant serpent who is the king of the snakes. He lived in a cave high in the mountains.

A young man called Purto became lost in the mountains and took shelter in Shah-Mar's cavern. Unknowing of the serpent's presence, Purto left an offering to Shah-Mar in return for his hospitality. The king of the snakes gave him a precious stone with which Purto paid off his debts. He then bought a flock of sheep and offered them to Shah-Mar who gave him a second stone. With this, Purto built a new family house. Word of Purto's good fortune got out and Kayen the ruler of Kilikia sent for him to ask him to use his influence with Shah-Mar to heal his sores. Shah-Mar prepared a cure as follows: he bade Purto eat a flower while Shah-Mar ate another one. Then he ordered Purto to give him some seven-year old wine and to decapitate him. He was to bury the body and make separate infusions from the left-and right-hand sides of the snake-king's brain. On returning to Kayen, Purto brought both infusions with him. The ruler's doctor wanted to try it first, so he drank some of the right-hand brain infusions that made the doctor die. The suspicious ruler had to be reassured that the left-hand infusion gave life instead of taking it. He drank and was healed, assuring that Purto was forever in favour. So it was that Shah-Mar gave up his life, although we must not say forever, for everyone knows that serpents regenerate themselves even from small parts of themselves. Somewhere in the mountains yet, Shah-Mar rules again, born of the body that Purto buried.

Shamir

In Judaic tradition, this is a tiny insect that can carve stone and wood and even break glass. It carved the Ten Commandments on the tablet of stone for Moses and one story tells how King Solomon sought to use its power to create a great temple.

In order to find the Shamir, King Solomon first of all used his knowledge of magic to bind one of the fearsome Afreet. With the help of this being, Solomon discovered that the Shamir was in the care of a woodcock that lived on top of a mountain. So Solomon sent his faithful servant Benaiah to capture the insect. Benaiah journeyed to the place where the woodcock had its nest, and there he found some of the bird's nestlings left alone. As his master had

instructed him, Benaiah placed a pane of glass over the nest and hid himself nearby. Soon the woodcock returned and found its chicks imprisoned beneath the glass. Screaming harshly, it hammered at the glass with its beak, but in vain. When it saw that this was of no use, the bird took the tiny Shamir from under its wing and laid it upon the glass. As soon as the insect touched it, the glass cracked into pieces. At that moment, Benaiah leapt out of his hiding place, seized the insect and thrust it into the lead-lined box. Then he set off for home. With the help of the wonderful insect, King Solomon was able to cut the stones he needed to build the great temple to the glory of God.

Shang Yung

Shang Yung is the fabulous bird of Chinese legend. Also called the Rain Bird, Shang Yung has only one leg. It was piously appealed to during droughts and it would appear to herald the rainy season. One story tells how it flew down and perched on the arm of the Prince of Ch'I who took counsel with Confucius on how to create a system of drains and canals. With the help of Shang Yung, the city was preserved from a terrible drought.

Sharama

In Hindu mythology, Sharama is the great dog that herds the cows of the sun god Surya towards the eastern horizon, causing the dawn each morning.

Shapeshifters

The ability to shapeshift was part of many of the cultures that depended upon hunting to survive. This primal ability is still seen among the Bushmen of Southern Africa, who not only follow in the tracks of animal prey but run like the animal they are chasing and make cries similar to it. Around the fire at night, before and after a hunt, they take the form of prey animals, imitating and embodying them. This behaviour has been part of human tradition from earliest times, when the sympathy between hunter and hunted was crucial for survival. Many traditions of disguising and masking derive from such pursuits. In Irish lore, the hunter's ability to blend into the landscape as an animal became a form of invisibility. Special shapeshifting spells of invocation called *Fith-Fath* were employed by Gaelic hunters in order to enable the hunt. Such pagan spells were even used by St Patrick who, when he was being pursued by enemies, invoked a Fith-Fath to change himself and his followers into the shape of deer in order to put scouts off the scent of their human prey. The remnants of this spell are left in the fairy-tale giant's cry of 'Fee, Fi, Fo, Fum'.

In world myth, the ability to shift-shape between animal and human forms is usually found in extraordinary individuals. Foremost of those in Irish myth is Tuan Mac Carill.

Tuan Mac Carill was called upon by Finnen of Moville, the teacher of the great saint Columba, to relate his lineage. Tuan came with the first colonists, the Partholonians, survivors of the Great Flood. When the Partholonians died out, Tuan passed from old age into the form of a stag and saw the coming of the Nemedians. When they died out, Tuan passed into the shape of a boar. In this form, he saw the coming of the Fir Bolg until the coming of the Tuatha de Danaan who overcame them, when he took the form of a hawk. Finally, he became a salmon and in this form was caught and served up as a meal to the queen of Ulster. When he was later reborn of her womb, he retained the memories of all he had lived through in previous forms.

A similar tradition is found in the case of the Hindu god Vishnu who is seen to shift shape through the many ages of the world. Each of his appearances is called an avatar or 'vehicle of manifestation' and he passes into these shapes whenever the world is threatened, for he is the preserving god of Hinduism who has appeared in the shapes of Rama, Krishna and Gautama Buddha. His earlier avatars include Matsya the fish, Kurma the tortoise, Varaha the boar, Nr-Simha the man-lion as well as Vamana the dwarf. This ability to shapeshift could be said to be in the nature of reincarnation. Although some of Vishnu's transformations are purposeful acts of rescue, taken as a whole they are the means by which the history of the world is preserved and extended. The final avatar, Kalki, will govern the Age of Strife that is still to come, punish evildoers, reward the virtuous, destroy the world and so create a completely new cycle of life.

Some shapeshifters do not wish to be caught and will use their skills to avoid entering into contracts or relationships. We see this in the myth of Proteus, the first man of Greek myth or, as he is also known, Nereus, the Old Man of the Sea, who when challenged takes the successive forms of a fish-tailed being, a lion, a stag and a snake. He was challenged by Aristaeus, the son of Apollo, who successfully out-wrestled him. Even within this myth, the whole memory of the world is seen to be embodied in one being whose very cells have come down via the ladder of DNA to their present pattern. In this way, the ability to take animal shape remains magically within each of us.

SHARK

The shark has acquired a modern, almost cult fascination, largely helped by the film *Jaws*, which has increased paranoia among swimmers and fishermen, and led to many naturalists making studies of shark behaviour, if only to disprove its reputation as a cold-blooded killer. In Polynesian territories, the shark represents the Milky Way and is called the 'Long-Blue-Cloud-Eater', the spirit who can become incarnate in successive chiefs, for just as the chief is to the tribe, so is the shark to the seas. This ancestral respect is also found on Hawaii where it is believed that sharks are ancestral spirits and the spirit-allies of *kahunas* (shamans). The King of the Sharks in Polynesian mythology is called Tumuiteretoka. Although sharks get a bad press, it comes as a surprise to hear of one actually acting in the role of a rescuer rather than as an aggressor.

On the north-west Pacific coast of America, a man and his wife went fishing for halibut. They found that their fishing line had acquired a heavy catch and so they paddled ashore in their canoe and wrestled the huge fish up onto the beach. They had never seen anything like it before, but the woman gutted it and hung it up to dry. But as she went back to the water's edge to wash her bloody hands, she was seized by the Killer Whales. In an attempt to get her back, her husband went to the house of the Fish Chief to ask where she had been taken. The Fish Chief told the fisherman that his wife had been taken to be the slave of the Killer Whales because the fish they killed had been their friend. The fisherman asked the help of any in that company to get his wife back and the only one to volunteer was the Shark. They travelled to the house of the Killer Whales where Shark hid the man behind the door. When the Whales asked for a brighter fire, Shark built it up with more wood. When they wanted more water, Shark went to fetch a bucket but as he hurried to wait upon the Whales, Shark slipped purposely and poured the water upon the fire. In the great hissing cloud of ash and steam, Shark seized the woman who had been serving the Whales and thrust her into her husband's arms, shouting at them to hurry away while he would cover their retreat. When the couple were nearly to the shore, they looked back and saw that a great fight was going on in the deep channel behind them. Shark was fighting the Killer Whales and ripping them to pieces with his sharp teeth.

SHEEP

The gentle and sometimes stupid sheep has frequently been taken as a symbol of docility and obedience. In Biblical lore, the sheep is the sacrifice acceptable to the Lord and is regarded more highly than the more wayward goat. When Christ judges the dead at Doomsday, the sheep will be parted from the goats, and the righteous sheep will enter heaven and the sinful goats will descend to hell, for he is the Good Shepherd. This shepherdly task is depicted by the bishop's crook, itself the kind of crook used by a shepherd to select animals or hook them out of danger; the congregation of a clergyman are accordingly known as 'his flock'.

In Chinese mythology, shepherds worshipped the sheep god Huang Ch'u Ping who might grant supplicants an increase of their flocks. In Madagascan lore, the sheep is believed to be the form in which some ancestors reincarnate, so they may not be eaten in those families. Throughout Europe, the shoulder blades of sheep are used for divination: the blade is thrown into the fire and then removed by the seers to determine where the bone has fractured. These lines are then studied to create the oracle to a given question.

It is not often that sheep are spoken of as weapons of mass destruction, but that is what they become in the Irish story 'The Siege of Druim', when the spell-working druids of King Cormac

Muy was married to a woman who gave him many strong sons, but whose last son was a lamb. Muy called his family together and explained that from henceforward, the family would no longer eat mutton, since they were now related to sheep. Muy obtained a young ewe from a stranger as a wife for his sheep-son. The ruler of that country required an animal from every household as a tax, but when each farmer or hunter came with the tax, the king asked, 'Where is my girl?' And so each family had to offer a girl to the king in addition to the animal. Soon it was discovered that the king was not marrying these girls but eating them.

When Muy went to offer a leopard he had shot with his bow, the king demanded his daughter. 'But I have only sons,' Muy said quietly. 'Then I will eat all your sheep instead.' At this threat to his youngest son, Muy raised his spear and killed the king. Muy and his family fled from the vengeance of the king's son but their way was blocked by a great river. Praying fervently for help before a tall tree, Muy was astounded to see the tree bend itself down and stretch out over the water like a bridge. Over it everyone ran as fast as they could, even the little sheep and his wife. When the king's son and his warriors got to the riverside, the tree sprang upright and a flood drowned them all.

send out three brown sheep against the enemy. The Munstermen are profoundly unmoved by these sheep until they look closer and see that each has a hard, bony head, a horny skin and a nose of iron. 'They had the swiftness of the swallow, the agility of the weasel, the rapidity of birds and were able to fend off a hundred warriors during a fray.' They are, in fact, three druidesses who have been transformed into monstrous sheep in order to terrify the enemy. The Munster druid, Mog Ruith, who is leading the assault on the opposing side creates a fire-breathing dog and two bitches to set the monstrous sheep's fleeces on fire.

SHEN LUNG

Shen Lung is the Chinese dragon that brought the rains. It was a five-toed dragon with a multi-coloured skin. The wearing of its image was forbidden to all but the Emperor himself, so sacred was Shen Lung.

SHOJO

In Japanese folklore, Shojo is a wild man in human shape but with red or pink skin and long red hair. Shojo dressed only in seaweed and lives on the seabed. Shojos are renowned for brewing medicinal potions and herbal cures and can make a shiro sake or brandy that is poisonous to the wrongdoer but tastes delicious to the good.

SIANACH

In Scotland, the Sianach is a giant deer that hunts humans in the mountains. This may be a faint memory of the prehistoric giant Irish elk that ranged across Europe until its extinction around 9,500 BC, which had an impressive spread of antlers spanning up to 12 ft across.

SILEN

The goat-footed man of Greek mythology, who is like a satyr but has the lower half of a horse and a horse's ears and tail instead of goat's legs and horns. The Sileni were led by Silenus. King Midas of Lydia once trapped a Silen by offering him wine. When the Silen was in his cups, the king asked him what was the meaning of happiness. To which the Silen responded, 'Not to be born at all is best, but having passed through the gates of birth, the next best is to die young.'

SILENUS

In classical myth, the oldest satyr was Silenus. He was attendant upon the god Dionysus as a fat old man riding upon an ass. In later Roman myth and in Renaissance iconography, he became a much more obese and comical character, but in earlier Greek myth, Silenus was skilled in the prediction of the future and the interpretation of the past. Any human being who could capture him and tie him up might ask questions about the past or future.

The Element Encyclopedia of Magical Creatures

Silimukha

In Indian tradition, Silimukha is the moon-king god of the hares who sent his eloquent messenger, Vijaya, to see if he could persuade the elephants led by Charudanta to seek some other place to drink for they had killed many hares. Vijaya climbed up onto a rock and spoke to Chaturdanta saying, 'I am the ambassador of Silimukha, the moon, who says to you that you have defiled the cool waters of my lake and killed my people. If you do this again, you shall receive my punishment.' Chanturdanta swore never to do this again, so Vijaya took him to visit Silimukha but instead led the great elephant to the still lake. Looking into the waters, Chanturdanta bowed low, swearing to keep his oath.

Simurgh

The Simurgh is a magical bird that appears in the legends of Persia and northern India. In many ways, it resembles the Phoenix in its longevity and the Roc for its huge wingspan. It is possible to see within the Simurgh elements of early Mesopotamian myth of the Anzu or Imdugud bird that roosts in the sacred world tree, as well as features of the Senmurv dragon.

In the 12th-century Persian poet Attar's *Conference of the Birds*, the birds meet together to discuss why they have no king. The hoopoe suggests the Simurgh as the king, while other birds suggest different kings. The Hoopoe responds by saying,

*So long as we do not die to ourselves
and as long as we identify
with someone or something
we shall never be free.*

The birds fly through seven valleys of quest, love, understanding, independence and detachment, unity and astonishment, undergoing many trials in order to attain the truth of this statement.

Sinaa

Among the Juruna people of the Xingu river in Brazil, the Sinaa is a being that is half jaguar and half human, the son of a giant jaguar father and a human woman. He was born looking ancient and had his eyes set in the back of his head. Like a serpent, he can pull off his skin, taking it over his head like a shirt when he goes to bathe. When Sinaa takes the forked stick that holds up the heavens away from the Earth at the end of time, the world will end.

Sinhika

In Hindu tradition, Sinhika is a female dragon who fought against Hanuman, the monkey god. He overcame Sinhika by leaping into her mouth and slitting her open from within.

SIRENA

Sirena is a huge and white winged serpent, mentioned in European bestiaries as existing in the Arabian Peninsula. Its air speed was so great that it could overtake a galloping horse and fall upon its victims. Its bite was so poisonous that its prey felt no pain. There is another Sirena in Spanish folklore who is a local variant of the Siren.

SIRENS

In classical mythology, the Sirens are women who have the lower halves and wings of birds. Some say that the Sirens were turned into their current shape because they had been playing with Kore, the maiden Persephone, when she was abducted by Hades, and Demeter was angered because they had not helped her daughter; she cursed them, saying, 'Begone and search for my daughter the world over.' But another story tells how Aphrodite turned them into bird-women because the Sirens stubbornly clung to their virginity, refusing to submit to man or god. The Sirens are flightless because they were defeated in a music contest by the Muses; the Muses pulled out the Sirens' wing feathers to make themselves crowns. And this is why the Sirens sing in a meadow among the bleached bones of sailors whom they have lured to their deaths. They are first cousins to the Harpies, living in a green island of their own. When the wind drops at midday, this is the time that people succumb to the Sirens. Homer speaks only of two Sirens, but other sources say there are three – Parthenope, Leucosia and Ligeia (Maiden-Face, White One and Shrill) – but yet others suggest an even greater number. The names given to them are Aglaope (Beautiful Face), Aglaophonos (Beautiful Voice), Molpe (Music), Peisinoe (Mind-Persuader), Raidne (Improvement), Teles (Perfect), Thelxepeia (Soothing Words) and Thelxiope (Persuasive Face).

Odysseus met with the Sirens on his return journey from Troy, but he was forewarned by Circe, who suggested that he plug the ears of his men with beeswax so that they might not be overcome by the Sirens' song. But Odysseus wished to hear their song and not succumb to it, so he asked his men to bind him to the mast, and refuse to untie him until they had passed their lands. Pairs of Sirens were carved upon classical tombs, much as angels are carved upon Christian ones. They were shown lamenting and singing dirges to the music of the lyre, but it is also possible that they have designs on the bodies of heroes buried in the tombs, since the soul was believed to leave the body in the form of a bird and, like the Harpies, the Sirens stood by waiting to catch the fleeing soul. The name 'Siren' seems to derive from *seirazein* ('to bind with a cord'), which describes the action of the Siren very well. In later European legend, the Sirens tended to be portrayed more in the manner of mermaids or with fishes' tails. Isidore of Seville was responsible for giving them scales and webbed feet.

The Element Encyclopedia of Magical Creatures

SIRIN

In Russian folklore, the Sirin is a bird-woman with the body of a brightly-plumaged bird and the head of a woman. It descended from heaven to sing wonderful melodies to those souls who were in a state of grace. This song would enable them to pass from earthly life and be received in heaven. It is clear that the Sirin ultimately derives from the classical Siren. The Sirin's partner is the Alkonost.

SISIUTL

In Haida legends of the Pacific north-west of North America, Sisiutl is a horned serpent or salmon with great fangs. It is depicted as a great head, with fangs that extend to create a huge body from which two snakes emerge. The gaze of Sisiutl is petrifying but, just as the classical warriors used the Gorgoneion emblem of the Gorgon upon their breastplates, so Sisiutl is in league with the war god Winalagilis to assist warriors.

SISUPALA

In Hindu myth, Sisupala is the weird offspring of a human queen and the god Shiva. Sisupala was born with unusual characteristics, having a third eye in his forehead and four arms. He was giantesque in size and the gods prophesied that he would be fortunate until the day he met the adversary who would kill him; this event would be heralded by the withering of his third eye and the extra arms; it finally came about when he met the god Krishna. Sisupala's human mother made Krishna promise to spare her son's life 100 times, but on the 101st occasion, Krishna called the sun from the sky, which caused Sisupala to be rent from head to toe. His flaming anger came boiling out of him in a river of rage, but Krishna absorbed it.

SKAHNOWA

Among the Seneca Indians of north-east America, Skahnowa is a gigantic turtle that lives in the pools and lakes where Doonongaes the horned serpent lives. Skahnowa acts as a kind of scout and hunter for Doonongaes.

SKINFAXI

In Norse tradition, Skinfaxi (Shining Mane) is one of the horses of the sun that bring the morning light to Earth. It is Hrimfaxi who brings the night. Snorri Sturluson, the 12th-century Icelandic writer who chronicled many of the Norse myths, writes of Dag and Nott (Day and Night):

Nott rides on the horse called Hrimfaxi, and every morning it drops dew onto the earth from its bit dripping with spittle; Dag's horse is called Skinfaxi and all the air and earth is lit up by his mane.

The Element Encyclopedia of Magical Creatures

Skirimsl

In Icelandic legend, Skirimsl is a giant sea monster or serpent that lives around Lagarfljot. It was believed to be harmless because Bishop Gudmund had used his spiritual powers to bind Skirimsl until Doomsday when, like a great many other serpentine sea monsters, it would break free and bring chaos.

Skoffin

The Skoffin is an Icelandic monster which is a bird with the qualities of a dragon or Basilisk. The Skoffin's glance is deadly – including to its own kind – which makes us wonder whether there can be any left upon the Earth, unless Skoffins mate while wearing a blindfold! In later centuries, Icelanders took the precaution of shooting at Skoffins with a silver button on which the sign of the cross had been engraved.

Skogs Fru

In Scandinavian tradition, Skogs Fru is the wild woodswoman who haunts the forest. She comes to the fires of hunters at night and tries to lure away the young men. She has a similar reputation and profile to certain nymphs or Rusalki who must be avoided rather than encouraged.

Skoll

Skoll (or 'Mockery') was the wolf who will devour the sun at the time of Ragnarok, the world's ending, in Norse mythology. He will be assisted by Hati, who pursues the moon in the same way.

Skookums

In the myths of the Pacific north-west of America, the three Skookums are spirits with long claws who live at the top of a mountain watching over the only fire in the world so that men should not steal it and become as strong as they.

Coyote stationed the fastest animals at intervals down the mountain when he went to steal fire. He seized the firebrand in his teeth and ran, hoping that as successive relay animals ran with the fire the Skookums would tire. When all that was left of the firebrand was a mere coal, Frog swallowed it and hopped away. However, the youngest Skookum seized his tail tight in her claws so frog hopped away leaving his tail behind, which is why frogs have had no tails ever since. Frog dived into a river but that did not stop the second Skookum from swimming after him. Too tired to jump further, the frog spat out the coal onto a piece of dry wood and the wood swallowed it. The three Skookums circled the piece of wood wondering how to take the fire out of it. Finally, they gave up and returned to the mountain top lodge. Coyote then showed the people how to rub two dry sticks together to create fire from the sparks that sprang out of it by setting woodchips and pine-needles nearby. This is how the Skookums lost part of their power and why you will always find fire inside wood.

SKRIKER

According to local Lancashire legend in north-west England, the Skriker is a dog with glowing eyes that is encountered by travellers in the dark. It comes up behind them with a squelching sound or walks beside them trying to lead the pace; if it appears ahead, then it is trying to get you from the pathway. In local parlance, a 'skriker' is a person who moans or complains, and this is exactly what the Skriker does. Since it is tantamount to death or disaster to beat it off or attack it, it is unclear just how much more bad luck might be had from ignoring it.

SKUNK APE

In the cryptozoological lore of Florida, the Skunk Ape, a kind of Bigfoot, was supposedly sighted during the late 1970s and 1980s. Some sightings consisted only of footprints but some have spoken of a large, reddish-brown creature. One busload of tourists reported seeing it standing in the cypress trees, shaking the branches as if to frighten them off. No one was able to photograph the animal, which some say might have been a bear. Those who have seen it say that the beast has long, ape-like arms and a repulsive odour that resembles that of a skunk.

SLEIPNIR

Sleipnir is the eight-legged horse belonging to Odin in Norse mythology. According to Snorri Sturluson, Sleipnir came into being when the gods were trying to build a wall around Asgard, their home. They contracted the giant builder Hrimthursar to complete the wall with the help of his horse Svadilfari in three years, in return for the sun and moon and the hand of the goddess Freya. Alarmed at his progress, the gods asked the trickster Loki for help. Loki changed himself into a mare in heat and caused Svadilfari to follow him. Hrimthursar ran after them. The progeny of the shapeshifted Loki and Svadilfari was the eight-legged Sleipnir whom Odin took for his own. Sleipnir's extraordinary stride enabled Hermodr to leap the wall around Hel. When Odin rides to Hel, he refers to runes graven upon Sleipnir's teeth. The eight legs of Sleipnir may refer to the eight directions of the heavens, alluding to the omnipresence of Odin when mounted upon him. Sleipnir grazes upon the world tree Yggdrasil.

SMOK WAWELSKI

In Polish folklore, Smok Wawelski is the dragon of Wawel Hill, Krakow, who lives in a cave on the banks of the Vistula. The cathedral and castle of Krakow stand upon Wawel Hill and the dragon is associated with the founding of the city.

It is said that Smok Wawelski plundered the land of livestock and killed indiscriminately unless it was given a young girl once a month. King Krak wished to stop this evil custom – especially as the only suitable girl left was his own daughter, Wanda. In the time-honoured fashion, Krak gave a proclamation to his people vowing to marry his daughter to any man able to defeat the dragon. A cobbler's apprentice called Szewczyk Dratewka stuffed a lamb with sulphur and left it outside the dragon's cave. After eating it, Smok Wawelski rushed down to the Vistula to slake the terrible thirst brought on by the sulphur. He became swollen with water and finally exploded. Dratewka subsequently married Wanda. The dragon's cave is now a tourist shop underneath the castle founded by Prince Krakus.

(*See also* Stoorworm.)

Snakes

Snakes and their larger relatives, the serpents and worms, have a central place in world mythology. Their ability to cast their skins and move about the world without feet has always made them appear in a magical or fearful light. In Egypt, the snake was believed to be one of the life-giving powers that was the sign of the four female members of the eight primordial gods – Naunet, Hehet, Keket and Amaunet – who represented water, space, darkness and invisibility respectively. The goddess of harvest, Thermuthis, was a snake or a woman with a snake's head. The evil snake Apophis was the opponent of the sun god Ra. But the symbol of the hooded cobra Uraeus was the emblem worn upon the brows of diadems of the Middle Kingdom, an emblem of kingship.

In Africa, the snake is believed to be a representative of the spirits or to be the actual spirits in snake form, so they are accorded great respect. Snakes come as messengers from the ancestors. There are frequent instances of people becoming possessed by snake spirits and falling down and writhing like them during trances. Snakes are drawn to music and dance, and can give oracles about diseases. According to Hindu tradition, the reason that snakes are able to renew themselves is traced back to the myth that tells how Kadru, the ancestor of the Nagas, enslaved Vinata, mother of the birds. In order to ransom her, the Garuda stole the elixir of immortality, the *amrita*, from the gods. But before the serpents could taste it, Indra retrieved it. As he fled with the *amrita*, some drops fell to Earth and the serpents slid through it, coating their skins with the renewing liquor.

In Navajo tradition, Snake is one of four creatures, along with Bear, Frog and Turtle who go on an adventure to procure a wife for Snake. They find a woman called Glisma who is enchanted by the lovely Snake who shapeshifts into a human man clothed in rainbow-coloured clothing. Despite her subsequent escape and recapture by Snake, Glisma learns from him how to make the sand-paintings by which people can be healed and the Hozoni chants that accompany this unique form of healing. Glisma's encounter with Snake and the Snake People is much celebrated as the source of the Navajo healing way.

Snee-Nee-Iq

In the legends of Kwakiutl peoples of British Columbia, Snee-Nee-Iq is a female cannibal who haunts the mountain passes looking for children who wander off on their own. Snee-Nee-Iq carries them off in her pannier and eats them later.

Solovei Rakhmatich

In Russian legend, Solovei Rakhmatich had the head and body of a man and the rest of him was a nightingale. He lived on a tree overlooking the pass between Cheringov and Kiev from where he overlooked all who travelled through it, giving his piercing whistle before swooping down and robbing them. It was the hero Ilya Muromets who shot down Solovei Rakhmatich and brought him back in a cage to the city of Kiev where Prince Vladimir ordered him to be beheaded.

SONARGOLTR

In Norse mythology, Sonargoltr (Sacrificial Boar) is the name given to the pig that was selected on Yule night. Those involved in the ceremony laid hands on the boar's back while swearing an oath. Then Sonargoltr was sacrificed in a *sonarblot* (blood sacrifice) to ensure a good harvest. The twitchings and entrails of the beast also provided an oracle for the year ahead. Boars designated as Sonargoltr were dedicated to the god Freyr.

SONG-SSEU

In Chinese legend, Song-Sseu is the name of the mythical bird with a human head and the body of a female pheasant. This divine pheasant was traditionally embroidered upon the ceremonial dance robe of a marriageable princess, for the first calling of the pheasant was a signal to young people that it was time to come out and dance.

SOPEDU

This Egyptian god was responsible for protecting the borders of the land. He was often shown in the form of a crouching falcon. According to the lore of Lower Egypt, it is Sopedu who acts as the instigator of the Nile inundation. He comes to the goddess Isis when she is her form of the star Sirius and impregnates her, so that she gives birth to the waters of the life-giving flood that enables the planting of crops to take place in the enriched mud of the Nile. The star Sirius is believed to be the herald of the annual Nile inundation. One of the epithets given to the pharaoh who has entered the after-life and become a star deity is 'the teeth of the king', a reference to Sopedu's presence as the predator who is invincible. Sopedu was worshipped at Saft el-Henna in the north-east delta of the Nile.

SORE-GUS

Among the Khoi peoples of Namibia in Africa, there is a Sun Ram called Sore-Gus who was found by a hunter called Giri who was amazed to see this glimmering golden ram. He shot it with his arrow and cut off some of the meat. On the way home, he suffered a terrible thirst, but whenever he found water, it immediately dried up. A wise man deduced that Giri had slain the Sun Ram. He instructed Giri to return to the ram's body and to replace the meat he cut out, praying that the Sun Ram might stand up and be restored. As soon as Giri uttered the prayer, Sore-Gus stood up and began to shine, and all the waters flowed back into their pools again.

Sothis

The Dog Star, Sirius was represented as a star goddess called Sothis in Egyptian mythology. The 1,460-year stellar cycle of Sothis was a reckoning of astrological measurement that made the year correct, since the Egyptians did not use the system of leap years to adjust annual calendrical slippage of days that cumulatively occurs without such adjustment. Sothis was shown as a great dog, as a woman crowned with a five-pointed star, or as Isis seated side-saddle upon a dog. Sothis was thought to be responsible for the annual inundation of the Nile upon which Egyptian agriculture was highly dependent. The 4th-century BC text known as the 'Lamentations of Isis and Nephthys' tells how Sothis unswervingly follows Osiris in his guise as the constellation of Orion across the sky. It is in the form of the male emanation of Sothis, that Sopedu comes to impregnate Isis and give rise to the Nile's inundation.

Sow

The female pig has long been associated with fertility, mainly because of the prodigious number of offspring that a large sow can give birth to and feed in one litter. The suckling pigs and their mother are frequently used as an image of the gravid moon that gives birth to a series of waxing and waning phases in European mythology. The ability both to give copious birth and to devour her young has given the sow a fearsome reputation in many cultures. Many goddesses have taken the form of a sow including Dorje Phagmo, who is also known as the great sow Vajra Varahi, the Tibetan bodhisattva whose squeal is said to evoke compassion. This red, fearsomely-tusked being appears as a woman with a sow's head and many human arms.

In British tradition, the goddess Arianrhod takes the form of a sow who seeks to devour her own offspring Lleu Llaw Gyffes when he is overcome by his wife, Blodeuwedd. In the Welsh Triads, a great sow called Henwen is pursued by King Arthur because of a prophecy that she will be the ruin of Britain. In different parts of the land she gives birth to a grain of wheat, a bee, and a grain of barley before giving birth to a wolf cub and a young eagle as well as Cath Palug whose depredations harmed Britain until it was overcome by Arthur's warrior, Cei. This strange assorted set of births at once give the gifts of agriculture as well as the predators which undermine civilization. And this is why the pig has been seen as the prime sacrifice of farmers for fertile fields, as it was by the Romans when Mars was still a god of agriculture rather than of war. Roman treaties and alliances were marked by the sacrifice of swine. The sow was also sacrificed at the Eleusinia and Thesmophoria, the Spring and Autumn rites of the Greek Eleusinian mysteries as offerings to the Underworld. They were thrown down deep fissures in the earth, mimicking the journey that Persephone, the daughter of Demeter, took to the underworld.

The Element Encyclopedia of Magical Creatures

Sphinx

For the Egyptians, the statues that represented kings or gods with their animal counterparts in one being were called *shesep-ankh* ('living statues'); this word became transmitted via the Greek as 'sphinx'. Sphinxes with different animal heads or bodies were often arranged in double rows along the approaches to temples as guardians, notably the ram-headed sphinxes that line the way to the temple of Amun at Karnak. The Egyptian Sphinx or Androsphinx, known widely from the Great Sphinx of Giza near the pyramid of Cheops, probably represents Harmachus or Horus of the Horizon, with its man's head swathed in a nemyss (headdress) and its leonine body. Over 240 ft in length, it has a stele between its paws that tells how Prince Tuthmosis was out hunting one day when he fell asleep in its shadow. The Sphinx prophesied that he would have the throne of Egypt if he promised to clear away the sand from the almost desert-entombed Sphinx. Tuthmosis became the fourth pharaoh of that name, reigning between 1425–17 BC. Such a long period of time has elapsed since then, that we are reminded of the Arabic saying, 'The world fears time, but time fears the pyramids.'

The Egyptian Sphinx was a benign embodiment of sovereignty and was male, unlike the Greek Sphinx, which is usually female and malign or antagonistic in nature. The Greek Sphinx had a woman's head and the body of a winged lioness. It challenged wayfarers on the road to Grecian Thebes. Its most famous dialogue took place with Oedipus, the king who unwittingly killed his father and married his mother. Asking the question she set to all travellers, she posed him this riddle:

> *What goes on four legs, on two and then three,*
> *But the more legs it goes on the weaker it be?*

Oedipus guessed the answer was 'Man', for he goes on all fours when a baby, on two legs when he is adult but on three legs when he uses a stick in his old age. This correct answer helped Oedipus destroy the Grecian Sphinx.

Spider

The spider is one of the great creating creatures, feared and respected the world over. As the weaving goddess of fate, she makes the web of all life, spinning the thread from her own abdomen, stretching through time and space. In both Greek and Norse myth, the spider is associated with the weavers of fate, the Moirae and the Norns. In Africa and the Caribbean, the spider is associated with Anansi the Trickster.

Among the Abron people of the Ivory Coast, Spider is a healer and a dancer. One day Spider met a woman covered with sores who was singing and dancing. He requested to learn the song and the dance and she showed him. But as the spider danced and sang, so the sores upon the woman's body began to heal up. As they left her skin, so they began to appear on Spider's body and soon it was in great pain. The woman went home but Spider continued singing and dancing. People in villages all around came to acclaim Spider. It showed them all how to dance and sing, exactly as the woman had originally shown Spider. As they learned the song and dance, so the sores left Spider's body and appeared on those of the villagers.

The bite of the spider was said to cause outbreaks of tarantism, an epidemic of dancing that afflicts those who suffer from it with extraordinary, wild dancing, which goes on for hours. Tarantism is centred upon Southern Italy where it is part of the ancient mysteries that have become incorporated into Catholicism, especially the rites of the Virgin and certain local saints. Sacred ecstatic and purification dances from early times are still found in these regions. Those who fall into tarantism, which can manifest as a manic or catatonic state, are believed to have been bitten by a spider and need to be attended by musicians who create the correct rhythms and cadences to match the afflicted person. Music that accompanies the tarantella dance is a ceaselessly spinning melody accompanied by violins, tambourines and castanets. On hearing the music, the tarantata (the one afflicted) will immediately dance to the rhythm until the affliction is worked out. Afterwards, the tarantata is an initiate of the spider-knowledge, quite calm and self-possessed again. Those who have been bitten by a poisonous spider in any part of the world – and lived to speak of it – often report strange, web-like dreams and preternatural knowledge of things.

According to the Andamanese Islanders in the Bay of Bengal, Da Tengat was the great hunting spider created by Biliku. He discovered the first fire and cooking methods but when he killed the Cicada, the first night fell. Da Tengat lit the darkness by finding blocks of resin and showed his people how to make torches. Finally, all their torches caused the dawn to come again. From that time onwards, day has followed night and night day. The Andamanese still dance into the night believing that their dances cause the sun to rise again. In the creation myths of the Nauru people of the South Pacific, Areop-Enap was the Ancient Spider who created the Earth and heavens by prising apart mollusc shells. Areop-Enap's son was Areop-It-Eonin (Young Spider), who created fire by bringing it from the abode of the thunder and lightning.

The Element Encyclopedia of Magical Creatures

In the Koran, the spider is seen as the symbol of a polytheist because its web is easily destroyed, however, during his flight to Medina, the Prophet Mohammad sheltered in a cave over whose entrance a spider wove a web which hid him away. Similar stories are told of Jesus who, on the Flight of the Holy Family to Egypt, hid from the soldiers of Herod in a cave where a spider obligingly wove a covering that obscured their presence from the murderous soldiers. King Robert the Bruce of Scotland is associated with caves and spiders in another folk tradition, which states that while he was hiding from his enemies in a cave he fell into despair over the many trials and setbacks of his cause during the struggle for Scottish sovereignty. He is supposed to have watched a spider continually reweaving its web and taken heart from this.

In the legends of Greece, the origin of the spider is said to have been the human woman Arachne whose weaving skills were so legendary that she entered into a contest with the goddess Athene. The goddess was annoyed with Arachne's skills and so she turned her into a spider forever.

SPIDER WOMAN

In the traditions of the Hopi Indians in south-west America, Spider Woman created all humans and animals. She led the migration northward to the Back Door of the World, leading the five clans through tropical lands to icy zones. On the way, they planted crops of fruit and vegetables. When they reached impassable ice and snow, she bade the clans push on to break through because this was the Back Door of the Fourth World. The Spider Clan agreed to persuade the other clans to help do this. The Blue Flute Clan created the Locust, a humpbacked flute-player to bring tropical warmth with his flute-playing. The Fire Clan summoned fire from the centre of the Earth. The Sun Clan implored the sun to shine brighter and the Snake Clan got the Snake to send vibrations along the world's axis from the depths of the underworld. All these attempts to melt the snow failed until Sotuknang, nephew of the Creator, told Spider Woman that if the clans had succeeded the world would have come to an end. He admonished her and said, 'You were given eternal life and beauty because you created these creatures, but now we let your thread run out.' The thread of Spider Woman unwound until she shrank to a ugly old woman, and the Spider Clan were ordered to return southwards where they would breed wickedness and evil.

In Japan, there is another Spider Woman, but she is less beneficent than the Hopi creator. Japanese Spider Woman lived in a mountain hideaway with her rundown human servants. When the hero Raiko was travelling at night, he saw a mysterious skull flying into a cave. Going to investigate it, he found himself caught in a huge sticky web. The weaver of the web seemed to be a human woman of great loveliness but it was really the evil Spider Woman. He struck out with his sword and the woman fled. Raiko's servant Tsuna rescued his master and together they discovered the white Spider lying with a sword sticking out of her distended body. As the hero split her open, the skulls of her many human victims tumbled out, followed by her spider children. Raiko and Tsuna had their work cut out to kill each of these monstrous offspring. Elements of this story will sound familiar to any reader familiar with Frodo's encounter with Shelob or Ungoliant in Tolkien's *The Lord of the Rings*: in that story also, the hero's servant, Sam, rescues his master.

Ssu Ling

In Chinese mythology, the Ssu Ling are the four spiritual creatures who stand at each point of the compass. The Ki-Lin or Chinese Unicorn with its deer's body, ox's tail, horse's hooves and single horn stand in the West. In the South is the Phoenix. In the North is Gui Xian the tortoise, while in the East is the Lung or dragon.

Stag

Wherever deer roam in the world, the male deer or stag is taken for a symbol of sovereignty and virile male strength. The stag also appears to be associated with the watchfulness of a celestial guardian, for in Norse mythology four stags representing the four winds stand about the world tree Yggdrasil, while in Chinese myth it is the emblem of Shou-Hsien, the God of Immortality. In Japan, it is the Celestial Stag, while in Greek mythology it is said that that chariot of

the virgin priestess in whom Artemis was embodied was drawn by stags.

In Hungarian mythology, the founders of the Magyar people, Hunor and Magor, followed a white stag that led them into a new land which was then called Scythia. From Hunor came the Huns and from Magor the Magyar people. The many-antlered stag with its head turned back over its shoulder remains an important emblem for Hungarians today. The stag is one of the oldest and most prevalent figures of Celtic tradition. This can be demonstrated by the astonishing number of antlers found in graves and pits where offerings were made. In one such, at Colchester, archaeologists digging at a shrine to the local god, uncovered a bronze figurine of a stag on which the inscription read *Silvanus Callirius* (Woodland King). The fact that stags grew and shed their antlers in spring gave them a significant role as harbingers of death and rebirth, and it is as such that they often appear in both literature and iconography.

There are a number of appearances of stags in stories throughout Celtic mythology and folklore. In the Irish Fionn cycle, the hero chases a stag which is Donn – the god of the dead and protector of crops and cattle – in disguise. He later marries a woman of fairy origin who often takes the form of a deer, and their son Ossian is considered half human and half deer. A song is recorded in which he addresses his mother thus:

If thou art my mother, a deer thou
If thou art my mother, a deer thou,
Be on guard from deeds of dogs.

Again and again, as in the story of 'Pwyll, Prince of Dyfed' from The Mabinogion, in which Pwyll encounters a stag that is also pursued by Arawn, stories of Otherworld visitations begin with the hunting or chasing of a stag. In the story of 'Culhwch and Olwen' from the same source, the stag is one of the mighty beasts with whom Culhwch is able to communicate and who helps the young hero to capture the boar Twrch Trwyth.

In one of the most famous poems of Celtic literature, 'The Song of Amairgin', there is the line 'I am a stag, of seven tines'. The number is important, emphasizing not only the sacred number, but also that the stag is full grown and powerful. The stag's antlers were seen as symbolizing the spreading branches of the wood, and it is for this reason that horned gods such as Cernunnos and the Lord of the Animals are so depicted. In the early medieval *Vita Merlini* (Life of Merlin), Merlin comes to the remarriage of his wife with a new husband riding upon a stag, an emblem of unrestrainable wildness. In his prophetic frenzy, he hurls a bone and kills the bridegroom before his ex-wife can be remarried, then returning to the Caledonian forest where he abides.

In Christian mythology, the European myths of St Hubert and St Eutachius tell how the saint was out hunting as a carefree young man when he cornered his quarry in the thicket. Before he could shoot the stag, Hubert and Eustachius saw that between the stag's antlers was the cross of Christ with the Saviour living upon it. He spoke words of restraint and called the young man to the spiritual quest instead.

STALLO

A Stallo is a Golem-like creature that Sami shamans make in Lapland. A Stallo was made from a piece of peat-turf upon which no human foot had ever stepped. From this piece, the shaman would cut pieces and lay them out upon the ground in the shape of man. To make the Stallo stand up and move, the shaman had to breathe out slowly and evenly over the turf. Then he called out in a loud voice that the Sami who had placed him there would give the Stallo half his strength and half his life, and now the Stallo would stand up and be ready to serve the shaman. In the days when shamans fought fellow shamans for influence – or just out of trickery or spite – they would send each other a Stallo or 'visitor', which is what the word means. The Stallo would then proceed to irritate and upset his master's enemy by tipping food from his plate, hiding his skies or making his fire go out. After this kind of procedure had happened time after time, the rival shaman would realize that he had a Stallo in his home. The Stallo was often given away by the low whistling that he made. This whistling was the signal that a Stallo would take shape. (In the far north, whistling is a form of magic all of its own.) When it became visible, the Stallo would then challenge the rival shaman, threatening to take his goods in a combat if he won, or else, if the rival won he would kill the Stallo and possess all that he had – which was half of what the sending shaman had! If the rival won, then the sending shaman would fall sick, since half his life-power would instantly leave him.

A Sami story tells how Isak Barfi went to hunt for reindeer and found a lonely tent where lived the quarrelsome Rasmus Gargo. It was getting late and he needed shelter so Isak asked and Rasmus had to accept rather than break the Sami tradition of hospitality. The next few days, Rasmus suggested that he and Isak hunt together and that they share the proceeds between them. Isak was the better hunter and caught nineteen reindeer to Rasmus's meagre eight. Having agreed to a fair distribution, Isak knew he could not back down, but he did argue for more. Rasmus then threatened him saying he would sent Isak a 'visitor'. Shortly afterwards, Isak was plagued by a series of small inconveniences that grew steadily worse: his axe vanished, his cauldron broke over the fire, tipping the contents out, his skies broke. He then knew that he had been sent a Stallo. Finally that summer, he heard a whistling and there in front of him was a Stallo. They fought until the Stallo was on the ground. He begged not to be killed with Isak's knife but offered his own silver knife. Isak knew that the silver knife would probably turn against him so he thrust his own knife into the Stallo. Sure enough, later that day Rasmus fell very ill as the Stallo took half his life with him when he died.

STHENO

In Greek mythology, Stheno was one of the Gorgons. Her name means 'strong'. When the hero Perseus cut off the head of her sister, Medusa, Stheno and Euryale were unable to catch him.

STOLLENWURM

In Swiss folklore, Stollenwurm is a huge lizard with the face of a cat. It has dragon scales, a long tail and a dorsal ridge along its body. It can raise itself upon its hind legs in order to stand better over its prey. It is reported to live in the Alpine passes. It is also called Tatzelwurm.

STOORWORM

According to the legends of Britain and Scandinavia, the Stoorworm was a giant serpent whose body was so large it could cover the face of northern Europe. It lived in the North Sea, but when it emerged it flooded the islands and coastal regions of Britain. Sacrifices were offered to the beast, until only the king's daughter would serve to propitiate it. The king offered half his realm if someone could kill the Stoorworm.

Assipattle, the outcast who lived in the ashes, was the only taker for this task. He kept a slow-burning fire of turf going and when the Stoorworm opened its mouth, he shovelled in peat after peat until the monster writhed and thrashed in its death agonies. These agonized twinings caused Denmark to be cut off from Sweden and Norway, and its vomited teeth formed the Orkneys and the Shetland and Faroe Islands. The residue of its burning body became Iceland. The Stoorworm may be a memory of the drowned land between Britain and Europe that was once called Doggerland but which is now called Dogger Bank, that was submerged in prehistoric times.

STORK

The stork was the subject for much myth and speculation since it migrated from place to place in a mysterious fashion. Pliny held that the last stork to arrive for the annual migration would be torn in pieces before the others could proceed, imputing the Greek custom of sacrifice to these birds. But the Greeks did recognize that the superior organization of storks, especially the fact that they were supposed to care for their elderly family members, led to the framing of a law that took its name from the stork. Before roosting, storks, like cranes, were said to post sentries who held a stone in one upraised claw so that, if they became drowsy, the stone would drop and wake them up again. This vigilance was recognized among Christians who saw the stork as a symbol of spiritual watchfulness and brotherly love.

Leonardo da Vinci wrote of the stork:

This creature drives away evil from itself by drinking salt water. If it finds its mate has been unfaithful, it abandons its partner. When it is old, its young nurse and feed it till it dies.

The faithfulness of the stork made it an emblem of Hera and Juno, the Greek and Roman goddesses of marriage. For most people in Europe, the stork is the traditional bearer of newborn human babies, as baby-welcoming cards still depict it carrying a baby in a triangularly folded white cloth held delicately in its beak.

Stealing the Sun and Fire

In the far northern hemisphere, where the sun's yearly circuit brings it below the horizon, giving several dark months for the most northerly latitudes, there are many myths about the stealing of the sun. These myths are most common in North America, where the act of stealing the sun is often accomplished by a culture-hero who has animal attributes or is in animal form such as Coyote who partakes of both natures. These legends speak not only of the solar cycle of the sun's return after midwinter when the days become longer and the nights shorter, but also of the primal gift of light that enables civilized, ordered and ordinary actions to take place again. In the light of this, it is ironic that the ones bringing order are most often the tricksters such as Xhuuya or Raven who, in Haida legend, stole the sun from the gods. We see many midwinter festivals or ceremonies that lead up to midwinter which recall the sun by festivities involving lights, such as the Hindu Diwali, the Jewish Hanukkah and the festival of Christmas where, liturgically, we celebrate the birth of Christ as the Sun of Justice who will bring resurrection to the world.

The theft of the sun is part of a wider genre of stories and myths that are called 'the theft of wisdom or knowledge'. Those who attempt to bring wisdom or technology from the possession of the gods invariably suffer physically like the frog of the North American Karok people, which once had a tail but lost this as a result of stealing fire for humanity (*see* Skookums). Sometimes the sacrifice becomes a badge of honour, as when the fox becomes burnt by the sun, forever afterwards being recognized by his burning tail. The stealing of fire is ultimately associated with the coming of technology, enabling the cooking of food, the firing of clay into pots and the smelting of ores into metals. This is why, in Greek myth, the theft of fire by Prometheus is punished so severely by the gods who resent the loss of wisdom to humanity – Prometheus is tied to a rock and has his liver plucked out daily by an eagle. Interestingly, it is a half man, half animal, the centaur Cheiron who, unable to die and already being in severe pain from the poisonous arrows that Hercules inadvertently shot, takes the place of Prometheus in an extraordinary act of self-sacrifice.

STORSJOODJURET

In Swedish legend, Storsjoodjuret is a lake monster that inhabits Lake Storsjoin in Jamtland. It takes the form of a horned serpent or a serpent with long ears. The legend of its presence is long-lived, for a runestone was placed on the lake's only island in an attempt to keep its powers at bay. There was an early attempt to catch or lure the Storsjoodjuret in 1894 when a metal cage was baited with dead pigs. The museum of Osersund still shows this contraption, together with the harpoons that were made to spear the Storsjoodjuret. In a marvellous example of hope over invisibility, the Storsjoodjuret was officially given legal protected species status since 1986.

STVKWVNAYA

In the Seminole Indian myths of North America, Stvkwvnaya is a serpent with a long horn that lives in the deep waters. If you wish to make a powerful aphrodisiac, you must summon the Stvkwvnaya from the depths by singing to it; when it is enchanted by your singing, then you can pare some of its horn to create your aphrodisiac.

STYMPHALIAN BIRDS

In Greek mythology, the Stymphalian Birds lived in the north-eastern region of Arcadia near the swampy Lake Stymphalos. The birds were in the shape of winged maidens with birds' feet. They had feathers so sharp that they wounded whoever they stooped upon. But they were most feared because they were maneaters. The Stymphalian Birds also lured people into the swamp, acting like sirens of the marshes. They were so numerous that when in flight they blotted out the sun. Hercules' fifth labour was to overcome the birds. He climbed up a slope overlooking the swamp and startled the birds by swinging a great bronze rattle or bird-scarer: the sound was so terrific that the birds flew up from the lake. The ones not scared off by the rattle, he shot at with his sling and bow. Some escaped to the Island of Ares in the Black Sea. The god Ares originally reared them and they were under his protection. The surviving birds were later met with by the Argonauts who accompanied Jason on his search for the Golden Fleece.

SUCCUBUS

In medieval clerical lore, a succubus is a female spirit who comes to men at night and sleeps with them. The succubus was supposed to be the cause of wet dreams and was sometimes associated with the nightmare.

Sughmaire

The Irish 'sea sucker' appears to be a form of the Muirselche. It was summoned by the hero Fionn Mac Cumhail to dry up a lake that needed to be drained. He brought the Sughmaire from the land of India, together with druids from Germany and female warriors from Britain and France. Irish legend says that there are nine Sughmaire throughout the world who made the currents ebb and flow in every harbour.

Suhur-Masu

Suhur-Masu is the Sumerian goat-fish that has the head and body of a ram and the tail of a fish. The earliest formulations of astrology were found in ancient Chaldea, where the skies were continuously clear at night. The Chaldeans codified the prototypes of the Western zodiacal figures, but Suhur-Masu is one of the zodiacal animals who has barely changed for he is still identifiable as the constellation of Capricorn the goat-fish ever since early times.

Sun Birds

In the legends of Zimbabwe, the Sun Birds are golden birds, statues of which were found in the excavations of the city of Great Zimbabwe. These birds are in fact swallows whose swift flight is praised in Bantu tradition, where storytellers relate how the Sun Birds fly better than even the eagle. Among the Shona, the Sun Birds originally belonged to the great goddess, Dzivaguru. According to legend, the first man and woman lived in darkness because the sun had not yet been found. The god Nosenga caught the Sun Birds in his trap and from then on the sun shone upon the Earth.

Sun Hou-Zi

In Chinese myth, Sun Hou-Zi is the divine monkey who was born from an egg impregnated by the wind. This extraordinary birth equipped him with magical powers and a swift wit so that he could trick the gods. He obtained the peach of immortality from them. He is also called Sun Wu-Kung.

Sun Wu-Kung

Sun Wu-Kung is the Chinese name of the Monkey King. Monkey was a small monkey with a furry body and tail, although he could stand more upright and resemble a human being when he chose. He went on to wear a golden suit of armour, given him by the Dragon Kings. Kuan Shi-Yin later gave him a silk robe that he wore with a tiger pelt about his waist. His eyes became red and diamond hard after he had been in her cauldron. He was born from the primordial egg that had been impregnated by the sky, and ruled over a realm of monkeys on a remote island where he called himself the Handsome Monkey King.

In a search to discover the secret of eternal life, he set out on a quest, arriving at the mountain where a Taoist priest lived. The monk taught him the martial arts, in which Monkey became very adept indeed. The Taoist priest renamed him Monkey Wu-Kung or 'pilgrim'. Returning home, Monkey discovered that his island home had been overrun by demons. He appealed to heaven for help and demanded divine recognition, whereupon the Jade Emperor of heaven granted him the post Pi Ma-Wen or 'Stable Boy'. Monkey was happy with the title until he discovered its menial meaning. Irritated at being mocked by the gods, Monkey disrupted the order of heaven and ate the peaches of immortality that the gods had reserved for a festival, and by eating the immortality pills that the great female Bodhisattva, Kuan Shu-Yin had prepared.

Now as an immortal, Monkey returned to his island where he overcame the demons. But he was hampered by the pursuit of the gods who tried to subdue him. Although captured and held under sentence of execution in Lao Tsu's cauldron, the immortal Monkey was only rejuvenated and refined by this. Finally, Jade Emperor called upon Buddha's help and Buddha had him trapped under a mountain for 500 years.

Kuan Shi-Yin helped release Monkey to become a bodyguard for a holy monk, Tripitaka, who was travelling from China to the Western Heaven to receive the scriptures from Buddha personally. Because of his extreme virtue, many demons sought to eat his flesh that would grant them immortality, making him a supreme target for trouble. Monkey's skills and tricks had only been honed during his imprisonment and he was able to shift his shape and size in such a way that only the gods could discern that it was he, while Monkey himself could immediately discern who was a disguised monster. His special weapon was a metal staff with which he could perform mighty feats and which could multiply itself, though the staff itself could become as small as a toothpick behind his ear. Monkey watched over Tripitaka for most of the journey, becoming his pupil, along with Chu Pa-Chien, the Sha Monk and the Dragon Horse. Buddha was able to give the scriptures to Tripitaka and in return for Monkey's great help, Buddha made Monkey the Buddha of Victory Through Strife.

The Element Encyclopedia of Magical Creatures

Surabhi

In Hindu mythology, Surabhi or 'Fragrant Rain' is the primordial cow who is the nurturer and mother of everyone living; her milk was churned by the gods. According to one tradition, Surabhi is the mother of the Nagas who were fathered by Kasyapa, the sage of vision. Surabhi was the mother of many cattle, chief of whom was Kamadhenu, the wish-bestowing cow.

Surma

In Finnish folklore, Surma is the monster that guards the gates of the underworld where the goddess Kalma lives. Surma was a perfect guardian for all who go this way to the land of the dead since it would let them in, but if any had the temerity to try and leave, it would tear them into pieces with its long fangs and swallow them down into its capacious, bottomless stomach. Although we are not told exactly what kind of monster Surma was, we may assume that it bore a singular resemblance to the mouth of a cave, if not to the mouth of hell itself.

Supporters of the Earth and Sky

In many myths the Earth is not able to stand by itself without supporters, many of whom turn out to be in animal form. Among the Kato Indians of California, the Earth was thought of as a great horned serpent that wound slowly southwards through the primeval waters with the creator Nagaicho standing upon its head steering it. Among the Iroquois, the Earth rests upon the back of a turtle (specifically the box turtle, *Cistudo carolina*) who is the only animal capable of such stability. This belief is also found in Hindu tradition where Kurma the turtle, one of the avatars of Vishnu, holds up the Earth.

There are also many traditions about a primordial man or being from whom all material creation is fashioned. Their very being is everything that we see around us. This myth is extensively told in Hindu tradition and is found throughout Indo-European myths, from the Norse Ymir to the Mesopotamian Tiamat. It is a tradition still embodied within the mystical lore of the Jewish kabbalists who believe that Adam Kadmon is the one who represents the microcosmic world, which is itself a reflection of the macrocosm, which is all that is. Very often there is a primal pillar, tree or support that keeps Earth and sky separate that is venerated as the support of creation, which is what we find in Norse myth with the world tree Yggdrasil. Yetl, the raven culture-hero of the Tlingit people of the American north-west Pacific coast, discovered the way to prop up the Earth. He drained a pool of seawater at low tide and killed the beaver who lived there, cutting off its foreleg to act as a prop. Then he put Hayicanke, the Old Woman Who Lives Under the Earth, to administer the prop. When her attention slips and she falls asleep we suffer earthquakes that usually wake her up again. The beaver is also a world prop in Welsh tradition as the Afanc.

The other common supporter of the Earth is the giant. This myth is most familiar to us from the image of the Greek Atlas holding the globe of the Earth upon his back, but in fact it stretches back much further. In Hittite myth, the giant Ubelluri is the original supporter. In the course of conflict between the storm god Teshub and a defeated deity, Kumarbi, the latter creates the rebellious Ullikummi to challenge Teshub. Kumarbi plants his son on the shoulder of Ubelluri where he grows prodigiously until he is 9,000 leagues tall. The gods are alarmed at his sudden appearance and cannot overcome him, so they send Ea, the god of wisdom to the supporter of the world, Ubelluri, who says,

> 'When they built heaven and earth
>   upon me,
> I knew nothing.
> But when they came and they cut
>   heaven and earth apart with
>   a cutter,
> This, too, I knew not.
> Now something makes my right
>   shoulder hurt,
> And I know not who he is,
>   this god!'

When Ea heard those words, he went around Ubelluri's right shoulder, and there the Basalt (Ullikummi) stood on Ubelluri's right shoulder like a shaft. The end of this myth is missing, but we note that Ullikummi is described as a basalt pillar while Ubelluri sounds like an antique Atlas, too busy doing his job to know much about what goes on above him. It is significant that pillars of basalt are the product of volcanic eruption, which could make this myth a distant memory of earth's upheaval.

In Norse tradition, Ymir is the progenitor of all the giants. He was formed of the ice blocks from the streams of Niflheim, the icy north, and the sparks from Muspellheim, the fiery south, which mixed together in the primordial void of Ginnungagap, and he was nourished by the cosmic cow Audumla. Odin and his brothers Vili and Ve killed him and rolled his corpse back into Ginnungagap where they made the earth from his body, the seas from his flesh and the heavens from his skull. It is said that Ymir's eyebrows are supported by four dwarves whose efforts allow daylight, moonlight and starlight to penetrate to the surface of the Earth. If this is indeed so, then these four dwarves should be given thanks for holding up the mere eyebrows of a giant to give us light, for they do no less than hold up the sky for us. This same myth is alluded to in the Welsh compendium of primordial myths, 'Culhwch and Olwen', where the eyes of the giant Yspaddaden are held up by forks.

Svadilfari

In Norse mythology, Svadilfari was a magical horse who carried the giant Hrimthursar to the land of the Aesir. The Aesir were in the process of enclosing Asgard with a wall and Hrimthursar offered to do it in three winters in return for the sun and moon and the hand of the goddess Freya in marriage. Svadilfari was allowed to help but the giant got on so well that it became obvious to the Aesir he would soon finish and that they would soon lose their means of light during day and night, as well as the lovely Freya, so they called upon the trickster Loki, to help slow him down. Loki changed himself into a pretty mare in season and drew near to Svadilfari who soon trotted off after her, pursued by an angry giant. From the union of horse and mare was born Sleipnir. After the birth, Loki resumed his shape but Hrimthursar was much delayed. Thor threw his magical hammer Miolnir at Hrimthursar, breaking his head open. The name 'Svadilfari' means 'he who makes an unfortunate journey'.

Svara

In Armenian legend, Svara is a yellow dragon that has a horn upon its head and a venomous capacity to poison whatever came near it. Svara was finally killed by Keresapa.

Svartalfar

In Norse mythology, the Svartalfar (black elves) lived in Svartalfaleim, which was also the world where the dwarves resided. It is possible to see the same division in the elvish world between the well-disposed and the malignant elf as there is between the fairy courts of the *Seelie* (Blessed Court) and the *Unseelie* (Unholy Court).

Swallow

Swallows make their lengthy migrations from hotter to cooler countries every summer in the temperate zones, becoming a welcome harbinger of good weather for those living in the north. For the peoples of southern Africa, the returning swallow appears at the beginning of October, heralding the spring when the new flowers respond to the rainfall by blooming in great profusion. The oldest story of their return is told in the Babylonian Epic of the Flood where a swallow returns with the dove after they have been sent out with the raven to find dry land. In Egyptian mythology, the swallow helped Isis when she had learned of the death of her husband Osiris. It sped up to heaven and informed the gods who were immediately able to lend their assistance. According to some traditions, Isis took the form of a swallow herself, lamenting about the sacred pillar which, in one version of the story, held the body of Osiris.

The Chinese Shang dynasty is said to have been founded by a swallow. It was told how K'o had two wives, Chiang Yuan and Chien Ti. Both women were bathing in the river when a swallow dropped an egg from its mouth. The egg had five colours upon its shell and the wives squabbled for it. Chien Ti caught it and swallowed it, becoming pregnant with the founder of the Shang dynasty. In China, swallows were emblems of fertility.

In Finland, 18 May is St Eric's Day when St Eric is supposed to arrive with the migratory birds. He carries a cuckoo under one arm and a swallow in his hand. This was the traditional sign that the sowing of oats must be completed and the barley sowing begun. The Swedish hold that the swallow beat its wings to cool the suffering Christ while he hung upon the cross calling 'Svala' ('Consolation'), which is why the bird is called swallow.

In the Haida myths of the northwest Pacific coast of America, the swallow Taadlat Ghaadala has a contest with Kkuuxuuginaagits ('Plain Old Marten'). They run a race from the depths of the Earth to the apex of heaven, creating a link between the two. This line, and the totem pole that is associated with it, can both provoke as well as measure earthquakes. The Christian bestiaries call the swallow 'Hirundo', saying that its high-minded devotion and attention to duty make it a symbol of the hope that descends from heaven into the heart of Christians. The *Physiologus*, the 2nd-century book of creature lore complied in the city of Alexandria, suggests that the swallow's absence is the result of a long winter sleep and that its awakening in the Spring is a emblem of the resurrection of Christ. For Moslems, the swallow is an emblem of the *haj*, the pilgrimage to Mecca, where it builds its nest in mosques and other holy places like the tombs of the saints. Gilbert White in his *Natural History of Selbourne*, reports the common belief that swallows nest at the bottom of ponds, and that explains their winter absence.

The swallow makes a cameo appearance in the film, *Monty Python and the Holy Grail*, where its speed and ability to carry objects to and from Africa is a strongly contested issue between King Arthur and his knights, especially the pedantic Sir Bedivere. This is a late mythic reference to a European belief that the swallow had within it two stones: a red stone that could cure and a black stone that could bestow luck.

SWAN

The abiding myth of the swan is noted by Leonardo da Vinci who wrote:

The Swan is pure white, without spot, and sings sweetly as it dies, dying upon the very strain of its song.

This myth of the dying swan derives from classical sources which see the swan as the symbol of the Muses. Early in the 20th century, the dying swan acquired a different connotation when Anna Pavlova made world famous the dance of the Dying Swan from Tchaikovsky's ballet *Swan Lake.* The swan was the emblem of Apollo, who is shown flying upon it. However, for the Hindu, the swan Hamsa bears the god Brahma upon its back, although this is sometimes said to be a goose. In Greek myth, Zeus takes the form of a swan in order to seduce Leda, whose children are not born viviparous from the womb, but instead hatch out from eggs. One of these egg-born children is Helen of Troy, ex-wife of Menelaus of Sparta, whose fatal beauty caused the downfall of Troy when Paris bore her away. Two great swan myths are found in Irish folk tale.

The four Children of Lir are cursed by their stepmother Aífe and turned into swans. The eldest, Finnguala retains the power of speech. They spend three terms of 300 years in different locations, during which time their fate is realized and Aífe is punished by being turned into a vulture, though other sources say she becomes a demon. Gradually, the Children of Lir are forgotten until their singing is heard by the monk Mo Chaemoc, a disciple of St Patrick. He takes them in and links them together with a silver chain. The new queen of Connacht Lairgnean hears about the singing swans and commands that she possess them, but as they are led away from the monk's cell, the term of their transformation comes to an end and they return to their human forms. Unfortunately, their eternal youthfulness only remains while they are still swans and the 900-year-old Children of Lir are baptized by Mo Chaemoc prior to their complete dissolution into dust.

Sylph

The god Oengus Mac Og falls into a love-sickness upon seeing a beautiful woman in a vision one day. She comes and plays upon a *tiompain* (hammered zither) and he falls into a trance from which none can help him. No one can tell who or what the reason for this sickness is until the great doctor Fergne divines the cause. He bids Oengus's mother Boann to seek for a woman who answers the woman's description. Boann discovers it is none other than Caer Ibormeith (Caer Yew-Berry) the daughter of the fairy king Bodbh. Bodbh cunningly offers Boann to let Oengus go down to the lake where Caer and her 150 maidens are to be found. If they can identify Caer, then Oengus can have her.

When they bear him to the lake, Oengus recognizes her but has no strength to take her. His family try to coerce Bodbh into letting them marry, but he is adamant. However, he lets slip that Caer and her attendants will alight upon the lake called Bel Dragon at next Samhain (Hallowe'en.) When Oengus is brought to that lake, Caer and her attendants are in the form of swans. He recognizes her again and, taking the form of a swan himself, he joins Caer and flies away with her.

In European magical lore, a sylph is an elemental spirit of the air. The name was first used by the Swiss metaphysician Paracelsus in the early 16th century, derived from the Latin *silva* (wood) and the Greek *nymphe* (nymph). The leader of the sylphs, who are invoked in magical workings where the cooperation of the winds is required, is called Paralda. The 19th-century ballet *Les Sylphides* portrays the spirits of young women who haunt graveyards: they are really more like Vili than sylphs, although both kinds of spirits are associated with the air.

T

Taadlat Ghaadala

In the Haida myths from the north-west Pacific coast of America, Taadlat Ghaadala the swallow, has a contest with Kkuuxuginaagits ('Plain Old Marten'). They run a race from the depths of the Earth to the apex of heaven, creating a link between the two. This mythic trajectory of Taadlat Ghaadala's race with his opponent is associated with a primal totem pole that is understood to provoke as well as measure earthquakes.

Tamdrin

Tamdrin is the name of the Tibetan horse king who is usually known as Hayagriya. He is one of the Dharma-palas who protect the teachings of Tibetan Buddhism. He takes the form of a man with a horse's head.

Tangaroa

Tangaroa is the Polynesian god of the ocean who breathes only once in 24 hours, causing tidal motion. In Tahuata (the Marquesas Islands) he is known as Tanaoa, the god of primeval darkness. In fine weather, Tangaroa turns into a green lizard.

Tangghwan Llaana

Among the Haida peoples of the north-west Pacific coast of America, Tangghwan Llaana is the 'Sea-Dweller' who is the god of wealth. He has a large amorphous body and two elongated eyes that have double pupils. He lives at the bottom of the sea in a house of great beauty, surrounded by seals that are its spirit-messengers.

Tangie

A sinister water horse from the folklore of the Shetland Isles. Its name derives from the Danish word for seaweed, which covers it like long shaggy hair. Sometimes Tangies have been known to appear as old men, but they are most frequently seen as horses that invite unwary travellers to ride upon them, after which they gallop off into the nearest deep water. A ferocious robber named Black Eric was said to ride a Tangie, giving him extraordinary powers and strength. Eventually he fell from the creature's back over a cliff known as Fitful Head, but the Tangie continued to terrorize the area.
(*See also* Kelpie.)

Taming the Animals

Throughout world mythology, the power of magical creatures lies in their untameable natures, for we seldom invest domestic animals with such mighty powers. Stories of the domestication of animals for meat are part of the early myths of civilization and animal husbandry in all cultures. We see how pigs have healed people of diseases, how the cow opens the way to abundance and so on. However, the most enduring myths of animal taming are not so much about domestication but of subduing the animal passions of human nature. Prime exemplars of this tradition are Buddha and Lao Tze, both of whom are depicted as riding upon a buffalo.

In the Book of Genesis, Adam is given the guardianship of all animals by God, who commands him to name the animals. This is movingly illustrated by William Blake's 'Adam Naming the Beasts', and was excitingly recast in C.S. Lewis' book *The Magician's Nephew* from the 'Narnia' series. The act of naming is also an act of knowing the inner nature of something. In the case of the Greek hero, Orpheus, it is the music of his lyre that speaks to and subdues wild animals, making them biddable and harmless. Music is the universal language that is understood by both men and beasts. In ancient Chinese myth, it was the raven-nosed emperor Yu who rid the land of harmful animals and who could capture and tame beneficial ones a hundred animals a time. He beat loudly upon a dance drum and all the animals obeyed the rhythm in the Dance of the Hundred Animals.

Taniwha

The Maori people of New Zealand describe this creature as a lizard-like dragon that preys on humans. The hero Pitaka, with the help of some fearless companions, managed to trap and kill several of these creatures. When they were cut open, the bodies of the people they had eaten spilled out, apparently undigested.

Tanngniortr and Tanngrisnir

Two supernatural goats that draw the chariot of the god Thor in Norse tradition. Their names mean 'Tooth Gnasher' and 'Tooth Grinder'. It is said that Thor and Loki stayed overnight with a farmer. In the evening, Thor slaughtered his goats, skinned them and threw the meat into a cauldron. When they were cooked, Thor and his companions sat down to eat, inviting the farmer, his wife and children to join them. Thor spread the goatskins away from the fire and told the father and his family to throw the bones onto them. The farmer's son took the thighbone of one of the goats and split it with his knife in order to get at the marrow inside. Thor stayed the night, got up at daybreak, raised his great hammer and blessed the goatskins. At once, the goats stood up again, but one of them was lame in its back leg. Thor saw this and asked if the farmer or a member of his family had damaged the goat's legs. The farmer's son admitted his fault and his father calmed the god's anger by offering him his children as recompense. They accompanied Thor thereafter as his servants.

Tanuki

In Japanese folklore, Tanuki is a badger with a mischievous spirit. Sometimes he takes human form, but at others he can appear as a bottle of saki.

T'ao Tieh

The most noticeable feature of this creature, which is found in the traditions of China, is its enormous head, cavernous mouth and serried rows of dagger-like teeth. Not surprisingly, its name can be translated as 'Glutton', and its appetite is legendary. It can take several different forms, including that of a human being and a tiger, but whatever creature the head represents also dictates the body under it. Thus a T'ao Tieh with the head of an animal has the foreparts of that animal; but in each case it has two hind parts and two stomachs. Sometimes it is painted on the inside of dishes to warn diners of the effects of overindulgence.

Tarasque

According to the medieval legends of France, the Tarasque sprang from the monstrous Leviathan who mated with a Bonnacon – a cow-like creature with the mane of a horse and enormous horns found amid the deserts of Asia. Despite the fact that it is classed as a dragon, the Tarasque is said to have the body of an enormous ox, and legs and feet like a bear. It terrorized the region of Aix la Chapelle until a local saint named Martha tamed it and drove it out of the country. Since then, the Tarasque has been paraded in the town's festivals.

TARBH UISGE

A giant water bull in the traditions and folklore of the Celts. In both Scotland and Ireland, it was described as a vast black creature with fiery red nostrils. It lived in the ocean and along the shores of its margin, emerging at night from the waves and rampaging across the land to mate with local cows. The progeny of such matings were called Corc-chluasask ('split ears'), for they were born with only a half an ear. In the traditions of the Isle of Skye, these creatures were killed immediately to prevent the bringing of bad luck. On the Isle of Man, the Tarbh Uisge (known there as the Taroo-Ustey) is considered less vicious than other creatures of this kind such as the Each Uisge, but is still best kept on the right side of.

A cross-grained farmer at Sulby found the Tarbh Uisge grazing with his herd. He recognized it by its round ears, but instead of treating it gently he gave it a sharp blow with his stick, driving it into the sea. His wife prophesied that this would cause their crops to be blighted and indeed this was the case. This made the farmer angry, and next time he saw the creature grazing with his herd, he crept up behind it with a long loop of rope and lassoed it, but the bull easily pulled the rope from his hand and returned to the sea. This time the farmer's potatoes were blighted. Finally, he agreed to go and see the fairy-doctor as his wife had advised, but he still paid no attention to the doctor's advice about treating fairy beasts with deference. He learned one thing however – that a stake cut from the rowan tree had power to subdue the Tarbh Uisge. So he cut such a stick and next time he sighted the bull he crept up behind it and drove it with the rowan wand into his shed. In due course, he took it to market and offered it for sale.

It was a beautiful beast and there was nothing to tell it from a normal animal except for its round ears, but no one would bid for it – until at last a simple fellow began to show some interest, saying he would purchase it if the farmer would ride on its back as he had claimed he could do.

The Element Encyclopedia of Magical Creatures

The farmer climbed on and gave the bull a smart tap with his rowan stake. The creature stepped out at a gentle trot; but then the farmer dropped the rowan stick and at once the bull set off at a gallop, heading for the sea with the farmer clinging to its back. He had plenty of time to repent his uncivil ways as he went. On reaching the shore, the bull went straight on and plunged into the sea, and with his last strength the farmer leapt from its back into the deep water. More dead than alive he struggled back to the shore; after which he was a changed man.

Tartaro

In the Basque folklore of Spain, Tartaro is a Cyclopian being described as a giant with one eye in the middle of his forehead. However, in some stories he becomes a grotesque animal, misshapen and vindictive. In most of the stories told about him, however, his victims easily outwit him.

Tatosok

The name given by the Abenaki Iroquois people of North America to a type of horned serpent known locally as Champ. It dwells in the depths of Lake Champlain between Quebec in Canada and Vermont in the United States. Frequently sighted, it is said to be around 30 ft long with several humps along its back and a horse-like head. It seems to be similar to the Loch Ness Monster, and some cryptozoologists have considered it as a possible leftover from the prehistoric period.

Tatzelwurm

In the folklore of Austria, the Tatzelwurm appears as a hybrid lizard-like creature with the head of the cat. Agreement as to its exact nature and appearance is hard to come by, and few agree as to the number of legs possessed by this creature – or indeed whether it has any at all. Its body may be smooth, rough, scaly or covered in hair. In Switzerland, it is known as the Stollenwurm. Both creatures are considered aggressive and they attack travellers in the mountains without warning.

Tawadi

Among the Makiritare people of the Guyanan highlands in Venezuela, Tawadi is the spirit of a Nacunda nighthawk (*Podager nacunda*) that lives in sixth heaven with Mudo and Hothottu.

Taweret

In ancient Egypt, the hippopotamus is a goddess, Taweret, wife of Set, and is usually shown standing upright with a hippopotamus's body but with human arms and legs. She carries an emblem called a *sa* (a rolled-up papyrus shelter) for herdsmen who are out tending flocks. She also carries the life-giving *ankh* (torch) symbol with which she expels typhonic forces. She was the matron of women in childbirth.

Tcipitckaam

One of the great number and variety of lake serpents in the traditions of the native people of North America. In this instance, the Tcipitckaam, which is also known as the Unicorn serpent, is described as a snake-like creature with the head of a horse and a single yellow spiralling horn emerging from its forehead. Variations on this describe it as having the form of an alligator, once again with a horn sprouting from its head. It is reported as inhabiting Lakes Utopia and Ainslie. At times, the Tcipitckaam has been known to take on the form of a young man, in which shape it lures young women to its home beneath the waters.

Tecumbalam

This Mayan bird was the one that broke the bones and muscles of the first men who were destroyed when the Hurakan god visited his anger upon the world. He was one of the four great winged beings who attacked the wooden bodies created by Gucumatz and Tepeu that were intended to become the first living humans. They each attacked a different part of the body to prevent the pollution of the primordial world. The others were Camazotl, Cotzbalam and Xecotcovach.

Teehooltsoodi

A creature from before the Flood, this water monster from the traditions of the Navajo people of North America resembles a very large otter with smooth fur and horns on its head like a buffalo. In one native story, Teehooltsoodi's child was stolen by Spider Woman; so angry and desperate was Teehooltsoodi that he caused several rivers to overflow, flooding the land for miles around.

Teelget

A dark and terrible monster from the traditions of the Navajo people of North America. The Teelget preyed upon humans for many years since it was finally brought down by an arrow made of chain lightning that was fired from the bow of the hero Nayenygami.

Telchines

In the Graeco-Roman tradition, the Telchines are an ancient race of beings, responsible for the invention of metalworking. They were associated chiefly with the islands of Rhodes, Cyprus, Chos and Crete, though in the writings of Pausanius there is mention of Athena Telchine who was worshipped in Boetia. The magical skill of the Telchines caused them to be accused of sorcery and the blighting of crops with their sulphur and foul water. Hence their reputation became that of a spiteful, jealous race of gnomes that Zeus scattered through the world after they attempted to kidnap Aphrodite. Some accounts describe them as like men, but with thick, flipper-like arms and legs, while in others their heads resemble those of dogs and their eyes hypnotize anyone who angered them. They were responsible, among other things, for forging the Trident of Poseidon and the sickle with which Cronos castrated Uranus.

TENGU

In Japanese mythology the Tengu are a race of monsters with human bodies, glowing eyes, sharp red beaks and birds' wings. The female Tengus are slightly different, being depicted as human in shape but possessing an animal head with huge fangs and enormous ears and noses. There are several types of Tengu, including the Karasa and Konoha. All of these creatures are extremely aggressive – and skilled in martial arts. They lived in a fortress in the dark forests of Mount Kurama near Kyoto, and in the past warriors travelled in the hope of encountering a Tengu and learning its skills. However, any traveller who dares to go to the home of one of these evil-natured creatures is more likely to be driven mad by fear. One of the best-known Tengu is Birdman, generally depicted as humanoid but with the head of a cockerel, complete with wattles and comb, but with human ears. It has long attenuated wings to which are attached human hands.

TE TUNA

A sea monster in the traditions of the people of Tahiti. At one time, it was the husband of the Great Universal goddess Hina before she mated with Maui, the Ulysses character of Polynesian mythology. Te Tuna is usually described as a huge eel-like creature.

TEUMESSIAN VIXEN

In Graeco-Roman mythology, the Teumessian Vixen was a giant fox who terrorized the countryside in the land of Cadmeia. Because she was immortal, she could not be caught, and to make matters worse she demanded a child to be sacrificed to her every year. In desperation, the people turned to the immortal hunter Laelaps, who was destined to catch anything he pursued. The resulting chase lasted for many months – and was obviously destined to continue forever. Zeus finally settled the matter by turning both hunter and hunted to stone.

The Element Encyclopedia of Magical Creatures

TEYU-YARGUA

According to the Guarani people of Paraguay, this is the name of the jaguar-lizard who guards Paititi, the fabled land of gold, which is situated in Lake Cuni-Cuni and ruled over by El Gran Moxo.

TEZCATLIPOCA

In the Aztec and Toltec myths of South America, Tezcatlipoca was a god of the sun and the wind, who took the form of both the jaguar and the ocelot – the other big cat of South America. Before the deities had reached their final form, there were simultaneously four aspects of Tezcatlipoca, which marked the four cardinal points of the compass and each were very different. In his northern aspect, Tezcatlipoca was black, in his Eastern aspect red, in his Southern aspect blue, and in his Western aspect white. Later, following the diversification of Aztec and Toltec cultures, these four aspects separated into distinct beings, each with a different name. The blue Tezcatlipoca of the South became Tlaloc, the god of rain; the red Tezcatlipoca of the East became Xipe Totec, who represented the sun; the white Tezcatlipoca of the West became Quetzalcoatl; while he himself remained in the North with the colour of darkness. After this, Quetzalcoatl became the central deity of both the Aztec and the Toltec, having conquered the three Tezcatlipocas of the other cardinal points.

Subsequent celestial myths and creation stories described mighty struggles between Tezcatlipoca, Quetzalcoatl and the other gods, who fought for the mastery of the world. One of Tezcatlipoca's favourite disguises during this period was that of the turkey, and he is sometimes shown in this form, but missing one foot which, according to various accounts, was either bitten off by the Earth monster, to be replaced by a mirror, or caught in a door that led to the Underworld. Other accounts associate Tezcatlipoca with the spider, and relate that he came to Earth along a spider's web. He was also recognized as the patron of magicians and the maker of the first sun that was called *nahui ocelotl* (from which we get the word 'ocelot'). The sun was knocked out of its orbit during a cosmic dance combat fought between himself and Quetzalcoatl. After this, Tezcatlipoca became the jaguar constellation we call Ursa Major. Tezcatlipoca's name means 'smoking mirror', derived from his emblematic mirror from which a spiral of smoke ascended. He wandered invisibly, noting wrongdoing and punishing it, and also presided over festivals and banquets.

THELGETH

In the traditions of the Navajo people of south-western North America, these are a tribe of hairy, headless, maneating monsters who were believed to be born to virgins who indulged in unnatural acts. Though they resembled the European Blemyahs, the Thelgeth were far

The Element Encyclopedia of Magical Creatures

more vicious, and preyed upon human beings. They are related to the Binaye Ahani and the Tsenahale with whom they form the tribe of monstrous creatures known collectively as the Anaye.

Thoth

The Egyptian moon god, who also presides over scribes and is seen as a fount of all wisdom. He is most often represented in human form with the head of an ibis, but he can also appear as a baboon. In each case, he wears a crown representing the crescent moon containing the full moon within it. Both these aspects of the god can be interpreted in terms of lunar symbolism; the ibis with its long curved beak which hints at the crescent new moon, and whose black and white feathers can be seen as indicating its waxing and waning. Baboons make agitated chattering sounds and rise up on their hind legs at dawn and this was understood as a greeting to the rising sun by creatures sacred to the moon god. The baboon is consistently shown in Egyptian art in an attitude of prayer. As 'Lord of the Sacred Words', Thoth gave to the Egyptians the gift of knowledge, and how to communicate by using hieroglyphics. He came to represent the embodiment of all scientific and literary skills, and was said to look after the sacred books contained in the House of Life, which included medical manuals, mathematical scrolls and instructions in social behaviour.

Thunderbird

In indigenous North American tradition, the Thunderbird is a major figure for all tribes. As a personification of thunder, he appears among tribal groups from the north Pacific coast to the plains and eastern woodlands. The Thunderbird or birds are powerful supernatural creatures, which not only produce thunder but also make war with other beings and forces, causing disturbances above and below the Earth – particularly with the powers beneath the water, the horned serpents or water snakes. The Thunderbird most often takes the form of an eagle with outspread wings. Among the Iroquois, the leader of all Thunderbirds is Keneun, who guards the sacred fire stolen by Manabusch. Among the Woodlands Iroquois, another Thunderbird is Oshadagea or 'dew eagle' who lives in the western sky and carries a pond of dew in the hollow of his back. If the Earth is attacked by fire, he releases life-giving dew to help it recover its fertility.

Tiamat

The great cosmic dragon in the mythology of Sumer and Babylon. According to the Babylonian 'Epic of Creation', after the division of heaven and Earth the only creatures in existence were Abzu and Tiamat. Abzu personified fresh water and Tiamat salt water. The pair were envisaged as male and female, though it is said that 'their waters mingled together'. They engendered a

The Element Encyclopedia of Magical Creatures

family of troublesome gods whose activities so disturbed Abzu that he planned to destroy them, despite Tiamat's protests. When Abzu was slain by Ea, Tiamat vowed revenge and created eleven monsters including Musmahhu, the Usumgallu and the Basmu – all types of horned serpent. In addition, she gave birth to Mushassu the Snake Dragon, Lahamu the Longhaired, Ugallu the Great Storm Beast, Uridimmus the Mad Lion, Girtabilli the Scorpion Man, Umu Dabrutu, whose name meant 'fierce storms', and Kulullu, a kind of mythical bison. All of these monstrous creatures were defeated by the god Marduk in a great cosmic battle. Tiamat was then slain and the disjointed parts of her body used to create the cosmos.

TI-CHIANG

A strange celestial bird in the legends of China, the Ti-Chiang has neither eyes nor beak, though it is possessed of the most splendid scarlet plumage and three pairs of feet.

TIETHOLSODI

A water monster from the traditions of the Navajo people of North America. This creature dragged two women down to his kingdom. A man and woman went down into Tietholsodi's realm to rescue them and were secretly followed there by Coyote, who kidnapped two of the monster's children. When the monster discovered his loss, he flooded the world in which the Navajo were living at the time, forcing them to flee upwards into the next world, the Earth as we know it today. However, the floodwaters began to rise so far that they entered the upper world. Fortunately, the kidnapping was discovered just in time by the rain and fire gods and the monster's children were thrown back into the world below, whereupon the waters receded.

T'IEN KOU

A great celestial dog in Chinese astronomical myth, the T'ien Kou is described as a huge dog with a tail of fire like a comet. Its home was in the heavens, but it sustained itself by descending to Earth every night and seeking out human children to eat. If it could not catch any children, it would attack a human adult and consume his liver. If it failed to eat, it would go back to the heavens and attempt to consume the moon. At which point, Hou I, the Celestial Archer, would come forth and shoot down the T'ien Kou to preserve the lunar orb. However, the T'ien Kou was reborn again next morning and the whole process would begin again.

TIGER

In the East, the tiger takes the place of the lion as the king of beasts. It represents royalty, fearlessness, ferocity and anger and is always a symbol of power. In India, it is an emblem of the warrior caste known as the Kshatriyas, and there is a legend of tigers being descended from the Hindu gods Shiva and Durga.

According to Korean legend, two animals desired to become human, the tiger and the bear. They prayed daily to Hwanung, the son of heaven, and he told both animals to retire to a cave for 100 days, eating only mugwort and garlic. The tiger was impatient and could not keep to this regime, but the bear continued faithfully, eventually becoming a beautiful woman who married Hwanung; their offspring founded the first Korean dynasty of kings.

The tiger is extremely important in Chinese myth, where it is representative of authority, courage, prowess and military valour. It was originally considered one of the Four Auspicious Creatures but was later replaced by the Ki-Lin. In Chinese myth, the tiger is sometimes depicted with wings to indicate its unearthly nature. However, the symbolism of this creature can be ambivalent, for when it is in conflict with the celestial dragon the two denote the opposing forces of spirit and matter. The Goddess of the Wind rides a tiger and in this form the animal represents the constellation of Orion. When an ordinary person encounters dangerous elemental forces, he or she is said to be 'riding the tiger'.

In Malaysia, the tiger must not be mentioned by name as this may invite it to attack. It is therefore known by such titles as 'Hairy Face', 'Striped One', 'Grandfather' or 'Lord'. Were-tigers are considered particularly ferocious and the soul of a wizard may enter the body of one. In Sumatra, were-tigers are powerful but friendly and the souls of the

Shiva is often portrayed as wearing a tiger skin about his shoulders. He obtained it when he went to visit the *rishis* (sages) in order to teach them some of the basic truths of the universe. He went in disguise as a young woman together with the god Vishnu. However, the rishis showed no interest in receiving two women or learning from them, so they released a savage tiger to frighten their unwanted visitors away. This tiger had been forged from sacrificial tigers and was invincible – or so they thought. Shiva subdued the tiger and removed its pelt by slitting it off the animal with the nail of his little finger, flinging the skin about his neck. The rishis then sent a serpent after him, which he made into a garland. After Shiva had overcome his last adversary, a black dwarf called Muyalaka, the god stepped over the creature's back and began dancing. His dance opened up the vault of heaven to reveal Chidambaram or Tillai, the centre of the universe, and the other gods came to watch Shiva establish the rhythms of the universe. At this point, the rishis cast themselves to the ground to worship the god. Ever after, Shiva wore the tiger skin as a sign of this event.

The Element Encyclopedia of Magical Creatures

dead can incarnate within them. In Graeco-Roman myth, the tiger can be substituted for the leopard, and as such draws the chariot of Dionysus, who is also shown riding a tiger. The skin on which Hermes placed the infant god is variously referred to as that of a tiger, a leopard or a fawn.

TIKOLOSHE

A strange hairy monster from the traditions of the Xhosa people of South Africa. No taller than a baboon, and walking with the same odd gait, with long arms trailing, the Tikoloshe once lived only in the rivers of the Transvaal, but in more recent times has been seen in the Natal and even in the city of Johannesburg. The creature can make itself invisible or appear like a human being. Jan Knappert, in his book *African Mythology*, gives the following story, which was told to him by native people.

A woman saw the Tikoloshe while she was out getting water and firewood by the river. The Tikoloshe rose from the deep water, stared at her, then leapt onto the bank. The woman fled, leaving her bundle of firewood behind; the Tikoloshe picked it up and capered after her, easily keeping up, until she was home. It was so quick that she could not fasten the door in its face, so it slipped in, jumped on her back and started mating with her. At this moment, her husband came home from a hunting trip. He tried to thrust his spear into the Tikoloshe, but it was so quick that the spear went into his wife's back and killed her. While the husband stood in shock, gazing at her bleeding body, the Tikoloshe jumped down from its perch on to his back and fastened its long black fingers around his neck.

Subsequently, a number of murders were committed which baffled the police. Most of the victims were women who had been raped prior to being strangled, but some were rich men whose money was stolen. No one saw the murderer even though one man was killed in broad daylight. It was believed that this was the woman's husband, still acting under the influence of the Tikoloshe.

TINMIUKPUK

The great Thunderbird in the mythology of the Inuit people of Alaska. Resembling a gigantic eagle with mighty talons, it is large enough to carry off a whole caribou, which it takes back to its lair in the mountains. It is also not above preying on humans if it cannot get any other food.

TIOMAN

In the mythology of the Malayan people of West Malaysia, Tioman was at one time a human princess who fell in love with the son of a neighbouring king. However, when her love was not returned she became so overwhelmed with tortured thoughts that her outer appearance changed into that of a dragon with horns and a mighty tail. In this form, her despair grew and she fled to the South China Sea where she brooded upon the waters for so long that she again became transformed. Her mighty shape became an island called Pulau Tioman, while her horns metamorphosed into the twin peaks of Bali Hai – the setting for the mythical Island in the musical 'South Pacific'. Her tail became the swirling waters of Salang.

TIPAKA

A beautiful winged horse in the folklore of Thailand. So fast could Tipaka travel that it could reach its destination before its rider had finished speaking the name of the place to which he wished to go. The horse became the mount of the legendary King Sison.

TISHTRYA

In the Zoroastrian mythology of ancient Persia and Iran, Tishtrya is the spirit of the Dog Star, Sirius. As a star which appeared in high summer it was said to bring cooling showers to reverse the actions of the demon Apaosha, who had carried off all the waters of the Earth and hidden them in place called Vourukasha. A great battle finally took place between these two powers in which they each took the form of horses: Tishtrya became a beautiful white horse with a gold harness, while Apaosha appeared as a great black horse without hair. At their first encounter Tishtrya was beaten back, but he attacked again and drove Apaosha away from Vourukasha. Their battle caused the imprisoned waters to overflow, and the rains descended again upon the Earth. It is said that this battle is repeated every year. Worshippers of Tishtrya were required to sing hymns to give him the strength to return again and defeat Apaosha, filling the rivers with rain.

Tisiphone

One of the Eumenides (Furies) from Graeco-Roman tradition. Tisiphone, whose name means 'retaliation', was the avenger of murder. She sat at night at the entrance to Hell armed with a whip with which she inflicted cruel punishments on criminals. She wore a bloody robe and had serpents instead of hair.

Tiuh Tiuh

In the mythology and beliefs of the Cakchiquel people of Guatemala, Central America, Tiuh Tiuh is a hawk responsible for the creation of the first humans.

Tiuh Tiuh killed a coyote and mixed its blood with that of a tapir and a serpent, kneading them with flour from ground maize. He is said to have created thirteen men and fourteen women who united and multiplied. They then separated into seven tribes. The warriors of these tribes set out under the command of Tiuh Tiuh and soon reached the coast. However, they found themselves unable to cross the sea. The two eldest warriors fell asleep on the seashore and were drowned, but the rest survived because they had in their possession a red staff that they had brought with them from the Place of the Sun. The other warriors struck the sea with this, causing the waters to divide so that they could cross to the far shore by walking along the seabed.

Titans

The name Titan originates in Graeco-Roman mythology but Titanic beings are found in most of the great mythological cycles of the world, where they are identified with powerful elemental forces, likely to cause disruption.

Today, Titans refer to beings of great size and strength, who are likely to be arrogant, powerful and violent. In Graeco-Roman mythology, the Titans are the twelve gigantic children of Uranus and Gaia, consisting of six sons and six daughters. The sons were named Coeus, Cronus, Hyperion, Iapetus, Oceanus, and Crius; the daughters (known as the Titanides) were Mnemosyne, Phoebe, Wrhea, Tethys, Theia and Themis. Uranus was also the father of the Cyclops and the Hecatoncheires or hundred-handed giants. The last-named caused him such anguish that he thrust them back into the womb of their mother the Earth. For this reason, Gaia urged the Titans to emasculate Uranus and establish Cronos as ruler of all the gods. Later, they aided Zeus in dethroning Cronos. When the Titans made war on Zeus, he vanquished them using weapons forged by the Cyclops who were famous metalworkers, and imprisoned all save Oceanus into the Underworld of Tartarus.

The word 'Titan' can mean simply 'Lord' or possibly 'to stretch', indicating either that they stretched forth their hands, causing lightning and disruption, or that they were stretched on an underground wheel, causing earthquakes and volcanoes. Their overthrow by Zeus equates with Odin's conquest of the Frost Giants, who were also Titanic. There is even a word – *Titonomachia* – that refers to the war of the Titans against the Olympian gods and to this day it stands for any violent insurrection against the forces of goodness and order.

A second group, also known as Titans and often confused with their giant kin, came together to slay the god Dionysus Zagreus. Dionysus Zagreus tried to escape by shapeshifting, but when he assumed the form of a bull the Titans killed and ate him. However, the goddess Athena rescued his heart, which she fed to Zeus, allowing Dionysus to be reborn from the union of Zeus and Semele. Zeus then destroyed this group of Titans and from their ashes created mankind, thus causing the good/evil aspect of human nature.

TLALOC

Also called Chac, this Central American rain god lived at the top of mountains where he ruled over a realm for those warriors who died in battle and those women who died in childbirth. He was the ruler of the drowned and the one who brought fertility to the maize fields. He had a head formed from two intertwined serpents.

TLASOLOTL

In the Aztec mythology of Central America, this great horned owl is an omen of the very greatest evil. He dwells within the temple of Itzlacolohqui, the god of the obsidian knife, who represents the iciness of death and great obstinacy.

TLATECHTLI

In the Aztec mythology of ancient Mexico, Tlatechtli is a gigantic frog whose cavernous mouth represents the entrance to the Land of the Dead. He often accompanied the serpent goddess Coatlicue.

TLOTLI

In Aztec mythology, this is the name of a hawk sent by the gods to see why the sun had stopped moving across the sky and to request that he resumed his journey once again. The sun refused to do this unless all the gods sacrificed themselves, which they did once they had recognized that the sun was their superior.

TOAD

Perhaps because of its unlovely appearance, the toad features extensively in world mythology. From the earliest times, the toad was associated with the moon and as such it came to represent resurrection because of the way the moon was perceived to renew itself constantly after it had dwindled to nothing. However, the toad can also be considered evil and represent death. In the West, it was assumed to be venomous and to spit poison. The great Roman naturalists, Pliny and Aelian, both maintained this, but Aristotle did not agree. Like the serpent, toads carried a precious jewel on their heads, known as the Borax stone, which had the power of detecting and acting as an antidote to poison.

In the Zoroastrian religion of ancient Persia, the toad is a servant of Ahriman, the power of evil, and it represents greed, envy and avarice. Among the Peruvian Incas, it was one of the four sacred animals, together with condor, llama and serpent. The Incas worshipped the Milky Way and Toad was associated with the part of this star system known as the Southern Cross. In this form, it was considered one of the gateways to the Sun.

In North America, Toad was the hero of the Huron creation story.

In the beginning there was nothing but water and sky for the animals to live in, so they decided that they needed a place where they could crawl to dry off or play. So they got together to work out how best to create land. Turtle, floating like an island in the sea, pointed out that there was dirt at the bottom of the ocean, and he volunteered his back as a platform from which to collect it. But this meant he could not dive to get to it himself because each time he did, he would lose everything that had been collected. Otter tried to dive down, but lost his breath before he could reach the bottom. Beaver took a turn, and even mighty Muskrat tried, but it was only Toad who was successful. Again and again he dived down, bringing back more and more earth, which he fashioned into land on Turtle's back. Finally, he was so exhausted that he died, using his dying breath to spit up the last morsel of earth. Thus he sacrificed his life so that others might live, and to this day toads are honoured among the Native American people.

The toad can also represent the dark Manitou and the powers of darkness are overcome by the great Manitou. In Mexico, the toad depicts the Earth and the toadstool is equated with the sacred mushroom, which gives enlightenment.

The toad God, sitting under a toadstool, portrays the mushroom God; the two poisons together, those of the toad and the mushroom, act as an hallucinogen and provide power for the shaman.

Among the Dakota and Lakota people, Gnaska is the name for the toad and they see him as a god as well as a trickster who has command over water. Although the name Gnaska is generally used for frog, most descriptions point generally to the toad, which in the common speech of the Lakota is *netapheha*.

In Britain, toads have been associated with witchcraft since the Middle Ages when witches were believed to have toad familiars. Toads were often hanged or burned along with the witch. Yet the toad was not always credited with evil. For example, it was believed that if a toad crossed the path of a wedding party, the couple would be fertile, have many children and be prosperous and happy.

The toad's lunar nature is seen in the story, from Chinese mythology, of the three-legged toad called Ch'ang O. At one time she was the wife of the Celestial Archer, Hon I, who was the guardian of the gods and the brew of immortality. Having stolen the elixir, Ch'ang O flew to the moon to hide. But the elixir transformed her into a hideous three-legged toad. She remains there to this day, on the face of the moon, which she eats away in her hunger, causing the moon to shrink to the sliver of its last quarter – though it is always renewed.

In Japan, it is said that a little girl, whose father had promised to sacrifice

her to the Rain Serpent if it made the rain come, managed instead to kill the serpent. That same day she met an old woman, who was really the Mother of Toads, and expressed gratitude to the girl for having disposed of the dangerous killer of toads, all of whom were her great-grandchildren. She gave the girl a toad skin, by means of which she could disguise herself in any shape she wished. The girl went to the royal palace disguised as an old woman and was taken on as a cook. In time, she revealed herself in her true shape to a Prince, who fell in love with her and married her immediately. A similar story of toad-charm is found in Kenneth Grahame's *The Wind in the Willows* where Toad wheedles his way out of prison by charming the gaoler's daughter into helping him escape disguised as a washer-woman – an inverse kind of shapeshifting for the transformatory toad!

TOATOATATAVAYA-O

In the mythology of Fiji, this is the name of a giant cockerel that ruled over all other fowls in distant times.

One day, Toatoatatavaya-o called his subjects to accompany him to the reef to gather juicy worms, clams and shellfish. Spreading their wings the birds flew behind their leader until they came to the reef. There Toatoatatavaya-o strode about proudly, grabbing all the worms before any of his subjects could get to them. As he strode about with his head in the air, Toatoatatavaya-o stepped onto a clam that was lying there. Immediately, the clam closed up catching the bird's foot. Then the tide began to rise. It crept up Toatoatatavaya-o's legs, then up to his body, and presently reached his neck. He was terrified and struggled to free himself, but was caught fast. In terror, he begged the clam to let him go. 'Perhaps you don't know who I am,' he said. 'I am the chief of all the fowls and it is time to lead my subjects back home. Please hurry up and let me go before I am drowned.' But the clam refused, saying that the fowls should have stayed inland and not robbed the shore of its tasty worms. The frantic rooster went on begging for mercy while the rest of the birds flew around him, calling his name and begging him to come home with them. But the tide rose steadily until the chief of all the fowls was drowned. To this day, the roosters crow and the hens still call his name when the tide is rising.

The Element Encyclopedia of Magical Creatures

TOMPONDRANO

In the traditions of the people of the island of Madagascar, Tompondrano is described as a huge sea creature covered in thick plates similar to a crocodile but much more powerful. Its head glows in the dark and it can be seen under water as well as when it surfaces. Though no one would be considered foolish enough to linger in its presence, fishermen in the area have reported the glowing shape of Tompondrano's head.

TOMTE

Creatures similar to the brownie in Scandinavian tradition. The name Tomte (or Tomtra) comes from the word *tomtgubbe*, meaning 'Old Man of the House', and this is how they most frequently appear. They are said to take great pride in a well-kept home, and will torment lazy housekeepers. Unless everything is kept clean and tidy, they will leave, which is unfortunate because a happy Tomte ensures a prosperous home. There are a number of elaborate rituals designed to keep the Tomte happy. It is best rewarded with a cosy fire and food, but some say that the creature should be fed at ten every evening and again at four in the morning. He should never be tormented or disturbed with excessive noise such as the sound of chopping wood. If he gets annoyed he will play tricks – pinching children, waking sleepers during the night and letting the cows out of the byre. The Tomte takes every Thursday off and on that day should be given extra food and butter in his porridge. At Christmas, he should be given a little piece of grey cloth, some tobacco and a shovelful of clay. The Tomte are usually described as wearing brown clothes and a green cap. They are extremely good fiddlers and like to dance under the moon. As they look after farm animals, they occasionally steal either hay or milk as payment for this.

TORE

Among the pygmies of Zaire, Tore is Lord of the Hunt, taking the form of a leopard. He is responsible for storms, when he is not hiding in the rainbow. Tore oversees initiation rites.

TORNGARSOAK

A huge polar bear spirit in the traditions and folklore of the Inuit people of the eastern Labrador coast. He inhabits a cave in the black mountains at the north of the peninsular which is called *Torngait* ('Spirit Mountain'). As Torngarsoak ('The Great Torngak'), he has supreme control over the spirits. One myth tells that he was originally a devoted father who changed upon the death of his children into a vicious spirit preying upon mankind. Elsewhere he is a creator who made man from nothing. Another story tells how at one time it was much harder to hunt the caribou because they were particularly keen-sighted and fierce. However, Torngarsoak caused one of the caribou to sew up the eyes of the rest, diminishing their sight and making them tamer. He is also considered to be the master of all seals and whales in the area of Ungava Bay.

TORTOISE

Though often overshadowed in myth by the turtle, stories of tortoise are widespread and fascinating. While the turtle is a sea-going creature, the tortoise is a land animal. The tortoise is also said to be highly promiscuous and sexually potent. In Graeco-Roman mythology, it is sacred to both Aphrodite and Hermes and has strong erotic connotations.

In Hindu Mythology, the tortoise is the second of Lord Vishnu's 32 avatars – forms which he takes in order to act in the physical world – and is known as Kurma, 'Old Tortoise Man', and is regarded as the progenitor of all living creatures. In the traditions of Himalayan Buddhists, the tortoise is considered an aspect of Manjushri, the Bodhisattva of Wisdom. Both in this tradition and that of Hinduism, the tortoise supports the universe and is depicted with its head to the south, floating on the primordial sea that surrounds the continents of the world. According to this view, the original materials from which creation is made up dry out in the wind, at which point Manjushri emanates a gigantic cosmic tortoise that floats on the primordial sea. In his wisdom, he recognized the need for a solid basis on which humanity could live, and rising into the atmosphere he shot a golden arrow,

which struck the tortoise in its right side. This caused the tortoise to turn over and sink, dripping blood from its wound and vomiting fire. These substances mixed with the elements dissolved in the water and hardened into the crust of the Earth, forming a foundation for the universe.

In Chinese tradition Nu Kwa, the great Naga, used the toes of a cosmic tortoise to mark the four cardinal directions. These become four animals with – in the north, ruling over winter – a black tortoise referred to as the Black Warrior. In an alternative Chinese cosmology, the creator Pan-gu emerged from a great cosmic egg, and created the universe with the assistance of a dragon, a Phoenix, a Unicorn and a tortoise. The shell of the tortoise forms the vault of the heavens and the creature itself is recognized as one of the celestial emblems, later perceived as a symbol of longevity and wisdom. The union of the tortoise and the snake is said to have engendered the universe in its current form. It is also held that when the tortoise has lived for 1,000 years, it is able to speak in human language and tell the future.

Another Far Eastern myth says that there is a huge tortoise in the depths of the ocean. It has one eye on the underside of its body. Once every 3,000 years it rises to the surface and turns over so that it may see the sun. A Mongolian variant of this says that at the end of creation, the Golden Tortoise which supports Mount Meru, the foundational peak of Eastern mythology, will suffer from the heat of the sun's last moments and turn over in its agony, thus bringing about the end of the world.

Curiously, in some parts of the East, the tortoise was considered to represent bad luck. When a new temple was erected in Shanghai in 1882, it was noticed that the new building resembled a tortoise. At once there was a great outcry, which was only resolved when the priests filled in two wells which were part of the complex, maintaining that these were the eyes of the animal and that now, having been blinded, it could do no further mischief.

Among the Zuni people of North America, both the turtle and tortoise were believed to house the souls of the ancestors. Once every year the men would leave the village, returning a few days later with captive turtles. How each animal reacted to its release in the homes of each family predicted events to come. Thus, if the turtle ran away and refused to return, the future was considered bleak; while if it came to hand to be fed, good luck was certain to follow. When the creature died, its bones were returned to the river. This process created a link between turtle and man, living and dead. At midsummer, a similar ritual was held by the Zuni in honour of tortoise to help ensure the return of the rains.

The tortoise is one of the oldest mythological animals of West Africa, and represents feminine power (with the snake as masculine). The tortoise is considered to be the origin of all ju-ju, and symbolizes fertility. Most African traditions declare that the tortoise cannot be defeated, which makes it extremely lucky. Naturally, its slow movements and wrinkled skin give it the appearance of age and wisdom, and there is a Swahili song in which the tortoise sings: 'I move house and yet I never move house. I carry my home whenever I travel.'

> A lion caught a tortoise, and the tortoise said to the great hunter: 'If you are wondering how to soften my shield and make me easier to eat, just put me to soak in the river.' The lion thought this was a good idea and put the tortoise in the river, where of course it escaped and hid in the mud.

TOTOIMA

In the mythology of Papua New Guinea the Totoima is a monstrous boar similar to the Western Twrch Trwyth and the Graeco-Roman Calydonian Boar.

In the stories of the Orokaiva people, the Totoima takes a human wife, appearing to her at night like a human male. During the day, however, he became a monster again, and whenever she gave birth to a child, he would seek it out and destroy it. In time, the woman gave birth to twins and this time managed to hide one of the two, a girl, while the boy was eaten. With the help of a local shaman, the wife caught up with the Totoima during the day, and the shaman revived the boy inside him, which at once grew into an adult and burst out of the side of the Totoima. The mother then gave permission for the shaman to marry her daughter, and at the ensuing feast the body of the Totoima was divided and eaten. To this day in Papua New Guinea, whenever a pig is consumed this story is retold.

TREFUILGNID TRE-EOCHAIR

A cosmic giant from the mythology of the Celts. According to a medieval text called 'The Settling of the Manor of Tara', an assembly of all the kings and lords of Ireland, together with all their principal storytellers, were brought together on the day of Christ's crucifixion. The text reads as follows:

We beheld a great hero, fair and mighty, approaching us from the west at sunset. We wondered greatly at the magnitude of his form. As high as a wood was the top of his shoulders, the sky and the sun visible between his legs, by reason of his size and his comeliness. A shining crystal veil about him like unto raiment of precious linen. Sandals upon his feet, and it is not known of what material they were. Golden yellow hair upon him falling in curls to the middle of his thighs. Stone tablets in his left hand, a branch with three fruits in his right hand, and these are the three fruits which were on it, nuts and apples and acorns in May-time: and unripe was each fruit … 'I have come,' he said, 'from the setting of the sun, and I am going unto the rising, and my name is Trefuilgnid Treochair.' 'Why has that name been given to you?' said they. 'Easy to say,' said he, 'because it is I who cause the rising of the sun and its setting.' 'And what has brought you to the setting, if it is the rising you must attend?' 'Easy to say,' said he, 'a man has been crucified today in the East, and because of this deed the sun has not shone upon the place where this event occurred. That is what has brought me to the setting of the sun to find out what ailed it; and thus it has been revealed to me …'

Trefuilgnid says of himself that he is 'a truly learned witness who explains to all everything unknown.' He then reveals to the most learned men of the five provinces the entire history of the land.

TRELQUEHUECUVE

Possibly the full name for the sea monster known as Cuero, a giant octopus with claws at the end of its tentacles and huge ears covered with eyes that can be made either large or small at will. Information about this creature is sparse, but the name Trelquehuecuve may also represent a tribe of evil spirits without particular form who are feared as Hide (or Huecuvu) throughout South America, especially in Argentina and Chile.

TRIPODEROO

Another of the marvellous creatures known as the Fearsome Critters, who appeared in the folklore of lumberjacks and forest workers in California during the 19th and early 20th centuries. The Tripoderoo's appearance is suggested by its name. It is a small creature with a long prehensile snout, which it is able to extend. It has only three legs, which are also telescopic. It hunted its prey through the brush and when it came close enough shot a quid of clay through its snout, knocking out its victim.

TRITONS

In classical mythology, the Tritons are mermen who have dolphin-like tails on their human bodies. They have yellow/greenish hair with gills and pointed ears. They escort the Nereids and attend Poseidon, announcing his coming with blasts upon their conch shells and spiral-shell horns. They are the sons of Poseidon and Amphitrite, living under the sea in golden palaces.

TROLL

The name 'troll' means simply monster in Old Norse, and these beings are certainly monstrous in the various forms in which they are found throughout Scandinavian mythology. They can sometimes be described as hostile giants, though in the literature of the Middle Ages they appear more often as fiends who are sometimes responsible for black magic. In later medieval Icelandic texts and West Scandinavian folklore, trolls play a greater role than giants. They are described as larger than people but extraordinarily ugly. They live in mountain caves and prey upon humans. In Swedish and Danish folklore in particular, 'troll' is a name used to mean a kind of brownie. In fact, there is almost no agreement as to their appearance, so that in Denmark trolls are more like ogres with humps on their backs and extremely large noses. In Norway, trolls are described as malicious hairy ogres, though the female of the species can appear as beautiful, with long red hair. They are said to live in burrows under the hills, filled with treasure.

Trolls hate noise and can be driven away by the sound of church bells. They are known to steal women, children and property and have even been described as cannibals. They are considered expert metalworkers, and can bring about almost miraculous hearing by the use of herbs and magic. Generally they are only ever seen between dusk and dawn and are turned to stone if the sun strikes them – for which reason many standing stones throughout the Northern world are said to be petrified trolls. In the Faroe Islands, the trolls are known as Foden Skemend (Hollow Men). In Finland, there is a particularly evil creature known as Sjotroll, which is only held beneath the water by the presence of two stones carved with runes that are placed at each end of the lake that the troll inhabits. In the Shetland and Orkney Islands, trolls are called 'trows' or 'drows' and there are three distinct families: the land trows, the Peerie trows and the sea trows. Jesse Saxby, the author of *Shetland Traditional Lore*, who was herself the ninth child of a ninth child, wrote of the Kunal-Trow, who were human in appearance, though morose and sullen by nature.

They wandered in lonely places after the sun had set, and were seen at times to weep and wave their arms ... They marry human wives, and as soon as the baby trow is born the mother dies. No Kunal-Trow married twice, so their period of matrimonial bliss is brief ... He seems to have found his solitary life unendurable, and met the advances of some humans with a certain amount of pleasure that his love of mischief usually brought all friendly overtures to an abrupt conclusion. A witch who craved to know the secrets of Trow-land was assiduous in courting the bachelor, and persuaded him to marry her on the assurance that her art would show him how to prevent the death he dreaded ... It was said that from this union sprang the Ganfer and the Finnis. The Finnis is the being who appears before a death, personating the dying person. The Ganfer is what we – in modern days – would call an astral, who is ever waiting to enter into some human being and align himself to the physical life.

In both Greenland and Canada, trolls appear in the folklore of the Inuit people and resemble the more ancient concept of the giant hairy Scandinavian troll. They are described as huge ugly creatures with enormous hairless stomachs that drag along the ground and talons on their fingers so sharp they resemble knives. More recently, the troll has become familiar to us from the writings of J.R.R. Tolkien. In *The Hobbit*, Bilbo Baggins encounters a group of extremely loud and boorish trolls who are turned to stone when the morning light strikes them. Those who have seen the first film of *The Lord of the Rings* trilogy will almost certainly remember the huge Cave Troll who attacks the heroes in the mines of Moria.

TSENAHALE

One of a group of monsters known collectively as the Anaye in the traditions of the Navajo people of North America. The Tsenahale are generally described as huge, feathered creatures that resemble the Harpies of Greek Myth. They were filled with malice towards all other creatures, upon whom they preyed whenever they could.

The Element Encyclopedia of Magical Creatures

TSISKAGILI

The Cherokee people of North America say that the Tsiskagili is the Red Crayfish, who got his colouring and inedible flesh when the primordial animals first set the sun in the sky, but it set so near to him that he was badly scorched.

TSOPO

A type of Unicorn mentioned in the traditions of Tibet. Unlike its European cousins, it was said to be savage.

TSUCHI-GUMO

A giant malignant spider from the folk traditions of old Japan, Tsuchi-Gumo is described as a creature so huge that it was believed impossible to kill. It hunted humans for sport as well as food and destroyed everything that crossed its path. In the end, it was killed by being trapped in its own cave. A huge mesh of steel wire was stretched across the cave-mouth, then the people built fires so that it was roasted to death.

TSUCKINOKO

A kind of huge snake found in Japanese mythology and folklore. Also known as Bachi-Hebi in northern Japan, the creature is usually described as much larger than an ordinary snake, able to jump distances of 3 ft and apparently possessing a liking for alcohol. There have been many reported sightings of the Tsuckinoko.

TULE

Tule is the spider god of the Zande and Sudanese-Zaire people of Africa.

Just as one may see a real spider descending from a tall tree, so Tule descended from the sky on a rope spun from his abdomen. When he first arrived from heaven, he carried in his bag the seeds of all plants and trees, for at this time the Earth was still empty and dry. Tule scattered the seeds in all the countries of the world, then he rose up to the sky again and began playing his drum. Soon all the seeds germinated. But at that time there was no water anywhere, and the new growth began to wither, so Tule went in search of water. Finally, he came upon a hut where an old woman lived. She had discovered yams and planted them to grow as food. Tule asked her for water but she said she did not have any. Tule knew she must need water for cooking, so he changed himself into a spider and crept up the wall. From there he saw jars full of water, so he pulled a reed from the wall and sucked water from them. The woman saw him and threatened him with a knife. Tule knocked over the jar as he tried to escape and the water flowed over the Earth.

Tule then resumed his human form and made peace with the old woman, promising he would dig her fields for her if she would cook him a meal.

She cooked him some yams while he made the first hoe and the first axe to cut trees and hoe the fields for cultivation. Then he made a bow and arrows and went into the bush and shot a deer that he gave the old woman to cook. The old woman, whom one may guess was not an ordinary woman, was pleased with this, so she gave some fruit from the Zamba-Lindi tree and told him to throw it on the ground at the crossroads and then look behind him. He did and saw a lovely woman whom he married.

Tumi-Ra'i-Fuena

In the traditions of the Tahitian people, the Tumi-Ra'I-Fuena is described as a vast octopus with a spotted skin. No ordinary sea monster, this creature has tentacles that reach to every part of the Earth and heaven, and perhaps even hold them in place. The god Rua tried to make the Tumi-Ra'I-Fuena release its grip on the world, but to no avail.

Tumuiteartoka

The king of the sharks in Maori and Polynesian mythology. Stories are told of Tumuiteartoka's encounters with human beings, including the hero Ngaru (Wave) who dared the Shark King to race on a surfboard that he had just invented.

Turtle

The mythic history of the turtle is a long and colourful one. In Australian Aboriginal legend, Porcupine was the brother of Turtle, but one day, he and his friends ganged up against Porcupine and thrust their spears into him. Which is why the porcupine has a spiky coat and why the turtle and his kind are forced to swim underwater, having no power upon earth.

In Sumerian myth, the turtle features as a symbol of the water god Ea (or Enki), who superintended all sweet fresh waters. When the Tablet of Destinies was stolen from Ea by the Imdugud bird, the storm god Ninurta recovered it but was unwilling to let it go again. Ea then made a clay turtle and brought it to life. The turtle dug a hole and covered it over, and Ninurta fell into the hole. When Ninurta helplessly bellowed to be let out, Ea mocked him with, 'So where are your brave deeds now?' Ninurta accordingly gave back the Tablet of Destinies, returning the sovereignty of heaven to Ea.

Among the Kalabari people of Nigeria, the tortoise is called Ikaki, 'The Old Man of the Forest'. He is a supernatural tortoise who lives behind the ancient village of Olomo, rarely allowing himself to be seen.

Ikaki made forays to the edge of the forest to dance, but whenever he did so, people came to watch him. He always sang a warning song to them, 'Remember my words. Don't anyone touch me. I am Chief Tortoise, Chief Grey Hair.' But the people enjoyed his dances so much they kept calling him back. Eventually, he danced and sang, 'Amegage. Human meat, yum-yum. Amegage. Human bones, yum-yum.' Then, as he raised his right legs, all the people in the East died; and as he raised his left legs, all the people in the West died. Ikaki went back into his shelter of the deep forest never to be seen again. However, the few survivors left on Earth came together in order to imitate the great tortoise's dancing. They were uneasy about the part where they must lift their legs, though, and so they consulted the oracle of Chuku, which told them to modify their movements to avoid further deaths. This dance was enshrined as the Tortoise Masquerade, performed annually at Olomo until the town was destroyed in war. The dance spread to New Calabar at Buguma where the dance of Ikaki is still performed. A man wears a tortoise shell on the top of his head, accompanied by the master of the drums. People still remember the part about lifting the legs and what resulted, but now the dancer makes fun of that original dance, for people tease him about the size of the calabash between his legs. The more they tease, the sooner the dancer removes a pair of testicles from under his robe and dangles them before the women. Ikaki is the powerful dancer whose magic can have destructive or creative effect.

To the Native American people, particularly the Navajo, Turtle is one of four animal spirits that travelled to an undersea village with the intention of taking two young women captive. Bear, Snake and Frog accompanied Turtle. He and Frog were elected to enter the village and kidnap the maidens, but they were spotted as they tried to leave with the young women whom they quickly killed and scalped. The villagers then tried to roast the kidnappers, and when they were unable to do so, attempted to drown them. Frog and Turtle made good their escape and soon rejoined their comrades.

TURUL

A mythological bird of great symbolic importance to the Hungarian people. It is said to represent the power and will of God and was recognized as an ancestor of Atilla the Hun. Representations of the Turul can be found in many different places, often represented as carrying a flaming sword. One legend tells the story of the wife of the hero Ugyek, a descendant of Atilla, who had a dream in which Turul appeared. In this dream, a crystal-clear stream sprang from within her, and as it flowed westward it became a mighty river. This dream was said to represent a symbolic impregnation of the woman by the Turul, and to indicate that she would give birth to a line of great kings.

Twrch Trwyth

A monstrous semi-divine boar from Celtic tradition. Its story is told in the 14th-century collection of ancient tales *The Mabinogion*. The young hero Culhwch is given the task of recovering a comb, razor and shears that were embedded in its thick pelt. In order to carry out this task, Culhwch requests the help of the hero Arthur and his warriors. Twrch Trwyth was already well known and feared among the Celtic peoples. Also known as Porcus Troyt or Troyn, it had originally been a king who was transformed into the shape of a boar because of some unspecified act of evil. Together with his sons, Grugyn Silver Bristles and Llwydawg the Hewer, he had ravaged the whole of Ireland. Once Arthur took up the hunt it continued across the whole of the country, along a line that can still be traced on a modern map. One by one, the family of boars were killed. Finally, Grugyn Silver Bristles was cut down,

followed soon after by Llwydawg. In the end, Arthur and Culhwch cornered the beast by the banks of the River Severn where they seized the razor and shears. At this point, the boar broke loose again and fled into the county of Cornwall where it continued to ravage the land until finally being chased over the cliffs into the sea. At the last moment, Culhwch seized the last of the treasures, the comb, from behind its ear. It was last seen swimming towards the horizon and was never seen again in the land of Britain. (*See also* Ysbadadden Pencawr.)

Typhon

In Graeco-Roman mythology, Typhon is a monsterous adversary of Zeus. It had a hundred snake-like heads, each with eyes that blazed fire, and serpents for arms. Typhon was the last offspring of Tartarus and Gaia, created so that he could attack and destroy the Olympian fortress. Zeus used an adamantine sickle to wound Typhon, but was himself overpowered, his sinews cut out and both he and his sinews put into the Corycian cave. Hermes and Agipan stole the sinews and restored them to Zeus. After this, the Fates (Moirae) made Typhon drunk and Zeus drove him down into the underworld below Mount Etna, from where he continues to be the source of hurricanes (he is the origin of the word *typhoon*) and occasionally causes the mountain to erupt.

TYLWYTH TEG

The name for the fairy race in Wales. Their name means 'The Fair Folk' and they are extremely attractive to look at, always dressed in white and having long fair hair. According to some accounts, they are ruled over by the underworld god Gwynn ap Nudd, while others say that their master is the magician Gywdion. In the past, these fairies were considered dangerous and children were brought up to fear and respect them. They especially liked to steal babies or older blonde children and leave a changeling called a *crimbil* in their place. Their own children are said only to mature at 100 years of age, when they leave to up communities of their own. They are especially fond of singing and dancing in fairy rings, though a human should be wary of joining them. Tylwyth Teg are visible only at night, and visit human houses after dark. For this reason, country dwellers in Wales used to tidy up and stoke their fires before retiring, so that the Fair Folk could make themselves comfortable. If they were pleased they might leave a present for the family, though this would disappear at once if spoken of openly.

The Fair Folk used to visit markets and exchange the money in farmers' pockets for their own, which disappeared when the farmer got home, or turned into dry leaves. The folklorist Edward Davies, writing in 1809, related the story of a lake near Brecon associated with the Tylwyth Teg.

An island rose from the middle of the lake, and it was observed that no bird would fly over it and that sometimes strains of music could be heard drifting from it over the water. In ancient times, a door in a nearby rock would open every Mayday, and those who entered would find themselves in a passage that led to the island. There, to their amazement, they discovered an enchanted garden full of the choicest fruits and flowers, inhabited by the Tylwyth Teg, whose ethereal beauty was only equalled by their courtesy and affability. Each guest would be entertained with music and told of whatever future events the fairies deemed right to tell them. The only stipulation was that the island should be considered sacred, and nothing must be taken away. One day, an ungrateful man pocketed the flower he had been presented with. This did him no good, for as soon as he touched the shore the flower vanished and the man himself fell senseless. The Tylwyth Teg were so angry at this sacrilege that the way to the island was closed forever. One man tried to drain the lake to see what was there, but a horrible figure rose from the water and commanded him to stop.

U

Uadjit

In Egyptian mythology, the cobra goddess Uadjit (also Wadjet or Edjo) was worshipped in pre-dynastic times at the north-west Delta town of Dep which eventually fused with Pe, the official residence of the kings of Lower Egypt. Uadjit was seldom depicted in human form like the other gods, but was always shown in snake form. The sun disk of Ra was depicted with the cobra of Uadjit curled around it that led to the cobra being thought of as the Eye of Ra which could spit fire against enemies of the king. Uadjit's symbol of the Uraeus, the upraised cobra, was placed upon the royal crown over the brow as a symbol of sovereignty's protection.

Ubelluri

In Hittite myth, the giant Ubelluri is the original supporter of the world. In the course of conflict between the storm god Teshub and a defeated deity, Kumarbi, the latter creates the rebellious Ullikummi to challenge Teshub. Kumarbi plants his son on the shoulder of the giant Ubelluri where he grows prodigiously until he is 9,000 leagues tall. The gods are alarmed at his sudden appearance and cannot overcome him, so they send Ea, the god of wisdom to the supporter of the world, Ubelluri, who says:

'When they built heaven and earth
upon me,
I knew nothing.
But when they came and they cut heaven
and earth apart with a cutter,
This, too, I knew not.
Now something makes my right
shoulder hurt,
And I know not who he is, this god!'

When Ea heard those words, he went around Ubelluri's right shoulder, and there the Basalt (Ullikummi) stood on Ubelluri's right shoulder like a shaft. The end of this myth is missing, but we note that Ullikummi is described as a basalt pillar while Ubelluri sounds like an antique Atlas, too busy doing his job to know much about what goes on above him.

Uccaihshravas

Uccaihshravas or 'Loud Neigh' is the white horse of the Hindu god Indra. He was created when the gods churned the ocean of milk upon the back of the tortoise Kurma along with many other wondrous beings.

Ugallu

The Ugallu was the Babylonian demon known as the 'Big Weather Creature'. He appears as a man with a lion's head, donkey's ears and birds' feet, with one hand raised to strike with a dagger and the other holding a mace. He wears a short, fringed kilt and has a curly lion's tail. The Ugallu acted as a protective spirit against demons and illnesses, and clay Ugallu figurines have been found in the foundations of houses.

UGRASURA

In Hindu tradition, Ugrasura is a serpent who belongs to the *asuras* (non-gods) who are continually at war with the gods. While the god Krishna was still young, Ugrasura swallowed him whole in an attempt to divert the god's powers from becoming fully mature. While inside Ugrasura, Krishna put on a rapid spurt of growth, becoming fully grown. Ugrasura exploded into pieces and Krishna escaped.

UMAI-HULHLYA-WIT

Among the Diegueno Indians of California, Umai-Hulhlya-Wit is a primordial serpent who lived in the cosmos. When Earth was peopled by the gods, Umai-Hulhlya-Wit came closer to see what was happening. His huge size caused widespread panic, so the gods urged people to make a brushwood dwelling for the serpent. Slowly it wound its way inside its new house until he was coiled within it when the people set fire to the brushwood shelter. As the fire took hold, Umai-Hulhlya-Wit exploded into pieces. Wherever those pieces fell, so understanding of rituals, stories, arts, music and languages spread through the tribes.

UMA NA-IRU

In Mesopotamian myth, the storm god Ishkur (or Adad) rides upon a Lion Griffin that has the foreparts of a lion and the hind-legs, wings and tail of a bird. Its name means the 'Roaring Weather Beast' and from its mouth is issued rain. The storm clouds that herald rain in that desert region were known as Adad's bull-calves.

UNCEGILA

Among the Sioux Indians of North America, Uncegila is a great female serpent who lived in the oceans. Covered with flinty scales and with a heart of rock crystal, she annually swam into the Nebraska river causing tidal waves so turbulent that the waters were muddied and unfit to drink.

Two young hunters decided to overcome the serpent Uncegila and so they found out where she was most vulnerable. When they confronted her, Uncegila reared up and threatened to seize them, but the young hunters had learned a spell from their medicine man and while one recited it, the other shot her through the seventh joint of her neck. The sun immediately dried everything out and made the land dry where it had been previously waterlogged. The hunters removed from the creature the crystal heart that had the ability to inculcate the power of prophecy until the time when uninitiated peoples despoiled it when this power was lost.

UNDINE

In European magical lore, an Undine is an elemental spirit of the water. The name was first used by the Swiss metaphysican Paracelsus in the early 16th century, derived from the Latin *undas* ('wave'). Undines are invoked in magical working requiring the cooperation of the waters. The leader of the undines is called Necksa.

UNICORN

The power of the Unicorn rests in its singularity. Despite variations in the mythology relating to this most elusive and remarkable of creatures, a persistent aspect of Unicorn lore is that there is only ever one of them. This adds to the mystique which has always surrounded this most extraordinary beast, and makes it the object of passionate quest by generations of mystics, who see in it a universal symbol of the greatest prizes of all – enlightenment and spiritual transformation.

The Unicorn is generally described as looking like a small horse. But it is a feature of its fabulous history that it changes shape with time, appearing now in one form, now another. Its size and shape varies enormously, from a kid or gazelle to an elephant. The Roman historian Aelian (*c.* AD 220) says that in India it is the size of a mature horse,

[it] possesses a mane and reddish hair ... it excels in swiftness. Like an elephant it has spatulate feet and has a boar's tail and one black horn projecting from the eyebrows, not awkwardly, but with a certain natural twist and terminating in a sharp point. It has, of all animals, the best and most contentious voice.

Even the shape of the Unicorn's feet differ: the medieval Vertomannus wrote: 'Unicorns have feet divided in two much like the feet of a goat,' while according to such classical luminaries as Aristotle, Pliny and Solinus they were solid. The horn too varies greatly in length and colour and can be either straight or twisted. The conventional Unicorn of heraldry, with which most of us are familiar, has the head and body of a horse, the tail of a lion and the legs of a stag, with a single horn on its forehead. The 2nd-century Alexandrian

The Element Encyclopedia of Magical Creatures

Physiologus, which describes the shapes and forms of the animal kingdom, notes 'it is a small animal, but exceedingly strong and fleet, with a single horn in the centre of its forehead.'

The mythology and symbolism of the Unicorn dates from earliest times and is virtually worldwide. One tradition said that it lived in ancient times but perished in the Flood. The Unicorn's antiquity is attested right back to the early Indus valley cultures of Harappa and Mohenjo-Dara of over 5,000 years ago where it appears frequently on the mud tablets that served as contracts in that culture. That wonderful assembly of lies, history and myth, the *Histories* of Herodotus, mentions the Unicorn as living· in Libya. The Roman historian Aelian says that it lives in India and that the Brahmins call it the Cartazonon and say that it reaches the size of a large horse when mature, that it frequents desert regions and wanders alone and solitary. Ethiopia was also said to have Unicorns – fierce and impossible to capture, while the Hereford *Mappa Mundi* depicts it in the upper Nile region.

According to Vertomannus, travelling in Arabia in 1503, the Arabs had a well-developed Unicorn tradition that said that it was to be seen in the Temple of Mecca. Egypt has versions of the animal in Abyssinia, and missionaries and travellers testified to its existence there and in Central Africa. The Roman emperor Julius Caesar said it dwelt in the Great Hercynian Forest and was the size of a bull and shaped like a stag. A Chinese traveller of the 11–12th centuries said that Unicorns occurred in great numbers in Tibet and that Genghis Khan met one on Mount Diadanaring.

In the 19th century, a French priest and traveller named Abbé Huc said, 'The Unicorn really exists in Tibet and is known by the name of Serou, or Kere in Mongolia.' In 1820, a British Major named Latta said that he had found one in Tibet and that it was called the one-horned Tso'Po. In the New World, the Unicorn is referred to by the conquistadors, by Sir John Hawkins in Florida, and by a Dr Dappe in 1673 as living 'on the Canadian border'. In each case, the description fits that of the conventional Unicorn.

The Unicorn is drawn to water. Its horn, called the Alicorn, is able to detect and counteract poison and was greatly sought after and prized. Kings and princes had drinking vessels made from it to detect poisoned wine. To test whether the horn was genuine, a circle was inscribed in the earth and a scorpion, spider or lizard placed in it; if genuine, the creature could not escape the circle. It has been suggested that the horns traded throughout the world during the Middle Ages were probably those of the narwhal. The belief in the medicinal value of the horn can be traced back to the 4th century BC, when it was believed to prolong the act of love and the life of the individual.

Perhaps the most fascinating and romantic belief attached to the Unicorn is that it could only be captured in a particular way. The Roman writer Mysiologus gives an account of this, describing it as the Holy Hunt or Virgin Capture. This is achieved by:

… decking a chaste virgin with beautiful ornaments and seating her in a solitary place in the forest frequented by the Unicorn, which no sooner perceives her than it runs to her and laying its head gently in her lap, falls asleep. Then the hunters come and take it captive to the King's palace and receive for it much treasure.

The Virgin with a Unicorn resting on her lap was a common feature in ecclesiastical architecture, particularly in stained-glass windows. It appears there because it was seen as symbolizing the triumph of chastity. Other traditions say that the virgin had to be naked and in some instances she was depicted as tied to a tree. Medieval poets used the virgin capture theme to represent the lover being lured to destruction. Christian theologians preferred to see it as depicting the defeat of the Devil, who can only be overcome by purity and innocence.

Associating the Unicorn with the Virgin Mary further extended such symbolism, but its chief association was with Christ, who, according to St Ambrose, 'is the only-begotten Son of God'. It is also that aspect of Christ who 'raised up the horn of salvation'. The horn as an antidote to poison is seen as representing Christ's power to destroy sin. In the earliest translations of the Old Testament (Septuagint), the Hebrew *Re'em* is translated as 'monoceros' (one-horned), but in later versions this becomes the Unicorn or wild oxen and is a symbol of fierceness. In Hebrew, it represents royalty, power and strength.

Probably the oldest form of the Unicorn is the Chinese Ki-Lin, a one-horned animal that is said to have appeared to the sage Fu Hsi about 3000 BC, emerging from the Yellow River. It appeared again at the death of the Emperor Huang Ti and at both the birth and death of Confucius. In Chinese symbology, it is described as one of the Four Spiritually Endowed or Auspicious Creatures or Ssu Ling, and is the essence of all five elements. It is also seen as embodying the union of the yin and yang, the Ky being masculine and the Lin feminine.

In the West, the Unicorn is almost always depicted as white or silver in colour and is strongly associated with the moon. This almost certainly derives from Graeco-Roman lore relating to moon goddesses, especially Artemis and Diana, whose triumphal chariot is drawn by eight Unicorns. In general, it represents gentleness, chastity, purity, virginity and strength of mind. It is also closely associated with royalty, the single horn being symbolic of unlimited and individual power. This is prominent in heraldry, in which the Unicorn appears frequently with the lion as representative of both solar and lunar energies.

UNWABA

When the Zulu sky gods wished to convey the wondrous message to Earth that human beings had been granted eternal life, they sent Unwaba, the chameleon. But he was so slow that the message did not reach them in time and humans and other creatures had already entered into their mortality.

The Element Encyclopedia of Magical Creatures

For this reason, the chameleons forever change from green to brown in mourning for Unwaba's dilatory message.

UPIR

The Upir is a vampire or werewolf in Russian tradition. The name seems to derive from the same root as the Serbian *vampir* and the Turkish *upir*.

URAEUS

In Egyptian mythology, Uraeus is the name of the sacred upraised cobra that is worn upon the brow of ruler's crown. It comes from the Greek word for cobra, *ouraios*. It is an image of the cobra goddess Edjo, also known as Uadjit. The uraeus was the image of sovereignty and protection. It is thought that Cleopatra, rather than killing herself with an asp, took a cobra to die with dignity rather than walk in the triumphal victory procession through the streets of Rome when her reign was overturned by the Emperor Augustus.

URIDIMMUS

The Mesopotamian lion man is shown as a man above the waist and a lion below. He stands upright and carries a staff. He is called Uridimmus or 'Mad Lion'. He may represent the Sumerian god Utu or the Akkadian god Samas who brings the beneficent light of the sun to Earth. He is the god of truth, justice and rectitude, a destroyer of evil

and a protector of kings. As Samas, he enabled King Etana to free an eagle that had been trapped in a pit by a serpent. Samas brought the plant of life to the childless Etana and enabled him to fly to heaven on the eagle's back. On the way, Etana lost his nerve and fell, but Samas rescued him and brought him safe to Earth where the king lived 1,560 years and had a successor, his son Balih.

URISK

The Gaelic Urisk of Scotland is a form of satyr with the top half of a human man and the lower half of a goat. Urisks, like their Greek counterparts, were amorous in nature and given to chasing women. They lived in the wild Highlands, especially round Loch Katrine in the Trossachs, although others lived at the waterfall of Glen Lyon as well as at the mountain Beinn Dorain. Urisks helped farmers with the herding of animals, and though they often followed travellers at night, they would do no harm.

URUS

In medieval European lore of the bestiaries, the Urus was described as a huge bull with saw-toothed horns that it used to cut down trees. The only way to capture an Urus was to wait until it accidentally drank seawater, which strangely disorientated it so that it became confused, stabbing the ground with its horns or else by becoming entangled in the trees which it was attempting to fell. This extraordinary myth may point to the extinct aurochs that were already on the endangered list when agriculture and the slashing and burning of forests began.

UTIU

In Mayan tradition, Utiu the Coyote was one of the four animals who helped bring maize to the gods so that they could form mankind.

UTU

Utu is the Sumerian sun god who is equivalent to the Akkadian Samas. He opens the doors of the sun and has as his emblem the pruning saw by which he tends the crops. He is invoked as the patron of extispacy (liver-divination), which was an exact science under the Sumerians who studied the shining mirror of the liver in scrupulous detail. When Utu is in animal form, he goes as Uridimmus the lion man. Unlike Samas, Utu has a more earthly and urbane nature. He tried to seduce his twin sister Inanna by getting her drunk. Inanna rebuffed his attentions by feigning ignorance of sexual matters, even pretending not to know how to kiss.

UTUKKU

In Assyrian mythology, Utukku were believed to be the vampiric souls of the dead or else evil spirits who had emanated from the bile of the god Ea. The Utukku were men who had animal heads, claws and horns. They lived in caverns, cliffs and ruins. Many spells against the effect of these vampires have been found by archaeologists, appealing against the seven demons of whom the Utukku is one form.

UWARBAMI

In Japanese mythology, Uwarbami is the great serpent with wings who was given to swooping down on unsuspecting people and carrying them off. It was finally killed by the hero Yegare-no-Heida.

V

Vahana

In Hindu tradition, the *vahana* is the vehicle by which a deity moves about. Many vahanas are mounts or chariots for the gods. Brahma rides upon Hamsa the swan or goose; Vishnu rides Garuda the eagle or peacock; Shiva rides his bull Nandi; Yama rides a buffalo, Agni upon a ram; Shani rides a vulture; Durga has her tiger; Vayu rides an antelope; Indra rides on an elephant, and Kamadeva has Makara the sea serpent.

Vajra Varahi

Also known as Dorje Phagmo, the great sow-headed Vajra Varahi is a Tibetan bodhisattva – an enlightened being who has sworn to return through many incarnations to Earth until the last blade of grass has also received enlightenment. Her pig's squeal is said to evoke compassion.

Valaha

In Tibetan Buddhist belief, Valaha is the gigantic horse king who flies through the air. It was the form taken by the gracious bodhisattva, Chenresi or Avalokiteshvara (the divine being who is believed to be reincarnated in the form of the present Dalai Lama). 'The Mirror of Royal Lineage' relates how Chenresi took the form of Valaha in order to give an example of how to reject wrongdoing and follow virtue.

There were once a group of merchants who were cast up upon the island of the *rakshasis* (demons) after a great storm. The rakshasis took the form of beautiful maidens and the grateful merchants believed them to be goddesses. They gladly set up house, each with a rakshasa and raised families. But the captain of their ship knew what kind of island they had come to and one night he dreamt he came to an iron house from which howling and crying emanated. He cried out, asking who was within. The men inside the iron house said that they were merchants who had been blown by storms and entered into relationships with demons. They told him that there was only one means of escape. If he followed a narrow pass and came to a golden strand with a turquoise pool rimmed by a green meadow, on the evening of the fifteenth day, a moonbeam would shine down, bearing the beautiful horse king, Valaha, who could carry 100 men upon his back. After the horse had drunk from the turquoise pool and grazed in the emerald meadow and rolled three times upon the golden strand, he would invite everyone to climb onto his back and he would miraculously bear them all away.

The captain awoke and realized what he must now do. On the evening of the fifteenth day when the moon was full, the captain did as instructed. He gave narcotic food to the rakshasis, when they were asleep, and he was on Valaha's back, he called the merchants to come from their imprisonment. They were told to close their eyes and not look back. But the narcotic dream that had been given to the rakshasis and their children by the merchants had worn off and they began to cry after the escaping men. All but the captain succumbed and turned back and they all fell to Earth and were preyed upon by the rakshasis who resumed their original hideous form. The captain was the only one who returned. Valaha taught him the doctrine of the Four Noble Truths and bore him homewards. To all the relatives of the lost merchants, he imparted teachings which would ease their grief and help them to avoid the fate of the merchants.

VALKYRIE

In Norse mythology, the Valkyrie are the female beings who carry away the souls of warriors slain in battle. Their name derives from the Old Norse *valr* 'battlefield-corpse' and *kjosa* 'to choose'. This implacable sisterhood of nine women ride through the air over battlefields to bring back those warriors most fit to enter the warriors' paradise of Valhalla. They were close to Odin and were sometimes called *Odins meyar* (Odin's maidens) or *Oskmeyjar* (Odin's wish-fulfillers). The numbers of Valkyrie vary according to successive layers of their myth; some 36 are attested of whom 13 named maidens serve the *einherjar* (the warriors of Valhalla): Hrist (Shaker), Mist (Cloud), Skeggjold (Axe-Age), Hildr (Battle), Thrudr (Power-Woman), Hlokk (Battle-Noise), Herfjotur (Army-Fetter), Goll (Battle-Cry), Geirolul (Spear-Charger), Randgridr (Shield-Destroyer), Radgridr (Bossy) and Reginlefir (God's Daughter). In

later myths, they also interfere in the course of battles and determine the outcome. Some fall in love with mortals, like the Valkyrie Sigrdrifa, (Inciter to Battle) who is known better by the name Brynhilde (or Brunilde). In Richard Wagner's *Ring Cycle* operas, which draw upon the Volsung saga and less upon the early mythological texts, she appears as the daughter of Erda and Wotan expelled from Valhalla.

VAMANA

In Hindu belief, Vamana is the dwarf who is one of the avatars (manifestations) of the preserving god Vishnu. When Bali, king of the *asuras* (non-gods or genii) had gained dominion over the three worlds through ascetic practices, the gods were deprived of their abode and no longer received the fumes of sacrifice. They came to Vishnu for help and so the preserving god became born of the sage Kasyapa (Vision) and his consort Aditi (Primordial Vastness). He was born as Vamana, a priestly dwarf who went to the asura King Bali with a request. 'Give me as much earth as I can cover with three steps,' he begged. Bali graciously granted this request, but was soon downcast as Vamana encompassed first the early world, then the heavens and thirdly, there being no space remaining, stepping upon Bali's head and pushing him down into the lowerworld where he had to acknowledge his defeat. However, because Bali had accomplished virtue through his efforts, Vishnu granted him the dominion of the lowerworld.

The Element Encyclopedia of Magical Creatures

VARAHA

Varaha is one of the avatars (manifestations) of the Hindu god Vishnu. Varaha is the form of the boar that Vishnu took when the Earth was submerged by the great inundation. Varaha dived to the depths of the ocean to overcome the demon Hiranyaksa who had thrown the earth to the bottom of the sea. Varaha then rescued the earth, floating it upon the ocean like a great ship. After planing the earth with his tusks, the great boar set up the mountains and divided the earth into seven continents. After this had been done, the god Hari, remover of sorrows, took the shape and form of the four-faced Brahma and created life. The same story is told of Prajapati, the lord of being, who took the form of a boar to rescue the earth and who, as the architect and world-builder Vivakarman, planed the earth which was then called Prithivi ('the extended one'). Prajapati and Prithivi are seen as the Adam and Eve of Hindu culture.

VASUKI

In Hindu belief, Vasuki is one of the three great Naga kings. He was the serpent who the gods used as a rope to twist about Mount Mandara at the Churning of the Ocean, from which many prodigious and wonderful beings arose, including the goddess of abundance, Laksmi, mother of Ganesh. Vasuki was fearful that Garuda would annihilate all the snakes and so he sent one snake to the bird every day in order to propitiate him. This agreement between them still holds good, for Garuda has stuck to his daily diet of only one naga. According to Punjabi legend, the daughter of Vasuki brought *amrita* to cure him of leprosy when he went once in human form. She rubbed the sacred healing ointment all over his body but forgot his thumb. While going to fetch a little more amrita she was captured by one of the Pandava brothers who married her, leaving Vasuki's thumb to remain leprous, which is why this disease is still the scourge of the Punjab today.

VELI

In Fijian legend, the Veli are the gnome-like fairies who inhabit the kauri and kabea trees in Vuniwaivutuka near the Navua river. The Veli have thick woolly hair tied back in pigtails and wear clothes made out of tapa cloth – a malleable papyrus-like cloth made of beaten tree bark. Each of the male Veli have several wives who do most of the work. They have a tendency to steal iron tools. Their favourite diet is the fruit of the tanuka and the boai, which Fijians take care not to chop down or the Veli will jump on them and beat them. They drink *yaqona*, a form of kava beer made from the wild pepper. Generally, the Veli live at peace with their human neighbours who take care to preserve their forest houses.

Vampire

Vampires are the living corpses of the undead who, instead of giving back their bodies to the earth, fire, air or water and decomposing in the usual way, are animated by their own or another spirit to drink blood or draw energy, goodness or virtue from the living. Those who have been bitten and thus infected by a vampire become vampires themselves when they are dead. Vampires are thus predatory upon the life-energy of the living and have a vested interest in maintaining their own half-life by such methods. In European lore, vampires return to their coffins at daybreak, when the cockerel crows or when church bells ring. The strongest vampire craze struck Hungary in the 18th century, and middle and southern Europe from Poland to Albania and Greece still harbour these traditions.

Vampirism is found in many parts of the world, including China, Malaysia, Indonesia, Africa and the New World. From ancient times onwards, there are vampires in different forms from the Babylonian Utukku, the classical Lamia and the Empusa of Hecate down to the gypsy Mullo, a dead spirit that becomes vampiric on the living and sucks blood when death customs have been given scant respect, such as keeping rather than burning the deceased's possessions – a custom which allows no resting place for the dead to return.

Not all vampires are human in form. In Japanese folklore, in the story of the 'Cat of Nabeshima', the Prince Hizen had a mistress who was really a vampire cat. She put a spell on the prince's guards and entered his bedroom each night sucking out some of his vital energy. As the prince's condition worsened and it looked as though he would die, a brave soldier called Ito Soda vowed to stay awake, resorting to the terrible expedient of piercing his own flesh with a dagger in order to stay wakeful. The mere sight of his vigilant eyes rendered the vampire cat powerless and she stayed away from the prince, who recovered.

When the Spanish conquistadors invaded South America in the 16th century and began to explore its legends and fauna, they discovered both the bat-god Camazotz who lived in underground caverns and sucked the blood of the living, as well as the real vampire bat, which does in fact suck the blood of animals – though rarely that of humans. The word vampire did not come into the English language until the 18th century after various well-attested cases of human vampires had been reported in Europe. In cryptozoological studies, vampirism seems to be the central feature of the Chupacabra or Goat Sucker that preys upon the blood of livestock. Some vampires have the ability to prey on those with whom they form partnerships without actually taking their life: in this respect, they behave like Incubi or Succubi, visiting women or men at night.

The standard methods of discovering vampires are the sudden death of livestock, the blood-emptied condition of the living or the strangely blood-engorged bodies of corpses whose graves have been opened or examined. A number of methods of destroying vampires have been employed, including decapitation, burning, exorcism and the good old stake through the heart, which is supposed to strike them dead or render them unable to function.

The wearing of religious emblems such as crosses, the stuffing of one's nostrils with garlic and other remedies are also supposed to ward off their attentions, but these methods are not foolproof, especially if the vampire is of another faith to yours (see Roman Polanski's film *Dance of the Vampires* for the famous scene in which the myth of the protecting crucifix is exposed as untrue). More recent research has associated vampirism with the historical figure of the 14th-century Transylvanian prince Vlad the Impaler, whose bloodthirsty retribution involved the staking of enemies who were laterally transfixed upon a pole set upright in the ground and left to die.

Vampires in fiction and drama are very much a growth industry among those who like to take their stories with a pint of blood. Since the publication of Bram Stoker's novel Dracula in 1897, vampires have swarmed into fiction and on to the screen, creating many memorable films and cementing vampiric clichés from the silent film *Nosferatu* down to TV series such as *Buffy the Vampire Slayer* and *Angel*.

Velue

In French folklore, the Velue is a shaggy beast known also as the Peluda. It has green fur with long tentacloid suckers coming from its skin, which sting whatever it attacks. It also has huge feet, a long tail and a snake's head. It was believed to have survived the Flood and, in the fashion of a dragon, ravaged the land by burning it with its breath and eating livestock. Whenever men set out to hunt it, it would dive into the river Huisine and cause an inundation of its own. When it stole a beautiful young woman who was to be married, her beloved tracked it down and sliced off its tail – its most vulnerable part. The Velue died as a result of this rescue.

Veo

In the cryptozoological reports of the island of Rintja in the Micronesian archipelago, the Veo is a creature the size of a horse, with large claws and a long head. Its body is covered with overlapping scales. It only appears at night when it feeds on termites and ants. Apart from its size, the Veo sounds very like a pangolin, except that the ancient 8-ft pangolin (*Manis paleojavanicus*), which once lived in the nearby islands of Java and Borneo, died out millennia ago.

Verethragna

In Hindu mythology, Verethragna is the ravaging boar that no one dared approach. Verethragna was the ultimate threat to mankind that the god of brotherhood and friendship, Mithra, held ready should men not show sufficient brotherly love to each other. The boar is thus an instrument that teaches the errors of ingratitude and complacency.

Vetala

In Hindu tradition, the Vetala is a vampire. Vetalas are the spirits that animate dead bodies to act in vampiric ways, feeding off the living. Vetala is also the word used to describe a magician who works by necromancy.

Viddofnir

In Norse mythology, Viddofnir ('The Far-Shouting One') is the cockerel who sits in the branches of the tree Mimameidr at Menglod's house. Menglod is a maiden who lives surrounded by a wall of fire, a clay wall and is guarded by the giant Fjosidr and two ferocious guard dogs. The meat of this cockerel is the only thing that can calm these dogs down, which is what happens when the god Svipdagr comes to woo Menglod. This myth has cosmological allusions within it, for Svipdagr means 'The Suddenly Dawning Day' and the presence of a cockerel within this story suggests that the long wooing

The Element Encyclopedia of Magical Creatures

and finding of Menglod is about the power of the day overcoming a long darkness.

VIDYESVARAS

The Vidyesvaras are the masters of knowledge created by Shiva in Hindu belief. They take the appearances of forest spirits, satyrs, nymphs, fairies and guardian angels. They are presided over by Pasupati, the Lord of the Animals who acts as a herdsman and guardian to all living things, much as Pan does in Greek mythology. The inhabitants of the sylvan forests are also clear seers of all that passes.

VIJAYA

In Indian tradition, Vijaya was the ambassador of Silimukha the hare god of the moon. He was sent to persuade the elephants led by Chaturdanta to seek some other place to drink after the elephant herd had trampled many hares to death. Vijaya climbed up onto a rock and spoke to Chaturdanta saying, 'I am the ambassador of Silimukha, the moon, who says to you that you have defiled the cool waters of my lake and killed my people. If you do this again, you shall receive my punishment.' Chaturdanta swore never to do this again, so Vijaya took him to visit Silimukha, but instead led the great elephant to the still lake. Looking into the waters, Chaturdanta bowed low, swearing to keep his oath.

VILA

The Vila or Vili (plural) are the names of the Slavic fairies who live as nymphs in the woods, streams, fields and lakes. They are thought to be the spirits of virgins and children who leave their graves at night to dance. This is a common motif to do with the unquiet dead who, because they have not fulfilled their life's mission, are unable to rest. Anyone who joined their dancing rings was doomed to dance continually until he died. Many of the Vili made human marriages and bore children. In some places, the Vili appear as fairy-godmothers who prophesy the birth of children and bestow their fate upon them like the Moirae. (*See also* Wili.)

VIRABADRA

In Hindu tradition, Virabadra is the monster that Shiva created when he was insulted by his father-in-law Daksha Prajapati. Virabadra had 1,000 arms and feet and 1,000 flaming eyes whose heat will consume all living things on the day of the world's ending. He has tusks sticking out of his sides and is so big that he crushed the moon god with one of his toes. He plucked out the eyes of Surya the sun god and cut off the hands of the fire god Agni, so that no fire could be kindled. He chased away Garuda and made Indra's strong warrior arm stiff and unmoving. He came against Daksha to avenge the insult upon Shiva of making offerings to all the gods but Daksha was ready to back down and apologize, which Shiva handsomely accepted.

The Element Encyclopedia of Magical Creatures

VISHAP

In Armenian folklore, Vishap was the dragon who lived on the peaks of Mount Ararat. The legend surrounding the dragon caused many warriors to make the attempt, not out of the glory of subduing or killing it, but solely to gain the gift that Vishap might uniquely convey to them. For it was said that Vishap's blood was so poisonous that any weapon that came into contact with it would partake of its venom, rendering all subsequent blows with that weapon completely deadly.

VISHNU

The Hindu god Vishnu is the limitless Pervader, the supreme cause of all. Vishnu spans the whole history of the present creation through his ten avatars or incarnational vehicles of manifestation, four of which are animal forms. The number of vehicles or avatars varies according to different accounts. His animal forms are Matsya the fish, Kurma the tortoise, Varaha the boar, and Nr-Simha the man-lion. In addition, he manifests as Vamana the dwarf. Each of these avatars is concerned with the preservation of the world in some way, which is Vishnu's task. Whenever the world needs a champion, Vishnu sends himself into the body of one who will help it. He has incarnated as Rama and Krishna, as well as Gautama Buddha whose teachings are believed to be the perfect vehicle in this present era of time to help men control their own destiny. His next avatar, Kalki the tenth avatar, is yet to come; he will appear riding upon a white horse during the age of strife when, with a sword blazing like a comet, he will re-establish a golden age, punish evil-doers, comfort the virtuous, destroy the world and from its ruins create a new humanity. (*See* Shapeshifters.)

VODIANOI

In Russian folk tradition, Vodianoi of Vodnik is a very strange creature indeed, appearing in many shapes. Vodianoi is variously seen as an old man with a blue face, white beard and green hair; a floating log covered with moss; an old scaly or furry old man with paws, glowing eyes, horns and a tail; or a giant and ugly fish. Depending on the phases of the moon, Vodianoi would appear younger or older. He lived in deep waters and often tried to lure people to come and join him there. Every being was at risk from his attentions except those whose occupations involved water, like fishermen and millers who took care to propitiate him with a cockerel. Vodianoi was particularly busy in the millrace and would lurk near the millwheel in the hope of someone slipping into the waters.

Vritra

In Hindu tradition, Vritra is a dragon serpent with three heads that surrounds the whole world. Being a creature that brings drought, Vritra is continually at war with the rain god Indra. Vishnu sought to bring a truce between them by promising that neither should attack the other with iron, stone or wood that was wet or dry by night or day. This contract lasted until Indra caught sight of Vritra one evening at twilight when it was neither night nor day. Entering the foam of the water's edge, Indra compounded together a weapon that was neither wet nor dry being a thunderbolt spear formed by the divine smith Tvastra from the bones of the seer Dadhici. With this he decapitated Vritra and released the cloud-cattle or the rains that Vritra had trapped within the mountain. (*See* Ahi.)

Vulpangue

In Andean tradition, Vulpangue is a great serpent that has the head of a fox. Other reports state that it is nearer in form to the Hide or Cuero, being a flat body with eyes about it on all sides that floats in the water. Whoever attempts to bathe in or cross the waters where the Vulpangue lurks is unlikely to emerge again.

Vulture

The vulture is one of the great scavengers of the earth. Not only eating carrion, it is also an official undertaker, called the Compassionate Purifier by the Parsees whose dead bodies are not buried or burned in the customary way but which are excarnated or exposed in Towers of Silence for the vultures to devour.

In Egyptian mythology, the vulture goddess Neckhbet embodied the protective and motherly aspects to such an extent that goddesses and queens wore the vulture-headdress, which was like a vulture's wings wrapped around and over the head of the wearer. The Egyptian priest Horapollo wrote of the vulture,

It is the type of a merciful man, because if food cannot be obtained for its young it opens its own thigh and permits them to partake of its blood, so that they do not perish for want.

This same legend is also ascribed to the pelican. In Greek myth, some legends tell how it was a vulture and not an eagle that perpetually ate the liver of the fire-stealing Prometheus. The Harpies also have the bodies of vultures. In one version of the Irish story of the Children of Lir (*see* Swan), the stepmother who enchants her stepchildren into the shapes of swans for a term of 900 years is changed into a vulture.

Vu-Murt

Finland is a land of a thousand lakes and, in legend, Vu-Murt is the spirit who inhabits them, the Man of the Water. Naked with long black hair, he can be seen combing it next to the waterside by those women who venture near when he is out of the water, but for those men who are nearby he may appear in the form of a woman. It is not considered to be a good omen to view him. However, fishermen, millers and others whose livelihood depends upon the water, offer him sacrifice. The Votjak peoples venerated him so that they might receive his favour by way of rain, the avoidance of disease and securing the fertility of people and animals.

Vuokho

In the traditions of the Sami peoples of northern Scandinavia and Finland, the Vuokho is a monstrous bird with great wings whose flappings displace the air so much that the sound is deafening. It preys upon the unwary. Samuel Taylor Coleridge wrote about Vuokho in his poem 'The Destiny of Nations':

> ... *that Giant Bird*
> *Vuokho, of whose rushing wings the noise*
> *Is Tempest, when the unutterable Shape*
> *Speeds from the mother of Death and utters once*
> *That shriek, which never murderer heard, and lived.*

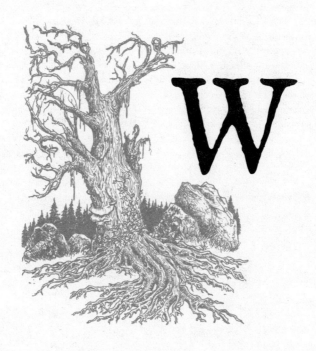

W

Wabus

In Menominee Indian traditions of North America, Wabus is the Great Hare who originally came from the blood of Nokomis, which her son Flint took. When Wabus grew up he became a man called Manabusch, the great hero and trickster.

Wagtail

The wagtail appears in the myths of the Abron peoples of the Ivory Coast where he is called Nconzo Nkila.

Wakandagi

In the stories of the Omaha and Mohawk peoples of North America, Wakandagi is a water serpent with deer-like antlers on its head and hooves on its feet. It lives in the waters of the Missouri river and the surrounding lakes. Usually seen only through a mist, Wakandagi is shy and difficult to see. It is jealous of its waters and throws up balls of suspended water against anyone venturing into its territory. These water-balls have to be thrown back or else they suddenly burst, flooding boats and canoes.

A powerful princess called Nzambi Mpunga was the creator of the world, but she neglected to make the drum and so people could not dance. Nconzo Nkila the wagtail made the first drum and beat it with his tail, causing Nzambi Mpunga great envy. She sent the antelope to beg the wagtail to lend it to her so she might dance. The antelope pretended that the drum was for himself: instead of dancing to it he stole it and the wagtail ordered his tribe to kill and cook the antelope. Then Nzambi sent the hyena Kivunga to fetch the drum. Having heard what happened to antelope, Kivunga rushed back to Nzambi and told her what had befallen. She then sent the ox Mpacsa to get the drum, but he went the same way as the antelope. Finally, an ant promised to fetch it. When everyone was asleep, the ant stole Nconzo Nkila's drum and bore it triumphantly to Nzambi who danced to its playing. But the wagtail was made unhappy by this theft and sent to the Prince of Neamlau to judge the case. He said, 'Nzambi is the mother of all things, but Nconzo Nkila made the drum, so it belongs to him.'

Wakinyan

Wakinyan is a type of Thunderbird in the lore of the Dakota peoples of North America. These huge birds whose wings protectively hover over the horizon appear in different ways. There are four main Wakinyan: those with bright red feathers, Thunderbirds with huge beaks and black feathers, blue-feathered Wakinyan without eyes or ears, and yellow-feathered ones that have no beaks. The Wakinyan operate at the four directions of the far horizon and their calling is the sound of thunder.

Walutahanga

In Melanesian folklore, Walutahanga is the water monster whose name means 'Eight Fathoms', after its deep-sea habitat. Walutahanga was originally born to a human woman as a female snake and was hidden away for fear of what her father might say. The mother kept the Walutahanga hidden, finding that the snake was useful to oversee the next child to which she gave birth. But the father saw what he took to be an ordinary snake near his baby and chopped Walutahanga into pieces without realizing who she was. After that, it rained for eight days and Walutahanga's chopped-up remains reunited, only to be chopped up again. Finally, Walutahanga was cooked up in a stew of which everyone ate save one woman and her child, her mother and sibling. Walutahanga appointed herself as the guardian over these two abstaining humans, bringing them good luck.

Wargar

Among the Papuans of Keraki, the first beings were animals called the Gainjin who originally came from the sky world. Wargar the crocodile and his companion Bugal the snake were the two who chose to remain on Earth after the other animals decided to return home after the first creation.

Washer at the Ford

In Celtic legend, the Washer at the Ford is found in Irish, Scottish, Welsh and Breton legend. She appears as an omen of death to warriors who encounter the Washer at the Ford washing blood out of linen. The clothes she washes are usually those of the observer. The Washer at the Ford is thus a form of the Death Goddess whose task is to take the worn-out bodies of the slain and wash the blood out of their garments, making their souls clean again. The Washer can appear as a beautiful but sad woman or as an ugly hag. In Ireland, the Morrigna sisterhood take this role, though it is most often Badb. In Wales, the goddess Modron appears in this guise to Owein ap Urien and becomes the mother of his twin children. In parts of Ireland, the Washer is associated with the Banshee. In Brittany, the Washer has companions who are called collectively *Les Lavandiers de la Nuit* in French or *Tunerez Noz* in Breton, which both mean 'The Night Washers'.

The Element Encyclopedia of Magical Creatures

WATERLORD

A pregnant woman whose co-wife had insultingly filled her water jar with mud, prayed at the water's edge for help, offering to dedicate her unborn child in return. As the words fell from her lips, Waterlord rose out of the waters, cleaned her jar and placed it on her head. That night she gave birth to a daughter whom she called Jinde Sirinde ('She Who the Waterlord Will Claim').

When Jinde was grown up enough to carry a full water jar upon her head, her mother sent her to fetch water morning and evening. As the girl was cleaning her jar, Waterlord dragged her by the ankles to the deepest part of the river where she had to live with him. Waterlord allowed her the space of one day to go back to say goodbye to her mother for the last time. Jinde was swimming back to the bank when Waterlord changed his mind. Jinde's mother would not open her door for her daughter, since a woman belongs to her husband and not to her parental home. So Jinde ran to her lover's house who came leaping out with his father's sword, risking his life to defend his girl. Down by the river, he could already hear the tumultuous waters as Waterlord broke from the waters, his seven heads rearing up. The lover raised his sword and severed each of the seven heads and Jinde was saved.

Among the Fulani of Mali in Africa, Waterlord is a kind of Hydra with seven heads to whom offerings are brought regularly to encourage it to continue the flow of the river. If it feels insulted, Waterlord will arrest the waters, causing drought.

WATER SERPENTS

The multiplicity of water serpents in world mythology is truly astonishing. Many of these myths arise from the troubling nature of water itself, which occasionally breaks from its channel and overflows, bringing flood, or dries up, creating drought. Many myths associate serpents and dragons with the locking up of water. Each stream, well, river and lake has its own attendant spirit and myth associated with it, a living entity who must be appeased and attended to, never ignored. Our ancestors' respect and fear of water are based upon its helpfulness and destructiveness. Spates of waters that swell when fed by the ice-melt of mountain springs, rivers that burst their banks at times of heavy rain, tidal bores that swarm like water dragons up estuaries, deep lakes that hide unknown monsters and catastrophic sea-going beasts of gigantic size all contribute to these water serpent stories. The multiplicity of such tales speak of crocodile-like beings, antlered or horned serpents and dragons and lake monsters that seem to hark back to extinct ichthyosaurs, especially in the case of monsters such as Champ and the Loch Ness Monster, which live in water channels so deep that few have plumbed them.

The Element Encyclopedia of Magical Creatures

WEEWILMEKO

In Algonquian legends of North America, Weewilmeko is the horned serpent, said to be a sturgeon with spines or else an antler-horned snake. These antlers were much desired by sorcerers as a source of great power.

WENDIGO

In North American legend, the Wendigo is a monster that takes different forms, according to the locality in which these legends are collected. Among the peoples of Canada, around the Berens Lake near Ontario, the Wendigo is an amphibious monster like an alligator with bear's feet or cloven hooves. Among the Ojibway, the Wendigo or Windigo is known as an ogre, which is invoked to ensure compliant behaviour from children. But among the Algonquin Indians it is the spirit of a lost hunter who now preys upon humans in a cannibalistic manner. This latter form is perhaps more widely known due to urban legends bringing the Wendigo to more popular notice, as has horror writer Algernon Blackwood's story *The Wendigo*.

WEPWAWET

In Egyptian mythology, Wepwawet is the Opener of the Ways who ushers the dead into the Underworld. He is in the shape of a jackal but is distinguishable from Anubis, the main conductor of the dead, by his white or grey head, which may suggest that he was originally a wolf. He was worshipped as the oldest god at Abydos and at Lykopolis (Wolf City), which is presently called Assiut.

WHALE

There are many species of cetaceans swimming the oceans of the world. It is only recently that science has discovered that their mysterious whale-song is not actually a language of communication between pods of whales (although it may also have that function) but is employed most often in charting the oceans and navigating between coastlines. The whale sends its ultrasonic call to hit certain coastal sea-mounts in order to get an impression of the shape of the coastline and sea bed by sound alone. Whales make tremendous journeys following shoals of fish and plankton, returning to particular coastal waters year after year in extraordinary migrations. This remarkable animal has been the source of many myths and legends. Every seaman's map used to sport a whale in one corner of the map to indicate the presence of sea monsters. Early sailors such as the Irish St Brendan, who some believe to have discovered the Americas on his voyage to the Land of Promise, found himself beached upon an island near Easter Sunday and decided to celebrate mass thereon, only to discover that the island was none other than Jasconius the whale.

The whale plays an important part in the myths of world cosmology, for it is believed that Leviathan tries forever to turn his head and tail towards each other to form a circle and that if he ever succeeds then the world will come to an end. Some whales, notably the narwhal with its long spiked horn jutting from its forehead, have been hunted to provide European rulers with their own Unicorn's horn. Such horns are still treasured as aphrodisiac medicine, although they are more often carved by Inuit craftsmen. There are several legends that relate how the whale was once a human being. This is an interesting myth since the whale is indeed a sea-going and social mammal that gives birth to its young. An Australian Aboriginal myth tells how the creating creatures included the whale.

The animals wanted to cross the waters and got Starfish to distract Whale so that they might be ferried to Australia by taking his canoe. When Whale discovered what Starfish had done, he tore it to pieces where it still can be found in the rock pools. Starfish tore a hole in Whale's head, a mark he still bears today. The other animals kept paddling as Whale chased them, mostly aided by Koala. As they came ashore, their many feet broke the canoe and they struggled to shore to become animals and animal-men, from whom all beings are made.

The miser Kondole, the only possessor of fire, refused to share it to light the night for a ceremony. Several performers were incensed at his selfish behaviour and refused to listen to reasonable methods of forcing Kondole to share fire. One lost his temper and thrust his spear through Kondole's skull. At that instant, all those present at the ceremony were transformed into animals. Some became kangaroos, opossums, rodents and other land animals, while others became birds or fish. Since Kondole was the biggest man present, he became the whale and since that time has spouted water from the spear-wound in his skull.

Among the Haida peoples of the northwest coast of Canada, the gods of the strait between their island and the mainland are the Qqaytsgha Llaanas, a pod of killer whales. They are led by Hlghan Xhiila ('Pierced Fin') and Hlgahan Ghaging ('Floppy Fin'). The Haida have many stories about Sghulghu Quuna ('Big Surf'), a heroic killer whale, who is the uncle of Xhuuya, the trickster raven. The muses of the Pacific coast, the Sghalanggaangas, are in the form of orcas or killer whales.

A similar story is told from the Encounter Bay region of Southern Australia.

The Element Encyclopedia of Magical Creatures

Werewolf

The name werewolf comes from the addition of the Old English wer 'man' and the word 'wolf'. A werewolf is a human being who has the ability to turn into a wolf, although the term can also be used generically to describe a human who turns into another kind of animal under conditions of sorcery or enchantment. Werewolves act entirely like a wolf while they are in that shape, and will prey upon any human or other animal.

The ability or misfortune to become a werewolf was conveyed in different ways: by curse, enchantment, sleeping in the light of a full moon, being conceived under a new moon, eating wolf meat, drinking where wolves have drunken or putting on a wolfskin. The werewolf effect takes place in the hours of darkness and subjects conceal their wolf skin and hide their activities during the day, completing the Jekyll and Hyde persona of werewolf existence. Those who are injured as werewolves may be easily discovered the next day since the human subject will have a wound in the same place, thus rousing suspicion of those who had not already noticed the tell-tale signs of werewolfdom – the hairy brows that meet in the middle, the variegated eyes, the long canine teeth and generally vulpine appearance. Once a werewolf, there are very few remedies to help you achieve a cure. Being shot with a silver bullet or arrow-head will probably put you out of your misery the quickest, although some werewolves pray to St Hubert.

The Greek god, Zeus, was said to have caused Lycaeon, the founder of Arcadia, to turn into a wolf after having unwisely sacrificed his own child to Zeus Lycaeus or the Vulpine Zeus. This unpleasant behaviour so disgusted the Olympian god that he determined to wipe out humanity by sending the Great Flood from which only Deucalion and Pyrrha escaped. The wolf-cult of Zeus Lycaeus was said to have still been practised as late as the 1st century AD, when a member of the Antaeus family told Pliny the Elder that he had been a Lycanthrope for nine years, having drawn lots with the rest of his clan to partake in these secret rites. The fear of werewolves reached its height in 16th-century France where many thousands of people were executed after being accused of witchcraft and lycanthropy.

Lycanthropy is the medical term for when the supposed victim believes himself to be a wolf, behaving in gait and appetite like one who is indeed transformed. In historical record, many warriors, including the famous Germanic and Scandinavian berserkers called *Ulfhednar*, who prepared themselves for battle in magical ways to receive the spirit of their totem animal or spirit within them, may possibly have led to some reports of lycanthropy. Burchard of Worms, writing in AD 1000, speaks of werewolves, and the wearing of a wolfskin in medieval Scandinavia was believed to be the means of becoming a werewolf. It is known that the Picts of Alba (now Scotland) went into battle naked so as to show and perhaps activate the woad-tattoos of clan totems upon their bodies; their fearless manner of throwing themselves upon their enemies unprotected by any armour made a distinct impression upon their foes.

Were-bears, -boars, -crocodiles, -dogs, -foxes, -hares, -hyenas, -jaguars, -leopards and -tigers are also found in different parts of the world. Werewolves have been popular at the cinema from the time of the black and white classic *The Wolfman* (starring Lon Chaney Jr) to *Harry Potter and the Prisoner of Azkaban* where Harry's teacher Professor Remus Lupin turns into a werewolf. The 2003 film *Underworld* dealt with the war that rages between werewolves and vampires, thus giving vampire-watchers and lycanthropes alike a double dose of enjoyment.

WHIST HOUNDS

Whist or Wish Hounds are spectral hounds who run over the south-west of England, especially in Dartmoor and Cornwall. They are a form of the Wild Hunt, led by the devil, so says folklore, but the leader of the hunt and chief whipper-in of the hounds is no less a personage than Sir Francis Drake, the first circumnavigator of the globe. He is said to lead a phantom procession of headless hounds that precedes the hearse of the dead.

WHITE BUFFALO CALF WOMAN

Among the Lakota peoples of North America, the source of much Lakota culture and ceremonial derives from White Buffalo Calf Woman. (*See* Ptesan-Wi.)

WHITE HART

In European folklore and heraldry, the white hart is a magical white stag whose appearance signifies the beginning of extraordinary adventures. White harts draw adventurers deep into the forest where lie the margins of the Otherworld, as we see in the Welsh tale of 'Pwyll, Prince of Dyfed', where Pwyll chases such a stag only to find that he is after the same quarry as Arawn, Lord of the Underworld of Annfwn, the In-World. He has to agree to spend time in that Lord's country while Arawn rules in Pwyll's stead in Dyfed. The white hart appears in a notable episode of Sir Thomas Malory's *Le Morte d'Arthur*, signalling the beginning of King Arthur's reign.

THE WILD HUNT

The Wild Hunt is a spectral phenomenon common to the Celtic and Saxon peoples of Britain. It consists of a pack of ghostly hounds who ride with their leader across different parts of the country. In south Wales, it is led by Gwyn ap Nudd, the king of the Underworld who with his Cwn Annwfn, the white hounds with red ears, rides over the Vale of Neath. Gwyn is said to have his palace under Glastonbury Tor from whence he was ousted by St Collen. There is also Herne the Hunter who rides with his hounds in Windsor Great Park. Both Wild Hunts ride after those who have committed unavenged wrongs upon the innocent. In the West Country, the Gabriel Hounds or Gabriel Ratchers ride on the same errand. They were said to have been heard in the 1940s on Hallowe'en night, riding through West Coker, near Taunton.

WILI

In Slavonic legend, the Wili is the name given to the spirits of young women who as nymphs live in fields, ponds, coastal regions, trees and clouds. They are the same as the Vili (*see* Vila), although as the Wili they are best known from the ballet 'Giselle', which was first danced in Paris in 1840. The Wilis in that story are the spirits of young women who died before their wedding night and show an almost vampiric propensity to act as succubi. They gather for midnight dances at the crossroads to lure young men to their deaths. In Bulgaria, these beings were called Samovily and were believed to be the souls of female children who died unbaptized. Puccini's little-known opera *Le Villi* draws upon this legend.

WILL O' THE WISP

The phantom marsh lights that are seen after dusk over swampy ground, the results of escaping gases of decomposing vegetation, are called Will o' the Wisp in Britain. This phenomenon is internationally known as the Ignis Fatuus or 'the Jesting Light', which seems to beckon the traveller from his path, often resulting in wet feet if not immersion in a bog hole. People have understood this phenomenon to be the result of spirits. Will o' the Wisps are also known in Japan where they are called a variety of names: 'Buddha lights', 'badger blazes', 'demon lights', 'fox flames', 'ghost fires', 'flash pillars' and 'flaming birds'. In J.R.R. Tolkien's *The Lord of the Rings*, the treacherous Gollum leads Frodo and Samwise through the Dead Marshes, which are not only lit by spirit lights but whose depths still hold the dead bodies of men, elves and dwarves from ancient wars with the dark lord Sauron.

Wildman

The Wildman appears throughout world mythology as a semi-feral being in whom the chief human characteristics are dominated by more bestial features such as long shaggy hair on his body, a tendency to be secretive, live in wild and unfrequented places and who has neither education nor refinement. In one of the oldest myths of the world, Gilgamesh befriends the wild man Enkidu and introduces him to a prostitute that he might understand himself as a man.

Some Wildmen have become utterly feral and so lost to their humanity that they prey upon their own kind. These cannibalistic myths are persistent throughout world mythology, stories born of hearsay or perhaps of less savoury and indiscriminate times when survival of the fittest was the order of the day.

The medieval world was fascinated by the Wildman, believing the forests to be full of such feral humans, when there were probably more outlaws and heretics surviving there than any such beings. The Wodewose or shaggy-coated Wildman was frequently depicted in tapestries and carvings complete with club in hand and female partner as the hairy inhabitants of the sylvan glade, quaint reminders of primitive and possibly mythical beings. Later in the 16th century, the poet Edmund Spenser, who served in the horrific colonization of Ireland with fellow Elizabethans and witnessed the severity and starvation endured by the native Irish who were forced to eat bark and grass in order to survive, included cannibalistic wild men in his pretty fable, *The Faerie Queene*. Shakespeare's Caliban in *The Tempest* is based more upon the reports of native peoples from the New World while the uncivilized Yahoos of Jonathan Swift's *Gulliver's Travels* were a parody of the European Wildman and a satiric take on what was to become the cult of the Noble Savage as outlined by Jean Jacques Rousseau later in the 18th century.

Some Wildmen are nearer to being Lords of the Animals, like Pasupati or Rudra, an aspect of the Hindu god Shiva, who roams naked through the forests and mountains as a friend of all the world, teaching the arts of music, drama and dancing by which means wisdom can be brought to the crowd. See Yeahoh, Yeren, Yeti, Yowie and the 'Epilogue'.

WISHPOOSHI

Among the Nez Perce Indians of Washington State in North America, Wishpooshi is the ancient giant beaver who lived at the bottom of a deep lake. Unable to stand its depredations any longer, the people called upon Coyote to help them. Coyote went to the lake with a great spear and a knife and fought Wishpooshi. By inserting a spear into the beaver, Coyote managed to hang on while Wishpooshi attempted to shake him off by diving into the depths. As they struggled, waterways, channels, chasms and gorges were carved out. Finally, Coyote became a floating log, which drifted into the mouth of Wishpooshi. Once he was within, Coyote became himself again and stabbed the beaver's heart. From the body of the beaver, Coyote made the Klickitat people whom the French colonists called New Perce.

WODJANOI

In Slavonic legend, Wodjanoi is a male water spirit who lives in whirlpools. He had a palace at the bottom of the sea full of the spoils of sunken ships. Fishermen would propitiate him with a pinch of tobacco, or by the gift of the first-caught fish or some butter poured into his pool. Wodjanoi was believed to pair with Rusalki or to have them in his service. It was believed that millers, beekeepers and fishermen were protected by Wodjanoi.

WODWOSE/WOODWOSE

Also known as Wild Men of the Woods, these are a curious species that appear as denizens of the woodlands and who live wild and separate from their human neighbours. Sometimes associated with the troll, they are widely represented in the literature, art and philosophy of the Middle Ages as human in shape but with leaves or long hair apparently growing on their bodies. They are often seen as a personification of those aspects of nature rejected by humankind in its espousal of civilization. The Wodwose, like the Wildman and the Green Man, thus came to represent some of the most deep-seated fears of the medieval Christian world, and for this reason they were banished to remote corners of the land. A proliferation of carvings representing these beings appears notably in medieval churches throughout East Anglia.

WOLF

The wolf excites a variety of emotions, prime of which is fear. As pack animals that have a tribal order with pack leaders and subordinates, wolves and humans have competed for the same territory and sometimes the same food, making the wolf a suitable object of projected blame and a symbol of rapacity.

There are many legends in which the wolf is the devourer of the light. In Hindu belief, the wolf of darkness swallows the quail that heralds the return of the sun; the divine twins, the Asvins, who are representatives of the day and night help revive the quail. In Norse myth, the wolf is one of the three creatures responsible for the bringing about of Ragnarok, the ending of the world. The fast-running Wolf was one of the animals who helped Coyote steal fire from the Fire People in a story from British Columbia in Canada.

Wolves appear in the foundation myths of many peoples, notably in the story of the foundation of Rome in which the twins Romulus and Remus, the sons of Mars and a Vestal Virgin, were set adrift on the Tiber to die. They washed up near the cave of Lupercal where a she-wolf found and suckled them. When they became the founders of Rome, the wolf was not forgotten; the popular festival of Lupercalia, celebrated on 15 February was held in honour of the fertility of flocks and fields. It involved two noble youths, smeared with blood, who struck everyone they met with strips of skin from a sacrificed goat to make them fertile. In Irish tradition, King Cormac was fostered by wolves.

Many beliefs view the wolf as evil, like the Zoroastrians for whom the wolf is a symbol of Ahriman. In Norse myth, Fenris the wolf is one of the beings created by Loki to bring trouble to the world, while Odin's two wolves Skoll and Hati, whose names respectively mean 'Repulsion' and 'Hatred', pursue the sun and moon trying to bite pieces out of them to plunge the world into darkness. The Christian tradition sees the wolf as the fierce and insatiable adversary of the meek and biddable Lamb.

The cleverness of the wolf is also celebrated however, and the stories regarding Ysengrim and his contests with the fox Reynard were immensely popular in medieval Europe. Many Native American tribes look to the wolf as a brother and teacher, one who shows the way beyond death. Kawatilikalla was the first being of the Tsewatenok people of north-west Pacific peoples of North America. He and his wife were wolves. One day when it was raining heavily, he said to her, 'I don't see why we should remain animals. Let us take off our skins and keep them only for dancing.' The Nootka people of that region believe that the wolf was the one who taught people how to dance.

Yanamhum was a youth whose people did not believe he was man enough, so he purified himself and visited the land of wolves. He obtained a magical club from their sacred temple and lived among them for a year, becoming one with them. His family had thought him dead but when he re-emerged from the forest, they did not recognize him and attacked him. When he uncovered his great club, every person fell dead. He sprinkled water upon those who had believed in him and raised them from the dead; those who had disbelieved in him he left for dead. The Wolf Dance is danced in honour of the strength that the youth found among the wolves.

The Element Encyclopedia of Magical Creatures

WOLPERTINGER

The Wolpertinger seems to be a German equivalent to the American Jackalope, a portmanteau animal that lives in the forests of Bavaria. It has a small mammalian body, but sports wings, antlers and fangs, so that it looks a bit like a horned rabbit or squirrel. Makers of tourist souvenirs specialize in making Wolpertingers as stuffed animals, to help boost tourism to those areas of Bavaria where people will regale you with tales of many sightings.

WOODPECKER

Among the peoples of Africa, the insistent tapping of the woodpecker is the harbinger of rain. Whenever people dance rain-dances, they place woodpecker charms inside the hollow drums to help hasten rainfall.

WORM

In north-west European tradition, 'worm' is the name given to many dragons: it comes from the Old Norse *wurm* or 'dragon'. Wherever the Vikings settled, this word has followed. Worms usually have serpentine bodies with horns. The most famous worms are the Laidley Worm, the Lambton Worm, the Loathly Worm and the Stoorworm.

WREN

The diminutive wren is the possessor of a wealth of lore concerning its abilities and it is the main player in an ancient ceremony that is still enacted in Celtic countries. The primary folk story of the wren, found across Europe, concerns a conference of birds who assemble to discover who shall be their king. The post will be awarded to the bird who flies the highest. All the birds in the contest take to the skies, each attempting to outfly the other until only the eagle is left in the race. Having outdistanced every other bird, the eagle begins to proclaim itself the king of the birds when the wren, who has been concealed in the eagle's feathers on his back, pulls himself to his full height and chirps, 'Behold your king!' Some trace the roots of this story back to Sumerian mythology. The Greeks call the wren *Basiliskos* ('little king'), while in Latin it is *Regulus* ('king'); in Welsh it is *Dryw* ('druid') or *Bren* ('king') – from which the word 'wren' is derived – and in Manx and Irish Gaelic it is still remembered as *Drui-en* ('the druid bird').

Up until the 19th and early 20th centuries, the custom of Hunting the Wren was found in Ireland, Wales and Brittany. This custom took place on St Stephen's Day, 26 December, when groups of boys and men went out with sticks to hunt and kill a wren, finally placing it in a 'wren house', a beribboned and decorated box, in which it is borne through the streets accompanied with songs. Some wren processions involved knocking on doors and asking for money, others involved the sale of a single wren feather to be placed in one's hat. Finally, the wren was buried with reverence. This custom is of great antiquity, relating back to the turning of the year and the fact that the wren's native name is associated with the druids who saw the wren as a bird of omen. It is evident that the druids saw the wren as the symbol of the old year and that its ritualized death and funeral procession was a necessary ceremonial to lay the old year to rest.

WUTE

In the stories of the African Cameroons, Wute is the name of the chameleon who God sent to tell the people the wonderful message that they would not have to die like the animals but that they would rise from their graves to live again. He set off slowly and carefully but the snake knew the message and arrived more speedily. Jealous of God's favouritism to the people, the snake told them that God's message was that they would remain in their graves forever after they died. When Wute finally arrived, the people called him a liar. Unable to gain their trust, Wute and the snake returned to God for true judgement as to the correct message. God agreed that the snake had lied and misrepresented his message, however because his word had been given to the people in this way, death would be able to kill many people who would never rise again. But the punishment for the snake was that people would fear and hate him forever and would kill him whenever they saw him.

WYVERN

In European lore and heraldic legend, the Wyvern is a beast with a dragon's head, the body of a serpent, a bat's wings and two forelegs, and a serpent's tail ending in a dart-like point. The Wyvern is associated with pestilence, war, envy and spite, although it can also use these qualities to protect those who have the Wyvern as their heraldic emblem.

The Element Encyclopedia of Magical Creatures

X

Xanthos

In Greek mythology, Xanthos is a horse who, with his brother Balios, is the off-spring of Podarge, one of the Harpies and Aeolus, god of the winds. Xanthos and Balios were both given to Poseidon to draw his chariot through the skies. Later, this chariot team turned up to draw the chariot of Achilles when he was fighting in the Trojan wars. It was behind this chariot that the Trojan prince Hector was dragged in victory by the victorious Achilles. When Achilles' cousin Patroclus was killed, Achilles mourned and blamed Xanthos and Balios, who he held could have saved him. But Xanthos said that Achilles should not question the gods in this manner and prophesied that the hero himself would be slain by a god. Apollo afterwards guided the bow of Paris to shoot Achilles in his vulnerable heel. Then the Erinyes made Xanthos dumb so that he might utter no further prophecies.

Xecotcovach

The Mayan bird who tore out the eyes of the first men, who were destroyed in the flood sent by the god Hurakan. He was one of the four great winged beings who attacked the wooden bodies created by Gucumatz and Tepeu that were intended to become the first living humans. They each attacked a different part of the body to prevent the pollution of the primordial world. The others were Camazotz, Tecumbalam and Coztbalam.

Xexeu

Xexeu was the giant bird of the Cashmawa people of South America. Like the Thunderbirds of North America, the Xexeu are responsible for assembling storm clouds.

Xhuuya

Among the Haida peoples of the north-west Pacific coast of Canada, Xhuuya is the name given to Raven, the great trickster. He is the son of Floodtide Woman and his uncle is Sghulghu Quuna ('Big Surf'), a killer whale. Xhuuya stole fire from the gods and was a frequent visitor to the beds of women, but he also brought light, water, berries and fish to human beings. He positioned the sun and moon in the sky and, in consultation with a dog, organized the shape of the calendar. With his glossy blue-black feathers, he is a sleek, plausible creature of extreme cunning and cleverness. His rites are celebrated among the Haida especially at midwinter when they re-enact the return of the light.

The Element Encyclopedia of Magical Creatures

Xhuuya flew around looking for a place to land after the deluge when the world was covered by sea water. He flew over the places where the new-born gods lay like pods of sea cucumbers about one rock that projected from the sea. As he did so, Xhuuya saw a bright light in the north and pushed himself through into a region of the Otherworld where he found a village. In one house, the chief's daughter had just given birth. Seeing the child unattended, Xhuuya skinned the child and crawled inside its skin, taking the baby's place. He was suckled by the mother, but did not take much nourishment from that, since he was really an adult raven with a grown-up appetite. While people slept, he slipped out of his skin and brought food back to the fire to cook it, returning to the cradle before they awoke. But one morning, several people awoke to find they were missing an eye. The people got wind of what was happening and surrounded the chief's house calling for the mother to bring her baby outside. Then they bounced him up and down while they sang and watched what happened as they dropped him. As soon as he hit the ground, he flew out of his skin and became a raven again.

XIANG YAO

In Chinese folklore, Xiang Yao is a monster with nine human heads and the body of a serpent. It goes about in the company of a black dragon called Gong-Gong. Their dung befouls watercourses turning them into stinking swamps.

XOLOTL

In Aztec mythology, Xolotl is the dog of the underworld. When the sun ceased to move, it was Xolotl who sacrificed the gods – with the intention of sacrificing himself also – in order to help the sun resume its cycle. However, Xolotl did not keep his part of the agreement and transformed himself into an irregular or mutant twin-stalked maize plant. In this refusal to agree to death, he is like Coyote. Xolotl then transformed from maize plant to the maguay cactus Mexolotl and finally into the larvae Azolotl before he was finally made to submit to his contract.

Xolotl was also the god of twins and of abnormal births: such people were considered to be deformed and irregular in Aztec society so that when an eclipse came along they were sacrificed to help the sun regain its strength to continue moving. Xolotl presided over the ball game *tlachtli* (a form of divine squash), which was played on the divine court of the sky. Aztec burials were often attended by the burial of a dog, for the animal's soul was thought to accompany the deceased, just as Xolotl faithfully accompanied the sun through

The Element Encyclopedia of Magical Creatures

the sky. It is thought that Xolotl was a pre-Aztec deity from the earlier Chichimec peoples who were said to be descended from a man and a bitch, the only survivors of the Flood. Xolotl seems to be closest to the North American Coyote in the way in which he is referred to as a creator. When the first semi-divine beings were born of a stone knife, the offspring of the Earth mother Citalicue, they asked their mother if they might create mankind to help them. Citalicue agreed and sent Xolotl to Mictlan, the Lord of Death, to obtain some ashes or bones of the dead. Xolotl returned with a bone but when he stumbled on reaching Earth, the bone broke into two unequal pieces. He picked up the fragments and put each into a bowl sprinkled with the blood of the gods. Four days later, a man emerged; four days on, a woman was born; these were the first people.

Y

YAC

In Mayan tradition, Yac the forest cat was one of the four animals who helped bring maize to the gods so that they could form mankind. The other creatures who assisted in this creation were Hoh the crow, Quel the parrot and Utiu the coyote.

YAKSHA

The Yakshas are forest spirits in Hindu belief. The word means 'mysterious ones'. They take the form of ugly black dwarves with pot bellies. The chief of the Yakshas is Kubera. The Yakshas are protective spirits who can take what shape they please, often appearing as ordinary trees. They protect palaces as well as houses, and people called them *Punyajana* ('Friendly Folk'). They are the protectors of earth's treasures, in the same way that the European dwarf is said to keep precious gems and golden treasure.

YAKSHINI

In Hindu belief, Yashini is a forest goddess or dryad who appears like a shapely, smiling woman on the pillars of temples and gateways, inviting the worshipper in. But in wild places they take the form of Ashvamukhi or 'horse-faced' beings with the bodies of women and the heads of horses. The Svetambara sect of Jains hold that Su-Tara ('the Good Star'), an aspect of the goddess Tara, is a Yakshini. Prince Vijaya

once came upon a Yakshini who enchanted his men to stillness. He pursued her into the deep forest where she turned into a beautiful girl called Kuvanna. In a story that seems straight out of Homer's *Odyssey*, she promised to release his men only if he married her.

YALE

In European legend, the Yale, which is also called the Centicore and Eale and is related to the Yali, is described as a horse-sized beast, having the body of a goat, with the tail and tusks of a boar, and with multi-coloured spots all over its hide. But it is also said to have the head of a goat, the tail of an elephant and the feet of a Unicorn. Its horns can move in their sockets to defend itself from attack from in front or behind. It may derive from the Yali and from the Hebrew word *ya-el* (goat). In heraldry, the Yale is the one of the Queen's Beasts.

YALI

Pliny the Elder mentions the Yali as coming from the Middle East and India, for it certainly shows a direct relationship to the European Yale, which may derive from it. In Hindu and Buddhist legend, this lion-bodied beast with the tusks of an elephant is found most often nowadays in the supporting pillars of Hindu Temples. However, different kinds of Yali are found with lion heads (*simha-vyala*), horse heads (*ashva-vyala*) dog heads (*shvana-vyala*) and

The Element Encyclopedia of Magical Creatures

human heads *(nir-vyala)*. This great diversity reminds us that the Yali is related to the sphinxes of Egypt and Mesopotamia that lie just a short sea voyage away from India. The Yalis symbolize the powers of the chakravartin ('world emperor'). The word Yali or Yalli derives from the Sanscrit *vyala* ('fierce monster').

YANG JING

In Chinese mythology, Yang Jing is the goat god to whom peasants make sacrifices so that their livestock may be free of the depredations of wild beasts. Yang Jing is depicted wearing a goat's-head mask and a goat skin. We find a close relationship here with the animal herdsman-god, the satyr Pan.

YANN-AN-OED

In Breton lore, Yann-an-oed (or Yannig) is a sea monster that swims off the coast in the hours of darkness to find prey. It makes the cry of an owl. Those who are tempted to reply immediately give away their location to the Yann-an-Oed who will sneak up and devour them. During the hours of daylight, it lives in the deep sea.

YEAHOH

The Yeahoh is the Kentucky name of Bigfoot. A man called Lee Maggard reported the following account in the 1950s.

A man got lost while out hunting and came across a big hole in the ground into which he lowered himself. Inside was a female Yeahoh with deer-meat hanging up along with other home-caught supplies. The Yeahoh was unconcerned and cut the man some raw meat, but the hunter could not eat it so he made a fire from the flint in his pocket and roasted it, giving the Yeahoh a piece. Everytime the Yeahoh moved or communicated she said, 'Yeahoh, Yeahoh', over and over. The man spent the winter there and he and the Yeahoh had a child. Whenever he tried to escape, the female Yeahoh would fetch him back. He finally made it to a river where a boat was ready to dock. He jumped on board only to see the Yeahoh and their child following behind. As he floated away downstream to his own kind, the hunter saw the Yeahoh tear the baby in half and cry, 'Yeahoh, Yeahoh'. Versions of this story appear up and down the Appalachian range.

YECH

In Indian folklore, the Yech is small fairy-like being, the size of a cat, who wears a white shell-shaped cap that renders him invisible. If you are able to secure a Yech's cap and put it under a millstone, the Yech will become your servant. Although it is supremely powerful, being able to shift cities and mountains, the Yech is unable to shift the millstone without hurting his fingers. A Yech who is not in service is likely to be found leading travellers astray.

YEREN

In Chinese cryptozoology, the Yeren or Yeh'ren is the equivalent of Bigfoot or the Yeti. The word Yeren means 'wildman'. It is described as being about 6½ ft tall with red fur all over its body. It walks upright and its footprints measure about 16 ins long. The biologist Wang Tselin claimed to have examined the corpse of a female Yeren in 1940. He said it looked like a cross between an ape and a human. Several sightings have been noted by Chinese officials, including one in 1976 when a car carrying six local government officers saw a Yeren attempting to get off the road by climbing a steep embankment from which it fell back in front of the car, transfixed by the car's headlights. One frightened official threw a rock at it and it ran off. This sparked an investigation into the Yeren by the Chinese Academy of Sciences, which has so far been inconclusive in its findings, but the hands and feet of an alleged Yeren were passed to the Academy in the 1980s. These appendages were examined by Zhou Guoxing who at first thought them to be an unknown species of monkey, but he later decided that they were the hands and feet of a macaque. However, it is clear that Yerens are not macaques but something much bigger and bipedal. It is assumed that the Yeren is a surviving *Gigantopithecus*, an otherwise extinct primate that lived in China over 300,000 years ago.

YETI

The Yeti is a species of Bigfoot that lives in the Himalayas. The word derives from the Sherpa *Yeh-The*, which only describes one of three species of Yeti, the others being called the Dzu-The, which is the largest and attacks yaks, and the Meh-The, although European explorers called it 'the Abominable Snowman' since it lives usually above the snowline. In 1938, a Captain d'Auvergue, curator of the Victoria Memorial in Calcutta in India, was travelling in the Himalayas when he became snowblind. He says he was saved from exposure and hypothermia by a 9-ft Yeti who nursed him back to health. The first European explorer to see and record it was NA Tombazi, a Greek photographer on a British geological expedition. He saw a creature moving across the mountain slopes, clearly standing upright, which stopped and picked at dwarf rhododendron bushes as it went. What clinched the sighting for the photographer was that the creature wore no clothes. Unable, in those days of early cameras, to set up a shot of the creature, nevertheless he went after it, camera in hand, to take photos of its footprints, which he found to be 7 ins long and 4 ins wide, with 5 distinct toes.

The Element Encyclopedia of Magical Creatures

The instep was clear but not the heel, due to the slope that the creature had been traversing. The prints were 1½–2-ft stride. The locals said he had seen the 'Kanchenjunga demon'. The best tracks were found by Eric Shipton and Michael Ward in 1951 who found them on the slopes of the Menlung Glacier between Tibet and Nepal at an altitude of 20,000 feet. These were clearly bipedal footprints, 13 ins wide and 18 ins long; even allowing for the sun spreading the melting snow of these prints, there was no creature that could have made them in the district, for what man would walk in the snow barefooted? Sir Edmund Hillary and Tenzing Norgay, the first people to climb to Everest's summit, also found giant footprints on the way up their triumphant ascent in 1953.

The King of Nepal keeps a court official whose task is solely to keep up with sightings of the Yeti. A recent expedition in the 1990s was guided by the Nepalese Yeti Finder to a tree in a wild and unfrequented part of the deeply-gorged forests where hunters have reported hearing the humanoid. Samples of hair were taken for analysis from the tree where the Yeti seemed to have rubbed itself. Back at the laboratory, the hair did not match with any known DNA hair samples of animals from that district. It was concluded that, although the scientists had been unable to catch sight of a Yeti, they had indeed found some of its coat. On the same expedition, they were introduced to an elderly woman who, it was said, had lived with a Yeti as its wife. She spoke a language which the Yeti Finder said was no known dialect of the region; the people in the village treated her with care and respect, entirely believing that her long absence from the village had been due to her sojourn with the Yeti.

YETL

According to the north-west Pacific coast peoples of the Tlingit tribe, Yetl is the name given to the hero Raven. His parentage is disputed. Some say that he is the son of a being called Nascakiyetl who lived in a lodge in which he kept the sun, moon, stars and light. Others say he is the son of Nascakiyetl's sister who had borne several previous children whom her brother had destroyed for he feared a prophecy that his sister's child would overcome his power and authority. Taking counsel with Heron, the woman swallowed a red-hot stone; when she later gave birth to Yetl he was first named Taqlikic ('Hammer-Feather') because of his extreme resilience. Other stories make him the son of a man, Kitkaositiyiqa, who gave him the ability to form a separate creation. Yetl transformed himself into a splinter of hemlock that Nascakiyetl's daughter swallowed. When he was born of her, he stole from the lodge the sun, moon, stars and light. After that, he created the winds, the people and turned one fast-running man into a dog so that he might go even faster on four legs than on two. He cast water, which he had stolen from Petrel, upon the earth to make the rivers and lakes. But Petrel lit a fire underneath Yetl as he

The Element Encyclopedia of Magical Creatures

tried to run away, which changed his feathers from white to black. He persuaded the old woman who regulates the seas to make them follow a pattern of tides, which they still do till this day. He was also responsible for capturing all the killer whales but one and rendering them down for oil. Yetl was helped in this task by a man who became incensed when Yetl tried to take his share of oil. The man trapped him in a box and threw it over a cliff. But since Yetl had taught him to fasten boxes with straw, he was soon free again. He also brought death to the world by killing the bear and cormorant with whom he had gone hunting. He also killed the bear's wife by tricking her into consuming some halibut bladders that he had previously stuffed with hot stones, and then he made a pit-trap for a deer, and so by these acts he introduced hunting and meat-eating to humanity. Yetl also discovered the way to prop up the Earth. He drained a pool of sea water at low tide and killed the beaver who lived there, cutting off its foreleg to act as a prop. Then he put Hayicanke, the Old Woman Who Lives Under the Earth, to administer the prop. When her attention slips and she falls asleep we suffer earthquakes which usually wake her up again.

YING LUNG

Ying Lung is the Dragon of Proper Conduct in Chinese Confucian lore. This is the only Chinese dragon to have wings.

YLLERIONS

In the letter supposedly written by the priest-king Prester John in the 13th century to the Christian princes of Europe, Yllerions is described as the Lord of the Birds who has flame-coloured plumage and feathers that are razor sharp. This fabulous creature is rare, for there are only two alive at any one time, each living for 60 years. They then lay 2–3 eggs that they incubate for 40 days before they hatch, after which the parents drown themselves in the sea, accompanied by a vast assembly of birds who take on the responsibility of raising the hatchling Yllerions. Prester John was a legendary king living in a fabulous foreign land. The fact that he was believed to be a Christian and might thus help European Christians against the Turks gave great hope to Europe, though it is clear that the letter was a wish-fulfilling hoax and that Yllerions is a near-relative of the Phoenix.

Ymir

In Norse mythology, Ymir is the primordial giant who gave his body to create the world. He was born of the melting ice of the primordial void of Ginnungagap and grew to huge proportions, nurtured by the great cow Audumla. All the giants were born of Ymir from his sweat. After the first gods were born, including Odin, Vili and Ve, Ymi was killed by them. All the giants drowned in the exudation of his blood except for Bergelmir and his wife who escaped the flood on a raft. The primal gods took Ymir's body to the centre of the Ginnungagap where they separated it to create the world: his blood became the sea and the waters, his flesh the earth, his bones the mountains, his teeth and bone the rocks, his skull the sky. From his hair came the trees and from his brain the clouds. The middle-earth of Midgard, the world of men, was formed from his brows. Ymir is also considered to be the ancestor of the dwarves. Ymir is connected to the Sanskrit Yama, and the Avedic Yima who, in Zoroastrian belief, is another primordial progenitor of everything. (*See* Supporters of the Earth and Sky.)

Yofune-Nushi

Yofune-Nushi was a Japanese sea serpent of huge size that preyed upon the islands of Japan making the life of fishermen particularly hazardous. They kept it in check by offering it a maiden every 13 June. One very courageous maiden called Tokoyo equipped herself with a sharp knife while she was waiting to be seized by the serpent. When it was close enough she stabbed out its eyes, killing it.

Yowie

In Australian Aboriginal legend, the Yowie is a monstrous humanoid with a hairy pelt. It was known for centuries by the aborigines who say that when their ancestors came to Australia, there was a race of savage ape-men who they fought. Because the Yowies had no weapons, the Aboriginal ancestors were successful and pushed their foes to the edges of the habitable regions. The Yowie has no neck, broad shoulders, longish hair that can be red, dark or black over its body and large feet. Their height ranges between 5–14 ft. The commonest sign by which you know you are in the vicinity of a Yowie is the stench. The Aboriginal word for the Yowie is '*Youree*' but the white settlers to Australia called these creatures 'Yahoos' after the sub-humans invented by Jonathan Swift in his *Gulliver's Travels*. But it is the Aboriginal term that is now used. The first sighting of a Yowie by white settlers was recorded in 1881. Scientists have insisted that no placental species were indigenous to Australia, but recent discoveries of fossil *Homo floresiensis* in the Flores Islands have caused some to think again about the spread of early hominids of whom the Yowie may be a survivor. (*See* 'Epilogue'.)

YSBADADDEN PENCAWR

The giant Ysbadadden Pencawr ('Hawthorn, the Chief Giant') is a central figure in the Welsh myth of 'Culhwch and Olwen', a compendious story with its roots in 6th-century oral memory.

This story has a lot to do with the coming of age of a young prince, for in Celtic tradition an untried noble is 'a piglet', while a tried and tested king is 'a great boar'. Ysbadadden has an exterior soul, hidden in the barbering implements on the back of Twrch Trwyth. His impossible tasks all have to be accomplished sequentially until Arthur's men arrive at the capture of the boar, but once the giant's hair and beard are reunited with the implements, Ysbadadden's power is no more.

The young hero Culhwch is made to fall fatally and irrevocably in love with the daughter of Ysbadadden by his stepmother who clearly hopes that his suit will be met by certain death, since none have ever overcome the giant. But Culhwch knows the odds against him and he travels to the court of his cousin King Arthur where he begs that Arthur cut his hair – the initiatory act by which boys are recognized as men. Then in the names of all Arthur's men, women and servants, he calls upon Arthur's help to accomplish his wedding to Olwen. A deputation of warriors goes with Culhwch to the court of the giant to ask for Olwen's hand in marriage.

They lodge with Custennin, the herdsman of the castle; he was once a landed noble, but is now enslaved. His wife opens a cupboard to reveal a young boy hidden within. Cei (the later Sir Kay) is incensed about this, but the women explains that she hides the boy Goreu in a cupboard for his own safety since Ysbadadden has killed 23 of her sons already. In order to be able to see his prospective son-in-law, Ysbadadden orders his servants to prop up his eyebrows. After the men make their request on Culhwch's behalf, he throws three poisoned darts after them which are caught by Bedwyr (Sir Bedivere in medieval tales) who returns what to him are spears, striking the giant in the knee.

When the wooing party returns the next day, another set of darts is thrown after them which Menw catches, striking the giant in the breast. The third time, when Ysbadadden's servants prise open his eyes to look upon the supplicants, Culhwch himself seizes the spear that is thrown at them and pierces the giant's eye. Having passed the preliminary discussion phase, the giant gets down to brass tacks. He agrees to the match providing that Culhwch can accomplish 39 impossible tasks, including finding the barbering implements by which he can be groomed for the wedding day. The other tasks involve the finding of mythical characters to accomplish certain tasks, which is where all of Arthur's court become involved, for each is occupied in retrieving objects, finding gods and heroes long dead and finally catching the ravaging boar, Trwch Trwyth, a feat that is fraught with danger, for the chief barbering implements are attached to the hair behind the boar's ears.

While these tasks are being carried out, Arthur sails to Ireland to fetch the hero's cauldron, an act which is an early correlative of the search for the Holy Grail in later medieval legend. When all the conditions have finally been met, Ysbadadden must submit to his barbering. The wild Pict, Kay, shaves the giant of beard, skin and flesh from ear to ear. He finally agrees that Culhwch has fulfilled all the impossible tasks, carping that he had the help of many to accomplish them, before Goreu, son of Custennin seizes him by his neck hair and drags him off to behead him, putting the great head on a stake, thus avenging the deaths of his brothers. Culhwch marries Olwen (who seems to be of a normal human size) to great rejoicing.

YSENGRIM

In medieval European legend, the wolf Ysengrim appears in the epic of Reynard the Fox. Ysengrim continually tries to catch Reynard. In one tale, Reynard persuades the wolf to eat some of a passing farmer's ham instead of himself. Reynard stretches himself out upon the road pretending to be exhausted, and the farmer lays the ham down in order to catch him, but Ysengrim runs off with it. As a pay back, Reynard persuades Ysengrim to dangle his tail through a hole in the ice in order to catch fish. While he patiently sits there, Reynard steals the priest's chicken and leads the pursuit to where the wolf is by now trapped, his tail encased in the ice. Before they are able to kill him, an old woman cuts off his tail and he scarpers off. Another tale tells why there is enmity between wolf and fox.

The Element Encyclopedia of Magical Creatures

Reynard persuaded Ysengrim to enter a monastery because monks always eat well. While the wolf was away from home, Reynard urinated in his lair where the cubs were. Hersent, Ysengrim's wife, tried to chase him away but Reynard raped her. Ysengrim's behaviour at the monastery was so outrageous that the monks beat him and cast him out. When Ysengrim's novice master attempts to teach him Latin for saying the Divine Office of prayer, Ysengrim says *'Cominus ovis'* ('Sheep, come hither') rather than *'Dominus vobiscum'* ('God be with you!'), and when instructed to say 'Amen' at the ends of prayers, Ysengrim utters *'Agne'* ('Lamb'). The monks put down his strange pronunciation to a heavy country accent.

In a sequence of terrible bad luck, Ysengrim loses his skin three times due to Reynard's interventions: once he has it flayed off at the court of Noble the Lion who rips it off and every time he gains another skin, he is destined to lose it again in a wolfish equivalent to the cat's nine lives. The theme of Ysengrim dressed as a monk preaching from a pulpit was frequently depicted in carvings, illuminations and other decorations by masons and clerks, since the ecclesiastical depredations of the clergy, to whom all people paid a tithe of their income, were exceedingly unpopular. A wolf in monk's clothing seemed a particularly apt image during the Middle Ages.

Yu Lung

In Chinese lore, Yu Lung started out as the celestial carp but when it leapt the Dragon's Gate waterfall, it transformed into a dragon with the head and fins of a carp instead. Yu Lung was the emblem and metaphor of students who had passed their examinations, and thus passed from being mere students into masters of their subject.

Yurugu

Among the Dogon of Mali, Yurugu the jackal fox is the son of the creator Amma. He is the representative of god's difficulties, the solution-finder but also one who sows the seed of division and disorder in the world. He taught men to dance and to divine. Yurugu comes to the Dogon late at night to dance in the sand of their divining tables. Those who act as diviners have to study for five or six years because the process of laying out the divining table with the six cosmic zones of the universe is very complex: the foot-steps of Yurugu are not clear to all to understand. The diviners must learn how to manipulate the twine, pebbles, shells, leaves, twigs and grain that call Yurugu.

The Element Encyclopedia of Magical Creatures

Yurugu wanted to learn speech and he attempted to lift up the skirt of Mother Earth that had been woven by the Nummo. Mother Earth became an ant but the incestuous jackal followed. No hole was deep enough for her to hide and Yurugu mated with her, which gave him the speech he desired. Because he was the first to speak, he was afterwards able to reveal to diviners the will of god. While Amma was asleep, Yurugu thought him dead. He began to mourn him in the first funeral rites that ever existed. Dressed in the fibrous skirt of his mother, Yurugu danced and spoke. The fibres of the skirt were full of words and water, and as he danced, he left traces of dust on the terrace: there were three tracks lengthwise and three tracks crosswise, which represented the roof of heaven, the inside of the roof, the altar-room of the dead. In so doing, Yurugu spoke the first words and outlined the future of the world. The terrace where he danced became the first divining table, which later diviners copied in the sand. To this day, diviners write their questions on the sand of the divining table and jackals come by night, lured by the bait of the question, to write their answers.

Z

Zagh

In Islamic literature and folklore, the Zagh appears as a fabulous bird that has the face of a human being. It has the ability to converse in human languages. It is very similar to the Roc and appears in many stories and poetic allusions as an emblem of divine intelligence.

Zantegeba

Zantegeba is the name of the baboon who struts about the forests of the Bambara people of Mali. His exceedingly lascivious antics are represented annually by a dancer who uses two small sticks to act as forelegs. He darts into the crowd focusing especially upon female spectators who scream and run away in case Zantegeba comes to rape them. Zantegeba's name means 'he of the big paws'.

Zlatorog

In Slovenian folklore, the Zlatorog is a fabulous beast that has the body and pure white coat of a chamois but with horns of gold. It grazed upon the topmost peaks of Mount Triglav and often lured treasure-hunters after it through dangerous ravines and defiles where the less cautious fell to their deaths. Only one hunter was able to wound the Zlatorog, though he failed to obtain its golden horns. Nevertheless, the blood spilt from the wounds formed a red flower, the carnation, which is now the emblem of Slovenia.

Zmag Oghjeni Vuk

In Bosnia and Serbia, the Zmag Oghjeni Vuk ('Fiery Dragon Wolf') is a werewolf associated with the 15th-century ruler Despot Vuk. He was born with a birthmark in the shape of a sabre and was able to breathe fire. He had a tuft of wolf hair that gave an inkling of his werewolfish capacities. He grew prodigiously and was the only person able to overcome the fiery dragon that was said to have fathered him. He was able to turn into a werewolf at will at night and when the sun was overcast for long periods.

Zmei Gorynich

In Slovenian and Russian folklore, Zmei Gorynich is a serpent with the head of a human being, or a human being that is a snake from the waist downwards. This monster was often associated with Baba Yaga.

Zombies

Originally in African lore, a zombie was any person who had come under the magical will of a sorcerer, although nowadays it tends to mean a dead human being whose own soul is absent but whose body can be inspirited by the will to work. The word comes from the Kongo *zumbi* or *zombi* which means a 'fetish' or 'enslaved spirit'. The following story was told to Jan Knappert in Natal.

The Element Encyclopedia of Magical Creatures

A Zulu man called Sipo told how his brother Vamba suddenly became ill, walking like an old man or, as people say there, 'walked zombie'. Shortly afterwards he died, but when they went to bury him, Vamba's body did not go through the normal process of rigor mortis but was entirely soft. Suspicious of magic, Sipo was uneasy. The next morning, the grave was open and the body had vanished. Now everyone knew it was sorcery that had caused Vamba's 'death'. Sipo searched the townships and villages all around, asking if there was a powerful sorcerer in the district. Eventually, in hushed tones, one particular man was pointed out to him, an influential man with a large farm. He waited at the gate until dusk, the time when ordinary people stop work and return home, when he saw 'an army of silent labourers come shuffling to the fields'. They even worked silently, without singing the usual work-songs by which labour is leavened throughout Africa. Sipo recognized his brother as he searched each face. He looked grey and depressed, nor could he talk for his tongue had been slit. Sipo carried his featherlight brother home where, shortly after, he died for a second time, this time exhibiting all the usual signs of deathly decay.

The term 'zombie' is known primarily to the world from the Haitian vodoun religion which is largely misunderstood by outsiders. Some vodoun priests (*books*) used the nerve poison tetrodotoxin from the puffer fish to produce the effect of death: in minute doses this poison does not bring actual death, just the suppression of the signs of life for up to 48 hours. The one who has taken it can recover. It is held that if a zombie eats salt or sees the sea, he will return to his grave. But there are much more disturbing stories that tell of zombies being turned into animals and slaughtered for meat. Haitian tradition states that those people who are dug up to become zombies are alive, but mentally impaired by a lack of oxygen after being buried; they say that zombies were used as slaves to labour in Haiti's vast sugar plantations. The capturing of people's spirits in order to keep them in eternal bondage seems to be an ironic reversal of the slave populations of Haiti who were brought to serve colonists in creating economic capital: those descendants of the slaves who act in this sorcerous way merely repeat history.

Zombies are not exclusive to Caribbean shores, since they appear also in the legends of Ireland and Britain, especially in the Welsh story of Branwen, daughter of Llyr, in which dead warriors are put into a cauldron to be brought back to life to continue as battle fodder for the conflict. In their fight against the Fir Bolg, the Tuatha de Danann similarly cause their dead warriors to come alive again at the Well of Slaine so as to replenish their army. The warriors who emerge can fight but cannot speak, since it is forbidden for them to speak of what lies beyond death.

The genre of zombie film started back in the 1930s and 1940s, and now the robotic dead, torn from the grave, still steadfastly tromp through city streets as the stock of many horror films – including the epitomy of the genre, George A Romero's *Night of the Living Dead* and the more recent wonderfully awful satiric spoof, *Shaun of the Dead* by Edgar Wright and Simon Pegg.

Zu

In Mesopotamian mythology, Zu was the great bird with an eagle's head and lion's body who was one of the creatures of Tiamat. He stole the tablets of destiny from Enlil, flying with them to the top of the Sabu Mountains where he put them in his nest. Enlil sent Ninurta his son to fetch the tablets back. With his storm birds, Ninurta surrounded Zu with clouds and tore off his wings, decapitating him. Zu is also known as Anzu.

Epilogue —
and One Last Entry

Just when we thought we were finished, another late entry came to light that seems to bring our exploration full circle. The subjects of people's beliefs and myths about magical creatures have been greatly disputed by rationalists and others who like to prove such tales to be merely hearsay or nonsense. But some discoveries go beyond fantastic speculation and are shown to be authentic memories of creatures which once lived – none more so than the following:

EBU GOGO

In the legends of the islands of Flores in Indonesia, the Ebu Gogo were believed by the islanders to be a dwarfish people who lived in the bush, ate raw meat and communicated in their own language. The Dutch settlers of this island who colonized Flores over 100 years ago thought these stories akin to the 'little people' legends of Europe and dismissed them. However, there is now substantial

and incontrovertible evidence to the contrary after paleoanthropologist Peter Brown, from the University of New England in New South Wales, revealed the findings of a recent excavation. The bones of a miniature hominid previously unknown to science were found on an island. The skeleton was of a 30-year-old female, 3 ft tall, weighing 55 lbs, who died about 16,000 years ago. In the same sediment in which her bones were found were stone tools, and the bones of dwarf elephants, giant rodents and Komodo dragon lizards that were larger than the current 10-ft species still living. Scientists immediately dubbed this discovery 'the Hobbit', after J.R.R. Tolkien's invented species of little people in the book of that name.

It is thought that this species, which has the scientific title *Homo floresiensis*, was still living on Flores until 13,000 years ago when it became extinct and had lived there since about 95,000 years ago. The stone tools discovered showed a complete understanding of the butchering of animals for they included blades, points, perforators and chopping tools. *Home floresiensis* was a bi-pedal, upright human with opposable thumbs and not merely an ape-like ancestor. It is thought that this hominid evolved from *Homo erectus* over 840,000 years ago. The size of a 3-year-old child but with a brain capacity one third as large, it had arms slightly longer than ours, with a hard brow-ridge, sharply-sloping forehead and no chin.

In refutation of the myth that the Ebu Gogo ate raw meat, it was clear that the *Homo floresiensis* used fire to cook the stegodon, the small but still significantly large dwarf elephant that weighed in at over a ton. The stegodon bones found suggest that this Hobbit-like creature chose to hunt the smaller juveniles, but that they also ate fish, snakes, tortoises and rodents as well as birds and frogs. The remains were discovered beneath a 12,000-year-old layer of volcanic ash. The dwarfing of mammalian species on the islands around Flores and elsewhere is usually due to adverse environmental changes where adaptation to a smaller size is essential for survival. The colonization of these islands by hominid species was previously thought to have taken place only 11,000 years ago. But the fact remains, while *Homo floresiensis* was living on the island, early modern humans like us, *Homo sapiens*, were already around – we survived together for over 30,000 years!

'If the gods bring it about, no marvel ever seems beyond belief to me.'
Pindar, 'Pythian Ode 10'

Bibliography

Adkins, Lesley and Roy, *Dictionary of Roman Religion*, Facts on File Inc, New York, 1996

Allardice, P., *Myths, Gods, and Fantasy: A Source Book*, Prism Press, Bridport, UK, 1991

Andersen, Hans Christian, *Danish Fairy Legends and Tales*, George Bell and Sons, London, 1891

Ashton, J., *Chapbooks of the Eighteenth Century*, Skoob Books, London, 1992

Barber, Elizabeth and Paul T., *When They Severed Earth From Sky*, Princeton University Press, 2004

Barber, Richard, (trans.), *Bestiary*, Folio Society, London, 1992

— *Bestiary (1220–1250): Being an English Version of the Bodleian Library Oxford Ms. Bodley 764*, Boydell Press, Woodbridge, UK, 1993

— *A Companion to World Mythology*, Kestrel Books, London, 1979

Barber, R. and A. Riches, *A Dictionary of Fabulous Beasts*, Boydell Press, Ipswich, 1971

Barclay, Reverend James, *Barclay's Universal Dictionary*, James Virtue, London, 1848

Baring-Gould, S., *A Book of Folklore*, Collins, London, 1890

Bayley, H., *Archaic England*, Chapman and Hall, London, 1919

Berndt, Ronald and Catherine, *The Speaking Land: Myth and Story in Aboriginal Australia*, Penguin Books, Victoria, Australia, 1987

Bett, Henry, *English Legends*, Batsford, London, 1950

Black, Jeremy and Anthony Green, *Gods, Demons and Symbols of Ancient Mesopotamia*, British Museum Press, London, 1992

Bleek, W.H., *Zulu Legends*, J.K. van Schaik, Pretoria, 1952

Borges, J.L. and M. Guerro, *The Book of Imaginary Beings*, (trans. N.T. di Giovanni), Jonathan Cape, London, 1969

Borsje, Jacqueline, *From Chaos to Enemy: Encounters with Monsters in Early Irish Texts*, Brepol Publishers, Turnhout, 1996

Bibliography

Bozic, S. and A. Marshall, *Aboriginal Myths*, Gold Star Publications, Melbourne, 1972

Brewer's Dictionary of Phrase and Fable, Centenary Edition (ed. Trevor Evans), Cassell, London, 1978

Briggs, K., *The Anatomy of Puck*, Routledge and Kegan Paul, 1959

— *British Folktales and Legends A Sampler*, Paladin, London, 1977

— *A Dictionary of Fairies*, Allen Lane, London, 1976

— *The Vanishing People*, Batsford, London, 1978

Briggs, K. and R.L. Tongue, (eds), *Folktales of England*, Routledge and Kegan Paul, London, 1965

Bringhurst, Robert, *Being in Being: Collected Works of A Master Haida Mythteller, Skaay of the Qquuna Quughawaay*, University of Nebraska Press, 2001

— (trans.), *Nine Visits to the Mythworld by Chandl of the Qayah Llaanas*, University of Nebraska Press, 2000

— *A Story as Sharp as a Knife*, Douglas MacIntyre Ltd, Vancouver, 1999

Brown, M.E., and B.A. Rosenberg, *Encyclopedia of Folklore and Literature*, ABCCLIC, Santa Barbara, California, 1998

Bullfinch, Thomas, *The Age of Fable*, Everyman, London

Bullfinch's Complete Mythology, Hamlyn, London, 1964

Burland, C., *Myths of Life and Death*, Macmillan, London, 1972

— *North American Indian Mythology*, Hamlyn, London, 1965

Burland, C., I. Nicholson and H. Osborne, *Mythology of the Americas*, Hamlyn, London, 1970

— *Mythology of the North Americans*, Hamlyn, London, 1970

Carew-Hazlitt, W., *Faiths and Folklore: A Dictionary*, Reeves and Turner, London, 1905

Carlyon, Richard, *A Guide to the Gods*, Heinemann, London, 1981

Carrington, R., *Mermaids and Mastodons: A Book of Natural and Unnatural History*, Chatto and Windus, London, 1957

Cavendish, R., (ed.), *Legends of the World*, Orbis Publishing, London, 1982

Charbonneau-Lassay, Louis, *The Bestiary of Christ*, Parabola Books, New York, 1991

Cherry, John, (ed.), *Mythical Beasts*, British Museum Press, London, 1995

Cooper, J.C., *Symbolic and Mythological Animals*, Aquarian, London, 1992

Cotterell, Arthur and Rachel Storm, *The Ultimate Encyclopedia of Mythology*, Hermes House, London, 2004

Coughlan, R., *The Illustrated Encyclopaedia of Arthurian Legends*, Element Books, Shaftesbury, 1993

Curran, Bob, *The Creatures of Celtic Myth*, Cassell, London, 2000

Dale-Green, P., *The Cult of the Cat*, Heinemann, London, 1973

Danaher, Kevin, *The Year in Ireland*, Mercier Press, Dublin, 1972

Daniélou, Alain, *The Gods of India*, Inner Traditions, New York, 1985

— *Shiva and Dionysus*, Inner Traditions, New York, 1984

Day, D., *A Tolkien Bestiary*, Chancellor Press, London, 1979

The Element Encyclopedia of Magical Creatures

Dixon, E., (ed.), *Fairy Tales from the Arabian Nights*, Dent, London, 1893

Dixon-Kennedy, Mike, *Encyclopedia of Russian and Slavic Myth and Legend*, Cassell, London, 1998

Dixon-Kennedy, Mike, *European Myth and Legend*, Cassell, London, 1997

— *Native American Myth and Legend*, Cassell, London, 1996

Elston, Catherine F., *Ravensong*, Norland Publishing Co, Flastaff, 1991

Enchanted World Series, *Night Creatures*, Time Life Books, Amsterdam, 1985

— *Spells and Bindings*, Time Life Books, Amsterdam, 1985

— *Water Spirits*, Time Life Books, Amsterdam, 1985

Encyclopaedia of Comparative Religion, Everyman, London, 1965

Epstein, P., *Monsters: Their Histories, Homes, and Habits*, Doubleday, New York, 1973

Everyman's Dictionary of Non-Classical Mythology, Everyman Reference, London, 1965

Feldmann, Susan, *The Story Telling Stone: Traditional Native American Myths and Tales*, Dell Books, New York, 1965

Folklore Myths and Legends of Britain, Reader's Digest, London, 1973

Franklin, Anna, *Illustrated Encyclopedia of Fairies*, Vega, London, 2002

Frayling, C., *Vampires: From Lord Byron to Dracula*, Faber and Faber, London, 1991

Frazer, J.C., *The Golden Bough*, Papermac, London, 1987

Funk and Wagnall's Standard Dictionary of Folklore, Mythology and Legend, New English Library, London, 1975

Gainsford, J., (ed.), *The Atlas of Man*, Omega Books, 1987

Galembo, Phyllis, *Vodou: Visions and Voices of Haiti*, Ten Speed Press, Berkeley, California, 1998

Gaselee, Stephen, *Stories from the Christian East*, Sidgwick and Jackson, London, 1918

Gaskell, D.S., *Dictionary of Scripture and Myth*, Dorset Press, New York, 1883

Gaynor, E., (ed.), *Dictionary of Mysticism*, Wildwood House, London, 1974

Gerritsen, W.E. and A.C. van Melle, *A Dictionary of Medieval Heroes*, (trans. T. Guest), Boydell Press, Woodbridge, England, 1998

Gheerbrant, A., *The Amazon Past, Present, and Future*, Thames and Hudson, New York, 1992

Gill, S.D. and F. Sullivan, *Dictionary of Native American Mythology*, ABCCLIO, Santa Barbara, California, 1992

Gill, Walter, *A Manx Scrapbook*, Arrowsmith, London, 1929

Godwin, Joscelyn, *Mystery Religions in the Ancient World*, Thames & Hudson, London, 1981

Gordon, Stuart, *The Encyclopaedia of Myths and Legends*, Headline, London, 1993

Gould, C., *Mythical Monsters*, (1886), Studio Editions, 1995

Gregory, Lady, *The Voyages of St Brendan the Navigator*, Colin Smythe, Gerrards Cross, 1973

Bibliography

Guerber, H., *Myths and Legends of the Middle Ages*, Harrap, London, 1948

Guss, David M., (ed.), *The Language of the Birds*, North Point Press, San Francisco, 1985

Gwynn Jones, T., *Welsh Folklore and Folk Custom*, Methuen, London, 1930

Hall's Dictionary of Subjects and Symbols in Art, Murray, London, 1979

Hargreaves, J., *Hargreaves New Illustrated Bestiary*, Gothic Image Publications, Glastonbury, England, 1990

Harland, J.A. & Wilkinson T.T., *Legends and Traditions of Lancashire*, Routledge, London, 1873

Hamer, M.J., *The Livaro: People of the Sacred Waterfalls*, Robert Hale, London, 1973

Hart, George, *A Dictionary of Egyptian Gods and Goddesses*, Routledge and Kegan Paul, London, 1986

Hayes, Will, *The Book of the Cow*, Order of the Great Companions, Dublin, 1930

Henderson, W., *Folklore of the Northern Counties of England and the Borders*, Longmans Green, London, 1866

Hill, D. and P. Williams, *The Supernatural*, Aldus Books, London, 1965

Hippisley-Coxe, Anthony D., *Haunted Britain*, Pan, London, 1973

Hole, C., *A Dictionary of British Folk Custom*, Paladin, London, 1986

Howie, M. Oldfield, *The Encircled Serpent*, Rider, London

Hyslop, Robert, (ed.), *Echoes from the Border Hills*, Pentland Press, 1992

Ivanits, Linda J., *Russian Folk Belief*, ME Sharpe, New York, 1989

Jacobs, Joseph, (ed.), *Celtic Fairy Tales*, David Nutt, London, 1895

Jones, G., *Kings, Beasts, and Heroes*, Oxford University Press, London, 1972

Jones, Reverend Henry and Lewis Kropp, *The Folk Tales of the Magyars*, The Folklore Society, London, 1889

Kaul, Flemming, *Thracian Tales on the Gundestrup Cauldron*, Najade Press, Amsterdam, 1991

Keightley, Thomas, *The Fairy Mythology*, Whittacker Treacher, 1833

Kendall, L., *Shamans, Housewives, and Other Restless Spirits*, University of Hawaii Press, Honolulu, 1985

Ker Wilson, Barbara, *Scottish Folktales and Legends*, Oxford University Press, London, 1954

Kerenyi, C., *The Heroes of the Greeks*, Thames and Hudson, London, 1974

Kerven, R., *The Mythical Quest: In Search of Adventure, Romance, and Enlightenment*, Pomegranite Artbooks, 1996

Killip, M., *Folklore of the Isle of Man*, Batsford, London, 1975

Knappert, Jan, *The Aquarian Guide to African Mythology*, Thorsons, Wellingborough, 1990

— *The Encyclopaedia of Middle Eastern Mythology and Religion*, Element Books, Shaftesbury, 1993

— *Indian Mythology: An Encyclopaedia of Myth and Legend*, Diamond Books, London, 1995

— *Myths and Legends of the Swahili*, Heinemann, London, 1970

— *Myths and Legends of the Congo*, Heinemann, London, 1971

— *Pacific Mythology: An Encyclopaedia of Myth and Legend*, Diamond Books, London, 1995

The Element Encyclopedia of Magical Creatures

Knatchbull-Huggeson, E., *River Legends*, Daldy Ibister, London, 1875

Lang, A., *Custom and Myth*, Longmans Green, London, 1898

Lawrence, Elizabeth A., *Hunting the Wren*, University of Tennessee, Knoxville, 1997

Layard, John, *The Lady of the Hare*, Faber and Faber, London, 1944

Leach, M., (ed.), *The Dictionary of Folklore*, Funk and Wagnall, Chicago, 1985

— *The Standard Dictionary of Folklore*, Funk and Wagnall, Chicago, 1972

Leacock, S. and R. Leacock, *Spirits of the Deep*, Doubleday, New York, 1972

Legey, E., *The Folklore of Morocco*, (trans. L. Hotz), Allen and Unwin, London, 1935

Leonardo da Vinci, *Prophecies*, Hesperus Press, London, 2002

Lipsanen, Anneke, *The Finnish Folk-Year: A Perpetual Diary and a Book of Days, Ways and Customs*, Otava, Helsinki, 1987

Lonsdale, Steven, *Animals and the Origins of Dance*, Thames and Hudson, New York, 1981

Lurker, Manfred, *Dictionary of Gods and Goddesses, Devils and Demons*, (trans. Campbell), Routledge, London, 1989

Lyon, P.J., *Native South Americans*, Little Brown, Boston, 1974

Macdowall, M.W., *Asgard and the Gods: Tales and Traditions of Our Northern Ancestors*, (Adapted from the work of Dr W Wigner), Swan Sonnenschein, London, 1902

MacKillop, J., *Dictionary of Celtic Mythology*, Oxford University Press, London, 1998

MacKinnon, J., *Scottish Folk Tales in Gaelic and English*, JMK Consultancy Publishing, Edinburgh, 1991

Maple, Erie, *Superstition and the Superstitious*, W.H. Allen, London

Marven, Nigel, *Incredible Journeys*, BBC, London, 1997

Matthews, Caitlín, *The Celtic Book of the Dead*, Connections, London, 2001

— *King Arthur and the Goddess of the Land*, Inner Traditions, Rochester, Vermont, 2002

— *Mabon and the Guardians of Celtic Britain*, Inner Traditions, Rochester, Vermont, 2002

Matthews, John, *The Celtic Shaman's Pack*, Element Books, Shaftesbury, 1995

— *Celtic Totem Animals*, Gothic Image Press, Glastonbury, 2001

McLeish, K., *Myths and Legends of the World Explored*, Bloomsbury Press, London, 1996

Menger, M. and C. Gagnon, *Lake Monster Traditions: A Cross-Cultural Analysis*, Fortean Times, London, 1988

Merkur, Daniel, *Powers Which We Do Not Know: Gods and Spirits of the Inuit*, University of Idaho Press, Moscow, Idaho, 1991

Mollet, J.W., *An Illustrated Dictionary of Antique Art and Archaeology*, Omega, 1927

Moon, B., (ed.), *An Encyclopaedia of Archetypal Symbolism*, Archive for Research on Archetypal Symbolism,

Bibliography

Shambhala Publications, Boston and London, 1991

Morrisson, S., (ed.), *Wm. Cashen's Manx Folklore*, G.L. Johnson, Douglas, Isle of Man, 1912

Mowat, E., *People of the Deer*, Readers' Union, Michael Joseph, London, 1954

New Larousse Encyclopaedia of Mythology, Book Club Associates, London, 1973

Newman, P., *Gods and Graven Images*, Robert Hale, London, 1987

Nigg, Joseph, *The Book of Fabulous Beasts*, Oxford University Press, London, 1999

— *Wonder Beasts: Tales and Lore of the Phoenix, the Griffin, the Unicorn & the Dragon*, Libraries Unlimited, Englewood, Colorado, 1995

O'Hogain, Dr D., *Myth Legend and Romance: An Encyclopaedia of the Irish Folk Tradition*, Prentice Hall, New York, 1991

Opie, R. and I. Opie, (eds), *The Oxford Dictionary of Nursery Rhymes*, Oxford University Press, London, 1977

Orbell, Margaret, *Traditional Maori Stories*, Reed, Auckland, 1992

Owen, W., *Strange Scottish Stories*, Jarrold Press, Norwich, 1983

Palmer, Jessica D., *Animal Wisdom*, Thorsons, London, 2001

Paré, Ambroise, *On Monsters and Marvels*, (trans. J. Pallister), University of Chicago Press, 1983

Parry-Jones, D., *Welsh Legends and Fairy Folk Lore*, Batsford, London, 1953

Payne, A., *Medieval Beasts*, British Library, London, 1990

Pennick, Nigel, *Crossing the Borderlines: Guising, Masking and Ritual Animal Disguises in the European Tradition*, Capall Bann, Chievely, 1998

— *Dragons of the West*, Capall Bann, Chievely 1997

Pennick, Nigel and Helen Field, *A Book of Beasts*, Capall Bann, Chievely, 2003

Piggott, J., *Japanese Mythology*, Chancellor Press, London, 1969

Poignant, R., *Myths and Legends of the South Seas*, Hamlyn, London, 1970

Porteous, A., *Forest Folklore*, G Allen and Unwin, London, 1928

Porter, J.R. and W.M.S. Russel, *Animals in Folklore*, D.S. Brewer, Cambridge, 1978

Price, Simon and Emily Kearns, (eds), *The Oxford Dictionary of Classical Myth and Religion*, Oxford University Press, 2003

Reader's Digest American Folklore and Legend, Reader's Digest Association, Pleasantville, 1978

Reed, A.W., *Aboriginal Myths, Legends and Fables*, Reed, Chatsworth, NSW, 1993

— *Maori Myth and Legend*, Reed Books, Auckland, New Zealand, 1983

Reed, A.W. and Inez Hames, *Myths and Legends of Fiji and Rotuma*, Reed Books, Auckland, New Zealand, 1967

Rider Encyclopaedia of Eastern Philosophy and Religion, Rider, London, 1986

Risdon, J., A. Stevens and B. Whitworth, *A Glympse of Dartmoor–Villages, Folklore, Tors, and Place Names,*

Peninsular Press, Devon, England, 1992

Robbins, R.H., *The Encyclopaedia of Witchcraft and Demonology*, Bookplan/Hamlyn, London, 1959

Rockwell, David, *Giving Voice to Bear*, Roberts Reiner Publishers, Niwot, 1991

Room, Adrian, *Room's Classical Dictionary*, Routledge and Kegan Paul, London, 1983

Rose, Carol, *Giants, Monsters and Dragons*, WW Norton, New York, 2000
— *Spirits, Fairies, Leprechauns and Goblins*, WW Norton, New York, 1996

Rose-Benoit, W., (ed.), *The Reader's Encyclopaedia*, London, Book Club, 1974

Royal Pageantry, Customs, and Festivals of Great Britain and Northern Ireland, Purnell and Sons, London, 1967

Ryan, J. and G. Bardon, *Mythscapes: Aboriginal Art of the Desert*, National Heart Foundation, National Gallery, Melbourne, 1989

Saggs, H.W.F., *Civilization Before Greece and Rome*, Batsford, London, 1989

Saunders, Nicholas, *Animal Spirits*, Duncan Baird Publishers, London, 1995

Saxby, Jesse, *Shetland Folk Belief*, Norwood Editions, 1974

Scheub, Harold, *A Dictionary of African Mythology*, Oxford University Press, London, 2000

Screeton, Paul, *The Lambton Worm*, Zodiac House, London, 1978

Senior, Michael, *The Illustrated Who's Who in Mythology*, (ed. G. Paminder),

MacDonald Illustrated, London, 1985

Sheppard, Paul and Barry Sanders, *The Sacred Paw*, Arcana, New York, 1985

Simek, Rudolf, *Dictionary of Northern Mythology*, DS Brewer, Cambridge, 1993

Skeat, W.W., *Malay Magic*, Oxford University Press, 1889 (reprinted Singapore, 1984)

South, Malcolm, *Mythical and Fabulous Creatures*, Greenwood, New York, 1987

Spence, Lewis, *A Dictionary of Mythology*, Cassell, London, 1910
— *The Minor Traditions of British Mythology*, Rider, London, 1948
— *Myths and Legends of Ancient Egypt*, George C. Harrup, London, 1917
— *North American Indians, Myths, and Legends*, Bracken Books, London, 1985

Squire, C., *Celtic Myth and Legend*, Gresham, London, 1889
— *Celtic Myth and Legend, Poetry and Romance*, Gresham, London, 1910

Stalder, Valerie, *Legends and Folktales of Lapland*, Alden and Mowbray, London, 1972

Steubel, C. and Brother Herman, *Tala o le Vavau*, Polynesian Press, Auckland, 1976

Stevens, W., *Giants in Those Days*, University of Nebraska Press, Lincoln, 1989

Swinburne-Carr, T., *A New Classical Lexicon of Biography, Mythology and Geography*, Simpkins Marshall, London, 1858

Bibliography

Thompson, Stith, *Tales of the North American Indians*, University of Indiana, Bloomington, 1929

Travels of Sir John Mandeville, (ed. N. Denny and A. Filmer-Sankey), Collins, London, 1973

Walters, D., *Chinese Mythology, An Encyclopaedia of Myth and Legend*, Thorsons, London, 1992

Warner, M., *No Go the Bogeyman: Scaring, Lulling, and Making Mock*, Chatto and Windus, London, 1998

Werner, A., *Myths & Legends of the Bantu*, Harrap, London, 1993

Westwood, Jennifer, *Albion: A Guide to Legendary Britain*, Grafton, London, 1992

— (ed.), *The Atlas of Mysterious Places*, Guild Publishing, London, 1987

White, T.H., *The Book of Beasts, Being a Translation from a Latin Bestiary of the 12th Century*, Jonathan Cape, London, 1954

Williams-Ellis, A., *Fairies and Enchanters*, Nelson, London, 1933

Wirtjes, Hermeke, (ed.), *The Middle English Physiologus*, Early English Text Society, Oxford University Press, 1991

Yeats, W.B., (ed.), *Fairy and Folk Tales of the Irish Peasantry*, W. Scott, Dover, 1992 (reprint)